History of
Bishopstone
& Bunshill

Written & Published

By

John Macklin

Best Wishes
John.
30 7 2011

This book is dedicated to my parents Cecil and Kathleen Macklin

First published by John Macklin 2011

ISBN 978-0-9568943-0-4

Printed in Great Britain by
Orphans Press Ltd
Arrow Close, Enterprise Park, Herefordshire, HR60LD

Acknowledgements

The vast majority of the primary research for this book was undertaken at the Herefordshire Record Office and I am indebted to Mrs Elizabeth Semper-O'Keefe and Mr Rhys Griffin and their staff for their assistance, expertise and courtesy throughout my researches. Robin Hill and the staff at the Reference Library Broad Street, Hereford Museum, Woolhope Club Library and Hereford Cathedral Library for their permission to quote from some of their journals and copy illustrations. The staff at The National Archives Kew, British Library and English Heritage Swindon also Major David Davenport for allowing me access to his private records and for using some material as illustrations. My father Cecil Macklin, Mrs Elinor English, Donald Watkins and Bob Carrington sadly no longer with us for sharing their memories of Bishopstone with me. The many villagers present and past who helped with photo's and information: Ian and Pat Astley, Frank Betambeau, Joyce Bradley (nee Montague), Ginny and David Carrington, Joan Clark (nee Cartwright), Sir John Cotterell, Andrew and Ann Culley, Phyllis Daniels, Rose Davies (nee Carpenter), Mr and Mrs Eagling, Muriel Holmes (nee Jones), Pat Jenkins (nee Suff), Sylvia Jenkins (nee Baugh), Janet Jones (nee Bradley), Bev Kelly, Alan Knott, Bob and Helen Matthews, George Phillips, Sylvia Price (nee Tippins), Tom Prosser, Jim Roberts, Jeff and Marg Smith, Audrey Tozer, Dave Verry, John Verry, Shirley Wadley (nee Rounds), Viv Waters (nee Alderton), John Watkins, Peter Watkins, John Wall, Margery Webb (nee Rudd) Audrey and Nora Wintour and Molly Young (nee Hill)

I am most particularly indebted to my good friend Sue Hubbard for her expertise and kindness in transcribing many early Latin documents especially the early Bunshill Court Rolls written in very rural Latin and for reading through the draft copy and advising on contents. Martin Turner my brother-in law for also reading the draft copy. Jake Macklin my grandson for designing and producing the cover. Last but not least my dear wife Josephine, for her encouragement, putting up with my years of research and obsession in writing this book and for helping with proof reading.

Foreword

In 1987 my father Cecil Macklin wrote about his memories of the village in the 1920's which I have included in this book. Afterwards in his latter years he started to research the History of Bishopstone and wrote a small leaflet on the subject, his enthusiasm has passed on to me. So now I have tried to complete the job with a more detailed study of the history of Bishopstone. My Grandmother had told my father her mother had attended Bishopstone School as a child in the 1860s, what he did not discover is that the association with Bishopstone parish goes back a further two generations. What the parish records show is my great, great, grandmother was baptised in Bishopstone Church on October 21st 1821 when my great, great, great grandparents were living in Banbury Hall. My great, great grandparents married in Bishopstone Church on May 27th 1848 as did my great grandparents who lived for a time in Scaldback, and over the next 150 years the family have lived in several different homes in the parish. My grandparents on my mothers side, John and Sarah Wall moved into Bishopstone in 1905 living initially in the Old School House and then Stonehouse, John Wall my grandfather served the parish as overseer of the poor, parish clerk and chaired the Parish Council for a brief period a position I now hold 80 years later, my father and mother were married in Bishopstone Church where in later years he served as a church warden another position I find myself holding in 2010 it is from this background I have developed a great affection and interest in the parish. It has taken over 8 years of research to write this book, studying many thousands of documents on the parish, deciding what information to leave out was difficult.

The parish had gone from holding a high esteem and importance within the county of Herefordshire in the 14th century down to a low position when it formed part of Foxley Estate throughout the 18th and 19th century. There have been many discoveries during my research; possibly the most exciting were uncovering Bunshill's very comprehensive Court Rolls that included written records for the year 1349, when the Blackdeath ravaged the Manor. These are held at the National Archives Kew. Inevitably in writing a book like this, involving so much translation, transcription, deciphering, interpretation and people's recollections I am sure some errors will be found for this I apologise in advance.

Contents

Chapter 1

Geology

Bishopstone lies at the eastern end of the most southerly group of hills, on the northern edge of the Herefordshire central plain. Together with Wormsley Hill and Dinmore Hill it is one of a little group of detached portions of the Black Mountain mass that have been left standing in isolation by erosion from the last Ice Age 12,000 years ago.

The last glacier pushed down from mid Wales past Kington gouging out what is now the Wye valley, enclosing a limestone hill we now know as Garnons Hill but leaving a ridge on its lee side. Along this ridge the village of Bishopstone sits today. The ice cap came nearly to the top of the hill; a geological survey carried out by Rev B B Clarke of the Woolhope Club in the late 1940s confirmed this. The lip of the glacier reached Breinton and Eaton Bishop leaving the escarpment we can see today with a tree-lined bank stretching from Sugwas House to the Camp Inn. When the ice retracted the Bishopstone area was left with a deep layer of clay. The benefits of this are still evident today, in providing a high water table with good productive agricultural soil, which man has made use of for the last 4000 years.

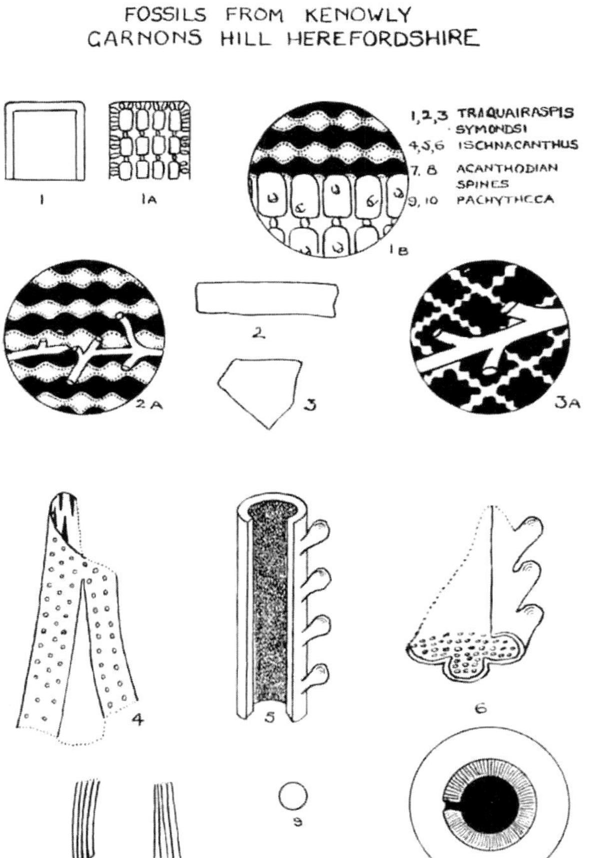

The height of Garnons hill is 763 ft above sea level; the base is 400 ft above sea level leaving a mass of 363 ft of rock and soil exposed on the hill.

The retreating ice left one other important feature: a spring had formed on the top of the hill, feeding a small stream running down to the valley. Although this was insignificant for thousands of years, it was the one necessary factor needed for man to settle in the area later to form the axis of Bishopstone village

(Figure 1) Fossils found by Rev Clarke in Bishopstone

Rev B B Clarke's survey also revealed a large find of fossils in the small quarry at Kenowly. The survey found that the hill consists of several bands of sandstone sandwiched between limestone. To extract this stone, quarrying was widespread and seven main quarries and hundreds of smaller ones were found.[1]

The purpose of the quarrying was

1 Building stone: the sandstone (in some of the bands are hard grits with the most delightful shades of pink and pale green) which can be seen in the Church, Bishopstone Court, Lena Cottage, Scaldback and many walls in the parish.

Earl Harold (later to become King Harold) in AD1060 surrounded the whole city of Hereford with a wall built of stone. He also built Hereford castle and rebuilt the Cathedral after it had been burnt down by the Welsh king Gruffydd ap Llywelyn and the English Earl Aelgar. As such a large quantity of stone would have been needed at this time, historians think some of this stone came from the Bishopstone quarries, the stone was probably dragged down to the river then floated downstream by raft.

2 Marl: there were hundreds of old marl pits up to twenty feet deep. The marl, being highly calcareous is rich in digested lime, and so forms an excellent dressing for agricultural land (some was used for building stone).

3 Limestone: This was quarried for burning to make lime, and also as a road material. Most of the limestone on the hill is very hard, which made it very suitable for repairing roads.

It was used extensively for the turnpike road from Hereford to Bredwardine; the Hereford Times in 1853 describes an application from the surveyor to the Hereford Turnpike Trust for the continued extraction of limestone for the purpose of road repairing.

4 Roofing tiles: some of the sandstone on the hill split naturally into tiles about an inch or a little more in thickness and these were once quarried extensively for roofing. Bishopstone Church and the Pleck Cottage are the only two buildings in Bishopstone where these tiles are still in use. From previous records Court Farm House, Bishon Farm, The Old Almshouses and Stone House had originally used these stone roofing tiles.

From this survey we can conclude that man had extensively quarried the hill since the arrival of the Romans in AD 43 until the 19th century.

Hunter Gatherers

The first evidence of occupiers of the land comes from the Mesolithic period around 5000 BC. Known as Advanced Hunter Gatherers they followed the river valleys. They stayed until the food supply was exhausted in that area and then moved on. We know they visited Bishopstone because a blue flint rounded thumb scraper was found in an arable field there in the 19th century and handed in to Hereford Museum.[2]

When the Channel Four programme excavated the Roman river crossing at Kenchester in 2006 an electronic sweep was carried out on the river plain and archaeologists were very surprised at the amount of activity that showed up. The area was literally dotted with campfire sites from the Mesolithic period.

Middle Bronze Age 1600-1000 B C

Within this period the first permanent settlers in this area arrived, they were the first farmers. The heavy clay soils gave rise to thick oak forests, which presented them with many problems, and necessitated the clearing of large tracts of woodland for their crops and herds. As evidence of their occupation, they left behind an axe [3]and a food scraper, again discovered in the 19th century. They were passed to the then lord of the Manor, the Rev G H Davenport, who kept the axe for his own private collection but handed in the scraper to the museum in Hereford where it is still kept. On an aerial photographic survey funded by the Woolhope club for their 2000 celebration,[4] two crop circles in the area were discovered, later identified as circular Bronze Age compounds. Both were situated on the village boundaries, one just over the Yazor brook in Mansel Lacy, the other at Bridge Sollers to the east of the new road leading to the main A438.

(Figure 2) Bronze Age food scraping flint found in Bishopstone

These early settlers appear to have farmed an area around the Yazor brook; it is likely that this area would have been continually farmed from this period, and it is interesting that the 18th estate century maps still referred to the area as the "old lands". The circular compounds identified by the photographs were used by the settlers to keep themselves and, perhaps more importantly, their cattle safe from attack by other tribal groups. Areas outside the compound were cultivated to grow wheat and barley.

The Iron Age farming community would have cleared more land to support a growing population. These were part of the Silures, a tribe who inhabited South Wales and the Welsh Marches for at least one thousand years before the Romans landed in Britain, but though a Welsh speaking people, they were not of Celtic origin. They would have worked in family units but by 390 BC locals from the tribe started to build the hill fort at Credenhill[5] where experts say each farming family was responsible for building and maintaining their section of the fortified ditch. It was built because the fort provided a safer area for people and their livestock from raiding tribes.

Credenhill could be described as a forerunner of the later fortified Norman towns. It was a large trading place for goods and livestock and also an administration centre. The chief and his administrators would have lived there. Excavation by archaeologists has shown that the fort contained a large grain store plus a building they described as a town hall. They also uncovered the footings of buildings with square floor plans, this is unusual because other forts of this period had only round huts. Experts say that as many as three thousand people could have occupied the site. There is little doubt that farms in the Bishopstone area would have contributed greatly to the building and maintenance of the Credenhill hill fort.

The Roman.Period A D 48-410

The Bishopstone of today sits either side of the former Roman road leading from Kenchester (Magna) to the legionary Forts at Clyro and Clifford. This was built as a marching road used normally by the army, (but later in the Roman conquest commercial trade was important so many travellers used the road). When the sewer was installed through the village in 1973-4 no evidence was seen of the original Roman road. Jim Gough who lived in the village during this period and had an interest in local history, spent two years looking into the excavations and told me afterwards he never saw any trace of a Roman road. But with nearly two thousand years of use it would be unlikely to find any evidence of the road. When the Romans built it, it would have been built above ground level. With years of cart traffic, mud dug out, stones laid in, dug out again the results of this activity has left the surface of today's road, in places, five feet or more below the level of surrounding fields. The road was not covered with a layer of tarmac until the 1940s, and there is written evidence that the road was so bad in the 1920s that the villagers walked in the fields adjoining the road to avoid being covered in mud.

(Figure 3) When the Roman Road was uncovered in 2008, before a new Bungalow was built on the site in the centre of the village, the line of the Roman Road was 15m south of the present road. This provides evidence of how the Anglo-Saxon ploughing had over the centuries pushed today's road north.

While writing this book new evidence has been found about the course of the Roman road. When excavating the footings of a new bungalow, 15 metres south of the current road, the Roman road was discovered roughly 4 feet under the ground level.

This movement north of today's highway can be attributed to the Anglo-Saxons ploughmen and their oxen ploughing teams. With eight beasts per plough they needed a huge headland to turn; over many centuries of ploughing the turning oxen would have pushed the headland of the field northwards.

Roman Villa

A Roman pavement was discovered in the parish in 1812 when a new rectory was being built.[6] The site Rev. Walker picked for his rectory was in the old medieval open field called North Hoarstone. It was to be built on high ground overlooking the church, replacing the old rectory down by the Church, which was said to be always damp. If any other site had been selected for the new rectory the remains of the Roman Villa may have never been found. The Hereford Journal reported the find on October 7th 1812 *"A large tessellated pavement has been discovered in digging the drain of the new parsonage at Bishopstone"*

(Figure 4) Illustration of a Roman Villa in Britain possibly similar to one built in Bishopstone

The discovery unearthed part of a pavement (mosaic floor) which originally would have been 30 feet square; it was lying 16 inches below the surface, and had been damaged by the plough.

The discoveries caused much interest, so much so that Rev. Walker was forced to employ a guard to watch over the site day and night to prevent bits of the pavement from being stolen.

The next week on October 14th 1812 The Hereford Journal reported, "The pavement has been covered over, and will be uncovered as soon as the house which is being built within a few yards of it, is in a state to be inhabited".

Thomas Bird, Esq. F.S.A. (who was an authority on Roman antiquities at the time) visited the site in the summer of 1829; he says the discovery was made in 1812 when digging a principal drain for the parsonage house. He observed that as the pavement was laid on a bed of clay, without foundation, it was in great danger of being destroyed by worms or by persons treading upon it in wet weather. He had a plan taken and an experienced draughtsman produced a drawing. The centre part was entirely destroyed and also the north side. Also in 1821, in the kitchen garden a foundation wall three feet wide and three feet deep was unearthed and was traced for fifty five feet, it was substantially laid but without cement. On the east side of the house was a twenty-inch foundation wall strongly cemented. Only three coins where found but a beautiful drinking cup was discovered and is now a major attraction in the permanent Roman display in Hereford Museum. Considerable quantities of black earth were found along with fragments of urns, and also a quantity of bones at a general depth of sixteen to eighteen inches. These are from the usual Roman funeral urns.

(Figure 5) Roman drinking cup discovered in Bishopstone

The site was left uncovered for about twenty years and it attracted many visitors including William Wordsworth who wrote a sonnet on the "Roman Antiquities discovered at Bishopstone"

While poring Antiquarians search the ground
Upturned with curious pains, the Bard, a Seer
Takes fire:-The men that have been reappear;
Romans for travel girt, for business gowned,
And some recline on couches, myrtle-crowned,
In festal glee: Why not? For fresh and clear
As if its hues were of the passing year
Dawns this time-buried pavement. From that mound
Hoards may come forth of Trajans, Maximins,
Shrunk into coins with all their warlike toil;
Or a fierce impress issues with its foil
Of tenderness-the Wolf, whose suckling twins
The unlettered ploughboy pities when he wins
The casual treasure from the furrowed soil[7]

(Figure 6) Drawing commissioned by Thomas Bird of Bishopstone pavement made in 1829

In a cottage garden next to the site a headless statue in blue and white porcelain from the Roman period has been unearthed within the last thirty years and has now been handed in to Hereford Museum.

Sir Humphrey Davy's opinion on the site in 1820 stated that the surface of England rises by natural causes, about an inch every century. Now given that the Romans left the neighbourhood eighteen centuries ago, this seems to bear out his theory.
The nave, south and north walls of Bishopstone church built in the 12th century are said by experts to be built from Roman stone possibly salvaged from the rectory site or Kenchester. The stones are fairly small and square, typically Roman, as Romans liked to transport their stone from the quarries by packhorse. The mason has laid the stones in courses to resemble the Roman style. There are also four corner stones made from Roman tufa stone built into the top of the 13th century extensions of the church.
The Woolhope Club in their field visit to Bishopstone on June 26th 1913 went to visit a Roman roadway opposite the church, Mr Jack their Roman antiquities expert said it was probably a private way to the Roman villa erected where the rectory now stands. It could be they were looking at the road closed in the 1820s, which is explained in chapter 9.

The Roman villa or farm at the Rectory site shows there was a significant Roman presence in the area. This is one of only four possible villas found in Herefordshire The buildings were fairly large, and must have been occupied over a long period of time to have such a large number of funeral urns found on the site. The pavement had been laid on the clay, which was unusual, because they are normally laid over a ducted heated floor.
Does this mean that it was firstly a farm, then taken over by a General or area administrator? Archaeologists tell us that there were other Roman buildings in the Bishopstone area; a brooch of the period was found in the field between Bunshill lane and the Roman road.[8]
The expert Thomas Bird's opinion was "*The distance the Villa stands from the station of Kenchester is nearly a mile and a half. This is directly east of the site at Bishopstone which was probably the commanding situation of the Praetorium, for the General had Kenchester, Crendenhill, and Dinedor perfectly under his eye from this spot*"[9]
What did the local tribes-people think? They would have been fascinated to see a building with foundations, timber cut and fixed with iron nails, a tiled roof and mosaic floor set against their crude huts, thatched roofs and dirt floors. Also the Roman soldiers with smart colourful uniforms, marching by in tight units were one of the spectacles they had never seen before. And as a parting thought I like to imagine the local Governor or General in his praetorium on a warm summer's evening looking over Bishopstone drinking wine from his cup made in the Nene valley, which is now in a glass case in Hereford Museum.

Dark Ages and Anglo Saxons A.D.410-1060

After the Romans left in A.D.410 the order they had imposed disappeared and the area reverted back to tribal territory Bishopstone became part of an area known as the frontier lands, suffering from many raiding Welsh tribes. The Anglo Saxons' control of the Kingdom of Mercia, of which Herefordshire was a part, consolidated somewhere round A.D.584-90. In around A.D.750 the famous King Offa united the local tribes and to add to the security of his kingdom built a dyke to separate it from Wales. King Offa gave a warning that if any Welsh man were found on the English side of the dyke without permission, he would have his hand cut off and if caught again the other hand would be removed. The southern end of this section of the dyke finishes at the river just above Bridge Sollers Bridge. The only part of Offa's Dyke visible today in Bishopstone can be seen by the side of the Steps House, where it rises up through the wood and follows a direct route over the centre of Bishopstone Hill and forms part of the western boundary of the parish. It looks today just like a deep ditch with a mound on one side. It must have taken many years and man hours to build, and would have been a very large ditch for the remains of it to have survived over a 1000 years.
Salt was a very important commodity in early medieval times. At the southern end of Offa's Dyke stood a homestead called the Salt Box.[10] (This was demolished around 1860 but snowdrops can still be seen in the A438 verge where the house once stood). Historians think it was a place where salt was exchanged with the Welsh tribes (after Offa's threat).
With Offa's Dyke in place the area settled down and the people of Bishopstone concentrated on farming. By the end of the 9th century the village geography had taken on more or less its present look. It was around this period that an early Saxon village was formed around the stream running down from the hill There was possibly a wooden church and manor house. The hundred systems were used to settle disputes and helped with the general smooth running of that area, Bishopstone being part of the old Saxon hundred (administrative area) called Stapel.

The hundred courts were held at "the hundred pit" inside the Iron Age hill fort at Credenhill where representatives from each parish would meet regularly to punish wrongdoers, settle disputes and receive orders passed down from the king.

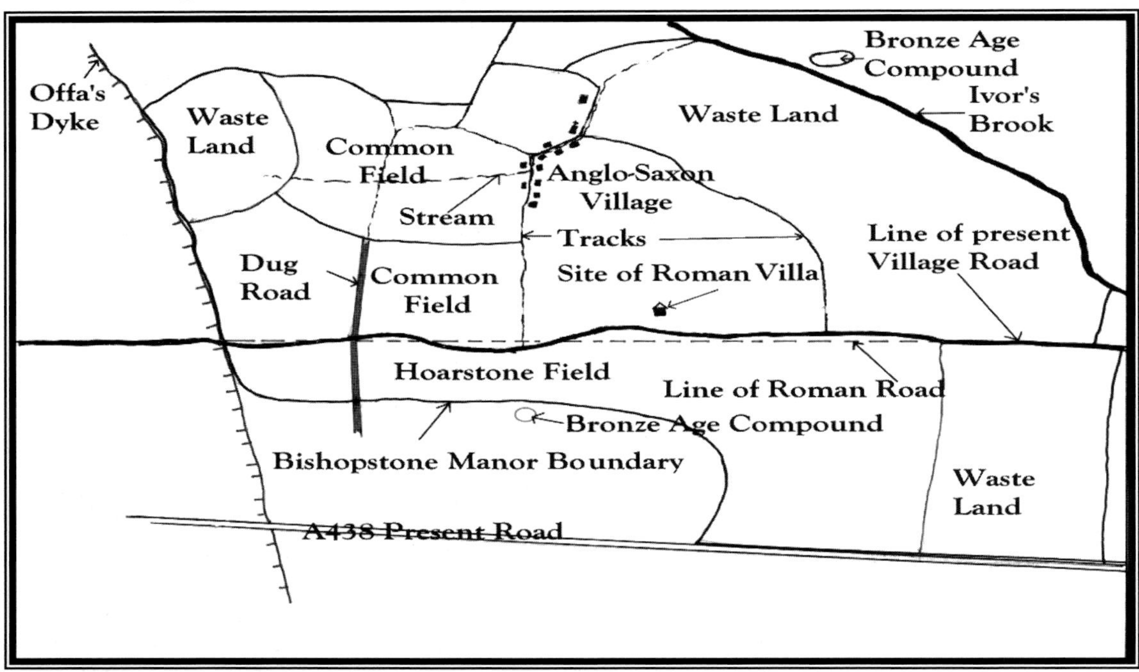

(Figure 7) Map showing locations of the Roman and early British sites, the curved line of the present village road was caused by the Anglo-Saxon ploughing methods.

(Figure 8) Alfred Watkins' photograph of the Dug Road in the 1890s

The dug road[11] which leads down from the south corner of Bishopstone Hill about 300m on the west side of Downshill Coppice crosses the Roman road at Downshill House and continues down to the river, this road dates to the Anglo-Saxon period or earlier. The banks down its length are about 2m high and 1.5 wide, the road itself is about 1.5m to 2.5m wide. Archaeologists believe the movement of stone and logs caused the wear on the road, (possibly when Offa cleared the hill of trees to build the dyke and give a good view to Wales). It seems that he could have had the trees dragged down to the river so they could float downstream and be used to build his castle and city wall around Hereford in A.D.760, which were recorded as being built of wood.

The hill stayed as a green grazing common from this period right up until the 1811 Enclosures Act. Another piece of evidence of Anglo-Saxon occupation comes from the name of an open field called Hoarstone, an Anglo-Saxon word meaning a prehistoric standing stone. These standing stones were used as boundary markers or to mark the presence of a chambered tomb, but no trace of standing stones or tombs have survived Hoarstone Field[12] in Anglo-Saxon times was a huge open field covering approx 100 acres which straddled the Roman Road running from the back of Stonehouse up to Downshill House.

The boundaries of the parish were set in the 10th century when the Saxon kings made the payment of tithes compulsory, which meant a contribution of 10% of the villagers' produce went for the upkeep of the church. To determine which church you paid this to, parish boundaries were established, and as most of the new churches were serving an estate it was logical that the parish boundary would follow the estate boundary.

The church would have had an endowment of land when founded, called glebe land, the income from which was intended to support the priest. The villagers also had to pay to bury someone in the churchyard, while the lord of the manor would be able to appoint a priest of his choice to look after his flock. There is no doubt a wooden church was built in Bishopstone around this period; the site where the church now stands was reputedly used for pagan rituals and by building the church in this place it would have stopped the pagan worship taking place and also encourage the use of the church.
Great changes occurred in the ownership and layout of agricultural land in this period, the reason for and the details of which are still not clear today.
Alongside these changes in ownership of the land there was a gradual conversion from an enclosed network of fields farmed mainly by family units, to an open field system worked by a community. The important element of this so-called open field system was co-operation within the new community centred on the village. The old fields would have been opened up into usually two or three great fields, each of which would have been subdivided into furlongs. These in turn were broken down into individual holdings of land or strips, which were tenanted by the peasant farmer who would hold a number of them scattered around the fields. The community as a whole would meet and decide the crops to be grown in which field and when.
At the time of the Norman Conquest in 1066 Bishopstone was already farming open arable fields close to the village and further grazing land beyond

Norman period

After the Norman Conquest the surviving Saxon lords kept their lands, but after a series of rebellions their land passed to Norman successors including Norman Bishops. This was certainly the case with Bishopstone; where a Saxon lord originally controlled the whole area called Malveshille (gravel or sandhill) the Saxon name given to our hill.
The Domesday Book is England's oldest national record surveyed in 1086, and records that Malveshille was now divided, into military units of five hides each between the Bishop/Canons (Bishopstone), Grufydd ap Maredudd (Mansell Gamage) and the de Lacys (Mansel Lacy). There was still left a moiety of one hide (120 acres) lying between Mansel Gamage and Bishopstone in the Shetton area. The Domesday book records it as belonging to two Saxon gentlemen, Godwin and Uhehetel, their demesne (own) land valued at thirty shillings in 1066, reduced to ten shillings by 1086. Whether these were the original Saxon owners, or descendants of a Saxon Lord? We will never know.

(Figure 9) **Entry in the Domesday Book "Bissopestona (Bishop's estate) part of Malveshulle"**

(V hidae geldabiles.) **5 hides that pay tax**

One hide is around 120acres, which indicates the Manor contained around 600 acres.

(In dominio est una carruca et alia ociosa) **In Lordship 1 plough and another idle**

This refers to the ploughs owned by the lord of the manor, in this case the Bishop of Hereford.
"Another plough idle" means the Lordship had more ploughs than ploughable land. The survey carefully matches the area ploughed with each plough. There are only a few entries listing an idle plough, one each in Cambridge and Dorset and only one other, in Preston on Wye in Herefordshire.

(IX villani) **9 Villeins (Villagers)**

Villeins were peasant tenant farmers of higher economic status than borders; they were unfree because they and their possessions belonged to the lord of the manor. They each held around 30 acres of land that could be passed down with each generation. Their land, held in the common fields, was not fixed but moved yearly as decided at the manor court meetings. They paid their dues and services by working the lord's land. This entry indicates that a small Saxon village of nine households with about forty five people including children lived around the church. Each villein would have a piece of enclosed land around his cottage of up to 5 acres, as well as land in the open fields. They would have a garden, fruit trees in an orchard, hens, pigs, geese, a few sheep and a cow.
The livestock, including the oxen used for ploughing, would be turned out on to the waste and fallow open fields in the day but always brought in at night.

(prepositus) A Reeve

The person employed by the Bishop of Hereford to supervise the running of the Manor.

The Reeve set the days on which the villeins and bordars worked the land for the lord, normally ploughing services and reaping. He would live in the manor house where the court and village meets were held, possibly on the site of Court Farm today. This manorial system is normally associated with the Normans, but in Bishopstone was already well established in the Anglo-Saxon period.

(iiii bordarii cum vi carrucis et dimidium) 4 bordars with 6½ ploughs

Bordars (from borde-wooden hut) were of a lower economic status than a villein, also called cottagers, they had up to 5 acres of land for which they paid only small rents, and were often tradesmen like a carpenter or a smith because their land wasn't enough to support them.

The number of plough teams depended on how many oxen the community could provide. They were usually light ploughs pulled by just two oxen. Half a team could mean there was one spare ox left and so they could not complete a team. These ploughs could not plough very deep, unlike the Lord's eight ox team plough.

(i ancilla) One female slave

Domesday book recorded 739 slaves in Herefordshire but only 16 females. It is thought that they were mostly the descendants of the original Britons when the Anglo Saxons conquered Herefordshire or possibly Welsh people captured during one of the punitive raids carried out by the Earls of Hereford before and after the Conquest The value of a slave was one pound and they could be bought or sold like livestock. A horse was more expensive at 30 shillings, a mare one pound, an ox 30 pennies, a pig 8 pennies, a sheep 1 shilling and a goat only 2 pennies. Some slaves were Saxons who had sold themselves into slavery in times of crisis to ensure their family did not die of starvation. Slavery was also a penalty for certain crimes. The single slave listed in Bishopstone's returns would probably have been a domestic servant, working for the Reeve.

(vi acrae prati) 6 acres of meadow

These meadows were in the vicinity of the village where the present day church now stands. These meadows unlike the open fields were fenced and protected by a ditch. They were a vital part of the village economy, and were carefully enclosed for a period after Christmas until the crop had been taken off them in the summer. These meadows like the open fields were held in common, and each man had his portion allocated to him, either by rotation or by drawing lots. After summer the cattle and livestock were let on to the meadows, which made then more secure, they were the most valuable commodities the villagers owned as each was looked on as having more value than a slave. There was a continual threat of Welsh raids, carrying off women, slaves and most importantly livestock.

(Tempore regis Edwardi valebat iii librae et post et modo iiii libre)
In King Edward's time it was worth £3 and afterwards and now £4

After the Norman Conquest a survey was carried out in 1066 to value all their newly acquired land for tax purposes. The Domesday Book survey carried out in 1086 was more detailed so there was a more accurate account of the land value. The 33.3% increase in value Bishopstone had acquired over that period, could mean more acres had been put under the plough or it was undervalued in the first survey.

There were very few recorded churches in the survey as they were not taxable, but it is generally agreed by historians that most manors had a church of timber construction with a nave and chancel and a thatched roof. I am sure this was the case with Bishopstone.

Who were these nameless poeple who first lived and built the village of Bissopestona and how did they live? From the many studies over the years we have a good idea. They built the original village on both sides of the small stream fed by the spring on the hill; even today it never dries up and so would have provided fresh water for all their needs. It is estimated that around forty-five people including the men, women and children and extended members of their families would have occupied the village. Their responsibilities were limited to obeying orders, their requirements were minimal: a few faggots (bundles of wood) for their firing, a few branches for their roof, a meagre pannage for their pig. They did not have to plan; the Reeve did that for them, and simply following routine solved most of their problems. They did not have to think. All they had to do was work; starting their working life at about the age of six, they went on working until they dropped dead from fatigue, illness, hunger or old age, old by the time they were about forty.

Their houses or "cots" hovels would be a more appropriate word were strung out along the stream; single-roomed structures of timber, wattle and daub, roofed with straw or reeds laid over branches; no windows, no chimneys, no floor other than the earth. In fact there was precious little difference between these huts and those which had been built a thousand years before.

The walls were rather higher. The smells were much the same, for the sheep, pigs and chickens in most cases and for much of the year shared the accommodation with their owners.

Their furniture consisted of stools, benches and tables (boards to be exact), which they made themselves. They likewise made their clothes and footwear, from homespun wool and home-tanned skins. They made their wooden platters, bowls and cups, their tools and implements, the latter with a little help from the smithy and the carpenter in the village.
Cooking was done in rough but admirably tough earthenware vessels on open wood fires. The hearth consisted of two or three large stones, out of doors for most of the year, and only brought indoors in the worst weather. They ate coarse bread, gruel, cheese, vegetables, pease, boiled mutton and boiled bacon whilst it lasted, with occasionally a chicken, eggs, perhaps a rabbit now and then, though it is not at all certain that they were widespread in England at this date, roast beef never. All of them (except the slave) held some land, and it is surprising what can be grown on even one acre. Their basic drink, for young and old, was almost certainly ale, a weak brew made with fermented barley and the water from the stream. This was certainly the style of living for the occupants of Bishopstone and many other similar villages in Herefordshire.

The Medieval Village

In the reign of Henry 1 (1100-1135) Bicopeston was included in the new Norman Hundred called Grimwrosue (Grimsworth).
Forty-nine years after the Domesday Survey, in 1135, the first written record of Bishopstone spelt Bicopeston appears, in the Liber Niger de Scaccario (Black Book of the Exchequer).
Manor in tenancy of John. This is the first recorded name of a person who lived in the parish, not surprising because he was the lord of the manor and accountable for the tax to be paid. John was a knight or man-at-arms and would have been of Norman extraction. The Bishop's practice was to replace the Saxon reeves with fighting men. John carried the estate name as was traditional then and was known as John de Bicopeston. Having obtained the tenancy around the year 1125 he rebuilt the church in stone and his own manor house next to it. Expert opinions now differ on the moat, as to when was it dug. Some are of the opinion that it surrounded the original wooden Saxon manor house, others say it was dug at this time. The moat was used in a defensive role to keep out the raiding Welsh but also used as a fishpond to supply fish for the table on Fridays. What we do know is the stone to build both was probably salvaged from the Roman villa site 400m to the east and some possibly from Kenchester.
The stone from the ruins of the villa would still have been lying around because Saxons were very suspicious of Roman sites, which they believed would bring bad luck to the community if touched. The Normans did not share these beliefs so the site was cleared of useful stone to build the church and manor house, and the site turned back into plough land. It was incorporated into Hoarstone field and stayed a large open field for 700 years till the Roman floor and footings were uncovered when the new Rectory was built there in 1812.

(Figure 10) Roman stones reused in the building of the church.

The church was built to a simple design consisting of a nave 50ft by 20ft, with a small chancel on the east end approached through a narrow arch. The main parts of the north and south walls of the nave are original but the early chancel was removed in the 13th century when the new chancel and north and south transepts were built. It's worth looking at the walls, which are faced with small square hard grey sandstone blocks evenly coursed which experts have identified as Roman, they were second-hand and over 700 years old when used to build the church.
To celebrate the church being built from Roman stone could be the reason why the church was dedicated to St Lawrence after the Roman martyr.
When we consider the people who lived in the parish at this period it is perhaps not surprising that what little documentary evidence there is relates almost entirely to the lords and their manors.
In 1135 the Bishop of Hereford on the marriage of Princess Matilda with the Duke of Saxony gave the couple the services of one knight, who was John de Biscopeston [13]

When her father King Henry 1st died later in that year Matilda was his heir, but Stephen her cousin claimed the throne as the nearest male kinsman. The result was civil war so John with his servants left his home in Bishopstone to carry out his duty on the battlefield in support of Matilda. Herefordshire was in the front line and saw plenty of action; the town and castle were held by John and his comrades for three years, but was finally unable to withstand Stephen's forces. This civil war was intermittently waged for years until a compromise was reached whereby Stephen would reign for his lifetime but accept Matilda's son Henry as his heir later to become Henry 11. It's not known if John de Biscopeston survived this campaign.

Henry 111 in 1216 granted fourteen estates including Bicopeston to Alexander le Secular of Sutton.

1236 saw the Statute of Merton by which the lord of the Manor was entitled to enclose certain fields as long as enough waste was left for the villagers. Alexander is recorded as enclosing 100 acres of land around the manor house in Bishopstone.

On the death of Alexander, Nicholas his son and heir took over the estates but he died at a young age in 1272 before he could marry and produce an heir. The estates were split up between his five sisters. Alexander's second daughter Cecilia, inherited the manor of Bishopstone when she was around 20 years old. She then married Sir John Daniel a knight from Tydeswell, Derbyshire who had come to Herefordshire to help Edward 1 repel the Welsh, and the couple moved into the Bishopstone Court.

With John and Cecilia came money and the Manor became an important place in Herefordshire. The lives of the villagers would have improved as Sir John would have needed extra workers to maintain his charger, packhorses and for domestic duties. The normal pay for a villager (peasant) working the fields for the Lord was 1 penny a day and that was only when there was work, but to assist and travel with the knight into battle the pay trebled to 3 pennies per day. In 1278, shortly after their arrival, Sir John and Cecilia acted as patrons to the church for the first recorded rector of Bishopstone whose name was William.

Knights were the elite of medieval society, but this did not necessarily assure Sir John of an easy life, his practical skills would be acquired only after long and rigorous training. A detailed document[14] dated 1282 records that Edward 1 ordered the Bishop of Hereford to provide five knights to fight under the command of Roger Mortimer to help with his conquest of Wales. One of the five knights the Bishop provided was Sir John Daniel of Bishopstone, he was away fighting for 40 days and reached Builth (Builth Wells). When the town had fallen he followed Roger Mortimer back to Kingsland where he was discharged. On his return each knight was presented with a barbed horse.

Sir John Daniel died on April 14th 1286 and left a will leaving his part of the manor to Richard his eldest son, who was only 13 years old. Sir John was buried in Bishopstone church. After his death Cecilia rebuilt the east end of the church and founded a chantry by the deed given below. This all took place before 1288 as at that date she is listed as having paid a fine of £20 to marry at will. She then married her second husband Sir Richard de la Bere in that year. She died in 1292 aged about 40 years old. She left four sons from her first marriage, Richard aged 19, John, Nicholas and William who were all younger, and a daughter Rose aged two from her second marriage. I have included the full transcript of the foundation document as it gives a good insight into the society and agricultural life in Bishopstone in the 13th century.

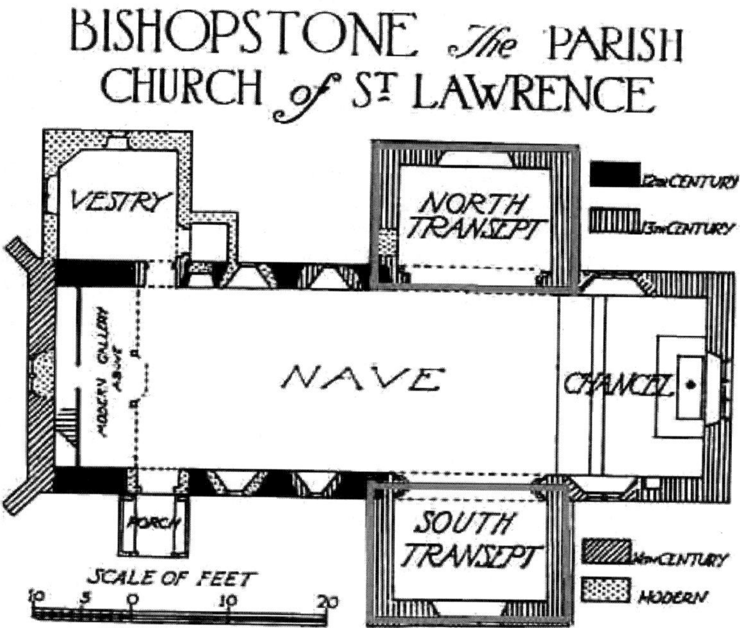

(Figure 11) North and South Transepts were built by Cecilia as Chantry Chapels.

Foundation of Chantry in Bishopstone Church[15]

I Cecilia de Secular an independent widow have granted for the upkeep of one chaplain to celebrate mass for the virgin Mary in Bishopstone church for my soul and the souls of Walter de Secular my lord (father), my children, my forebears and all those from whom I have received good, one messuage and curtilage [a dwelling house with small courtyard] with a croft and 17 acres of land in the village and area of Bishopstone. Also 6 seams (sacks) and 10 trugs (shallow baskets) of good well winnowed wheat and 16 trugs of well winnowed oats. 3 of the seams are to be given by Thomas le Porver and his heirs at 3 feasts viz one at the feast of St Denys (9th Oct), one at Purification (2nd Feb) together with 8 trugs of oats, and one at the feast of St Ethelbert (20th May), for the lands which he holds, viz for 14 acres of land assigned for that service. Adam son of Richard is to give 3 other seams of wheat and 8 trugs of oats for 13 acres of land which he holds, at the same terms, and Richard de Brugge is to give 10 trugs of wheat at the feast of All Saints, for the 3 acres of land which he holds in the vill of Newton. Also I grant to the said chaplain 14d of annual rent, which Walter Welsh pays for a certain meadow, which he holds, half to be paid at Michaelmas and half at the Annunciation.

The said Chaplain shall also have pasture for 4 cows, bulls or bullocks with my cows, but not in my garden nor in my meadows until the hay is carried. He shall have 40 sheep in my pasture with mine, except as above. He shall have 10 pigs with mine except in my wood of Wormesley. His own herdsman shall keep all these beasts. If it should happen that my heirs or I should not have beasts at pasture in the vill of Bishopstone, the Chaplain may still do so.

Also I grant that the said chaplain shall feast with me and my heirs four times a year viz for 3 days at Christmas (Christmas Eve, Christmas Day, Boxing Day), for 3 days at Easter, 3 days at Pentecost and 3 days at the feast of St Lawrence (10th Aug); if it should happen that the chaplain is not with us at those times he shall have for each feast 1 trug of wheat, 4 gallons of good ale and 4 dishes of cooked food from my kitchen.

The chaplain shall also have the straw from 10 selions (strips) of land wherever in the field he chooses. But if it should happen that the chaplain thus appointed by me or my heirs should behave very dishonestly or gossip or be a fornicator or adulterer or be litigious, or frequent taverns, or commit serious theft, or hold the divine office in contempt, then I and my heirs shall at once remove him and another suitable chaplain shall be presented to the Bishop of Hereford. If I or my heirs do not present another chaplain to the Bishop within three months of the death or removal of a chaplain, the Bishop may present a suitable person, but if I or my heirs find him to be doing wrong we will remove him and appoint another in his place. After the death or removal of a chaplain all the goods belonging to his holy office shall be assigned to my heirs and me until the appointment of another, but we shall not remove or take away any of them.

I will that in the mass of the Blessed Virgin, after the first prayer, the chaplain shall say the prayer for the dead for my soul and the souls of my Lord Walter and my children, my ancestors and all those from whom I have received good. The chaplain shall at his own cost provide the communion bread and wine and candles as required. If my heirs or I cannot find a chaplain to carry out this service in return for all the goods named above we may take them back into our own hands and maintain a chaplain ourselves.

And I bind myself and my heirs to faithfully and truly observe this and assign it all into the hands of the Bishop of Hereford so that he may enforce it without any conflict or dispute whether in common law or civil law. And I will warrant all things assigned for this service and quit them from all exaction, demand, suit of court, relief, heriot or service to the crown. And I have set my seal to it with these witnesses:- Warin de Grendon, Richard de Clehonger, Simon de Bridge (Sollars) Richard de Kinnersley, John Russell, Thomas la Power of Bishopstone, Richard New of the same, Richard de la Weir (From the Old Weir) William of Bunshill and many others.

This deed was rewritten in 1531 after a dispute arose over endowments and is entered in the register of Bishop Charles Bothe. The original document must have been in a damaged condition, the copyist misread Alexander as Walter so jumped to the conclusion that he was her husband. She is more likely to have asked for prayers for her father than her brother-in-law; the only Walter who could have appeared on the document is Cecilia's brother-in-law, Walter de Fresne, Lord of Moccas who was married to her elder sister and co- heiress Alice. The original may have been written in French as all the surviving documents relating to Cecilia are recorded in French, so we can only presume it was her native tongue and that she was of Norman descent. From the deeds we can learn that Cecilia had many servants, a kitchen contained in a separate building away from the house, a garden positioned on the land between the church and the house where she did not want to encounter livestock on visits to her private chapel, which she would have entered by her own private door on the north side. This garden would have included a carp pond, which is referred to in later documents.

There were no woods recorded in Bishopstone at this time. There are records of small woods at different times but Bishopstone stayed mostly wood free until the planting of the hill in the late 19th century. The woods at Wormsley that Cecilia refers to, appear to be part of Bishopstone Manor, as records from the rents book of 1704 list how many logs tenants of Bishopstone removed from Wormsley wood, and another 16th century document refers to Bishopstone pigs kept in Wormsley woods.

Why did Cecilia want to set up this Chantry? It was a general belief in the thirteenth century that prayers shortened your time in purgatory. and speeded your journey to heaven The only sure way to make this happen was to set up your own chantry foundation. It was a financial provision for the "chanting" of masses by a priest in memory of the founder and their family. It also extended the services available in the parish in a number of ways. Chantry priests frequently helped in the administration of communion at Easter time. They also provided more occasions on which parishioners could attend mass by officiating over the early morning "morrow mass" for the benefit of working folk. There was a very full daily round of prayer in churches before the Reformation, which meant they were used much more than now seems possible. The chapel in the north chancel was dedicated to Mary the Virgin, and provided an extra altar used mainly for the lord of the manor and his family. The south chancel was a chapel dedicated to St Ann (mother of the Blessed Mary) and used by the labourers. These chapels were in use right up until the Reformation when all the chantries were closed. Protestant ideas took hold, chantry priests were prevented from saying traditional Catholic mass for the dead, and the Protestant perception was that the prayers of others were not the means of salvation, which must rest on personal faith and actions.

(Figure 12) South Wall of the Chapel, the lower part was built with local sandstone, followed by a section of Roman stone recovered from the original Chantry

It is worth looking at the north and south chapel in the church, built by Cecilia. It's evident that the building of the walls of the chapels was started without disturbing the original chancel.

The north chapel was dedicated to St Mary in a service taken by John Bromfield on November 7th 1322.

With Cecilia's sudden death, it's not known if the work was completed before she died, but the chapels are a legacy, which she has left for us all to see and use today. This chantry deed was to support a chaplain who would have assisted William the Rector with services held at church

The executors of Cecilia's will[16] were Brother John, the Prior of Wormesley, Sir Ralph who was serving as chaplain of St Mary's Bishopstone by 1310 and Sir William de Brugge (Bridge). A court held in Hereford in 1310 lists the above people as creditors of the will for the sum of £8 and 1 mark. William the rector appointed by the Bishop in 1278 would have been a farmer and a priest, he would have to support his family and workers from the glebe farm and land on the south side of the church and glebe strips in the open fields, which totalled 18 acres. This would mean working along side the villagers at busy times such as ploughing and harvest.

After Cecilia's death there were many court cases over the estates of John Daniel and the le Secular family. Because John's eldest son and heir Richard was under age the crown took over his part of the estate until he was 21 years old. The Burghope family related to the Le Seculars took over some of their lands in Bishopstone, but they were never recorded as ever living in the manor, they lived in Burghope, a large estate now part of Wellington parish. The Daniels family were in a litigation battle with the Burghopes who took over the roll as patron to several Rectors for the parish.

Richard Daniel and his wife Rose had three children, Elizabeth born 1298, Katheen born 1300, and Joan born 1303. He died soon after his last daughter was born leaving the estates to his brother John.

This Sir John Daniel, like his father before him, served as a knight for service due from his manor in Bishopstone with the royal army fighting in Scotland in 1304. He was summoned to serve as one of the knights of the shire of Herefordshire in parliament in 1316.

John Daniel[17] gave land in Widemarsh for the erection of a Priory for the Preaching Friars which still stands today and is known as Blackfriars. His last campaign as a knight was with the barons fighting against the Despencers but he was captured and beheaded at Hereford in 1321.He was 46 years old and never married. He was possibly buried at Bishopstone Church.

Nicholas and William Daniel died without heirs so on January 23rd 1328, Rose their half sister went back to court to claim she was the rightful heir of Bishopstone, rather than Richard's daughters. On 30th March 1328 the estate was awarded to Rose and her heirs.

Going back to October 17th 1308 [18] the Sheriff of Hereford issued a writ against John Cobb who was a tenant farmer holding 45 acres in Bishopstone. At a full meeting of the Grimsworth hundred John Cobb was charged with violent crime and not attending court. It was proved that he had not been seen for a year and a day so the farm was placed into the king's hands. Felony was a hanging offence in those days so no wonder he disappeared. Afterwards a dispute arose as to whether these lands were part of the Manor belonging to Agnes, widow of Walter de Burghope, or of Roger Devereux, the dispute was settled in favour of Roger. It was recorded that the farm John Cobb held stood on the east end of Bishopstone Hill.

After much legal fighting the manor of Bishopstone was split into three as a result of an inquisition in 1316, which certified the three lords of the manor as John Daniels, Adam Fitzadam and Roger Devereux. From this point the parish lost its status in the county by not having a serving knight resident in the manor house. It would be 250 years until Humphrey Berrington in the sixteenth century, through inheriting part of Bishopstone and purchasing the other parts, made it back into one Lordship; only then did Bishopstone regain its status.

John Daniels held the lands east of the manor house centered on Bishon, Adam Fitzadam held lands on the west around Downshill, and Roger Devereux lands north west of the manor house up onto the hill.

John Daniels' portion was the largest, 284 acres of farming land plus the use of the common land.

The first recorded murder or manslaughter took place in Bishopstone in 1326. The case was heard in Hereford on September 28th .[19] It states that William son of John le Waleys (Welsh) of Bisshopeston killed William son of John in the Hale of Bisshopeston. The court gave William a pardon on condition he joined the king's army.

The Waleys (Welsh) family settled and lived at Bishon for many centuries afterwards. There was always tension between the Welsh and English, could this ill feeling be the cause of the dispute which ended in Williams' death? We can only speculate. It's ironic that by forcing William into the King's army he would at some time be fighting his kinsmen. There were not many Welsh people living north of the river at this time and this was still the case 200 years later when a survey carried out by Henry V11 showed only 5% of the population living in Grimsworth Hundred were of Welsh descent as against an average of 30% south of the river.

Going back to Rose Daniel she was a widow by 1327 so she called on the Devereux family to provide a knight for the Bishop. On March 24th 1327 Thomas (Devereux) of Bisshopstona was called by the king for service overseas with Vincent de Bergeveny parson of the church of Bisshopestona. With nine others they were called upon to accompany and provide protection for the Bishop on his journey to France.

Thomas Devereux of Bissopestona appeared in court in Hereford on June 20th 1334[20] after his return from France, when it was claimed that he and others, Henry de Brunshope, Thomas de Brunshope, (Henry's son) and Baldwin de Brugge (Bridge Sollers) with his brother Edmund and nephew Walter de Brugge broke into the deer park at Credenhill, hunted there and carried away deer. They were all pardoned. The king had granted to the manorial lords of the thirteenth century the right of free warren which gave them the right to hunt wild animals on their lands but prevented anyone else from doing so. But on the other hand, to follow and hunt deer, in such circumstances, was no trespass, for deer were "beasts of the forest", and not beast of the warren. So it seems in this case deer were wandering on to the manor's grounds. Thomas Devereux set up a hunting party with his neighbours and used this right to hunt the deer back to the park in Credenhill and kill them. It would have been easy to chase deer in the fourteenth century around Bishopstone as there were only a few meadows and fields around the manor house and church which were enclosed by hedges of fences. Mostly the countryside consisted of large open fields and wide common lands either side of Yazor brook. On horse back you could take a direct route to your destination between different local villages and manor houses.

Beasts of the warren were rabbits, hares, wild birds and doves, the peasants were not allowed to kill or take any for their own use as they were only for the lord's table. The doves were a nuisance to the peasants, the lord's dove house holding hundreds of birds would descend onto the peasants' fields taking their fill and fattening themselves for the lord's table at his men's expense.

The earliest deed relating to Bishopstone is held at Hereford Record Office. Dated 1345 it is written on sheep skin and is in excellent condition. It records the changing ownership of land in Chutinton (Shetton) and Bichopeston.[21]

I, Walter son of Godfride of Buford, grant to Roger Pichard son of Sir Roger Pichard for 27 shillings sterling paid into the hands of the said Walter by the said Roger, a certain messuage with crofts, curtilages and other appurtenances, which I formally held from Sir Roger Pichard of Standun {Staunton } and which lies in the vill of Chutinton. Together with free rents in the vills of Chutinton and Bichopeston as follows

1d	*(p a) from John Russel and his heirs*
6d	*from Henry son of Thurbarin of Chutinton*
3d	*from John son of of Chutinton*
1d	*from William son of Walter of Chutinton*
6d	*from William Faber {Smith} of Bichopeston (Blacksmith)*
2d	*from Adam of Hewe of Bichopeston*

Roger is to pay Walter a rent of one rose at the Feast of the Nativity of St John the Baptist [Midsummer Day]

Witnesses: Adam the Clerk of Staunton; John le Bonde; William de Mere; John Broche; John Russel of Chutinton and many others

The document is only a record of what has taken place, Walter would have met up with Roger at all the land referred to, together with all the witnesses; Walter would have picked up a handful of soil and put it into Rogers hand, after this had taken place the final act was for Roger to hand over the 27 shillings.This was carried out in front of many people, and legally the lands exchanged hands at this point. Hence the legal term "livery of seisin" which is still used today? The event was then recorded in a parchment document that was then placed on the altar in the church with Roger's dagger laid on top for everyone to see who now owned the land.

Walter wanted to keep some control of the land so a payment of one rose had to be carried out by Roger personally each year on Midsummer's day. Similar to what we call today leasehold, this was quite a common practice in those days. The other interesting fact is the mention of Walter the blacksmith at Bishopstone.

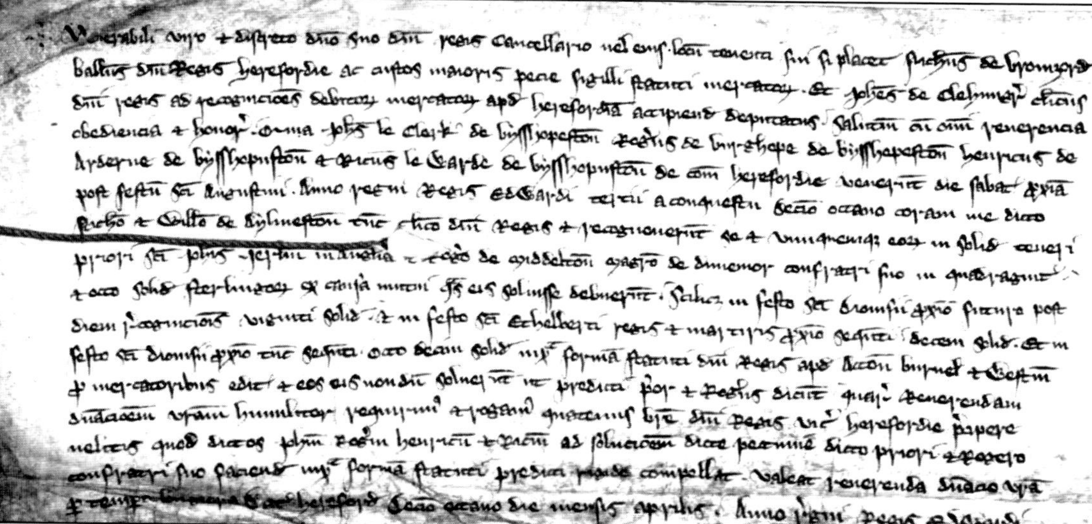

(Figure 13) Copy of original document dated May 1344

A document relating to Bishopstone, held in the National Archives, states that the Rector, John, together with Roger Burghope, Henry Ardene and Richard Warde had borrowed 48 shillings from the Knights of St John of Dinmore in May 1344 (possibly to repair the church). They had not made the repayments, so a summons was sent for them to appear before the court of Chancery in London. The Knights were the equivalent to modern banks in the 14th century. [22]

Chapter 2
Medieval

The Black Death arrived in Herefordshire in 1349. Within nine months the plague had swept across the county; records show that 40% of the clergy and between one-third and one-half of the people died. The only reference to Bishopstone in that year states that William de Radenore, the Sheriff of Herefordshire, died of the plague on the 6th June. He held lands in Bisshopeston consisting of[1]
A curtilage (Dwelling house and yard) yearly rent 4d; 25 acres of arable land, yearly rent 2s 1d (tenant Henry de Bishopeston; 3 acres of arable land, yearly rent 3d (tenant Walter de Stradhull).
We also know that the parson, Bartholomew Tynel, probably died of the plague Thomas Myles his "acolitus" (assistant) survived and was presented as the new Rector in early 1350, a position he held until 1359 when Sir John Eylesford persuaded John Pykering, a man of considerable wealth, to fill the vacant position as Rector of Bishopstone. John Pykering held the post until 1385. He was of a higher social standing than any previous rectors. John appears in four court rolls while he was Rector, taking different people to court for non-payment of debt in cases that involved large sums of money for this period.[2]

Ralph de Ferriers (Knight) & William Chamberlyn	April 20th 1355	100marks.
Thomas de Wandsworth	May 30th 1356	40marks
Thomas de Were (Skinner) citizen of London	May 10th 1370	80marks
John de Berley of Essex	May 28th 1375	200 marks

(One mark was valued at 13s 4d)
John was a well-travelled man, often staying in London and does not appear to have spent much time at his Rectory in Bishopstone. To cover his absences Sir John Eylesford put forward Hugh Harper, former Rector of Buildwas a parish near Bridgnorth in Shropshire, in 1380 to carry out the pastoral duties.
On July 14th 1384 Hugh was instituted as the new Rector of Bishopstone under the patronage of Sir John Eylesford and John Pykering himself. The reason for Hugh's investiture was that John Pykering had received a commission from the Bishop of Coventry and Lichfield, to travel to Rome. Travelling to Rome in the 14th century was not an easy assignment; the whole journey would be made on horseback, complicated by having to cross the channel on a small boat. John travelled with a large party, but it was still a hazardous journey with a high risk of being attacked, robbed or even killed. The party reached Rome in early January 1385 after travelling for six months but John died in Rome on January 22nd 1385.[3] Not knowing this, and not having received a resignation from Pykering, the Bishop of Hereford refused to recognize Hugh Harper as Rector, he served notice for John Pykering to return by October 30th 1385. After an enquiry it was discovered that the names on the commission and the subsequent institution to Bishopstone had been accidentally obliterated. Hugh Harper's institution as Rector of Bishopstone was finally and officially recognised on May 28th 1388[4] when the patron was Johanna widow of John de Burghope.
While John Pykering benefited from wealth and travel, the peasants of Bishopstone suffered hardships like all country labouring folk. The following verse comes from "Piers Plowman's Crede" written in 1394 which helps us understand their suffering.[5]

"And as I went by the way, weeping for sorrow
I saw a poor man by me, on the plough hanging
His coat was of a clout, that cary (coarse cloth) *was called*
His hood was full of holes, and his hair cut
With his knobby shoes, patched full thick
His tongue peeping out, as he the earth trod
His hosen overhung his gaiter, on every side
All beslobbered in mire, as he the plough followed
Two mittens so scanty, made all of patches
The fingers were worn, and full of mud hung
This fellow wallowed in the muck, almost to the ankle
Four heifers before him, that weak had become
You could count all their ribs, so wretched they were
His wife walked by him, with a long goad
In a coat cut short, cut full high
Wrapped in a winnowing sheet, to cover her from the weather
Barefoot on the bare ice, but the blood flowed
And at the end field lay, a little bowl
And on it lay a little child, wrapped in rags
And two of two years old, on another side
And they all they sang a song, that was sad to hear

Records show that between 1060 and 1349 the population of the average manor doubled, and so we can guess that between eighty to one hundred people were living within the manor of Bishopstone when the plague struck. With up to half the workforce dead, without enough labour to work the land, a lot of the open fields in Bishopstone, would have returned back to waste.

Bunshill has a wonderful set of court and manorial rolls from this period, which are held at The National Archives at Kew. When you come to the Bunshill section later in the book, these will give you a vivid account of the Black Death, and how it affected Bunshill. As it is in such close proximity we can only presume that it had a similar consequence in Bishopstone.

The other notable effect of the Black Death was the change in social structure due to the scarcity of labour. There simply were not enough survivors of the plague left to work the land, so those who had survived could demand more wages, or they simply moved to a different village where they were offered more money for their labour. The legal ties of servitude to their lord started to break down. We can deduce from the rent roll of 1385 that Bishopstone had followed this trend; it lists eighteen freemen and women living in the parish. Without a resident lord of the manor, there was very little interest paid to Bishopstone. The three owners of the lordships would have had enough problems dealing with their own respective home manors after the plague. Bishopstone land was rented or sold to anyone who was willing to work it.

The results of the Black Death can be seen in the 1377 poll tax which lists only 48 persons over the age of fourteen in Bishopstone liable to pay tax. It's been calculated by experts that in the 14th century with the immense dangers of childbirth and such a high level of infant mortality, a small village like Bishopstone would take five years to add just one new individual to its community.

On a 1379 tax document four names are recorded with holdings valued over 100s who were liable to pay tax in Bishopstone, John New (Court Farm), Walter Welsh (Bishon Farm), John Norris (Bishon) Edward Smith (Townsend Farm).These surnames can be found in documents relating to Bishopstone for the next 200 years as land ownership passed from father to sons.

John New de Bisshopeston appears as Clerk of the King's court from 1362-1394, sitting in the Hundred Court, his name appears on many documents of the period.

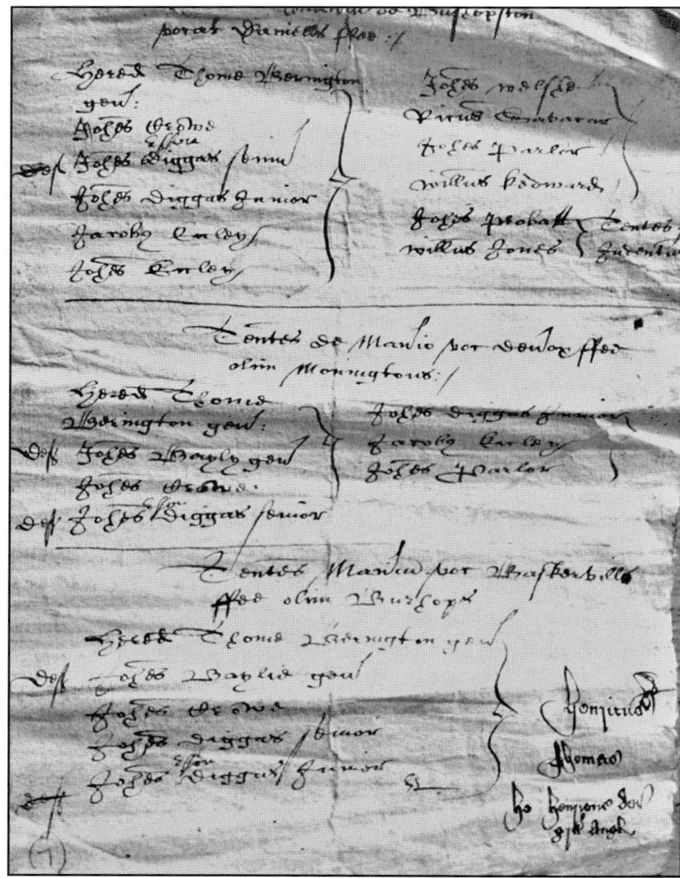

(Figure 1) Rental Roll of Bishopstone written on animal skin this one has survived in good condition

The Daniel rent rolls of Bishopstone are some of the earliest manuscripts held in the Foxley collection, there are six rolls dated 1385, 1436, 1468, 1500, 1520 and 1590. They all relate to the one third of the Manor originally in the ownership of Richard Daniel who in his will of 1327 list the rental value of his messuages and lands in Bishopstone as £4. All the names on the list are freemen and women except the clergy, some are ambitious villagers who survived the plague and have risen to join a new social rank, that of the yeoman farmer. The rent paid is called the chief rent, which all freeholders paid to the lord of their manors. Historically this set of rent rolls is invaluable because it enables us to trace land ownership in Bishopstone throughout the 14th and 15th centuries. The Daniel family had lived in the manor house for three generations, but when Rose Daniel died, it was let out to John le New who occupied the house until he died in the 1390s. William Daniel, a distant relative who lived in Burghill, inherited Rose Daniel's lands in Bishopstone. After the death of John le New, William and his family moved into the manor house, his descendants continually occupied the house until around 1490 when the Gomonds of Byford inherited the Daniel part of Bishopstone.

Byshopeston[6] Rental of William Danyell made 9 Richard II [1385]

1385		Around 1415
Walter Walsch	5s 8d	now Thomas Walsch
Roger Walsch	2s 10d	now John Walsch
Henry le Taylour	8s	now Richard Smyth
John Norrys	1¼d	now John ap Ithell
Edward Smythes	2s 2d	now Margaret Edwards
Thomas Macke	2s 4d	now Margaret Edwards
Henry le Smyth	3d	now Richard Penour
Margery Robynes	13s 4d	now Richard Smyth and Margaret Edwards
John Clerk	18d	now Thomas Watkyns and Richard Penour
Joan le New	2s 6d	now John Walsch
Joan Breye	10d	now to the altar of St Mary
John Smyth	23d	now John ap Ithell
John le Grand	2s 6d	now John Peer
Walter le Clerke	2s 6d	now Thomas Watkyns
John Bernes	12s 4d	now John Walsch
Giliana Heynes	4d	now the said John Walsch
William Shipward	2d	now Richard Penour
John le Newe	2d	now John ap Ithell
John Kynardysley	8s	now Richard Smyth
Roger Symond	3s 8d	now Matilda Parlour
Total	£2 18s 1¼d	

The names in the left column relate to the year 1385, the right column was written when updating the roll in around 1415. Interestingly the holdings of twenty people in 1385 were condensed to just ten in thirty years, this could relate to a change in farming practice or the general decline in population experienced in most villages.

The land William Danyell collected rent from was mostly east of the lane to the church including Bishon, 287 acres in total. The division of manors left a messy and complex system of land ownership, between the different manorial lords, this certainly was the case with Bishopstone where there were no definite boundaries and some of their strips in common fields and enclosed plots could be in other parts of the parish. There were four main farmers in Bishopstone and they all rented or owned lands from the three lordships; and from these rolls it is clear that the farmers and smallholders of Bishon started to segregate themselves from the main village. They enclosed land around their properties; developed their own open field system, and common land. This situation arose from the devastating effect of the Black Death, the few villagers who survived could only cultivate the open fields around the village, leaving the outer fields to return to waste. A few enterprising farmers, smallholders and villagers bought the freehold land around Bishon from the Daniel family.

Edward Smith had gained the freehold of the Townsend Farm and enclosed some plots of land around it. The other two lordships combined held the original open field systems running around the eastern side of the hill with their common on top. This segregation caused some problems and jealousy at the manor court meetings because Bishon fields were flat and easy to work, whereas some of Bishopstone fields, because of the slopes of the hill were awkward and difficult to work. The Daniel rolls list four messuages (farms), seven smallholders plus six cottages in the village by the church. The cottagers were only paying a few pennies rent per annum, John Norrys paid 1¼d rent on one such cottage. Next came seven smallholders paying around 2s to 3s for between six to ten acres of land, these smallholdings were scattered out from the village along the road to Bishon. Margery Robynes farmed one hundred and twenty acres in Bishon paying a rent of 13s 4d per year. The Walsh brothers occupied Bishon Farm; the cellar of their medieval farmhouse is still in use today as the cellar of Bishon Farm.

Let me explain: When Bishon Farm house was built in the 1670s on the site of the original medieval house they reused the cellar, which is much older than the present 17th century farmhouse. The 20th century 240 acre Bishon farm, was in the 14th century divided into two main farms and many smallholdings.

The surnames on the list are worth a second look. Before 1250 peasants generally had no surname. Surnames became necessary when government introduced personal taxation called poll tax. They are of interest to us, not merely because we still have them but because in their origin they tell us something about the person who bore them. They tell, for instance, where a person came from, Bishopstone's Walter and Roger Walsh's family originally came from Wales as their surname suggests; John Norrys's family lived in the north of the village.

Other surnames originate from a person's occupation, such as John Clerk and Walter le Clerk (both men of the church), William Shipward (Anglo Saxon for a shepherd), Henry le Smith (blacksmith in Bishopstone), Edward Smith (descendant of a blacksmith), Henry le Taylor (tailor in Bishopstone, John le Grand (French name for a large man), who occupied the New Inn site, paying 2s 6d a year rent, and finally John le New so named because he was a new John who had come to live in the village.

Another illustration of how names developed from the places people lived in the parish comes from a deed dated 1399, that graphically demonstrates this theory.[7]
1 Richard Wodende of Bishopstone
2 Richard of Exale of Bishopstone
Quitclaim of a farm and ½ virgate of land in Bishopstone at the Wodende place
Witness William May, Henry Smyth and others.
From this point on Richard Woodend and his family would always carry the surname Woodend, born from the fact that he occupied a farm at the end of a wood in Bishopstone in the 1390s.

A deed dated March 20th 1389 states that John Devereus and Philip Holgot, Lords of Bishopstone Manor grant to Phillip Strode and Agnes his wife for their life a messuage called Arnaldus and six acres of land lying in Oxfield, Windmill field and Puckwell field. Witnesses, John De Eylesford knight and others[8].

(Figure 2) Post type 14th century windmill, Bishopstone's windmill would have been of a similar design.

This was the first mention of the windmill at Bishopstone, which is recorded as working for the next four hundred years; it was blown down in the great storm of 1799, when 200 windmills in England were destroyed, of which Herefordshire lost 38. The Bishopstone windmill was positioned in Lower Hill Field (See map chapter 3) the best position to catch the prevailing wind from the southwest. It was a post mill that was operated by turning a tail beam manually so the sails would face the wind.

The power of the Bishopstone lordships, changed throughout the 14th century as the Daniel family's importance waned, and that of the Devereux family grew. The Devereux lands in Bishopstone made up only a small part of their large holdings of estates, with Bishop's Frome as its main base.
Sir John Devereux [9]in 1369, with a military tenure at Bishopstone, fought with the Black Prince in France and rose through the military ranks to hold the military posts of Constable of Dover Castle and Lord Warden of the Cinque Ports. He added £100 to the chantry endowment of Bishopstone church in 1385 and died in 1392. In his will each poor man who attended his burial was given a penny to pray for him, he gave 11 marks to the Greyfrairs, and as soon as possible after his death he ordered 1000 masses to be said for his soul and the souls of his father and mother. His son John died without heirs in 1397.
His sister Joan, wife of Walter fifth Baron Fitzwater, owner of the Castle and Manor of Lentales and Dorstone inherited the Devereux estates including one third of Bishopstone.
Another third now belonged to Philip Holgate who was a lawyer in the county and had purchased estates including Bishopstone from Sir John Eylesford.. Sir John had inherited the estate from the Burghope family.
William Daniels owner of the last third lived in Bishopstone Court house.
In 1400, Bishopstone Manor was split into these three lordships: Philip Holgate (Burghill), Joan Fitzwater (Dorstone) and William Daniel.

The preceding paragraph relates to the Lords of the Manor, but what about the villagers for whom no such records exist? We know around eighty adults lived in the parish before the Black Death, all worked the land except for the blacksmith, carpenter, tailor and a few other skilled workers.
Their cottages were of simple cruck construction, with main timbers of curved uprights (crucks) placed opposite to each other and a ridgepole running the whole length of the house and holding the various pairs of uprights firmly. On this a rough framework of hedgerow timber was used for the roof and walls. The walls had sticks placed between the uprights, twigs were woven in and out between them forming a sort of crude latticework, and on this was thrown the daub (a mixture of mud and cow dung) till it reached the required thickness.

Finally the roof was thatched. Such a cottage was easily built with the help of the village carpenter and required no great skill in setting up. There was no chimney and smoke from the fire escaped the best it could from the door, windows and crevices. The fire was made on the bare floor usually in the centre of the room. This type of cottage had a life expectancy of around fifty years until it needed rebuilding, and this pattern of building lasted well into the 18th century.

Many of the priests in Herefordshire during this period were described as from peasant stock. Bishopstone church with its two chapels was a prominent church in this period, with 18 acres of glebe land, a rectory, tithes money from the manor, rich patrons, two chantry priests to assist with the services, all this added up to make Bishopstone an attractive parish for a rector. The chantry priest of Saint Mary's Chapel also had many benefits, a house and a very attractive package of land and goods from Cecilia's endowment.

After Sir John Devereux was beheaded, Rose Daniel inherited the living of Bishopstone and took over the patronage of the church. Rose paid Walter de Hurtsley to study, so he could become the new Rector. The Bishop granted him two years to study and he was Ordained in Wigmore church on May 29th 1333 as an acolyte (assistant priest) and then instituted as Bishopstone's rector on September 18th 1333.

Diocesan visitation reports of Herefordshire in 1397[10] are regarded as one of the most complete records of parish life in the 14th century. It was important to the church to find out how well a parish was run, as well as reporting on the state of the church buildings and parsonage houses. The visitation process was a formal and well-organised regular event, 281 parishes carried reports. 44 of these the parishioners reported, "all is well." In the remaining parishes the main offenders are the laity, but with surprising frequency the clergy are involved, there are sixty mentions of clerical offenders. Rectors and vicars are again and again denounced as fornicators and adulterers, keeping women from their husbands, while some parsons were recorded as drunkards and tavern haunting.

The Bishopstone entry is no less incriminating with parishioners saying that Sybilla wife of John Norris, is a common defamer of her neighbours, where she has stirred up scandal in the parish; and especially that the same Sybilla falsely and maliciously defamed Rose Daniel, grandmother of Alice, wife of Edward Smythe, asserting her to be an adulteress, to the effect that the said Alice, heiress of the said Rose, lost her inheritance, owed to her by law.

This statement was verified the next year in 1398[11] when, Margaret widow of Sir John Devereux (Tillington) and Phillip Holgate (Wellington) the other Bishopstone landowners brought an action of ejectment at the Hereford assizes, against John Northfield (Chaplain) and Alice Smythe, grandchildren and heirs of Rose Daniel. It was claimed that their mothers were the illegitimate daughters of Rose Daniel and that they had obtained possession of the properties and land by deceit. The jurors discredited this statement and the verdict was given to John and Alice. Edward and Alice Smythe lived in Townsend Farm; John the priest lived in Saint Mary's House standing next to the churchyard.

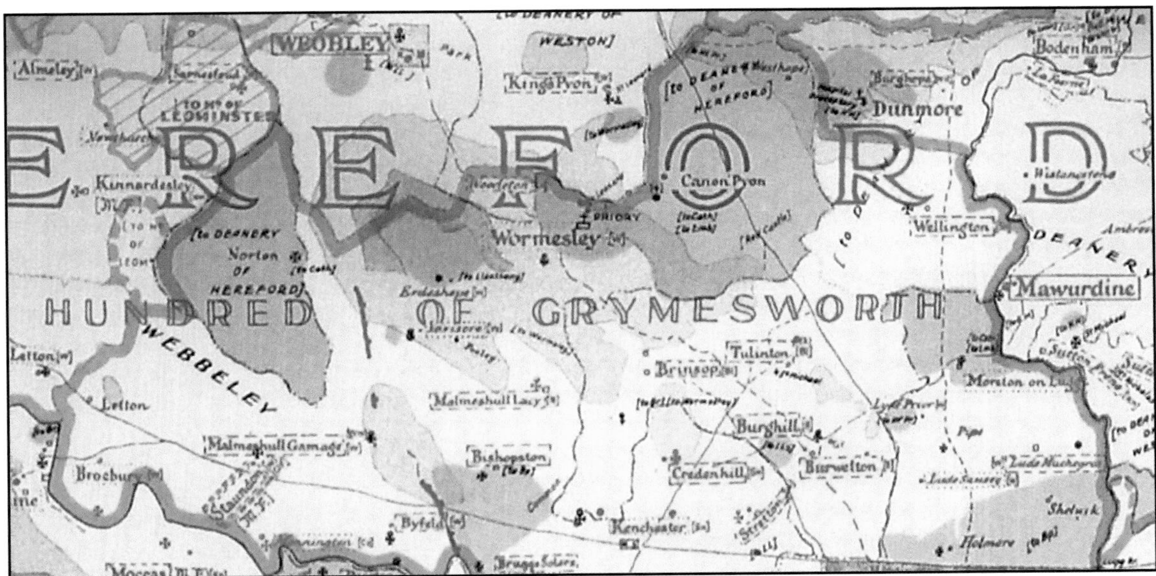

(Figure 3) Map of Grimsworth Hundred in 1400, area shaded in blue were Manors belonging to the Church either the Bishop of Hereford or Deanery. Note the Roman road marked on the map as the main route to Kington.

1400

(Figure 4) KING HENRY V

The new century brought a time of unrest for Herefordshire. The Welsh had begun a rebellion against the English in 1401 and by 1403 the Welsh army had advanced into the west of the county and were threatening the city. To counteract this, Henry V arrived in Hereford that summer and assembled an army. On the September 15th 1403 he led his army out of Hereford. Records state that he headed to Eardisley Castle, following the river Wye but staying on the north side, and based on this information the King would have led his army through the parish of Bishopstone that day. This is the only record I have found of a king leading his army through the parish. The cottagers on the edge of the Bishopstone Common and the peasants working in hill field would have had a good view of the approaching army led by the king.

Joan Fitzwater[12] (owner of a third of the manor of Bishopstone) died in 1412 and because her son and heir Humphrey was under age the King held the land on his behalf (this was the usual practice and when he reached the age of twenty-one the title deeds were handed back). During this period their portion of Bishopstone was let to John de Bodenham at a rent of £4 per year out of which he gave 13s 4d to the King while the remaining £3 6s 8d went to support the incumbent.

In 1422 Humphrey Fitzwater came of age and inherited one quarter of Bishopstone. It appears that part of the Fitzwater holdings must have been sold off, as his land holding in Bishopstone had been reduced from one third to a quarter. Philip Holgate[13] seems to have increased his holdings in the parish as he is now listed as patron of the church. As a lawyer he split his estates into trusts. His son and heir Thomas who died in 1468 was M P for Herefordshire in several parliaments and listed Bishopstone as part of his estates, which were inherited by his two daughters Eleanor and Alice. The subdivision of ownership in this manner increased by intermarriages, caused such uncertainly as to the right of presentation to the rectory, that on two occasions the aid of jurors, under a writ, was required to settle claims.

Alice Holgate, the younger daughter and co-heiress of Thomas Holgate, married Hugh Monnington of Westhide and on his death she married Richard Walwyn who was given the right of presentation on June 14th 1448.

The bitterest of civil wars, The Wars of the Roses between the houses of Lancaster and York dominated Herefordshire in the fifteenth century. Most of the barons in Herefordshire fought for the cause of Richard Duke of York, the Earl of March who had inherited the earldom through his mother, the daughter of Edmund, the last of the male line of the Mortimers who died in 1425.

Part of Bishopstone, through intermarriage appeared in the hands of Edmund Mortimer at the time of his death. The King claimed Edmund's lands, this was disputed and on June 5th 1431 at the Chancery Court. John Duke of Bedford (who was warden of England, as the king Henry V1 was only 17 at the time) appointed John Meverall Squire of Throwley (Staffordshire) to seize the Bishopstone lands, eject the occupiers and keep the same for his use until further orders. John Meverall appointed his son Sampson Meverall Knight and Isabel his wife to hold the manor. A letter dated June 28th 1431 confirmed that this had been carried out.

In 1432 Thomas Daniels residing at Bishopstone Court is recorded as trying to bring Robert Bromwich to the Chancery Court, a royal court that the Archbishop of Canterbury, as chancellor of England, presided over.[14]

To the most reverend father in God and gracious lord the Archbishop of Canterbury, Chancellor of England.

Showeth meekly your poor orator Thomas Danyell of Herefordshire him grievously complaining upon one Robert Bromwich of the said shire how he and other two of the Marches of Wales unknown as yet, by the said Robert entreated and hired, oft times have lain in wait in divers places, armed in manner of war with jacks, sallets, gleyves, spears and daggers, to have slain the said Thomas Danyell in his own several grounds in Bishoppeston in the said shire. And for they could not meet with him after their intent, they in the same array went and entered the place of your said suppliant of Bishoppeston aforesaid and there they found him hacking with an hatchet in his hand and none other weapon upon him but as a naked man standing, and thought none harm to them nor to none other.

And they upon him made assault and him wounded in two places of his body, the one wound into his lights fast by his heart and the other into his body, the which were horrible and grievous, and him there left for dead. And from him forthwith they went to a sawyer of your said suppliant standing at his work in the said place and him grievously wounded in two places of his head and left him also lying there for dead, and it is openly known in all the country thereabouts. Wherefore your said poor orator in the most humble wise beseecheth you of your most reverend fatherhood and gracious lordship to grant a writ sub poena in the straightest wise of your gracious avise to make the said Robert Bromwich to appear afore you in the Chancery in all hasty time as is most goodly, and him to examine of this matter and then to see straight execution therein as the case requireth, in example to others for the love of God in way of charity. Considering gracious lord that the said Robert is flitting and voiding into the Marches of Wales and hath no substance of livelihood to abide upon within the said shire and also is greatly allied within the same shire and useth such riot and misgovernance and supportance of March men that your said suppliant dare not nor may not sue nor prevail against him at our law.

Simplified this means:

To the reverend father lord the archbishop of Canterbury chancellor of England.

(Figure 5) 15th century soldiers

Your humble servant Thomas Daniel of Herefordshire would like to bring a civil action against Robert Bromwich of Herefordshire and two unknown persons from the Welsh marches hired by the said Robert to kill me.

They were dressed in jacks (sleeveless padded tunic worn by foot soldiers), sallets (light metal helmet with outward curving rear part) and armed with gleyves (swords) spears and daggers. They lay in wait in several places within my own ground in Bishopstone but without success, they then came to my house dressed as above, where I was hacking wood with my hatchet and no other weapon on me, and was no threat to them. They attacked me, wounding in two places on my body, one to my intestines by my heart leaving me for dead. From me they went to my sawyer and grievously wounded his head in two places. Please can you issue a writ to make him appear before a Chancery Court very soon as he is moving in and out of the Welsh March (the border area where the normal law of England was not enforced as it was subject to "Marcher Law"). To bring this action proves that Thomas Daniel did not move in the circle of the powerful landowners of Herefordshire, so his only course of action was to appeal to the Chancery Court. Nothing happened because the order to reclaim the manor came from the highest authority in the land, the Duke of Bedford. It appears that Thomas Daniel could have been the victim of mistaken identity and because he was living in the manor house, the soldiers presumed he was the lord of the manor, since the other lords who had claimed Edmunds Mortimer's land in Bishopstone were not living in the parish. It may just have been an episode in a long running dispute between Bromwich and Daniel which took place then because Mortimer had died and so his tenants were seen as easy game, or part of something larger aimed against the Mortimers, or just part of the general mayhem on the Marches which at that point were a seriously scary place to live. Thomas must have recovered from this ordeal as we see him collecting rent for his lands in 1436, and also in 1451 he signed as a witness to a deed for a Thomas Penbrugge of Mansel Gamage whose wife inherited land in Bishopstone. He had died by 1486 when his wife Joan had taken over the rent rolls.

Rental of Joan Danyell lately wife of Thomas Danyell made 8 Ed IV [1468/9][15]

John Walsch with others	18s
Richard Smyth and Elizabeth his wife	22s ¾d
Joan Walsch	5s 8d
Henry ap Howell chaplain late Matilda Parlour	3s 8d
Thomas Smyth chaplain with others	2s 6d
Hugh Ragon clerk with others	9s ½d
William Botte chaplain with others	10d
John ap Ithell and Cecilia his wife	23d
Walter Melyn and Richard Watkyns	3s 3d
William Botte chaplain with others	14d
Thomas Nycoll for 1 messuage which he holds at will	16d

When Thomas Holgate's wife died in 1468, the part of Bishopstone, which she had inherited, passed to Thomas Holt and his wife Isabella. Isabella was Thomas Holgate's granddaughter. The clergy from the church had increased their land holdings as stated in the 1486 Daniels' rent roll, it lists three Chantry priests and the Rector Hugh Ragon as all expanding their holdings. John and Joan Walsh and Richard and Elizabeth Smith were occupying the two large farms in Bishon. We also have the first record of the Bythel family living in the parish John ap Ithel and his wife Cecilia (ap Ithel was an early version of the surname Bythel).

Thomas Smith a chantry priest who occupied the New Inn site plus 6 acres, The Church Ale was probably brewed on this site; the landholders would have given barley, to the church as tithes payment. This would have been brewed into ale and sold to raise money for the upkeep of the church; there were more than a hundred saint's days in the church calendar before the reformation, which might be celebrated. This enterprise would have developed over time into an Alehouse and when the Church distanced itself from the selling ale, the property was let out to tenants. A New Inn was built on the site in 1590. Thomas was the brother of Richard Smith owner of the Townsend Farm, descendant of Cecilia who left the Chantry endowment.

William Botte, chantry priest, lived in a cottage with 1acre in the village.

Hugh Ragon the Rector rented 52 acres from the Daniels plus 50 acres of glebe and church land, which meant he was farming 102 acres. Over the centuries; land had been left to the church so that the total church landholdings had increased to 50 acres by 1468.

(Figure 6) Artists impression, Bishopstone's 15th century Bowmen leaving the Church on a Sunday after divine service to walk up through the village to the practice ground.

On February 2nd 1461 the battle of Mortimers Cross in Herefordshire took place. We have no record of any of the residents of Bishopstone taking part, but we do know that by law every male in the village over 14 would have to practice with the longbow every Sunday after church service. The men and boys would walk up the village and practice on Bowman's Croft, a long meadow put aside for this purpose, which was situated on the left side of the lane leading to the church, opposite the Townsend Farm, and still carried that field name in the nineteenth century.

Chapter 3
1400-1600

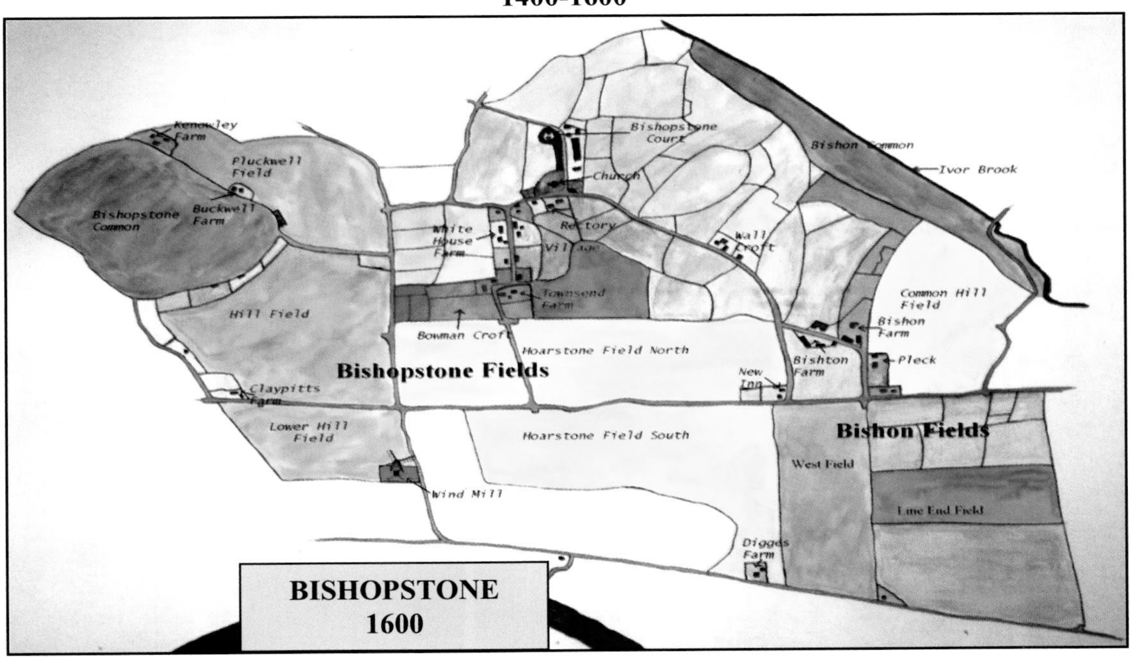

Documents relating to Bishopstone during the 15th century are scarce, although the Manorial Court met twice a year and the proceedings had to be recorded by law, no records of these meetings appear to have survived. Bunshill again has a wonderful set of records for their courts. For Bishopstone I have only found three court rolls, two in the 17th century when the manor was under the stewardship of Humphrey Berington, and another for a court dated 1554, recorded with other rolls of manors belonging to the Bishop of Hereford. The ecclesiastical records are comprehensive and go some way to make up for the lack of other documentation.

The Bishop still collected a small rent, plus a knight's service (to provide a fighting man for the Bishop when needed) from the three main landowners, Daniel, Monnington, and Baskerville. The Daniels had increased their holdings in the manor by 1460, their freeholders paid 2p per acre, this rent charge per acre stayed the same from 1386 until 1610.

The chief rent *(freehold land)* of **Danyells Fee** and after Gomonds Fee and after Byritons *(Beringtons)* Fee [this heading was written c 1590, the rental which follows written 1530[1]]

The lords of the manor of Byshopston be discharged of suit to the Bishop's court by a fair deed

The chief rent of Crowes land	*22s 5d*
The chief rent of Dyggas lands	*18s 00d*
The chief rent of Faukeners lands	*9s 00d*
The chief rent of Pennours lands	*14d*
The chief rent of Welshes lands	*5s 8d*
The chief rent of Parlours lands	*3s 6d*
The chief rent of Furges lands	*14d*
The chief rent of Mellyns Close	*9d*
The chief rent of Mellyns lands	*2s 6d*
The Close in the tenure of John	*6d*
The rent of Pers lands	*2s 6d*
The Lady's Close	*10d*

All of the messuages (farms) from the preceding rental have long disappeared, although the land on which four farms of the above stood can be traced and are listed below.

Crowes lands and Dygges lands today make up Bishon Farm

Mellyns Close relates to Pleck Cottage and Pers lands to the Stonehouse. (New Inn).

When Joan Daniel died, William Gomond from Byford inherited the Daniel lands; he also owned part of the manor of Byford. William married Elizabeth (granddaughter of Alice Holgate) and this further increased their holdings in Bishopstone as she was co-heiress of all the Monington lands. After their marriage they moved into Bishopstone Manor house; William died in 1503.

Elizabeth married her fourth husband John Chabner on November 9th 1509 in Bishopstone Church.[2]

The Church 1400-1600

If you had attended Bishopstone Church before the Reformation in 1549, you would have seen outside the church a large stone statue of St Lawrence, and a large cross high above the Church.

As you stepped inside the church, your eyes would have met a sea of colour, wall paintings illustrating stories from the bible and images of saints around the walls. The east end of the church was cut off by a large wooden partition of trelliswork elaborately carved, called the rood screen. Beyond this against the east wall stood the high altar where mass was celebrated, to the left and right were the chapels, each with a chantry altar, all these altars were covered with embroidered and jewelled cloths. There are decorative clothes on all the images, which are lit by candles burning around their bases, many more large candles would have been burning on the altars and stands, the whole inside of the church would have been glittering and flickering. Against this background you would have heard the priest and chaplains celebrate mass, hear confessions, say prayers for the dead, and petitions to the saints that underpinned people's lives

(Figure 1) This 1850 water-colour painting by Charles F Walker, illustrates how the Church would have looked in the 15th Century excluding the Yazor Church porch added by Rev Lane Freer in 1841. Note! The large cross on the east end and the St Lawrence griddle above the bell turret. Rev Lane Freer installed a new Victorian turret in 1854.

The priest was regarded with great respect, as a person by training and ordination set apart from ordinary people for holy duties. He was therefore not allowed to marry.

This all changed when the new Church of England held its first service in the church on Whitsunday 1549; gone was the glitter, although looking at the records it was a slow process of change in Bishopstone.

Rectors and chantry priests of Bishopstone between 1400-1600.[3]

1388-1412 Rector **Hugh Harper**

1412-1415 Rector **Hugh Ponyysbury**

1415 Rector **Walter Wales**, instituted as Rector of Bishopstone on August 17th 1415; Walter was a local lad, son of John from Bishon Farm. He would have been sent away to study, paid for by his patron Alice Edwards and Henry her son.

Alice Edwards was granddaughter of Rose Daniels who owned part of the manor of Bishopstone and had lived in the manor house. Henry her son married Margaret Pychard whose father owned the manor of Staunton on Wye.

1416 Chaplain **John Fourches,** instituted as Chaplain of the Blessed Virgin Mary's Chapel Bishopstone on June 26th 1416, John is also recorded as sitting on the jury to elect the new rector of Monington.

1428 Rector **Walter ap Ithell** (Bythel) Patron William Hare and Hugh Ragon

1448 Chaplain **Hugh Ragon,** instituted as chaplain on June 14th 1448, supported by Richard Walwyn, whose wifw Alice was heiress of Hugh Monington, landowners in Bishopstone

1465 Rector **Hugh Ragon,** Hugh the Chaplain became Rector of Bishopstone and Eton (near Sugwas). Patron the Bishop

1470 Rector **William Waters,** Patron Richard Walwyn and Alice widow of Hugh Monnington

1481 Rector **John Gough,** Patron John Baskerville in right of his wife Eleanor daughter and heir of Thomas Holgate. Reason resignation of Hugh Ragon

1488 Rector **Walter Waters**, Patron the fee of Joan Daniels. Joan who lived in the manor house had just died so her monies collected from rentals were used to support a rector. Reason resignation of John Gough

1490 Rector **Sir Walter Waters**, **Richard Smith** chaplain

Sir was a title used for priests as a mark of respect.

In 1542 an enquiry was held because there were four claimants for the right of patronage to the Church.[4]

1. John Chabnor, in right of his wife, widow of Gomond
2. John Chamberlain, in right of his wife Joanna the elder daughter of Elizabeth Gomond
3. John Patershall, son and heir of William Patershall, in right of his mother, Sybil, the younger daughter of William & Elizabeth Gomond
4. Thomas Monington

The result of this enquiry was that John Chabnor and his wife Elizabeth and her heirs were entitled in right of their moieties of the lordship of Bishopstone to two turns of the presentation in succession, and that at the next vacancy the right would devolve upon Thomas Monington and his heirs.

1542 Rector **Thomas Carpenter,** Patron John Chabnor and Elizabeth his wife. John Chabnor and his wife Elizabeth had died by 1546 so Thomas Monington then exercised his right as Patron.[5]

The following 1546 Visitation Return and Chantry certificate still survives.

Thomas Carpenter Rector
Sir John Matthews has the cure
John Phelpotts sen, Thomas Ellismor, Walter Crowe, Walter Digges
They want a bible on account of poverty ("Great Bible" (English) published in 1539), *the chancel is ruined, the chapel of St Mary (north) is ruined by default of Thomas Monington and Thomas Havard and the chapel of St Ann (south) is ruined. Each chapel is ordered to be repaired by Michaelmas*

The upkeep of the church fabric was important, so the Bishop inspected churches regularly; Bishopstone Church from the return above was in a very poor condition. The Bishop issued his instructions on the spot; these were entered into a "register" in which a record of the visitation was made so the Bishop could check up next time to make sure the recommendations were carried out.

Basically this is how the system should work. The lord of the manor as patron appointed the parish priest who was given a house and glebe land, and received annually a tenth part (tithe) of the produce of each parishioner's land. In return he was bound to keep his church and parsonage in good repair and carry out his religious duties. The upkeep of the nave was the responsibility of the parishioners, while the chancel came under the jurisdiction of the clergy and the patron looked after the chantry chapels. The church was in a poor state of repair and because of the long running dispute over patronage, nobody would take on the responsibility. Walter Crowe and Walter Digges were the churchwardens; both were freeholders owning farms at Bishon.

In 1547 Edward VI came to the throne at the age of nine years. A Council of sixteen nobles ruled the country, with a protestant leader, the Duke of Somerset. The accession of Edward VI speeded up the protestant reformation of the church and this resulted in the end of the chantry chapels

Bishopstone like all other parishes were ordered to produce a Chantry Certificate to estimate its value.[6]

Chantry Certificate 1548

The parish of Bishopstone ; houseling people (over 14yrs old) 68
A stipendiary priest within the said parish church there called Our Lady Service
Certain lands and tenements given by one Cecile Seculer to the intent towards the maintaining of a priest to celebrate in the said church to pray for her ancestors Incumbent:-none
The lands and tenements belonging to the same be of the yearly value of 20s 9d
Plate weighing by estimation 8 ounces, Ornaments valued at 3s 4d

Because most of Herefordshire still held to the Catholic faith, many valuable items were hidden by the parishioners in the hope that they could bring them out later, although Bishopstone did comply with the orders by taking some of the listed valuables into Hereford. Somerset's government then sold off chantry lands (in Bishopstone consisting of St Mary's House and land and Mellyns Close (The Pleck) with its land). Bishopstone parishioners painted over the wall paintings and removed the rood screen so when the officers came to inspect, it looked as if they had carried out the government requirements.

The stone altar was also supposed to be removed and replaced by a wooden table but some ingenious person in Bishopstone enclosed the top in a wooden frame to disguise it. This stone top, still used today has five roughly carved crosses; a symbol of the five wounds of Christ, I believe it is the orginal altar top and dates from before the Reformation. They also hid their Catholic chalice.

On Whitsunday 1549 the Rector of Bishopstone Thomas Carpenter carried out for the first time the new service using the new English prayer book.

The commissioner reported in 1553 that the church goods consisted of chalice and paten silver gilt, weighing 12.5 ounces, with two bells. The same year Queen Mary succeeded to the throne and as she was a devout Catholic, the chantry chapel was reinstated and catholic worship was again taking place in Bishopstone Church.

1554 Nicholas Philpot was appointed as the new curate with Richard Monnington as patron.

Queen Elizabeth 1st succeeded to the throne in 1558, new laws were introduced which said every person had to go to church on Sunday morning and stand there quietly till the service was over, they had to receive the sacrament at the major feasts. If they did not appear, or take sacrament the churchwardens could fine them.

(Figure 2) These three vessel holders used in Roman Catholic worship are still present in the Berington Chapel (North transept) of Bishopstone Church (they would have been originally above an Altar). In St Anne's Chapel (South transept) you can clearly see the marks in the east wall of three holders, these were removed in the 1548-49 period, broken off possibly with the help of a large sledgehammer.
Photo 2010

Rev Wilmot in an article written for the Woolhope Club in 1912 writes, "Local tradition has it that the north transept, which was the Berrington Chapel was used for Roman Catholic worship concurrently with the reformed Church in the nave, access being through a door at the west end." This arrangement seems to have carried on for the next 100 years or so especially with the Beringtons as Lords of the Manor being of a very strong Catholic faith.

1580 John Price was appointed the new rector with John Berington as patron

The 1582 Bishop's visitation report of Bishopstone[7]
Moryce Pope Churchwarden, Thomas Welshe Churchwarden, Richard Crowe Parishioner, James Eckley Parishioner
They present that the parson was absent from his benefice for four score days together.
That they want and lack monthly and quarterly sermons.
That Thomas Bridges Gent does not come orderly to church nor has received communion three times in a year.
The chancel is decayed and wants glass in default of the Rector, to be repaired and certified by Michaelmas on pain of 10s. Another chapel is decayed in default of John Chamberlain Gent as above.
They want a Communion cup, in default of the Rector.
(This may mean that they are still using the old Catholic chalice which had been ordered to be destroyed 33 years earlier)
Pain means a find that had to be paid to the diocese if the work was not carried out in the time specified

In 1584 Nicholas Philpotts is recorded as the new rector
1584 Bishop's visitation report
Nicholas Philpotts Rector.
Thomas Bridge and John Digges Wardens
We do present the church is in decay of tiling and glazing in default of the parishioners.
Midsummer to amend the same on pain of 3s 4d and to certify at Hereford the Saturday following upon the pain.
That the chancel is in decay of glazing in default of the parson, midsummer to amend on pain of 3s 4d and to certify in Hereford Item we had not our quarter sermon Otherwise all is well

Although John Berington was now Lord of the manor and had brought some wealth to the parish, the Church was still in need of repairs. There appears to have been some animosity between John Berington and Nicholas Philpotts the rector. Nicholas was also vicar of Bridge Sollers, where he lived; the glebe land and parsonage of Bishopstone, were let to Thomas Berington, John's brother. [8]

Parish of Bishopstone 1589 (Glebe Terrier)

To the 97 we do present John Berington Esq to be the patron of the Church, Item there belongeth to our parsonage first 10 acres in Eydon Croft which shooteth upon one meadow of his own being 2 acres of ground. Item in Powckehole Fylde 3 acres of arable ground shooting upon the Dingle Lane and at the other end of the same 5 acres more. Item in Elborlane [Ebborlane?] 2 acres shooting upon Parllors land. Item 3a shooting up to Bishopstons Hill. Item in the Hill Fylde 10a shooting down to the highway leading towards Hereford. Item in Upper Hill Fylde 4a shooting upon the land of Mr Dalahaie at both ends of the same.

Item 4a shooting down upon the highway leading towards Hereford. Item 1a at the head of the same. Item in the Lower Hill Filde, 1a at the Cley Pitts. Item 4a in the same length of land shooting upto the highway and shooting upon the land of James Eccley at the other end. Item 2a shooting upon the Mill Fylde and to the highway aforesaid. Item 2a more shooting upon the same Mill Filde. Item in the Horestone Filde 5a in the Sand Pittes and abutting on one meadow of John Digas. Item 2a abutting upon one croft of the parson's and 2a more at the head of the same. Item 1 other acre at the Horestone abutting upon the highway. Item 3a in Prestle abutting upon the land of Richard Crowe. Item 4a shooting upon one croft of John Phelpotts called the Pewe Croft. Item 4a abutting upon the land of Mr Dallahaye at both ends. Item 1a shooting upon Downeshalles Gobbett. Item 1 dwelling house, 2 barns and 1 outhouse for cattle, and Thomas Berington gent is tenant to the parson and no more to this article we cannot depose. Richard Ornell and Richard Savicour churchwardens Richard Crowe, James Eccley and John Watkings sidesmen.

(Figure 3) 1589 Glebe terrier

This glebe terrier, the first of only three surviving terriers for Bishopstone, gives the first real details on the parsonage, which really was a working farm with some 12 acres around the house and barns opposite the church, and the remaining 55 acres in the common open fields. The parsonage lands can still be found on the 1770 estate map and are easily identified. The field names Hoarstone, Hill, Pluckwell, Lower Hill and Claypitts still existed as open common fields in 1770 although, as in many early records, the spelling differed depending on the writer.

The new lord of the manor of Bishopstone came from the very wealthy Berington family. Humphrey Berington built a new manor house in Bishopstone between 1560 and 1565; he demolished the old medieval house built in the 13th century to build his new house within the moat enclosure.

John Berington became the patron of the new rector John Price in 1580, he appointed a new rector Humphrey Duppa in 1589 as the sole presentee to Bishopstone Church.

Digges of Bishopstone

An entry in the Bishop of Hereford's rentals dated around 1400, from the lands of John Danyell at Bishopston 7s, from 1 messuage of Walter Dugge 20d, from 1 tenement of John Dugge 10d, 8d paid. Dugge appears to be a form of Dygges. This was the first record of the Digges family living in Bishopstone, they played a major role in Bishopstone for the next 300 years as churchwardens, freeholders, and large landholders, building a squire's house and ending up as gentlemen of the same social status as the Beringtons. Their story is recorded in over 100 deeds and bonds held in the Foxley Estate records, retained after the Digges' land holding in Bishopstone was sold to Robert Price of Foxley in 1709.

Throughout the 15th century the Digges family are recorded as occupying two small freehold farms in Bishopstone, but at the beginning of the 16th century the family decided to expand and bought most of the Welsh's freehold land. In a deed dated February 5th 1530, Walter Digges purchased 2 messuages (farms), 120a of arable, 6a meadow and 6a pasture from William Bradford, Christopher Digges, and Thomas Williams in east Bishopstone called Bishen.

When Walter died in 1542 Nicholas his son inherited the Bishopstone lands, which he leased to a William Watkins. Nicholas died in 1552 and he left a will.

I find there is nothing morbid about wills but they are rather fascinating, not as symbols of death, but to find out more about the person who left them, and their family and friends left behind. They throw light on the houses and the customs of the time. It would not do to print all the Bishopstone wills that I have recorded in full, as they would become boring. I will use some extracts, or the will in full sometimes if it represents part of the parish history. The wills of this time were normally written in the last few days of the person's life, and with a little imagination one can see those old or infirm people lying propped up in bed, one can hear the quill of the Rector, in this case Thomas Carpenter scratching the parchment. From the following will it's possible to tell that Nicholas was not married and he does not appear to be very religious, although he left money to the Cathedral. Normally the wills start with "First I bequeath my soul to God Almighty" and if they were Catholics this was followed by "To his mother Saint Mary and unto all the holy company of heaven". It could be that because it was made just after the reformation, Thomas Carpenter was not sure of the correct wording.[9]

An abstract of Nicholas's Digges Will dated July 1552.

"I bequeath my soul to the Trinity, St Mary and all the saints".
I am Sick in Body, whole in mind and of perfect memory, my body to be buried in the enclosure at Bridge Sollers Churchyard. To Hereford Cathedral I leave 6d.
William Baylye gent of Bridge Sollers, Thomas Carpenter the parson of Bishopstone and James Carpenter of Kinnersley as appointed in my deed of feoffment are to stand seized of my messuage, lands and tenements in Bishopstone, to pay my debts and funeral expenses and then to pay the profit arising from the said messuages to my brothers John Digges and Thomas Digges and Katherine and Margaret my sisters for 6 years, and then to my brother John Digges and his heirs forever. If John dies without heirs, then to Thomas my second brother and his heirs.
Whereas I have leased all my said lands in Bishopstone to William Watkins, if it pleases God the said William to occupy the same lands at a yearly rent, except one house called Over House in which George Hughes now dwells to Katherine Digges, this was rented to the said William for 4s
To Thomas my brother 1 heifer, To Elinor Caldicote 6s 8d
William Baylye and James Carpenter to be my executors
Witnesses, Hugh Rumsey clerk, Thomas Barold, William Watkins, William Caldiott. John Price

The Digges' did not appear in the Henry VIII tax entries for Bishopstone, which appear to list owners/occupiers and tenants living in the villages, not the landowners.
They do appear in an entry in the Calendar of Patent Rolls 1549, which is a list of all the land and property giving tithe money to chantry chapels:-
The yearly rent of 14d and service from lands called Dyggaseland in the parish of Bysshopton in Grymswood hundred, Hereford in tenure of Richard Watkyns, the yearly rent of 3d. and service from the lands called Mellens lands in the tenure of George Eccle (Eckley), The messuage with curtilages containing 45acres arable land, in the common fields of Bysshopton parish in the several tentures of Thomas Waters, John Chamberleyn and John Phylpott, and the lands called Meddell Wood, in the late service of St Mary in the parish church of Bysshopton.
By 1550 John Digges was back in Bishopstone as one of the main freeholders paying rent. In 1551 an inventory was carried out on all the malt and corn held in the city of Hereford. One entry of interest records,
John Dyggas of Busshopston supplied to one George Elyott" Eight busshells of good sweete and merchauntable whete and eight busshells of good sweete pure clene and merchauntable rye of Hereford mesure"
Hereford measure was a larger measure than in other shires. Rye was a very common crop grown partly for the use of its straw for thatching as well as the grain for brewing.
Marriage settlements were common agreements in the 16th and 17th centuries, land was often settled by both parents, a dowry was given by the bride's father and a jointure agreed for the woman's maintenance if she became a widow. In the case of John Digges yeoman of Bishton, son and heir of John Digges, and Joan Knap daughter of Henry Knap of Canon Pyon, in their 1598 marriage agreement the dowry money was given to John Digges senior to settle land to his son and daughter in law with conditions. .
All Digges lands in East Bishopstone, Bishopstone and Brinsop settled on John junior and Joan, John senior and his wife to retain the capital messuage and to have one third of the produce of the land and of the milk, cheese and white meat and of the kine (cattle) on the farm.
In the 1630 court rolls for Bishopstone John Digges held two freehold farms containing 120 acres and he also rented from Humphrey Berrington 90 acres of land leased for 21years at £17 5s per annum.
There appears to be at least four generations of John Digges in the preceding documents. John purchased Townsend farm and other smallholdings in Bishopstone he had two sons Richard and Humphrey.
In 1646 Richard Digges takes out a mortgage of £200 on Bishen farm where his father lives, a smallholding with 6 acres at Clay pits, and the Townsend farm with 6½ acres, which was rented by Roger Penner. He takes out another mortgage in 1654 for another £300 and buys Wormsley Grange.
On June 1st 1657 John Digges son and heir of Richard Digges of Bishopstone entered into a marriage settlement with Dynah Graves of Stoke Orchard Gloucestershire.[10]
In consideration of £200 paid by Dynah's family the following lands are settled on John and Dynah.
1. Messuage (Bishen) in occupation of Richard and John
2. Smallholding at Claypitts with 6 acres in occupation of Thomas Williams
3. House and garden (Townsend) with 6½ acres late in occupation of Roger Penner, now George Powles
4. Tenement and 4 acres (Hill), in occupation of Richard Boulcott
Subject to payment of an annuity of £23 to Elizabeth Knapp of Canon Pyon (Aunt)

John and Dynah to have the hay, the corn crop and all the old standards about the house, bedsteads, tables, furnace, two beds, 6 hogshead of beer or cider, ploughs, wains, harrows.
Also 1 additional feather bed and some of the brass, pewter, sheets, table napkins, table cloths, blankets, some wool, 4 oxen, 1 horse, 4 cows, 4 young beasts, 40 sheep, 2 pigs or 2 pigs in bacon.
John to pay Richard £200 for all the above.
Richard to provide meat and drink to John and Dynah for one year until they can provide their own at Bishopstone.
From the records it would appear that the Digges family had a comfortable life considering this was just after the Civil War. Richard Digges moved from Bishopstone in 1658 and purchased a property in Dilwyn called Solers for £200.
Humphrey, Richard's younger brother lived in Hereford where he had become a wealthy and important man. He was a Royalist and supported the King in the Civil War and records show that on December 23rd 1645 Humphrey Digges was an officer of the works in Hereford.
When the Scotch army under General Leven came to assist the Parliament forces who were besieging Hereford, he escaped and his property was impounded. Later in the war when Colonel Birch was in command he paid a ransom of £10 to reclaim his house; after the War in 1657, he was appointed under sheriff of Hereford. In 1660 the Sheriff of Hereford, William Powell, on current parliamentary views of past political incorrectness; recommended Humphrey Digges as Viscount Scudamore's deputy as steward to the Dean and Chapter of Hereford.
Church records show that on January 9th 1660, Humphrey Digges son of John and Dynah was christened in Bishopstone Church, shortly after Dynah inherited an estate in Corse, Gloucestershire. John and Dyah with their family left Bishopstone, selling all their landholdings in the parish to brother Humphrey for six hundred pounds. In 1664 Humphrey was living in a very large house in St Owen Street and all four farms in Bishopstone were let out to tenants.
Humphrey married Eleanor Thomas, daughter of Michael Thomas Gent of Michaelchurch, she was the granddaughter and heiress of Epiphan Howarth who owned most of the manor of Vowchurch. Humphrey was now very wealthy; he lent money through bonds to Marshall Bridges of Tiberton so he could develop business interests including the trade in slaves for the colonies, Humphrey received good returns on his money. Humphrey and Eleanor decided to build a new house complete with the appropriate stabling, buildings and gardens at Bishon to show off their newly found wealth. The old farmhouse was knocked down and replaced with an H section house with two wings, joined by a centre section. It was of timber frame structure three stories high; standing on a first floor made from solid stonewalls: most large houses in Herefordshire constructed in this period were built by this method. The house today contains the west wing and part of the centre section of this original Digges house, the east wing was demolished in 1780. A new coach house, stables and brew house were built and formal gardens were laid out, a new cobble stone drive with fancy iron gates and a lodge house built to guard the entrance. (the stone from the foundations of Digges entrance walls, pillars and a lodge house were excavated in 2009 and reused in the building on the new entrance to Bishon Farm). The total cost of all this reconstruction came to £700, a lot of money at the time. This work was all carried out during the period 1665-70.

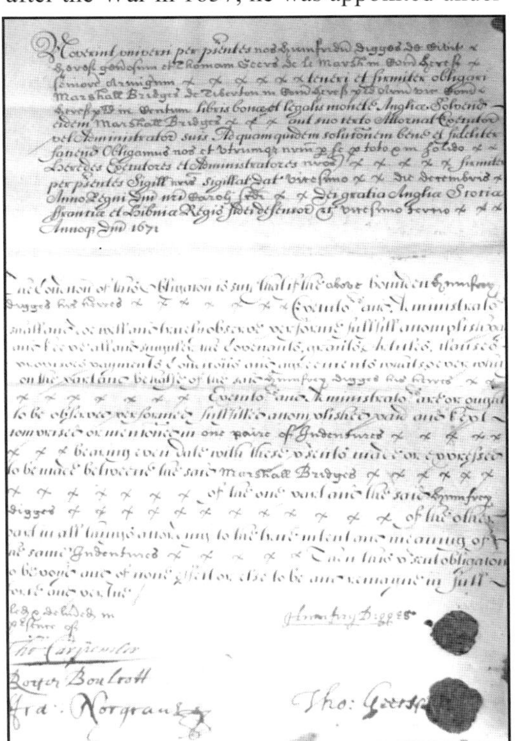

(Figure 4) Bond between Humphrey Digges Thomas Geers and Marshall Bridge 1671

Humphrey was then known as a Gentleman of Bishton Herefordshire, he received many of the Herefordshire gentry including Lord Hereford, Viscount Scudamore and George Coningsby from Hampton Court, whom he used as witnesses on many of his documents and deeds. As Under-Sheriff he presided over many court cases in Hereford brought about by the civil war.
From reading his paperwork, it's easy to imagine him to be a typical cavalier, a King Charles look-alike, and flamboyant, with a fancy signature.

Humphrey continued to buy freehold land in Bishopstone including a smallholding known today as Bridge Ash and a smallholding on Bishon Common.

He died on December 5th 1681 and was buried in the chancel of Bishopstone church on January 7th 1681; the flat stone marking his grave was covered over when the Rev Lane Freer renovated the church.

Humphrey left his holdings to his wife Eleanor, who tried to collect some of the debt owed to Humphrey from his brother John, who then brought a court action against Eleanor. He contested the will, saying that his own son Humphrey was the rightful heir of the Bishen estates, as Humphrey and Eleanor had no children. A long court case followed with the outcome that Humphrey junior was awarded the bulk of the estate while Eleanor was awarded the houses in Hereford, Bridge Ash in Bishopstone also parcels of land in Bishopstone, Brinsop and Mansel Lacy. All the court records of this case are deposited at Kew including the original probate inventory that has unfortunately suffered water damage.

(Figure 5) Sketch of Bishton Farmhouse

The Inventory of Humphrey Digges of Bishton Hereford gent deceased exhibited on May 2nd 1682 by Francis Nixon, notary public, acting on behalf of the executor, put a value of £436 17s 10d on his possessions making him a wealthy man when he died. (Inventories never record properties or lands owned by the person). His inventory with its list of goods and value gives a snapshot of life at Bishton farmhouse in the 17th century. The inventory lists 8 lower rooms and 9 bedrooms.

The great parlour contained 18 leather chairs, 1 couch, 2 tableboards, 2 carpets, hangings(curtains) and one looking glass, value put on all the items in this room £10 9s 0d. Two little parlours contained chairs; chests, coffers and a tableboard in each, one square, the other round

Humphrey's silver plate included two large cups, two lesser cups, one tunn, one nutmeg cup lipped, one silver tobacco box and thirteen silver spoons value £17 1s 8d

The kitchen contained many brass pots and dripping pans, two iron pots, one pot of brass and 6 brass candlesticks the dairy house contained cheese value 40s, 5 tubs of butter 30s, flour 18s grinding stones and other implements 80s.

Cheese chamber containing all types of cheese value 30s, in the store chamber yarn, 2 dozen of round hemp and flax unspun, 1½ stone of candles and 1 bushel of salt.

In the kill house, bacon 30s, 2 flitches of beef and beef hanging 7s, the cellar is recorded as full of cider of all kinds plus 2 casks of beer valued at £14 4d the highest valued room in the house.

The 9 bedrooms included a blue chamber containing bedstead, feather bed couch warming pan, trunks and hangings value £3 19s 10d, a new chamber lists 2 feather beds, 6 chairs, 1 sideboard, 1 dressing table and hangings value £6. The inventory lists, a total of 15 beds, maids' chamber (2 beds), servants chamber (3 beds) clerks' chamber and Mr Herbert's chamber. Not everyone had a bed some still slept on straw mattresses.

Outbuildings included a boulting house with 3 hogshead of cider and a large brew house containing one furnace, one pewter steele, seven vats, two trinds, one washing tub, three old hogsheads and three hogsheads of vinegar £2 8s 10d, 7 sacks of old hops £2 16s.

Granary, 6 bushels of wheat 15s, Malt House, one bushel of dried malt 10s, ten bushels of barley 20s, malt in the vat and on the floor 31s.

Wheat in the barn un-threshed £12 5s, rye in the home barn £4 10s, wheat in the other barn un-threshed £3, barley there un-threshed 25s, peas un-threshed £2.

The cattle, eight oxen £24, thirteen cows one bull £32, six heifers and one bullock £10 10s, four; three-year old bullocks £7 10s, eleven small calves £5 10s, two old fat cows £3 10s, six year old beasts £8.

Sixty and odd sheep £9, two saddle horses £10, six old cart horses with their gear £20, two weaning colts 30s, two two-year old colts £6, thirty swine of all sorts about the house £10 10s, five hogs in the house feeding £3 9s.

Corn on the ground, fifty six acres of corn, barley and kimridge growing £38, hay in the houses £10, one cyder mill with the appurtenances £1 10s.

One dysle cart, one dung cart, one dysle wain, one dung wain and one dung crib £8 10s, one wagon £4, one charriott and its harness £4, the ploughs, yokes, tewes, ralls, and other implements 20s.
Humphrey also owned properties in Hereford; in the deceased's barn at Aylestone, a small quantity of barley and peas, un-threshed, a small parcel of hay and a little furnace in the house £3 6s 8d.
In a house near All Holland [I think he means All Hallows = All Saints] in Hereford
In a room above stairs, one bedstead, one tableboard, four stools, two chairs, one stand, one little table cloth, the hangings about the room and one little hanging shelf 21s 4d. In the same house below stairs one square tableboard, six leather stools, one chair, one old press, one other little table board and fourteen sacks of old decayed hops £4 8s 6d.
A small quantity of hay in a room by the Red Lyon stable in Hereford 10s.
Item debts due to the deceased by book which are hopeful (i.e. they are likely to be paid up) amounting to the sum of £80.

Just a few notes on the inventory; the use of carthorses for farming work was still fairly rare, it was still believed that to plough Herefordshire clay you needed the strength of oxen. The chariot listed was a fancy four-wheeled coach used by Humphrey and Eleanor. Francis Mowgrove was Humphrey's live-in clerk, Mr Herbert was the farm manager, and the house would have always been busy because the farm servants and indoor servants all lived in, around twenty people.
Eleanor, Humphrey's wife remarried Delabere Winston who owned the Blakemere estate, after her death she was buried next to Humphrey in the chancel of Bishopstone Church on August 7th 1691.
In her will she left her lands in Bishopstone, Hereford and Mansel to her new husband. She was a lady of class who had never borne any children. All these details are recorded on the flat stone over her grave in the chancel of the church now covered over. She left her best gowns to her stepdaughter as shown in part of the will that follows.
I bequeath to Thomas Winstone my husband's son a silver tankard and a gold ring.
I bequeath to Mary Winstone my husband's eldest daughter my silver petticoat.
I bequeath to Fortis Winstone my husband's daughter my satin petticoat and another gold ring.

Humphrey junior moved into Bishton in 1684, he was 24 years old. He worked the farm for just four years, but he was no farmer, not surprising really as he trained as a lawyers clerk as a young man, paid for by his uncle at a cost of £40. He was continually selling off and mortgaging land to keep solvent and eventually rented the farms out and moved to Hereford where he became a shoemaker.
One surviving rental agreement dated 1704 shows that Humphrey rented Bishton to one John Knott for six years at £50 per annum. This document gives a good description of house and gardens in 1704. Listed were a main farmhouse, brewhouse (where the ale was made), stables, coach house, barns, outbuildings, pigscotts, cowsheds, cottage, boulting house (mill house) with one chamber above, parlour garden with its fruits, the walk leading to the rear of the house containing an avenue of trees and the drive to the house with fruit trees in the hedgerows, plus all the farm field names.
This agreement was never completed because Humphrey appeared in court before Sir Robert Price in January 1708: he was in debt and arrears to the tune of £1000.
I don't know if it was coincidental but Sir Robert purchased the estate shortly afterwards.
Humphrey Digges entered an agreement on December 4th 1708 to sell Bishton, Townsend Farm and Berkley tenement to Robert Price of Foxley for £1220 and final deeds exchanged on January 16th 1709. The ownership of all Digges freehold lands in Bishopstone totalling over 200 acres had now passed into the hands of the new lord of the manor, Sir Robert Price of Foxley. Thomas Winstone inherited Eleanor's lands in Bishopstone including "Bridge Ash" and a smallholding on Bishon Common; he sold some of his holding to Robert Price in 1710.

Bishopstone in the reign of Henry VIII

John Chabnor was an important man in Herefordshire in the beginning of the 16th century. He was the chief collector of taxes for Henry VIII covering the Grimsworth Hundred he also collected other taxes for the king during the period 1512-1543. Although not particularly liked he brought a higher profile to the parish after his marriage to heiress Elizabeth Gomond when they moved into the Court manor house.
On September 24th 1535 Thomas Cromwell, on the instructions of Henry VIII, ordered by letters patent the owners of the Townships of "Eton Busshop", "Were", Kenchester, "Brugg Canon", "Brugg Solers", Credenhill, "Breynton", "Bisshoppeston", "Bronyll" and "Tuppyreley" to destroy two fulling mills one at Sugwas the other in Hereford plus two corn mills. The owners of Bishopstone were listed as James Baskerville Knight and Thomas Monington
The reason for these ordered were navigation of the river combined with local clergy opposed the changes he was making to the church. It was recorded that great distress was caused in the city and the named townships and the woollen industry was destroyed never to recover.

Valuation of Bishopstone 1543 for Henry VII Taxes[11]

John Chabnor	*Property & land (Court & New Inn)*	*£80*	*Tax paid 20s*
Walter Crow	*Property & land (Bishon)*	*£60*	*Tax paid 6s 8d*
Thomas Parlour	*Property & land (Blacksmith)*	*£47*	*Tax paid 6d*
John Welsh	*Property & land (Bishton)*	*£47*	*Tax paid 6d*
Hugo ap Thomas	*Property & land*	*£46*	*Tax paid 7d*
Thomas Waters	*Property & land*	*£44*	*Tax paid 2s*
Walter Waters	*Property & land*	*£44*	*Tax paid 2s*
John Phepotts	*Property & land*	*£42*	
John Waters	*Property & land*	*£05*	*Tax paid 20d*
Thomas Chabnor	*Property & land*	*£05*	
John Hewes	*Property & land*	*20s*	
George Hewes	*Property & land*	*20s*	
Thomas Elmore	*Property & land*	*20s*	
William Forge	*Property & land*	*11s*	
John Carpenter	*Property & land*	*11s*	
John Smith	*Property & land*	*11s*	
John Llanyo	*Goods*	*20s*	
Christian Carpenter	*Goods (Parson's sister)*	*11s*	

Out of the 28 parishes in the Grimsworth hundred, Bishopstone paid the 21st highest payment of tax, Bishopstone Court occupied by John Chabnor was one of the highest taxed properties in the hundred, indicating it was also one of the largest. Besides the Court, Bishopstone Manor contained eight main farms, eight smallholdings and possibly another six to eight hovels that were valued under 20s and not liable for tax.

(Figure 6) Early illustration of the Bishops Palace

On October 22nd 1554 a Court leet for the manor of Bishopstone was held at the Bishop's Palace in Hereford before Anthony Washburn Gent. To give an idea of how the parish system worked in the 16th century, I will try to describe the proceedings. Attending this court would have meant a long walk for the villagers as only a few could have afforded the luxury of a horse.[12]

Imagine the scene, our villagers arrive at the Bishop's Palace, a place of grandeur to local peasants, they would have been hustled into the Great Hall which to our parishioners must have looked spectacular with its expensive decor. Firstly the jurors from the village were sworn in, then the village spokesperson stood up and said Elicius Dyke had still not cleaned out the ditch from St Mary's house to Hill road as he was ordered to at the last court hearing, water was still flooding on to the village road. The spokesperson informed the jurors that Elicius Dyke had not attended the court today, as it was his duty to do so. The court fined Elicius Dyke 2d for non-appearance, and fined him a further 3s 4d for not cleaning out the ditch.

Next up was Thomas Welshe from Bishon Farm, he explained to the court that he had a stray red pig on the farm, which he had kept for one year; no one had come to claim the pig which he valued at 12d, the court decided to sell the pig to Thomas for the value he had placed on it. Hugh Serrell and Thomas Parlor both stood before the court, Thomas was the village blacksmith; they had both been charged with trantery (buying and selling goods without a licence) at the last court and were fined, neither had paid their fines. So they were fined another 4d by the court for non-payment. With a manor court you could not get away with anything, even if you did not attend the court you were fined in your absence. The noise in the Great Hall suddenly intensified, a disturbance, Thomas Hopton "gent" one of the Bishopstone jurors had for some reason walked out of the court while it was still in session. If he disagreed with the verdict given to the last case it's not clear. The villagers all gave their opinions, a discussion then took place involving all, and after this the jurors decided that Thomas had left without permission, so he was in contempt of court and is fined 6d. There would have been much gossip between the villagers on their way home that afternoon and among the village for the next few days, on the outcome of their manor court.

Just a few explanatory notes; Elicius Dyke had purchased the land and chantry house from the Crown after the closure of the chantry chapel in 1548. This was the house and land Cecilia had endowed 250 years earlier to house and support a priest for St Mary's Chapel.

He was responsible for the ditch that ran down the village but it was blocked, meaning that the water was spilling out and running down the road. Elicius Dyke sold the house and land shortly after to Humphrey Berington.

Thomas Parlor the Blacksmith made a will on February 2nd 1557 leaving his tools to his son John so he could carry on the family business. The family had been Bishopstone's blacksmiths since the 1400s. This will made by Thomas on his death bed, starts by him saying "Sick in body but in perfect remembrance" this statement made at the start of the will is to prove although seriously ill, Thomas was still mentally capable of giving instructions on his estate to Parson Nicholas Phelpotts bending over the table board in the gloom of the cottage, writing down Thomas's instructions on to parchment with a quill pen. Nicholas writes "*To my son John 2 hammers, one anvil, 2 pairs of iron tongs, a pair of bellows and one "wreste" of iron". To Alys my daughter a red calf and a brass pot. The residue of my goods to my wife Elizabeth. My wife and my son Richard to be my executors. Witnesses Nicholas Phelpotts, George Hewes and many others.*"

The other prominent family who moved from the village in the early 16th century were the Smiths who farmed Bishon with 120 acres of land. They were the direct descendants of Sir John Daniels (13th century). One of the brothers, John Symth leased the Manor of Bunshill.
A deed dated November 6th 1527 records[13] *John Devereux, Edward Lawton and William Smyth of the Were, conveys to Margaret Crowe all their lands, tenements farm and rents in Bishopstone and Mansel Lacy. Then to Walter Crowe, son of Margaret and his wife Katherine.*
Bishon farm was now in the hands of the Crowe family who originated from Court Farm, Kenchester.

(Figure 7) This early Victorian painting called "A view from Bishopstone Hill" shows White House farm, the building to the right of the Church.

James Baker was a yeoman farmer who owned the freehold of White House farm situated in the centre of the village. He died leaving three young daughters and made provision for them in his will. Soon after he died his wife Katherine sold the farm to Richard Carpenter brother of the rector.
Abstract from the Will of James Baker of Bishopstone March 16th 1577
"To the church of Bishopstone I leave 3s 8d, To my 3 daughters all the profit to come of a lease that I have from Thomas Feror, To Margaret Foote 1 sheep, To my maid 1 sheep, To my man Bunde 6d. All the residue of my goods, together with an agreement I have for the tithes with the parson of Bishopstone for 3 years. I give to Katherine my wife, who is to pay ten pounds to each to my daughters when they reach 21 years. If any of my daughters should die, her share to go to the survivors. My wife shall keep my daughters until they are 21 and give them their "Chamber" and array for their marriage I make Katherine my wife executor with Thomas Carpenter parson of Kinnersley and Thomas Foote.

The main part of the Manor passed to Joanna Chamberlain, William Gomond's granddaughter and heir. She married Humphrey Berington, grandson of William Berington of Stoke Lacy, in 1548. Between 1560-65 they built their manor house and moved in. They had two sons, John and Thomas. Humphrey died before 1580 and John inherited the Manor, the full history of the Beringtons is covered in the1600-1700 section of the book. Importantly by 1590 John had purchased the other two lordships of the manor, and was now the sole lord of the Manor of Bishopstone. The headings of a rent roll written in 1590, demonstrates how the lordships had been divided, *"The rent roll of John Byrtition (Berington) of is manor of Byshopston called Danyells Fee and after Gomonds, The rent roll of John Byrtiton of his manor of Byshopston called Baskervilles Fee, The rent roll of John Byrtiton of his manor called Monnington Fee",* the roll also reveals many of the farms and smallholdings having land that overlapped between the three lordships.

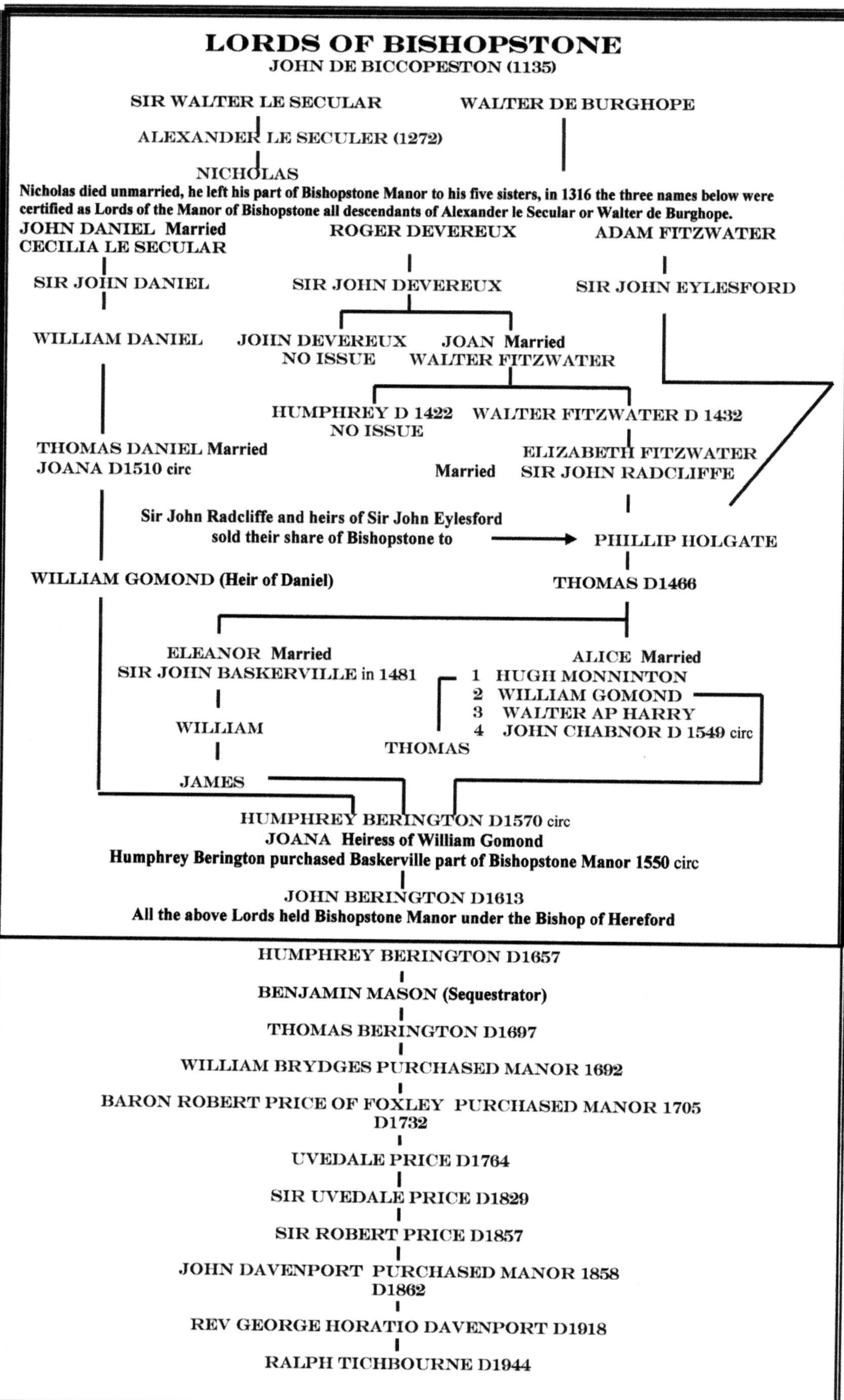

LORDS OF BISHOPSTONE
JOHN DE BICCOPESTON (1135)
SIR WALTER LE SECULAR
WALTER DE BURGHOPE
ALEXANDER LE SECULER (1272)
NICHOLAS
Nicholas died unmarried, he left his part of Bishopstone Manor to his five sisters, in 1316 the three names below were certified as Lords of the Manor of Bishopstone all descendants of Alexander le Secular or Walter de Burghope.
JOHN DANIEL Married CECILIA LE SECULAR
ROGER DEVEREUX
ADAM FITZWATER
SIR JOHN DANIEL
SIR JOHN DEVEREUX
SIR JOHN EYLESFORD
WILLIAM DANIEL
JOHN DEVEREUX NO ISSUE
JOAN Married WALTER FITZWATER
HUMPHREY D 1422 NO ISSUE
WALTER FITZWATER D 1432
THOMAS DANIEL Married JOANA D1510 circ
ELIZABETH FITZWATER Married SIR JOHN RADCLIFFE
Sir John Radcliffe and heirs of Sir John Eylesford sold their share of Bishopstone to
PHILLIP HOLGATE
WILLIAM GOMOND (Heir of Daniel)
THOMAS D1466
ELEANOR Married SIR JOHN BASKERVILLE in 1481
ALICE Married
1 HUGH MONNINTON
2 WILLIAM GOMOND
3 WALTER AP HARRY
4 JOHN CHABNOR D 1549 circ
WILLIAM
THOMAS
JAMES
HUMPHREY BERINGTON D1570 circ
JOANA Heiress of William Gomond
Humphrey Berington purchased Baskerville part of Bishopstone Manor 1550 circ
JOHN BERINGTON D1613
All the above Lords held Bishopstone Manor under the Bishop of Hereford
HUMPHREY BERINGTON D1657
BENJAMIN MASON (Sequestrator)
THOMAS BERINGTON D1697
WILLIAM BRYDGES PURCHASED MANOR 1692
BARON ROBERT PRICE OF FOXLEY PURCHASED MANOR 1705 D1732
UVEDALE PRICE D1764
SIR UVEDALE PRICE D1829
SIR ROBERT PRICE D1857
JOHN DAVENPORT PURCHASED MANOR 1858 D1862
REV GEORGE HORATIO DAVENPORT D1918
RALPH TICHBOURNE D1944

Chapter 4

BERINGTON, OF BISHOPSTONE.

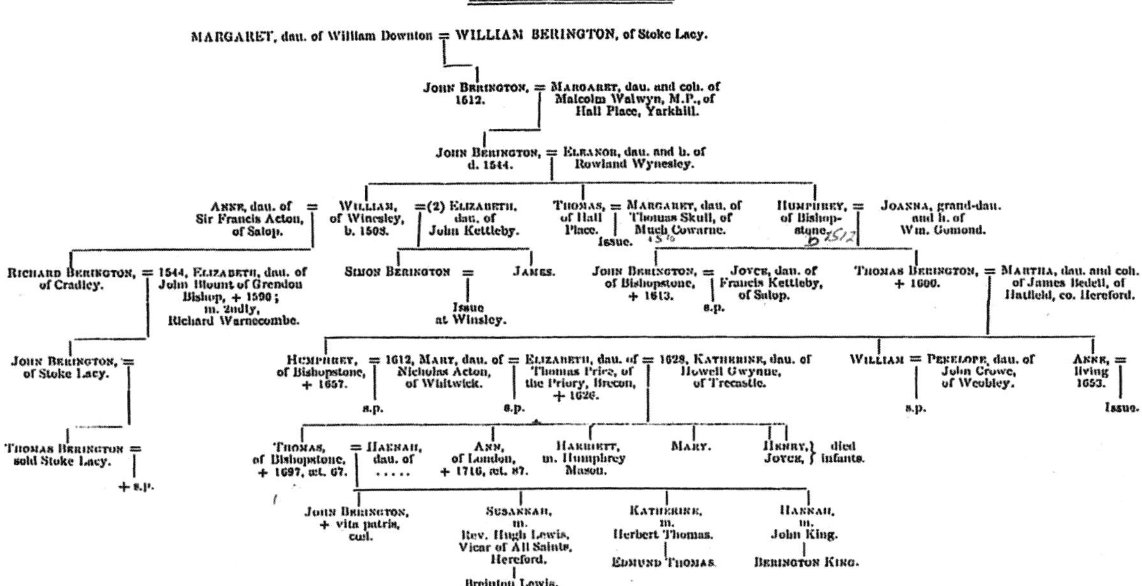

Humphrey Berington was the 3rd son of John Berington of Stoke Lacy; he married Joanna Chamberlain around 1550. Joanna was the granddaughter and heir of William Gomond of Byford who had acquired a large portion of Bishopstone through inheriting the Daniel and Monningtons parts of the manor. Humphrey was about 40 years old when he married Joanna and had acquired wealth from commercial pursuits. Through a marriage settlement with Joanna he acquired the moated manor house but not the land, which was rented out, by her father and his nephew who were the other benefactors of William's will. The medieval house was old, possibly 13th century and in a poor condition. I have found no written evidence as to when the original house was built, but this could have been the second or third house to occupy the site. The only evidence that an earlier house may have occupied the site, are the names of the lords of the manor of Bishopstone who presumably lived there throughout the preceding centuries.

(Figure 1) **Berington Coat of Arms**

In 1558 Elizabeth 1 came to the throne; this was the start of the so-called "golden age" in which prosperity was enjoyed by the upper classes and the middle/merchant classes as well, quite a lot of whom bought in to Herefordshire estates.

Against this background Humphrey decided in circa 1560 to build a new manor house in true Elizabeth style, which was described at the time as "a commodious residence with a fine gateway".[1]

Most of the timber taken from the old medieval manor house was used as piles to support the foundations of a new house. The old cellars were retained and the new house was three stories high having a stone built ground floor, topped by a timber frame for the next two floors, covered with a stone tiled roof. It was originally larger than the present house with a central courtyard bordered by another wing and separate kitchen block. (This discovery was made in 1920 when the house was being restored by Captain Hinckes of Foxley and recorded at the time by Alfred Watkins, Herefordshire's great historian).

Silas Taylor the 17th century antiquarian on his travels described the house *"as a pretty royalty and a neat seat haueing all things fitt for a house about it selfe"*

(Figure 2) Author's impression of the newly built Bishopstone Court in the 16th century.

A handsome gateway protected the residence at the end of the moat bridge, a piece of renaissance work that must have reflected the quality of the main house. This gateway had the top removed in 1894 for safety reasons, the photo on the right was taken in 1890 by Pilley, note the crack in the centre of the arch. Humphrey died in the late 1570s and the manor passed to his eldest son John, who married Joyce Kettleby from Shropshire; she came from an old distinguished family with a very elaborate crest
John was Sheriff of Herefordshire on two occasions, in 1588 and 1604, but was exposed to annoyance and expense on account of his Catholic faith. His name appears on official returns of "convicted popish recusants". He also held the manors of Pixley and Catley in Bosbury but his main residence was Bishopstone Court.

In 1590 with John purchasing the ancient Baskerville Lordship interest in the manor, together with his mother's inheritance, Bishopstone was now in the ownership of one single individual "John Berington" for the first time in over 500 years. John didn't farm his lands himself; as Lord of the Manor and Sheriff he held a high status, dealing with county affairs and his other manors. The demesne lands attached to Bishopstone manor were let to John Dalahaie. Thomas Berington, John's brother was a farmer who lived in the parsonage by Bishopstone church and farmed the 82 acres of glebe land. It was not unusual for the clergy, rectors or lay rectors, not to live in the Parsonage, but to receive the rent and tithe payments, and also many clergy had independent means. In this case the Rector of Bishopstone was also the Vicar of Bridge Sollers where he lived in the Vicarage.

(Figure 3) Gateway in 1890 before the top section was removed.

John and Joyce had no children but had gathered great wealth in their lifetime.

John died on February 5th 1613 a copy of his will follows:-

Will of John Berington of Bishopstone March 22nd 1612[2]

In Dei nomine Amen the two and twentieth day of March in the year of our Lord God one thousand six hundred and twelve I John Berington of Bushopston in the county of Hereford esquire being of good and perfect remembrance and not sick in body (thanks be given to God) yet being uncertain when or how soon it shall please God to alter and determine the state and course of this my temporal life do therefore ordain and make this my last will and testament in manner and form following.

First I bequeath my soul unto almighty God my Maker hoping to be saved by the Death and Passion of his dear son Jesus Christ my only Redeemer and by none other manner whatsoever. And my body I commit to be buried in the chapel adjoining to the chancel of the church of Bushopston aforesaid called the Lordes Chappell.

Item I bequeath for and towards the reparation of the parish church of Bushopston aforesaid the sum of 6s 8d and for and towards the reparation of the parish church of Pixley in the said county of Hereford 6s 8d. Also whereas I have heretofore conveyed and assured all my manors, lands, tenements, tithes and hereditaments with their appurtenances unto Sir Francis Ketilby knight, William Dansey, Bryan Crowther, John Ketilby and Richard Pearle esquires, to the uses, intents and purposes in the said conveyance and assurance mentioned, expressed and declared, now my will is and I do hereby devise and bequeath unto the poor people of the Almshouse of the Sickmans in the suburbs of the City of Hereford and to their successors for ever one annuity or yearly pension of 6s 8d.

Item I do give and bequeath unto Humphrey Berington my nephew, son and heir of my brother Thomas Berington deceased, £100 of good and lawful money of England to be paid unto the said Humphrey Berington when he shall accomplish the age of one and twenty years. Also I do give and bequeath unto the said Humphrey Berington my signet and brooch of gold to be delivered unto him when he shall accomplish the age of eighteen years. And if the said Humphrey Berington shall happen to die in the meantime then I give and bequeath the same signet and brooch of gold unto William Berington brother of the said Humphrey Berington to be delivered unto him when he shall accomplish the like age of eighteen years. Also I do give and bequeath unto the said Humphrey Berington all my glass, wainscot, table boards, bedsteads, cupboards, benches, forms and join stools at Pixley to be delivered to the said Humphrey Berington when he shall accomplish the age of one and twenty years.

And also I do give and bequeath unto the said Humphrey Berington all my glass, wainscot, table boards, bedsteads, cupboards, benches, forms and join stools at Bushopston aforesaid to be delivered unto the said Humphrey Berington immediately after the decease of Joyce Berington my now wife so as she the said Joyce Berington doth not sell, exchange, spoil or ill use the same but occupy and use it in good sort and so leave the same at her decease unto the said Humphrey Berington or his assignes to whom this my will is the same shall then come and remain.

Item I do give and bequeath unto William Berington brother unto the said Humphrey Berington £100 to be paid unto the said William Berington when he shall accomplish the age of one and twenty years. Item I do give and bequeath unto Anne Berington sister of the said Humphrey Berington and William £200 to be paid unto the said Anne Berington when she shall accomplish the age of one and twenty years or else be married. And also my will is that Joyce my now wife shall find provide and allow sufficient meat, drink and apparel and other necessaries best befitting their birth and education according to the discretion of Joyce my said wife and my appointed overseer unto the said William Berington during the life of the said Joyce and unto the foresaid Anne until she shall be married or else accomplish the full age of one and twenty years, bringing them both up or causing them to be brought up in such learning and qualities as shall be fitting to their several ages, sexes and estates. And also my will is that my said wife shall have the use of all my plate during her natural life and after her decease then I do give and bequeath two parts of my said plate unto the said Humphrey Berington and the third part thereof unto the said William Berington, the residue and remainder thereof to be bequeathed and disposed at the will and discretion of my said wife. Item I do give and bequeath unto my godson William Ashfeild an angel in gold. Item I give and bequeath unto John Sheppard son of Thomas Sheppard late deceased one young cow and two sheep.

Item I give and bequeath to Bridget Evans the daughter of Rebecca Evans twenty nobles. Item I give and bequeath unto every one of my servants which shall be in my service at the time of my decease one half year's wages according to their several wages over and above the arrearages of their said several wages of any such shall be due unto them or any of them at the time of my decease, these last recited legacies to be paid within one quarter of a year after my decease. This the within written will was published by the testator John Berington, in the presence of the persons subscribed William Ashfeild, Mary Caple, Robert Wolfe, Thomas Tanner, John Sheppard.

Proved 14 May 1614 by the oath of Joyce Berington.

The "Angel in Gold" John bequeathed to his godson is a gold coin worth about 10s. Interestingly he leaves to his nephew Humphrey Berington "my glass, wainscot etc"; glass making was expensive before 1589 when a new method was introduced to lower the cost. It was also difficult to transport in a county renowned for its rough roads.

The Court contained many glass leaded windows, which were fashionable in the Elizabethan period and the expensive wooden panelling (wainscot), John mentioned these in his will before the manors and houses. This panelling could have possibly come from the old house that he pulled down as it was at its most popular in the thirteenth century.

Thomas Berington, John's younger and only brother, died in 1604 leaving a wife and three young children, Humphrey aged 4, William aged 3 and Ann aged 2. They were all born in Bishopstone Rectory but after Thomas's death they were taken into the manor house and brought up by John and Joyce. John gives his gold broach and signet ring to Humphrey when he reaches 18 years old and he is to inherit the estates at the age of 21 years. John left provision for his other nephew and niece. He called the north chapel in the church "The Lord's" meaning that it belonged to the lord of the manor and this is where he was buried. Joyce commissioned a wall tablet in his memory and an altar-tomb over his grave. This was very elaborate and very expensive, the sides have three carved coats of arms of the families, and effigies of the husband and wife in the costume of the period lie on top, each holding a bible. Whether or not they are lifelike images of John and Joyce is not known, but the dog at the man's feet is definitely a greyhound which is the type of dog used on the Berington coat of arms. The base was painted in very bright colours. The tomb would have originally stood in the middle of the chapel over John's grave but Rev Lane Freer had it moved into a corner when he restored the church in 1841.

(Figure 4) Berington's tomb in Bishopstone Church

The king held wardship of Humphrey's lands until his 21st birthday a normal legal procedure. Humphrey married Mary Acton on September 25th 1613 when he was only 13 years 9 months old; Mary's age is not recorded. In the 16th century such marriages were legally arranged with children as young as twelve in order that land settlements could be agreed at an early stage. This practice gradually faded out in the early part of the 17th century. After the wedding ceremony the children returned home to live with their parents or guardians, waiting until they reached a more mature age before setting up home together. To clarify their position an inquisition was held in Hereford. An inquisition post mortem was held after John Berington's death at the City of Hereford on March 23rd 1614[3] to establish what lands the deceased held from the Crown and who was his heir, so the king could get his entry fine from the heir on his inheritance

John Berington at the time of his death was seised in his demesne as of fee in the manors of Bushopston, Catley and Pixley with all messuages, tenements, etc etc in the county of Hereford in the parishes of Bushopston, Mauncell Lacy, Mauncell Gamage, Bosbury, Monesley, Stretton, Yarkhill, Aylton, Pixley and Ledbury; and in a certain parcel of wood called Maynes Wood with appurtenances (60a.) in Ashperton; and in the chapel of Kynaston with part of the tithes thereof in the parish of Much Marcle; and in another parcel of wood called Le Grove in Eaton Bishop; and in the moiety of a burgage in Bromyard. And that the said John Berington being so seised, together with his wife Joyce, on the 25th September 10 James I (1613), in consideration of a marriage to be held between Humphrey Berington (heir of John, being son of his brother Thomas) and Mary Acton, one of the daughters of Nicholas Acton, and in order to increase the jointure of the said Joyce, made a settlement of the said properties to trustees – Francis Ketherough of Cotheridge co. Worcs, kn., William Dansey of Brinsop esq, Brian Crowther of Knighton co Rads esq, John Ketilbie of Cotheridge esq, and Richard Pearle of Dewsall esq. [The trustees were to hold the property of John Berington for life, then to Humphrey and Mary and heirs and in default of such heirs to William Berington and heirs and in default of such heirs to various other Beringtons and heirs in succession. Also recites settlement on the Sickmans Hospital].

And they say that the said Joyce survived John and has a life tenancy in the said properties. And they say that the manor of Bushopston is held of the Bishop of Hereford but by what service they do not know and the yearly value after deductions is £3-6-8, John Berington died on 5 February last past and his heir is Humphrey Berington who at the time of John's death was aged 13 years and 3 months and was in wardship of the king by virtue of the lands held of the king.

(Figure 5) Plaque in Bishopstone Church

Joyce had a life tenancy on the properties after John's death, these would pass to Humphrey and Mary after her death. Joyce died in January 1616 and made the following will from her deathbed.[4]

In Dei nomine Amen the eighteenth day of January in the year of our Lord God one thousand six hundred and sixteen, I Joyce Berington of Bishopston in the county of Hereford, widow, late wife of John Berington of Bishopston aforesaid Esquire deceased, being sick in body but of good and perfect remembrance, thanks be to God therefore, do make and ordain my last will and testament in manner and form following. First I bequeath my soul unto almighty God my maker hoping to be saved by the Death and Passion of his dear Son Jesus Christ my only Redeemer and by no other means whatsoever. And I commit my body to be buried in the chapel adjoining to the chancel of the church of Bishopston aforesaid called the Lordes Chapel. Item I give and bequeath unto the poor of the parish of Bishopston aforesaid £6 and towards the reparation of the parish church of Bishopston aforesaid 6s 8d. Item I give unto my cousin William Ashfeild the 20 marks he oweth me. Item I give unto my cousin James Coren the £5 he oweth me by bill and the £5 I paid for him which he borrowed in my name. Item I give unto my cousin William Parry 20 nobles. Item I give unto my cousin Anne Parry one feather bed, one bolster and one dozen of flaxen napkins. Item I give unto my cousin William Berington one nag or £3 to be disbursed or paid unto the said William Berington when he shall accomplish the age of eighteen years. Item I give unto my cousin Anne Brace one feather bed, one bolster, one pair of large flaxen sheets, one tablecloth, one dozen of flaxen napkins and one coffer lying at the bed's foot in the chamber over the hall. Item I give unto my goddaughter Joyce Ashfeild the £4 which my cousin John Ashfeild and my cousin Michael Ashfeild do owe me. Item my will is and I do hereby ordain that my cousin Nicholas Acton shall have all the oxen, kine, horses, young beasts and all other manner of cattle with all the tacklings and implements of husbandry at Bishopston aforesaid in the same manner at the same rates and values as now he hath the same until such time as my cousin Humphrey Berington, son and heir of Thomas Berington deceased, shall accomplish the full age of one and twenty years. And after the said Humphrey Berington shall accomplish the said age then my will is and I do hereby give and bequeath all the aforesaid cattle with all the tacklings and implements of husbandry or their several rates and values wholly unto the said Humphrey Berington to be then paid and delivered unto him by the said Nicholas Acton. Item my will is and I do hereby likewise ordain that my cousin Nicholas Acton shall have and keep all manner of household stuff and utensils at Bishopston aforesaid in as good plight and form as the same now are until such time as the aforesaid Humphrey Berington shall accomplish the full age of one and twenty years and then to deliver the same unto him. Item I give unto my goddaughter Joyce Duppa one cow two swine and two sheep. Item I give unto Briget Evans the daughter of Rebecca Evans £12 and one bed. Item I give unto Stephen Sheppard £3, one bed and one pair of sheets. Item I give unto John Sheppard 40s. All the rest of my goods, chattels and cattels unbequeathed, my debts and legacies paid and my funeral expenses in worthy and beseeming manner discharged, I do give and bequeath wholly and entirely unto the said Humphrey Berington when he shall accomplish the full age of one and twenty years. Item I do constitute and ordain my trusty and well beloved cousin Nicholas Acton Esquire my only and sole executor of this my last will and testament and for his pains herein I give him the sum of 20s. Item my will is that whatsoever I shall at any time or times hereafter during my life add to, affix or annexe to put out or alter in this my present will, the same shall stand in form and effect and be part and parcel of this my last will and testament. In witness whereof to this my present last will and testament I have subscribed my name with my hand and put to my seal the year first above written. Joyce Berington's mark. With these witnesses, James Goode, William Rogers, Roger Jenkyns, Heugh Powell. Proved at London in the PCC court 26 April 1617 by Nicholas Acton Esquire.

She was buried next to her husband in the Berington chapel.
One of Joyce's beneficiaries Joyce Duppa, was the daughter of Bishopstone's rector Humphrey Duppa. Nicholas Acton, Humphrey's father in law proved the will in London. He lived at Whitwick which was an ancient manor within the parish of Yarkhill. What happened to Mary, Humphrey's first wife I have been unable to discover except the fact she died at a young age, possibly in childbirth, this being the most common cause of death in young women.
Humphrey Berington was patron of the church in 1623 for the new rector John Hawkyns and at around this time he married his second wife, Elizabeth Price of the Priory Brecon who died in childbirth two years later together with her baby.
He was one of the squires of the county who in 1626 refused to contribute to a loan for the expenses of the coronation and was fined £10. Knighthood was a tax imposed upon every gentleman of a certain estate (an income of over £40 per annum), by which he was compelled either to take that order upon him or pay compensation in money. Considering that Humphrey was such a royalist it's difficult to understand why he refused to pay. He appears to have been very strong-minded and to have wanted his own way, a characteristic that eventually brought the downfall of the family.
In 1628 Humphrey married his third wife, Katherine Gwyne of Trecastle, and their first children were born in 1630, twins Thomas and Ann, and then came Harriett, followed by Mary and lastly Henry and Joyce who both died in infancy.
Ciceley Bethell, half sister to Humphrey, died at the manor house in Bishopstone, which at this time had become the home of a large extended family. From the will of Ciceley made on August 19th 1626 we know that there were maidservants working at the house because she left them 2s each. Ciceley's will also records that the Berington family were members of the higher echelons of society by the emphasis placed on mouring her death, "*To John Hawkyns 50s to buy a mourning cloak, To my sister Penelope Berington 5 mourning gowns, To my brother Humphrey Berington and Elizabeth his wife £6 to buy each of them a ring to wear for my sake*". Ciceley also left "*To the poor of Bishopstone 16s to be divided between them at the discretion of my brother Humphrey Berington*". Ciceley a wealthy spinster had inherited farms and land in Brinsop which she left to her half brother and sister with money and gifts for the rest of the family.
This period in history was recorded as good times. It was a time of great and growing prosperity with an extravagant lifestyle for the country gentlemen. Men lived with a splendid enthusiasm, with their elegant beards and colourful clothes, Humphrey as a cavalier would certainly have looked this way. Little did he know what events would befall the family in the future through his strong royalist beliefs: he was never to enjoy the same standard of living again.

Humphrey Berington

Humphrey Berington's name is recorded in numerous Parliamentary papers, more than any previous resident of Bishopstone or anyone since. He first came to the notice of the authorities in 1626 as previously mentioned. But more serious events were to follow when he, like many other Herefordshire gentry, objected to the payment of the so-called Ship Money. Charles 1 had come to the throne in 1626 and he brought in a tax levy called Ship Money without the consent of Parliament on February 11th 1628. This was to raise money to build a fleet of ships to secure the country against France, and each county was given a figure to raise. Every year the tax was collected, and every year the gentry of Herefordshire were getting more rebellious until it eventually became the main cause of the Civil War.

On May 10th 1637 Humphrey Berington heard that John Giffard who had a contract with the Commissioners of Saltpetre and Gunpower to produce 9 cwt of gunpowder a week for the Admiralty, was intending to send his workmen to Bishopstone to dig out the material to produce saltpetre. Gunpowder is made from three main ingredients: saltpetre, charcoal and sulphur. Part of the procedure to make saltpetre involved boiling the waste from stables or dovecotes; collectors would scour the countryside for suitable sites and one such site was found in Bishopstone.

Humphrey with a kinsman called Mr Parry and his servant Henry Thomas paid a visit to John Giffard's new works in Hereford. He asked John Giffard's workmen John Abington and Guy Andrews, if they intended to come to Bishopstone and on being told that they did, he swore they would find no work there. He first asked his kinsman, Mr Parry to throw down the tubs of saltpetre but he would not. He then ordered Henry Thomas to empty the tubs of saltpetre which he did. Humphrey told the workmen to take away their tubs and do what they would, for he would make no satisfaction (compensation)
The Commissioner asked Humphrey to compensate John Giffard for his loss but Humphrey refused. He was then sent a summons to appear before the Lords of the Admiralty.

An entry dated Charles I 21st May 1637 in the Calendar of State Papers Domestic records the start of the case.[5]

Petition of John Giffard, Saltpetreman, to the Lords of the Admiralty. Petitioner's works being now settled at Hereford, and his servants at work in the country adjacent, Humphrey Berington, of Bishopstone, when two of petitioner's servants had made a load of liquor ready to be sent to the boiling house, on the 10th inst., caused a servant of his, called Black Harry, to throw down all the tubs, to break some of them, and to spill all the liquor; and afterwards, his Majesty's commission being shown to him and satisfaction requested, he obstinately refused. Petitioner being now in London attending on the Lords, his servant has come above 100 miles to certify the truth, as appears by the annexed affidavit. Mr. Berington being a man of worth in the country, by whose example others are encouraged, petitioner prays that he may be sent for, and order taken that his Majesty's service in petitioner's charge may go on again, and that Mr. Berington may satisfy petitioner his loss.

Humphrey had set out for London taking with him Henry Thomas alias Black Harry. Henry Thomas was a local lad: imagine his trip to London when his normal travelling distance as a farm labourer would hardly extend beyond Hereford. What he saw in London was a ramshackle city full of timber houses and narrow streets (this was London before the great fire of 1666) and it must have been an eye-opening experience for the country lad. On June 12th 1637 Henry Thomas stood before the court and said " The destruction was the order of Berington against the persuasion of his wife"
John May, servant to John Giffard who had also travelled to London as a witness said that the loss to his master was £50. The court after hearing all the evidence issued the following order.

June 17.Whitehall. Order of the Commissioners of Saltpetre and Gunpowder, upon the complaint of John Giffard, saltpetreman, against Humphrey Berington. After reciting the facts as stated in papers before calendared, and that the damage to Giffard had been above £40, it was ordered that Berington should forthwith pay £30. to the saltpetreman, and also the messenger's fees, and stand committed to the custody of the messenger until he humbly acknowledge his sorrow for his fault and performed this order.

Humphrey was imprisoned until the June 21st when he finally apologized and raised the £30; it was a large sum of money to find and was sufficient then to buy a 10-acre farm.

1637 June 21st Humphrey Berington, of Bishopstone, co. Hereford, to the Lords of the Admiralty. According to an order of the 17th inst., I acknowledge that I am very sorry for my fault in the said order mentioned.
June 21st Entry on the Admiralty Register of the appearance of Humphrey Berington this day. Having acknowledged his sorrow for his fault, and performed the Lords' order, he was discharged.

This was the first of three imprisonments Humphrey suffered in his lifetime; his involvement in the English Civil War is covered in the following chapter.
Humphrey died in 1657 aged fifty-seven years, he appears to have been a broken man following his last long spell in prison. He left all his possessions and debts to his only son Thomas.
Humphrey was buried in the north transept (Berington chapel), a flat stone marks his grave now under the choir stalls.
Thomas was 27 years old when he inherited the estates. He was married to Hannah who gave birth to a son John, on August 13th 1661. They already had three daughters Katherine, Hannah and Susana. Their last child Mary was baptised on October 20th 1662 but was buried on February 7th 1663. Thomas spent the next 29 years living in Bishopstone, borrowing money against the estate and selling off parts of it. He travelled to London regularly, attending the House of Lords courts trying to recover the Pixley estates, which he claimed Benjamin Mason had taken from his father under threat in the Civil War. After Benjamin Mason's death these disputed estates passed to his widow and children. The House of Lords finally settled the case on March 19th 1696 two years before Thomas's death.

Whereas this Day was appointed for hearing Counsel upon the Petition and Appeal of Dodington Mason Gentleman, from a Decree of the Court of Chancery made 7° Julii 28° Car. Secundi, in a Cause there depending, between Thomas Berington Esquire, Son and Heir of Humphry Berington Esquire deceased, Plaintiff, and George Mason Esquire and Sarah Mason Widow, the Petitioner's late Brother and Mother, deceased, Defendants; as also upon the Answer of the said Thomas Berington put in thereunto:
The Appellant's Counsel acquainted the House, "That the Appellant was willing to make a Conveyance of the Estate in Question, and deliver all the Writings in his Custody or Power touching the same, upon Oath."
Judgement affirmed.

There were many mortgages taken out on the farms in Bishopstone using the deeds as security to finance this long running court case. Thomas finally sold the Manor of Bishopstone in 1692 to William Bridges of Colwall, a mercer from London, for £3100 to settle his debts. The Manor consisted of the Manor Farm, Old House Farm, Whitehouse Farm, Claypitts Farm and several smallholdings amounting in all to 360 acres plus 75 acres of common land over which he had rights.
Thomas and Hannah had three daughters and a son John, their heir who died unmarried within the lifetime of his parents. All the daughters married, Susana to Hugh Lewis, Vicar of All Saints Church in Hereford, Hannah married John King from Weobley and had a son called Berington, and Katherine married Herbert Thomas.
Thomas Berington moved to the manor house in Pixley where he died, he was buried in Bishopstone church on October 16th 1698 aged 67. His wife Hannah was buried on February 4th 1709. Both were buried together in the north transept (Berington chapel) and their grave marked with a flat stone.
The last of the Beringtons, Ann (a spinster) who was Thomas's twin sister, died in the City of London and her body was brought back to Bishopstone for burial on July 19th 1716 at a cost of £40. The journey took seven days due to poor roads and the slow speed of the horse and cart used to transport the coffin. In her will she left £1000 to build almshouses for the poor of Bishopstone. In her memory an oval tablet of white marble is on the wall in the north transept of the church inscribed thus

(Figure 6) Ann Berington tablet Bishopstone Church.

Ann Berington, Spinster

One of the daughters of Captain Humphrey Berington, of Bishopston, Esq, eminent for his loyalty and affection to his King and Country, who raised a Company of Foot at his own expence for the service of the Royal Martyr, King Charles 1, by whose cruel and bloody fate he and his children were ruined. But Providence raised his beloved daughter, Mrs Ann Berington to be a comfort and support to his family, by assisting her brother and his son in all their difficulties: they dying, and in them all the males of the family, she made a generous provision for some of her nearest relations, and out of a pious and religious zeal for the poor of her native County, did by will give to the Hon. Mr.Baron Price and Timothy Geers Esq. (her Executors and Trustees), £1000., to be by them disposed of in charity, and for the relief of the poor of Bishopston, in such manner as they should think fit, and did thereby enjoin them faithfully and conscientiously to see her will performed. She died 12th July 1716 A.D., aged 86 years.

There's more on Ann and her life in the chapter covering her charity and the building of the Almshouses. Humphrey Berington was responsible for the break up of the Manor of Bishopstone: if he had changed sides in the English civil war like many of his contemporaries, the Berington family would have left their influence on Bishopstone today, possibly with a model village by the church together with a large country house of classic structure sited under the hill and an 18th century landscaped park complete with drives and lodges.

Chapter 5
1600-1700

A long court suit between William Kedward and Humphrey Duppa (Rector) would have dominated the talk in the Bishopstone at the turn of the 17th century. William Kedward lived in Byford but he owned an enclosed plot of land in Bishopstone that lay beside the lane leading up to Bishopstone common. The dispute was about the tithe payment or non-payment to the Rector. The parishioners were on the side of William Kedward, because if the Rector had won his case they all would have to pay tithes on their seeds. I have included the entire record of the case as written up by the clerk of the court, because I think it gives a wonderful look at the social life, and the characters that lived in Bishopstone on the turn of the 17th century. It reads like a book, describing how the tithes were worked out and left in the church porch. How they relied on the elders of the parish to uphold traditions, and how the women worked the fields together.

(Figure 1) Palace yard entrance door, circ 1900 the same entrance the villagers, would have used in the 17th century.

The consistory (church) court was held in the Bishop's Palace in Hereford and most of the witnesses would have walked the seven miles to give their evidence. The grandeur of the court setting, standing in front of the court giving evidence, recorded by the Clerk of the Court with his quill pen scratching the parchment was an ordeal these country folk would never forget.

Main Characters in the case are John and Mary Crowe (Bishon Farm), Thomas Crowe (John's brother), John and Ann Digges (Bishton Farm), John Walsh (New Inn), James Eckley (The Pleck), and his brother Walter (Walle Close). All these freeholders were representing William Kedward as witnesses. Anthony Barnes, Henry Delahay, John Ireland, William Jones and Elizabeth Howells, all poor labourers, were the witnesses put forward by the Rector.

Witnesses on behalf of William Kedward against Humphrey Duppa March 20th 1600[1]

Thomas Crowe of Bishopstone, yeoman, aged 70

Said that for most part of his life he had lived in the parish of Bishopstone and knows Anthony Barnes, Henry Delahay and Elizabeth Howells well. He knows that they are very poor, needy and simple people of little or no credit or regard among their neighbours and such acquainted with them. And the said Anthony Barnes having no other means to maintain himself only with his hard labour doth live very poorly and often in times in very great want when work faileth him. And as for Henry Delahay the witness says that the said Henry is commonly reputed and taken to be a bastard and is found and maintained by the parish and hath no trade or course of life to get his living but in an idle and uncertain manner without pains taking, for the most part getting some small maintenance and relief at the hands of the parishioners of Bishopstone aforesaid. And he taketh the said Henry to be such a manner of person that he is not fit to be a witness or give testimony in any cause or to be credited upon his oath. And so this witness is persuaded in his conscience that the said Henry is also of others commonly accounted, reputed and taken. And this witness further sayeth that the said Elizabeth Howells hath been commonly reputed and taken for a lewd woman of a sorry, loose life and bad conversation for which cause Thomas Howells her husband departed from her divers years past and so at this present continueth as this witness truly thinketh. And further he taketh this Elizabeth to be no fit witness in any cause or matter nor to be believed upon her oath. And as for William Jones this witness sayeth that he is but a poor man having little to live upon save only his hard labour and so is commonly accounted, reputed and taken by such as known him.

Mary Crowe wife of John Crowe of Bishopstone, husbandman to whom she has been married 25 years and she is aged 44

She has heard from credible witnesses that Anthony Barnes hath been suspected to have come lightly by or stolen a hat. She was at the birth of John Ireland and as far as she can now recall he is not above the age of 20 years, if he be so much. And she well knew the said Ireland when he served Humphrey Duppa as his household servant, continuing with him for the space of a year or thereabouts.

John Digges of the parish of Bishopstone in the county of Hereford, husbandman, aged 60
Sayeth that for all or most part of the time that he hath been and lived within the parish of Bishopstone aforesaid, which hath been most part of his lifetime, Anthony Barnes, Henry Delahay and Elizabeth Howells have been very poor and needy and do live upon the relief of the parish being otherwise not able to maintain themselves. And the said Jones is a poor man having beside his labour little to maintain himself withal. Henry Delahay is a bastard with no certain trade hath of late gone from house to house and hath by same been at certain times set at work or maintained. And Elizabeth Howells is of loose life and bad behaviour, Thomas Howells her husband did forsake and leave her company. They are all unfit witnesses.

Ann Digges wife of John Digges has been married to him for 40 years and is aged 54 or upwards.
Anthony Barnes, whom she as known for 20 years is accounted and taken to be a pilfering fellow and to have stolen away from places where he wrought and been entertained divers and sundry things as napery ware, a hat from one James Godsall being his wife's hat, for which cause and for the opinion that is generally almost within the whole parish of Bishopstone conceived of him the said Barnes of his pilfering, stealing and bad behaviour this witness says that divers (people) have refused to use him for work.
And she has known Ireland almost since he was born and to her best remembrance he is not above the age of 17 years if he be so much, And the said Ireland was lately household servant to Mr Duppa and hath continued with him in service for the space of 2 years.

John Walshe of Bishopstone, husbandman, aged 40.
He has known William Jones, Anthony Barnes, Henry Delahay and Elizabeth Howells for these 12 years last past or thereabouts during all which time and now at this present day they have been and are persons of small credit or estimation among their neighbours and such people accounted of that if there debt were paid they were not worth a farthing. And Henry Delahay is a very poor man who liveth upon the alms of the parish. Elizabeth Howells hath been and yet is accounted to be a lewd woman of her body and a very bad person for divers other of her lewd and ill qualities and demeanour and so bad and disordered a woman that her husband hath forsaken her company and gone away from her.

Richard Savacre of Mansell Lacy husbandman, has lived at Mansell for 3 years, previously at Bishopstone for 4 or 5 years, aged 48.
For the space of 16 years last past has well known William Jones, Anthony Barnes, Henry Delahay and Elizabeth Howells and for all or the most part of that time they were poor or needy folk of idle or no regard within the parish of Bishopstone where they remain. And further sayeth that William Jones and Anthony Barnes are day-labourers getting there living with their sore labour, not having any other help or means to live, and are afraid of Humphrey Duppa lest he should trouble them or otherwise vex them with suits. And the said Delahay is commonly accounted to be a bastard and hath been an idle person and wandering vagrant about Bishopstone for many years not settling himself in any good course of life but shifting from house to house for food and maintenance, And he has known Elizabeth Howells for 30 years and for all that time she has been accounted to be one of lewd life and unchaste conversation and her husband forsook her company, after whose departure the said Elizabeth had one or two children by others as it hath been spoken of and reported as well in the parish of Bishopstone as other parishes and places near adjoining. And so they are not credible witnesses.
And further he has heard it creditly reported that Anthony Barnes did steal and purloin a hat out of the house of James Godsall and the said Godsall affirmed as much unto this witness and that it was most true that he had so done and that the said Barnes was enforced as he said to restore the same hat unto him again, And further sayeth he hath heard that the said Barnes hath bin given to filching and stealing.
John Ireland is not above 15 years respecting his statue and countinance whereof this witness hath taken good regard. And well remembers that Ireland was Mr Duppa's boy and drove his plough and continued in his service above a year. And he served the said Mr Duppa when he was sworn a witness in this cause and for that reason he favoured his said master and not an indifferent witness.

John Welshe of Bishopstone, husbandman aged 40
He has well known Anthony Barnes for 12 years and hath late heard it reported by some whose names he cannot now call to remembrance that the said Barnes hath been suspected of felony. He hath known John Ireland almost from his childhood and is verily persuaded that the said Ireland doth not exceed the age of 17 years. And further sayeth that he knew him when he served Humphrey Duppa as his household servant and he remembereth he served him above the space of 2 years and departed out of his service about Candlemas last past.

The case continued at a hearing in the Bishop's Palace 18 months later September 25th 1601

(Figure 2) Early engraving of the Bishop's Palace Hereford

Walter Pember of Bishopstone, labouring man, lived in Bishopstone for 30 years and is aged 76
He has lived in Bishopstone for 30 years last past and for all those years has never heard or known of any tithe on hemp demanded or paid in Bishopstone either to the now parson or his predecessors. He very well knew Parson Phellpotts and Parson Carpenter, predecessors of the said Humphrey Duppa, Parson of Bishopstone, in whose time no tithe of seeds of hemp or flax was paid, and being a parishioner and inhabitant he would not have been ignorant of it. It has always been the custom in Bishopstone that after the parishioners and inhabitants have watered and dried their hemp and flax they have paid tithe on it to the parson. But whether in lieu and consideration of the watering and drying thereof no tithe nor tenth of the seed due thereof this witness for that he never knew the matter in question knoweth not.
He thinks the tithe of the apples is not worth speaking of, nor can he give any valuation thereof.
As for Anthony Barnes, Henry Delahay and John Ireland are and have been for anything this witness heard to be contrary accepted as honest poor folk. As for Elizabeth Howells she hath been accounted a person of bad life and conversation.

John Phellpotts of Much Mansell (Mansel Lacy) day labourer. Has lived there for 20 years, before that he lived in Bishopstone from his birth, aged 75
For his whole life he has been a parishioner of Bishopstone or Mansel Lacy and has never known tithe on hemp and flax to be demanded or paid. The parishioners of Bishopstone have been accustomed, after they watered and dried their hemp and flax, to pay the tithe to the parson there. But he cannot say whether in consideration of the watering and drying they never paid tithe on the seed thereof, since to the best of his remembrance the matter has never come into question. The tithe of apples is not worth speaking of, nor can he give a valuation thereof.
William Jones, Anthony Barnes, Henry Delahay, Elizabeth Howells and John Ireland have been and are, far as he knows or has heard, poor honest and true people and he is persuaded in his conscience that they will not depose a falsehood upon their oaths nor forswear themselves.

James Eckley of Bishopstone, yeoman. He has lived there for 40 years, he is 70 years old.
He has been a parishioner in Bishopstone for 40 years and has never known Humphrey Duppa or any of his predecessors demand tithe of the seed of hemp or flax, nor any tithe thereof paid by any parishioners or inhabitants of Bishopstone. And he further sayeth that during the said time and until the beginning of this suit there hath been and now is within the parish of Bishopstone a use and custom holden and kept and never contradicted that the parishioners and inhabitants in consideration that they rippled, watered and dried their hemp and flax growing within the parish ought to pay no tithe of any seeds of hemp or flax. And the same was often affirmed by very ancient and substantial men of the parish who have said that the same custom has been kept within the parish all their time.
He can give no valuation of the tithe of 5 apples as it is not worth speaking of. William Jones and Anthony Barnes are honest poor men living upon their sore labour, as he verily thinketh. Elizabeth Howells has been a woman of bad and lewd life and conversation, Henry Delahay and John Ireland are boys of little or no credit.

Mary Crow wife of John Crow of Bishopstone, yeoman, has been married 25 years.
She has been a parishioner and inhabitant of Bishopstone for 11 years during which time she never paid nor heard demanded any tithe of the seed of hemp or flax. The custom is that the parishioners and inhabitants ripple, wash and dry their hemp and flax and in consideration of their labour bestowed there abouts they pay no tithe of the seeds to any parson. She has heard it credibly declared by divers People ancient and substantial men of the parish who have affirmed that this is the custom.
She is well persuaded that in the year mentioned William Kedward had no flax growing within the parish of Bishopstone for being at the tithing of the hemp she could not see where any flax had grown in the said Kedward's ground, which she thinks she should have seen if any had been, nor did she hear any mention thereof. And she further sayeth that the tithe of the winter hemp was delivered to Kedward's wife to be paid unto the said Humphrey Duppa who carried the same towards the parsonage house. And she thinks that the tithe of the 5 apples is so small and slender that it is not worth speaking of or fit to be in question.
She was tithed for the hemp and the tenth part was set apart from the other nine parts on the hedge which enclosed the ground where it grew. The hemp was not put in water to be watered but only on the hedge and so watered by the dew and rain.
The winter hemp, after the tithe was taken out, was offered by Kedward to be sold to Ann Crow for 2d or 3d but she refused to buy the same at that rate.

Ann Digges of Bishopstone wife of John Digges of the same whom she has been married for 40 years, Aged 54 or upwards
She has been a parishioner and dweller in Bishopstone for 33 years and during that time neither she nor any parishioner paid tithe on the seed of hemp or flax to the party in this case or his predecessor, Sir Nicholas Phellpotts. For all that time the use and custom is and hath been and never violated or sought to be infringed before the beginning of this suit, for the parishioners of Bishopstone to ripple, water and dry their hemp and flax and then pay the tithe thereof to the parson, But whether in consideration of their labour in rippling, watering and drying the same hemp and flax the parishioners have had and enjoyed all the seed thereof without paying tithe thereof she does not know.
In this years and months covered by this case Kedward had no flax growing in Bishopstone; she knows all this grounds in the said parish and would not have been ignorant of it, in the year 1599 Kedward did not sow nor convert to his use any hemp within the parish of Bishopstone. And further she says that in the year 1600 she heard Nicholas Parlor, then servant to Humphrey Duppa, say and confess that he had received from the said William Kedward the tithe of the summer hemp which was growing that year in Kedward's grounds, and so she is fully persuaded that the same was paid.
And further she says that at the request of William Kedward she and Mary Crowe did truly and justly set out the tithe of the winter hemp growing on his grounds in Bishopstone in 1600, which tithe was afterwards delivered to Elizabeth, wife of William Kedward, Margaret Crow, Elinor Rose and Katherine, servant of John Digges who intended and meant, as they said, to carry to the parson Humphrey Duppa and she afterwards saw the same tithe, being 7 handfulls lie in the church porch of Bishopstone, and therefore she is persuaded that it was paid.
She can give no estimate or valuation of the apples, it being in her opinion not worth demanding.
She and Mary Crowe set out the tithe of the hemp on the place or ground where it grew, being set up against the hedge enclosing the same ground.
Winter hemp was never watered otherwise than by the rain and dews that fell from above. It is an easy matter to discover watered hemp from unwatered by the colour.
The winter hemp, after the tithe was paid, was offered for sale by William Kedward to Ann Crowe for 2d, but she offered him 1½d for it which what this witness thinks it was worth.
William Jones, Anthony Barnes and Elizabeth Howells are persons of no good name or fame within the parish and not fit or credible as witnesses, Henry Delahay and John Ireland are poor boys.

John Crowe of Bishopstone, Gent. Has lived there almost from birth and is aged 70.
It hath been a custom and use in Bishopstone for the inhabitants to ripple, water and dry the hemp and flax and then pay tithe of it. And he is fully persuaded that in consideration thereof and of their labour employed thereabouts no tithe of seed thereof has been paid. In his remembrance to these 60 years past no parson has ever demanded tithe of seed nor has any parishioner paid it.
Kedward had no flax growing in Bishopstone in the years in question.
The tithe of the apples are of such small value that they are not worth speaking of.
John Ireland was a boy who drove Humfry Duppa's plough.

Witnesses for Humphrey Duppa

William Jones of Bishopstone, labourer aged 40
He has been an inhabitant in Bishopstone for 24 years. As long as he has known it the right of receiving the tithes these has belonged to the parson of Bishopstone. For the same 24 years the parson there has been in possession of the tithes.
In the year 1600 William Kedward had hemp growing in Bishopstone which the witness estimates to be worth 8d and the seed thereof worth 4d and the tithe worth respectively after that rate.

Anthony Barnes of Bishopstone, husbandman aged 60
For 20 years he has been a dweller in Bishopstone and for a long time he has known that the right of having the tithes belonged to the parson.
During 1600 William Kedward had growing in Bishopstone hemp worth 10d and the seed thereof worth 3d, and the tithe worth according to the rate.
And in the said year passing the ground of the said William Kedward in Bishopstone he did see (to the quantity of) 5 apples or thereabouts growing on a tree within the said grounds worth a farthing or thereabouts.

Henry Delahay of Bishopstone, tailor aged 20
Says that William Kedward is from the parish of Byford.
For these 10 years last past he has known that the right of having and receiving the tithes belongs to the parson.
In 1600 William Kedward had growing in Bishopstone hemp worth 7d and the seed worth 3d and the tithe worth rateably.

Elizabeth Howells of Bishopstone, wife of Thomas Howells of the same aged 80.
William Kedward is from Byford.
For 40 years past she has know that parsons of Bishopstone lawfully and peaceably enjoyed the tithes without let or interruption until the present contention between the now parson and the defendant William Kedward.
In 1600 Kedward had growing on his ground in Bishopstone hemp worth 4d and the tithe rateably. But whether the hemp had any seed she is ignorant. She did see 3 apples growing upon the said William Kedward's trees in Bishopstone in 1600.

John Ireland of Bishopstone, aged 17.
William Kedward is from Byford.
He has known Mr Duppa to be the parson of Bishopstone for 7 years past and to have received the tithes belonging to the parsonage of Bishopstone.
A little before harvest last past he saw hemp growing on Kedward's land in Bishopstone but what it was worth he knoweth not. He did hear Humphrey Duppa to require William Kedward to pay him the tithe of this hemp which he did grow in the parish of Bishopstone in the year 1600 and Kedward answered that he should not have it before the seed was of it.

There is no verdict recorded of the outcome of this long case, talking to historians they say it's not unusual for this type of case to peter out, but I think Humphrey Duppa the Rector never received his tithes on the hemp and apples, which proves the freeholders had power and input over the parish affairs.
By law every person over the age of fourteen had to attend church, and take the sacrament, if you failed to carry out your legal requirements the Rector would report you to the authorities. It would result in an appearance before the church court, where the judge would either give out punishment or dismiss the case; this was then recorded in the volumes of Acts of Office[2]. I have picked out a few entries for Bishopstone in the date range 1598-9 just to illustrate the wide range of power the Church had over its parishioners. Punishment ranged from penance (standing in front of the congregation in church holding a candle wearing a white robe, explaining in detail why they received the penance, and afterwards declaring repentance for one's sins) or excommunication (banned from attending church or associating with your neighbours).
Most cases concerned non-attendance at church like John Crowe, who was charged with not frequenting Church: his case was dismissed. Sometimes people attended a church outside their own parish. Robert Smith was reported for being absent from evening prayer in the previous October but in Court he said that he went to Mansel Church instead; again the case was dismissed.

Another offence heard in the court, was for working in the field at the time of the church services, Richard Ornell was reported for gathering corn on St James Day at the time of evening prayer and having been absent from evening prayer previously. He denied gathering oats but admitted his absence. The court's punishment was one day's penance.
John Crowe was accused of causing his son to carry bands to lay between the reapes of corn on a Sunday in time of divine service. He was also ordered to come to church on September 16th, but only came in at the end of the service and Mr Berington ordered the vicar to complain about him. John was dismissed with a warning. It seems odd that Mr Berington thought he had a Vicar instead of a Rector but it could have been the Vicar from Bridge Sollers who was taking the service.
Other reasons for which you were summoned to court were personal activities, which were deemed not acceptable by the Church. Take Margery Smith for instance, she appeared for "abusing the minister and giving him very unreverent speech" and saying "thou art saucy". She denied it, and was dismissed with a warning. Thomas Carwardine's case was a little more interesting, he was charged with "bordarholding" a whore in his house, He confessed that there was a strange woman in his house who had stayed there about a month, during which time she was delivered of a child whose father was John Newton of the city of Hereford as she herself confessed. As this was a more serious offence Thomas was ordered to do two days penance in Bishopstone and Byford, and to certify it at the next court. He also had to do one day's penance in Mansel Church and certify as above, because he had complained in the court that he had been unfairly treated. It was a waste of time because at the next court Thomas Carwardine didn't bring in his certificates.
Humprey Duppa the Rector in 1600 appears to have become annoyed by the Court case and the parishioners who opposed him in court as he started reporting these people to the church court for some very minor offences, "Ann Digges for a negligent comer to church and for a common sleeper in time of divine service, she promised to amend her fault and was absolved". "Mary Crowe wife of John Crowe for not taking the sacrament on All Saints' Day; on May 6th 1601 she appeared and produced a certificate to show that she had taken sacrament at Christmas and Easter". Mary was also absolved. Catherine wife of John Welshe. "Absenter from Church and not receiving sacrament, she bought in a certificate", also absolved.
It was now the turn of the parishioners who in 1602 reported Humphrey Duppa, Rector, for admitting Catherine Welshe to church to hear divine service and receive the sacrament while she was excommunicated and had not done penance. The Rector tried to cover himself by bringing Catherine before the court and providing her with a certificate to say she had received the sacrament. "Catherine, wife of John Welshe, for not receiving the sacrament at All Saints or Christmas 1600, or since then. She brought in a certificate to say she had received the sacrament at Christmas and was dismissed with a warning". After this the friction between the Rector and his parishioners settled down with far less entries appearing in the church court records.

Humphrey Duppa the Rector died in 1611. In his will dated October 14th 1611[3] he left £5 each to his four children Palle (Paul), Joyce, Sibell and Elizabeth, and the rest of his goods to Alice his wife.

Glebe Terrier, Rectory Farm and House

The term Glebe Terrier is specific to the Church of England. A terrier is a written survey, or inventory, of land (the word derives from the Latin terra, land), Bishopstone has three surviving copies from this period. The glebe is the land or other property held by the incumbent for his support.
In the 1589 glebe terrier of Bishopstone it lists, a Parsonage Farm sitting in 2 acres of enclosed land, containing one dwelling house, two barns and one outhouse for cattle, one 10 acre meadow adjoining the barn plus 47 acres of strips in the common fields.
More details were given in the 1611 terrier.[4]
Inprimis one house, 5 rooms tiled ,together with a little garden. Item 2 barns, one of 5 rooms thatched and the other of 3 rooms thatched. Item 1 close of an acre joining to the house and one orchard of an acre joining to the churchyard
The house would have been timber framed with a stone tile roof, five rooms all on the ground floor, hall, parlour, two other rooms fitting into four bays (usually 12ft square) with a lean-to buttery on the back. A very substantial house, considering that the vicarage at Bridge Sollers in 1608 had only one room. Most of the cottages would have two rooms, a hall and parlour with a buttery on the rear; the latter was where the brewing was done. Rooms and bays were of a similar meaning as the barns are listed as 5 rooms and 3 rooms with a thatched roof.
The glebe land attached to the Rectory was now listed as 82 acres, with accurate descriptions of where the strips are located in the open arable field, naming those who owned the land on either side. The original glebe land was 50 acres, the additional acreage appears to be land either bequeathed to the Church or put at the disposal of the rectory by the lord of the manor.

The arable land listed is in the three main Bishopstone common fields, Hoarstone, Hill and Pluckwell. Interestingly there is none in the Bishon Fields, proof that the glebe arable lands predate Bishon, they originated from the three Anglo-Saxon common fields, when Bishon was mostly waste or moor.
Let's just look at one common field, Hoarstone, as an example of detail in the terrier.
Item the arable land in Horestone Fyelde,(Hoarstone Field) 5 acres, Mr Berington's land joining on both sides. Item 3 acres between the lands of William Pennar on the one side and the lands of Richard Crowe on the other side. Item 2 acres between the lands of William Pennar on the one side and Mr Berington on the other. Item 1 acre between the lands of Mr Berington on one side and the lands of John Diggas on the other. Item 1 acre between the lands of Mr Berington on the one side and Richard Crowe on the other. Item 3 acres between the lands of Mr Berington on the one side and William Pennar on the other. Item half an acre Mr Berington's land joining on both sides. Item half an acre between the lands of Mr Berington on one side and the lands of John Diggas on the other. Item an acre between the lands of Mr Berington on the one side and John Proberts on the other. Item 2 acres between the lands of Mr Berington on one side and the lands of John Diggas on the other. Item an acre between the lands of Mr Berington on the one side and William Pennar's on the other. Item an acre between the lands of George Philpots on the one side and William Pennar on the other. Item 3 acres, Mr Berington's lands lying on both sides.

These strips of land were marked in the common Hoarstone field by mere (marking) stones. Hoarstone field covered an area of approx 100 acres split in two by the Roman Road.
The old Rectory was extensively rebuilt around 1620, as shown by the last glebe terrier of Bishopstone made on September 26th 1636[5] which lists the house as now having a cross wing containing the great chamber with a chimney, plus two lodging chambers, one hall, one little parlour, one buttery and three little lower rooms adjoining the garden and one other room as an entrance into the house, with one corn loft over the entry. The Rectory was now a ten-roomed house, this rebuild was carried out by the lord of the manor Humphrey Berington, to accommodate the new Rector John Hawkyns in 1623. The outbuildings were also improved with two barns containing 8 bays, one beast house, one sheepcote, and one stable. The glebe land had grown by 5 acres to 87 acres. Five parishioners witnessed the 1636 terrier; Richard Digges and William Berington could write and sign their names while Nicholas Parlour "blacksmith", John Probert "church warden" and Thomas Welsh who ran the New Inn could only make a mark.

The 17th century started with high hope for the villagers of Bishopstone. John Berington as Sheriff of Herefordshire brought wealth and prosperity to the whole parish. The village by the church still had nine enclosures left from its medieval past, seven were freehold and two belonged to the manor. The most noticeable difference from the previous centuries is the use of written deeds and records; previously it was exclusively for the upper class and the church but now the system records all classes down to the paupers.
One or two of the large freeholders could sign their names on documents. But the majority of the parishioners were illiterate.
Bishopstone commoners must have wanted to learn to read and write, we have our first mention of a school in Bishopstone, given in the Acts of Office dated February 1635, although it was short lived
"John Sitting Curate of Bishopstone was asked to appear before the Bishop for not having a certificate for teaching a school at his house. He did not appear (he is ill)."
I have found no further record of the school, the Bishop must have refused John a certificate, but he was in further trouble in November 1636 when he was sent to appear before the Bishop again for not wearing a hood or cap during the church service.
The last entry in the church court book for Bishopstone was made in November 1638 it states Humphrey Berington had not paid the church rate, he did not appear. More interestingly Elizabeth Parlour was accusation of fornication with John Gough, although she didn't appear to answer charge, a note written said she will appear at the next court and plead her good character.

In 1643 Parliament passed an ordinance designed to strip the churches of everything that represented the Anglican faith. Oliver Cromwell's Commonwealth government had started to take power; the Church of England didn't exist for the next 18 years. The parishioners did not get off lightly, the puritans were as strict as their predecessors and among the many new laws over this period, Christmas could not be celebrated.
Relating to the seventeenth century I have copies of over four hundred documents of people and places in the parish, from the sale of one strip in a common field to the manor itself. It was a very turbulent century for Bishopstone mainly as a result of the Civil War.

To help understand how a parish class system in the seventeenth century; I have listed the inhabitants of Bishopstone in a so-called pecking order.

(1) The Lords of the Manor were the Berington family, they held the manor under the Bishop of Hereford for which they paid a peppercorn rent of £3 6s 8d per year plus a military tenancy on the land (see the Court Rolls 1630) on condition that they provided knights when required. The military tenancy and Bishop's Manor status were abolished in early 1660, one of the last acts passed by the commonwealth.

(2) The freeholders: they held the largest area of cultivated land, 380 acres. Two of the biggest landholders were the Crow and Digges families. The Digges family owned 2 farms and 120 acres at the beginning of the century that increased to 3 farms and 150 acres by the end of the century. After the Civil War they were mostly known by the title of gentlemen Their home in Bishopstone was called Bishton, it was rebuilt in the late 1660's, the second largest house in the parish after the Court.

The Crowe family came to Bishopstone in 1511 when Walter Crowe bought Bishon farm which passed to John Crowe his son, who died in May 1610 aged 80. He left the farm to his wife Mary (who was a lot younger than John), his son Richard and daughters Penelope and Marie. John also owned a farm in Tillington, through a marriage settlement on his wife. Mary Crowe remarried, handing the farm over to her son Richard Crowe who died suddenly in 1627. John, Richard's son, was only 17 when his father died and the farms were taken into the wardship of John Monnington till he came of age. He also added more land by buying half of William Berington's farm for £138.

Next in order came the Eckley family who originated from Mansel Lacy. James Eckley bought 40 acres of land and a farm in the 1570s from the Crown, as explained previously, this was originally chantry land owned by the Chapel of St Mary. He built a new house called the Pleck replacing the old tenement called Mellin.

John his brother also built up his holdings in the parish by buying land in the common fields, a smallholding on the edge of the common on the hill, and a farm called Walle. He sold on a smallholding described as a messuage barns and an orchard situated on Bishopstone Hill totalling 4 acres, to Thomas Scandett in 1612 for the sum of fifty one pounds of good English money.

John appears to have caused a stir, as recorded in the manor court rolls for 1628, by letting three tenants build cottages on his freehold land without the court's permission. The Eckley family were freeholders and tenants in Bishopstone all through the seventeenth century.

Other freeholders included Margaret Welsh with a farm of 30 acres, John Parlour the blacksmith with a smallholding of 10 acres on the hill, Nicholas Parlour with a 15 acre farm in the village, John Thomas who was the village carpenter built a cottage on the hill, John Ornald held a cottage on Bishon common, David Pugh a house (later part of Burcott Row) and land in Bishon, John Savaker the New Inn, and lastly Thomas Geers (Gent) Marsh Farm, Bridge Sollers who owned 3½ acres, (eventually this become part of Garnons estate). Besides the Gents hardly any of the others could sign their names, most documents were endorsed with a shaky cross.

(3) The tenant farmers. Some leases were for the lives of a husband and wife, some for 21 years, and a few (only two I know of in Bishopstone) were for 99 years. These were John Snead who negotiated a 99-year lease with Humphrey Digges for 3 acres out of Linning field so he could build the blacksmith's shop, and Thomas Forris who in 1647 also obtained a 99-year lease from Humphrey Berington on Clay Pitts Farm. William Berington, the younger brother of Humphrey lived in the village and farmed 20 acres for an annual peppercorn rent of two shillings. Stephen Powell a smallholder with 6 acres also lived in the village; there were 14 tenant farmers in 1630 holding between 1 acre to 90 acres.

(4) The cottagers also had a legal right to land, usually a strip or two in the common fields, a leftover from the original medieval system. These cottages also carried common rights so they could let their livestock onto the common and open fields at agreed times. One cottager was Thomas Sheppard who was a weaver with a cottage in Bishon, which carried all common rights.

(5) The squatters, they had cottages built on encroachments on the commons: Bishopstone appears to have had only a few around the common fringes. These, like the servants, are by and large the nameless ones with few records of their names.

(6) The servants who lived in on the farms.

The whole system in Bishopstone revolved around agriculture.

It is important to remember that no farmer, however large his holding, or his social position, was at liberty to cultivate his strips in any of the common fields as he pleased. The jury of the manor court would decide the system of cultivation for him. This court jury was made up from all classes from the village who owned common rights, from a cottager Thomas Sheppard with one strip up to the largest holder John Digges. The court decided on all aspects of agriculture, from which seeds were to be sown in different fields to the dates at which the fields were opened and closed as common pastures. The manor court also settled disputes over land and the maintenance of the ditches.

There appears to be only two of these court rolls surviving for Bishopstone; they are nice examples of how the manor system worked in the early part of the 17th century. These meetings took place in the main hall of Bishopstone Court.

The first in 1628 appears to be an emergency meeting called because of the death of John Eckley who had sold land before he died causing disputes about land ownership, and several new owners were building cottages without the court's permission. The second court roll is a record of the annual meeting in 1630.

Manor of Bushopston[6]

Court Baron of Humfrey Berington esq. held there 23 Chas I [1628] before Thomas Lawrence esq steward there. **(Thomas Lawrence was Humphrey Berington's agent, Humphrey like his uncle never farmed any land in Bishopstone and every part was let out except the Manor House and stables)**

Essoins: John Bridges gent, and John Thomas by Mary Debitott and John Ornall **(apologies for not attending the court)**

Homage sworn **(The names listed below had to formally acknowledge they were tenants to the Lord of the Manor Humphrey Berington**

John Diggas
John Probert
Stephen Powles
Thomas Taylor
Richard Walshe
Francis Pillinger
Walter Eckley
John Savacre
Philip Savacre
John Thomas

First they say on oath that Thomas Geers gent (2d), Nicholas Parlor (2d), Thomas Savacre (2d), John Parlor (2d) free tenants of this manor owe suit of court and have made default on this day, therefore they are amerced. **(The four named above should have attended the court; because they failed to turn up they were fined 2d.)**

Item they present that John Eckley, now deceased, during his lifetime alienated to John Arnold by deed 4 acres of free land held of the lord, of which ½a lies at the common, upon which a cottage has been recently erected in which the said John Arnold now lives, ½a in le Merefeild, 1½a in Lyneing (Linning) Field, 1½a in Horeston (Hoarstone) Field and ½a in Lower Hill Field. John Arnold is ordered to appear at the next court to do fealty and other services under a pain of 20s. He holds by suit of court, knight's service and heriot.

(Suit of court; The duty to attend the lord's court.

Heriot; A payment that lord of the Manor could claim from the heirs of a dead tenant (essentially a death tax) which was forgiven if he died in battle.

Knight's Service. Part of the tenure of land was to provide soldiers with weapons and armour to fight for their lord on behalf of the sovereign

Item they present that John Eckley in his lifetime alienated to Thomas Savacre 5a lying together in Lower Hill Field. Therefore the said Thomas Savacre is ordered to appear at the next court to do fealty and other services under a pain of 20s. He holds by suit of court, knight's service and heriot.

(If Thomas Savacre did not carry out the court's instructions, by appearing at the next court to do fealty (swear allegiance to the lord of the manor), and other services he would, like John Arnold, have to pay 20s which was around four months wages)

Item they present that the said John Eckley in his lifetime alienated to Philip Savacre 1 cottage and 4a land of which 1a lies in Lyneing Field, 1a in Horeston Field, 1a in Over Hill Field and 1 close containing [gap] acre. The cottage is called Walle Close. (See map)

Philip Savacre is ordered to appear at the next court to do fealty and other services under a pain of 20s. He holds by suit of court, knight's service and heriot.

Item they present that the said John Eckley in his lifetime alienated to John Thomas 1 cottage and 1a land on the south part of Bishopstons Hill. John Thomas is ordered to appear at the next court to do fealty and other services under a pain of 20s. He holds by suit of court, knight's service and heriot.

(John Thomas was the village carpenter)

To this court came John Diggas and in open court acknowledged that he holds of the lord 2 messuages and 120a land by annual rent of 21s 11d of which 18s to the said manor called Daniels Fee and 8d to the manor. He holds by suit of court, knight's service and heriot and other services. And he did fealty.

(John Diggas, Bishton Farm)

To this court came Richard Walshe and in full court acknowledged that he holds of the lord 1 messuage and 24½a of land by annual rent of 5s 8d, suit of court, knight's service and heriot and other services. And he did fealty

(Richard died soon after this court, but because the farm was under a life long tenancy with his wife Margaret , she carried on farming after his death).

Item to this court came Walter Eckley and in full court acknowledged that he holds of the lord 1 messuage and 40a land by annual rent of 5s 8d suit of court, knight's service and heriot. And the said Walter requested that John Arnold, Thomas Savacre, Philip Savacre and John Thomas should make contribution with the said Walter towards the rent of the said property because they had separately obtained part of the lands belonging to the said messuage totalling 14a as shown above.
To this court came John Savacre and acknowledged that he holds of the lord 1 messuage called Walleclose and 4a free land, part of the land of John Eckley, by annual rent of 5s 8d suit of court, knight's service and heriot and other services. And he should make contribution with the said Walter Eckley for the said rent of 5s 8d. And he did fealty.

(John Eckley had left his house and remaining land to his son Walter, and because his father had not declared selling off some of his free land to the manor court, the court made Walter still liable to pay the Lords rent.)

To this court came Thomas Sheppard and acknowledged that he holds of the lord 1 cottage and 3a free land by annual rent of 4d and 2 chickens, suit of court, knight's service and heriot and other services. And he did fealty.

(Thomas Sheppard's annual rent of 4d and 2 chickens at Christmas, was a normal part of the tenancy by the end of the seventeenth century, but the chickens were sometimes specified as capons because some of the tenants were giving the lord the 2 oldest and toughest birds.)

Item they present Thomas Bithell (12d) of Byford, Thomas Smith (12d) of the same, William Jenkins (12d) of Shutton for staff driving in the common called Bishopstons
Common therefore they are amerced.

(These three lived outside the parish but held land in the manor and so were covered by the court)

And they present William Maddocks (6d) for carrying away fern outside Bishopstons Common.

(Fern from the common on the hill was cut as winter bedding for beasts, temporary roofing material, medical properties and in winter burnt on the gardens for potash; what William Maddocks' needs were we don't know)

It was ordered that no tenant henceforth should keep their beasts in the cornfields except on their own land under pain of 7s

(No livestock was allowed into the common field).

It was ordered that no tenant henceforth should cut fern in Bishopstons Common before Lammas without a licence from the lord under pain of 7s.

(Lammas [1st August] date set when fern could be cut.)

It was ordered that Mary Debitott or the tenant of John Bridges gent should scour the ditch in Smithes Meadow before next Michaelmas under pain of 7s.

(John Bridges snr (gent) from the Ley in Weobley had bought the farm formerly belonging to the chantry, he was the father of Mary Crowe of Bishon Farm, and this John was Mary's brother. His tenant Mary Debittott was liable to maintain the ditches that ran through her land and keep them clear, if it was not done by 2nd February she would be fined seven shillings)

Item it was ordered that before the next feast of All Saints the jurors should inspect encroachments and the removal and putting down of mere stones and should give their verdict under a pain of 7s for any juror who does not do so.

(Mere stones marked the boundaries of the strips in the common fields and were commonly moved to gain more land. All the jurors met in the field and a majority verdict was made on the repositioning of the stones. If any juror did not turn up they were fined seven shillings)

Affeerers John Diggas, John Probert
By me, Thomas Lawrence

There is no record of Bishon farm in these Court Rolls, since Richard Crowe of Bishon Farm had just died, and his son and heir John was underage and could not appear. This next meeting is more representative of the usual annual meeting of the Court, where declaration of land holdings and maintenance business were discussed. There were often smaller meetings when the parishioners with common rights in that particular field met and discussed and agreed on what crops could be planted, also setting the date when the field would be opened for grazing. From this record it is possible to work out the freeholders from the tenants and the land they occupied. In 1630 Bishopstone parish consisted of 17 listed farms of various sizes, and three cottages, 361 acres of free land, 304 acres of demesne land and 75 acres of common. This is the only surviving court roll of Bishopstone from which we can extract enough information on what was happening in the parish before the Civil War, so for this reasons I have included the full transcript with some explanatory notes.

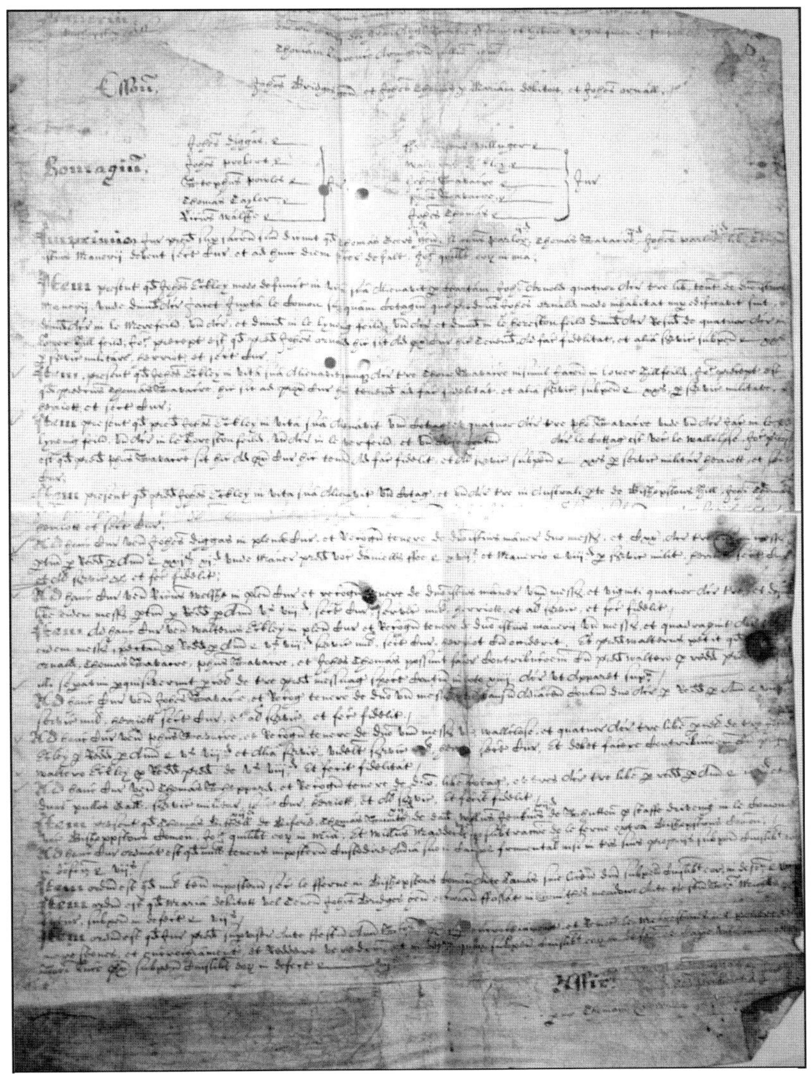

(Figure 3) 1630 Court roll of Bishopstone

Court Rolls of Bishopstone 1630

Court Baron of Humfrey Berington held there 25 Oct 6 Chas I [1630] by Thomas Lawrence esq., steward. Essoins none. Homage sworn, William Berington gent, John Probert, John Diggas, John Colcombe, John Parlor, John Thomas of New Inn, Nicholas Parlor, John Thomas of Hill, Stephen Powell, John Savacre, Thomas Taylor, Thomas Sheppard, Richard Lewys and Philip Savacre.

First the jurors say on oath that Margaret Walsh (2d), James Davies (2d), and Thomas Geers (2d) have made default of suit of court and so are amerced.
Item they present that Alice Savacre and John Savacre since the last court have alienated to William Gomond gent 7a of arable land held of the lord of this manor by annual rent of 2d, knight's service, heriot and other services.
To this court came John Diggas and acknowledged that he holds of the lord 2 free messuages and 120a of land belonging by annual rent of 21s 11d, knight's service, heriot and other services and he claims common of pasture in Bistons Common and Bishopstons Hill appertaining to his tenements as is accustomed.
William Berrington gent claims to hold 1 messuage and 30a land by annual rent of 2s, suit of court, knight's service, and heriot and he claims to hold common of pasture in Bistons Common and Bishopston.
John Parlor acknowledged that he holds of the lord 1 free messuage and 9a land by annual rent of 7s, suit of court, knight's service and heriot and he claims common of pasture in Bistons Common and Bishopston.
Nicholas Parlor acknowledges that he holds of the lord 1 messuage and 15a free land by annual rent of 2d, knight's service, and heriot and he claims common of pasture.
Stephen Powell claims to hold by indenture 1 messuage and 6a land for the life of the said Stephen, Ann his wife and John Powell, by annual rent of 33s.
Thomas Taylor claims to hold by indenture for 21 years 1 messuage and 3a land by annual rent of 28s.
Richard Lewys claims to hold by indenture by right of his wife 1 messuage and 30a land for life of Alice his wife by annual rent of 13s 4d.
John Probert claims to hold by indenture for term of the life of himself and his wife Elianor 1 messuage and 10a land by annual rent of 46s.
The same John Probert holds for 21 years 90a land by annual rent of 19s.
(John Probert although a churchwarden could not read or write his name, how he carried out his duty of keeping a written record of baptisms and burials is a mystery, he is yet to discover his misfortunes in the pending civil war)

John Colcombe holds by indenture 1 messuage and 5a land for term of his life by annual rent of 10s.
John Catchmey holds by indenture 1 messuage and 1a land for life of himself and wife Elizabeth by annual rent of 13s 4d.
John Thomas of New Inn holds by indenture for life of himself and wife Eleanor 4a land by annual rent of 20s. **(John Savacre was the freehold owner of the New Inn, There were now two John Thomas's living in the parish, if they were related is unknown)**
Walter Eckley in full court acknowledged that he holds of the lord 1 free messuage and 40a land belonging to the same by annual rent of 5s 8d, suit of court, knight's service and heriot. **(Walter lived in The Pleck)**
John Thomas acknowledges that he holds 1 cottage and ½a free land by annual rent of 1d, suit of court, knight's service and heriot. **(John Thomas the carpenter lived in the cottage he built on Bishopstone Hill)**
John Savacre holds 1 messuage and 6a free land by annual rent of 8d, suit of court, knight's service and heriot. **(This smallholding stood at the end of the bridle path next to the present A438)**
Margaret Walsh has alienated 2 parts of a messuage and 30a free land to George Eckley and holds the other part herself by annual rent of 5s 8d, suit of court, knight's service and heriot and other services.
(Margaret Walsh had sold some of her freehold land to George Eckley after her husband Richard had died)
Thomas Sheppard holds a 1 cottage and 2a free land by annual rent of 2d, suit of court, knight's service and heriot. **(Thomas was a weaver)**
Alice Savacre holds 1 messuage and 15a free land by annual rent of 2s 8d, suit of court, knight's service and heriot. **(Alice was John's mother, her farm house stood on the Burcott Row site)**
John Savacre holds by indenture for 21 years 1 cottage and 1a land by annual rent of 14s.
Item they present that Thomas Geers gent holds of the lord 3½a free land by annual rent of [gap] suit of court, knight's service and heriot. **(The jurors recorded Thomas Geers holdings [landowning gentry of The Marsh Bridge Sollers and Garnons]because he was not present)**
Item John Diggas acknowledges that he holds 1½ virgates of land containing by estimation 90a by indenture for 21 years by annual rent of £17-5-0. **(It appears John Digges forgot to declare he was renting 90 acres from Humphrey Berington when he first stood up.)**
Item they present that John Crowe holds 1 free messuage and 120a of land by annual rent of 42s, suit of court, knight's service and heriot and that the said John is under the age of 21 years and is in the wardship of John Monnington by the lord's grant. **(Because John was under age he was not allowed to appear at the court)**
Item it is ordered that no-one henceforth shall keep beasts in the corn fields before harvest except on their own land under a pain of 7s each. **(If any of the tenants let their livestock into the common fields before the harvest the court would fine them seven shillings)**
Item it is ordered that John Diggas shall scour the ditch next to the house of John Arnold at Bistons Common before next Michaelmas under a pain of 7s.
(John Digges ordered to clean out the ditch at Bishon Common by February 2nd or the Court would fined him seven shillings, four hundred years later there are still problems with the same ditch)
Affeerers William Berington, John Diggas
By me T Lawrence, steward there.

The New Inn changed hands on July 15th 1637. John Savacre senior appears to have died, so his sons John from Dinedor and William from Sutton sold the Inn by feoffment (early form of conveyance) for £38 to Phillip Gwilliam. Phillip lived in a smallholding in Bishon, he let out the Inn to Thomas Welsh. Phillip was a bachelor who soon found himself in debt and sold the New Inn and his smallholding to Humphrey Berington. When he died in 1671 he did not leave a will. On October 17th 1672 David Pugh of Bishopstone appeared before the Bishop and swore that Phillip Gwilliam had died intestate and that he was his nearest cousin, and administration was granted to him. An inventory taken at the time of his death lists, 5 kine (cows) value £8, all his wearing apparel and household stuff worth 20 shillings,a debt due from William Clarke by bond £2 10s, due from Richard Smallman by bond £5. Total value of estate £16.10s.
In 1655 William Berington sold his farm at the Townsend to John Crow for £120. What can be confusing is that John Digges also owned a farm called Townsend, so we have two farms of the same name. The farms stood either side of the road down to the church hence both referred to as Townsend Farm, similarly named farms were found in nearly every village or township in Herefordshire. William Berington had married Penelope Crow, John's sister in 1640, they were both Bishopstonians.

Bishon Farm was a centre of disputes from 1627 to 1645; it started when an ageing Mary Depal late wife of John Crow sold part of Bishon Farm to her brother John Bridges of the Ley, Weobley. Bridges sold it on to James Davies but John Monnington's widow disputed this sale.
I have listed below some of the transactions on Bishon Farm to show how complex land ownership could be over a short period of 56 years.

1627 Court settlement on the death of Richard Crowe, Mary Depal late wife of John Crowe, mother of Richard Crowe, settled three messuage 130 acres of land to John Crowe (grandson) for life. Two smallholdings were leased out.

1630 John Crowe under age (in wardship of John Monnington) held 1 free farm 120a (Court Rolls)
1631 Mary Depal (grandmother) sells part of farm to John Bridges
1632 John Bridges sells Bishon farm to James Davies
1632 John Crowe settles an annuity of £10 secured on Bishon farm to his mother Joan
1640 James Davies owned under dispute with widow Monnington (Council of Marches)
1645 John Crowe of Weobley (cloth merchant) repurchases farm for £90 as per court instructions
1655 Edward Baker Gent rents Bishon farm.
1656 Richard Foote rents Bishon Farm
1666 John Crowe, Vicar, sells Bishon Farm to Ann Martin
1676 John Crowe Vicar of Upton Cresset, Salop sells Townsend farm)
1683 Ann Martin dies leaving Bishon Farm to trustees to form a charity
1683 Richard Foote now tenant to Ann Martin Trust

Ann Martin Bread Charity Bishon Farm[7]

Ann Martin, a wealthy spinster from Hereford, purchased Bishon Farm from John Crowe in 1666. Ann's will dated December 9th 1683 is a very long detailed document on the settlement of her estate.; in which she instructed that part of the rent received from Bishon farm, £27 per year, should endow a charity for the poor women of All Saints, Bishopstone and Burghill on her death.
Ann's executors were Robert Price of Foxley and his brother-in-law Thomas Carpenter of Credenhill, (both men had inherited parts of the Foxley estate by marriage to the Rodd sisters). They set up a bread charity for the poor women, £10 per year to All Saints, £5 to Burghill and 40 shillings to Bishopstone. "A penny loaf after divine service to be given to poor women, monies left over to be divided up between the poor women on the four principal feast days forever". This applied to each of the parishes named.
It is of interest to Bishopstonians because the charity on Bishon farm ran for 311 years until 1994 when Donald Watkins finally paid it off. During this period it remained the same yearly payment of 40s until decimalization came in, when it turned to £2. The payments to All Saints and Burghill appear to have lapsed many years ago.
These are some of the interesting points extracted from the will. She made the will in the thirty-fifth year of Charles the second whom she named as King of England, France, Scotland and Ireland. Ann lived at Bovine a large house in the vicinity of the old Victoria Eye Hospital; she left goods and property to many friends Today a wooden plaque on a wall in All Saints Church Hereford records these facts.

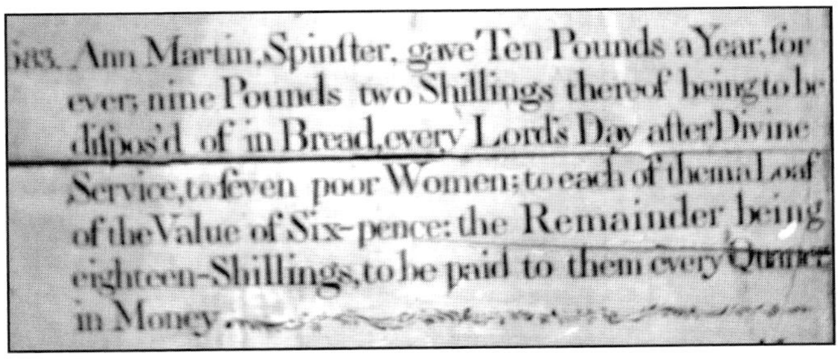

Ann Martin, Spinster, gave Ten Pounds a Year, for ever; nine Pounds two Shillings thereof being to be dispos'd of in Bread, every Lord's Day after Divine Service, to seven poor Women; to each of them a Loaf of the Value of Six-pence: the Remainder being eighteen-Shillings, to be paid to them every Quarter in Money.

(Figure 4) Ann Martin recorded on the charity board hanging in All Saints Church.

Ann was also very generous to her two maids who nursed her in her illness, Sarah Thomas and Sybil Downing to whom she left her house, the greater part of her estate and 40s a year each to be paid out of the rent of Bishon Farm.
Her distant relatives disputed this part of her will but a court settlement went in favour of the two maids. Sarah Thomas, one of her maids, went on to marry John Eckley from Bishopstone, possibly meeting him on visits to Bishon farm with her mistress.
Ann was buried in Hereford Cathedral next to her sister, she left £100 for a decent interment, out of which money was used to pay for thirty grey gowns with hoods for thirty women to wear when accompanying the coffin to the grave, together with scarves and gloves for the bearers of her pall, and the Custos and Vicars Choral of the College of Hereford to attend her corpse and say and sing the divine service.

Chapter 6
Civil War & Commonwealth (1641-1661)

There's no doubt that twenty years of civil war and Commonwealth rule changed the fortunes of the parish for ever, it would never be able to recover financially after this conflict, resulting in Bishopstone Manor being sold in 1698 by the then lord of the manor Thomas Berington, who was bankrupt after his father Humphrey's involvement in the Civil War.

As with any war this one created confusion. I have tried to piece together individual pieces of information to make sense of what happened in Bishopstone during this period and to understand these records it is important to look at Herefordshire as a whole and the chain of events that took place over this period[1]. Most of the gentry in Herefordshire supported the King, like Bishopstonian Humphrey Berington and Humphrey Digges. In 1641 Humphrey Berington had signed his name on a paper to support the King with many other prominent Herefordian gentry, but to their dismay on October 2nd 1642 the Earl of Stamford entered Hereford unapposed with his parliamentarian troops. He was appointed Governor of Hereford and his troops plundered many royalists estates in Herefordshire including Garnons and Bishopstone. Mrs Joyce Jefferies, a royalist, kept a diary of the events. She had fled Hereford on September 23rd 1642 for her safety, escaping to Garnons the dwelling house of Francis Geers before the Parliamentarians arrived, as an extract from her diary helps to explain.

My place of refuge proves to be insecure, for on October 6th Captain Hammond and the barbarous company plundered Mr. Geer's house, both them and me, of much goods, took away my two bay coach mares and some money and much linen, and Miss Eliza Acton's clothes.

On March 27th 1643 she records, *"this Monday morning the men of Little Mansel and all the company of Herefordshire went to Ross to meet the other army"*

I am not exactly sure what happened at Humphrey Berington's house, Bishopstone Court when the troops came to plunder. The only written evidence I have seen records, "*when the troops left the house the side wall of the house had fallen into the moat"* Humphrey would have put up some resistance to protect his property by closing the gate over the moat etc., the troops could have left a mine (an explosive device made from gunpowder commonly used by the Parliamentarians troops) under the wall as a parting act; it seems to me very little else could have brought the side of the house down. The other possible explanation for the damage caused would be to bring in a small cannon and aim for the corner of the house. It appears Humphrey was so enraged by this action he immediately set about recruiting his own private army of a hundred men and paying for them out of his own pocket. To help finance this army he borrowed £1,200 from Thomas Geers and as security against the loan he put up Catley Manor. Joyce Jeffries' diary entry, which refers to the Little Mansel men, said they left on March 27th 1643. That date ties up nicely with Humphrey Berington, proof that he must have assembled his foot soldiers within six months of the plundering of his house. Little Mansel was part of his estate lying just over the Bishopstone boundary in Mansel Lacy, and from there he would have led his foot soldiers to Ross then on to Higham in Gloucestershire where on April 1st the Hereford gentry including Humphrey and the Welsh took part in a major battle against Sir William Waller's parliamentarian troops. The Royalists lost the battle and Captain Berington was taken prisoner. From other documents we can name three or possibly four Bishopstone parishioners who fought in the civil war beside Humphrey Berington.

John Probert was one; he was listed in the 1630 court rolls as a farmer and churchwarden. John never married. He returned after the war to his farm in the village and the 1661 tax assessments list John as the tenant of the ten-acre farm with others living with him. In 1672 John Probert's [2]name appears in a Hereford court statement. "*Ordered that the elders of this county do pay unto John Probert of Bishopstone who has been a soldier for his late master and was wounded in his service ye yearly sum of 40s to be paid quarterly as is such cases be asked. And ye same to begin in course according to ye propriety of the admission as is asked in ye alike cases."*

John died in 1674 and was buried in Bishopstone Church.

Thomas Welsh was another soldier. His name appears in Hawkening v Berington, a court case[3] held in 1680 over the ownership of the New Inn. In part of Thomas Berington's statement he says, *"Thomas Welsh made a lease with Humphrey Berington for the New Inn, he lived there and ran an Alehouse for many years before Humphrey died. Thomas is now paid maintenance by the parish. His mother and father kept the Alehouse before him. Thomas Welsh did live with Humphrey as a servant, also the said Thomas Welsh was for sometime confirmed as a soldier under the command of the said Humphrey in the time of the late civil war."* Thomas Welsh died in 1686.

Henry (Harry) Thomas known as "Black Harry" as previously recorded lived with Humphrey as his servant and was made famous in the neighbourhood for tipping over the saltpetre in 1637 on his masters instructions. Unlike the previous two named soldiers Harry had a wife, Catherine, and two children Edmund and Elizabeth.

The other possible candidate for service in the royalist army is Thomas Forris who appears to have been rewarded by Humphrey Berrington who gave him a 99 years lease on Claypitts Farm, one house, garden and orchard, one acre croft at Down (Downshill), a four acre plock called Cockshells old lands, two acres in Lower Hill Field, and two acres in Upperhill Field for 20s per year. This cheap 99-year lease could be a favour for his services to the Royalist cause. Humphrey signed this agreement on March 7th 1647 although as the estate was under sequestration by Benjamin Mason he took a personal risk of more punishment by making this lease. The agreement stood the passage of time with the rent staying at 20 shillings for 99 years as shown on later estate records.

After the battle of Higham Sir William Waller carried on advancing with his army to Hereford where he persuaded the Royalists to give up the town, so on April 24th 1643 parliamentarian troops entered Hereford for the second time. He left Hereford with his troops on June 6th and immediately afterwards a strong garrison of Royalists reoccupied the town.

Humphrey Berington appears back in Bishopstone by 1644, it's unclear if he escaped prison or paid a fine for his release. The war had escalated in the county by 1645, the royalists had improved the defences of Hereford which was now described as having a strong stone wall around it and some cannons.

King Charles 1 reached Hereford on June 19th 1645 and held a reception where many of the gentry came to pay homage possibly including Humphrey Berington and Humphrey Digges. This appears to have been the first time they could have met the King. On July 10th the King left Hereford for Abergavenny attended part of the way by Herefordshire gentry including Captain Berington. Whilst in Hereford the King's Troops were stationed at Brinsop Court, the home of Roger Dansey. Humphrey Berington and Humphrey Digges returned to Hereford where they prepared to defend the town against the approaching Scottish army under the Earl of Leven. On July 30th 1645 the Scottish army began their siege of Hereford. The two Humphreys from Bishopstone plus their soldiers were trapped in the town for a month with the defenders repelling all the Scots threw at them including a mine at Fryers Gate and their cannon fire hitting St Owen's church. With the gentry trapped inside the town, they could offer no protection for their manors and the Scottish army who had to live off the land for provisions to feed themselves and their horses plundered many parishes including Bishopstone taking anything they needed and more.

Existing official records show that of the 106 parishes in Herefordshire, 70 claimed against the Scottish army for houses rifled, and doors, chests and trunks broken open. Several families had most or all their cattle, horses and goods taken, many lost plate, jewels and all kinds of rich household stuff, including rings, linen, and books. Many parishes had the plate and linen of their churches taken. Bishopstone claimed £218 11s 2d. We know the Scottish army for a time camped at Byford so Bishopstone was within easy striking distance. On the August 1st 1645 His Majesty approached Hereford from Worcester with his army. The Scottish Army on hearing this by the next morning had dispersed and vanished out of sight. The King entered the city in triumph and held another reception where it is possible the two Bishopstoneians met the King again. The enemy were now closing in on the King. On the September 6th the King was in Weobley. It was a cat and mouse war: with 2,000 Roundheads on horse back at Leominster the king's whole Army met at Arthur's Stone near Dorstone Castle on Wednesday 17th September, the last time Humphrey Berrington could have seen the King.

Colonel Birch hired six men with a constable and disguised them as labourers who were sent to help repair the town walls. Early in the morning of the December 18th 1645 they killed the guard and let the drawbridge down at the Bye Gate and after a freezing march through the night Birch's army retook Hereford with little bloodshed. Meanwhile Humphrey Berington with the other Hereford gentry retreated to Goodrich Castle, where they held out until July 31st 1646 when the castle fell and 50 officers and 120 soldiers were taken prisoner including Captain Berington for the second time.

(Figure 2) Goodrich Castle showing the extent of the damage caused by Colonel Birch's army.

Charles 1 was put on trial on January 1st 1649. After being found guilty he was beheaded on Tuesday 30th January and the monarchy was abolished on 6th February. The Royalists who supported the King in the war had to appear before the Committee for Compounding.

Humphrey Berington was taken before the Committee on May 1st 1649 for "assisting the King in the beginning of the late troubles"[4]. He returned to court in March 1650 and was fined one sixth of the value of his estates, £632 6s.

Having failed to raise the money Humphrey was arrested and imprisoned 12 months later, he was then taken to Gloucester prison, which was located in the castle. The conditions were atrocious there, it was overcrowded, housing up to 1500 prisoners with very little food. He was trying to sell his manor at Catley to raise the fine but times were so uncertain that property had no value. The family put together several petitions for his release; Ann his wife went before the Committee and begged for the income from one fifth of the estate, claiming that she and her children were starving. In December Humphrey's daughters Joyce and Anne returned before the Committee asking for an allowance to be paid, saying that they had received nothing, had run out of charity from friends and there were five children who would certainly perish if an allowance was not given. They also added that the estate had been sequestered for 6 years, their father was still in prison and the County committee had let out the estate worth £300 per year for only £50.

The Committee was petitioned again on July 6th 1652, where William Lynn offered to pay Humphrey Berington's fine if he was allowed to hold the estate as security until he was reimbursed. The Committee ordered this case to be represented to the Army Committee and Parliament. Fifteen months later in October 1653 the fine was raised to £650.

Humphrey Berington was released from prison on November 8th 1653, after his fine had been paid. He had spent two and half years in Gloucester Prison. This period in prison had undoubtedly taken its toll on Humphrey because he died in Bishopstone four years later in 1657, at the age of fifty seven. Because Humphrey had borrowed money to fund his soldiers and help the war effort he was effectively bankrupt.

Francis Geers of Garnons was the main claimant on the estate.

March 1653. Fras. Geeres, sen., of Garnons, Hereford, begs reference to counsel of his title to the tithes of Much Marcle and chapel of Kinaston, co. Hereford, with glebe lands, conveyed to his brother Thomas in 1638 by Berington, as security for 400l. (£400) loan, with interest; also Catley Manor, conveyed for 264l. (£264) in 18 Charles, for which sums Berington in 1642 entered a statute of 1,200l. (£1200), yet unpaid, and the premises which are come to petitioner are sequestered for Berington's delinquency.

This debt of £1,864 was repaid by the conveyance of lands to Thomas Geers and the advowson of Bishopstone church, the Rectory and the glebe lands, with the right to present a clergyman to the parish church. More concerned about his own church at Bridge Sollers, Thomas installed John Cutler into the Rectory in Bishopstone in 1655 and presented him as Vicar of Bridge Sollers. This large rambling house and land would have been an attractive residence for a country clergyman, compared with Bridge Sollers' one room vicarage, which had been plundered by the Roundheads.

Bishopstone church would have been used in the period 1655-61, but only for Presbyterian services, which didn't include recording baptisms. Following the restoration in 1660 of the Anglican Church, services were held again with John Cutler installed as the Rector

The first and oldest surviving entry in the parish register transcripts of Bishopstone church was the baptism of John Berington on August 29th 1661; he is described as John son of Thomas and Hannah Berington born August 13th 1661. Thomas must have rejoiced to see the Anglican rite restored in time for the christening of his son.

The Geers family held the patronage of Bishopstone church until Price of Foxley purchased the manor. Throughout this period Bridge Sollers vicars and Bishopstone rectors were the same person although they always lived in the Rectory in Bishopstone.

Benjamin Mason sequestrator of Bishopstone

On December 18th 1645 Colonel Morgan and Colonel Birch had retaken Hereford city for Parliament, Captain Benjamin Mason and Captain Silas Taylor were appointed Sequestration Commissioners for Herefordshire. Colonel Birch was always suspicious of Benjamin Mason, for example when they met he commented on his dress saying he was dressed like a flamboyant "Royalist," he did not wear the plainer clothing usually worn by Parliamentarians. He was right; at the start of the war Mason fought for the Royalists and then changed sides but his two brothers remained loyal to the King. He was only interested in lining his own pocket and immediately confiscated Humphrey Berington's estates along with those of many others Royalist gentry, these estates were rented out to parliamentarian supporters. When Humphrey returned to Bishopstone he was in for a shock, Benjamin Mason was already holding manorial courts in Bishopstone and he had moved into Humphrey Berington's Manor House at Pixley. There was nothing he could do, all the powers he held as Lord of the Manor had been stripped from him. Benjamin Mason also sold all the lumber (trees) in Bishopstone and Pixley and pocketed the money.

The Bishopstone estate was let out at a very cheap rent of £50 per annum, unsurprisingly to Mason himself. This only came to light on September 22nd 1653 when Silas Taylor brought Mason before the Committee for Compounding *"Mason confessed to signing Taylor's name on a certificate of control because two names were needed and Taylor was away". Capt Taylor was surprised when he was told by George Lynn the clerk, that Mason had signed both names to gain control of Humphrey Berington's estate. He would have only agreed if the estate would be let at £180, the full value.*
Parliamentary papers record that *Captain Benjamin Mason during the Commonwealth was lord for a time of Bishopstone and held manorial courts there between 1646-53.*
What happened between Humphrey Berington and Benjamin Mason is unclear but in 1650 Humphrey Berington signed over all his estates to Mason on a 99 year lease. His son Thomas fought for many years in court cases to have the deeds returned. The Compounding Committee had just fined Humphrey £632 with the threat that if he did not pay, imprisonment would follow: he could not pay his fine because he had no money. His son Thomas in a later court cases wrote, "Humphrey his father made the lease and signed the same under distress". If this transaction was made at sword-point or as a result of promises by Mason to save Humphrey from prison is unclear, but it could explain this one sided agreement. Humphrey went to prison and Benjamin Mason held the lands until 1661 when the monarchy was reinstated, and the Court of Chancery returned all sequestered estates to their original owners, in this case Thomas as Humphrey's heir, but Benjamin Mason did not return all the deeds. In 1698 Mason's children were ordered by the courts to return all paperwork and deeds for the Berington estates.
Benjamin Mason also bought a piece of freehold land in Bishopstone from Thomas Welsh according to a set of deeds held in the Hereford archives. His family held the land until 1678 when it was sold to Humphrey Digges. It was an enclosure of land next to the New Inn land, bordering the old road to the church and for many years after it was called Mason land. There was a legacy on the land to pay charity money to old soldiers; this was still being paid in 1704 as recorded in the rent book[5].
On March 22nd 1654 at the Haberdashers' Hall, the Commissioner for Sequestration to the County Committee for Monmouth, brought Benjamin Mason's integrity into question again; in his defence he presented this evidence to the committee. *Petition of Capt. Ben. Mason of Pixley, co. Hereford, to the Protector. Has been engaged in his service. In 1642 at his own expense of £800, raised a troop of horses for Parliament, for which, though promised, he received no satisfaction*
He moved on to Somerset and Bristol but court cases and controversy followed him.
He was appointed as a JP for Somerset in March 1660 and married the daughter of George Doddington of Nether Stowey, Somerset. He died on January 1st 1672 at his home of Beauchamp Roothing in Essex.

The freeholders not involved with the military carried on as usual throughout the war. The value of the farms and cottages was at an all-time low, Thomas Sheppard (weaver) and his sister Elizabeth purchased Crabtree Cottages, a double dwelling, from John Love of Kenowley for just £11.[6] (The cottages were located next door to Kenowley Farm)
The church had jurisdiction over testamentary matters; probate of wills was dealt with the Bishop's court. The court granted probate in the wills of people with properties solely in that diocese. This system applied before 1642 and was reinstated in 1661 after the Commonwealth and Civil War period.
With the Anglican Church effectively closed down wills of any substance were now sent to London to be proved. During this period Bishopstone had three wills sent up to London. All these were newcomers to Bishopstone.
Elizabeth Scaundrett had moved with her brother into a farmhouse later converted into three cottages to be called Burcott Row. She was a friend of Humphrey Digges and like many other Royalists she moved out of Hereford and kept a low profile from the Parliamentarians. Another Royalist, Edward Baker, was leasing Bishton Farm from Humphrey Digges for the duration of the war. Elizabeth,who was unmarried, made her will[7] on March 3rd 1653: she was wealthy, leaving bonds to the value of £300 and two cows to her niece. She named her executors as Humphrey Digges and Simon Tranter from Bunshill.

John Farmer was another newcomer to the parish during the war period, he purchased Nicholas Parlour's freehold farm in the village. Whether the sale arose from Nicholas' involvement in the war is not recorded. John Farmer died in 1656 soon after he moved into the farm.
All seemed to be straightforward with his will[8] until it was contested by Aubrey Smith of Byford, who claimed he had given John Farmer a loan of £20 against which Farmer had given him two deeds, and that Farmer had also made a will leaving all his holdings to Aubrey who was going to be his executor. This was because John Farmer was at one time a servant of Aubrey's father in Kenchester to whom he owed a great benefit and advantage. John Farmer had changed his mind and left everything to his wife.

In her defence Elizabeth said she had never seen Aubrey give John any money, the deeds for the properties were in her house and she would not give then to Aubrey as he had no right to them. The value of the farm in Bishopstone including 15 acres and the holding in Wormsley were not worth more than seven pounds.
This little court case is interesting because it demonstrates firstly the extremely low value of the properties and land during the Civil War and also the case was heard in front of "The Right Honourable the Lords Commissioners for Keeping the Great Seal of England," the short lived court of the Commonwealth. Elizabeth Farmer was given the court's decision and she is listed as still living on the farm in the 1664 hearth tax list.

James Alderne the other newcomer to the parish had taken on the tenancy of Whitehouse farm. He was the brother-in-law to John Welsh, formerly of Bishon Farm who had gained in status during the war, going up from a yeoman farmer to a gentleman living in Hereford. As they each gave five hundred pounds to the Royalist cause it seems likely James Alderne was keeping a low profile in Bishopstone. He was listed as a gentleman, his brother Thomas was Sheriff of Hereford and for a time the family home was at Monnington. I have put in part of his will with explanatory notes because it contains a few characteristics written into the wills of that period.

Will Of James Alderne Gent[9]

James Alderne of Bishopstone in the county of Herefordshire being infirm in body but of perfect memory makes this last will and testament. First I bequeath my soul unto almighty God and I request that my body be buried at the discretion of my executors.

Item I give to my beloved wife for her livelihood and maintenance so long as she shall continue unmarried six pounds a year paid by my executors. (James knew that as long as she stayed a widow she would need money, if she remarried her new husband would support her. He is making sure that she can survive when he is gone.)

The sum of £100 I bequeath unto my daughter Jane on her marriage. And my will and desire is that if my daughter Jane shall marry in my lifetime that I shall hand the said £100 to my executors to pay to my said wife six pounds a quarter divided into equal parts. (If Jane married in his lifetime James would have made a settlement on her. The £100 would be used to provide a dowry if he is dead by the time she marries.)

Items I give to my said wife all the goods she bought with her and two silver spoons, a bedstead, one bed furnishing and two pairs of sheets. (The bed and its furnishing were still the most valued possession in the house.)

Item I give and bequeath to my daughter her mother's trunk and all things within, two silver spoons, one bedstead and bed furnishing, and two pairs of sheets.

(Figure 3) 17th century spinning wheel

Item I give and bequeath unto my said daughter the sum of ten pounds to be paid in a form of fifty shillings a year upon the feast of St Michael. Item I give and bequeath unto my said daughter two of my best kine (cows), the ones that were formerly given by Christen Thomas. (His wife's trunk would contain the entire dowry she brought with her when they married)

Item I give and bequeath unto my said wife and daughter all the flax and hemp which grow in the present year at Bishopstone to be equally divided, and to each of them one spinning wheel. (First record I have seen of spinning wheels in any of the Bishopstone wills.)

Item I give and bequeath to my son John Alderne the sum of ten pounds to pay for an apprenticeship and indentures, to be paid by my executors.

(Apprenticeship had to be paid for, John was still a boy; apprenticeship usually began when you were about 14)

Item I give and bequeath to my son John Alderne, two silver spoons, one bedstead and bed furnishing and two pairs of sheets.

Item I give and bequeath unto my son Thomas Alderne all the residue of my goods and chattels after my debts and funeral expenses.

(Thomas collected all outstanding money and was left all the farming equipment and livestock. He must have been farming elsewhere, as James didn't leave him the lease on Bishopstone Farm.)

Item my will and meaning that if any of my children shall die before their portion be paid to them accordingly to the terms before limited and appointed, then the sum payable to the deceased party be equally divided between my surviving children

Item I give and bequeath unto my brother John Walsh gentleman the remainder of my lease of Bishopstone, whom I appoint to be my executor of this my last will and testament (After James's death John Walsh sub-let the farm to Richard Colley. What happened to the other Alderne family members is not known)
Twenty ninth day of May 1658 Witnesses Thomas Berington and John Astley
The will is interesting because it differs from the normal practice, where the wife would be the main benefactor and on her death the children would inherit. Because this appears to be a second marriage the whole family was split up. Thomas Berington witnessed the will, which helps to verify that he was living at the Court House after his father's death.

The Poor Law

Common Law was written in English from 1594 instead of Latin. In 1601 the Poor Law Act was passed. This ordered the churchwardens and overseers of every parish to levy a poor rate on the landowners of the parish. Each parish was responsible for its own poor people the elderly, sick, blind, orphans and those not able to work for whatever reason. Every person had one parish, and one parish only, in which he or she had a "legal place of settlement" which entitled them to parish relief. The criteria for gaining this included it being their birthplace or the fact that they had lived in the parish for over three years. A labourer if hired at a local hiring fair would only be on a contract for 11 months in order to prevent them from gaining a settlement in the parish they were working in. The burden on the parishes was felt for the next 225 years until it was changed to a system of area workhouses in 1835. Fierce quarrels broke out between parishes including Bishopstone over claimants for relief. These claims were resolved through the Quarter Sessions court. In 1669 James Preece claimed for poor relief from Bishopstone but the overseers there said he was born in Staunton-on-Wye and was a vagrant. A date for the two overseers of Bishopstone and the claimant was set to meet at the Quarter Sessions May 9th 1669 but James Preece did not turn up and it was reported that he was now thought to be living in Letton

A more serious case in 1678 was that of William Taylor who appealed to the overseers stating that he had paid rent for a cottage in Bishopstone for 16 years and had a wife and five children. The house had fallen to the ground six weeks ago and the family were living in the open. The Justices in Quarter Sessions ordered the parish to build a house on the waste ground (common land on the hill) to accommodate the family.

This was an unusual case where a poor man had taken on the parish and won. He lived the rest of his life in Bishopstone, his eldest son William occupied the cottage after his father's death, both were classed as labourers. The cost to rebuild the cottage was £19 14s, no doubt they used some of the old material although they used 50 new wooden uprights, the carpenter's fee was £2 2s 6d. He would have sawed and joined the timber; all the joints were mortice and tenon, secured by a dowel peg about an inch thick which needed special facilities and tools. The rest of the cottage would have been built by a village labourer, probably by William Taylor himself and the straw for the roof would have been provided by his employer, a recognized practice of the period.
In the same year at the next Quarter Sessions Bishopstone clashed with Burghill over Thomas Llewellyn, both saying he was a vagabond and not from their parish.
The Justices ruled that more proof was needed and ordered him to appear at the next Sessions Meanwhile, Thomas Llewellyn was sent to the house of correction (prison) and the overseers of Bishopstone were ordered to pay the 1s 6d a week charge for his food. If it was proved he came from Burghill then that parish had to pay back the money. Nevertheless at the next Sessions Bishopstone lost out and he was returned to the parish.
Charles II returned to England in 1660, the Commonwealth ended.
The parish records started again on August 29th 1661. All the previous records were lost, because the Anglican clergy were ousted and the rites weren't held. Civil registrars were appointed to record births and marriages so they didn't use the registers; local people hid them away for safety, because they felt that they had a religious significance. In some cases the new Presbyterian minister destroyed them if he got hold of them.
Bishopstone's records for some unknown reason never survived. Many of the diocesan records were lost, probably burnt by Parliamentarian soldiers occupying the cathedral after the siege. Short of money the King started to raise money through taxes, the first was the Military Tax of 1661. Bishopstone had 27 properties with land, which were taxed as valued over one pound, and 6 cottages, which were under that value.

Tax 1661 milita Accessments [10]	**£**	**s**	**d**
Mr Berington (Court House)	80	00	00
John Culter Rector (Rectory)	36	00	00
John Adams (Smallholding next to Rectory)	2	00	00
John Parlor (Stocks Farm)	3	00	00
Bartholonew Pillinger (Godsell's Cottage 1700)		13	4
Richard Colley & Co (Whitehouse Farm)	6	00	00
John Probert (Smallholding in village)	2	15	00
John Powle (Smallholding in village)	2	00	00
Widow Berrington (Smallholding in village)	2	00	00
Widow Farmer (Smallholding in village)	2	15	00
William Mathews (Townsend Farm No1)	7	00	00
George Powle (Townsend Farm No2)	4	00	00
John Williams (Cottage Brierly close in village)	1	00	00
David Merediff (Cottage on hill)		15	00
Francis Bassett (Cottage on hill)		10	00
Richard Savaker (Claypitt Farm)	2	00	00
George Painter (Cottage by Claypitts)	1	00	00
Thomas Green (Gent) (Cottage by Claypitts)	1	00	00
George Eckley (Bishton Farm)	24	00	00
Richard Foote (Bishon Farm)	24	00	00
John Scandrett (Burcutt Row)	3	00	00
Walter Eckley (John son) (The Pleck)	6	00	00
Phillip Gwilliam (Farm next to New Inn)	3	00	00
The Widow Halling (Bridge Ash)	2	0o	00
Thomas Welsh (New Inn)	1	00	00
Walter Arnell (Ornell) (Cottage Bishon Common)	1	00	00

In 1661 when this survey was taken there were thirteen properties in the village by the church, five in Bishon, and three around Claypitts Farm plus a scattering of cottages mainly on the commons.
Best known of the commodity taxes was the hearth tax or chimney tax, first levied in 1662, by which all householders were rated at two shillings a hearth. Bishopstone's first entry appears on Michaelmas 1662 with 37 hearths in 22 households but no details. Lady Day 1664 listed all the names of the householders, one cottage had disappeared since 1662, leaving 21 properties with chimneys and 12 without, ranging from Thomas Berrington (Bishopstone Court) 8, Richard Eckley (Bishton Farm) 4, John Cutler (Rector) 3, Richard Foote (Bishon Farm) 3,Thomas Welsh (New Inn) 2. The following had only one hearth. John Adams, John Parlor, Richard Colley, John Probert, Roger Pennor, Richard Savaker, Elizabeth Farmer, William Mathews, George Powle, John Williams all lived in the village. James Bithell, George Jones and Sarah Farris lived in cottages around Claypitts, Phillip Gwilliam, Walter Eckley and John Scandrett lived in Bishon. The last returns on Michaelmas 1671 lists the same number of households, 21, with chargeable hearths, the only differences from the original 1664 entry, are that Bishopstone Court had two additional chimneys making ten in total; two householders had built an extra chimney on their cottages but two cottages had blocked up their hearths to avoid paying the tax; the number of exempt had dropped to ten meaning that two cottages had fallen down and not been replaced.
By comparison Credenhill was a smaller village in 1664 with only 5 households paying hearth tax and 16 were exempt.

The early part of the 17th century between 1600 and 1642, was a relatively prosperous period for agriculture, and Bishopstone witnessed some house building similar to a lot of villages all over England. John Ornell and Phillip Savacre both built cottages in 1630, one on Walle Close and the other on Bishon Common, we presume by using the old traditional way, reusing old timber for the frame and topping off with a new thatch roof, no chimneys. By 1705, when Baron Price bought the Manor both cottages were missing, they either fell down or were dismantled, reinforcing the expert's option that cottages built this way had around a 50 year life expectancy.

Other cottages and farms stood the test of time and are still with us today. The New Inn (now Stonehouse) was built in 1590 for Paul Delahay (Gent) just before the turn of the century making it one of the oldest houses in the parish along with the Pleck. Bishopstone Court was built about 30 years earlier but very little of the original building survives, as it was mostly rebuilt in the middle of the eighteenth century.
Stonehouse still has its original timber frame. It carries carpenters' marks in the timbers, from which experts can date it within a time span of 30 years. The building appears on the Daniel's rental roll of 1590, listed as the New Inn, which gives an accurate date for the building. Originally single storey it was modified around 1680, the roof raised to make it into two storeys, a central chimney built and an extension to house animals added on the west side. It possibly replaced an inn or alehouse, which was originally on the site, the land can be traced back to 1385 when it was rented by John le Grand. Stonehouse had many owners in its early years until Baron Price purchased it in 1705 as part of the manor after which the property stayed part of Foxley estate until 1920. It was licensed as an inn until 1825 when the closure of the road to the church killed off any trade.

(Figure 4) The carpenters who built quality timber framed houses would carve a mark into the timber as a way of identifying the houses they had built. Experts can identify these marks to within a 30-year time span. This 2008 photo shows the identification mark the carpenter carved into the Pleck around 1575.

The Pleck was built for John Eckley around 1575, possibly by John Thomas the village carpenter. Its frame was built from straight oak timber and stone tiles were used for the roof similar to the New Inn and Bishon farm. The use of stone roofing tiles is one of the reasons these houses are still with us today, they lasted longer than the thatch roof and although more expensive initially, the roofs were almost maintenance free. The tiles would have come from the quarry on Bishopstone Hill.
John Thomas the carpenter also built a house for himself on Bishopstone Hill, this house stood for over 300 years, it was eventually purchased by Garnons Estate and demolished in the late 1800's.
The parish records of 1661-99 reflect the state of the parish. Thomas Berington lord of the Manor was bankrupt. A lot of the houses, cottages and farms were in poor repair. The Old House Farm sitting in Walle Close had fallen down by 1673; a lease dated 1674 between Thomas Berrington and John Savacre lists barns, beast house, sheepcotes and stables, no house. It appears to have been unoccupied when the hearth tax was assessed, as it is not listed. The two cottages next to the farm had also disappeared by 1705. Three other cottages in the village had also disappeared in the same period. Walle Close is an Anglo-Saxons name for a piece of land containing a well, which could mean the site was occupied in the Anglo-Saxon period. In 2008 Bob Carrington told me it was always wet in the place where the farm and cottages formerly stood even though it was land-drained.
Six of the men listed as the main occupiers from thirteen cottages and farms in the village, had died before 1671, showing an aging population; reinforced by the fact only sixteen children were baptised during this ten year period less than half the usual figure.
Between 1661 and 1699, 52 boys, and 47 girls were baptized in Bishopstone Church, 9 boys and 8 girls dying within their first year. There were 59 different families in the records for this period. 15 burials of unmarried servants and labourers, who were hired to live in and work on the farms. The Parlours and Eckleys with 11 entries each were the largest family surname followed by the Pillingers 10, Taylors 7, Pugh, Evans and Willmoors 6, Hargest and Colley 5, Bethel, Foote, Forris and Millichamp 4, etc. The most popular names for girls were Elizabeth with 12 entries, followed by Ann 8, Mary 7, Margaret 6, Elinor 3, Hannah and Joan 2, Joyce, Janet and Marie, Alice, Judith, Fanny, Jane 1.
The most popular boys' names were John 23, James 9, Francis 5, Humphrey 3, David and George 2, Alex, Anthony, Arthur, Benjamin, Berrington, Edmund, Edward, Horace, Hugh, 1.

All parishes had to send a certificate to the church authorities declaring who in the parish had not taken the Holy Sacrament at Easter. John Cutler the Rector sent his certificate in for Bishopstone dated June 22nd 1665, he said that Joyce Romfall was a Quaker and also Elizabeth Parlour *"who is now and then a little franticke"* (which I take as meaning she has a mental health problem) did not take the Holy Sacrament. It was signed by John Culter Rector and John Adams Church Guardian

The Church Courts were again in full control of their parishioners by the 1670's, the Acts of Office entries for Bishopstone appear to be nearly identical to the period before the Commonwealth dealing with non Church attendance and social problems. These are just a few of the entries to give a flavour of the courts' coverage.

Acts of Office 1673-1686[11]

1673 George Powles, churchwarden for not taking his oath and not exhibiting his presentment. He didn't appear to answer the charge and was excommunicated (banned from attending church). This was repeated for the next four years and it was never resolved as far as I can see. The Church or Rector appears to have had a disagreement with its officers, the next year it was the turn of David Meredith.
1674 David Meredith, churchwarden to receive orders for mending the church and churchyard fence. Summonsed three times, didn't appear, excommunicated. In March 1675 he produced a certificate of the repairs and was absolved. (It was very important to keep the fence or wall around the church in good repair. The church law right into the early 19th century stated that a wall or a fence was to be used on the churchyard boundary, certainly not a hedge. The main reason was to keep out the pigs, if they entered the churchyard they would soon dig up corpses and eat them as most people could not afford a coffin and were buried in shallow graves wrapped only in a cloth shroud.)
1679 John Wontoon for boasting that he had carnal knowledge of the body of Susan Meredith and for saying that she was a whore and his whore. On November 4th 1680 he appeared in court and admitted that he had copulated with Susan Meredith. He was ordered to do public penance in the churches of Bishopstone, Byford and Bridge Sollers the parishes where he had committed the acts. In December he produced a certificate to say he had done the penance. (I suspect the churches would have been full when he carried out his penance to hear his boastful details.)
1680 Margery Pugh, alias Ridgley to answer an accusation of incontinence (lacking self-restraint in regard of sexual desire) with William James, her servant. She didn't appear to answer the charge and was excommunicated. In December 1680 she appeared and apologised for her non-appearance before and was let off the excommunication. She denied the accusation and produced witnesses to her good character so the accusation was dropped.
Timothy Millichapp the Rector, to receive orders to repair the outhouse and barns belonging to the parsonage, which were decayed. He said that it wasn't his fault because his predecessor had let them get into that state, but was still ordered to repair them and produce a certificate to prove it.
1681 Margery Pugh alias Ridgely to receive orders to render an account for the administration of probate of her late husband David Pugh. She brought in the account on 12th October and was dismissed.
Thomas Bythell for encroaching on the glebe lands, he produced a certificate from the incumbent and was dismissed.
Thomas Berington for not paying the church rate of 7s 6d in 1680 and not paying in 1681. Summonsed three times, didn't appear so excommunicated. In April 1682 his representative appeared with a certificate of payment and the case was dismissed.
This little selection taken from the court records gives an idea of the wide range of power the court possessed.

David Pugh

David Pugh yeoman whose wife Margery was mentioned in the court records appears to have been an intriguing and interesting character; he came to Bishopstone in 1668 having purchased John Scandrett's sixty acres of freehold land and its main farmhouse which stood on the Burcutt Row site. He was a churchwarden in 1669, the year his son Phillip was born. His first wife Phyllis died in 1672 shortly after she give birth to a daughter called Elinor. David then married his second wife Margery Ridgley. In 1679 David and his son Phillip, who was now aged eleven, became ill; David died and was buried on November 12th 1679 at Bishopstone Church, Phillip survived. David who was in his late thirties when he died probably thought he would recover from his illness so did not make a will. The paperwork left after his death is intriguing, the inventory carried out shows up nothing unusual, it was a seven-room house with four lower rooms and three under the thatch, and comfortably furnished for a yeoman farmer. *In ye hall, one table board, one form, four stools, one warming pan, three pewter dishes, two small brass pots, value £2. In the parlour, one table board, one form, one coffer and one cupboard, 13s 4d. In the chamber over the parlour, one feather bed and bolster, one bedstead, one rug, one coffer, one sack of hops, about six bushels of rye, about three bushels of barley, value £2 8s.* (Gathered crops and cheese were stored on the first floor to protect them from vermin). *In the chamber over the hall, one bushel of wheat, two ripes and seven cheeses, 16s. In the buttery, three hogsheads of cider, two empty hogsheads, one barrel, one old furnace, one trind, two flitches of bacon and a tub of butter, £3 17s.* (The buttery would have been across the rear of the house, traditionally where the beer or ale was brewed, hence the furnace. (One hogshead of cider is approximately 54 gallons.)

In the lower chamber, one bedstead, one feather bed and bolster, one blanket, one rug, one set of curtain, three blankets, and two coffers, £2. (This was the main bedroom traditionally on the ground floor; the curtains were used to enclose the main four-poster bed.) *In the chamber over the lower chamber, one bedstead,one feather bed and bolster, one blanket, 10s. In the barns, lumber about the place and one acre of rye, £1. cattle, about five horses, one mare, one cow, two small bullocks, one small heifer, twenty two sheep, three sows and six small store pigs, £11. Two acres of corn on the ground 13s 4d, one old cart 10s.* *Total £29.11.00*

When making these inventories everything was priced on the low side and to justify this they would use the terms small or old. The valuation was usually done by neighbours or relatives, in this case parish officers carried out the inventory, which was just a coincidence. You usually had someone who knew what they were talking about so a farmer would do a farmer's appraisal, a craftsman's tools would need a similar craftsman to do it. One would need to be able to read and write, as in this case John Parlour signed his name but Richard Foote (Bishon Farm) could not write and like Margery Pugh made a mark. John Parlour was a churchwarden, Richard Foote was parish constable. There is no record of any money or silver plate on the inventory, which was not unusual.

Margery did not produce her account of the administration of David's estate until the court ordered her to do so, two years after his death and it makes interesting reading.

*The account of Margery Pugh alias Ridgley. "**The Charge**" the sum of £29 11.00 being the true value of all the goods, chattels of the deceased in according with an inventory held by this court.*

The Discharge. *Dated October 12th 1681; Paid for the funeral of the deceased and to the doctor for Phillip, £9.* (Doctors were very expensive only a few could afford them). *Paid for the watching and attending the deceased in his sickness, 5s.* (This is quite normal and would be the local midwife or similar person and neighbours who helped out with the nursing.) *Paid to the workmen and servants for wages, £1. Paid a bond in goods to Mr Digges, £10 12s.* (Paid in livestock possibly the 5 horses)

Paid for a heriot, £1 13s. (Freeholders and copyholders paid heriots on death to the lord of the manor, traditionally it would have been the best beast, but now the payment was made in money). *Paid for a sword, 5s.* (One mystery I cannot understand, why a dying man in the last few day of his life would purchase a sword; was he under threat? Of course David might have ordered it before he took ill and she had to pay for it.) Margery paid out £29 14s 00d settling outstanding bills.

How did Margery survive, with a young family and stepson Phillip who was still only thirteen? Well she employed a male servant William James to help with the farm, with whom she became too friendly, that attracted the attention of the Church, as recorded earlier in the chapter, she also sold land to Thomas Berrington, and Timothy Geers.

Good arable land could be sold for £4 an acre. What was left of the freehold land passed to Phillip (David's son) on Margery's death. He was recorded as a freeholder in 1705 and his widow was still holding the land in 1742. The farmhouse at Burcott eventually passed on to Phillip's daughter Eleanor. Pugh's lands are shown on the 1770 estate map in many of the common fields; the enclosed lands are listed in the 1839 tithe map by the crossroads leading to the church.

The other significant will is that of James Bythell cooper of Bishopstone. David Pugh and James Bythell died within five months of each other; both were middle aged and respected members of Bishopstone community, serving as churchwardens. James was also a tenant farmer as well as a cooper, renting both a house at Claypitts and Whitehouse Farm from Thomas Berrington. He also appears to have died suddenly and away from home, his simple will was witnessed by a Matthias Parham and Humphrey Tokeley, surnames I have not found recorded locally.

Will of James Bythell of Bishopston, cooper. April 12th 1679[12]

All my goods to my wife Mary Bythell, all my goods and chattels and cattles with all my corn on the ground and all goods I now possess, and at her discretion to be disposed of to my three sons.

The mark of James Bythell; Witnessess- Matthias Parham. Humphrey Tokeley

James had been fairly comfortably off, coopers were in constant demand as barrels were the standard form of storage. The witnesses of the inventory could all sign their names. Humphrey Digges was a gentleman from Bishton, John Parlour was church warden and a witness to many of the inventories in Bishopstone because he could read and write. John Macklin was a yeoman farmer from the Knapp Farm Bridge Sollers; William Llewellin could have been a relative. It is a very long inventory covering two pages so I will only include some of the more interesting points.

Tools and instruments belonging to the trade £2. Barrel staves and spokes and hoops, timber belonging to his trade £5. In his hall of his dwelling house at the Clay Pittes, one table board and frame, one stool, one trind, one little ladder, five pewter dishes, one pewter flagon, one pewter can, one candlestick, one salt, two brazen dishes, one pair of handirons and pot links with other trumpery10s. (One little ladder indicates there was no stairs in the house, this was used to access under the thatch)

In the solar over the hall, five bushels of wheat, one flitch of bacon, part of one flitch of beef. £1. In the cellar one hogshead of cider, four empty hogsheads and four half hogsheads, £2 6s. Other items at the Claypitts, forty sheep valued at £4, ten pigs £2, and corn in the barn which came off four acres, plus two acres of kimridg and seven acres of lent grain.

(Figure 5) Part of the garden wall to Whitehouse Farm, located in the hedgerow down by the church is all that remains today of the farm.

At his farm called Whitehouse in the hall there one table board, one form, one stool, four milk trinds, two pails, one churn, three brass kettles, one brass pot, one posnet, with other trumpery, £2. In the chamber there, one feather bed and two bolsters, two blankets, one covering, one rug, one bedstead, seven pairs of coarse sheets, two tablecloths, six napkins, £4. (Tablecloths and napkins were not commonly used by yeomen farmers) *In the chamber over the hall there and other chambers by, sixty bushels of wheat and rye, £7.*

All the rooms upstairs were used as storage, other items on the inventory included six small plough bullocks value £15, the highest value on the inventory (the use of horses for ploughing was still a century away) five kine (cows) £10, six young beasts £9, three calves £1 10s, five swine £2 10s. One nag and one bay mare and colt £5, the bay mare would have been James personal mount to reflect his status. Farm implements had little value as they were mainly made locally with the help of a wheelwright. One corn wain, one dung wain with ploughs, yokes, loones and other implements of husbandry £6. The barns were full of wheat, rye, barley, peas and pulse and eight loads of hay. The total amount of the inventory came to £121.6s.

Roger Penner another ex-churchwarden, died on April 12th 1679; in his will he left all his goods, cattle, chattels and household stuff to his wife Mary. Roger lived at Penners Farm in the village, it appears that small farmers could not survive on farming alone and all needed extra income. David Pugh was a horse trader, James Bythell was a cooper, Roger Penner also had a trade as a cobbler. His inventory lists the usual household goods, plus seven sheep, one sow and four pigs, one cow, one mare, three acres of corn, one acre lent corn, plus; *I pair of boots without tops, 1 pair of slippers, 4 pairs of shoes, 10s. Lasts and boot trees and tools in the shop, 2s 6d.* The total value of his goods £11.17s.2d

Roger could only make his mark. His son, another Roger, was occupying the farm in 1705; he was the last of the Penners to live on the farm before it was demolished. After his death in the 1730s Penners land was incorporated into Court Farm but Penners Orchard where the farmhouse stood is listed on the 1839 tithe map. The farms listed in the three different wills have now all disappeared.

(Figure 6) Blacksmith shop in 2010 parts of the building are original, dating back to 1694

In 1694 a 99 year lease was made between Humphrey Digges gent of Bishton and his wife Amiens with John Snead, *on land in Bishon Snead was to build a Smiths Shop, sixteen feet square, in a field called Linning Field on the side of the common road between Hay and the City of Hereford at the gate entrance, enclosed out of Linning Field, to another gate entry to an enclosed piece of land called Lowmoor Croft. Along the side of highway to plant a hawthorn hedge, set in the hedge a row of lime trees, Snead to maintain.*[13]

The blacksmith's shop still stands in the centre of Bishopstone although somewhat altered over the years; John Snead built Forge Cottage some years later. The wording in the lease suggests that the main highway passed through Bishopstone and it was only when the turnpike company developed what is now the A438 that the majority of the traffic moved away from the Roman road.

What was life like for a Bishopstone yeoman farmer after the civil war, what food did they grow? Thomas Powell of Bridge House Kenchester died in 1693, attached to his will were notes on husbandry dated 1688, possibly as a guide for his son and heir the timetable of planting and the type of crops grown would be similar to that of Bishopstone farmers, the notes were arranged by months and I think are very interesting. They list a large assortment of crops that were grown in the garden and the number of flowers grown, possibly for medicinal reasons. The whole system rotates around the phases of the moon, which has now revived itself as a modern gardening trend.

No potatoes were grown; it would be over a century before the first potatoes were grown in Bishopstone. The act of bleeding humans and animals appears to be common treatment advised for many ailments. Some of the words were illegible and the spelling incorrect by modern standards these I have left in.

January; In this month cut down timber and it shall not cleave nor be eaten by worms; in the last quarter of the Moon, set and sow kernels and bay trees, privet and box, set quicksets, rosetrees, peaches, philbets and plum trees; if the frosts be not too hard, prune and lop them; before full moon sow and set beans and pease; and dung land; in the last quarter geld cattel to rear, fallow land for wheat and rye, trench garden with dung; and remove bees; and for your own health keep your body warm; let good wholesome dyet be your physician, moderate exercise and labour yourself to cause appetite.

February; Sow all sorts of pease and other pulses; sow mustard seed, set and plant vines, hops gooseberries and any fruit that grows in bushes, prune and trim all sorts of fruit trees from moss and canker; remove superfluous branches, graft in the later end of the month, sow cold stiff land; take heed of cold; forebear phlegmatic meats.

March in the new of the moon (the wind anyway but South or West) graft pears, wardens or apple trees; make an end of sowing all manner of pulses, and begin to sow oats, barley, parsnips, onions, carrots, cucumbers, melons and all kinds of pot-herbs; slip hartichoaks and sage; ??? lambs; let blood according to strength and necessity but repair to the learned physician look what cannot be cured in spring by physick, will hardly be cured all the year after.

April; Sow barley, hemp and flax, pole hops; set and sow all kinds of garden herbs; open hives, and let bees labour for their living; let tanners now provide them with bark; and all good huswives look to their dairies; bleed and purge with advice, those that are troubled with itches and gout, let them go to the bath in this or the three following months.

May; Sow barley on the light lands and bearing grounds, and hemp and flax, and all manner of fine seeds and herbs; take lambs from their dams; stir land for wheat and rye; leave lopping of trees; teach hops to climb, but cut off the superfluous branches; rise early, walk the fields, especially by your running streams; sage and sweet butter now an excellent breakfast; sage and clarified whey, as also scurvy grass ale, and wormwood beer, are wholesome drinks to be drunk fasting.

June; Shear sheep, bring home fewel, weed corn and gardens, set rosemary, carnations and gilly flowers; sow lettice and radish feed three or four days after the full, for then they will not run to seed; make hay; carry sand, lime, marle and manure of what kind so ever; ???? your land; cut neither hedge nor tree in this and the two next months; beware of great thirst; use thin and light dyet, moderate exercise and chasts thoughts.

July; Making your hay and house it while it's fair weather; pull hemp that is ripe; gather garden beans; get rue and wormwood and gaul to strew your floors, to destroy moths and fleas; fence your copses; use moderate dyet, take heed of great thirst, for nothing brings the pestilence or pestilent diseases sooner than extreme thirst, and fervent heat and cold taken suddenly upon them, take no physic bleed not but upon violent occasions.

August; Follow close your corn harvest; sow winter herbs in the new of the Moon; gather garden seeds; mow barley and oats; gather your summer fruits; refrain from sleeping in the day time after meat; avoid riot and excess.

September; In the beginning of this moneth and end of former, gather hops when they wax brown, the weather waxing fair and no dew on the ground; kill bees; make verjuice; ???? and rye; move and set all slips of flowers, between the two put swine to mast; removed trees every new moon from September to February especially in the new of the Moon, the weather fair and wind south or west; use physick moderately; forbear fruit to ???? or rotten; avoided riot and excess of dyet.

October; Sow wheat and rye, the sooner the better for fear of rain; set acorns and nuts; gather winter fruit, the weather dry in the afternoon and in the wain of the Moon; cut rose trees if you desire to have score of roses, do this once in two years; refuse not any needful physick; ???? hands of the learned, use all moderate sports to revive the vital spirit.

November; Make malt; kill hogs; trench gardens with dung; set crab apple stocks; sow wheat and rye in exceeding hot sandy ground; cut down timber for plows, carts and other implements for husbandry; use wholesome meat and drink with good exercise to preserve health.

December; In this and the next months cut down timber in the last quarter of the Moon; uncover the roots of fruit trees; set beans and pease; cover all the best flowers and herbs from frosts and storms with rotten horse dung; look well to your cattel; water and keep moist your meadows; let horses blood; and drink good wine and strong drink; keep the body warm clad; thy house warm and dry; cast all care from you, and relieve those that are in want with thy charity. Thus I have ended these observations, which are laid down for thy advantage, make good use of them and give God the glory.

Chapter 7
1700-1750

William Brydges of Colwall who was a mercer from London, purchased the Manor of Bishopstone in 1692 from Thomas Berington for £3,100.[1] Thomas although destitute was clever enough to negotiate as part of the deal that he and his family could still remain living in Bishopstone. In 1696 the long running case over the ownership of his Pixley Manor was finally settled, the family left Bishopstone and set up home in Pixley. Documents held in Hereford Record Office show that his twin sister Ann who lived in London, paid the household running costs, and also paid off some of his creditors in this interim period. William Brydges never resided in Bishopstone, he set up a lease with Roger Penner in 1694 for his farm, garden, backside and orchard on a 21 year term; other than this lease I have found no other evidence of Williams's involvement with Bishopstone. William died in 1704, his eldest son returned to Colwall to run the family estates and he decided to dispose of Bishopstone Manor.

(Figure 1) Baron Robert Price who purchased the Manor of Bishopstone in 1705

On July 9th 1705 Baron Robert Price of Foxley purchased the ancient Manor of Bishopstone for a sum of money and an exchange of lands between himself and William Brydges. Baron Price had inherited part of Foxley by his marriage to Lucy Rodd in 1679; she was the eldest daughter and co-heiress of Robert Rodd who died in 1681. Through his wife, Robert Price came to hold a major part of the Rodd inheritance, which included the manors of Mansell Lacy and Yazor. He added to this central block by purchasing estates from a number of smaller gentry in the area, acquiring in particular properties of the Garnons family in Mansell Gamage, the Tomkyns family in Byford, and the former Berington manor of Bishopstone. Robert was a Baron of the Exchequer, Attorney General for South Wales in 1682 and later in 1726, a Justice of the Court of Common Pleas; as his wealth increased he purchased other manors and farms all over Herefordshire. In 1717 Robert built a new square red-bricked mansion at Foxley. He died on February 2nd 1732 aged 79 and was buried in Yazor Church. He had two sons and a daughter; his eldest son Thomas died when on the Grand Tour in Genoa in 1706, reportedly by unfair means, and the second son Uvedale succeeded to his father's estates. Uvedale married Ann, daughter and co-heiress of Lord Arthur Somerset, further increasing the family's wealth. His land agent for Bishopstone was William Brown who kept a detailed rent book[2], which lists all the tenants and freeholders and what land they occupied. Also the very helpful churchwardens of Bishopstone, when recording their entries in the Bishop transcript[3] gave the occupation of the people entered throughout the period 1695 to 1720.

(Figure 2) View of Foxley House April 1791

Tenants and Freeholders in Bishopstone whose names appear in the rent book after Baron Price acquired the Manor of Bishopstone in July 1705

Rent Charged	*£ s d*
The Main Farm (Court Farm) Dan Matthews	*142.00 00*
Whitehouse farm Thomas Bythell	*22.00.00*
John Parlour (Hargest lands)	*5 03 00*
Richard Foote Farm (Later Richard Snead)	*6 00 00*
William Godsell House and Land	*10 00*
Roger Penner House and Land	*3 00 00*
George Powle House and Land	*1 12 00*
Thomas Mathews House and Land	*16 00*
George Bythell.House and Land at Claypitts	*7 10 00*
Howel Evans New Inn and Land	*2 00 00*
More for Arnolds Land	*12 00*
Gyler Nicholas House and Lands	*2 04 00*

Freeholders Chief Rents (Freeholders only paid a small land rent to the Lord of the Manor)

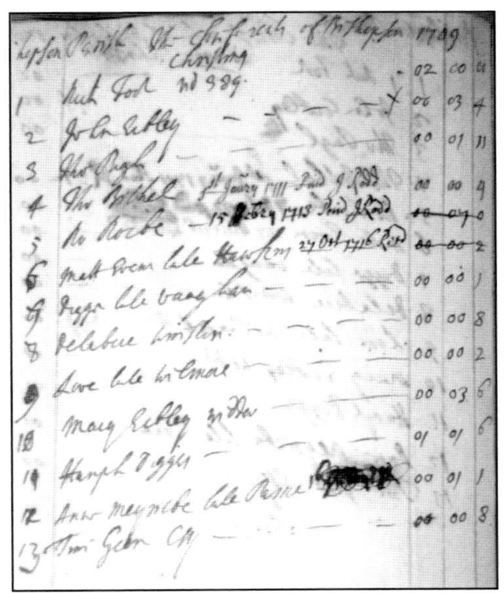

(Figure 3) Freeholders list 1709

	£ s d
Richard Foote Bishon Farm	*2 06 00*
Humphrey Digges Gent Bishton Farm Freehold	*1 01 06*
John Eckley for House and Lands	*3 04*
Phillip Pugh Freehold in Bishen	*1 11*
Thomas Bythell his Freehold in Claypitts	*04*
Roger Rocke Freehold	*7 00*
R Hawkin Freehold	*08*
H Vaughan now Digges freehold	*01*
Delabere Winstone Freehold	*08*
Mr Love late Wilmor Freehold	*02*
Mary Eckley Freehold	*3 06*
Anne Meyrick late Paine Land Freehold	*1 01*
Mr Tim Geers Gent Freehold	*08*

The farms, houses and cottages in the parish were in a poor state of repair after years of neglect, the advowsons and glebe land of Bishopstone were under the ownership of Timothy Geers of The Marsh, Bridge Sollers, a leftover legacy of Humphrey Berington's dealings. Baron Price purchased back the advowson of the Rectory in 1707 using his position as lord of the manor to regain the rights. Another problem emerged after Baron Price's acquisition of the manor, houses had been built on the common land, and land had been enclosed out of the common without permission. The Beringtons and William Brydges had turned a blind eye to these encroachments. On instructions from Baron Price his land agent reclaimed the land and the houses, and then charged rent to the occupiers for living in the properties that many had built. He was acting within the law, as lord of the manor. The perpetrators had no deeds or written proof of permission to encroach onto the common land; John Hargest, John Woonton and Matthew Evans would have had a good argument to keep their homes but without legal help they stood no chance against such a powerful figure as Baron Price.

The list of properties repossessed on Bishopstone Hill Common by agent Brown, includes Hargest's house garden and orchard, Wontnor's house, garden and close, one newly built house with garden and another house and garden both in possession of Matthew Evans, house and garden now Digges.

This period of time recorded in this rent book over a 15-year period, is just a blink of the eye in the lifespan of the parish yet it changed the direction of the village forever. It saw the start of the demise of the village along the church lane as well as the loss of power held by the freeholders. Maybe the fate of the parish was decided in 1316 when the court decided to split the manor in three, but the final phase happened between the years 1705-20. Although this was happening slowly throughout many villages in England, Bishopstone's changes happened suddenly, the agricultural system was in decline, freehold yeoman farmers were unable to make enough to survive, which inevitably lead to large landowners buying farming land cheaply.

Baron Price was a prime example of this trend, by 1720 over 240 acres of freeholders' land had been purchased; out of Bishopstone total acreage of 776 he now owned over 700. This obvious shift of power allowed Price to control and dictate the running of the parish; decisions were now made in Foxley mansion.

Freehold properties purchased by Baron Price 1705-1720

John Love's cottage and garden (Kenowley) purchased in 1709,

James Rowland's house and garden (Banbury Hall) purchased in 1710.

Digges Estate of 172 acres was purchased in 1710 for £1,250 this estate included Bishton farm, Townsend Farm and Berkley Place.

Winstone farm (Bridge Ash) of 15 acres purchased in 1710 (formerly awarded to Humphrey Digges wife, Elinor in 1682).

Mary Digges' house and land on Bishopstone Hill purchased in 1710.

Eckley's farm in Walle Close was purchased in 1712. The buildings were pulled down and the land incorporated into Court Farm.

Baron Price also purchased arable land in Bishopstone from Thomas Williams, Hugh Thomas and Mr Russell in October 1710, strips lying in Hoarstone Field, Upper Field and Ploughwell field totalling 32 acres plus 7 acres in Lower Hill Field from George Bythel.

Timothy Geers and his association with Bishopstone.

Timothy Geers, son and heir apparent of Thomas Geers Sergeant-at-law, inherited the Bridge Sollers Manor when his father died in 1703. Timothy first appears in the Hereford court records in 1694, when he was a younger man but still believed in his principles. This is a small extract from the court case;[4]

Samuel Lestoken sayeth, that when he was at the "Catherine Wheel" tavern, Pelham Corbett toasted King William's health to one (whom you believe to be Rowland Andrews) who refused the health, and when he was thereupon required to leave, declined to do so; and, calling for some ale, began a health to him, who had "Lost fifteen shillings" and wished that, if ever it came into his hand again he would play his game better. When he still refused to leave, the deponent threw a glass of cider in his face, at which Timothy Geers attacked James Leda with a pair of tongs and then confronted him with a drawn sword, giving rise to a general fracas among those present; Richard Andrews struck Pelham Corbett, and taking him by the neck cloth, almost choked him, Andrew's mother and her daughter and the maidservant attacked the deponent, tearing his cravat, and drawing blood from his hand and nose, after which, the company ran away.

The Geers family were still supporters of the Catholic cause, and being asked to drink to the health of a protestant King caused offence followed by this fracas. Queen Mary who had just died, had shared the throne with her husband King William, both protestants. This dispute arose at a secret meeting in the tavern, where Jacobite news letters were read, after a sentry was in place guarding the door. The toast to *"who had lost fifteen shillings"* refers to James II without directly speaking his name. The Catherine Wheel tavern was pulled down in the nineteenth century and the new Shire Hall was built on the site.

After this escapade Timothy settled down and married Mary Winsford in 1695. As part of his marriage settlement he lists Marsh farm in possession of Edward Eckley, and Knap Farm in possession of John Macklin. Timothy lived at the Marsh Farm but when his wife inherited Hatfield manor and other estates the family moved to a large new house in Hereford.

His association with Bishopstone started when his father died. Part of his inheritance was the patronage of Bishopstone church with its tithes, and the Rectory Farm. Adding to his holdings as mentioned earlier, Timothy purchased a messuage and land lying in Bishon from Martha Pugh and slowly acquired other parcels of land in Bishopstone from the Pugh family. In 1721 he oversaw the building of the Almshouses on Bishopstone Hill. Interestingly, in a marriage settlement for his daughter he lists Garnons Estate value at £100 yearly rent and Bridge Farm at £27 yearly rent. From his will dated August 17th 1751 he left Bridge Sollers to his son Thomas who died two years after his father. Thomas's sisters inherited the estate, one married a Mr Broome from Withington and they rented out the small farm in Bishopstone to Mary Guest from Monnington. On the decease of the survivor of these ladies, Bridge Sollers Manor and the Bishopstone Farm passed to their heir-in-law, Sir John Geers Cotterell.

Ann Berington Almshouses

Ann Berington, the second daughter of Humphrey Berington was the foundress of the Almshouses built on Bishopstone Hill in 1721. She was born in Bishopstone in 1630 with her twin brother Thomas, she lived throughout the Civil War in Bishopstone with her mother, brother and sisters. When her father died in 1657, Ann with her younger sister Mary moved to London; a shrewd businesswoman who appeared to be very dominant, she made her money through bonds, lending money at a high interest rate, normally 10%, which helped her and Mary live in London's higher society.

From Ann's will[5] written on the July 13th 1710 we can learn a lot about Ann and Mary's lifestyle. Living in a residence called the Brickhouse, St Martins in the Field, London, which was newly erected with a stable and coach house she secured a long lease from John, Lord Bishop of Winchester. They appeared to have many servants as her will provided money to some and a legacy to her personal maid. Ann's will was written in a very flamboyant way and in a very large hand leaving a large proportion of her entire estate to the poor of Bishopstone. Her executors were Timothy Geers of the Marsh, Bridge Sollars and Baron Robert Price of Foxley. Possibly because she had witnessed the suffering of the poor in Bishopstone during the Civil War, and what she had experienced herself, with her family having to beg for food to survive, and the help the parishioners gave the family throughout this period, she decided to repay her parish with this gift.

One line in the will of interest reads "the fathers and mothers of Berington King (her niece and nephew) shall not interfere with this legacy". She left legacies to several relatives and friends.

Ann died on July 12th 1716 at Brickhouse in London when she was 86 years old, Mary her sister had already passed on. Ann was buried in the Berington Chapel in Bishopstone Church on July 19th 1716. The funeral cost £40, this included bringing her body back from London - no easy task in the early eighteenth century with the state of the roads. There is a long inscription on a white marble tablet in the north transcript of the church in her memory as recorded in chapter 6. Just to clear up any confusion in the spelling of the Berington surname, during her time in London, Ann in her documents changed from using one r to two r's in her surname, after which she appears to have used the later version.

After the will was proved Timothy Geers and Baron Robert Price decided the best way to use the money was to build almshouses to house six poor people, and give each an annuity to live on with other benefits. This was their decision; nothing was stipulated in the will on how the money left to the poor should be used.

Timothy Geers became the main instigator overseeing the building of the almshouses and setting up rules and orders regarding who could qualify to occupy an almshouse.

Baron Robert Price gave the land situated on the hill: it is a mystery to me why the almshouses were not built in the village near to the church but possibly the thinking was that most of the paupers lived in cottages and hovels on the edge of the common so they would all be together. It was not an easy site to build on and a long way for the poor and infirm to walk to church, yet after it was built it must have looked a pleasing sight and could be seen for miles, although it must have been cold in winter, sat on the top of the hill facing north east.

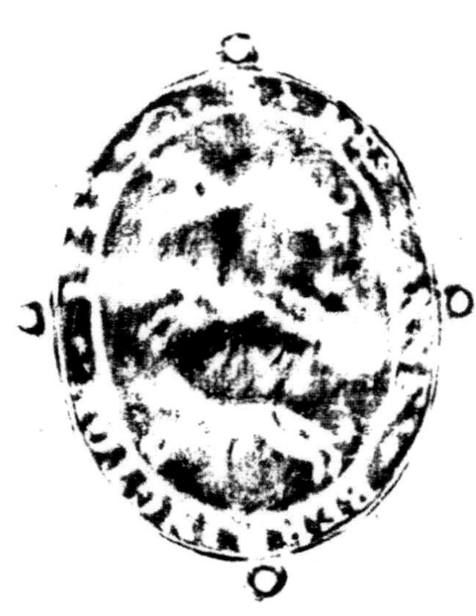

(Figure 4) Copy of a rubbing made in 1910 from the last surviving Almshouse badge.

Timothy Geers with the approval of Baron Price set up a trust consisting of Baron Price or his heir, Timothy Geers or his heir, the Rector of Bishopstone and the Vicar of Bridge Sollers as "trustees and overseers of the said Almshouse and Almspeople."

The rules and orders[6] are written over three pages so I have extracted some of the main points because mostly it is very repetitive.

An Alms person should be of the age of 50 years and upwards and whose poverty or infirmities should render them the greatest object of charity, wherein women should always have the preference to men. No one should be admitted into the Almshouse but such as should be a parishioner of Bishopstone where Ann Berington was born.

Each occupier was paid their annuity free from any deductions on the quarter days, March 25th, June 24th, September 29th, and December 25th.

Each Alms persons was given a cloak or gown to wear made from good grey or brown cloth with a proper trimming once every two years.

The persons who should be admitted into the said Almshouse must wear a badge of brass or copper-plate affixed on the outside of the sleeve of the right arm of their respective hospital-gowns or coats, with the coat of arms of the said Ann Berrington, viz., three greyhounds argent, stretched in a field sable, and the words and figures "Mrs. Ann Berrington 1723," cut or engraved thereon, to denote the foundress of the said Almshouse. (In 1723 the accounts record the first 6 badges cost £3). Mrs stood for "Mistress" and was used for single women as well as married.

When any of the poor people should die, the coat or gowns of such person so dying, with the badge or plate thereon, should remain for the use of the person who should next succeed the said deceadant in the said Almshouse; that anyone admitted into the said Almshouse should be of the communion of the Church of England; and that upon Sundays and holidays they should, in a decent manner, in their hospital-gowns and coats, attend divine service in the parish church of Bishopstone aforesaid; that none should be admitted into the said Almshouse but such as were single persons, and should live alone in their respective dwellings; and that no one should be permitted to live or cohabit with them, or any of them, in the said Almshouse, unless any of the said alms people by reason of age, sickness, weakness, or other infirmities, should need assistance, and then in such case a daughter or some near relation to such infirm person might be permitted to live in the said Almshouse, as an assistant to such persons, and in case any single person who should be admitted into the said almshouse should afterwards marry, then such person marrying should be removed from the said Almshouse, and some other single person placed therein, who, from the time of such marriage, should receive the said rent and charity-money appointed to be paid as aforesaid; that none should be admitted into the said Almshouse who should receive any bread, alms, or pay from the said parish of. Bishopstone, or go a begging or strolling about the country; and that in case any should, be admitted into the said Almshouse who had received any pay or relief from the said parish, then from the time of such admittance such parish-pay should cease, and be no longer paid; that none should be admitted into the said almshouse but such as should be of good report and behaviour, and not given or addicted to drunkenness, cursing, swearing, scolding, wrangling, abusive language, pilfering, or an idle and vicious course of life; and if any person after admittance into the said almshouse should be found guilty thereof, then (upon complaint) such person should be removed from the said Almshouse, and some other person of more civil and orderly behaviour placed in the room and stead of the person so removed, who should receive the benefit of the said charity; that none of the people in the said house should keep or feed any pigs, sheep, or goats, in the court or yard belonging to the said Almshouse, which might damage the said court, or be an annoyance to other the inhabitants in the said Almshouse; and that in case any the said alms people should commit or do anything in breach of the rules and orders therein before mentioned, then such person should be removed from the said almshouse, and some other person, under the qualifications aforesaid, should be elected in his, her, or their place.

Building the Almshouses

The original book of accounts[7] for the Almshouses, also gives a good record of its building.
On May 12th 1721 five years after Ann Berington's death a start was made on the building of the new Almshouses on the Hill under the supervision of Timothy Geers. The site size was 100 feet by 80 feet, enclosed out of the common. The position is still easy to identify today by the remains of the stone boundary walls that surrounded the site.
Hugh Dyer (you remember him from renting the limekiln), made a start levelling the site and Mr Lockley a professional surveyor was employed to set out the ground ready for the mason Robert Pritchard
Henry Gardiner from the Court provided some of the first timber on to the site, 2 ton and 45 foot of oak for which he was paid £1 6s 8d a ton already squared and sawn. David Moles the carpenter and Robert Pritchard the mason both lived in Mansel Lacy, possibly staying on in the parish after finishing working on the new brick mansion built for Baron Robert Price of Foxley in the years 1717-20. The Almshouses were the first brick building in Bishopstone and the local masons who had only worked with stone lacked experience to lay the bricks so Robert Pritchard with his expertise was given the job. The bricks came from the brick works at Stockley Hill and were hauled by John Snead the blacksmith who now appears to have gone into the haulage business, he also hauled material for the new mansion at Foxley. A good strong cart with a team of horses would be needed to ford the river at Bridge Sollers and climb the lanes up to the site; his first loads brought in 5,000 bricks at 14s per thousand. John also carted in the loads of sand and lime, one cartload of sand cost 1s. Local labour and material were used where possible.

(Figure 5) Artist's impression of the new Almshouses on Bishopstone Hill circ1730

George Powell the village carpenter and smallholder provided 700 ft of elm board at 11s 6d per 100ft. On October 30th 1721 John Hargest a labourer who lived just across the common was paid 2s 6d for cutting fern off the common and covering the unfinished site to protect it against the winter weather. The mason, Robert Pritchard did not return to the site until June 1722 nine months later. The only work carried out in this period was by John Hargest and Hugh Maddox who riddled the ground behind the Almshouses. The possible cause for the delay could be explained by an entry on June 2nd that John Snead was paid 1s 6d for haulage of the inscription stone from Tomkyns Hill. This was to be built into the front of the building as featured on our present Almshouses.

David Moulds like other 18th century carpenters was responsible for the timber, from selecting the tree to the final fix as recorded in the following entry dated March 30th 1722. First David visited Mr. Morgan of Swinmore to select the trees, he was paid 9s for falling, squaring and crosscutting the timber, after Mr Morgan was paid for the finished timber which amounted to 2 ton and 12 foot of elm board at £3 per ton. Oak timber was more expensive and for 1 ton and 5ft of oak board he was paid £3 4s 6d per ton. The price of the oak timber had more than doubled in 12 months, unless Henry Gardiner in the earlier entry had supplied second-hand timber. Then Richard Dean was paid 10s for the carriage of the timber from Swinmore back to Bishopstone. In June the carpenter was paid £1 for sawing 950ft of timber. In July 1722 with the river level at its lowest making it easier to ford, the final 6,920 bricks were hauled from Stockley.

Two thousand stone roof tiles were purchased from John Evans, the mason who lived at Stocks Farm, who at this point of time was operating the quarry on the hill; the tiles cost £2 5s 0d. Richard Pillinger was paid 1s 10d for gathering 6 bags of moss which was used as insulation between the ceiling rafters. The winter of 1722 appears to have had favourable weather as the work continued with no letup. In April and May of 1723 Robert Pritchard plastered out the Almshouses and Roland Evans from Berkley Close in the village fixed the 2000 tiles on the roof, this took seventeen and a half days and he charged 1s 3d per day making a total payment to him of £1 1s 10d. The paint cost 19s 8d for the colours and 3 quarts of oil. The glazier P Griffith supplied and fitted the glass and lead into the windows at a cost of £3 12s 0d. The main building was completed by the end of May 1723, John Evans finished off the outbuilding and courtyard. On September 9th 1723 five poor people moved in.

Hugh Dyer was building the boundary wall throughout the next year but he died in April 1725 before it was completed. The Almshouses were finally completed in August 1726, five years after the start, at a cost of £221 2s 1d.

The Almshouses consisted of six individual rooms, 12ft by12ft, joined in a row under one roof. Each room had a fireplace, door and window with painted walls and ceiling and a flagstone floor, a real luxury for the occupiers, who were used to draughty timber frame buildings and dirt floors. When it was finished in 1726, the site comprised a front courtyard containing a communal bake oven, coalhouse, cobbled yard, and rear gardens, the whole site contained within a 5ft high stone wall. The walls were needed to keep out the livestock that wandered loose on the open common.

(Figure 6) This inscription stone came from the original Almshouses, it was rebuilt into the front gable of new Almshouses.

Richard Garret was paid 17s 6d for making 2 seats in Bishopstone Church for the alms people. The labour rates charged on the building vary according to skills, on August 15th 1723 Mark Hadley charged 7d per day, similarly William Taylor and Fred Turner on December 10th for 10 days work were paid 6d per day totalling 5s 0d. Labourers rates appeared to have risen by March 1725 because Thomas Phillip was paid 10d per day, Hugh Dyer the resident labourer earned a total of £23 4s 2d over the 3yrs he worked on the site.

A skilled tradesman could charge up to 2s a day, four times the rate of a labourer; the mason, Robert Pritchard, was paid on piecework to lay the bricks at 10s per thousand plus a day rate of 2s per day for plastering. The carpenter David Moulds earned £16 9s 6d over the five years of building the Almshouses while Roland Evans the roof tiler charged 1s 3d per day.

The materials used in the building were 18,750 bricks at 14s per thousand, 2000 stone tiles and the total cost of the timber used came to £21 12s 0d.

After the building phase the account book records the annual accounts, which start on September 9th 1723 when the first five occupiers moved into the Almshouses. Widow Evans, Widow Hargest, Widow Turner, Widow Nicholls and William Taylor were each paid £1 6s 0d for their Michalmas quarter. Widow Wilcox alias Evans moved into the one remaining almshouse on November 11th and on the day she entered the almshouse she was given 13s. The winter coal allowance of half a ton each was delivered on November 16th by Stephen Garret who charged 7s 6d carriage for 3 tons of coal at 15s 2d a ton. On December 19th 1723 the six poor were paid £7 16s 0d for one quarter due at Christmas and they were also given 1s each "for the feast at Xmas" Here is just an example of the first entries.

Dec 24th	Paid Richard Cox for cloth for six gowns	£3 1s 6d
	Paid Phillip Warner for making and thread	11s 4d
Jan 4th	Paid Roger Wigley for six baskets for coal	3s 0d
	Paid Roger Wigley A pair of scales and horse to them	3s 0d
Jan 24th	Paid Thomas Jones for six pair of shoes	16s 0d
	Paid for six badges	£3 0s 0d

At the end of the accounting year 1723 the total amount paid out of Ann Berrington's legacy was £920 16s, Timothy Geers had personally paid out this amount for building the Almshouses, funeral expenses, the wall inscription in church (which cost £12), and legacies to the relatives.

Baron Price held the money arising from the estate of Ann Berrington which in January 1723 amounted to £2168 15s 7d.

After payment to Timothy Geers it left £1247.19s. From 1723 to 1736 Baron Price held the money, paying an interest rate of 4% which covered the cost of running the Almshouses throughout this period. At Christmas 1736 when the accounts showed a balance of £1302 16s, Baron Price and Timothy Geers decided to invest the money in property and purchased a farm and 170 acres of land in Credenhill costing £1218 9s from Edward Eckley who rented it back from them at £40 per year. This left a balance in the account of only £84 0s 6d.

The yearly accounts are fairly repetitive but there are a few interesting entries. For example the trust would pay for your funeral expenses as in the case of Ann Evans one of the original occupants.

February 8th 1737; -Paid Henry Gardiner for Widow Evans funeral expenses, laying out, coffin, for ye bell, making the grave 14s.

Another entry of interest; "December 9th 1764 3 ton coal at 15s, carrying from Hereford 19s, 3d for turnpike" (This is the first record of a separate turnpike charge, this coal was hauled from the tramway head situated over the Wye bridge or the wharf in Hereford.) The coal supplied to the Almshouses on December 28th 1757 came by coal barge up to Bridge Sollers and the entry states, "Three years coal at 15s per ton plus landing charge 4d per ton." Occasionally Uvedale Price ordered a six-ton barge of coal that was hauled upstream by a team of six to ten men. The last entry for barge coal was in 1762 where it states that 3-ton of coal landed at Bridge Sollers at 17s per ton. Before 1730 the barges provided a regular service to "The Wharf" Bridge Sollers to bring up coal, returning with cider and other produce.

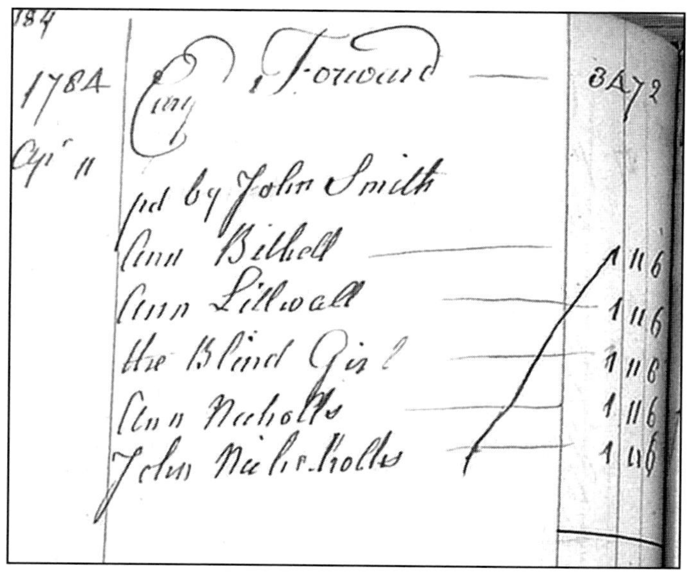
1784 Apr 11 — To Forward — 8A72
pd by John Smith
Ann Bithell 1 11 6
Ann Littwall 1 11 6
the Blind Girl 1 11 6
Ann Nicholls 1 11 6
John Nicholls 1 11 6

(Figure 7) Page from the Berrington Account Book 1784

After this date the wharf fell into disrepair, and an estate map dated 1730 shows the wharf but not in use.

The increase in quarter payments in 1775 is covered by a note "found it difficult to get silver to pay odd shillings I will now pay one guinea and half guinea per quarter".

In 1777 the title of the Almshouses was changed to a Hospital as the record states "*John Geers Cotterell, Trustee of Hospital*" and for the next hundred years it was called Bishopstone Hospital.

These next entries are also intriguing; Dec 19th 1784 deducted from blind girl, 10s 6d for coffin for Susan Parlour paid £1 1s instead of £1 11s 6d. (Why the blind girl had to pay for the coffin is a mystery.)

1796 Feb 9th Paid Edward Morris for his blind daughter after she was suspended £1 11s 6d
1796 July 9th Paid the blind girl (Mr Price's desire) £1 11s 6d
(The Morris family had a hereditary condition, which caused blindness, and there are several references to the family later in the book. The girl was removed from the Hospital without receiving her quarter payment but Edward Morris had approached Sir Uvedale Price's representative on the matter and Sir Uvedale had ordered payment.)
The Almshouses carried on operating in this way up until the latter part of the nineteenth century when decisions were made to build new Almshouses in Bishon. The full set of accounts can still be read, a wonderful record of the poor people who occupied the Almshouses over the years. The building of the new Almshouses is covered in chapter 14.

The rent book of 1705 records Bishopstone Common as being [blank] acres in size, having a well and quarries for paving. William Brown puts a value of ten pound a year rent to be collected from the commons and stone quarries. He left a blank on the acreage of the common presumably because he did not know it. The size of Bishopstone common is listed in other documents as being approximately 50 acres. Bishon common is recorded in the rent book as containing 25 acres with a note "can be enclosed by court". There were different legal jurisdictions on the commons; Bishopstone common was by far the oldest dating back to the Anglo Saxon period. Unsurprisingly there is no record of any money ever paid or charged for the commons' use.

I would like to take the reader on a walk through the parish in 1715, one of the last years the village by the church was fully occupied, making a brief historic account of the families living in the parish at this time, and showing where the farms and cottages were situated. The year 1715 is significant because it is recognised as the last year of a cycle of severe weather, often referred to as "the little ice age." which had lasted from 1645-1715. The Bishopstone parishioners were struggling to survive as the weather had a great impact on crop yields, causing the harvests to fail, and appears to be the reason for so many arrears in the rent book. The great storm of 1703 was probably the worst ever experienced in England, the only effect on Bishopstone appears to be the destruction of the windmill, never to be replaced. 1704 was the driest year recorded for 20 years; up to 1715 dry summers and cold winters became the normal weather pattern, after this date the weather returned to be more varied. 1708-09 recorded the coldest spring for 47 years when the frost lasted for 3 months with the Thames frozen over for 2 months. The parish register record appears normal through this period with the average of 2-3 burials per year.
King George 1 had come to the throne in the previous year, a German who did not speak a word of English. This new king would have held no interest for the parishioners of Bishopstone whose main worries would be the supply of food and keeping warm in the severe winters.
The numbers of the properties match up with the 1715 guide map printed at the end of this chapter.
(1) We start at the Manor House "Court Farm", Henry Gardiner had just taken over the tenancy of the farm in 1713 from Daniel Matthews. The farm and buildings were in a very poor state of repair. It is difficult to judge the size of the farm at this time, probably around 400 acres, because some of the enclosed land was still measured in math. Math is the old method of measuring land area, it is worked out by how much corn a man can cut with a scythe in a day i.e. a seven days mass field would take one man seven days to cut the corn. The rent book lists 41 days of mass in fields, 73 acres in enclosed fields, 128 acres arable land enclosed with 133 acres in common fields. There are 10 acres of orchards, 21 acres of woods including the Yazor Wood of 20 acres. The Manor of Bishopstone had owned this wood outside the parish for centuries as their medieval pig wood, a relic of Wormsley Priory. In 1715 tenants offset some arrears by paying in goods and cider, also repair expenses were charged against the rent.
Daniel repaired the well, he used 14 sacks of lime and seven bushels of hair to repair the manor house, Daniel also supplied Foxley Estate with 40 bushels of pulse (type of bean) and 20 bushels of peas, plus 8 hogshead of cider (a hogshead is 54 gallons) - 432 gallons valued at £2.8s 0d in 1715 works out to £316 in 2010 value = 9p a pint.
Daniel Matthews added more acreage by leasing Bishton Farm from Baron Price after the Baron had purchased the farm in 1710.
By 1713 Daniel Matthews, who paid £142 a year rent, was substantially in arrears. He appears to have left suddenly, though whether by mutual agreement or forced out by non-payment is not recorded. However his debt was not paid off according to the rent book. Henry Gardiner took over Court Farm by negotiating a reduced rent of £112 per year because farming was in a recession. He did not take on Bishton Farm, this was let to John Ashley. Henry came from a wealthy yeoman farming family; his father Henry farmed New House Farm in Brinsop. Henry and his descendants occupied Bishopstone Court for the next 128 years, they were the major employers in the parish, and at different times held all the parish officers' positions from churchwarden to overseers of the roads.

(Figure 8) The Court Farm shown in this 2008 photo is very different in appearance from the original timber framed house occupied by the Gardiner family. It is one of only five sites occupied in 2000 out of the 34 listed in 1715.

In 1716 Henry put carp in the moat and fishpond, cut and carried lumber, and also carried 18 loads of stone. Like many of Baron Price's tenants Henry Gardiner was called upon to provide material for the building of the new mansion house, in this case stone and lumber.

The next year he charged the estate 13s 3d for three bushels of corn for feeding pigeons and fish, both fattened for the table at Foxley, the fish pond and dovecote were essential food providers as they had been in medieval times. The round base of the dovecote was still visible in the 1950s, it was located in the centre of the farmyard. Bob Carrington removed it; he told me that at the same time he filled in what was left of the fishpond between the moat and church.

Henry had two limekilns built at a cost of £6 10s. The lime made from burning limestone quarried out of Bishopstone Hill was used to improve the soil quality by spreading it over the fields.

He also carried out repairs on the house, paying £7 10s for coating the great parlour and chamber (this seems expensive for lime wash: maybe the colours added were costly) as well as mending the chimney, roof, floors and windows; Henry also paid for rough casting the outer wall panels above the stone of the great parlour (This entry reinforces Alfred Watkins findings in the 1920's that the house had a stone ground floor with timber frame above). He also repaired the farm buildings, and made a new yoke house, the total repair bill for this year is £113 10s 2d which was more than the rent charge, this amphasises the poor state of repair the house and farm were in when he became tenant.

In 1715 the farm would have employed over 20 servants and farm workers. In Henry's inventory made after his death it lists the amount of livestock kept and crops growing on the farm which are impressive even by modern day standards. 14 working oxen, 6 carthorses, 40 cows and calves, plus a bull, 13 horses, 110 sheep and lambs, 27 pigs, 95 acres of wheat, corn and barley, 68 acres of peas and pulse.

By the time Henry died at Bishopstone Court in 1747 he had become a very wealthy yeoman farmer as we can see from his inventory.

The total value was £587, equivalent to roughly £940,000 in 2010; it's worth remembering that farm labourers' wages in 1715 were 5s (25p) per week.

Henry junior married Ann around 1730, John their eldest son and heir was born in 1734 followed by Ann (1735), Henry (1738), George (1739), Mary (1744), Elizabeth (1749) and finally William (1753). John died suddenly in 1759 aged 25; Elizabeth his sister died in 1772 aged 23 as stated on the wall plaque in the church.

Henry the second eldest son married Ann Hodges a widow from Brinsop on December 12th 1767 in Bishopstone Church. Henry was now heir following John's premature death and he inherited New House Farm at Brinsop where he lived out the rest of his life. Henry and Ann produced seven children, four died soon after birth. One child George born on March 4th 1769 was to return to Bishopstone in later life purchasing Bishon Farm in 1806.

(Figure 9) Gardiner plaque Bishopstone Church

George the third son married Elizabeth Barrell on February 28th 1780 in Bishopstone Church. When his father died in 1783 aged 85 he became the third generation to hold the tenancy on the farm.

George and Elizabeth had four children, Elizabeth (1780), George (1783), John (1784), and Thomas (1785). John died as a child, the other two boys never married; Elizabeth married the Rev David Williams.
George senior lived until his 95th year and was buried on March 4th 1834, George his son became the fourth generation to hold the tenancy after his father's death. We don't know if this caused friction between the brothers, but whatever the reason there was a tragic end to Thomas's life when he committed suicide.
The report from the Hereford Journal dated May 3rd 1836.
Suicide. On Wednesday last an inquest was held at Bishopstone before Thomas Evans Esq coroner for this county, on the body of Mr T Gardiner, who on the evening of the previous day shot himself with a small pocket pistol, in his bed chamber. It appears the unfortunate deceased who resided with his brother, had been in a low desponding way for three of four weeks. Through no apprehension was entertained he would commit suicide, at between six and seven on Tuesday evening one of the servants went into his bedroom to adjust the bed, when she saw him lying on the floor, and immediately called her fellow servant, who found him quite dead, and a quantity of blood cold and clotted on the boards near him. He had placed the pistol in his mouth when he committed the fatal act. The jury returned a verdict of insanity. The deceased was 51 years old.
He was buried on April 28th 1836 at Bishopstone Church.
George carried on farming Court Farm keeping up his interest in the parish, serving as the rector's churchwarden, overseer of the poor and road surveyor throughout the 1830s. 1841 was the last year he served as churchwarden for Bishopstone, the following year he left the Court Farm financially ruined although he had managed to keep a freehold cottage on Bishon Lane (Cherry Trees), which his father had bought in 1773, where he went to live. Still struggling financially he sold the cottage to James Pember in 1846 and rented The Cottage on Bishon Lane where he lived out the rest of his life, looked after by Fanny James, his illegitimate daughter. He died in 1859 and was buried in Bishopstone churchyard. The story of George his cousin who purchased Bishon in 1806 continues in the 1800 section.

Standing by the Church today it is so tranquil and quiet it's hard to imagine how busy the area would have been in 1715, looking up the dusty road leading through the village, you would have seen people going about their daily business, visiting one of the village tradesmen, the wheelwright, cobbler, saddler or butcher, farm labourers shouting, children playing in the background and the constant noise made by the many livestock gathered together in a small area as all the farms and cottages in the village would have kept pigs and chickens.
The church in 1716 is recorded as being in good condition, quite different to when Thomas Berington left the court. In 1695 the church was recorded as been in poor repair, glass missing, roof leaking, all the villagers had to contribute to its repair or face a fine.
The list of tenants and freeholders and how much they paid towards the repairs to the church still exists but it does not include the then new lord of the manor William Brydges. Twenty names appear on the list starting with William Morgan (Court Farm) 17s 6d, Humphrey Digges (Bishton) 13s 6d.right through to Bartholomew Pillinger 2d (day labourer) total sum raised £3 6s 7d. This money was only used to purchase materials not available in the parish; the stone roof tiles were raised from the quarry on the hill, labour was given free by the villagers, only the glass and other materials would have to be purchased.
The 1716 article of enquiry[8] regarding the church makes interesting reading,
Rector Timothy Millichamp is blind and living in Beckley in Gloucester, the curate who is the rector's son is not licensed. The Rectory is indifferent (meaning in poor condition) *and the barns are propped up to stop them falling. The bible is the old translation but the prayer books are new, churchyard is fenced but no hospital or free school. There is a donation to charity from Bishon Farm of £27 per year. There is an old lady from the village who teaches catechism in church. Prayers are 9 a.m. and 4 p.m. on a Sunday except winter. Children and servants have not been sent to Sunday school.*
The Rector's son acted as a curate although he was not licensed, Uvedale Kyffin, clerk and Jonathan Bick curate both appear in the Bishop's transcripts for 1715, and it's unclear who was running the church affairs while Timothy was living in Gloucester. The order book in 1716 instructed the churchwarden to buy a new bible for the parish to replace their "old translation"; on April 4th the new book was produced. By 1719 Henry Gardiner was the churchwarden and he was ordered to repair the reading desk; on July 26th the following year Arthur Humphrey gent was ordered before the court for not bringing his child to be publicly baptized.
The churchwarden's position carried responsibility, which could be expensive. On February 2nd 1724 John Evans was ordered to repair the church; he bought in a certificate on January 17th 1725 to prove he had carried out the work.

There were three burials in the Berrington private chapel at the beginning of the 18th century, firstly on June 1st 1700 Hugh Lewis, Vicar of All Saints Hereford, husband of Susannah Berrington, then Ann her aunt in 1716. The last person to be buried in this chapel was Hannah King on July 10th 1724. Susannah and Hannah were Thomas Berrington's daughters. Another entry that caught my eye from this register - on November 7th 1726, John a child born at David Morgan's farm was baptised. His mother never came forward because of the implications of being an unmarried mother so she just left him to be found on the farm. Who gave him the name John is unknown.

An incident outside the Church in 1724 reflects on the wide variety of situations which did arise regarding the poor. The overseer and churchwarden Henry Gardiner had the heavy responsibility of looking after the parish poor. Because of the downturn in agriculture the parishioners had very little money and were struggling to feed their families, they could not contribute to the poor rate which left very little money in the parish coffers. Paying out from this dwindling fund would often cause disputes that could only be settled by the courts. Jane Cook was such a case. She was a woman of strong character and on November 8th 1724 she was summoned before the church court for using "opprobious" language to a very high degree, to the curate of Bridge Sollers and his wife in the churchyard, immediately after divine service. She did not appear to answer the charge; remember that Bishopstone's Rector was blind and living in Gloucester and there was a dispute about his son taking the church services without being ordained, so it appears that the curate from Bridge Sollers had stepped into the firing line, regarding a parish dispute.

In the 1725 order book appears a court case; Jane Cook v Overseers of the poor in Bishopstone.[9]

Jane Cook nee Williams of Bishopstone shows she was born in Bishopstone and had a freehold there before she was married, and now wrongfully detayned and held from her, she married a husband from Taunton in Somerset who is now dead.

She is now asking for a house or habitation and 12d a week from the parish.

These court cases were always longwinded; Jane with her young son John had to live on the charity of her brother John, who lived in a hovel on the edge of Bishon Common, but finally a court decision was made three years after Jane arrived back in Bishopstone. This was read out in court to Henry Gardiner the overseer for Bishopstone on June 10th 1727.

Jane Cook of the parish of Bishopstone in this County widow.

Justice of the peace for this County to the churchwardens and overseers of the poor of ye parish of Bishopstone before me, thou court has made upon you providing for habitation and 12d per week for Jane Cook's maintenance.

Jane Cook challenged the parish and won. She would have been given part of a rented parish house on Bishopstone hill to live in. Her name appears on a set of deeds in 1765, James Tringham (tailor) of Bishopstone to Thomas Bythell (yeoman) all that dwelling house lately erected on land purchased by James Tringham from Jane Cook. Jane inherited her brother's land on Bishon Common after his death and sold it to James Tringham.

(2) Up the lane stands a very large timber-framed house "The Rectory" which was extensively rebuilt by Humphrey Berington in 1636. Next to the house stood the eight bay barn with chambers over for the servants to live in, a stable and a sheepcote. Timothy Millichamp's wife Judith died in June 1706 and his daughter in 1711. The Rector's son acting as curate lived in the rectory until Timothy was brought back to Bishopstone on June 21st 1727 to be buried. He was the last rector to live in this Rectory and was the last true farming rector to live in Bishopstone; afterwards the Rectory was only occupied by tenant farmers or farm workers until eventually it was demolished in 1813.

(3) Next to the Rectory stood the wheelwright,s shop and dwelling house, together with a garden, orchard, meadow and backside all attached to the property. Roger Rocke who lived next door at the Stocks owned the property. There were many tenants who rented the wheelwright shop in the early 18th century including John Howells who in 1715 is listed as the wheelwright. John would have also farmed the 4 acres attached to the property. He employed an assistant to work with him, the shop area would be covered with shavings and seasoning wood ready to be worked on. The workshop opened up onto the lane for easy access. John's work came from the local farmers. John Evans demolished this property in 1720 after he had purchased it.

(4) The freehold Stocks Farm on the corner of the lane was occupied by owner Richard Rocke, he was a saddler by trade and also farmed its 42 acres. The Stocks was a large timber framed house with a barn and pigsty. Richard who was married to Mary had two occupations like most of the small tradesmen and craftsmen working in small villages.

Richard appears to have struggled financially because he sold the freehold farm around 1720 to John Evans, a roof tiler from Mansell Gamage who had also purchased Townsend Farm. John was married to Ann, sister of Henry Gardiner from the wealthy farming family. John Evans inherited money through his wife Ann, which he used to purchase all the freehold smallholdings and cottages around him in the village, and he then let the buildings fall down; in effect he started the demise of the village. I have not found any evidence of stocks or the use of them in Bishopstone, though historically most villages had them; the farm name could have started out as Rocks Farm changing through the years to Stocks Farm.

(5) Roger Penner, a farmer, lived in the next smallholding up the lane, his family can be traced living in Bishopstone since the first rental was recorded in 1385. The name Penner derives from the person who was responsible for penning the stray animals in the village pound. Roger was married to Hannah and he obtained a lease on the farm from William Bridges in 1694 for 21 years. The smallholding had a garden, backside, orchard, four acres in common fields and two fields in Little Mansell, for this Roger paid a rent of £1 10s per year plus two chickens at Xmas. He had run up arrears of £5 7s 3d by1713 and gave up the farm when the land was taken over by Henry Gardiner, Court Farm who eventually demolished the house.

(6) George Powell farmer lived next door in a messuage (dwelling house with outbuildings), garden, two closes and an orchard with the usual two acres in each of Bishopstone's three common fields. The Powell family had lived in the parish for a hundred years. George and his wife Elizabeth had secured a lease for life on the smallholding from Thomas Berrington in 1676 at £1.12s per year. By 1715 George was 70 years old, he lived alone with his son John as Elizabeth had passed on. John took over the tenancy on his father's death. They were both good farmers and never fell into arrears. By 1740 the farm was taken over by Simon William, 10 years later it disappears altogether off the records.

(7) Briery Close on the corner of the lane was possibly one of the original old Anglo-Saxon one-acre plots, now containing an orchard, barns, backside and messuage. It was a freehold property belonging to William Matthews gent, the tenant in 1715 is not recorded but the deeds show that after William died his wife Mary sold the holding to Rowland Evans (roof tiler) in 1725 for £75. Rowland was a brother to John Evans who purchased the Stocks Farm. The title deeds of the property run from 1669 when John Savarce owned the dwelling through to 1828 when Sir John Geers Cotterell purchased the house from Annie Archer's executors and demolished it. With the property came 2 crofts enclosed out of Hoarstone Field.

(8) A newly built cottage stands across the lane, Thomas Ferris built this cottage on a 1 acre plot of ground enclosed out of the Townsend lands, he paid a yearly rent of 5s. Thomas was a butcher who operated the Killing House for Thomas Morgan where animals were killed and butchered. John Evans purchased this property in 1720 with the Townsend Farm.

(9) The Townsend house has a very long history going right back to the 13th century when the house was occupied by Alice daughter of Sir John Daniels who had married Edward Smith. After this and for the next five hundred years the land associated with the house was known as Smiths land. Townsend means the last house in the township, which it was in the 16th century. The deeds list the owners from 1676 when John Crow (Vicar of Upton Cressett in Shropshire) sold the farm to John Williams, whose heir Robert Tyler of Tillington sold the farm plus other cottages to John Evans in 1720 for £200. The property consists of a large timber framed main house with two barns, cider house and stables and 10 acres of lands. John Evans moved into the farmhouse with his wife Ann. The house was occupied until the beginning of the 20th century.

(10) The Killing House was used by Thomas Ferris as a Butcher's shop. Butchery in 1715 was not a very nice profession; the animals were killed by slitting the throat with a large knife; hauling themover a beam and letting the blood drain into a large vessel. Some of the poor animals had a long slow death, the noise and smell coming from this building situated in the edge of the village at times must have been unbearable.

(11) The next farm standing on the lane back towards the church was called Whitehouse Farm. When Robert Price purchased Bishopstone in 1705 Thomas Bethell was the sitting tenant. This was the second largest tenant farm in the Manor containing 100 acres. Thomas had taken over the tenancy from his father, he paid £22 a year rent for a house, garden and backside, 12 acres of meadow, eight days math of meadow and 28 acres in Hoarstone field, 28 acres in Puckhall Field and 26 acres in Hill field.

Thomas left the White House Farm in 1709; shortly afterwards he built his new house called the Steps on the turnpike road next to Claypitt Farm. Thomas and his son, another Thomas, appear to have come into money for they changed their titles from yeomen farmers to gentlemen in the early 17th century. The Bethell family had lived in the villages of Bishopstone and Byford for many generations, the last of a very long line of Bethells left Bishopstone in the 1940s. The Whitehouse Farm can be traced back to the 13th century. David Morgan was the new tenant by 1709 with his wife Ann paying a rent of £22. He also rented the land at Digges's Townsend Farm at £6 per year plus Hargest lands at £5 3s. By 1712 he also had fallen into arrears and started supplying goods to Foxley estate instead of rent money. Eight hogshead of cider for Foxley, allowance 1s; 20 bushels of peas for Foxley allowance £3 6s 8d; 13 bushels of barley for Foxley £1 10s 4d.

(12) Next door to Whitehouse Farm stands Godsell's House, so called because William Godsell had been the tenant for many years until his death in 1714; William had never been in arrears with his rent. After William's death, the house was rented by David Morgan (Whitehouse Farm) until 1740 for the use of his farm workers, sometime after this date the house and outbuildings were demolished.

As we leave the noise of the village and make our way up the lane towards the Mansel road, we turn left up towards the hill. Now we leave the enclosed lands behind and see directly in front one of Bishopstone's common fields called Hillfield. This field dates back to the Anglo-Saxon era along with Hoarstone and Puckwell making up the three common field system for Bishopstone village. Hoarstone was the largest field at nearly 100 acres, followed by Puckwell and Hillfield, 80 acres each. Bishon's three common fields had evolved in the 12th century. The five hundred year old three-year rotation system was still being used in 1715; spring planting, followed by winter planting in the second year and the third year left fallow. These fields were still managed by a very elaborate, complex and ancient procedure. The arable land was divided into strips, these could and did run in different directions within the main field. Hillfield was a prime example of this, divided into Downset and Hill Furlong running at ninety degrees with each other in the same field. It's important to remember that no farmer, however large his holding or property, or however important his social position, was at liberty to cultivate his strips as he pleased.

The road comes to a T junction, the left leading to the river crossing and ferry at Bridge, the right lane leading around the outside edge of Puckwell field to Mansel Gamage. As you look up, directly in front is Bishopstone Hill, the top half is grass covered with fern patches dotted around. Fifty acres of this make up Bishopstone common, a ribbon of cottages and houses mark the east and south edge, with one or two enclosed plocks within the common itself. What in the 17th century was described as "a fine stonewall" marks the Bishopstone boundary around the north and west to enclose the common. Originally the common had no boundary wall, only marker stones, but following disputes with Byford and Mansel Gamage whose commons covered the rest of the hill, a wall was built.

The cottages were mainly freehold; they all owned "rights of use" on the common, if you could call them cottages, probably more like huts, one room and a dirt floor. Some were the homes of the paupers supported by the village under the poor relief system. The village owned some of the properties while others were rented from owners by the village to accommodate the poor.

(13) The smallholding on the north side of the hill sitting on the boundary with Mansel Gamage was built in a disused quarry bed, called today Kenowley. In 1705 this house and surrounding land belonged to John Love, freeholder. John was a cobbler and farmer who died in 1709, his son Thomas, who was a miller from Hereford, sold the holding to Robert Price. Looking back at previous owners, Thomas Sheppard who owned the premises in 1639, was a weaver and built a double dwelling in the garden to house his workers. These were called Crabtree Cottages and cost just £16 to build; they must have been poorly built because by 1705 they had fallen down.

Giles Nicholas moved into the smallholding in 1710 with his wife Jane they had eight children two of whom died in infancy. Giles died in 1720; he was listed as a farmer and his eldest son, another Giles, who died in 1748 carried on the tenancy. In 1715 the smallholding consisted of a house, garden, orchard, half an acre of ground and four acres of arable in the lee of the house. Giles Nicholas' rent was £2 4s 0d per year and following the trend of the other small farmers, by 1717 he was in arrears of £4 9s 6d, amounting to over two years rent. To help out he supplied a hogshead of cider to Foxley for an allowance of 10s. Giles junior carried on farming until 1736 but with mounting arrears he could not pay the rent and was evicted; Giles fell on the mercy of the parish and was awarded relief from the overseer.

(14) Just to the south was Hargest's farm. John Hargest a young farmer of 25 and his wife Elizabeth must have been heartbroken when William Brown, Robert Price's agent, came knocking on the farmhouse door in July 1705. He told him that his farm had encroached onto the common and was to be reclaimed by Price as lord of the manor. His father William was living on the farm with John and Elizabeth and their two children. In 1690 the farm was listed as the fifth largest farm in Bishopstone, but land had been illegally enclosed over a period of years. The land attached to the farm was rented to John Parlour, while the Hargest family stayed on in the farmhouse and paid rent but with no income they soon fell into poor relief. When John died in 1727 aged 48 he was listed as a pauper and was buried by the parish, his wife Elizabeth moved into the Almshouse where she died in 1735. On a happier note John's son married Ann Gardiner in 1741, they had five children, Ann inherited wealth and their children and grandchildren were tenant farmers in and around Bishopstone until 1820. The farmhouse was demolished by 1737.

(15) Further south sitting in a niche on the edge of the common was a smallholding called Buckwell Farm consisting of four acres enclosed, plus strips in each of the common fields. This smallholding was farmed up until the early 1900s and the ruins of the farmhouse are still visible today. The rent book tells a tale of Richard Pillinger, a farm labourer, and how precarious life could be; lack of work or illness would mean that you and your family had to rely on parish relief to exist. Richard Pillinger and his wife Eleanor had eight children between 1687 and 1706, at which time he was a labourer renting Berkeley Close from Humphrey Digges. By 1706 he and his family were on parish relief listed as paupers. Robert Price gave Richard a chance by renting Buckwell Farm to him at £2 4s 0d per year. Richard died in 1720, he was listed as a farm labourer but thankfully he had worked his way off parish relief. His eldest son, another Richard, took on the tenancy of the farm and married Susan Weaver a year later in 1721. This Richard died suddenly in 1727 aged 40; in 1732 Susan married William Jones her farm servant, who then became tenant of the farm. William had appeared before the church courts in 1731 accused of fathering a bastard child on a certain Susan Lawrence.

Back down to the road we walk towards Bridge then turn up the green lane towards the common. If we look further along the road towards Bridge (now known as Bridge Sollers), there on the side of the road stands what remains of the village windmill, blown down in the great storm of 1703. Above this on the hillside stands the large stone-built limekiln owned by the manor and rented to Hugh Dyer for five pounds per year. The lease binds Dyer to keep the kiln in good repair and he is to have liberty of digging and burning for himself or his tenant. Hugh Dyer was a labourer who never married and lodged with other families. According to the rent book he never paid any rent in the years he occupied the site, he just built up arrears. When he left in 1715 William Brown's entry in the rent book states that there were five tons of lime left in piles and lists some of the goods allowed against Hugh Dyer's rent: *five loads of the lime delivered to Bishopstone Court £2 10s; one load of roof tiles delivered to David Evans for tyling (tiling) the beast house at Morehampton being four square £1 8s 6d.* The stone roofing tiles were a by-product, made from the harder stone removed to expose the softer limestone seams.

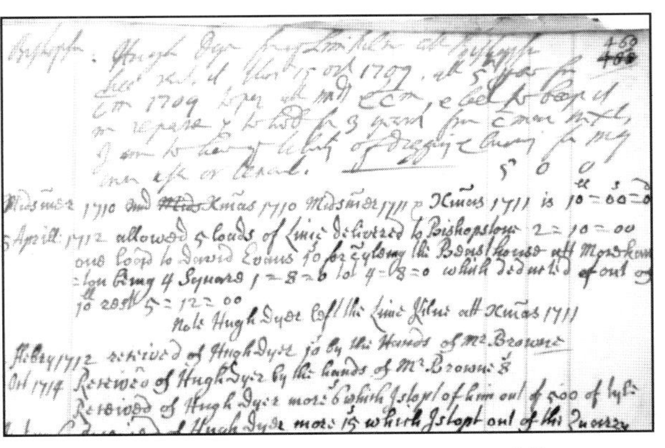

(Figure 10) Rent book entry of Limekiln

(16) At the top of the lane on the right bordering the common stands a very old house and an enclosure of 9 acres belonging to the Parlour family. The family had held this freehold smallholding for over a hundred years. They had traditionally been the blacksmiths of the village for many generations but James Parlour had broken the family tradition and was farming by 1715; James and his wife Bridget lived with his father John, now a village carpenter. The Parlours had lost out to John Snead the new blacksmith who had built a new smithy shop in Bishon in 1694.

(17) Opposite the Parlours' orchard is the proposed site of the new Almshouses, while further on towards the centre of the common stands Well cottage, a two-acre holding enclosed by a hedge, named after the only well on the common, which supplied the water for all the cottages, and livestock on the Hill. On one of the first maps of Herefordshire made by Taylor in 1754, only two features in Bishopstone are shown, the church and this well.

The only other well shown on this map is the holy well at Peterchurch, which makes me wonder if our well was of some significance in Herefordshire before the eighteenth century, but I have found no evidence to verify this. The only other water supply on the Hill was a spring, which served Kenowley farm. Well Cottage is today called Swiss Cottage; it was made into a folly for the Garnons estate in around 1804 and rebuilt to look like an Alpine house.

(18) Back across the common is another enclosed piece of land containing a cottage with three acres. John Wontnor lived here, again he received a knock on the door in July 1705 by the land agent, William Brown, to inform him that his smallholding was encroaching on common land and he would now have to pay rent. According to the rent book he never paid a penny and ran up arrears. John was a labourer always referred to by his surname for he carried the burden of his disgraced father, who in 1680 stood before the church courts and boasted that Susan Meredith was a whore and his whore.
Since then the family had been cold-shouldered but because of the workings of the poor system they could not leave the parish even if they had wanted to.

(19) The next cottage on the left was also an encroachment onto the common ground. Matthew Evans a labourer lived in one half of the cottage, if you could call it a cottage, cheaply built timber framed with wattle and daub walls, thatched roof and dirt floors, a single room with a fireplace at one end used for cooking. Internal wooden shelves were fixed to the top of the walls under the thatch; this is where the children slept. Matthew was married to Elizabeth, by 1715 they had five children, aged between ten and two. The other half of the cottage was occupied by William Taylor, a pauper who won a court case in 1675 to make the village overseers rebuild this cottage on the common for his family; now forty years on, the cottage was divided and occupied by two families on parish relief. This one double cottage was the home for sixteen individuals; highlighting the problems the poor were experiencing in these times.

(20) This cottage newly built by Matthew Evans was the home for two other pauper families headed by Francis Powell and Mark Handley. Francis Powell died in 1712 leaving a young son Francis aged only five. Young Francis is a good example of how the parish system works. In theory no matter what level of life you were born into, you could rise up or down the social ladder from a pauper to a gentleman. Francis was taken under the wing of his uncle William a carpenter who taught him the trade. In 1731 he and his uncle built a cottage, which still stands today on Bishon Lane called "Cherry Trees". Francis moved into the house in 1734, his mother Mary moved into an Almshouse where she died in 1745. Francis lived with Elizabeth Taylor in the new house and had an illegitimate child called John, in their childhood these two had lived next door to each other on the hill. They never married and were both excommunicated from church. After his mother died in 1745 Francis moved out of the parish, and leased the house to Elizabeth for 99 years for a one off payment of £19 15s. Who paid this money, or if it was paid at all is not disclosed but possibly it was a legal requirement so Elizabeth could remain living in the house with her son John.
The other tenant occupying Matthew Evans' house was Mark Hadley, "pauper". He and his wife Eleanor had three children, Mary born in 1705, and twins John and Elizabeth born August 1710. The twins both died and were buried in October 1711 aged only 14 months. It was unusual for twins to survive at all in the eighteenth century, infant mortality was high and these twins stood little chance, being born into a pauper family.
To help understand why these people were in and out of poverty it's worth looking at the national average wage for agricultural day labourers, which in 1720 was 7s per week. In Bishopstone the best day labourers only earned 10d per day, making 5s a week; and some only 6d per day (3s per week). So they were poorly paid against the national average but this appears the general trend for the whole of Herefordshire. The working week consisted of six days working all the daylight hours with Sunday off. It may sound incredible, but it is nevertheless a fact that a man could live on that wage, provided he earned it every week. Not only live, but also marry and raise a family. It is clear that it could be done, the Taylor and Pillinger famlies from Bishopstone were living proof. Sanitation and hygiene, for instance, cost the eighteenth-century workingman nothing, except the trouble of getting a bucket of water from across the common. Travel cost him nothing, since he walked. The rent for his house cost, at the most, a few pence per week if not paid for by the parish. There was always a garden in which he could grow vegetables, keep a few hens and perhaps a pig.
The staple diet of these men was bread, cheese, milk, eggs and beer. Meat, apart from that of their own pig, was out of the question, even at sixpence per pound; so were tea, sugar or any taste of sweetness other than those which could be picked from the hedgerows. Soup made from vegetables and bones would often constitute a main meal, reinforced by a hunk of bread.

Moreover, there was always a slack period after harvest and hay-time, when many workers were laid off, even the good workers. Through this period many had to rely on parish relief.
I think a poem written by Crabbe could easily relate to our parish houses on the hill.

There, in yon house, that holds the parish poor,
Whose walls of mud scarce bear the broken door;
There, where the putrid vapours, flagging, play,
And the dull wheel hums doleful through the day
Their children dwell, who know no parents' care;
Parents, who know no children's love, dwell there!
Heartbroken matrons on their joyless bed,
Forsaken wives, and mothers never wed;
Dejected widows with unheeded tears;
And crippled age with more than childhood fears;
The lame, the blind, and, far the happiest they!
The moping idiot, and the madman gay.
Here too, the sick their final doom receive,
Here brought, amid the scenes of grief, to grieve,
Where the loud groans from some sad chambers flow,
Mix'd with the clamour of the crowd below,
Here, sorrowing, they each kindred sorrow scan,
And the cold charities of man to man.

(21) Next cottage on the top of the hill was called Mary Digges' cottage; it was in poor condition when Robert Price purchased it in October 1710. Eleanor Blunt was the tenant, paying 16s a year rent. When she left in 1712, Henry Ireland, who had taken on the cottage, did not pay any rent. A note in the rent book explains, "Rent free till Henry Ireland repairs this house." Added to his problems the rent book lists James Watkins living in one bay of the cottage and renting the apple trees, he was a servant of William Thomas. Typically in the 18th century if you wanted more living space, you just built an extra 12ft bay on the end of your cottage. John Digges of Bishton owned the cottage originally and on his death his daughter Mary inherited it.

(22) Walking to the end of the common, turn left down the parish boundary lane towards the turnpike road, halfway down stands a smallholding named in some documents as Halfway House, in other deeds as Berkley Close. Purchased by Baron Price in 1710 as part of Humphrey Digges estate the smallholding was known locally as Richard Pillinger's house. Richard Pillinger and his wife Elena had seven children two of whom died in infancy. Richard was a pauper and lived on parish relief.

(23) Next door and lower down the lane stands a house, garden, backside, orchard and a one acre close called Matthews House. It carried a lease for life to Susana Catch, former maid to Humphrey Berrington, dated August 14th 1661 at 12s per year. Susana's daughter and husband had lived in the house until 1710. Henry Ireland had rented the house from 1713 together with Mrs Digges house (No 21). This house was also in poor repair as the rent book states "Allow him the first year rent for setting this house in repair".

(24) George Bythel farmer, lived in Claypitts Farm at the bottom of the lane, he was the son of George the Cooper who died suddenly in 1680 and left a very interesting inventory as listed in the 1600-1700 section. Claypitts farm was an old timber framed 14th century yeoman's house built on the side of the main road leading from Hereford to Hay. Built into the bank, it gave commanding views over the Wye Valley. From an earlier inventory we have a good description of the house. One large hall with a bedchamber going off the main room, a cellar under the house containing the usual hogsheads of cider. A room called a solar under the thatch and over the hall, no stairs but a little ladder to climb up into it. This is where the children or servants sleep with the food store of cheese, bacon, corn, etc. It was an important farm with a barn attached, a garden, 4-acre orchard also a 4-acre field called Cockshells Old Lands, (possibly named from finding fossils in the limestone scattered in the field) it was situated just under the limekiln on the hill. It was let under a 99-year lease set up by Humphrey Berrington on March 7th 1647 for a 20s a year rent. George married Mary Prosser in 1711 after his first wife Frances died in childbirth. James, his 19-year-old eldest son was living and working with them. By 1715 George and Mary were both in their late 40s and like everyone else they were in arrears of £8 2s 8d. After George died a John Davies was listed as the tenant in 1737 and in 1746 when the 99-year lease expired James Bythel who was now 52 years old purchased the property from Baron Price. The Bythel family lived there until 1818 when the Garnons estate purchased it. The farmhouse was demolished about 1885; the barns are still standing today converted into living accommodation.

(Figure 11) Bridge Ash rebuilt with a new brick first floor and roof, the original Digges Farmhouse stone lower floor can still be identified in 2010.

(25) Now follow the road towards Hereford bearing right down the dingle towards the Boat Inn and ferry past Bridge Sollers church, half a mile through Bridge Sollers parish we come to the Bishopstone boundary. Just on top of the bank is a smallholding leased to James Rowland. It was purchased by Baron Price in 1711 from William Winstone the son and heir of Delabere Winstone the last husband of Eleanor Digges. A typical sized 17th century yeoman's farm, it contains a house, barns, garden and orchard with 30 acres in the common fields. After Baron Price acquired the holding the 30 acres of land were split between John Foote (Bishon) and Daniel Matthews (Bishton), and added to their tenancy agreements. The sale agreement describes the house as falling down, but by 1712 James Rowland is paying a rent of £1 per year, so some rebuilding must have taken place. James must have been elderly as I cannot find any reference to him in any parish records. Baron Price sold the house, garden, orchard and some land to Matthew Evans in 1720. The Evans family owned the farmhouse until 1825, when it was sold to a James Hancock who had been a tenant for many years. The property was known as Winstone House until 1825, after that it became Bridge Ash. The common field next to the house was always called Bridge and with a large ash tree on the property it is easy to see where the name has come from.

(26) Travel west along the turnpike road to a point where a bridle path heads north towards Bishon and you will find another smallholding, owned by Timothy Geers from the Marsh. Timothy Geers had purchased this from Martha Pugh after her husband Phillip had died in 1713. The Pugh family had owned this smallholding from 1667 but never lived there, preferring to live in the much bigger house in Bishon. They let the smallholding to tenants, it came with 6 acres of enclosed lands plus strips in common fields. The holding was occupied until the 1850's when it was demolished after the exchange of lands between Foxley and Garnons estates.

(Figure 12) This tranquil setting of the Old Post Office in 2000 gives little clue to its past history.

(27) Turning left following the bridle track north through the common field of Bishon, with West field on the left and Lining field on the right, half way between the roads we cross a foot path still in use today, which is listed in many deeds as the boundary between strips in these common fields. On reaching the Roman road and looking east, we see the blacksmith's shop of John Snead. John came to the village through his marriage to Eleanor Foote daughter of John Foote of Bishon Farm. They were married on January 13th 1694 at Bishopstone church when John was 31 and Eleanor 21 years old. In 1694 John built himself a smithy shop as previously recorded and he lived with his wife Eleanor in the cottage just up the road, today known as the Old Post Office. This so-called smallholding with a garden, orchard and 30 acres in the common fields was on a lease made with Thomas Berrington in July 1664, for the lives of Richard and Eleanor Foote of Bishon farm. When Eleanor Foote died in October 1708, John Snead and Eleanor (her daughter) who were already sitting tenants took over the tenancy. Now in the ownership of Baron Price the rent was set at £6 per year and two capons (chickens) at Christmas. By 1715 John was in arrears of £9 16s 8d. He like many others in Bishopstone set off work against the rent. Allowance for shoeing horses from February 12th 1711 to June 24th 1715, £1 15s.

Shoeing oxen from February 4th 1712 to January 24th 1713, £3 6s 6d. Oxen were commonly shoed for walking long distances to markets even as far as Smithfield in London. Other blacksmith work carried out includes repairs to plough irons £2 11s 4d. The ploughs used in 1715 were still all made of wood except for an iron tip on the mould board that turned the furrow. Work at Bishon Farm for a pair of hooks and eye for Mr Ashley's barn door and for staples and slings for a manger 5s; for making 4 wedges and a spike to raise limestone 3s. By 1719 John was £22 10 7d in arrears and his 30 acres in the common fields were re-let to Bishon farm. He then turned to hauling to make ends meet. Allowance for seven cords of wood and 11 days hauling brick and rubble were 3d per day coming to 3s 7d

(Figure 13) John Snead's headstone Bishopstone Churchyard

The new brick-built Foxley mansion had just been finished and John was helping to clear up the site; 3d per day was a pitifully low rate of pay for a day's work including the horse and cart. He must have been desperate to put food on the table for his large family. In 1716 John and Eleanor had their final child, making a total of 11 children born over a twenty-year period, 3 of which died in infancy. John was now aged 54. Eleanor was 43 when she gave birth to her last child, James. She died in 1726 aged 53. Like many women she would have been exhausted by the constant struggle of bringing up a family in the early 18th century. With the help of his children John carried on working and living at the smallholding until 1736. He helped with the building of the Almshouses, the account book records him as a hauler carrying material up to the site with his eldest son William helping him. John Snead worked as the village blacksmith in Bishon until 1735 when at the age of 72 he handed over to the next blacksmith, James Hancock. John moved into the Almshouse and lived there until he died in 1757 aged 95. He was buried on February 26th in the churchyard on the side of the east path and his gravestone marking the site is still in good condition. Around 1735 Forge Cottage was built to house James Hancock, the new Blacksmith.

(28) To the west and next door to John Snead's farm stands a Herefordshire long house where Phillip Pugh lives. This had been the fourth-largest farm in Bishopstone in 1670. Phillip was never a successful farmer like his father David, he was listed as a labourer by 1715 and survived the economic recession by continually selling off parcels of his land to Timothy Geers, eventually ending up with just this house. Phillip died in 1727 aged 59 and was buried as a pauper. His only son John, also a labourer, never married and died young aged 25. In 1737, his mother Martha moved into the Almshouse where she died a pauper in 1743. We know from his father's inventory that it was a large six-roomed house with two rooms upstairs and his father had servants and workmen living-in. The house was in poor condition by 1715. Eleanor, Phillip Pugh's eldest daughter inherited the house, she had married Walter Dickens at Stretton Sugwas church on December 26th 1737.They moved in and started a family, and by 1745 they had 4 children, 3 girls and their only son Walter just born. This was an unlucky house for the Dickens family; Walter the father died in 1747 a poor man, as a labourer he could not work because of ill health. Eleanor struggled on with the children but died in 1753 leaving Walter her only son and heir aged 8. The next document dated September 18th 1754 names Timothy Mathews as the legal guardian of Walter Dickens who was under the age of twenty-one. He let the house to Samuel Stokes, and then in 1769 a court letter signed by Walter Dickens yeoman of St Ann, Westminster ordered the sale of the house, because he had been seized for debt. It was sold to John Clements an innkeeper from Hereford for £45. After many alterations this house was eventually divided into two, then three and became known as Burcott Row.

(Figure 14) The Pleck in 2008 now a Grade 2 listed awaiting restoration.

(29) Heading back west along the road opposite the blacksmith shop a lane leads down to Bishon Farm. Down the lane on the right-hand side stands the Pleck, a typical yeoman's farm with barn, outbuildings and stable plus 30 acres in the common fields owned by Sarah Eckley from Mansel Lacy who inherited it from her father John who died in 1707. John was the last of five generations of Eckley's to live in the ancestral home built by Walter Eckley in 1550-60. It is a fine example of a 16th century oak timber framed building using 9 inch square timber for the frame, with huge 12 inch corner posts, capped by a stone tile roof.

John Bishop and his son Thomas were tenants throughout the early part of the 18th century and on Sarah Eckley's death the property passed to her sister Lucy who was married to William Rogers, a yeoman from the city of Hereford. When Lucy died her son William, a silk painter from Middlesex sold the Pleck on January 20th 1740 to Edward Goode for £30. The houses and buildings stood in four acres, plus a one-acre paddock at Scaldback, and the 30 acres of common field tillage.

(30) Carry on straight down the lane and into Bishon farm. The tenant in 1705 was Eleanor Foote who carried the life tenancy in the name of her husband Richard who died in 1671 at a young age. The Foote family originated from Kenchester. The farm was listed at the time of Richard's death as a dwelling house, two barns, one stable, sheepcote, wain house, beast house and a garden plus enclosed land. Tillage in the common fields were 31acres in Linning Field, 31 acres in Hoarstone Field and 30 acres in Moors field. When Eleanor died in 1708, her son John Foote (yeoman) and his wife Elizabeth secured the tenancy of the 140-acre Bishon farm. John had married Elizabeth Godsell a local girl, daughter of William Godsell who lived in the village, John and Elizabeth had three children John, Hannah and Eleanor; he like his father and grandfather held the important position of constable.
English constables of this time were important local figures drawn from the more substantial members of the village, on a par with churchwardens and overseers of the poor. John held all three jobs at different times but he was always the parish constable.
John's duty to the parish was to keep order, acting as a mediator between the village and Crown. One duty John regularly carried out was to check if any vagrant had slipped into the parish who might steal something or, which was even worse, might die and have to be buried at the expense of the parish. Another regular task of the constable was to keep a list of men eligible for service in the Militia, to present the list to the Chief Constable every quarter, and to pay the statutory levy.
October 31st 1718, Lease between John Foote and Uvedale Price[10].
Bishon Farm with land in Bishopstone, Brinsop and 8 acres in Mansel Lacy £27 per year. John Foote to keep land well and not to plough up any pasture without permission of Uvedale Price.

(Figure 15) Stonehouse in 2008 very different in appearance from the timber framed Inn of 1715.

(31) Back up the lane onto the Roman road turn right and within 200 yards on a T-junction stands the New Inn. The site with its four acres of orchards and three acres in common fields can be traced back to the 14th century although this inn was built around 1595. Howell Evans was the innkeeper; renting the New Inn from Baron Price for £2 per year. He had taken on the tenancy in 1685 with his new wife Elizabeth. The Bishop's transcripts show their first three children were all baptized as Ann in 1685, 1687 and 1689; an explanation could be that the first two Anns must have died in the first few weeks of life, although there is no record of their burials. This does not appear to be uncommon, there are several records of babies being baptized with the same name in different years but no burial record. The churchwarden wrote up the Bishop's transcripts at the end of the year and it is likely that a lot of entries were forgotten; the transcript records are not always reliable. We know from the wills that a lot of Bishopstone churchwardens could not read or write, they were reliant on others to perform this task.
Howell and his wife Elizabeth carried on producing children, Mary in 1694, another Ann in 1697, Hannah in 1699, Edward in 1701, Martha in 1705 and Sibyl in 1707 making a total of nine children, three of whom died in infancy. This appears to be the average sized family as long as the wife kept in good health. The Inn was not very profitable and he had run up huge arrears. When he died in 1721 he was £14 2s 10d in arrears, equal to seven years rent. After his death Elizabeth took on the tenancy of the New Inn until 1731.
Howell's elder brother Royston was the last miller to work and live at Bishton mill, which closed in 1711. Apart from the arrears the rent book shows that Howell paid 3d a year bridge money, this was a local Herefordshire tax to keep the bridges in good repair.
He paid 25d a year to a "Masons Soldiers Charity" from land now attached to the New Inn originally owned by Benjamin Mason in the civil war.

(Figure 15) West wing of Bishton Farm the only surviving part of Digges original house. 2007

(32) Following the right fork the road leads down to the church and village, (one of the roads closed in 1820) and two hundred yards on the right stands the entrance drive to Bishton, guarded by a fine set of gates and wide enough to allow easy access to carriages pulled by a team of four horses. Humphrey Digges built this entrance around 1675, this was part of a building programme when Humphrey spent £700 (a huge amount of money equal to one million pounds in 2010) to change Bishton from a farm to a country residence fit to entertain his prominent friends. We have a good description of its appearance written in a 1704 lease: there was a well maintained hawthorn hedge lined with apple trees leading to the entrance gates, where stood a Bower (cottage), while other interesting items mentioned included a court yard containing stables and coach house, brew house, bouting house with chamber above, parlour, garden and walks leading down to the mill. This information was taken from a six-year lease that Humphrey Digges, shoemaker of Hereford, made with John Knott, yeoman on June 25th 1704, to let Bishton out at fifty pounds a year. This Humphrey had just inherited Bishton from his father, who was the nephew of the original house builder. The estate had fallen into disrepair by 1700 and the cottage by the drive entrance and the mill with its adjoining house had all disappeared by 1709. The mill operated when water from the top pond, was released down a channel to the lower pond driving the wheel. A small spring and stream fed the top pond. As stated previously Baron Price purchased the estate on December 24th 1709 for £1250 after Humphrey Digges had appeared before him in court charged with bankruptcy. It was purchased at a very low price but as part of the sale agreement Humphrey removed and retained the wainscot (carved wooden panelling) from the house and a furnace from the brew house.
By 1715 Mr John Ashley had tenancy of Bishton at £55 per year, he had taken over from Daniel Matthews who in 1710 was charged a rent of £56 per year.
These are some of the entries taken from the rent book when Daniel Matthews became the first tenant, *Townend house pulled down for three loads of hay,* this was the old farmhouse which stood across the road from Townsend Farm in the village. Two properties with the same name is nothing unusual, both properties were the last houses in the township standing opposite each other, one on the east of the road the other on the west.

Allow 20 cartload of Cumpos (manure) from buildings at Bishton	*10s 0d*
Allow 18 cartload of bushes cleared from ground at Bishton	*9s 0d*

These allowances for clearing out the farmyard and land show the farm had been neglected over many years. The farmhouse windows were glazed in 1717 at a cost of 8s 6d, and new weatherboards fixed over the windows costing 3s. John was still farming Bishton in 1720 when the rent book closed.
By 1737 Matthew Nash was farming Bishton Farm now containing 172 acres for a rent of £59 per year.

(33) Heading down the road towards the church, on the right stands an old house and buildings in Walle Close, neglected and empty. Forty years earlier Walle Close would have been bustling and busy, as the close contained a large farm called Old House Farm, and two smaller yeoman farms all grouped together forming a small hamlet. Now in 1715 only one remains standing, the smaller freehold yeoman farm with a house and barns standing within a one-acre enclosure. The Eckley family had owned the land since 1560, four generations later Rolland died in this farmhouse on November 12th 1711.
Married life for Rolland and Ann had started so brightly, for the first 10 years between 1662 and 1672 they had rented the old Bishton farm, at 140 acres the second largest farm in Bishopstone. Rolland and Ann had six children, two of whom died in childbirth.
In 1672 when Humphrey Digges started his rebuilding programme at Bishton, Rolland moved back to this family farm, and after Ann died in 1704, his daughter Mary looked after him.
In early November 1711 they both appear to have fallen ill. Mary died first and was buried on November 7th while Rolland lay in his farmhouse dying. It's easy to imagine the scene, propped up with pillows in bed, too weak to sign his mark, drifting in and out of consciousness, being attended to by his daughter Sarah. Worried by his worsening condition and with no will made, she sent her daughter Elizabeth sculling up the lane to fetch Mrs Foote and Mrs Astley from the farms to witness the will that he made from his death bed by spoken word on November 11th.

The will whispered out by Rolland was written down by Mrs Foote and they both witnessed the event. Rolland was buried soon after on November 16th. The Will states; *I give to my grandchildren William, Ann and George Eustance one sheep each. The rest of my possessions I give to my daughter Sarah Hosier and my granddaughter Elizabeth Smith*[11].

(Figure 16) John Jones headstone

(34) As we look back towards Bishon common, there stands one last smallholding belonging to John Jones, originally part of the Humphrey Digges estate. John Jones, a labourer, purchased the freehold property in 1710. He married Mary in 1718 and they had two children. There were possibly other cottages or hovels on the edge of the common but this is the only one mentioned in the rent book. John and Mary are both buried in Bishopstone churchyard, their gravestones recording that John died on June 20th 1754 aged 66, and Mary relict of John Jones on February 9th 1770.

It was a house of generous proportions and had a large bay attached. Before 1710 it was the home and place of work of John Macklin the weaver whose father held the tenancy of Knap Farm in Bridge Sollars. John's handloom would have measured at least 8 feet high and 12 to 13 feet long, too large to fit into a normal cottage. He rented the property from Humphrey Digges. As a man with a trade he would have been welcomed into the parish although his move to Bishopstone was a short tragic affair for his family. All his misfortunes are recorded in seven consecutive entries in the parish's records. On July 1st 1706 his son John was baptised; he was buried on July 7th 1706 just after he was born, but the next five entries have more harrowing undertones. March 1st 1707 daughters Ann, Margaret and Elizabeth baptised. March 3rd 1707 daughter Ann buried, March 7th 1707 daughter Margaret buried.

Their ages are not recorded, whether the girls were of different ages and were baptised together because they were suffering from a life threatening illness or possibly they could have been triplets, but these entries confirm the tragic suffering of child mortality at the time; if an infectious disease entered the family home there was very little that could be done. John with his wife Ann left the parish soon after their daughters were buried in the church, moving to a small farm in Mansel Lacy that still carries the Macklin name today.

From this imaginary walk around the parish in 1715 we can conclude that Bishopstone parishioners were struggling to pay their rents and to keep the houses in good repair.

The village on Church Lane had effectively disappeared by 1750 only five houses were left standing - the Rectory, Stocks, Birley Close, Townsend Farm and Whitehouse Farm.

A survey in 1705 listed 34 properties in Bishopstone, by 1720 this number had dropped to just 23, the lowest housing stock in the parish on record, yet the same numbers of families were living in the parish. Many of the day labourers and paupers, had to double up in the parish houses. Nine houses were demolished by 1750, five in the village plus Eckley's Farm in Walle Close, Hargest Farm under the hill, the Millhouse and Bower (cottage) both on Bishton farm.

New houses and cottages built in Bishopstone during the eighteen century were Forge Cottage (circa 1740), Old School House (c1750), Orphanage (Cherry Trees) (c1734). Thomas Bythell built The Steps (c1730); next door to the Steps William Bythell, built a row of three cottages in the orchard (c1747) and James Tringham built a house on Bishon common in 1765.

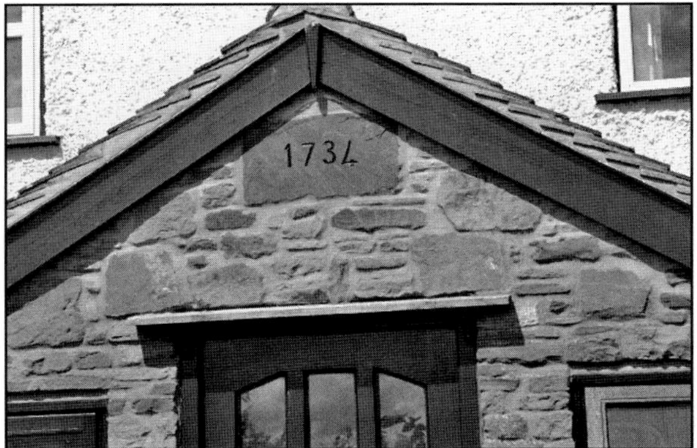

(Figure 17) Cherry Trees date stone
Photo 2009

Two of the above new cottages are well documented; in 1734 William Powell (carpenter) built the cottage now known as Cherry Trees (Orphanage) on Bishon Lane. It was built on the site of an old cottage that had fallen down fifty years previous called the Lower Well, which appeared on an exchange of properties and lands between Richard Digges and John Crowe on December 20th 1656.

The industrious William Bythell the carpenter had just finished building a row of three cottages in the orchard next to his farmhouse in Claypitts, the first occupiers of these cottages were Ann Butcher, Thomas Hayes and John Wyatt. William went on to build many more houses in the parish including a cottage destined to become the Nelson Inn. The area known as Claypitts for a period in the middle of the 18th century was a small hamlet of eight dwellings.

It was a pity that the houses in the village were not rebuilt after falling into disrepair after the Civil War. If they had been repaired, today we could be looking at a very nice compact village down by the church. But it never happened so the poor day labourers were forced to live on the hill in only what could be described as hovels while the rest of the parish stood in a time warp for nearly a century until the Enclosure Act of 1809.

1752 was the first year in England to officially begin on January 1st. Until the Calendar Act of 1752, the year in England began officially on March 25th (Lady Day) This act brought further changes in England which was some 11 days ahead of the Catholic European countries because in 1582 when other European countries adopted the Gregorian calendar, England being Protestant did not. In 1752 these days had to be cut out of the year to adjust the English calendar and therefore Wednesday September 2nd 1752 was followed immediately by Thursday September 14th. Bishopstone's overseer and churchwarden did not adopt the new system and for another three years they continued to use the old system, starting their year on March 25th. Also from 1754 a new register book for marriage was kept to comply with the Act of Parliament of the same year, that stated banns had to be called in the church three times before a marriage. During the period 1700-50 thirty-five marriages were registered at Bishopstone church.

On the death of Timothy Millichamp, James Allen became the new rector of Bishopstone, presented by Uvadale Price on August 3rd 1727; he was also the vicar of Yazor where he lived. Bishopstone Rectory and parsonage lands were let out to Henry Gardiner who used the Rectory to house his labourers. On February 11th 1730 James Allen was ordered to repair the parsonage house and rebuild the parsonage barn. On December 9th 1731when he brought in a certificate to say he had carried out the repairs, he complained to the court that the buildings had been neglected for 15 years due to the fault of the previous rector

James Allen BA (son of the previous rector) became the new rector of Bishopstone on February 23rd 1754 when his father retired; James had a younger brother Bennet, who was also a man of the cloth but whereas James was happy to be a country rector, his brother had a far more adventurous and interesting life.[12]

Bennet Allen was born in 1736. Following his brother to Oxford he obtained a BA at Wadham College in 1755, and unlike James he stayed on at Oxford for his MA. He was ordained in 1761, after which he developed a close friendship with Lord Frederick Balmore who had inherited the proprietorship of Maryland. With Fredrick's encouragement, Bennet left for America in October 1765 with his sister Elizabeth who became his housekeeper and by 1771 he ended up as Rector of All Saints Church in Fredrick Town. The church was rich from tobacco money and Bennet received over £1000 per year enabling him to purchase a house and employ servants, plus three curates to help run the church; he also owned a warrant on 1000 acres of land.

However he was a loyalist and suffered under the War of Independence. Bennet returned to London where he wrote articles against the Americans. As a result of these newspaper reports one Lloyd Dulany challenged him to a duel with pistols. On June 18th 1782 both arrived by cab at Hyde Park at 9.30 in the gathering dusk, the seconds paced out 8 yards and the duel took place with the outcome that Lloyd Dulany died three days later from a punctured lung. Bennet was uninjured.

Bennet Allen was put on trial for murder, but the charge was reduced to manslaughter by the judge and he was sentenced to 6 months in Newgate Prison. After his prison sentence he received £6000 for his losses in America from the British Government plus a pension of £300 per annum. His sister Elizabeth also received a pension. He became the chaplain for Lyford Hospital and died in 1818. James his brother remained rector of Bishopstone until 1776, when he resigned to become vicar of Mansel Lacy where he resided until his death in 1808.

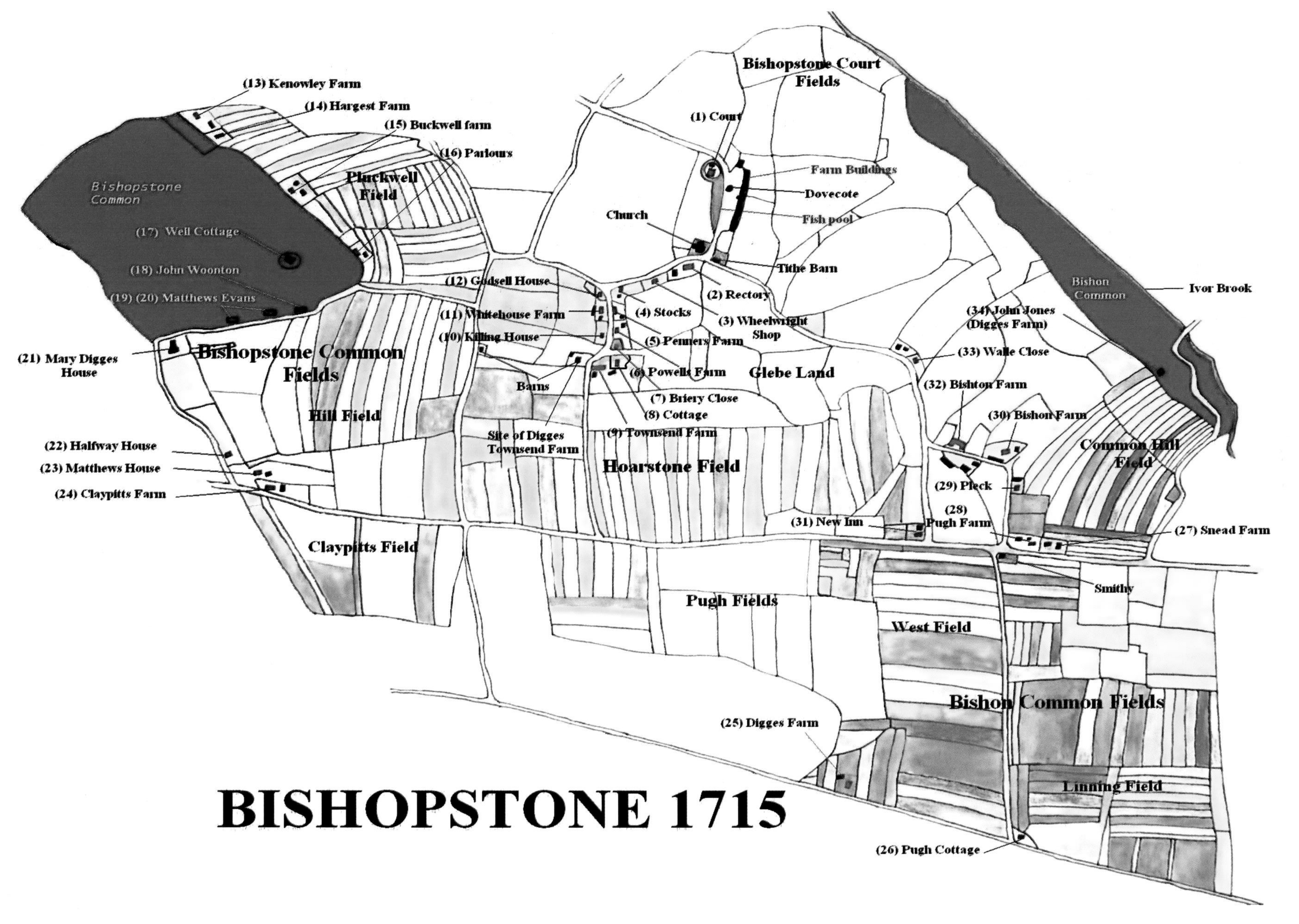
BISHOPSTONE 1715
Bishopstone Common
(13) Kenowley Farm
(14) Hargest Farm
(15) Buckwell farm
(16) Parlours
Pluckwell Field
(17) Well Cottage
(18) John Woonton
(19) (20) Matthews Evans
(21) Mary Digges House
Bishopstone Common Fields
Hill Field
(22) Halfway House
(23) Matthews House
(24) Claypitts Farm
Claypitts Field
(12) Godsell House
(11) Whitehouse Farm
(10) Killing House
Barns
Site of Digges Townsend Farm
Bishopstone Court Fields
(1) Court
Farm Buildings
Dovecote
Fish pool
Church
Tithe Barn
(2) Rectory
(3) Wheelwright Shop
(4) Stocks
(5) Penners Farm
(6) Powells Farm
(7) Briery Close
(8) Cottage
(9) Townsend Farm
Glebe Land
Hoarstone Field
Pugh Fields
(25) Digges Farm
Bishon Common
Ivor Brook
(34) John Jones (Digges Farm)
(33) Walle Close
(32) Bishton Farm
(30) Bishon Farm
Common Hill Field
(29) Pleck
(28) Pugh Farm
(31) New Inn
(27) Snead Farm
Smithy
West Field
Bishon Common Fields
Linning Field
(26) Pugh Cottage

Chapter 8
1750-1800

A detailed survey book[1] of Foxley Estate was made in 1742 following the death of Uvedale Price's wife Ann. Although Uvedale was the M.P. who represented Weobley, he resided in fashionable Bath where he died in 1764. His eldest son Robert lived at Foxley running the estate. This survey book lists the whole land holdings of the estate in great detail including Bishopstone. The 1705 rent book used by William Brown contained names of the meadows and fields, followed by his own rough measurements, that later proved wildly inaccurate.

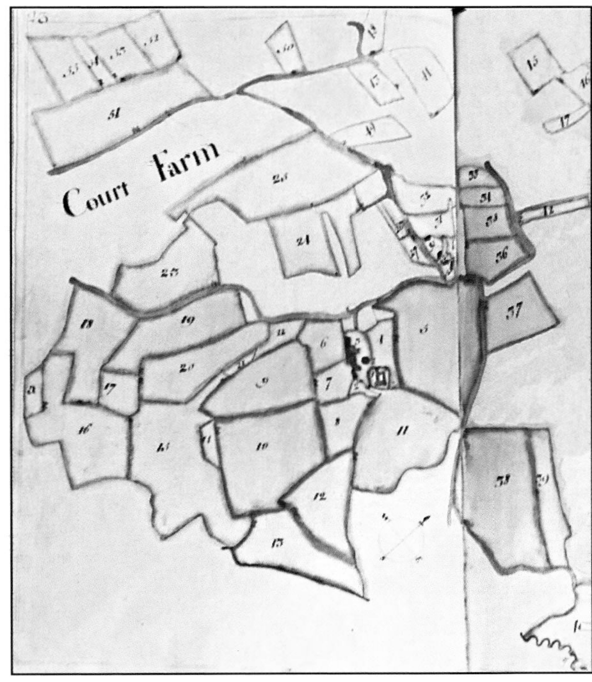

(Figure 1) Court Farm 1770

Bishopstone Court Farm;
Henry Gardiner £115 rent for the house, outhouse, barns, stables, cratchhouse, garden and fold.

Orchard	51 acres
Copse wood	02 acres
Meadow	29 acres
Pasture	114 acres
Tillage	147.½ acres
Total	**343½ acres**

Some of field names recorded in the survey book are worthy of a sentence or two, **Hoarstone** a Anglo-Saxon name for standing stone, **Wall Close** another Anglo-Saxon field name meaning a place where there is a well or spring, **Askors Gobbit** is named after a place where you would find lizards, **Cockshoot** meaning either a glade where nets were spread to catch woodcock, or alternatively could mean a hillside spring flowing through a spout, in this instance I would favour the second option. **Lords Croft** would have been associated with the administration and working of the medieval manor. **Lady Meadow**, land previously owned by the chantry chapel. **Bowman Croft**, where the medieval bowmen practiced their skills. **Linnards** an old name referring to an area where flax had been grown.

Whitehouse Farm; Thomas Morgan for Whitehouse Farm £22, a house, barns, beasthouse and other buildings, garden and orchard, half an acre of orchard lying in the east end of the farmhouse known by the name of Godsell's orchard. Orchard 7½ acres, hopground 1 acre, meadow 9½ acres, pasture 9 acres, arable 105 acres. **Total 132 acres**

for Townsend Farm £6, for Hargest Farm £5 3s, for Godsell House £1. Total £34 3s.

Powell Farm; Simon Williams late George Powell for his farm £2 10s, as follows a house, barn, beasthouse, garden and fold, ½ acre of orchard adjoining said house, 1 acre of orchard the other side of road against Thomas Morgan killing house, 2½ of tillage lying in three separate places in Shutton upper field, ½ acre lying in Shutton lower field not ploughed, 2 acres lying in Hoarstone field near the New Inn. **Total 7½ acres.**

Well Cottage; Henry Gardiner late Thomas Williams for a House, little orchard, 2 acres of tillage land behind the said house lying on the top of the south side of Bishopstone hill £1 10s

(Well cottage today is known as Swiss Cottage.)

Sneads Farm; James Hancock for part of Sneads Farm for the house garden, and one acre of orchard adjoining the Smithy shop by the roadside lying in Bishon. £3

(Sneads Farm today is known as Old Post Office.)

New Inn Farm; John Evans for the New Inn Farm £2 10s, extra tillage land 12s.

For house, barns, and garden lying in Bishon, orchard 2 acres, meadow ½ acre, tillage 3½ acres. **Total 6 acres** (New Inn today is known as Stonehouse.)

Claypits Farm; John Davis late George Bethel for a house and land by lease for 99 years which will expire in 1747 at 20 shillings and is as follows the house, garden at the Claypits.

5½ acres of tillage, 2 acres of orchard adjoining the house and tenement. **Total 7½ acres**

Land at Lower Field. Thomas Bethell for 7 acres of arable land lying in several places in the lower field called Winstone land. This being valued at £1 3s 4d.

Kenowley Farm; Giles Nicolas for House, garden and five acres of land adjoining the said house part of which is planted with apple trees lying on the north side of Bishopstone Hill with land adjoining to the said house. £2 2s

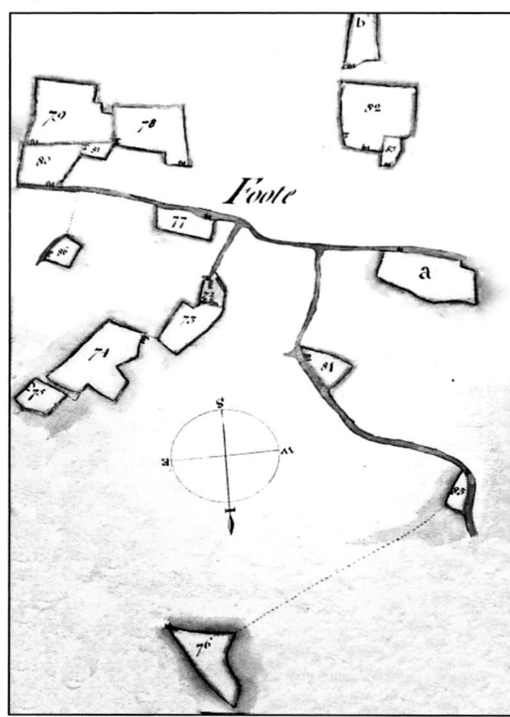

(Figure 2) This map of Bishon Farm was taken from the 1770 survey book

Buckwell Farm; William Jones late Pillinger for a house and garden lying off the northeast side of Bishopstone hill £2 3s. 1 acre of orchard adjoining the house, 1½ acres of tillage being 3 half acres_lying the north side of Line End field, 1 acre of tillage lying near the old clay pits near Hargest house, ½ acre the old close adjoins the Hargest house **Total 4 acres**

Bishon Farm; John Foote £27 a year to be given to charity, in bread to six poor women in All Saints Burghill and Bishopstone.

John Foote rents land off Uvedale Price Esq in Bishon not charity £4 16s, Total £31 16s

The house, barns, beasthouse and other buildings fold and garden lying in Bishon.

Orchard	4 acres
Meadow or pasture	22½ acres
Tillage	119 acres
	Total: 145½ acres

137 acres charity land, 8½ acres Uvedale Price.

Bishton Farm; Matthew Nash for Bishton Farm and part of Savakers land at £59 a year as follows, the house, outhouses and barns.

Orchard	19 acres
Meadow	9½ acres
Pasture	59½ acres
Tillage	86 acres
	Total; 172 acres

Freeholder Chief rents in Bishopstone.

Stocks Farm; John Evans late Rocks house and lands in Bishopstone	7d.
Pleck farm; Sarah Eckley house and land in Bishon	3s 4d
Pugh farm; Widow Pugh house and land in Bishon	5d
Timothy Geers for part of Pugh's	1s 6d
Thomas Bethell for land at Claypits	9d
Winstone Farm; (Bridge Ash) **Mathew Evans** house by the side of Hereford Rd	2d
Berkley Close; Rowland Evans for house and land in Bishopstone.	1s 1d
Total	13s 10d

(Figure 3) My impression of how the cottage could have looked in 1850 after Rev Lane Freer had built his brick schoolroom on the end of the cottage.

A new cottage was built in Bishopstone in the summer of 1753. William Evans had inherited Winstone Farm (Bridge Ash) from his father Mathew, and now he gave a piece of land measuring one and a half acres enclosed out of South Hoarstone Field to his daughter Mary as a wedding gift. The indenture dated July 14th 1753[2] specifies that Mary's new husband Simon Williams, a carpenter, should build a new cottage on the land to provide the newlyweds with a home. The cottage was extended in the 1850s to provide a schoolroom, today greatly extended it is a private house called Wiston House. The land given to Mary as a wedding gift, now contains six properties in 2010.

The population of the parish had been static at around 170 since the end of the Civil War, made up of around 36 families living in 30 properties ranging from Court Farm to the parish poor cottages on the edge of the commons. The survey book was used as a working document and references were made when tenants had died or property had changed hands. The last entry was made in 1773 referring to Snead Farm (Old Post Office) then in the hands of William Watkins.

The death of Uvedale Price our Lord of the Manor in 1764 started a chain of events whereby in the next 50 years the landscape of the parish would be changed dramatically. Robert Price, Uvedale's only son lived at Foxley; he died suddenly in 1761 at the age of 40, three years before his father. Robert Price was a gentleman artist interested in travel, landscape and aesthetic landscape improvement. Robert's son Uvedale[3] was seventeen years old when his grandfather Uvedale from Bath died leaving him the estates to inherit when he came of age. Uvedale was born at Foxley and was baptized at Yazor Church on April 14th 1747.

Uvedale was educated at Eton and Christ Church Oxford. As a young man he was a figure on London's social scene, and was described as the "macaroni" of his age. He made the Grand Tour in 1767 with his Etonian friend, Whig politician Charles James Fox and on his return he settled to run the estate at Foxley. In 1774 Uvedale married Lady Caroline Carpenter, daughter of the Earl of Tyrconnel, and he was made a baronet in 1827.

Uvedale's survey book contains 29 maps and 9 written surveys, with index and summaries, covering 5,321 acres, of which 4,579 acres lay in the Manors of Yazor, Mansel Lacy, Bishopstone and Mansell Gamage. Bishopstone's total acreage was recorded as 760 acres 3rods 7perches. It contained the very first detailed maps of Bishopstone divided into sections. The maps show buildings in block plan, fields or strips in open fields outlined in colour, orchards, woods, gates, streams, ponds and roads. Field tracks or footpaths are marked by pecked lines.

Bishopstone Hill Common is recorded in the concordance as 57acres 2rods 25perches, Bishon Common 12acres 2rods, cottages and waste 10acres.

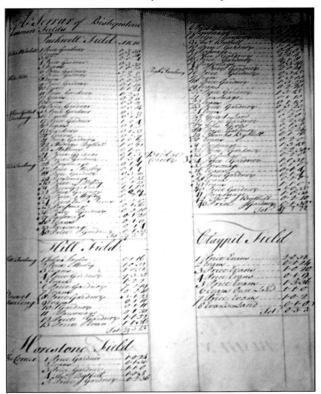

(Figure 4) List of all the owners and tenants of the strips in Bishopstone's three common fields; Hill field and Claypit field were originally one field, Hoarstone and Puckwell the other two. The main fields were also subdivided into smaller sections as listed above; i e Bridge Corner, Askors gobbet furlong etc.

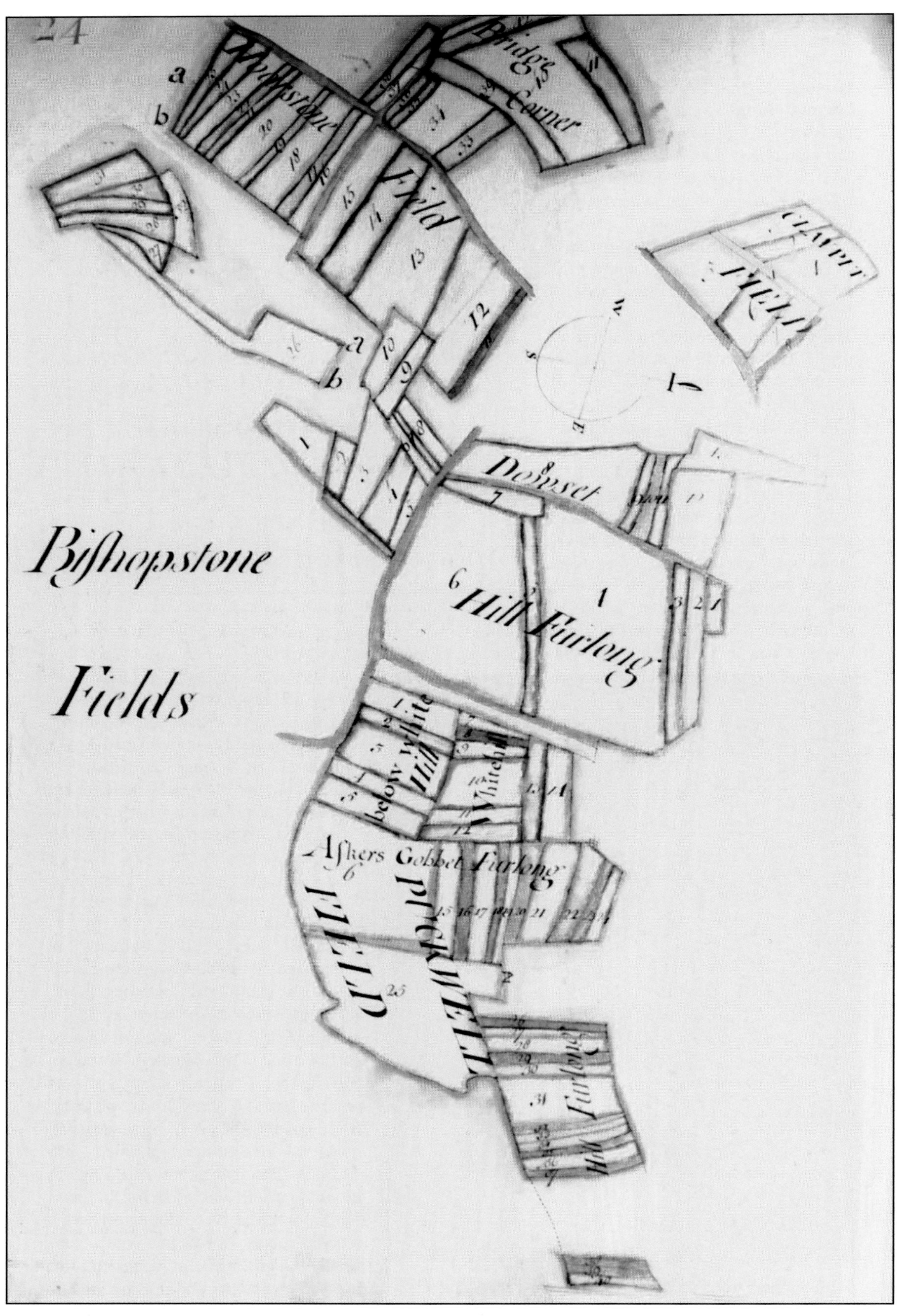

(Figure 5) A Terrier of Bishopstone three common fields, Hoarstone Field, Hill field, Puckwell Field. The different colours and numbers identify the farmers who worked the strips. Some were tenants of Uvedale Price others were freeholders.

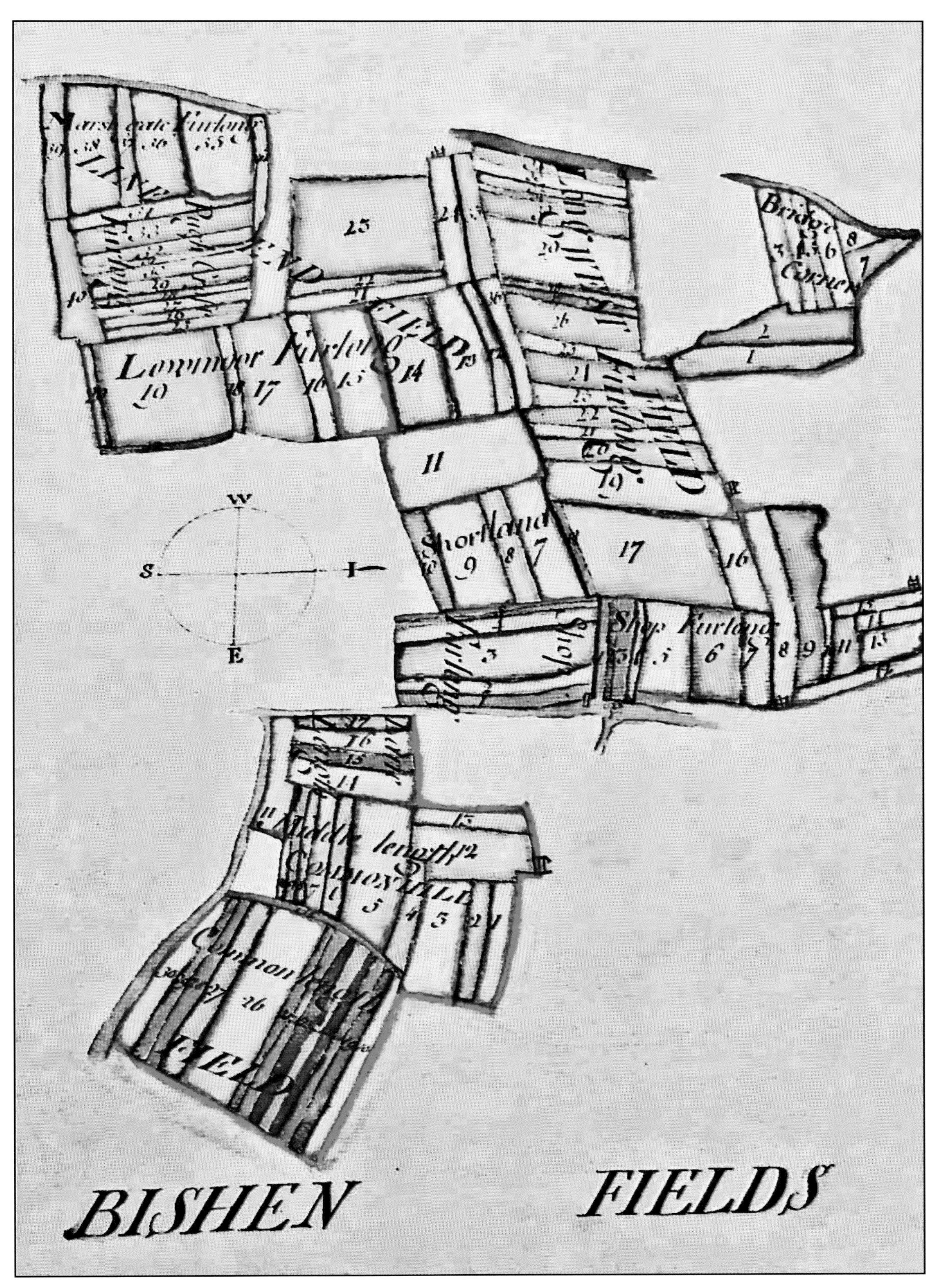

(Figure 6) A terrier of Bishen's three common fields Common Hill Field, West Field and Line End Field (which appears to be sometimes called Linning Field). Interestingly the lands in the fields are attached to the farms in Bishen which could indicated that at some point in its early history Bishen could have been a settlement in its own right.

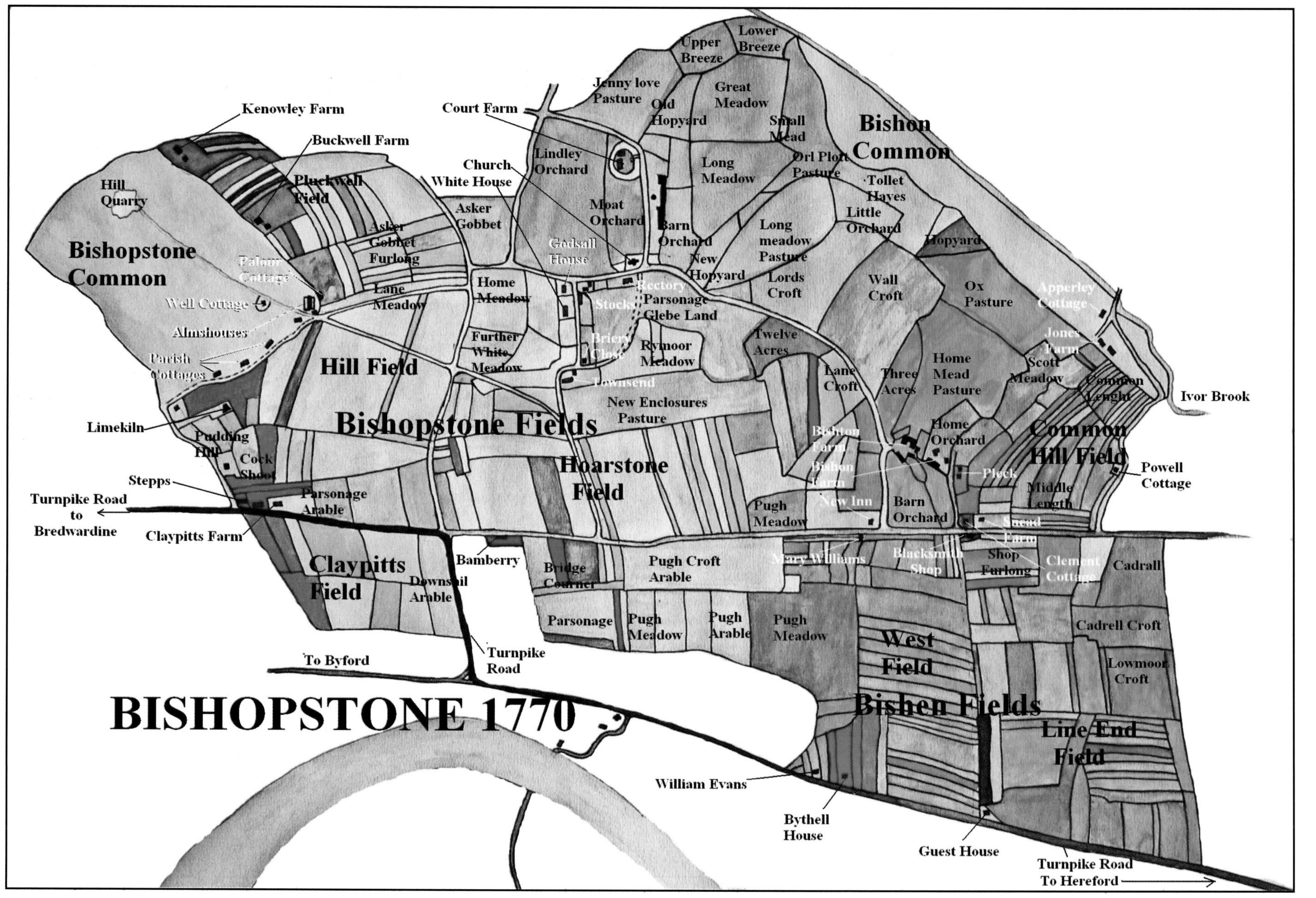

BISHOPSTONE 1770
Kenowley Farm
Buckwell Farm
Hill Quarry
Bishopstone Common
Plackwell Field
Asker Gobbet Furlong
Lane Meadow
Well Cottage
Almshouses
Parish Cottages
Hill Field
Limekiln
Pudding Hill
Cock Shoot
Stepps
Turnpike Road to Bredwardine
Claypitts Farm
Parsonage Arable
Claypitts Field
Downsell Arable
Bamberry
Turnpike Road
To Byford
Bishopstone Fields
Court Farm
Church
White House
Asker Gobbet
Home Meadow
Further White Meadow
Lindley Orchard
Moat Orchard
Godsall House
Jenny love Pasture
Old Hopyard
Upper Breeze
Lower Breeze
Great Meadow
Small Mead
Long Meadow
Barn Orchard
New Hopyard
Rectory
Stocks
Parsonage Glebe Land
Briery Close
Rymoor Meadow
Townsend
New Enclosures Pasture
Hoarstone Field
Bridge Courtier
Pugh Croft Arable
Parsonage
Pugh Meadow
Pugh Arable
Pugh Meadow
Bishon Common
Orl Plott Pasture
Tollet Hayes
Little Orchard
Long meadow Pasture
Lords Croft
Hopyard
Wall Croft
Ox Pasture
Apperley Cottage
Twelve Acres
Lane Croft
Three Acres
Home Mead Pasture
Jones Farm
Scott Meadow
Common Lenght
Ivor Brook
Home Orchard
Common Hill Field
Powell Cottage
Pleck
Middle Length
Bishon Farm
Pugh Meadow
New Inn
Barn Orchard
Snead Farm
Mary Williams
Blacksmith Shop
Shop Furlong
Clement Cottage
Cadrall
Cadrell Croft
Lowmoor Croft
West Field
Bishen Fields
Line End Field
William Evans
Bythell House
Guest House
Turnpike Road To Hereford

Colour on Map	Tenant of **Uvedale Price**		Acres	Rods	Perches
1	(1) Henry Gardiner	**Court Farm**	355	1	38
2	(2) John Foote	**Bishon Farm**	96	3	0
3	(3) Timothy Matthews	**Bishton Farm**	81	3	16
4	(4) John Pember	**New Inn**	4	2	29
5	(5) Willam Mosley	**Buckwell Farm**	4	1	30
6	(6) Edward James	**Kenowley Farm**	4	3	33
7	(7) Richard Cox	**Parlour Cottage**	1	1	24
8	(8) Ann Lilwall	**Bamberry**	0	2	0
9	(9) Richard Evans	**Claypitt Farm**	11	3	5
10	(10) John Hancocks	**Bishopstone Hill**	1	2	27
11	(11) James Hancock	**Blacksmith Shop**	1	1	16
12	(12) Joseph Guest	**Freeholder**	18	3	5
13	(13) Richard Evans	**Townsend, Stocks**	42	0	6
14	(14) Thomas & James Bethell	**Stepps & House**	13	0	27
15	(15) John Goode	**Pleck**	12	3	19
16	(16) Parsonage	**Rectory Farm**	18	2	7
17	(17) Bridge Poor	**Charity**	0	1	4
18	(18) Rowland Evans	**Briery Close**	1	0	28
19	(19) John Taylor	**Bishopstone Hill**	0	3	5
20	(20) John Clements	**Cottage**	0	1	36
21	(21) William Evans	**Bridge Ash**	1	1	17
22	(22) Mary Williams	**Cottage**	0	3	8

Nathaniel Kent[4] a 32 year-old land surveyor from North End Fulham London was responsible for changing the face of Bishopstone's agricultural landscape.

In 1774 Kent carried out a survey of all the land owned by Uvedale Price, on which he made comments concerning good husbandry practices, including the repair of buildings and fences, the maintenance of gates and stiles, drainage, liming and manuring, limitations on the acreage sown with corn and breaking up pasture, the cleaning of meadows and removal of ant-hills, planting withies on "Aquatic" land, demolition of unnecessary buildings and payment of rates and taxes. Kent's expertise after carrying out improvements to Foxley was much sought after, he worked for the Earl of Hardwick and Thomas Coke of Holkham in Norfolk.

From 1791 till he died in 1810 Kent worked for the King making two model farms in Windsor's Great Park and improving the King's estate in Norfolk.

One note in his survey book refers to Bishopstone's freehold farmer Richard Evans who owned Townsend Farm, and also rented Claypitts Farm from Uvedale Price. Nathaniel Kent writes "The premise are valued at £7 10s 0d. but he [the tenant Richard Evans] would not give it". Implying that he was a man, whom it would be imprudent for Mr Price to have any dispute with.

Richard Evans died in 1778. A plaque is mounted on the wall of Bishopstone Church to record his and his son's life: he appears to have been a formidable character.

The main change to Bishopstone parish on Kent's recommendation was the amalgamation of Bishon and Bishton Farms

These improvements gave Uvedale Price a better return on his farms. For example in 1770 Court Farm containing 355 acres returned a rent charge of £167 per year but after Kent's improvements in 1774, Court Farm was 357 acres and commanded a rent charge of £250 per year.

The same with Bishon and Bishton farms; in 1742 the two farms had a total acreage of 317 carrying a combined rent charges of £86 per year. By 1777 the two farms were joined together, Kent had reduced the acreage to 263 acres by removing Savakers land but still returned a rent charge of £160 per year. This was the end of Bishon, the independent charity farm carrying a low rent of £27 per year; the same yearly charity money was now extracted from the overall rent of the two farms. The old Bishon farmhouse was now used as a cottage to house farmworkers.

Uvedale Price followed Kent's advice and set up written leases with strict guidelines, the first time this type of agreement had been carried out between landlord and tenant in Bishopstone, previously it was only word of mouth followed by a minuscule written line.

Agreement entered into July 1st 1774 between Uvedale Price of Foxley esq. and George Gardiner of Bishopstone yeoman.

The said Uvedale Price agrees to let to the said George Gardiner for a term of 14 years from Candlemas next ensuing at the yearly rent of £250

The entire farm called Bishopstone Court as newly modelled and altered by Nathaniel Kent consisting of 357acres 2rods 11perches. To keep all buildings in good repair and also ploughboot and cartboot at £7 a year in lieu of the latter at his option.

To allow rough timber for gates and styles, to allow to take all pollard and alder which hasn't been cropped within the last 15 years except where they are in the middle of the field or separate from the hedge row and are under 6 inches girth 2ft from stem.

Not to crop under 10 years growth. To permit the tenant to sow and dispose of his wheat in the last year of his term leaving the straw and fodder for the benefit of the landlord or succeeding tenant. Not to plough any meadow or pasture without leave under a penalty of five pound per acre additional rent for every acre broken up. Not to sow more than two thirds of his tillage with any type of grain or corn in any one year nor sow more than two crops successively upon any part of the farm. To find straw for thatching and carry all materials for repairs. To pay all levies and taxes. To keep all straw and hay upon the premises during the whole term and leave all dung and compost upon the same at the end. To keep all the ditches and fences in good order and condition and to lay at his expense 75 perches of good effective covered drainage every year at least 3 foot deep and properly filled up with stone, till all the wet part of the meadow and pasture are laid dry. The said drains to be pointed out and approved by the landlord or his agent.

To mow all rushes twice a year, to lay all anthills within the first seven years, to lay down at least 20 acres of tillage with grass within the first seven years. The landlord will pay for the grass seed. To keep all the inside of the fields free from bushes, fern and rubbish. To permit the landlord to take away any pollard which stands in the open part of the field. Likewise to permit him to set up private gates and roadway through any part of the farm for his own use making reasonable allowance for all damage done. If the said George Gardiner shall choose to give up the premise by Candlemas 1776 he shall be at liberty to give Mr. Price six months notice.

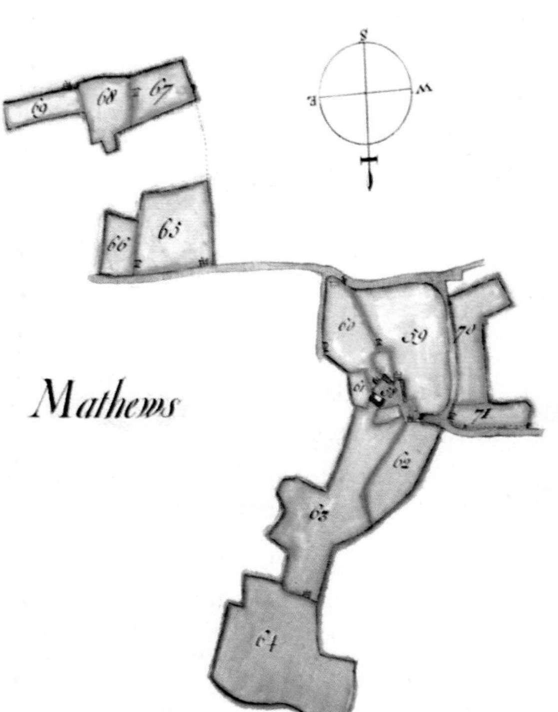

Lands at Bishen in the Occupation of Timothy Mathews

	Quantity A. R. P.	at p. Acre	Per Ann.
58 The Homestead	1-1-0		
59 Barn Orchard Arable	3-2-0	1	5-10
60 Home Orchard Pasture	2-2-1	1	2-10
61 The Garden	0-1-0		
62 The Three Acres Arable	2-1-4	12	1-7
63 Home Mead Pasture	6-1-1	1-7-6	8-11
64 Ox Pasture	8-1-24	11	4-11
65 Cadrell Croft Arable	3-2-16	11	2-2
66 Do. Pasture	1-0-32	11	12-6
67 Lowmeer Arable	1-3-11	12	1-1-6
68 Do. Meadow	1-3-8	1-4	2-2-0
69 Do. Arable	1-1-1	12	15-0
70 Lane Croft Arable	2-1-32	12	1-9-6
71 Do. Meadow	1-1-1	1-4	1-10-0
In Commonhill Field	6-1-6	10	3-1-6
In Line End Field	21-1-35	10	10-15-0
In West Field	18-0-33	10	9-2-0
Tot.	81-3-16		55-2-0

(Figure 7) Page 26 of the survey book shows the lands in Bishen in the occupation of Timothy Mathews, 82 acres Note! Timothy Mathews also rented 125 acres in Shetton, plus other land in Mansel Lacy from Uvedale Price part of which is still attached to Bishon Farm.

Timothy Mathews of Bishton Farm died in 1774, Mary his wife stepped into his shoes and farmed Bishton; Timothy had also rented Shetton Farm, and other land from Foxley Estate, he was farming 384 acres at the time of his death. I have not included a copy of his will due to its length. Here are some of its more interesting features. Timothy had no direct descendants, so he left his goods and chattels to his wife Mary in her lifetime then to his nephews and nieces. He leaves his best bed and furniture to his wife although there is no record of this in his inventory[5] dated April 5th 1774.

He also leaves to Mary *"the bureau, boxes and chairs and whatever else belongs to the rooms where the Captain formerly lay"* This reference to a Captain is intriguing. Was part of the house rented out to a Captain? If it was, I cannot find any documentary trace of a Captain living in Bishopstone; was Timothy referring to Captain Humphrey Digges who built the house? Or maybe Timothy himself had served in the military? The original house had thirteen rooms yet only six rooms were listed in his inventory, some rooms appear to have been left off the list, including the main sleeping chamber and the rooms formally occupied by the Captain. Timothy did not use the great room for entertaining guests, it appears to have been used as a storeroom housing spinning wheels and saddles; the kitchen must have been a large room to accumulate all the furniture listed, plus it was used for feeding all the servants and labourers, who would have sat and eaten together with Timothy and Mary, a common practice of the time. He also kept in the kitchen the clock that he had inherited from his uncle. Timothy's inventory is worthy of a few notes of interest. Josiah Ridgeway and Richard Evans who compiled the inventory listed 5 carthorses and harnesses and gear worth £40, yet 6 oxen and yokes are valued at £48 so the carthorse and oxen were valued the same at £8 each, regarded as equals as working farm animals. Cows came next in value at £6 each, a colt and cattle carried the same value of £3 10s, pigs were worth under a £1, sheep even less at 5s each. Farm implements were also valued cheaply, a plough 3s, cart £1, wagons £5 (these estimates were always valued on the low side). Total value of the inventory came to £279 14s.
Interestingly although Timothy had the use of carthorses he still used 3 teams of oxen for ploughing: it was commonly thought in Herefordshire that oxen plough teams were better suited to turn over the heavy clay soil. We know the brewhouse contained two furnaces plus thirty casks, a high quantity for the farm but he was possibly brewing on a commercial scale, selling to local alehouses.
As a comparison to Timothy Mathews complex will, this is the simple will of Abigail Bishop who died on December 18th 1765 at her home, Pleck Cottage.
I do give and bequeath unto my friend Elizabeth Matthews the wife of Daniel Matthews of the parish of Monnington on Wye all my said goods, chattels, my household goods other things and money and whatever can be found.
This is my last will and testament
Mark of Abigail Bishop.

Chattels of Abigail Bishop Widow of Bishopstone

Her wearing apparels	*10s 00d*
Bed Bedstead bolster	*£1 01s 00d*
Two pairs sheets	*5s 00d*
Two whelts	*2s 00d*
Dripping pan, spit, trenches	*2s 00d*
Two pots, one kettle, one tub, and a trind	*7s 00d*
One pail, 5 earthen dishes, one iron	*1s 00d*
Two cupboards, two benches, two chairs and stools	*5s 00d*
Two barrels, fire slice, tongs, flesh fork	*2s 00d*
Other lumber and things forgotten	*2s 00d*
	£2 18s 00d

January 3rd 1777 agreement between Uvedale Price and John Ashley of Pembridge for Bishton farm now in the occupation of Mary Mathews and Bishon farm in the occupation of John Foote 263 acres for a term of 14 years, insuring at the yearly rent of £160.

The agreement made between Uvedale Price and John Ashley for the combined Bishon and Bishton farms followed a similar line but with some differences which are listed below.
Allowance of four pound per year in lieu of plow, wain and wagon boot. To put all buildings into tenantable repair as soon as possible. To allow use of timber in the rough to repair gates, stiles, floodgates. To grow a coppice of four acres in Mansell Gamage and cut at six years. To carry out main drainage, pointed out by the landlord or his agent at an allowance of £10 a year till completed. To plant 10 willow in hedgerow by common for stake and poles. Allow two or three loads of stakes from Byford for the first three years. Also enough stone from Darkhill to make lime for the first three years. Allow John Foote to come on the land to reap crop of wheat planted at Michaelmas. And not to break up any pasture or meadow land, with a five pound per acre penalty. To keep a game dog in good hunting order for use of Uvedale Price. To permit Uvedale Price his friends or agent to come onto the premise to cut wood, make a saw pit and to hawk, hunt shoot and fish at their pleasure. To have 20 acres of tillage put down to grass, the landlord to pay for the seed.

(Figure 8) 1791 painting of the hill without tree cover shows Bishopstone common on the top right. This illustration was produced by Humphrey Repton, as one design for Sir John Cotterell's proposed new mansion house; it was one of the designs rejected

The marriage of John Geers Cotterell to Frances Evans, a local heiress, brought new wealth to the Garnons Estate and the newly weds asked Humphrey Repton to design and build a house with leisure grounds to match their newly found status.

Humphrey Repton was advising William Parry[6] of The New Weir Kenchester. In 1791 while Repton was still involved at The New Weir, John Geers Cotterell began a correspondence with him, which subsequently led to a survey in July of that year. Originally James Wyatt had been asked to produce a design for a new house, which is shown in the Red Book submitted by Humphrey Repton as a long straggling gothic structure, set against the woodlands of Garnons Hill. Wyatt, who always took on too many commissions, never provided the finished drawings, so Cotterell decided to defer the building of a new house for the duration of the war with France. This Red Book contained plans and sketches of the proposed house and parkland. One sketch shows parkland with a leisure carriage drive leading to a lodge in Bishopstone parish, east of the newly planned mansion, using land not yet in the ownership of the estate. The land needed in Bishopstone to carry out the landscaping drawn by Repton in the Red Book, would be purchased or obtained by exchange over a period of the next twenty years. . Another problem arose because the turnpike road passed directly in front of the newly planned mansion. The solution was to move the turnpike road south, where today it forms part of the main A438 trunk road.

It's worth elaborating on the turnpike road system, which first came to Bishopstone in 1730. The English road system in the late 17th century was in a terrible state, said to be fit only to move goods by packhorse as travel by wheeled vehicle was impossible in winter. The parishes were unable to provide the required standard of highway maintenance, so a nation-wide system of turnpike roads came into existence. These were established under individual Acts of Parliament for each stretch of road and were administered by local trusts whose trustees were made up of local landowners. The qualification to be a trustee was to own land with a rent value of £100, to be an heir apparent of an estate of freehold lands valued at £150 yearly, or have a personal estate valued at £4,000. Tolls were levied on people using turnpike roads in order to raise money for their maintenance.

Hereford Turnpike Act was passed in 1730; all major roads leading out of the city were covered by the Act, looking on a map like spokes of a wheel radiating out. The first meeting of around eighty trustees was held on July 1st 1730 at the Swan and Falcon, Hereford. The road that passed through Bishopstone parish was listed as the Hereford to Bredwardine Passage turnpike road; it follows roughly the line of the A438 to Staunton on Wye where it deviates left over Tin Hill to Bredwardine.

The trustees could erect and set up any toll-gate, bar or chain across any part of the said road, and also across any lane or way leading into or out of the same. They would provide a toll-house near to each toll-gate, for the collector to live in and a signboard was put on the tollhouse showing the table of fees.

These toll-Houses were soon built. Of the four built on this road, three are still in evidence today although modernized through the centuries. The first toll-house on leaving the City was positioned on Whitecross Road next to the junction with White Horse street, next came Stretton Sugwas toll-house, still standing by the war memorial, and the last one on Bredwardine Bridge. The only one now missing was positioned at Staunton on Wye.

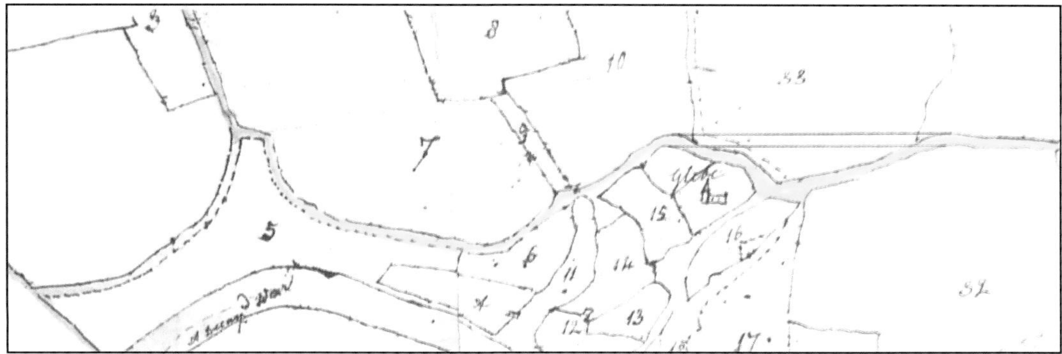

(Figure 9) This 1730 estate map shows the old road that I have highlighted in yellow, the lines drawn indicates where a new section of turnpike road was built by Bridge Sollers church. Another interesting feature is the decayed wharf shown on the river

The estate map of Marsh and Knap estates made in 1730 shows the road or track to be upgraded into the turnpike road. It was twisty and open sided in places and pencil lines drawn on the map show where it was straightened at a later date. The question must be asked why it did not follow the Roman road through Bishon, which until this time was used as a main route for travelling between Hereford and Hay. Early deeds and documents of properties in Bishon verify this fact. The answer I think lies with the major landowners who were elected onto the turnpike board. Their influence decided the line of the road, so just after the Kites Nest Inn the road followed the lesser track towards Bridge Sollers and the home of Timothy Geers, then back up on to the Roman Road past his Garnons House. The better-maintained turnpike road would make carriage travel to his residences quicker and more comfortable.

By 1791 this road system had improved considerably with two regular coach services passing along the road each week. They made a splendid sight and sound, with large bells on the collars of the two front horses and a boy blowing his horn to warn other traffic of their approach.

To create Repton's plan of a new mansion standing behind sweeping parkland it was decided to build a new section of turnpike road between Bridge and the Portway. Not everyone in Bishopstone was happy with this plan, especially Thomas Bythel who owned and ran the Flower de Luce Inn (The Steps), which stood on the original turnpike road. It left the Inn on a no through road with no passing traffic, the public road was closed just past the Inn and turned into a private drive leading towards the new mansion and gates were erected across the road so only estate traffic could pass through, these gates were in operation until the 1960s.

Country people did not like change and resentment could be passed down through the generations. It reminds me of a tale my father told me about my great grandfather James Whiting who lived in Bishopstone. To visit the doctor in Staunton on Wye he always walked the line of the old Roman Road that passed in front of Garnons Mansion insisting it was his right to do so which caused many arguments with the estate staff who tried to stop him.

In 1764, Berrington Almshouse paid 3d toll money to Henry Gardiner of Bishopstone Court Farm for hauling the coal from Hereford; looking at the old list of toll charges he must have used his broad wheeled farm cart to fetch the coal as a narrow wheel cart carried a 6d charge.

The new section of turnpike road between Bridge and Portway was started on August 1st 1791. Joseph Joynes carried out the building of the new road. A new quarry was opened up in Byford to provide the stone, marl was hauled out of Bishopstone Hill quarry and gravel was also used from the riverbed. For the record the road was 13ft wide, stone was impacted to 8 inches deep, and timber piles were used in the swamp areas. Joseph Joynes was paid two shillings three and a half pennies per yard to build the road and twenty pounds to fill in Bridge Dingle, and to build a stonewall on the lower side of the Dingle at least nine feet high and two feet thick. The total cost including land was £578 6s 4d with the last payment made on February 10th 1794 when I presume the new section of road was already open.

By 1871 Herefordshire had abolished the turnpike road system, they were unpopular and the introduction of the railways contributed to their failure.

Exchange of land[7] in 1793 between Garnons and Foxley Estates.

(Four cottages on Bishopstone Hill in occupation of Phillip Warwick, John Love, John Ashley and John Geers Cotterell. Two tenements in occupation of James Hancock, a smallholding on the hill and Clay Pits Farm of 9 acres 2 rods, adjoining the Hay to Hereford turnpike road. An oak coppice called Limekiln Coppice 1a 1r 30p on Bishopstone Hill, pasture land below the turnpike road in Clay Pits field. Parcel of land adjoining John Loves cottage, 1½acres. All the trees growing in the ditch belonging to the land and tenement on the hill. Occupier James Hancock had enough land on the southwest of said trees to fence and enclose. Except all mines and quarries of lime or stone that may in the future be discovered on the land now given to John Geers Cotterell and the right for Uvedale Price to remove same. John Geers Cotterell to build a stone lime kiln with arches capable of burning nine dozen bushels of lime at a time on a piece of ground called Pudding Hill adjoining James Hancock's tenement and to have liberty to burn lime for one year, also to clear enough ground to dig limestone for one year of the farms in occupation of tenants of Uvedale Price in Bishopstone.)

All the Bishopstone property and land in the above agreement was exchanged for land in Mansell Gamage, for the first time Garnons owned significant land on Bishopstone Hill. The old limekiln had obviously fallen into disrepair at the east end of oak coppice so as part of this agreement a new kiln was built on the west end of the coppice, this one acre oak coppice had for centuries provided fuel to burn the lime.

This exchange of lands plus changes in the poor law made in 1795 moved the parish from the stagnation of the last 100 years, to a new growth in houses and people. Firstly the change in the poor law allowed labourers to move out of the parish to find work without losing the right to parish money.

The common open field strips were also exchanged between landowners, so land could be enclosed into reasonable sized fields. This change produced the quilt pattern fields we still see today. Also many freeholders built on their allotments given in exchange for relinquishing their rights on the common lands, this alone increased the number of cottages and houses in the parish from a static thirty to over sixty.

In 1692 a new property tax was introduced. Initially intended as a tax on personal estates and land, it soon became a charge solely on land. Indeed, by 1702 it was being called a "land tax"[8]. By 1698 the tax had become stereotyped, the rate being fixed at the county quotas of 1692. Within the county the commissioners could apportion the rate as they saw fit. Between 1780 and 1832 these tax returns had to be deposited with the Clerk of the Peace since the tax was used as a means of identifying those who could vote for county MPs. Bishopstone's surviving returns are dated between 1783 and 1830, some historians thinks these are inaccurate, but I have found them extremely useful because the money charged on the land stayed the same throughout the period, making it easy to trace land ownership and give accurate dates on land exchange.

(Figure 10) Sir John Cotterell 1st Bart

George Gardiner appears on all the returns as collector or assessor and they were always witnessed by signatures of other taxpayers in the parish. Just one example of the interesting information to be gathered from these returns: the Geers land holdings in Bishopstone was tenanted to Joseph Guest in the 1770s and after the death of Timothy Geers the land ownership passed to James Broome of Withington who had married Timothy's sister Mercy Beta. After she died Sir J G Cotterell inherited the land and by 1830 Sir John owned thirty-one acres in small allotments spread all over the parish.

The invasion of the French, who landed on the Pembrokeshire coast in 1797 caused some concern to the people of Bishopstone, Uvedale Price visited the farms on his estate including John Ashley at Bishon Farm and George Gardiner Court Farm.

He wrote, *"All were trembling, unarmed, without confidence or connection, especially the smallholders and labouring poor, who can scarcely buy bread so will hardly buy arms."* He formed his own-armed company of troops made up of volunteers from his estate including Bishopstone parishioners.

Sir Uvedale Price was famous for his writings called "Picturesque Landscapes and Estate Management". He did not like straight marching roads but preferred the sunken lanes of Foxley made by the steady impact of men and livestock. Sir Uvedale spent much of his life's work on landscaping Foxley; he designed the water features and lakes, and planted many of the specimen trees that are still seen today at Foxley. His father had planted most of the encircling woodland and built three prominent follies on the highest points of his estate, one at Lady Lift, another called Ragged Castle on the ridge in Mansel Lacy and, across the valley on Bishopstone Hill, Fragley Castle. All three viewing points gave wonderful panoramic views of Herefordshire. Fragley Castle, the folly built on Bishopstone Hill, was converted into a worker's cottage and was awarded to Sir John Geer Cotterell in the Enclosures Act. Recorded in Sir Uvedale's woodland planting book dated 1746 "*a small coppice wood was planted below the tower on Bishopstone Hill*". In the final years of his life Sir Uvedale appears to have been a lonely man, suffering ill heath and worrying about his daughter Caroline's deranged state of mind. Many famous people visited Foxley during his lifetime, including Thomas Gainsborough who became a friend and would go sketching in the woods. William Wordsworth made two visits and on both occasions was shown round the estate by Uvedale. George Romney the famous portrait painter also visited to paint Lady Caroline.

(Figure 11) Portrait of Sir Uvedale Price

Sir Uvedale met Lord Nelson at a civic reception held at the City Arms on Monday August 23rd 1802 and because of his specialist knowledge of trees Lord Nelson appointed him superintendent of the Forest of Dean, to search out oak trees to build the navy's new war ships. This prompted him to plant more oak trees on the estate, and also to plant up a 12 acre oak wood on the north east side of Bishopstone Hill called Caroline Grove named after his wife or daughter. Although never used for the intended warships some of the mature trees were used in the restoration of Windsor Castle after the fire in 2001.

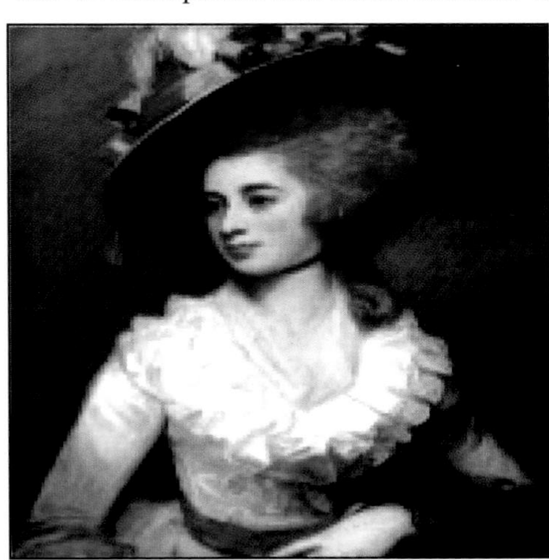

(Figure 12) Lady Caroline Price

Sir Uvedale Price also built Castle House in Aberystwyth as his seaside residence, a Gothic castellated style mansion designed by Nash on the west side of Marine Terrace. At times he resided at Croft Castle whilst his son Robert, who by 1815 was MP for Weobley, lived at Foxley running the estate. Uvedale Price was made a baronet in 1827 two years before he died.

In 1776 Bishopstone had a change of rector not once but twice. James Allen as previously recorded resigned on May 17th 1776. He was replaced by Thomas Kidley who resigned 14 days later when Thomas Evans took on the living of Bishopstone. What happened to cause this resignation is not recorded but here are some of the facts, Thomas Evans had gained a BA at Oxford on January 17th 1764 aged 20 years old, he had become vicar of Kings Pyon by 1767, and on June 1st 1776 the two swapped parishes, Thomas Evans now becoming the rector of Bishopstone. His appointment was a success and he went on to become a Prebendary of Hereford Cathedral and a local Justice of the Peace, appointing two curates for Bishopstone to help with his work, Barry Edmunds in 1777, followed by Thomas Dixon in 1782. Thomas Evans died in 1809.

Thomas Evans put his name to a document now held at the National Archives, Kew. It's a list of crops grown in Bishopstone parish which although undated was recorded around the turn of the 19th century: Wheat 129 acres, Barley 66 acres, Oats 5 acres, Potatoes 2 acres, Peas 50 acres, Beans 2 acres, Turnips 36 acres, Vetches 3 acres, total acreage under cultivation 293 acres.

Chapter 9
1800-1850

From 1800 onwards a national census was carried out in England every 10 years. The first four 1801, 1811, 1821, 1831 were called the population acts, and although not listing any individual by name they gave an accurate figure of the population and housing. They show that Bishopstone's population increased from 172 in 1801 to 278 by 1831, and the number of dwellings had doubled in the same period. Having studied in detail the first four surveys, I have come to the conclusion that the figures are misleading. Bishopstone's overseer George Gardiner carried out the first surveys, he counted all buildings as one unit where in fact the Almshouse contained six separate units and many of the cottages were double dwellings. This error appears to have been put right by 1821 but even allowing for the error there was a significant cottage and house-building programme carried out in Bishopstone between 1810 and 1830 not to be repeated again until the 1960s. The whole parish revolved round agriculture with the two main farms, Bishon and Court Farms employing between them 40 farm workers in any one period.
Within the Grimsworth Hundred Bishopstone parish had the largest percentage of increase in population over this period; Bridge Sollers increased from 53 to 71 persons, yet Byford suffered a decrease from 203 to 187.

Bishopstone 1801 Population Act. Houses 31, families 40, uninhabited houses 1, males 79, females 93, families employed in agriculture 42, families employed in trade, manufacture or handicraft 11, other persons not in above 119. **Total no persons 172.**
Bishopstone 1811 Population Act. Houses 38, families 51, uninhabited houses 0, males 97, females 111, families employed in agriculture 40, families employed in trade, manufacture or handicraft 9, other families not in above 2. **Total no persons 208**.
Bishopstone 1821 Population Act. Houses 63, families 63, uninhabited houses 1, males 117, females 153, families employed in agriculture 48, families employed in trade, manufacture or handicraft 14, other families not in above 1. **Total no persons 270.**
Bishopstone 1831 Population Act. Houses 61, families 62, uninhabited houses 4, males 126, females 152, families employed in agriculture 36, families employed in trade, manufacture or handicraft 12, families not in above 14. **Total no persons 278.**
1831 additional information gathered: Agriculture, 2 occupiers employing labour, 2 occupiers not employing labour, 33 labourers in agriculture, 17 employed in retail trade, handicraft, masters or workman, 3 employed in labour not agriculture, 6 other males aged over 20 years not servants, 1 servant aged over 20 years of age, 1 servant under 20 years of age, 15 female servants. 4 capitalists, bankers, professional or educated men

(Figure 1) First Ordnance Survey Map 1814

The four professional or educated men in the parish were the Rev Walker, Bishopstone Rectory, Mr Thomas Gough, Gent, Downshill House, George Gardiner, Court Farm and George Gardiner the younger, Bishon Farm. (George Gardiner of Bishon Farm was the nephew of George from Court Farm, to avoid any confusion in the parish records, during this period George of Bishon was usually referred to as the younger)
The population explosion in the parish coincided with twenty years of good growth in agriculture, this was followed by a decline between 1821 and 1831, which left twelve farm labourers and their families without any regular income and put extreme pressure on the overseers of the poor in Bishopstone. There were several reasons why this happened. When the country was at war with France agricultural prices kept rising until the battle of Waterloo ended the war in 1815. Prices slowly fell back until 1820 when there were disastrous falls, prices were less than a third of those of 1813, cows fetched £3 as against £15, ewes 25s against 72s, and farm workers' wages dropped from an average of 13s to 8s a week.

Farmers needed fewer labourers due to the increased usage of machinery, along with improved farming techniques. Oxen, the traditional farm working animals, became redundant and in Bishopstone there is no mention of them in any of the inventories after 1800; a carthorse could do the work of two oxen and at twice the speed, this meant less working animals on the farm and less acres to produce fodder.

An article reviewing agricultural in Herefordshire dated 1820 gives the average wages of the farm worker.

Shepherd	up to £30 a year
Dairy-Maid	£5 a year, plus keep
Labourer	from 9s to 15s a week
Harvest wages	from 13s to 30s a week, varying according to meals supplied.
Reaping	(per acre) oats 16s, beans 21s, wheat 7s to 21s
Mowing	(per acre) 2s 6d to 4s
Turning muck	one penny per load.

I might add that a "working week" was about 70 hours on average, sometimes much more, and payments for holidays, were neither given nor expected.

The one season of the year where even the labourers had a real sense of sharing in the bounty of the earth was the six or seven weeks at harvest time, when the men were fed at the farmhouse in communal style. What follows is a typical day's intake in the harvest period.

6 am.	1 pint of strong beer, bread and cheese
8 am.	Breakfast of cold meat and beer
11 am.	1 pint of strong beer, bread and cheese
1 pm.	Dinner. One day roast beef or mutton (pork will not do) and plain pudding, Next day boiled beef or mutton and plum pudding.
4 pm.	1 pint of strong beer, bread and cheese
7 pm.	Hot mash or mutton pies Hence each man has daily, seven pints of strong beer.

By 1815 taxation was overwhelming for the Herefordshire farmers - just look at the annual rates and costs of George Gardiner at Bishopstone Court.

	£ s d
Rent to landlord	250 00 00
Tithes	63 10 11
Poor rates	77 13 4
Land tax	16 13 3
Window lights	24 1 0
Cart horse duty (six)	14 4 0
Saddle horse duty (two)	5 6 6
Gig duty	6 6 6
Tenants duty for making 120 bushels of barley into malt	42 00 00
New rate for building Shire Hall.	9 00 00
Total	**£508 15 6**

The higher increase in rent for land, coupled with the low agricultural prices, made George Gardiner of Court Farm struggle financially, particularly after the death of his father in 1834.

His cousin George Gardiner of Bishon Farm never had the same money problems; in 1797 he married Sarah Tunstall of Lawson Hope, Canon Pyon. The Tunstall were a wealthy family who originated from the Potteries and Sarah brought money into the marriage. George Gardiner, purchased Bishon Farm from Foxley Estate on September 18th 1806, securing the farmhouse and buildings plus 100 acres of land while the other half of the farm, 150 acres, he rented from the estate. As land prices were very buoyant at this time, fetching around £25 per acre, George would have paid around £2500 for his half of the farm.

George appears to have been a farmer who embraced modern farming techniques using new machinery. He built one of the first threshing machines in the county around 1808 on Bishon Farm; it was housed in its own specially built barn at a cost of £300. The threshing machine with its complex gearing occupied two floors of the barn and was capable of working chaff cutters, grinders and turnip slicers. Power to drive the machine came from a horse engine, basically four horses walking in a circle turning a large shaft that rose into the top of the barn from which all the gears and belts could be driven. These machines caused much discontent among farm labourers because they were frightened of losing their livelihood; riots occurred in southern England where many machines were smashed.

We know about the existence of this threshing machine barn, because in 1826 William, George's son, lost his life to this machine when he was 21 years old. The inquest records into his death held at Hereford Record Office give a vivid description of the event.
Because William was to be buried in Canon Pyon church in the Tunstall plot his inquest was held in that parish in readiness for his burial. William Pateshall the coroner of the County chaired the inquest[1] comprising 12 jurors while John Stephens attended as Bishopstone parish constable. Thomas Mellin, a labourer from Bishopstone, gave a statement saying he was working alongside William at the time of the accident. Doctor John Griffith junior also gave a statement.

Thomas Mellin made his statement on February 3rd 1826.

"It will be three weeks tomorrow since he, with the deceased and three other persons, were employed at a barn in the said parish of Bishopstone, we were mashing and bossing clover with a threshing machine, four horses were working the machine. The horses and machine were the property of old George Gardiner of Bishen in the parish of Bishopstone who was the father of the deceased, that during the working, the gloves of the deceased had been torn from the hands of the deceased two or three times, afterwards the strap came of the idler of the machine, the same there being in motion by the working of the horses, that in attempting to replace the strap the left arm of the deceased became entangled by this strap and the said arm of the deceased was pulled up the shaft of the main wheel of the machine so that the arm of the deceased was nearly torn from the body and he was therein trapped, the horses were nearly in the act of stopping when this injury happened to the deceased. The deceased had called for the horses to be stopped but did not wait for them to be quietly stood before he made the attempt to replace the strap, the injury happen by accident."

John Griffith the Doctor's statement.

"That on Saturday evening in January the 14th I attended the deceased at Bishopstone, I found the left arm of the deceased broken in three places a very considerable wound, the muscles and shoulder very much lacerated and torn, together with a very considerable injury about he left side, it appeared that the arm had been forced around a small object with great force. I attended the deceased every day until the 24th of the same month, when he died from the injury befallen on him. The deceased was at his father's farm in Bishopstone from the day of his injury until his death."
The Reverend Davenport demolished the threshing barn in 1871 when he modernized the farm buildings

The siblings of William Gardiner are worthy of a note. Henry his eldest brother left Bishon at his coming of age and moved to Lawson Hope, Canon Pyon, his mother's 370-acre estate. Henry never married; he lived out the rest of his life farming the estate.
Sarah Gardiner his eldest sister married Joseph Hincliff Sunderland at Bishopstone Church on September 14th 1830; Joseph was the founder of Sunderlands, the Hereford based auctioneers. After the death of her brother George Henry, the Lawson Hope estate passed on to Sarah and her husband.
George senior died on August 20th 1834 at Bishon Farm, and was buried at Canon Pyon next to his wife Sarah who had passed on in 1831.
In his will proved in December 1834, he instructed his trustees to sell all his properties and divide the monies raised equally between his sons George of Lawson Hope, Benjamin of Hereford, and his daughters Mary and Ann. To his other daughter Sarah, wife of Joseph Sunderland, he left £600 and to his daughter Ann, who was living at home at the time of his death he left an additional £200, one chest and the bed she slept in.
The total value of his estate was valued at just under £2000, and because agriculture was at a low ebb the farm was never put up for auction but the trustees negotiated with the Foxley Estate to purchase back the farm with the condition that Benjamin, George Gardiner's son, could take on a new tenancy. Foxley Estate paid the going rate of roughly £10 per acre; the value of the farm had dropped by over half in thirty years.
Benjamin unfortunately was no farmer, unlike his brothers; he had opted for a more comfortable lifestyle living in a large house in Hereford after his marriage to Harriett Lawford. He arrived at Bishon Farm in 1835 with his wife and two young children; three more children followed, Sarah, Joseph, and William. By 1840 he had built up a large household staff and a governess to educate his children. All his correspondence was addressed to Bishon House since he had dropped the farm part from the address, possibly because he thought he was of a higher social standing than a farmer. Benjamin and the family disappeared from Bishon in 1843, he had attended the church vestry meeting on March 23rd of that year then there is no further paper evidence of Benjamin living in the parish.

What happened after they left the parish is a mystery; they appear to have both died before the 1851 census, the four surviving children according to the census were all living separately, George at Aston Ingham and Mary Ann living with relatives in St Nicholas, Hereford. Sarah age 15 was living with her aunt Mary Ann Hill, a farmer's wife at Weston under Penyard, and Joseph the youngest is listed as a boarder at St Owens Street boys school Hereford; after leaving school he moved to London.
Joseph Tunstall of Burton Court Burghill in his will dated 1855, left £500 in trust for the four children of his deceased nephew Benjamin Gardiner.

On August 12th 1809 the Reverend Adam John Walker was admitted as the new Rector of Bishopstone, the position was vacant due to the death of Thomas Evans. The National Gentleman's magazine carried Thomas Evans' obituary with anecdotes of a remarkable person, Prebendary of Hereford Cathedral, Rector of Bishopstone and for many years Commissioner of the Peace for Herefordshire. In his will he left his personal estate to his wife Sarah during her natural lifetime then to his five children. Part of the new conditions for Adam John Walker's appointment laid down by the Bishop of Hereford, stated that the new Rector must live in the parish. The Old Rectory Farm was rented out and farmed by John Ashley but in January 1810 it was inspected and was found to be unfit and unhealthy and was condemned. Not surprising, because Bishopstone rectors had not lived in the Rectory since Timothy Millichamp had left over a hundred years earlier. The Rectory Farm had been rented out over this hundred-year period to tenant farmers, but mostly to the Gardiner family of Court Farm who farmed the land and used the rectory to house their farm labourers. The Bishop was insistent on implementing the clause attached to the appointment by only issuing a licence for one year on March 18th 1811, stating although the parsonage home was unfit Adam John Walker would still have to reside in Bishopstone parish. So Walker selected a site for his new rectory on high ground west of the original rectory overlooking the church, on land which had just been awarded and enclosed out of Hoarstone Common Field as part of the Enclosures Act. Adam managed to secure a mortgage with the governors of Queen Ann's Bounty for £950; the total cost to build the new parsonage house. He signed the paperwork on August 29th 1811 and building work started. Whilst digging out the foundations the remains of a Roman villa were found as I mentioned in the earlier Roman section of this book. The rectory was finished in late 1812, a standard late Georgian house with a porch with Doric columns and fanlight.

(Figure 2) This 2000 photo shows part of the original Rectory built by Rev Walker.

1812 Hereford Journal

To be sold by auction on Monday thirteenth of April 1812 at the Rectory House, in the parish of Bishopstone. (Six miles from Hereford)
The following very desirable farming stock, and implement of husbandry property of Mr. James Ashley, who is quitting the farm, comprising of four cows and heifers in calve, two in-calf cows, one barren ditto, three draft mares, two of which are in foal, the one is aged four, the other six, one capital good saddle mare, two 2-year-old colts, twenty ryland ewes and lambs, and ten wether sheep, a little crossed with south down; two sows with pigs, one strong store pig, four smaller stores, one narrow-wheeled cart, with thripples and dash-boards, one broad-wheel cart, one narrow ditto, two pairs of harrows, one ground car, one roller, one lammas plough, one long plough, about five hurdles, one kiln hair.
The sale to commence precisely at 11 o'clock in the Forenoon.

After this sale the Rectory House with the farm buildings were pulled down; a glebe farm had stood on this site since the 13th century. James Ashley, the last tenant of Rectory Farm, was the son of John Ashley who had rented Bishon farm in the late 18th century from whom it appears he inherited a lot of farming stock, which might explain the large number of animals and equipment entered into the sale.

Whilst researching the newspapers of the time I also came across this advert placed in the Hereford Journal dated October 23rd 1811. Amusing because it illustrates the infancy of the banking system.

Lost on Saturday. *Lost on the Hay road five miles out of Hereford in the vicinity of the fifth milestone, small Moroccan pocket book containing a five pound bill, three one pound notes of the Hereford banks, and a few small papers, the number of the bills are known and payment stopped, whoever will bring the same to Mr. Bennett's Hotel, Hereford shall be handsomely rewarded.*
The fifth milestone has now disappeared; it was near the Bunshill turn on the A438 within our parish boundary. The Pigot Directory 1822 lists James Bennett as proprietor of the City Arms Hotel, he was also the Post Master for Herefordshire. Other interesting bits from the directory; Sir J G Cotterell and Robert Price Foxley were members of parliament for the County of Herefordshire. Conveyance by water, lists the following canals; Hereford to Gloucester, Kington and Leominster, weekly service to Bristol by river, John Easton's Barges, Castle wharf, William Cooke's and Swift & Co Commercial Wharf.

(Figure 3) Rev Adam Walker is looking at the telescope wearing a white wig.

Adam John Walker Rector of Bishopstone between 1809-39 was an interesting man; he was previously the curate of Leybourne Kent, second son of the highly regarded Victorian, Adam Walker, inventor and writer. He is also the earliest Rector of Bishopstone for whom we can see an image as he was part of a painting called the Adams Family, painted by the renowned artist George Romney between 1796 and 1801 and now considered a national treasure, presently hanging on permanent display in the National Portrait Gallery.
The family were acquainted with many artistic and literary friends. The Rector's father was a philosopher and lecturer who toured the country. His eldest brother William and younger brother Deane were both astronomers of some acclaim. Artist George Romney presented his painting of the family as a gift to Adam Walker senior; another friend William Turner, the famous landscape artist, presented Adam with a watercolour of Hereford Cathedral that he had painted in 1793. This painting is now part of the Hereford Museum collection bequeathed to the museum by his daughter Loveday. The poet William Wordsworth was an acquaintance and visitor and wrote a sonnet entitled Lesbia to Miss Loveday Walker. At Loveday's coming of age party in 1821 a tulip tree was planted in the garden to mark the occasion, where it still stands today and has turned into a very fine specimen.
The Rev Walker was the incumbent of Bishopstone for thirty years and his sudden death was reported in the Hereford Times.

Hereford Times January 13th 1839.
Awfully sudden death, on Tuesday morning last, the family of the Rev Adam J Walker Rector of Bishopstone in this county, were plunged into deep affliction by the sudden death of the Reverend Gentleman, Mr Walker had been indisposed for several days, and had experienced many attacks of angina pectoris. On Tuesday morning he went upstairs and on his descent suffered a fatal attack of the affliction, he fell down and immediately expired. The deceased was in the 70th year of his age, he was highly accomplished and his death has occasioned the deepest regret to his friends and relatives.

Enclosure Act

The General Enclosure Act of 1801 forced Bishopstone and Mansel Lacy parishes, under the lordship of Uvedale Price, to implement the act. The crops and cultivation of the late 18th and early 19th centuries differed little from those of the preceding centuries. Over vast areas of England wheat, rye and beans were sown in the autumn; barley, oats and peas or lentils in the spring; and roughly one third of the land was left fallow every year. New crops such as clover, rape, rye-grass, lucerne, sanfoin and turnips were known, tested and found advantageous. Nathaniel Kent had preached this to Uvedale Price late in the previous century. These new crops could not be cultivated on any worthwhile scale as long as the thousand-year-old system of open fields remained in operation. The abolition of the old system involved long and often bitter controversy, although it released up to 25% more tillage land. The enclosures of the open fields in Bishopstone were implemented over a period of years without causing a lot of controversy. Parts of the common fields had already been enclosed, many of the strips had been exchanged between freeholders, to form blocks of land; all this helped with a smooth transition.

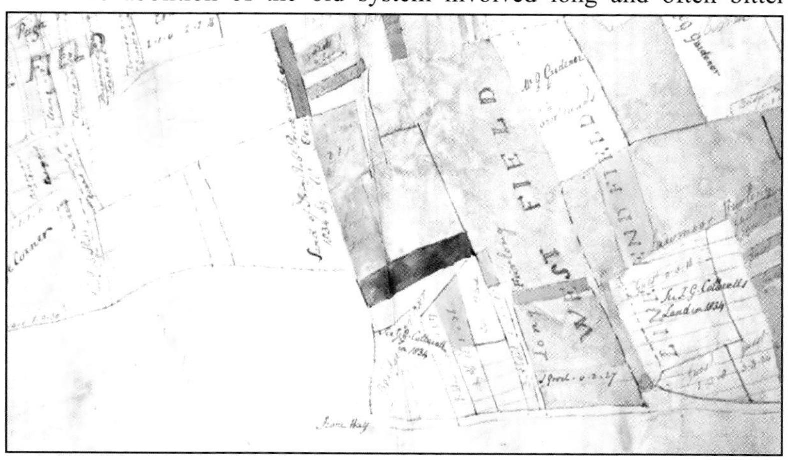

(Figure 4) Part of the 1790-1834 working map shows West Field in Bishon, only two strips are left in this Common Field, belonging to Joseph Guest and John Goode (Pleck) both freeholders. The main part of West Field coloured in blue is in the ownership of Robert Price of Foxley waiting to be divided up into smaller fields. Sir John Cotterell inherited Joseph Guest's land whose strips were all accumulated into a block of 13 acres at the lower end of Line End Field

A record of what was happening on the ground can be traced on the working map above used by Foxley Estate; it is roughly drawn with notes written on the map, but it is an invaluable record of the changes that were taking place.

On April 29th 1809 Uvedale Price put forward a loan of £150 for the purpose of implementing the Act[2]. Appointed by Parliament, James Cranstone of King's Acre Gent and Benjamin Wainwright of Hereford Gent were the Commissioners to oversee the Enclosure Act for Bishopstone and Mansel Lacy.

BISHOPSTON, AND MANSEL LACY INCLOSURE.

WE the Commissioners named and appointed in and by an Act of Parliament, made and passed in the 49th year of the reign of his present Majesty, King George the Third, intituled, "An Act for Inclosing Lands in the Parishes of Bishopston, and Mansel Lacy, otherwise Much Mansel, in the County of Hereford," *Do hereby Give Notice*, That we have appointed a Meeting to be held by us at the Lion Inn, at Yazor, in the said County, on Thursday, the Twenty-seventh day of July next, at the hour of Ten in the Forenoon; at which time and place, all Persons and Bodies Corporate and Politic, claiming any property whatever in, over, or upon the Commons and Lands by this Act directed to be Divided and Inclosed, are required to deliver a particular account in writing, of their respective claims, or they cannot afterwards be received.

Dated the Twenty-ninth day of June, 1809.

J. CRANSTON,
BENJ. WAINWRIGHT.

The first meeting was held on July 27th 1809 at the Red Lion Inn Yazor, all of Bishopstone's landholding parishioners would have attended. After many meetings most of the common land in the parish was divided up into allotments, the size of each allotment determined by a complex method of land and building valuation.

In 1810 a terrier of all the land and buildings in Bishopstone was ordered by the Commissioners, for the purpose of calculating the allotments' sizes. It recorded names of all the occupiers, field names, size, usage, (either orchard, meadow, pasture or a combination) and their rental value. Orchards had the highest value, followed by pasture and then meadows. The same applied for the houses, cottages and buildings; John Williams's three cottages on the hill were valued at £1. 10s each while the Court Farm house and buildings carrying a value of £10 18s 4d.

An advert was placed in the Hereford Journal February 12th 1810.

At the Greyhound Inn Hereford 11 o'clock sale of 15 acres of common land on Bishopstone Hill.
(Sir John Geers Cotterell purchased this No 3 allotment for £375 through his agent Mr Steadman)
Some of this money was used to build a new brick bridge over Ivors Brook at Bishon Common to carry a new public road.

By March 27th 1812 the six common open fields in the parish had disappeared, Hoarstone, Pluckwell and Hill in Bishopstone, Common Hill, Line End and West in Bishon; the strips were put together and the smaller freeholders were given blocks of land which they enclosed.

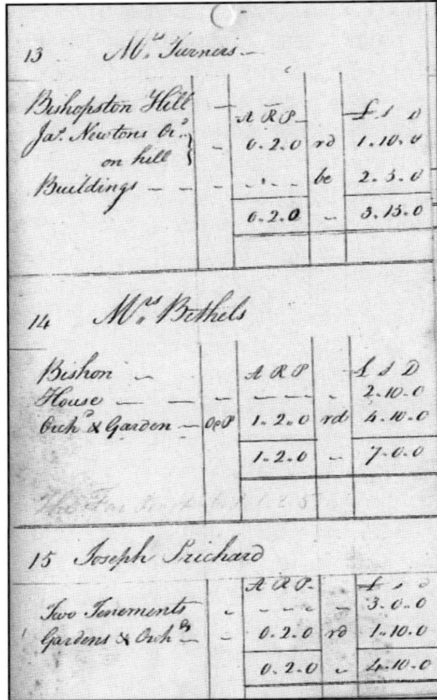

13 Mr. Turners

		A R P		£ s d
Bishopston Hill Jas. Newtons Cr. on hill	–	0.2.0	rd	1.10.0
Buildings	–	–	do	2.5.0
		0.2.0	–	3.15.0

14 Mrs. Bethels

		A R P		£ s D
Bishon House	–	–	–	2.10.0
Orch & Garden	0.0.P	1.2.0	rd	4.10.0
		1.2.0	–	7.0.0

15 Joseph Prichard

		A R P		£ s d
Two Tenements	–	–	–	3.0.0
Gardens & Orch	–	0.2.0	rd	1.10.0
		0.2.0	–	4.10.0

(Figure 5) Page from the 1810 terrier
13 Cottage on hill
14 Bethel's House pre Nelson Inn
15 Burcott Row

The commissioners were paid two guineas a day expenses for examining, hearing and determining the title to any land or tenement that was in dispute. If any persons were dissatisfied with their findings they could appeal and proceed to a trial in law. Within two years most of the common fields were agreed and enclosed mostly by exchange.
Uvedale Price purchased 12 acres of common land on Bishopstone Hill for £300 in 1810; he then reclaimed the £150 loan he had made to the commissioners plus interest.
The agreed enclosures were legalised quickly by the commissioners so that the normal business of farming, selling land or building a house on the newly acquired enclosures could take place.
The two commons proved a lot harder to agree on, and although some allotments were agreed and fenced, a few were disputed. Settling these disputes became a complex and arduous task for the commissioners, which carried on for many years. Twelve public enclosure meetings were held at the Lion Inn, Yazor before 1820, all advertised in the Hereford Journal; after this all meetings were conducted behind closed doors. A committee was formed to act for all parties involved, consisting of both the enclosure commissioners plus Sir Robert Price, Sir John Geers Cotterell, The Right Reverend Father in God Edward, Lord Bishop of Hereford, The Reverend Adam John Walker (Rector of Bishopstone), George Gardiner Gent (Bishopstone Court Farm), George Gardiner the younger Gent (Bishon Farm), Mary Bethel widow (The Steps) who replaced Thomas her deceased husband and William Bythel Butcher of Hampton Bishop replacing his grandfather William deceased (Claypitt). The first copy of the Act for Bishopstone and Mansell Lacy was released on January 14th 1833, 24 years after the first meeting. The final seal was not put on the document until December 15th 1859, 50 years after it started; even by 1833 many of the original parishioners had died.
As well as overseeing the enclosures the commissioners also defined and delimited certain parish roads. Bishopstone lost four ancient lanes and roads, and two new public roads were created. One new public highway gave access to the new allotments on Bishon common, the other new public highway was necessary to give access up to Bishopstone Hill.
A public notice appeared in the Hereford Journal on October 16th 1809 declaring that two public roads that crossed Bishopstone common were to be closed.
Number 1. *Public carriageway and drift road and highway extending from the north end of Steps Lane to the Almshouse Lane.*
Number 2. *Public carriageway and drift road and highway extending from the public road number one by Almshouse to the Hill Quarry.*

Other new laws were passed under the Bishopstone and Mansell Lacy Act because of concerns over where cottagers would keep any livestock now the commons had disappeared.
No person allowed grazing livestock on any highway or lanes under penalty of 20s for every horse or beast or 10 shillings for every sheep or goat. (This granted power for parishioners to impound the offending livestock if found and hold until the penalties were paid.) *All allotments awarded to be fenced in within seven years. No stock allowed into allotments unless owner or occupier erects fence to guard against young quick.* (hedge) *Glebe land to be set out and enclosed.*
To pay for repairs to ditches, build bridges and cover the cost of making new private and public roads awarded in this Act.

The maps illustrated on the next page are copied from the original Enclosure Act documents; it contains names of the parishioners in alphabetical order recording their land holdings and the number of their awarded allotment.

William Apperley, Bishon Common No 37
Thomas Bethel, The Flower-de-luce No 34
James Bethel, 5 dwellings Claypitts No 38
Mrs Bythel, Nelson No 39
John Cleeton, Bishon Common No 35
Sir John Geers Cotterell tenants;
(Hancocks, house and buildings (Claypitts)
William Jones, house No 43,47,48,49)
John Foot, house garden and orchard No 44
Glebe, Old Rectory by Church No 53
George Gardiner, Bishton Farm No 52
Hospital House, Bishopstone Hill No 51
John Nicholas, Birley Close No 32

(Figure 6) New public roads marked in yellow

Samuel Preece, Cottage Bishopstone Hill No.45
Uvedale Price Esq. Sundry farms tenants.
George Gardiner, Bishopstone Court. **Barnaby Pember**, Buckwell Farm. **George Gardiner**, Bishon Farm. **James Hancocks**, Smith Shop and cottage. **John Williams**, Kenowley Farm. **Thomas Bethel**, Bramberry Hall. **Mrs Pember**, New Inn Farm No 24,25)
Joshua Prichard, two tenements Burcutt Row No 28
John Smith, (heir of Mrs Turner) Townsend, The Stocks, Cottage on hill No 42
Benjamin Turner, Close of land on Steps Lane No 29
John Tringham, house, land, cottage let to G Phillpotts Bishon Common No.31
William Watkins, Pleck smallholding, cottage in Bishon No 26,27
John Williams, three cottages Bishopstone Hill No 50
Sarah Williams, Two Cottage in Bishon (Old schoolhouse) No 33
Mary Williams, Small holding Bishon Common No 36

Notes taken from the final Enclosure Bill
Awarded to **Mary Bethel** parcel of arable land 1acre 2rods bottom of Pudding Hill.
Awarded to **William Bethel** strip of land 1acre 3rods 23perches next to a messuage called the Nelson, also **William Bethel** purchased allotments 29,30,32,33,34, from Benjamin Turner, John Tringham, John Nicolas, Sarah William and Thomas Bythel.
Awarded to **Sir John Geers Cotterell** Pudding Hill Croft, 8acres 3rods 16perches Hill Field, 14acres 3rods 20perches and 7acres 12perches (common field), Croft of land 14perches bounded by road from Bridge Boat to Bishopstone.
Tenement known as Griffith Cottage (Swiss Cottage) with plock and wood 2acres 2rods 5perches.
Cottage or tenement called Fragley Castle and land 39perches.

(Figure 7) Painting of a Cottage on Bishopstone Hill by Lucy Davenport circ 1860.
Possibly Fragley Cottage, (Tithes map 31).
Lucy went on to marry Johnny Arkwright of Hampton Court

Following the 1820 Easter vestry meeting the parish clerk John Williams was instructed to apply to the courts for further road closures in Bishopstone.He was to report that the parish could not afford the maintenance required on all the parish roads.

Herefordshire

We Benjamin Biddulph and Edmund Pateshall Esquire, two of his Majesty's Justices of the Peace for the said county, at a Special Sessions held at the City of Hereford in the Hundred of Grimsworth in the said county on the eleventh day of March one thousand eight hundred and twenty, having upon view found that certain parts of a Highway within the parishes of Bishopstone and Bridge Sollers in the said hundred, the one lying between the turnpike road leading from Hereford to Hay at a place called Bridge Dingle and the village of Mansel Lacy, at a certain road leading thereout to Bishopstones hill, and containing in length 1326 yards or thereabouts; And another road leading from the said turnpike road near to Bridge Sollers church towards Bridge Sollers ford or ferry near the river Wye containing in length 154 yards or thereabouts; And another road branching out of a certain road leading from Kentchester to Byford at a place called Owen's Cottage and leading from thence to Bishopstones Court in the said parish of Bishopstone, and containing in length 1200 yards or thereabouts, and severally particularly described in the plan hereunto annexed, may be diverted, turned and stopped up so as to render the same more commodious to the public. And having viewed courses for new highways in lieu thereof through the lands and grounds of Sir John Geers Cotterell Baronet and Robert Price Esquire, the one of such highways being of the length of 587 yards or thereabouts and of the width of 20 feet or thereabouts and another of such highways being of the length of 88 yards or thereabouts and of the width of 20 feet or thereabouts, and which are respectively particularly described in the plan hereunto annexed.

And having received evidence of the consent of the said Sir John Geers Cotterell and Robert Price to the said new highways being made through their respective lands hereuntofore described by writing under their hands and seals we do hereby order that the said highways be diverted and turned through the lands aforesaid. And we do order an equal assessment not exceeding the rate of sixpence in the pound to be levied and collected upon all and every the occupiers of the lands, tenements, woods, tithes and hereditaments in the said several parishes of Bishopstone and Bridge Sollers. And that the said money arising thereupon be paid and applied in making recompense and satisfaction for the same unto the said Sir John Geers Cotterell and Robert Price.

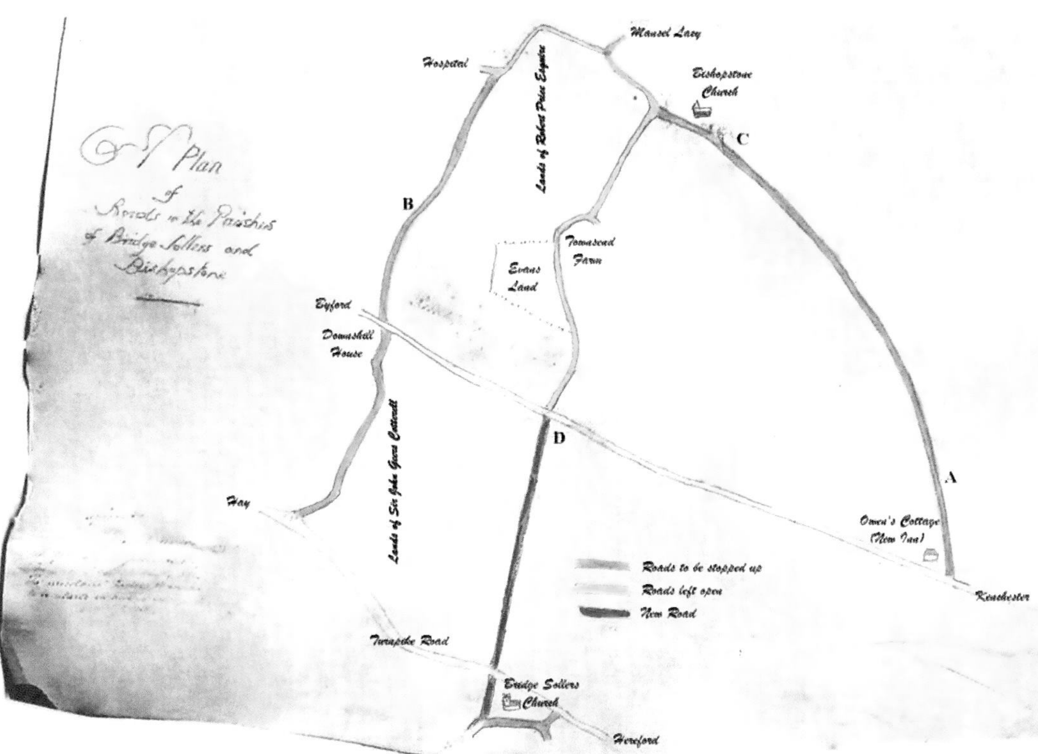

(Figure 8) Some of the writing on the map has faded. So I have copied over the original. The points marked A B C & D are the reference points for the photographs taken in 2010.

Public Alehouses in Bishopstone

New Inn

(Figure 9) Artist's impression of the New Inn early 19th Century

The New Inn was the only public alehouse recorded in the parish from 1590 until 1770s when a second alehouse opened called the Flower-de-luce. The New Inn stood originally on a junction where a road leading to Bishopstone Church joined the Roman road, as explained previously this road was closed in 1820. The alehouse is still standing today in the centre of the village; it is now a private residence called Stonehouse.

The first record I have found by name of the inn was recorded in the 1590 rentals, it showed Paul Delahay paid 2s 6d rent for his messuage and lands called Peers land, "now called the New Inn". It's worth remembering that when the New Inn was first built on the side of the Roman road it was the main highway between Hereford and Kington; this status only changed after the building of the new turnpike road in the 1730s.

I suspect there was an inn on the site before, because the 1468 rentals record Thomas Smyth the chaplain renting the property, and knowing how the church controlled the alehouses in this period it seems highly likely. The site is first recorded in 1385, when John Peer was listed as the occupier and John le Grand as the previous tenant. The rent charge of 2s 6d remained the same from 1385 until the last record in 1590.

In 1630 John Thomas and his wife Eleanor held the indenture of the New Inn for their life by an annual rent of 20s. Soon afterwards on July 15th 1637[3], John Savaker of Dynder sold the inn to Phillip Gwilliam for £58. Throughout the civil war Thomas Welsh was the keeper of the New Inn, he was also a soldier who fought with Humphrey Berrington on the Royalist side. His occupancy is recorded in a document[4] held at the National Archives Kew, titled Hawkening v Berrington. This featured a long court case involving the New Inn indentures lost by Benjamin Mason who sequestrated the Manor of Bishopstone from Humphrey Berrington in the time of the Commonwealth.

The rental book[5] of 1705 lists Howell Evans paying rent of £3 11s for house and land called the New Inn; by 1720 this rent had dropped to £2 per annum. The Evans family held the tenancy of the Inn until the 1760s; John Pember became the next tenant, he married Ann Hancock at Bishopstone Church in 1756 and they had 14 children. John died in 1804 and was buried at Mansel Gamage, his wife Ann carried on running the inn until April 1811 when her granddaughter, another Ann, heavily pregnant, married Herbert Pritchard at Bishopstone Church. Herbert became the next tenant, until 1819 when he suddenly died at the age of 46. Ann carried on for the next couple of years after her husband's death. Barnabus Pember, her uncle who was born at the inn, stood as guarantor. The last Alehouse Keeper recorded in 1825 was Thomas Powell, a friend of Barnabus Pember.

From the 16th century every keeper of an alehouse or inn had to enter into a bond, usually to the value of £10, binding them to keep an orderly house upon forfeit of the sum. This bond was in effect their licence and each bears the signature of two Session magistrates, this method of control ended in 1828 with the introduction of the 1828 Licensing Act.

The only surviving record of the Alehouse Keepers in the Grimsworth Hundred runs from September 1818 until 1828.

Alehouse Keeper	**Guarantee**
1818 Herbert Pritchard (New Inn)	*William Lloyd*
William Bethel (Nelson Head)	*Edward Powole*
1819 Herbert Pritchard (New Inn)	*William Gallowas*
William Bethel (Nelson Head)	*William Hancock*
1820 Ann Prichard (New Inn)	*Barnabus Pember, Thomas Bethel*
William Bethel (Nelson Head)	*William Pritchard*
1821 Ann Pritchard (New Inn)	*Barnabus Pember*
Richard Yapp (Nelson Head)	*Thomas Ludwick*
1822 James Burden (New Inn)	*Barnabus Pember*
Richard Yapp (Nelson Head)	*Richead Snead*

1823 John Bowers (New Inn)
Richard Yapp (Nelson Head)
1824 John Bowers (New Inn)
Richard Yapp (Nelson Head)
1825 Thomas Powell (New Inn) last year of operating
Richard Yapp (Nelson Head)
1828 William Jones (Nelson) last entry.

Thomas Hadcock
William Mead, James Powell
Thomas Hancock
William Mead
Barnabus Pember
Thomas Moore

Struggling to survive in its village location the New Inn finally closed its doors at Christmas 1825 after serving the parish since 1590. Three different alehouse keepers had tried to keep the inn open but they all failed.

Flower-de-Luce

(Figure 10) Artist's impression, sketch of the Flower de Luce early 19th century.

This Bishopstone alehouse is today a private residence called "The Steppes" reverting it back to its original name. It stands on the boundary with Byford.
Built around 1740 by Thomas Bethel on land he owned at the Claypits, the house was built in the base of an old quarry as its name implies. A new quarry was excavated just up the hill behind the house to provide stone for building the turnpike road. William Bethel, Thomas's cousin had bought the Claypits farm next door in 1747 and built a row of four cottages in the garden to provide homes for the quarry workers. Thomas senior died in 1777 and left the house to his son, another Thomas, who some time after set up the house as an alehouse called the Flower-de-Luce. All went well until the turnpike road was moved in 1791 leaving a rather isolated alehouse on a no-through road. It struggled to survive for the next twenty-five years before finally closing in 1816.
Several adverts appeared in the Hereford Journal naming the alehouse, one advert on July 10th 1811 reads, *For sale by auction a wheat crop to be sold at, the Flower-de-luce, in the parish of Bishopstone enquiries Mr Wheatstone at the premises.* I presume Mr Wheatstone was the alehouse keeper, he did not renew his tenancy, and had vacated the premises by December 1811, as shown by this advert in the Journal. To be sold at auction
At the Flower-De-Luce Inn, in the parish of Bishopstone seven miles from Hereford, on Thursday the 28th day of November 1811, and the following day, all the household goods and furniture, comprising bedsteads, with or without hangings, good feather beds, bed clothing, tables, chairs; bureau chests and chest of drawers, Pier and swing looking glass, clock and case, kitchen furniture; and excellent copper furnace; casks; brewing utensils, sundries and other articles
The sale to commence at 10 o'clock in the forenoon of each day.
I have not discovered who the next tenants were but an advert for a tenant was placed in the Journal on December 11th 1816, from which no new tenant was found.

HEREFORDSHIRE TO BE LET

And entered upon a Christmas next. That old established public house called the Flower-De-Luce otherwise The Stepps situated in the parish of Bishopstone between six and seven miles from the City of Hereford together with about nine acres of good land, and a part of it with orcharding and the land in good condition, with good cellars, good stabling, Brewhouse and cider mill on the premise, and the building in good repair, the situation lies well for a man in the dealing business.
For further particulars apply to Mr. Thomas Bethel near the Stepps House who will show the premises.
Thomas Bethel died around 1824 leaving the house to his niece Jane Hobby with the provision that his second wife Mary, whom he had married in1809, could occupy the house until she died. The Hobby family became insolvent, and tried to sell the Steps by auction at the Greyhound Inn Hereford on March 5th 1831 but were unsuccessful. It was rented out to agricultural labourers throughout this period. Jane Hobby eventually sold "The Stepps" to Sir J G Cotterell in 1845 for £1100, to include house, barn, cider mill, cottage above where Mary Bethel dwelt, timber, land and meadow. Sir John's new tenant was Ann Ellis who made cider on the site and advertised herself as a cider retailer. The house was extensively rebuilt in the 1880s.

Nelson Head Inn

(Figure 11) Artist's impression; The London to Brecon coach leaving the Nelson Head in the 1830s after dropping off the postbag. The service was called the Telegraph and ran every Tuesday, Thursday and Saturday. It arrived at the Nelson around 4.00pm.

In 1766 William Bethel, a carpenter of Claypits Farm, Bishopstone bought two plots of land between the Hereford road and South Hoarstone Field for £40 from Roland Evans, and soon afterwards he built a cottage on it. When he died in 1806 he left it to his son, another William who opened part of the house as the Nelson Head Inn around 1813. The Session records from Weobley are lost so it's difficult to give an exact date.

The first newspaper advert I have found referring to this inn appeared in the Hereford Journal on August 9th 1815 advertising a sale by auction to take place (*At the Nelson Head Inn, near Bridge Church.*)

This was a popular name at the time for an Inn, Lord Nelson was a national hero after his death at Trafalgar, but there may have been a more personal reason for the choice as the Bethels could well have been among the crowds who gathered to cheer Nelson when he visited Hereford in 1802 to receive the Freedom of the City.

The Inn became very successful, but this was short lived because of a tragic accident, reported in the Hereford Journal on November 1st 1820.

Melancholy accident- *On Saturday evening as Mr. Bethel who keeps the Nelson Head on the Hay Road about six miles from the city, was crossing the Wye on a pony with his son, from visiting some land he rented, owing to the depths of the water and the rapidity of the current, they both perished, leaving a wife and six children fatherless, the horse swam out.*

The story does not end there; looking through the burial records of Bishopstone Church an entry records, William Bethel buried December 12th 1820, age 48 years body decomposed. Note; drowned with his son James on October 28th 1820.

Seven year old James who perished with his father was buried on November 3rd 1820. William was in the water for another month before he was found, he would not have been a pretty sight.

William had built up a large property portfolio before he died, having inherited the five properties at Claypits, plus the Nelson on his father's death. He further expanded his portfolio, by purchasing a cottage on the hill in 1817 from John Smith (Townsend Farm) for £95 to add to three cottages he had already purchased up on Bishopstone hill. On enclosure allotment number 47 on Bishopstone Hill, he built two new stone cottages. When he died William left ten properties to his wife and children. After William's tragic accident, his wife Ann carried on running the Nelson Inn, not alone for long because on May 29th 1821 she married Richard Yapp just five months after she had buried her husband. They expanded their holdings by purchasing the Oxford Arms in 1826 and moving into Hereford leaving William Jones as tenant licensee of the Nelson.

Their eldest son, another William, who was a butcher together with his sisters sold Claypitts Farm with its four cottages to Sir John Cotterell in 1839, while the three cottages on Bishopstone Hill were sold to John Davenport of Foxley for £160 on October 5th 1859.
The Nelson Inn was sold to James Baker and John Perks who in 1856 sold it on to William Lloyd of Bishon Farm; he insured the Nelson for £200 on June 17th 1856.
On William Lloyd's death his executors tried to sell the Nelson by auction, it was advertised in the Hereford Times on January 25th 1868 but they were unsuccessful. Shortly afterwards the Rev George Davenport of Foxley purchased the Nelson with some other cottages in Bishopstone for £800 from William Lloyd's executors.
In 1871 the Nelson was rebuilt by George Davenport adding a cross wing on the east end and recording the fact for posterity with a plaque carrying the date and his initials which can still be seen on the gable end of the property facing the road.
The former timber framed house was encased in brick, new farm outbuilding were built and a further 30 acres of land were attached making it into a farm
When Foxley Estate sold its holdings in Bishopstone in 1920, the sitting tenant Rosana Bywater purchased the Nelson along with 40 acres of land.

New Housing and Land Sales

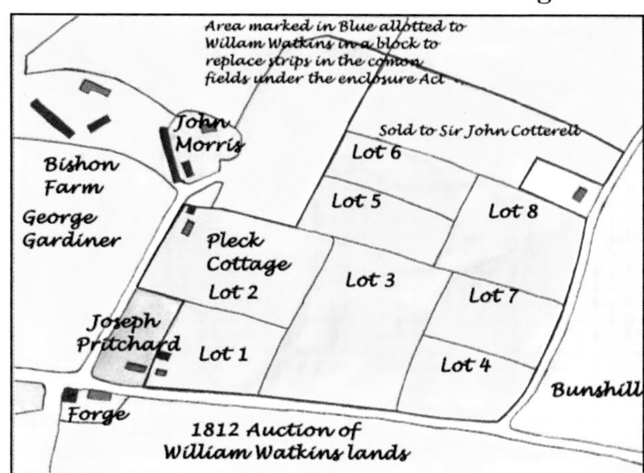

(Figure 12) This block of land marked out of the Old Common Hill Field was awarded to William Watkins in 1811, today in 2010 it contains twenty properties

There was no significant increase in the number of properties in Bishopstone parish between 1664 and 1810, but this changed after 1812. William Watkins was awarded a block of fourteen acres enclosed out of the Common Hill Field, Bishon, to replace the fourteen acres of strips held in the three common fields. William had purchased the Pleck from John Goode and the cottage (Old Post Office) from Uvedale Price of Foxley in 1773. He was now facing bankruptcy and so to raise some money he placed his holding in Bishon up for auction. This sale of freehold land along with the common allotments started a new cottage and house building programme in the parish of the like never seen before.

HEREFORDSHIRE
TO BE SOLD BY AUCTION

At the Greyhound Inn, in the city of **Hereford**, on Saturday, the Thirty-first day of October, 1812, at four o'clock in the afternoon, Subject to Conditions.
Lot 1; A neat cottage and garden in the occupation of Edward Preece, 1a 3r 9p.
Purchased by the William Davies farmer from Mansel Lacy.
Lot 2; A House, Barns, Building, and Garden, in the Occupation of James Morris, 2a 1r 12p.
Purchased by the Foote sisters ex Bishon Farm,
Lot 3; Part of a Piece of land, well planted with thriving and healthy Fruit Trees, 1a 2r 34p
Purchased by Jeremiah Apperley who lived on Bishon Common, He was a Carpenter and Wheelwright. Jeremiah built a brick cottage on the site soon after the auction, today the middle house of the Clovers Row.
Lot 4; The other or remaining Part of land, also well planted with Fruit Trees 1a 3r 6p.
Purchased by William Davies Mansel Lacy
Lot 5; Part or Parcel of an exceeding rich Piece of Land, 1a 2r 38p
Purchased by Jeremiah Apperley Bishon Common
Lot 6; Another Part of the same Piece or Parcel of Land, as now staked out, 1a 2r 29p.
Purchased by George Gardiner Bishon Farm
Lot 7; Another Part of the same Piece or Parcel of Land, 1a 2r 28p.
Purchased by William Davies Mansel Lacy
Lot 8; The other or remaining Part of the name Piece or Parcel of Land, 2a 7p.
Purchased by John Hancock Bridge Ash Bishopstone Shopkeeper
Lot 9; A Parcel of Land, allotted to the aformentioned Premises by the Commissioners, 2r 2p.
Purchased by Sir John Geers Cotterell

New Houses and Cottages built during this period

The Rev Adam Walker's New Rectory as recorded earlier had just been built in 1812.
Jeremiah Apperley built a brick cottage on plot 4 soon after William Watkins' sale around 1813. This was the first brick cottage to be built in the parish.

(Figure 13) 1970s photo of Apperley's brick cottage

After Jeremiah died in 1820 his wife Elizabeth had a timber framed and thatch cottage built on the east side of the plot to house her workman John Barnes, a wheelwright. In the 1880s a brick cottage was built on the south end of the original cottage to form a double dwelling.

Mr Benjamin Turner yeoman of Weobley built Downshill House between 1809-14 on a plot of ground called Dunsell Croft, purchased from Thomas Bethel in 1809 for £175.
Benjamin Turner, like so many other farmers, was in financial difficulties soon after he built the house, so he put the new house up for sale by advertising it in the Hereford Journal.

To be sold by Private Contract; *A neat, newly erected brick-built messuage, with slate covering called Downsell House. Comprising a Kitchen 15 feet by 14, with a Parlour of the same dimensions, Brewhouse, Pantry, underground Cellar, four excellent Lodging rooms on the first floor, with an attic storey over the whole which would make four more comfortable bedrooms; also a new Barn and Stable of stone, together with a pleasant Garden adjoining the house, and a piece of rich Land, part thereof planted with fruit trees; lying within a short distance from the Turnpike road leading to Hereford, and six miles distance therefrom.*
The premises are Freehold, and desirably situate in the parish of Bishopstone, near to Garnons, and command a beautiful extensive view over the most valuable lands in the county, and also of the River Wye, and the country abounds with game of every description.
The same may be viewed by applying to Mr. B. Turner, the proprietor on the spot. Possession maybe had immediately.

The house didn't sell, so Benjamin Turner approached John Smith of Townsend Farm Bishopstone who was also in financial difficulty and they agreed on a joint auction. Benjamin Turner put in Downshill House and John Smith some land, the auction advertised in the Hereford Journal was held at the Salmon Inn, Bridge Boat on April 11th 1814.
Sir John Cotterell's agent attended the sale and purchased Downshill House. The lease and release, an early form of conveyance dated May 26th 1814, states that John Geers Cotterell paid £530 to Benjamin Turner for the house, building and land.
John Smith did not sell any of his land that was offered for sale at the auction.
Benjamin Turner stayed on living in the house as a tenant until 1824, when Thomas T Gough, Gent rented Downshill House until 1839. The Reverend John James Skully, curate of Mansel Gamage Church became the next tenant, paying a rent of £25 per year. Rev Skully helped out with services at Bishopstone Church until the arrival of the new rector, the Rev Lane Freer. Throughout this period Sir John Cotterell was trying to link the livings of Bridge Sollers and Mansel Gamage together. Mr Skully resigned because of his wife's ill heath, and moved to Cleobury Mortimer; he wrote to Sir John on August 3rd 1846 asking for payment for curtains left at Downshill House, which the land agent Mr Blashill had promised to pay for. In late 1846 Rev Skully became the curate at Newent in Glos where he died on March 2nd 1848.
His death was recorded in the Hereford Journal of March 8th 1848.
At the Vicarage Newent, after a few days illness Rev John James Skully, curate of Newent, Chaplain to the Newent Union Workhouse in his 45th year, the deceased left a widow and seven small children.
William Pember, alehouse keeper from the Red Lion Inn at Yazor, son of John Pember, New Inn Bishopstone, purchased from the Foxley estate 30 acres of land plus Banbury Hall cottage at the beginning of the 19th century. He also purchased John Williams's old enclosures and allotment No 50, on which he built a new stone double cottage.

Hereford Journal

To be sold by auction at the Red Lion Inn Yazor on Monday 17th day of August 1818 at four o'clock in the afternoon subject to conditions of sale to be then and there produced in the following lots.

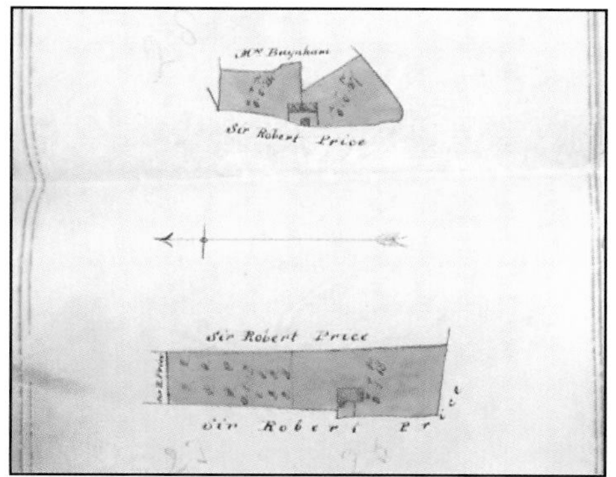

(Figure 14) Sale plan with tithe numbers written on in pencil.

Lot 1; Two new built stone Dwelling Houses and necessary building, under one roof in excellent repair, and two gardens adjoining in possession of John Holder and James Turner, yearly tenants.

Lot 2; Another Messuage Dwelling house, and building all in good repair, two gardens. In possession of John Butler.

The above premises of situate in the parish of Bishopstone in the County of Hereford on the south side of Bishopstone Hill in the midst of Sir John Cotterell's plantations and command a delightful prospect of the River Wye and adjacent country.

Similar to all the other auctions in this period, the properties did not sell. Soon afterwards William Pember agreed to sell 30 acres of land and one old cottage above Clay Pitts farm to Sir John Cotterell. On May 23rd 1821-he received £200 plus £48 for the standing timber from Sir John's solicitor; he still retained the possession of Banbury Hall plus the three cottages on the hill. After William's death these properties passed to his son George who sold all the properties to Garnons in the late 1880s.

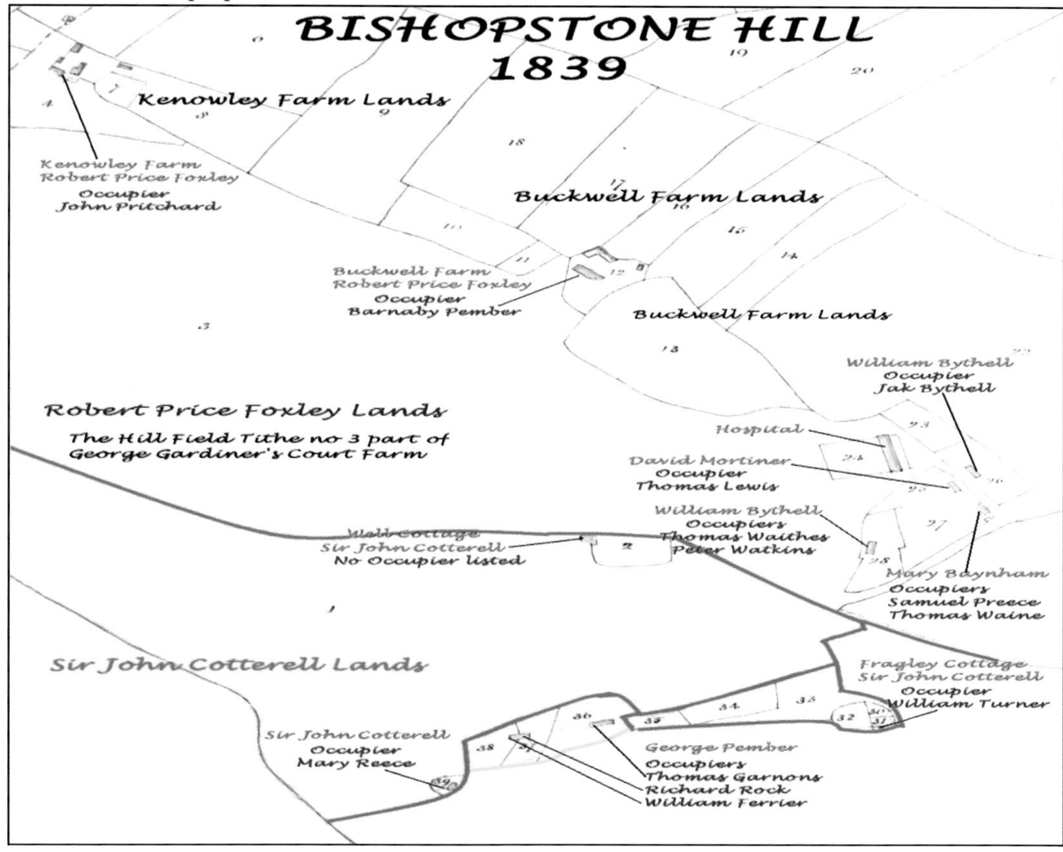

(Figure 15) Taken from the original 1839 Tithe Map with modern descriptions

It appears that alehouse keepers were the only people making money, because William Bethel and William Pember both built new cottages. The addition of these four new cottages made a total of fifteen cottages on Bishopstone Hill, the highest number ever recorded. When you add in the Almshouses, Buckwell Farm and Kenowley Farm it makes a total of twenty three homes occupied on the Hill in the 1830's, of which only one survives, Swiss Cottage now used as a shooting lodge by Garnon's Estate.

Bishon Common had an even more radical change throughout this period with many more houses built on allotments. Henry Edwards of Bunshill Farm saw the opportunity to supply housing for his workman. In the 1820s he purchased two allotments, numbers 27 and 29. On 29 he built a stone cottage followed by a pair of cottages on 27.

(Figure 16) 1970s photo of Stonehouse (142) Bishon Common. One of only two original cottages left from 1839.

Others followed Henry Edward's example, in 1820 Elizabeth Williams built a timber framed cottage on allotment 36, John Lewis and John Clayton built on allotments 35 and 40, William Vaughan also built a cottage on land he purchased from John Tringham. This added seven new cottages to the four already built, plus the pair of cottages in Brinsop, and another pair in Mansel Lacy making a total of 14 properties in the area of Bishon common.

John Smith Snr of Townsend Farm died in 1823. After his death his son John struggled to keep the farm solvent; he also became another victim of the agricultural recession forcing him into selling his farms and lands to Sir John Cotterell in 1827.

As part of the sale agreement he and his mother were allowed to continue living at Townsend Farm for the rest of their natural lives. John only lived another year and was buried in Bishopstone Churchyard on August 2nd 1828 aged just 37. After John's death, his mother Ann moved to Colwall to live with her daughter. The Smith family are remembered on a marble plaque in Bishopstone Church positioned in the south transept. This sale ended the family's ownership of the land that had started a hundred years earlier when Ann's great grandfather John Evans bought the farm.

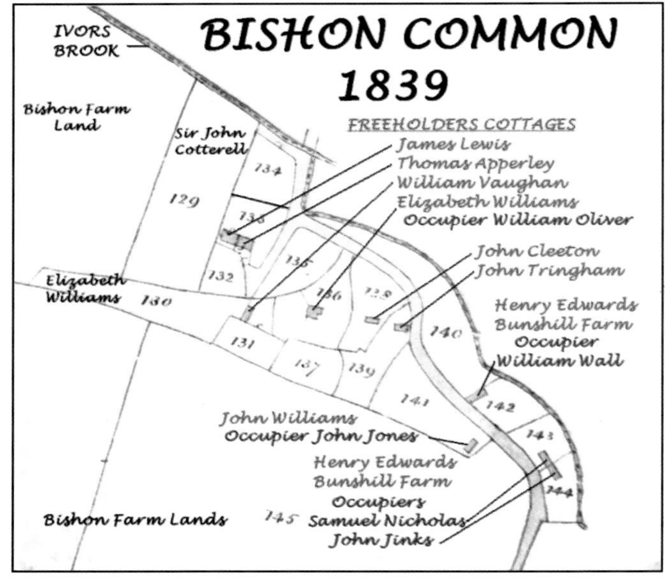

(Figure 17) Taken from original 1839 tithe map with modern descriptions.

Sir John Cotterell also purchased Birley Close from John Hope of Brecon in 1824, Birley Close stood next door and north of Townsend Farm, and was known locally as Annie Archer's Cottage as she was the last occupant. John Hope was a descendant of Ann Archer and had inherited the smallholding that was one of the original messuages left from the old medieval village. The deeds for the property go back to 1669 when one John Savaker occupied it; the latest deed described it as a messuage with barns and outbuildings standing on a one-acre plot. In 1669 Birley Close sold for £40 including the mandatory two strips in each of the three common fields; in 1824 Sir John Cotterell gave £80 for the cottage and buildings but it was never occupied again and pulled down.

After acquiring John Smith's land Sir John now had ownership of all the land between the Garnons mansion and Bishopstone Road, so the long awaited east drive could be built. Lena Lodge was built in 1828 to guard the entrance, but for various reasons the drive was never finished.

Lena Lodge was used to house estate workers. After the completion of the lodge, Garnons Estate built a pair of three bedroom stone cottages called Scaldback Cottages, named after the meadow they were built on, these were used as extra housing for their expanding workforce.

Samuel Powell built Rose Cottage in 1834, later called Peartree Cottage, on part of Joseph Pritchard's garden opposite Forge Cottage.

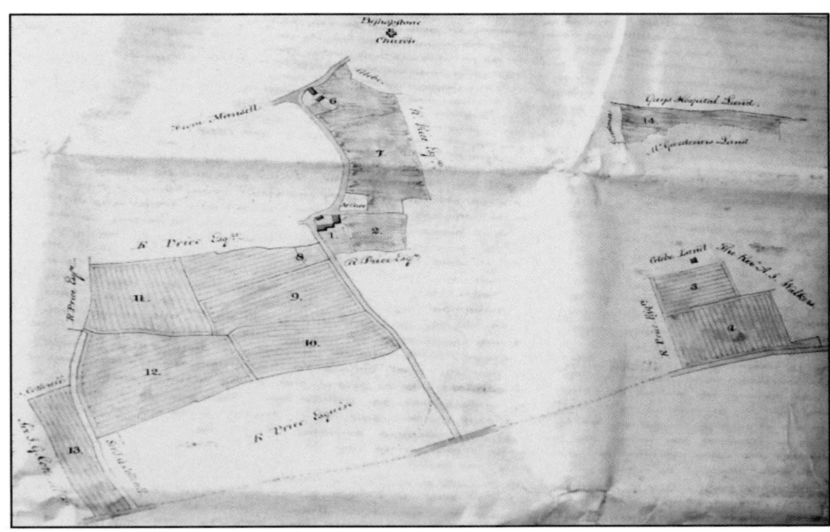

(Figure 18) 1828 sale map includes The Stocks, Townsend Farm and over 40 acres of land. John Smith had been the largest private landowner in Bishopstone. Scaldback Cottages were built on plot 4, Lena Lodge on plot 10.

George Proctor the carpenter built 'The Cottage' on Bishon lane in 1837 on land he purchased from John Hancock, the shopkeeper from Bridge Ash. Henry Edward of Bunshill Farm provided the £100 mortgage to build the house.
The Reverend Lane Freer built his new lodge, drive, and entrance gates in 1841.
Twenty-five new properties were built in Bishopstone parish over this thirty-year period.

(Figure 19) Lena Lodge

(Figure 20) Scaldback Cottages

Tithe Map

Tithes originated before the Norman Conquest; the essential purpose was to provide an income for the minister of the church but a portion might be used to repair the church or relieve the poor. This tax of one tenth of the yearly proceeds arising from the land and from the personal industry of the inhabitants was paid in produce gathered from the land.
The Tithe Commutation Act of 1836, which converted the duty into a money payment, finally ended payment in kind. The tithe record resulting from this act comprises three main elements, a large-scale map, an accompanying apportionment on which are listed the names of owners and occupiers of property together with the size of their holdings, and a file of material collected by the commissioners during the course of their work.
John Johns was appointed assistant Tithe Commissioner for Bishopstone parish just before Christmas 1835, a very detailed survey was carried out, and he held meetings in the parish to explain to the landowners the working out of tithe payments in money and in his words *"fairly presented the sum which ought to be the basi of a permanent commutation of paid Tithes".*
This legal document with detailed map gives the exact position of every house, building and details of land ownership in Bishopstone, naming the tenants and what land they occupied in 1839. As a historian it is an invaluable document.
Notes recorded by the commissioner.
I find that the Rector for the time being is entitled to the Tithes.
He declares he hereby awards an annual sum of £183 per annum to the provision of the said Act, and a further sum of £13 14s to be paid to the Rector in lieu of all the Tithes for the Glebe land.
Act passed June 7th 1839, Total due for Bishopstone £196 14s
This parish was actually measured to contain seven hundred and sixty seven acres plus the roads measurement of nine acres two rods twenty five perches.

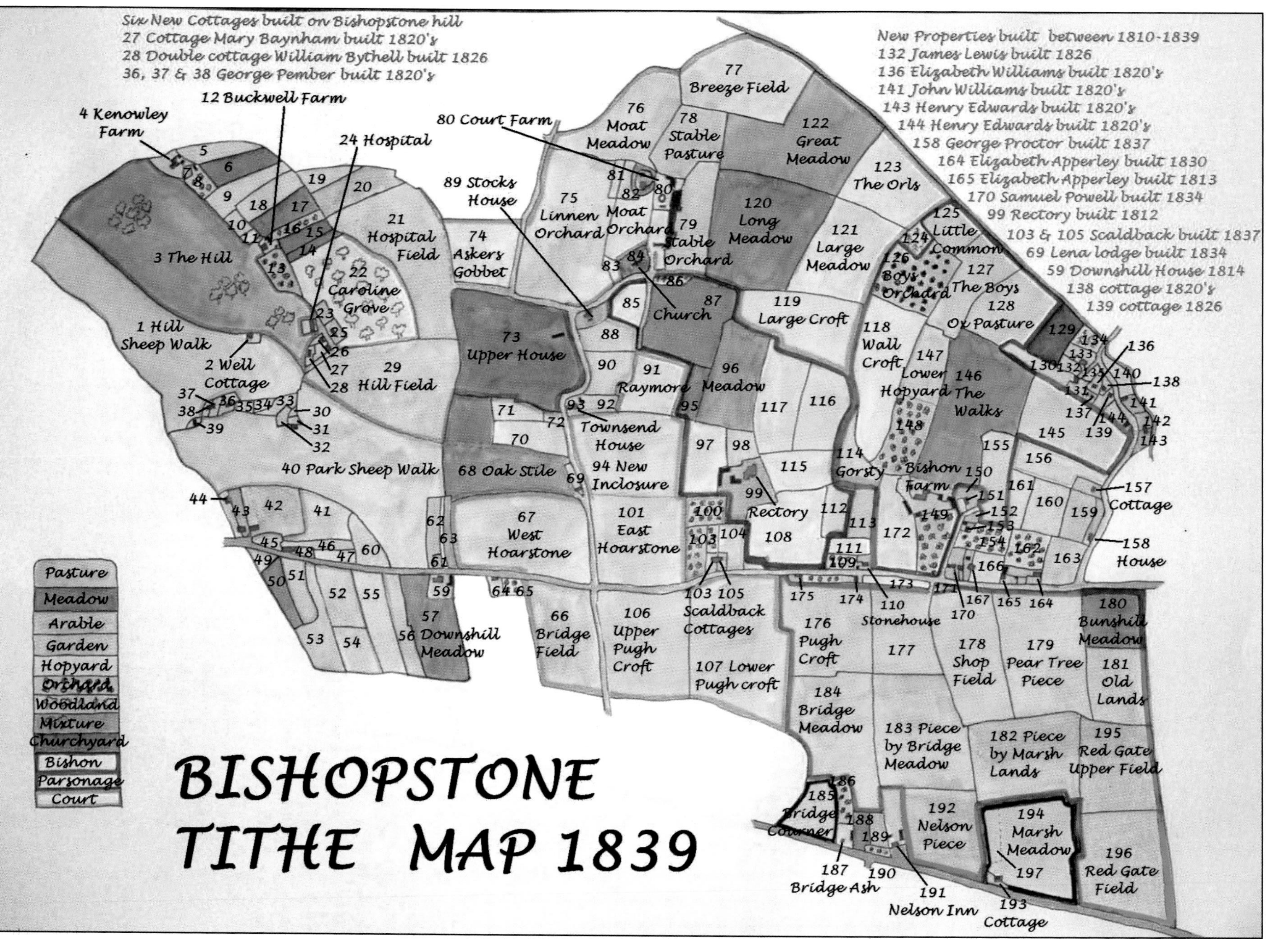
BISHOPSTONE TITHE MAP 1839
Six New Cottages built on Bishopstone hill
27 Cottage Mary Baynham built 1820's
28 Double cottage William Bythell built 1826
36, 37 & 38 George Pember built 1820's
New Properties built between 1810-1839
132 James Lewis built 1826
136 Elizabeth Williams built 1820's
141 John Williams built 1820's
143 Henry Edwards built 1820's
144 Henry Edwards built 1820's
158 George Proctor built 1837
164 Elizabeth Apperley built 1830
165 Elizabeth Apperley built 1813
170 Samuel Powell built 1834
99 Rectory built 1812
103 & 105 Scaldback built 1837
69 Lena lodge built 1834
59 Downshill House 1814
138 cottage 1820's
139 cottage 1826
Pasture
Meadow
Arable
Garden
Hopyard
Orchard
Woodland
Mixture
Churchyard
Bishon
Parsonage
Court
4 Kenowley Farm
12 Buckwell Farm
24 Hospital
80 Court Farm
89 Stocks House
1 Hill Sheep Walk
2 Well Cottage
3 The Hill
21 Hospital Field
22 Caroline Grove
29 Hill Field
40 Park Sheep Walk
56 Downshill Meadow
66 Bridge Field
67 West Hoarstone
68 Oak Stile
73 Upper House
74 Askers Gobbet
75 Linnen Orchard
76 Moat Meadow
77 Breeze Field
78 Stable Pasture
79 Stable Orchard
82 Moat Orchard
87 Church
91 Raymore
93 Townsend House
94 New Inclosure
96 Meadow
99 Rectory
101 East Hoarstone
103 105 Scaldback Cottages
106 Upper Pugh Croft
107 Lower Pugh croft
110 Stonehouse
114 Gorsty
118 Wall Croft
119 Large Croft
120 Long Meadow
121 Large Meadow
122 Great Meadow
123 The Orls
125 Little Common
126 Boys Orchard
127 The Boys
128 Ox Pasture
146 The Walks
147 Lower Hopyard
150 Bishon Farm
157 Cottage
158 House
176 Pugh Croft
178 Shop Field
179 Pear Tree Piece
180 Bunshill Meadow
181 Old Lands
182 Piece by Marsh Lands
183 Piece by Bridge Meadow
184 Bridge Meadow
185 Bridge Courner
187 Bridge Ash
191 Nelson Inn
192 Nelson Piece
193 Cottage
194 Marsh Meadow
195 Red Gate Upper Field
196 Red Gate Field

Easter Vestry Meeting

Like all other parishes in the early 19th century Bishopstone was an ecclesiastical unit, dating back to the Middle Ages. From a spiritual and social point of view the church exerted a great influence over the villagers' lives while in the 16th century the parishes' importance increased with extra administrative duties imposed on them by the government. The constable for instance, became an important executive officer as well as a law enforcement agent. In 1555 each parish was made responsible for its highways and a surveyor was appointed annually to oversee the repair of them. Overseers of the poor were also appointed annually; parish officials were normally chosen at an Easter meeting in the parish vestry. The parish rate was set to cover the costs of the highways, poor relief and the village constable. An entry in the earliest surviving minute book of Bishopstone vestry meeting dated March 30th 1841 illustrates how the system works.

Present Rev Lane Freer Chairman, Rector
Mr George Gardiner Churchwarden for Rector (Court Farm)
Mr B Pember Churchwarden for parishioners (Buckwell farm)
Mr Higgins (Townsend Farm, shoemaker)
Mr Benjamin Gardiner (Bishon Farm)
Mr Proctor (The Cottage Bishon Lane, carpenter)

Mr Higgins (Shoemaker, Townsend) and Mr Hancock (Shopkeeper, Bridge Ash) were elected overseers of the poor.
Mr George Gardiner was elected overseer of the roads.
Mr John Apperley (Wheelwright, The Clovers) was elected constable.
The parish rate was set at 5d in the pound.

These appointed officials looked after the basic day-to-day running of the parish taking over from the old manorial courts that had finished over a hundred years earlier. Basically the parish was bankrupt, the accounts show that in 1827 George Gardiner, elected overseer of the poor, was using his own money to keep the system working. The parishioners could not afford to pay their proportion of the poor rate. The same with the roads in the parish, the parishioners were struggling to keep them in good repair. Every parishioner had to give their time free to maintain the roads. Cartloads of stone usually picked from the fields by children, were tipped at strategic places around the roads and at the quiet times in the agriculture calendar men, women and children would work as teams under the supervision of the overseer digging out mud from the road surface and refilling with stone, while the largest stones were broken up with a napping hammer. This system with stone infill was used on parish byroads until The Local Government Act of 1894 saw the county council take over the maintenance of the roads.

Richard Lane Freer

(Figure 21) Richard Lane Freer

Richard Lane Freer was arguably the most distinguished person ever to live in Bishopstone; he was Rector for 24 years from 1839 until he died on August 11th 1863. There are two books written about his life, he also published a book about his sermons. The two books can be seen in the reference section of Hereford Library, well worth a read. I have included only a brief outline of his life, and some of the legacies he left in Bishopstone. Richard Lane Freer totally refurbished Bishopstone Church, extended the Rectory and built a new lodge. He was an academic and although he had a privileged upbringing his vocation in life was to help the poor. He was born in 1805 at Handsworth, Birmingham, the youngest son of the Reverend Thomas Lane Freer MA who was a direct descendent of Jane Lane, heroic daughter of Colonel Lane, who in the time of the Civil War assisted the escape of Charles II by carrying him before her on horseback from Worcester to Bristol where he succeeded in getting safely to France. His mother was the daughter of Nathan Wetherell, Dean of Hereford who could trace his genealogy through a direct line back to Gorman, King of the Danes in A.D.700.

Richard Lane Freer was educated at Westminster School, and then attended Christ's College Oxford where he graduated in 1828. In 1829 Dr. Cornwall, Bishop of Worcester ordained him deacon and he became curate to his father in his native parish of Handsworth. He carried on his studies and gained a M.A. in 1834. Whilst at the university he met Uvedale Price of Mongewell House, Oxford who became his best friend, he was the son of the Reverend Dr. Robert Price, younger brother of Sir Uvedale Price of Foxley. It was through Richard's friendship with the Price family that he was offered the living of the Rectory of Bishopstone and Vicarage of Yazor in 1839, and in 1841 the census lists Uvedale Price as a guest of Richard Lane Freer staying at Bishopstone Rectory. In 1848 when he was 43 years old Richard Lane Freer married his cousin Harriet, daughter of the Rev John Clutton D.D. Canon of Hereford Cathedral and Rector of Kinnersley. A report of the marriage appeared in the Hereford Journal dated May 17th 1848.

Marriage of Rev R Lane Freer with Miss Clutton, St Nicholas Church, on Tuesday morning last. Soon after 10.00 o'clock, crowds of persons assembled in the vicinity of the Church. His Grace the Archbishop of York who performed the marriage ceremony arrived on Monday evening when a peal of bells from the Cathedral and All Saints rang to mark his arrival. At 11.00 His Grace left the residence of Canon Musgrove Broad Street, to St Nicholas Church, crowds thronging the streets, the marriage party left the residence of the bride's mother in Castle Street, arriving at the church gate, in carriages and pairs. (where an immense crowd rendered the presence of the police necessary to clear a passage). Bridesmaids Miss Macmichael and Miss Rowden. Bridegrooms men, Rev J Lucy and Master Dowdeswell, immediately surrounding the communion rails were Sir Robert and Lady Price, Miss Cotterell, The Rev Canon Musgrove and Mrs Musgrove, Rev J Johnson, Rev J Rogers. The Cathedral bells rang at intervals during the day.

This abbreviated report gives a flavour of the day, it also reflects the importance of the couple in Herefordshire society.

When he arrived at Bishopstone Rectory in 1839, Richard brought his mother and six servants with him, including a butler and his gardener, William Wilson, who was Scottish. Richard's mother was a well-travelled lady who persuaded him to extend the Rectory at his own expense to produce one of the largest in the diocese. After it was finished the ground floor contained four reception rooms and a parish room, the dinning room, was extended to a length of 30 feet as specified by Richard's mother; he later reported "she needed a large dining room to accommodate her needs". Richard had a new south drive put in to join the Roman road complete with a new lodge to guard the entrance; the original drive down to Bishopstone church was now only used as a private carriageway for his own personal access to the church. The new drive and lodge were completed by 1841 as shown by the plaque on the wall of the lodge accompanied by Richard's initials.

With William Wilson's help he transformed the fields down to the church by landscaping them into parkland, planting many specimen trees.

In 1841 with the aid of the County surveyor John Gray he restored the church at Bishopstone at his own expense.

The ancient parish church was in a state of woeful dilapidation as stated in early nineteenth century documents. It was a typical country parish church with flagstone floors and stone interior walls, and in need of a lot of repairs.

(Figure 22) The church after the 1841 restoration showing the flagstone flooring, which was replaced by tiles in 1854. Note! The pulpit on the left and Dutch almsplate positioned on the Altar

Richard commissioned a new stained glass east widow by Warrington of London in 1841, the other windows were restored and the roof removed and some of the trusses replaced. The interior walls were plastered, false cross beams were fitted between the original trusses, and coloured sheet metal scrolls displaying texts from the bible were hung on the walls.

Sarah Lane Freer (Richard's mother) died while visiting friends in Southsea on January 11th 1842 aged 65. She was buried in Kingston Hampshire but always regarded her main residence as the Rectory in Bishopstone and Richard commissioned a stained glass window to her memory in Bishopstone church. This was installed in the small south window by the altar, and contained glass panels, which he had personally collected as a young man on his grand tour of Italy on his way to the Holy Land. He also commissioned a marble monument by Peter Hollins that hangs on the north wall of the chancel. Sarah left the bulk of her wealth to Richard, including a lot of silver plate, while the rest was split between her eldest son the Reverend John Lane Freer, who was a chaplain to the Marines, and her daughter Mary.

(Figure 23) 1841 date hidden in the east window

In 1844 Uvedale Price of Mongewell House, purchased a Father Smith organ that had originally stood in Eton College. This was enlarged and improved under the direction of Vincent Novello and Uvedale presented it to his friend Richard Lane Freer who placed it in Bishopstone church. Uvedale never saw the organ finally installed in the church as he died suddenly in 1844 aged only 40 years. There is more information about this famous old organ later on in the book.

In 1854 the interior of the church was completely gutted for the second time. The floor was re-laid with Godwins of Withington encaustic floor tiles, the first to be laid in this county. The seating was increased to seat 200, and the ancient porch from Yazor's old church was moved to Bishopstone replacing the original structure. When it was finished it had the most ornate and beautiful fabric of any church in the diocese. Uvedale Price had started to build a new church at Yazor; but because of his untimely death his friend Richard Lane Freer completed the project, building the spire and the internal decorations and putting in the stained-glass windows at his own cost.

After completely restoring these two churches, Richard was responsible in his lifetime for overseeing the erection of 18 new churches and 72 restorations in his role as Archdeacon of Hereford.

In Bishopstone church he maintained a 30 strong, well-trained choir with an organist/choirmaster that was the envy of the other parish churches, incidental expenses associated with the choir being paid for by Richard. The 1861 census lists John Whitney (Professor of Music) as the church organist living at the Rectory Lodge. James Hunt another organist died in 1845 aged 15, Rev Lane Freer mounted a plaque on the south church wall in his memory.

(Figure 24) Isambard Kingdom Brunel's Great Eastern liner

On August 16th 1862 Richard left Liverpool for a six-week voyage to America aboard the Great Eastern, a paddle and screw driven liner with six sailing masts and 800 people aboard. This was Isambard Kingdom Brunel's new liner, twice as large as any ship built before.

Richard wrote a complete journal on the trip, a copy of which is kept in the Hereford Library; it makes very interesting reading.

The ship hit a rock on Wednesday August 27th 1862 while approaching New York harbour, and started to list badly so all the passengers were evacuated by small craft to the nearest shore, in Richard's case Flushing Meadow. Whilst in America, Richard witnessed troops passing through New York travelling south to fight in the Civil War. He travelled to Alabama, Niagara then back to New York; because of the repairs needed to the Great Eastern after colliding with the rocks on the inward passage, her return voyage was delayed. So Richard went to the Cunard line and booked to come home on the Persia, a smaller ship, which left New York on September 10th 1862. After a rough crossing he decided to disembark at Cork onto the Robert Bruce, a small steamer that conveyed mail into the harbour. He disembarked on September 19th and caught a train back to Hereford.

In 1851 Richard became a magistrate and in 1852 the Bishop of Hereford, Dr. Hampden, appointed him to the office of Archdeacon of Hereford. After his marriage he encouraged his wife Harriet to start a school in the parish room at the rectory. Later in the book there is a section that covers a detailed account of Bishopstone School.
In January 1854 Richard gave a lecture to the Diocesan Education Association in which he says that his parish school educates the labourers' children, farming children and a child from a respectable solicitor. After a visit to one of his parishioners in Bishopstone he reflects *"it is really preposterous to go into a labourer's cottage, and find a man paid 7s a week, and then talk to him about educating his children. The poverty of these people, where every hand is so valuable that it is almost impossible for poor men or women to refuse to allow their children to go and work when a neighbouring farmer summons them".*
Richard was extremely proud of the new parkland he had created leading down to the church, called the Lawns; a footpath used by the villagers to walk to church skirted the edge which they had to stick to, they were not allowed to walk down using the newly laid stone drive. Richard was a smoker and enjoyed his pipe and cigars and was also a passionate cricketer.
In 1861, while yachting, a fall from a rope ladder injured the lower part of his spine. This caused a recurring problem that affected his health and was thought to have contributed to his death. In August 1863 he fell ill in Dover, and determined to return home he travelled to Malvern, stayed there to rest for a few days and finally arrived home at his beloved Rectory on Sunday 9th August. Sadly, Richard died two days later on Tuesday August 11th 1863.
Seventy clergy attended his funeral; the shops in Hereford were closed in the afternoon as a mark of respect.

HEREFORD TIMES AUGUST 22nd 1863

Funeral of the **Ven. ARCHDEACON LANE FREER,D.D.**

The remains of the Ven Richard Lane Freer D. D. Rector of Bishopstone and Archdeacon of Hereford, were deposited in their last resting-place on Monday afternoon last, in Bishopstone churchyard amidst the silent tears of very many, who evidently felt that a sincere friend and kind and good Christian pastor had been taken from them. In accordance with his express wish the funeral was to be as unostentatious as possible. Many of the villagers and people of the district congregated round the sacred enclosure, but to take a last look of all that remains of him whose memory, in connection with his good work in kindness of heart, will be cherished in grateful remembrance. Those who had known him longest loved him the most, and it seemed a generally expressed fear that his like will never be seen again in the Hereford Arch Deaconry. His demise is regarded as the most serious loss, which the Church in this county has sustained for many years; but it is hoped that he is a good example and the enviable name he has left behind will stimulate others to walk in the same steps.
Five o'clock was the hour named for the funeral, but an hour prior to that the church bell tolled slowly, indicating that someone is about to be borne to his last home. It seems difficult, however to bring the mind to believe that, on so lovely an afternoon, when all nature looked so pleasant and inviting, whilst the waving cornfields smiled and air seemed so balmy, it was he who being the chief spirit in the restoring the pretty church, he who being the village pastor and friend to the poor for so many years, he who was ready to give temporal as well as spiritual assistance, he who was beloved by everybody rich and poor, who had resigned his charge, and whose body was now about to be placed in the cold and silent earth in the midst of his parishioners, over very many of whom he had performed their last rites of the Church, another was now called to discharge for him. Yet so it was. The body was borne from the rectory on the shoulders of four of the labourers on the estate, and as the procession moved slowly down the pleasant walk towards the church, very many gave vent to their pent-up feelings and sorrowed over their personal loss.
The grave was a common earth one quite shallow, and when the last portion of the service was over, the majority of those present took a last look and departed in silence.

The coffin was made by Mr. William Jones, Mansel Lacy from oak grown on the estate. It was exceedingly well finished, the oak being beautifully polished.
The furnishings were of brass, and on the breast-plate were the words. *"In memory of Richard Lane Freer, D. D., Rector of Bishopstone and Archdeacon of Hereford. Died August 11th 1863, aged fifty-seven years".* A wreath of newly gathered flowers had also been placed on the coffin.

A stained glass window by John Hardman of Birmingham was installed in Hereford Cathedral in his memory at a cost of £1200 paid by public subscription. The largest stained glass window in the cathedral, called the great north transept window, it is easy to identify from outside, as it faces High Town. To really appreciate the beauty of the window and read the inscription written below it, it is best viewed from inside the Cathedral; it also gives a graphic illustration of the high esteem in which Richard Lane Freer was held in the county.

(Figure 25) *Above* North Transept window Hereford Cathedral. *left* Inscription stone to Rev Lane Freer situated below window

In his will proved December 8th 1863 he left just under £25,000, equal to a value of over £4 million in today's money, to his wife and charities. A portrait of Richard Lane Freer still hangs in the Masonic Hall in Hereford.

The Poor Book 1825-36[6]

The entries in the only surviving account book for Bishopstone's overseers of the poor highlight the struggle the poor experienced from 1825 through to 1836. The Poor Law Amendment Act was passed in 1834, to help relieve the financial burden placed on parishes. For some considerable time, certainly since the middle of the 18th century, the old Elizabethan Poor Law had proved to be inadequate. This was certainly true in Bishopstone where the parish overseers could not afford to sustain provisions of the Poor Acts. After the new act was passed the Bishopstone poor were grouped with the surrounding parishes and placed under the umbrella of the newly formed Weobley Union, where a new workhouse to cover this group of parishes was going to be built, yet the records show Bishopstone continued to rent two cottages for the poor until 1855 with money raised from a private rate. Bishopstone was more fortunate than many other parishes in having the Berrington Trust Almshouses, which eased the pressure on the overseers by accommodating six poor people. The account book is grim reading in places and brings home the fact of how destitute the poor were in the nineteenth century, depending on the parish for everything. The overseer paid for everything from housing, food, clothes and shoes to doctor's bills, coffin and finally funeral. The rules laid out in the Act were strictly followed. To qualify for relief you would have to be born in the parish, live for many years in the parish or serve as a churchwarden. After marriage a wife would receive relief from her husband's parish. Since 1601 the parish had looked after its poor as recorded by the few court cases I have mentioned earlier in the book. Reading through these accounts brings home the reality of how the overseers struggled to provide for the poor. The poor cottages built on Bishopstone Hill common by the lord of the manor 200 years earlier had disappeared, fallen down through lack of maintenance. The overseers were now renting cottages on Bishopstone hill from freeholders, the first entry in 1825 shows nine cottages rented to house the poor and by 1834 this had grown to eleven. This is basically one fifth of the housing stock. What struck me straight away in reading the accounts was the fact that people whom I had considered fairly wealthy, like Elizabeth the widow of John Foote Bishon Farm, whose family had held the tenancy on the farm for over 150 years, ended up on parish relief living in a rented cottage. The parish even rented a cottage belonging to Elizabeth's daughter Mary, who it appears had inherited the cottage from her father, leaving her mother destitute. John Williams (parish clerk) owner of three cottages on the hill in 1812 and tenant farmer of Kenowley, would by 1830 also be receiving poor relief, living in the one remaining cottage he owned. John had sold his other cottages to William Pember in 1820; he was eventually admitted into the Almshouse where he lived out the remainder of his life. His old cottage was in such a poor state of repair that by 1839 it had fallen down, only recorded on the tithe map as a garden. These facts show how easily a person could fall into poverty.

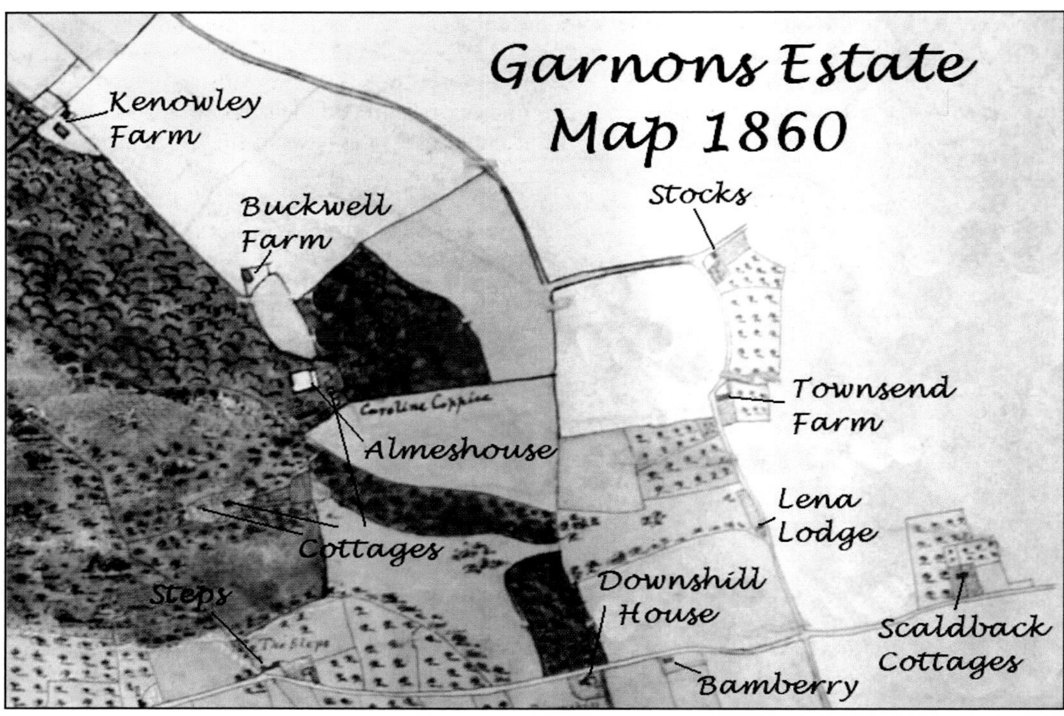

(Figure 26) Part of Garnons estate map shows their land holdings in Bishopstone.

Weekly relief was a payment made to help the old, the sick, widows, mothers with their newborn children and anyone in the parish who had no income. Depending on their circumstances, some received a few pence to help tide them over, where others were paid just enough to survive.

All of the names on the list carry a story of a poor person's predicament. If we pick just two names, Margaret and Ann Morris who each received 2s per week they are both worthy of further investigation. As the surname indicates they were related, Margaret was the Ann's auntie. The Morris family suffered from a genetic disorder which caused blindness in some of the family. Margaret Morris was born in Bishopstone in 1768 and her father Edward was a part time labourer. It's difficult to establish if she was born blind, or suffered the affliction early in her childhood. There are several entries in the Berrington charity records relating to Margaret as the blind girl. She moved into an almshouse as a young teenager after her mother died. In 1783 an unusual entry in the Berrington charity account book records that 10s 6d was deducted from her alms money to pay for the coffin of Susana Parlour a fellow alms person. The charity always paid for the coffins of their inmates; intriguingly was Margaret suspected in some way of contributing to Susana's death and money deducted as a punishment? We can only speculate.

The Disbursement of Tho.s T. Gough Overseer of the Poor of the parish of Bishopstone for 1825 & 1826

Weekly pay

	Weeks				
Mary Haines	52	1/-		4	4
Marg.t Morris	52	2/-	5	4	-
Ann Bedward	26	2/-	2	12	-
D.o D.o	8	2/6	1	-	-
D.o D.o	11	3/6	1	18	6
Ann Watkins	52	1/-	2	12	-
Tho.s Williams	52	2/-	5	4	-
Ann Morris Cl.d	52	2	5	4	-
Geo Philpott	52	4/-	10	8	-
Appeleys Child	52	1/6	3	18	-
Widow Foote	52	1/6	3	18	-
Mr Griffiths daughter	26	2/-	2	12	-
Jn.o Williams Boy	12	1/-	-	12	-
Llewellyns Child	52	2/-	5	4	-
Claytons Child	50	4	-	16	8
			51	7	6

(Figure 27) Page from poor book 1825-26, lists the elderly, infirme and 5 bastard children the parish provided for.

The records show that she was suspended and removed from the Almshouse in 1796 for bad behaviour, but what constituted bad behaviour is not recorded. It could have been for not attending the obligatory church services, or maybe because she was tormented by others because of her blindness. What I think is particularly sad throughout this period is that the Berrington charity records only refer to Margaret as "The Blind Girl". After her removal and some instruction from the lord of the manor, Uvedale Price, Margaret fell back onto the mercy of the parish, living on weekly relief in a parish pauper cottage. During this period Ann Morris, Margaret's niece, a servant girl working in the parish, became pregnant, a not uncommon event for servant girls. With her new illegitimate daughter she moved in with Auntie Margaret, which benefited both parties as both collected relief and Ann looked after her aunt.

The next event in Ann and Margaret's lives was reported in 1827:

"Ann Morris of Bishopstone Hereford having been brought before a magistrate for stealing a rail post, Margaret Morris her aunt in whose house she lodged, offered to swear that within the eight years during which her niece had been living with her she had never seen her bring any stolen article into the dwelling. On cross-examination the old hypocrite confessed that she had been blind for upwards of fifty years so of course she would not have seen anything."

The funny thing is although reprimanded by the court, Margaret was actually telling the truth.

Ann's illegitimate daughter Margaret (named after her auntie) died from smallpox in 1828 and Ann herself died in January 1835 at the age of 37. After Ann's death Margaret Morris was taken back into the Almshouse where she lived out the rest of her life; she died in 1851 aged 83 years after sixty-six years of parish relief. Margaret's nephew John was also struck down with blindness in his late thirties as reported later in the book.

(Figure 28) 1842 watercolour painting of Bishopstone Court gateway

Bishopstone's overseer rented cottages to house the parish poor; the list for 1825-26, records firstly who owned the cottage, followed by the name of the pauper who occupied it, and finally the cost to the parish for the year's rent. I have added the tithe map number for easy reference.

Rentals (cottages to house the poor 1825-26)	**Tithe Map No**	
Hobby's cottage for Thomas Haines (part of rent)	44	£3 04s.00d
Yapp's cottage for James Jones	28	£4 04s 00d
Yapp's cottage for Thomas Williams	28	£4 00s 00d
Mortimer's cottage for Samuel Preece	25	£4 00s 00d
Griffith's cottage for John Eckley (part of rent)	2	£3 14s 06d
Bethel's cottage for Ann Bedward	42	£3 03s 00d
Sir John Cotterell's cottage for Widow Foote (part of rent)	30	£1 05s 00d
George Gardiner's cottage for John Griffith	32	£4 00s 00d
Mrs Smith's cottage for John Jones	26	£3 03s 00d
	Total	£82 01s 00d

John Hancock the grocer, of Bridge Ash, was elected overseer of the poor at the Easter Vestry meeting in 1826 replacing Thomas Gough Gent of Downshill House. The Hancock family had lived in Bishopstone for over a century, they were well known and respected and John's brother James farmed Claypitts. The unpaid job as Bishopstone's overseer of the poor held high responsibilities. John's decisions on whether to give a relief payment could determine a life or death situation for some paupers. He would have experienced many a knock on the door, day and night asking for help. From the records it appears that John was more generous than previous overseers, spending £153.5s.10d in the year and only collecting £139 11s 3d in poor rates.

The list of defaulters on payment of the poor rates is interesting, Mrs Smith of Townsend Farm owed £6 10s 8d: we know she was in financial trouble after her husband John had died. William Wall, parish mason with a huge family to support, living in a rented cottage on Bishon Common, defaulted on 2s 4d; Elizabeth Powell the blacksmith defaulted on 8s 4d which indicates that tradesmen were also suffering in this depression. In 1826 John Hancock inherited thirteen poor people in the parish on weekly pay; every week they visited his shop to collect their money, ranging from 1s for Ann Boucher up to 3s 6d for Ann Bedward. The eight cottages rented to house the poor were also his responsibility.

The casual disbursements, cash paid to relieve the poor, needed decisions on the spot. John made eighty nine payments over his year in office, mostly as relief for illness, where those who could not work were paid a shilling a week. Other payments included laying out George Philpots for which a woman was paid two shillings. John Jones' wife received 5s for lying in, a term used for a payment made after giving birth. During the year clothes costing 10s 6d and a pair of shoes costing 5s 9d were given to Apperley's illegitimate daughter.

To add to the expenses in this year two more families fell into poverty. John Williams fell ill: in April 1826 the account book recorded that Phillip Bishop's boy was paid 1s 6d for going to fetch the doctor for John Williams. Betty, John's wife was paid 5s 6d to buy butter and flour during this illness. This appears to have been the standard procedure; flour was given so bread could be baked and faggots of wood plus coal were also supplied. John Williams died on May 17th and was laid out by Mary Preece for 2s. The doctor was called as a last resort; most paupers appear to die a few weeks after he was summoned. In September Betty Williams fell ill herself and Mrs Bishop was paid 2s a week to care for her.

Doctor J Morgan charged one bill of £6 in the year; the overseer only gave permission to fetch a doctor in very serious cases of sickness. With £6 the overseer could rent a cottage for eighteen months to provide housing for a poor family.

Thomas Haines and his family had been receiving poor relief for several years but in the winter of 1826-27 the family suffered; they had been receiving flour, oatmeal, wood and coal throughout the winter but on February 17th they lost their daughter, little Ann aged 2 years. The overseer paid out just 16s for her shroud and coffin made by John Stephens. The family were given clothes, flour and mutton after Ann's funeral. Thomas, who could not work full time for some unknown reason, met a tragic end; he was killed by a bull and buried on May 20th 1835, this placed his wife and children to be totally dependent on the parish. George Gardiner Bishon Farm settled up all the £20 arrears at the end of the financial year out of his own pocket. At the next parish meeting, held at Easter 1827, George himself was elected overseer of the poor, a position he held for the next six years; it needed a firmer hand to keep the spending under control.

Parish overseers always kept a weather eye on local unmarried females, because they were always concerned about illegitimate children; the parish was responsible for the upkeep of any such children born in the parish, which placed an extra expense on them. Margaret Hancock's was a typical case that began on January 7th 1832. The first step carried out by the overseer George Gardiner, after spotting she was pregnant, was called an examination, this was not a physical examination but more an interview to find out who was the father. If the woman was willing to name him a summons followed to ensure he paid for the upbringing of his child. Margaret Hancock never divulged who the father was, so George placed an order of removal from the parish on Margaret. She also refused to say from which parish she came. So George Gardener charged the parish 5s for a journey into Hereford to establish Margaret Hancock's home parish. He must have found out the information, as Margaret is not recorded as living in the parish after this date. There were many examinations of pregnant women in the eleven years the account book covers. Some never told the overseer who the father of the child was, unlike Elizabeth Morgan. After her examination on July 31st 1830 when she named the father as a former parishioner John Williams, a warrant was issued against him and John Proctor, the parish constable, was sent to serve the warrant. On September 15th John Williams was finally examined at a cost of 10s 6d to the parish, money paid to John Proctor for apprehending him and physically returning him to Bishopstone so George Gardiner could question him, when he confirmed that he was the father. John was up to his old tricks again in 1833; this time Charlotte Wiley named John Williams as father of her child and the overseer, George Gardiner, ordered his removal from the parish. John did not leave quietly, as on February 11th 1833 the overseer made a journey to Hereford at a cost of 6s to answer the complaint of John Williams. Often a removal order was obtained without serious intention of carrying it out forthwith but to force a settlement certificate, this procedure appears to have worked with John Williams.

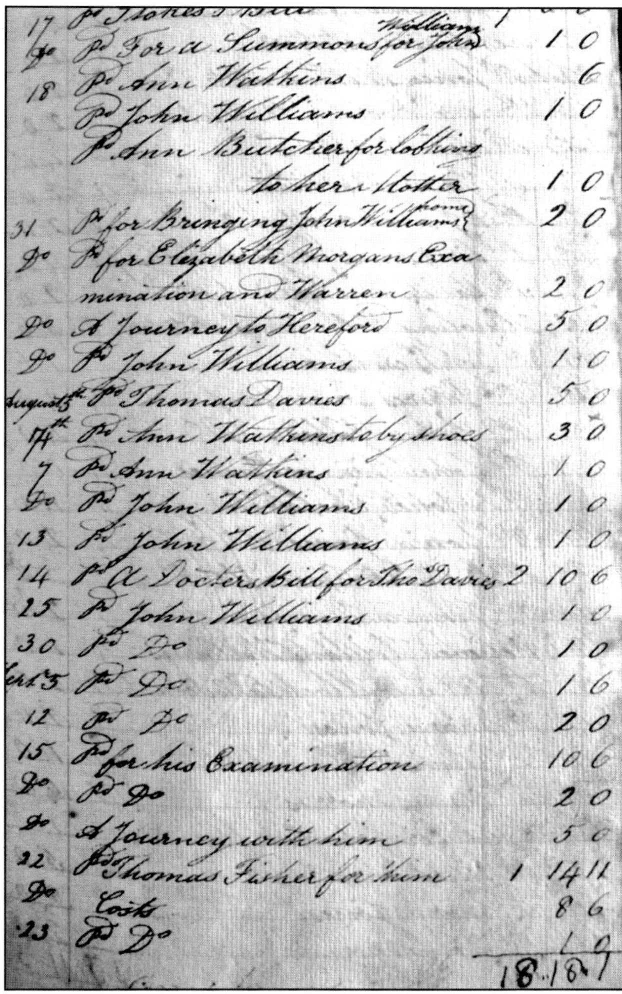

17 Pd Stones's Bill ...
do Pd For a Summons for John William 1 0
18 Pd Ann Watkins 6
Pd John Williams 1 0
Pd Ann Butcher for clothing to her Mother 1 0
31 Pd for Bringing John Williams home 2 0
do Pd for Elizabeth Morgans Examination and Warren 2 0
do A Journey to Hereford 5 0
do Pd John Williams 1 0
August 5th Pd Thomas Davies 5 0
7th Pd Ann Watkins to buy shoes 3 0
7 Pd Ann Watkins 1 0
do Pd John Williams 1 0
13 Pd John Williams 1 0
14 Pd A Doctors Bill for Thos Davies 2 10 6
25 Pd John Williams 1 0
30 Pd do 1 0
Oct 5 Pd do 1 6
12 Pd do 2 0
15 Pd for his Examination 10 6
do Pd do 2 0
do A Journey with him 5 0
22 Pd Thomas Fisher for him 1 14 11
do Costs 8 6
23 Pd do 1 0
18 18 7

(Figure 29) Page from the poor book 1830 recording the expense John Williams caused the parish by fathering a bastard child.

Reading between the lines it's easy to imagine some of the scenes. Take Ann Parlour, she had tried to obtain relief from another parish but was instructed to claim on Bishopstone. She arrives walking into the parish on December 4th 1833, and on asking where she can find the overseer; she is directed down to Bishon Farm. On her arrival George would have sent out a boy to fetch the parish constable John Stephens, who would have been working in his wheelwright shop behind his cottage (now called the Old Post Office). Ann appears in ill health and is accompanied by a three-year-old child. She explains that this is her husband's parish so she is entitled to relief, she was married in Bishopstone Church on April 4th 1825 to James Parlour, a volunteer, serving in the navy stationed at Gosport; further questioning reveals the little boy is of no parish as he has never been baptised. Alarm bells start ringing: who is the father of this child? George Gardiner sent a letter to Gosport on December 7th at a cost of 11d to check Ann's story, and a letter was received back on December 16th at a cost of 1s 1d. This must have verified her story because a horse was sent out to fetch the doctor at a cost of 3s to the parish. The story appears to have had a happy ending as Ann recovered, James returned to Bishopstone, and James their son was baptised in Bishopstone church on March 4th 1836 at the age of six years. I am impressed with the very efficient postal system it had only taken nine days for the return letter to arrive, considering that the letters had travelled by mail coach with many changes; interestingly a payment was also made on the receipt of the letter.

A few other entries in the accounts caught my eye. Hereford Infirmary is only recorded twice, firstly Catherine Boares' child was taken to the infirmary on March 29th 1832 at a cost of 16s 4d to the parish; and on May 22nd 1833, Thomas Morgan was taken to the infirmary at a cost of 2s 6d.

The parish constable armed with a warrant could operate outside his parish. For example George Jordan had stopped his payments to the parish for his illegitimate child so on December 17th 1831 George Gardiner went to the magistrates to obtain a warrant to approach him. Constable John Stephens was sent out with this warrant on January 7th 1832 as the book entry records

Apprehended George Jordan for disobeying the order of fileation 5s.

The parish also paid for coffins to bury the paupers; a child's coffin and shroud cost the parish 17s as in the case of Betty Wyatt's daughter on April 3rd 1830. Adults were more expensive: Ann Morris's coffin cost £1 while John Williams's coffin cost £1 2s when the parish buried him on January 16th 1831. John Stephens made all these coffins in his wheelwright's shop.

Unemployed able-bodied men on relief were found a task about the parish. Roads always wanted repairs, as happened in the case of Samuel Clark who came to the overseer for relief for himself and his family who were housed in a cottage on the hill with the rent paid by the overseer. The records show that Samuel was sent up to the quarry on the hill to raise stone for laying onto the roads. He started raising the stone in August 1833, with the parish overseer paying him 11d a yard, and by January 1834 Samuel had single handed quarried 24 tons of stone.

From May 24th 1836 the Weobley Union took over the administration of Bishopstone's poor as ordered by the Poor Law Act 1834. The parish book stops at this date and the Weobley Union minute book[7] starts, which records a first weekly payment for the poor of Bishopstone of 10s 1d. With an order to build a new workhouse to house the poor of the Weobley District, tenders were put out. Heather and Johnson of Hereford quoted £3,134 5s 0d and Collins of Leominster provided a quote of £2,678 0s 0d. Collins was offered the contract to carry out the whole job for £2,200 0s 0d which they accepted on June 21st 1836. George Gardiner was appointed as guardian of the Bishopstone poor and was elected onto the Board of Guardians who ran the Union. The new workhouse in Weobley was opened on March 25th 1837 when three paupers from Bishopstone entered it. Bishopstone was estimated to need 71 days of maintenance a year for their poor and were charged accordingly. The poor rate charged to the parish in 1837 was £49, roughly one quarter of the previous year, so the parishioners were very pleased to pay the smaller bills. A Medical Officer was employed by the Guardians at £15 a quarter to inspect the poor of the parishes. Some out relief was still distributed to the poor in the parishes; mostly clothing made in the workhouse. Bishopstone was charged £3 8s 4d for clothing in 1838, priced per article, shirts 2s 6d, trousers 6s, stockings 6d. Bread was also supplied to all the poor in the parishes by one contractor Mr Whiting who in 1837 charged £6 3s 0d per week for supplying bread to all the parishes within the Weobley group, but how it was distributed I am not sure.

A minute from the Weobley Workhouse account book dated June 25th 1838 records,

Inmates of the workhouse next Thursday, Roast Beef, Plum pudding with potatoes and cider-the master to make the pudding not to exceed a value of 12s, the order for meat to be increased in weight, and the cider given not to exceed 1 pint.

Considering most of the inmates were children a pint of cider seems quite excessive.

Weobley Union's Board of Guardians used the workhouse as relief for the poor of Bishopstone from 1837 until it closed in the 1940s.

(Figure 30) Weobley Workhouse note! two separate entrances for male and female

1841 Census

The office of the Registrar General was created in 1836 to oversee the national system of registering births, marriages and deaths. For this task the new Poor Law Unions of 1834 provided a handy organization as they invariably served as registration districts, hence Bishopstone came under the Weobley Union.

In 1841 the Registrar General assumed responsibility for collecting data for the decennial national censuses, which had begun in 1801.

Before 1841 the parish overseers of the poor only gathered a limited amount of information as referred to at the beginning of this chapter. The 1841 census was a much more thorough enquiry, a printed census form was delivered to the head of each household and was collected the following day, some people couldn't read so the census enumerator had to fill in the form for them. A few people were suspicious of the form and made false or vague returns. However reading through the Bishopstone returns they appear fairly accurate if checked by cross-referencing the data to other records.

The census forms were still fairly basic consisting of six main columns, (1) Place or name of the property, (2) Houses whether inhabited or uninhabited, (3) Names of each person of abode therein the preceding night, (4) Age and sex, (5) Profession, trade, employment or independent means.
(6) Born in this county.
The total number of people sleeping in the parish that night was 307, consisting of 150 males, 157 females, included in this total were children under ten consisting of 36 boys, 47 girls.
Bishopstone hill listed 16 properties of which four were uninhabited; Bishon common listed 14 cottages with one uninhabited, these 30 properties, some poorly built of wattle and daub were the homes of the thirty-five agriculture labourers who were in employment living independent of the farmhouse. Three farmers were listed, George Gardiner, Benjamin Gardiner and James Hancock, three wheelwrights George Payne, John Stephens and John Apperley. One butcher, Joseph Baynham; one cooper, Benjamin Lewis; two shoemakers, William Jenkins and Thomas Higgins, who employed one tradesman and two apprentices. Two carpenters, William Pember and George Proctor; one grocer, John Hancock; one publican, Mary Gower, Nelson Inn, with two female servants and four dealers staying at the Inn that night.
Bishopstone Court Farm contained 305 acres of land, Bishon Farm 240 acres making a combined total of 545 acres of agriculture land out of the parish total of 766 acres. These two farms provided the main employment for the agricultural workers. George Gardiner of Court Farm is listed as being between 50 and 55 years old and had never married, he lived on the farm with 3 female servants and 4 male servants; the youngest boy servant was John Harris who was 12 years old, the youngest girl servant Elizabeth Jones 15 years old. The census does not identify whether the servants were farm or domestic, possibly they could have been both.
Benjamin Gardiner, farming at Bishon, records the largest household on the census return with 16 persons staying on the farm that night: Harriet his wife and their 4 children, Ann Verry the governess, James Lawford a tailor, 4 male servants with the youngest William Haines aged 10, Charles Morris a horse breaker, 2 female servants and Mary Jones the charwoman.
There are no scholars listed on the return, proof the school had not opened in the parish yet.
The last question asked in the census was whether you were born in the county. 31 Bishopstone residents that night were born outside the county, which is a higher percentage than normal, mostly caused by Rev Lane Freer and his entourage, Rev John Skully and family at Downshill and a few visitors like the 4 dealers staying at the Nelson overnight. Also Elizabeth Apperley from the Clovers, had after the sudden death of her wheelwright husband John, recruited a skilled wheelwright called John Barnes from Worcester to run the workshop who brought with him his wife Martha and four children.
Before 1832 the right to vote was a privilege held by just 3% of the population, mainly from the upper and middle classes. The Great Reform Bill of 1832, made more men eligible to vote, adding two categories, freeholders who held property that could be let out for over 40s per annum and short term-lease holders who paid over £50 per annum rent. The Bishon Common freeholders were all descended from people who were awarded land under the enclosure act, the only two in the over £50 per annum rental category were the tenants of Court Farm and Bishon Farm. There were six female freeholders who would have been eligible to vote except for their sex. Elizabeth Apperley (Clovers) and Mary Baynham nee Foote (Pleck Cottage) just to name two. This discrimination carried on until 1918 when all males over 21 years and females over 30 years old were given the right to vote but not until 1928 was women's voting age dropped to 21.

(Figure 31) Foxley House seat of Sir Robert Price.

The voters in 1832 would have travelled to a polling station in Hereford, and then felt obliged to vote for Sir Robert Price the lord of the manor, their votes helped Sir Robert, hold his seat as M.P. for Herefordshire County. Sir John Cotterell another Bishopstone landholder had just stood down after serving nearly thirty years as M P, the two had represented the county for many years.

Voters List Bishopstone 1832

Name	***Abode***	***Nature of qualification***	***Name of property***
Apperley Thomas	*In this parish*	*freeholder*	*Bishon Common*
Bythel William	*In this parish*	*freeholder*	*Nelson Inn*
Clayton John	*In this parish*	*freeholder*	*Bishon Common*
Davis William	*Mansel Lacy*	*freeholder*	*Old Post office*
Gardiner George	*In this parish*	*tenant*	*Court Farm*
Gardiner Thomas	*In this parish*	*freeholder*	*Cherry Trees*
Gardiner Benjamin	*In this parish*	*tenant*	*Bishon Farm*
Hancock John	*In this parish*	*freeholder*	*Bridge Ash*
Lewis James	*In this parish*	*freeholder*	*Bishon Common*
Mortimer David	*Widemarsh street*	*freeholder*	*Bishopstone Hill*
Pritchard Joseph	*Moorhampton*	*freeholder*	*Burcott Row*
Pember William	*Red Lion Yazor*	*freeholder*	*Bishopstone Hill*
Tringham John	*In this parish*	*freeholder*	*Bishon Common*
Walker Adam John	*In this parish*	*Glebe Land*	*Rectory*
William John	*In this parish*	*freeholder*	*Bishopstone Hill*

I have used the properties modern names for easy identification, all the Bishopstone Hill and Bishon Common properties on the list have now disappeared.

A survey of Bishopstone was carried out on July 31st 1849. I have included parts of this record because of its historic value as it gives a very detailed survey of the church. This was all written up into a note book now held in Hereford library and the church record is interesting because it gives details of all the flat tomb stones visible in 1849, before Richard Lane Freer covered them over with his new floor tiles. The first paragraph deals with information I have already covered, except to say there were 61 houses in the parish and two daily schools. There was no communion rail above the steps in the chancel, but otherwise the church appears essentially the same as we see it today. The nave contained 22 open pews plus the church had a small gothic font.

The flat tombs in the centre of transept were,

John son of Henry Gardiner Court Farm died February 7th 1750 aged 24,

Richard Evans Townsend Farm died June 21st 1778 aged 48 and Ann his wife October 10th 1810 aged 76.

Flats in Chancel,

Eleanor Winston, wife of Delabour Winston died August 7th 1691 (Eleanor Winston was originally married to Humphrey Digges)

Eleanor wife of Michael Thomas of Michael Church Eskley and daughter to Epiphan Howarth died March 13th 1680.

Humphrey Digges, Gent, December 5th 1681 aged 64 years.

John Gardiner February 7th 1759 aged 23 years,

Henry Gardiner February 11th 1783 aged 85 years,

Ann Gardiner wife of Henry November 4th 1784 aged 79 years,

Elizabeth Gardiner July 7th 1797 aged 49 years,

George Gardiner March 4th 1834 aged 94 years.

Flats in North transept,

Thomas Berington December 17th 1697.

Flat stone with curious old cross marking, (old Berington grave)

Two flats were recorded in the old porch,

Eleanor Hardy February 3rd 1758 aged 81 years,

John Hargest April 15th 1777 aged 30 years.

Tombs recorded in the churchyard by the porch,

James Pember 1840 aged 84 years wife Ann 1841 aged 86, James Pember September 14th 1839 aged 47 years, William Tyler July 18th 1794, Lilwall 1831, Baker 1780, plus 2 illegible.

The two flat stones in the porch, Hardy and Hargest, were moved when the new porch was fitted around 1853 and some of the outside tombs listed have also now become illegible. Only the people who held high office in the parish or the rich (you had to pay for it) were buried inside the church, like the Gardiner family who had served as churchwardens and officials of the parish for many years. The next best burial plots were in the porch, after that it was preferable to be buried as close as possible to the entrance of the church. Hence in Bishopstone churchyard all the chest tombs surround the porch.

Chapter 10

1850-1870

Looking through the baptism records of Bishopstone from 1850-60, two entries caught my eye. The first entry records on November 5th 1853, Baptism; Eliza, bastard daughter of Sarah Hall, wife of transported felon; and the second entry on September 21st 1856 is more intriguing; Baptism; John, son of Sarah Hall wife of transported convict. Further investigation into Sarah Hall reveals that at the time of the 1851 census, Sarah and her two children were receiving parish relief, they were living with Valentine and Ann Williams her parents in a cottage on Bishopstone Hill. Sarah had married James Hall and they were registered as living in Wormsley where their first two children were baptized.

Just going back to the census, Sarah had entered herself as a widow in her status column, the inspector had crossed this out and written "Married": Sarah had tried to hide the fact that her husband was a convict.

The Easter Quarter Sessions held at the Shirehall Hereford[1] on Monday March 18th 1850 case, No 22/23 James and Thomas Hall charged with stealing one ewe sheep valued at one pound from William Drew of Tedstone Wafer on February 17th 1850, they did kill with a knife and carry off the carcass.

Both pleaded guilty, James aged 35, was the older of the two brothers, he had a previous conviction for stealing in 1842. James was sentenced to twelve years transportation. His brother Thomas aged 21 years was given a sentence of 12 months hard labour in prison.

James Hall was transported to Australia in 1850 aboard the convict ship Dudbrook, his convict records ends with one last entry, it states "Escaped December 8th 1852 from Freemantle." There is no further record of him.

This last entry may explain the fact that Sarah remarried, she was possibly informed of his escape, however this fact is not known. The records show that on June 20th 1857 she married John Lewis a farm labourer from Bishopstone at Hereford Registry Office. He was the father of her illegitimate son John, but there is no record of the father of her daughter Eliza. The 1861 census lists Eliza as a stepdaughter of John Lewis. Sarah and her new family were still living in the same cottage on the hill in 1861, with her father, plus an additional son called Thomas, making five children in total. John her second husband was still only 24 years old. James Hall's punishment may seen very severe by modern standards, although only a few years earlier he could have been hanged for the same offence. He offered no explanation in court as to why they killed the sheep, maybe the family were starving, James had been convicted before so he should have learnt his lesson.

The Quarter Sessions records[2] also listed Bishopstone in another case, this time in the year of 1857. There appears to have been some animosity in Bishopstone between Thomas Powell (farmer) of Buckwell Farm and his neighbour Benjamin Lewis (cooper) who lived in a cottage next to the Almshouses. It started in December 1857 when George Jones, Thomas Powell's farm labourer together with Benjamin's daughter Sarah, was accused of stealing 60 lb of wheat from the farm on December 9th. George Jones was a bachelor who lived with his parents in the Almshouses. The case is worthy of a mention because it demonstrates how the legal system worked in the mid 19th century. Thomas Powell would have gone to the local Justice of the Peace with his accusations, taking any evidence with him and also providing names of any witnesses to back up his claim; if the Justice thought there was a case, the accused would have been given a summons by the local constable (in this case John Christy) to appear before the next Quarter Sessions court.

They appeared at the next Quarter Sessions held on the January 4th 1858 in the Shirehall Hereford where George Jones was found guilty of larceny; because he already had a previous conviction George was sentenced to twelve-month's imprisonment with hard labour. Sarah Lewis was also found guilty and was sentenced to three months imprisonment with hard labour. The imprisonment of Benjamin's daughter Sarah, caused a bitter feud between the neighbours, followed by an argument: on June 30th 1858 when Thomas Powell accused Benjamin Lewis of stealing one chestnut plank. This plank Benjamin claimed was given to him by Thomas a year earlier to make a barrel. The case ended up in court. Benjamin pleaded not guilty at the Quarter Sessions held on October 18th 1858 but the court found him guilty of receiving stolen goods and he was given a sentence of fourteen days imprisonment.

The 1851 census forms were more refined than their1841 counterpart; the forms now included information on marital status and relationship to the head of the household, age had to be recorded exactly, plus details of where you were born and whether you were blind, deaf or dumb. Employers were also asked to specify how many people were in their employment. This additional information gathered by the 1851 census gives us a more detailed analysis of the parishioners who lived in Bishopstone at a time when agriculture was improving. It was the start of what was called *"The Golden Age of English Agriculture"* - 1852-63. There were now five farmers listed on the 1851 returns against three in 1841.

George Gardiner had given up the tenancy of Court Farm in 1842 and another bachelor, Joseph Plant, was now farming the 305 acres of Court Farm. He employed eight farm labourers plus the following people who lived in the farmhouse: Ann Wilson as his housekeeper, her husband John the farm shepherd, two house servants and three farm servants.

BISHOPSTONE.

BISHOPSTONE, a Parish situated about six miles W.N.W. from Hereford. There is a very pretty and by no means small CHURCH, in which are several beautifully stained windows. The Rev. Richard Lane Freer, M.A., Rector; Mr. Joseph Plant, Churchwarden; Mr. James Davies, Clerk. Service –11 a.m. and 3 30 p.m.

There is a SCHOOL, principally supported by Mrs. Freer. Average number of scholars, 30. Ann Fowler, Mistress.

CLERGY, TRADES, FARMERS, ETC.

Freer Rev. Richard Lane, M.A., Rectory
Appely John, wheelwright
Beavan John, boot and shoemaker, Bishon Common
Blashill Thomas, agent
Davies James, Parish Clerk
Ellis Ann, cider retailer, The Steps
Fowler Ann, Schoolmistress
Gardiner George, boot and shoemaker, Bishon Common
Hancox Barnabas, blacksmith
Higgins Thomas, shoemaker, The Stock
Lloyd Wm., farmer, Bishon
Perks John, victualler, *Nelson*
Plant Joseph, farmer, Bishopstone Court
Powell Thomas, farmer, Bishon Hill
Stevens John, wheelwright

(Figure 1) Extract from the 1851 Kelly's Directory

Benjamin Gardiner had also given up his tenancy on Bishon farm. William Lloyd was the new tenant on the 240 acre farm; he employed seven labourers, plus one dairymaid, one indoor servant and three farm servants all living in the farmhouse.

65-year-old Thomas Bayliss, farmed the 30 acre Kenowley Farm. Thomas lived with his two bachelor sons, Thomas the eldest helped out on the farm and John, his other son, was the last person to operate the big lime-burning kiln up on the hill.

Elizabeth Godsall farmed Townsend Farm, she was a widow aged 61 years and the farm came with 13 acres of land. All the above four farmers were tenants of the Foxley Estate.

Widow Ann Ellis, farmed the 60 acre Stepps Farm. She lived with her unmarried daughter and child, employing one farm labourer, plus she lists three lodgers as living in the house. Ann is recorded in the trade directories as a cider retailer.

It's worth noting that the old Claypitts farmhouse had now been demolished with only the barn left standing. The Claypitts land together with Bythel's and Smith's lands acquired by Sir John Cotterell were joined together to form a 60-acre unit.

Although the majority of the parishioners found employment on the five farms, ten parishioners were employed by parish tradesmen: Barnabas Hancock the blacksmith employed two men, Thomas Higgins of Stocks House, a shoemaker, employed two shoemakers plus one apprentice. John Apperley of The Clovers, wheelwright, employed one man and one apprentice; John Christy of Scaldback Cottage the tailor employed one apprentice (John Christy was also the parish constable); John Bevan Bishon Common was a master cordwainer employing one journeyman; John Perks of the Nelson Inn employed one servant.

Other non-employing trade persons living in the parish were John Hancock a shopkeeper from Bridge Ash, Joseph Baynham who ran a butchers shop from what is now Winton House, Benjamin Lewis, Bishopstone Hill who was a cooper and finally Richard Williams the first listed parish roadman in Bishopstone he lived in a cottage on Bishon common.

There were six women dressmakers plus two plain sewers all working from home, forty agricultural labourers living in cottages, ten labourers living in farmhouses, ten people were recorded as being on parish or hospital relief, one hundred and fifteen people were in employment. The census records the population of the parish as 269, 139 males, 130 females; it also listed sixty dwelling houses with only one house uninhabited on the hill. Surprisingly only eleven heads of household, out of fifty nine, were born in Bishopstone. These were George Gardiner ex Bishopstone Court now renting "The Cottage" Bishon lane; John Hancock (shopkeeper) of Bridge Ash; John Apperley (wheelwright) from the Clovers; Elizabeth Apperley, John's mother who lived in the cottage next door; Henry Meredith (gardener) who lived in Burcutt Row; Barnabas Hancock (blacksmith) at Forge Cottage, plus George Wall (mason), Benjamin Mosley (farm labourer), Mary Vaughan retired, George Payne (master carpenter); they all lived in cottages on Bishon Common.

For the first time in a census, 44 scholars were listed as attending the new school in the parish room at the rectory; the school headmistress was Mary Stephens who lived in the cottage now called the "Old Post Office," she was assisted by Ann Fowler aged sixteen. Mary Stephens was the widow of John Stephens former wheelwright and parish constable

Richard Lane Freer's rectory was the only house in the parish run as a gentleman's residence, with downstairs staff consisting of a butler, footman, cook, ladies maid, housemaid, kitchen maid and coachman. Thomas Blashill the land agent for Garnons Estates lived at Downshill House with his wife Ann and one house servant.

The biggest family in the parish belonged to George Wall, a mason who lived on Bishon Common in a two up two down cottage with his eight children.

John Morris was the only person registered blind on the census returns. Looking back into the records, it appears he was a normal hard working farm labourer until he reached the age of 42, living with his wife and three children, in the one cottage left on the old Bishon Farm site. In 1849 a note in the tithe collection book records "no charge, in Infirmary" against his name, he was suffering from the family's hereditary blindness. The Morris story is covered in an earlier chapter. The parish moved him into a cottage on Bishon Common where he received parish relief to support his family; he died in 1852 aged 45 and was buried in Bishopstone churchyard on October 3rd of that year.

John Apperley's Apprentice

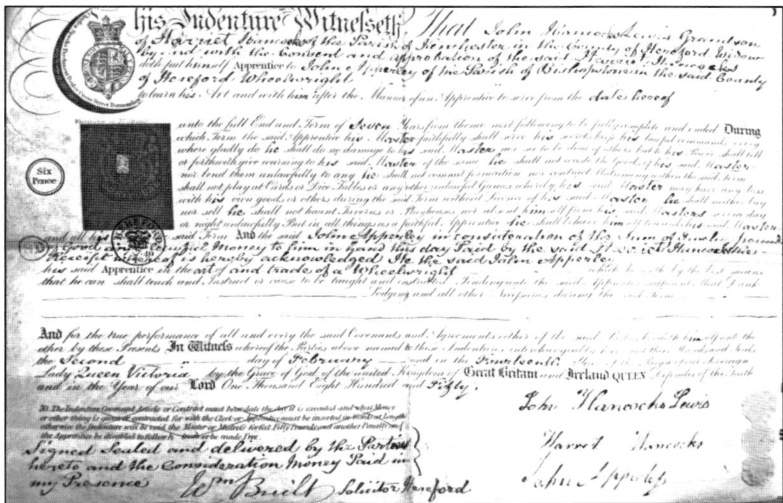

(Figure 2) Apprenticeship indenture between John Apperley "Wheelwright" and John Hancock Lewis

The only surviving 19th century apprenticeship indenture I have found naming a Bishopstone tradesperson, was made between John Apperley, a wheelwright operating from the Clovers with John Hancock Lewis. It was signed and dated February 2nd 1850, a legal document drawn up by a solicitor. In the agreement John Apperley will take on John Hancock Lewis for a seven-year apprenticeship and John as Master will teach him the art and trade of wheelwright. John Hancock Lewis was only 12 years old. The standard indenture document states that the apprentice must faithfully serve his master, shall not haunt taverns or playhouses, nor play cards or dice tables or any other unlawful games. Harriett Hancock who was John Hancock Lewis's grandmother paid £12 to John Apperley for the apprenticeship. What happened to John Hancock Lewis? Well, he worked out his apprenticeship in the workshop and yard attached to the Clovers house, until he reached the age of 19. John then dropped his Lewis surname, and became known, as John Hancock. He never appeared to carry on in his trade, he married at 21 and became the father of 12 children of whom 8 survived. His wife's parents left them £100 which they used to start farming at Orcop, John always used a pony and trap to drive to Hereford market, but during the heavy snows of 1881 he became trapped in Hereford. He tramped the 9 miles home on foot, returning at night, to find his sheep buried in the meadow adjoining his home. Trying to rescue them, he was overcome by weather conditions and fatigue, and died; his body was not found until the next morning. He was only 44 years old and his youngest child only 6 weeks old.

Steps Quarry Bishopstone

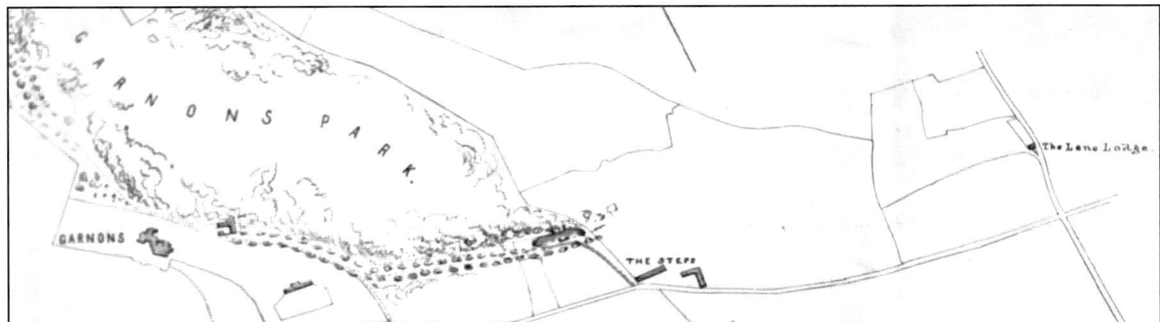

(Figure 3) Map showing position of the quarry and the line of trees planted to form an avenue originally intended to extend out to Lena Lodge.

The surveyors of the Turnpike Road Trust had power to raise stone to repair the roads under the Turnpike Road Act but the trustees of Garnons Estate challenged this in 1853. The matter came to a head when ornamental trees, part of the avenue planted from the drawings in Humphrey Repton's red book, had fallen into the quarry. These trees formed part of an avenue through which passed the drive that exited at Lena Lodge in Bishopstone.

At the Petty Sessions held in Weobley on March 3rd 1853[3] Thomas Blashill the steward of the estate gave evidence, stating that the quarry had become so large it had now spilled over into Byford parish. The quarry now provided enough limestone marl, Mr Blashill claimed, to repair most of the turnpike road between Hereford and Hay. Working under the turnpike surveyor, the men blasted and hauled large quantities of stone out of the quarry. The surveyor argued the case that the quarry provided the best stone for road laying, although it was more expensive, costing 4s a cubic yard, against gravel from Bridge dingle at 2s a yard; river gravel was charged at 1s 3d a yard and he could not give a price on stone picked from the field as he had not been offered any.

Mr Blashill argued his case, explaining that *"as far as his understanding of the Turnpike Act, it authorises the taking of stone only to repair the road in that parish or the parish adjoining the quarry, not to supply stone to other parishes"*. He also said that if the Petty Session gave the surveyor an order to raise stone for another two years; he would appeal against that decision.

Because the Petty Session authorised the surveyor to continue taking stone an appeal case was held in 1856 against this order made by the four magistrates of the Weobley district.

The situation had now intensified, with two counsels and a solicitor acting for both sides. The case started by the appellant Sir Henry Cotterell's counsel saying that the Steps Quarry was situated inside a park, the Act stating that the surveyor was not empowered to *"search for, dig, get, gather stone from a garden, yard, park, paddock or ground planted as a nursery for trees"*. The chairman dismissed this saying that knocking down a few hedges did not constitute a park. He continued *"although Mr Repton, a gentleman of considerable reputation as a landscape gardener, in his book prepared in 1791 says that Garnons is a park legally a park means an enclosed place where deer are kept"*.

Mr Blashill called as a witness said, *"he has been the steward of Garnons for the last sixteen or seventeen years. When he first went to the estate there was a grass road between the trees, which was used both as a drive and a ride; this road continues to the mansion, and from thence to the lodge at Bishopstone. He had planted a nursery alongside the quarry on instruction of Sir Henry in February last. Mr Shellard the surveyor had intensified the activity in the quarry moving stone along the private drive down through the lodge gates and leaving piles of stone on the roadside. He described generally the residential damage done to the estate by the working of the quarry, principally arising from the destruction of or injury to walks and drives commanding extensive and beautiful scenery, the danger of blasting, and the inconvenience of having quarrymen on the estate, with the privacy of which it unquestionably interfered; the blasting of the rock can be heard at the mansion"*. On cross examination Mr Blashill did admit that stone from the quarry had been used in the estate lime kiln, and for a new wing Sir Henry Cotterell was building on the mansion.

Mr William Mann a coachman was called to give evidence as an expert. He said that he was the driver of the coach between Hereford and Hay and it was his opinion that the gravelled part of the road was the soundest.

Sir Henry's gardener and gamekeeper also gave evidence of the destruction caused by the quarry. Edward George the gamekeeper said, "*He had known the eggs of the pheasants broken by fragments of stones from the quarry, thrown up by blasting, and a great deal of damage done by disturbing the birds in breeding time*".

Mr Cook, counsel for the Turnpike trust said, "*There was no desire to injure Sir H Cotterell; on the contrary, every disposition had been evinced to oblige him in every possible way. It was clearly shown that the estate of Garnons contains the best material for the purpose of road making. But in the nineteenth century- in this age of advancement and civilization- in this year of out Lord 1856, were they to have counsel brought here to tell them that the roads cannot be mended because a young Baronet cannot have his pheasants hatched? And because some inconvenience may possibly be experienced by the young ladies in their solitary rambles in a green lane?"*

A voting paper was passed round, after which the Chairman without stating the number of majority, said the order should be confirmed.

Although the Turnpike Trust had won this case the quarry was shut down soon after. I thought the case was useful to report on because it reveals one of the reasons the drive leading out to Bishopstone was never fully used.

Sale of Foxley Estate

On Tuesday August 28th 1855 the Times newspaper advertised the forthcoming sale of Foxley Estate[4], to be sold by Auction at the Mart, London, near to the Bank of England, comprising 4330 acres, Mansion House, £5,600 a year rental income, plus the advowson of Bishopstone & Yazor.

This must have been an uncertain time for the estate's seven tenants in Bishopstone, Joseph Plant (Court Farm), William Lloyd (Bishon Farm), Thomas Powell (Buckwell Farm), Thomas Bayliss (Kenowley Farm), Mary Owen (Stonehouse), John Morris (cottage next to Bishon Farm) and finally Barnabas Hancock (Forge Cottage, blacksmith).

HEREFORDSHIRE.

Particulars of Sale

OF

THE MANORS, ADVOWSONS,

AND

ESTATES OF FOXLEY,

SITUATE IN THE PARISHES OF

YAZOR, MANSEL LACY, BISHOPSTONE, MANSEL GAMAGE, NORTON CANNON, WEOBLEY, AND BRINSOP,

IN THE COUNTY OF HEREFORD.

THE ADVOWSON

OF THE UNITED PARISHES OF BISHOPSTONE AND YAZOR,

AND

THE ADVOWSON OF MANSEL LACY.

THE WHOLE OF THE PROPERTY IS FREEHOLD,

And lies nearly in an unbroken Ring Fence,

CONSISTING OF

4,330 ACRES

OF CAPITAL

ARABLE, MEADOW, PASTURE, HOP, & WOOD LANDS,

WITH

A FAMILY MANSION,

A SMALLER RESIDENCE, WATER MILL, FARM HOUSES, &c.,

PRODUCING AN INCOME OF NEARLY

£5,600 A YEAR;

Which will be Sold by Auction, by

MESSRS. FOSTER AND SON,

AT THE MART,

NEAR THE BANK OF ENGLAND, LONDON,

ON TUESDAY, 28th AUGUST, 1855.

AT TWELVE O'CLOCK,

IN ONE LOT.

Particulars may be had of Messrs. ROBINSON and TOMLIN, Solicitors, 48, Conduit Street, Hanover Square; of Messrs. BOYS and TWEEDIE, Solicitors, Ely Place, Holborn; CHARLES BLAKE, Esq., Solicitor, 49, Fleet Street; Messrs. FIELD and BIGNOLD, Solicitors, Norwich; Messrs. C. and J. ALLEN and SONS, Solicitors, Carlisle Street, Soho Square; J. T. COOKNEY, Esq., Solicitor, 5, Lamb's Conduit Place; Messrs. EDWARDS and FRANKISH, Solicitors, 11, New Palace Yard, Messrs. F. and C. BODENHAM and JAMES, Solicitors, Hereford; Mr. FOSBROOKE, Land Surveyor, Hereford; at the Mart, London; and of Messrs. FOSTER and SON, 54, Pall Mall.

(Figure 4) Sale poster advertising the sale of Foxley Estate

Sir Robert Price M.P. (lord of the manor of Bishopstone) was declared bankrupt to the sum of £288,207 in the London courts on October 1st 1855. He was described as an iron manufacturer and a dealer in iron. His address was given as Stratton Street, Piccadilly and Foxley in the county of Hereford. A detailed set of accounts for the last seven years were presented to the court, rental from estate in Hereford 1848-1855 amounted to £26,665 9s 6d; expenses at Foxley for repairs and alterations £17,311 12s 2d; personal and private expenditure during the period £30,121 16s 8d, but the losses for the period were a staggering £104,582 3s 10d. To try to cover the losses Sir Robert had borrowed money from his personal friend and fellow MP. Earl Fitzwilliam of Wentworth Woodhouse in the West Riding of Yorkshire. One of the richest men in Britain, who made his fortune from coal, Wentworth Woodhouse was the biggest stately home in Britain. As security Lord Fitzwilliam held the deeds for the Foxley Estates and it was he who put the estate up for auction.

Robert Price was born at Foxley on August 3rd 1786, the only son of Uvedale Price. He was educated at Eton and Christ Church, Oxford and went on to complete his studies at Edinburgh where he studied agriculture. Robert Price became a Whig M.P. for Herefordshire in 1818, holding the seat until 1841. In 1823, he married his cousin Mary Anne Elizabeth, daughter of the Reverend Dr. Robert Price, D.D., Prebendary of Durham and Canon of Salisbury. In 1845, he was elected Member for the City of Hereford (so for nearly 40 years he held a seat in the House of Commons). He also became the Chief Steward for Hereford, a position he proudly held. Robert set out with great vigour to become an iron master, but sadly with no experience, his enterprise failed. Things might have been different had he managed to hold out until the upsurge in the iron trade in 1854 due to the Crimean War.

On November 1st 1855 he surrendered to the bankruptcy court and listed numerous creditors that revealed the scope of business as well as his lifestyle.

Sir Robert died on November 5th 1857, at the age of seventy-one, one year after the sale of his beloved Foxley. The Hereford Times reported his death on Saturday, November 14th 1857 in a mourning black-edged obituary.

"His gentlemanly appearance, his cheerful temper, his uniformly kind and amiable manners, his ardent desire to serve his friends, his high sense of humour, and his real goodness of heart, endeared him to people with whom he associated, and rendered him deservedly popular with both the rich and the poor."

As Hereford's Chief Steward Sir Robert Price was given full honours by the city, when his coffin arrived by train at the Barrs Court station at 4.40 p.m., on Thursday, November 12th 1857. The Mayor, Corporation, and many civic dignitaries were present at the station to meet the coffin and say their last farewells. The following report was extracted from the Hereford Times. *"The hearse drawn by four horses, preceded by police officers bearing torches, and officers of the corporation, bearing mourning emblems, proceeded slowly through the city. All the shops were closed, and at private houses the shutters were either closed, or the blinds drawn. Vast numbers of people assembled in the streets to watch the melancholy procession.*

(Figure 5) Sir Robert Price Bart. M. P.

The procession passed through High Town, down Eign Street, to above Eign Bridge, where it parted in two rows, one to the left, the other to the right, as the coffin passed through and went out of the city limits and on to Bishopstone, to the home of his friend the Ven. Archdeacon Freer. The official party then turned, and marched in formation to the Guildhall."

It must have been an impressive sight as the long column proceeded by policemen holding lighted torches, slowly passed though Bishopstone in the dusk of a November day before turning down the Rectory drive.

The body of Sir Robert lay at rest at Bishopstone Rectory overnight; Sir Robert Price was buried the next day in the new Yazor church. At the same time, the bells of the City churches rang a muffled peal in token of the event, and those of All Saint's church rang out the age of the lamented deceased, an unusual compliment in recognition of the Chief Steward of the City.

Lady Price eventually moved to Lowndes Square, in London, and before her death managed to pay off all the debts. Sadly there were no children from the marriage.

The estate did not sell at the auction held in August 1855, but in the December of that year, John Davenport of Westwood Hall, Leek in Staffordshire offered £220,000 for Foxley Estate.

John Davenport was the eldest son of John Davenport who had made a fortune in porcelain; John never entered the family business and was a successful lawyer in his own right. He paid a £20,000 deposit on March 2nd 1856, which left £200,000 on a mortgage with Lord Fitzwilliam at a rate of 4%, and obtained possession.

(Figure 6) John Davenport

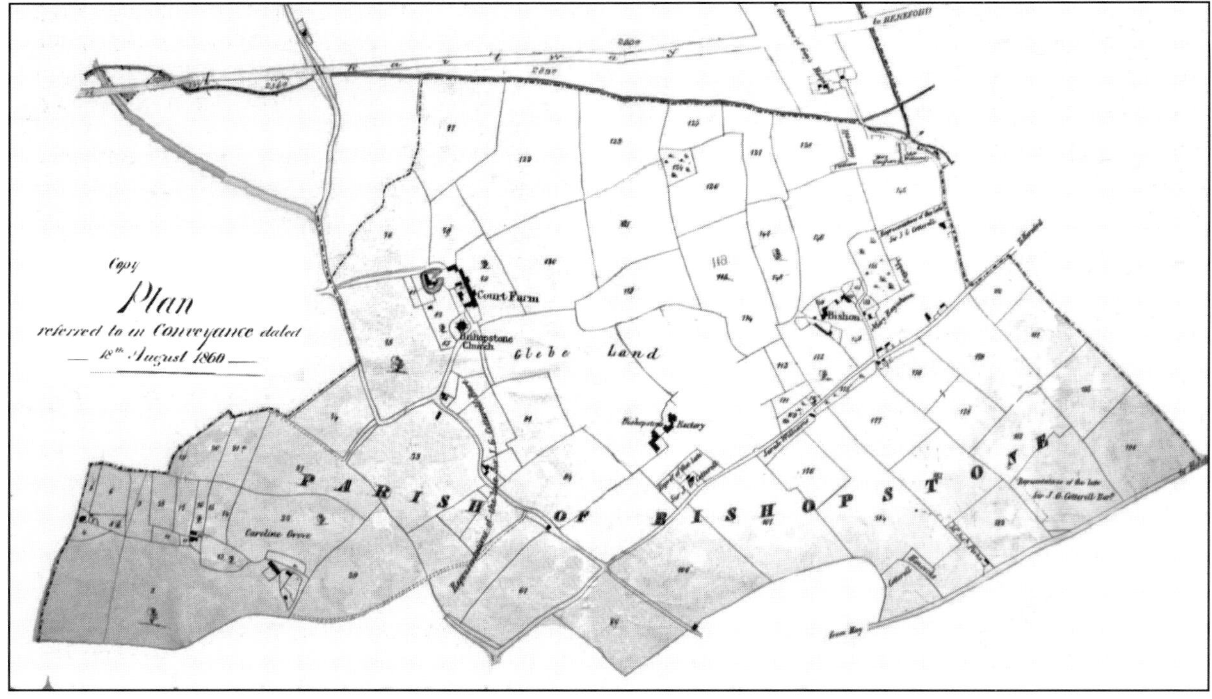

(Figure 7) Every parcel of land numbered on the above final Conveyance Map was included in the sale of Foxley Estate. Note! The road marked top left hand was to lead to a proposed railway station, which was never built. Note! The railway company had still not acquired the land through Bishon Common.

He paid £50,000 on June 30th 1856, another £50,000 on October 31st and the rest was paid off in lump sums over the next few years. The purchase did not appear to bring any luck to the Davenport family as John his eldest son, who was to inherit the estate, died on July 2nd 1858 aged 28 whilst serving with the 1st Dragoons. His father died four years later in 1862 aged 62 and the estate passed to a reluctant second son the Rev George Horatio Davenport who was 30 years old.

Bishopstone School 1849-1894

In 1839 the Council for Education was established and various Diocesan Boards of Education soon followed this. The Rev Richard Lane Freer was an original board member for the Hereford Diocesan Board and decided to start up his own school in Bishopstone: he was encouraged by his new wife to set an example for others to follow. This was the first Church of England school in the area. Lady Southampton opened Kenchester School in 1826 for 50 female scholars, but being a nonconformist school it was frowned upon by the Church of England clergy and from the 1841 census we know that no child from Bishopstone attended it. In 1849 Mrs Lane Freer started the school, using the large parish room in the Rectory as the classroom. 44 scholars aged between 4-14 years are recorded in the 1851 census as attending school either at the Rectory or, in the case of the more advanced children, receiving their schooling at Mansel Lacy. An entry in the 1851 Kelly's directory states "there is a school in Bishopstone supported by Mrs Lane Freer average number of scholars 30", and records Ann Fowler as the school mistress. The 1851 census reveals that Ann was then aged 16, living with her widowed mother and brother in the Rectory Lodge; Ann's brother worked as a groom for the Rector.

The masters and mistresses of the school appeared to change very frequently in its early days. The school proved so popular that the classes soon built up to over 50 pupils, outgrowing the Rectory's parish room.

In 1854 Archdeacon Lane Freer secured a tenancy on a derelict cottage in Bishon belonging to John Snead of Bridge Sollers. He converted the timber frame cottage, containing one room up and one down, into accommodation for the use of the teacher and then built a brick extension that contained a classroom and a small storeroom; outside wooden toilets were also built. He covered the whole building with a new slate roof, which he provided at his own expense. By todays standards it seems too small to house so many scholars, but then people were used to be living in confined spaces. With most of the cottages only containing two rooms up, plus two down, a family of up to ten could happily live in these conditions.

The 1861 census shows Miss Susan Charter living in the School House as mistress; Archdeacon Lane Freer employed her in 1856. In 1859 Susan was recorded as Bishopstone's first sub postmistress, carrying out both jobs from the School House. The post arrived at 11.00 am and departed at 2.45 pm by messenger. Eventually the postmistress job became too much for Susan so she gave it up - imagine teaching up to 50 pupils and dealing with the post at the same time. After the Archdeacon's death in 1863 the school became a National school for boys and girls. The new schoolmistress was Miss Leonora Drane who came from Ditchingham in Norfolk, she brought some much needed stability to the school, staying as its teacher for the next 24 years. Miss Drane who was born in 1832 always stated on the census return forms that she was younger than her actual age, usually by four or five years, she also signed her name Draue, possibly to stop the children making jokes about her surname.

In 1870, Forster's Education Act added an element of compulsion into the voluntary school system, this included keeping a school logbook.

Bishopstone School log book[5] is deposited in Hereford Record Office. It runs from November 1871 until the school closed in July 1894 and it's a wonderful record of the day to day running of the school, showing how outside influences affected the school and village affairs in general. But it must be remembered that it was written from the point of view of the teacher rather than that of the management committee. As the logbook contains 272 pages it would be impossible to include so much information here, however I have included some of the more interesting entries, with some additional notes by way of explanation or other informative facts.

The school hours were from 9 am until 4.30 pm with a one hour lunch break. The school had an infant class of children aged between 3-5 years old who were taught mostly by a school monitor, selected by the mistress from one of the older children who had just left the school. A logbook entry for January 1st 1872 revealed that Harriett Powell the monitor was paid 1s 6d a week, paid quarterly. The other children were split into four standards, increased to six in 1886. Most of the children left at 12 years old but a few returned to pass their last standard, like Alfred Lawrence from Kenowley, recorded in the logbook on October 14th 1890 *"Alfred Lawrence left this week to commence work but wishes to be presented to Her Majesty's Inspector for a certificate in proficiency at his visit in December".* (Alfred left the school on his twelfth birthday)

The children had an hour's scripture lesson every day; every year the pupils were given songs to learn as the school formed the basis for the church choir. Other lessons were arithmetic, spelling, geography, handwriting and needlework; the infants' sewing lessons were sometimes taught with the help of the rector's wife or his daughters.

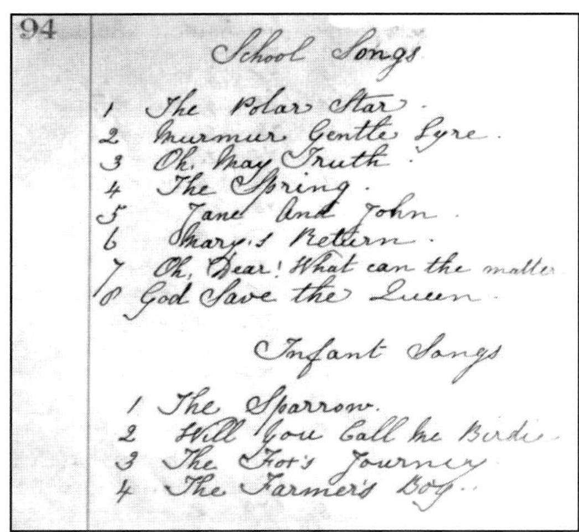
94

School Songs

1 The Polar Star.
2 Murmur Gentle Lyre.
3 Oh, May Truth.
4 The Spring.
5 Jane And John.
6 Mary's Return.
7 Oh, Dear! What can the matter
8 God Save the Queen.

Infant Songs

1 The Sparrow.
2 Will You Call the Birds.
3 The Fox's Journey
4 The Farmer's Boy.

(Figure 8) School songs for 1884

After 1892 history lessons were introduced. A school inspector from the Education Authority would arrive every November to examine the children to their standard and then send his report in by February the next year.
On February 3rd 1872 three new children were admitted into the school, followed by three more on the 5th, as recorded in the logbook. Each year at Candlemas Mr Plant and later Mr Like from Bishopstone Court Farm, and Mr Barnett of Bishon Farm would hire new labourers, so every year the school logbook would record three or four families, and occasionally as many as seven, leaving Bishopstone and new families replacing them, there was always a continuous movement of agricultural labour.
Traditionally Archdeacon Lane Freer would take the children on school trips, sometimes by train from Credenhill station; his successor Rev Robins carried on with this tradition. On June 27th 1872 a holiday was given so the mistress could take the children to Aberystwyth, this was the last recorded trip made by the whole school. You can only imagine the excitement among the children travelling by train to the seaside, a trip some of their parents would never be able to make in their lifetime due to the poverty in the rural workforce.
However they could show off their gardening skills by exhibiting at the Bishopstone Flower Show held on August 1st 1872 in the rectory grounds when the children would be given a day off school.
The Hereford Journal reported on the event.

BISHOPSTONE ANNUAL FLOWER SHOW

The annual show for the districts of Yazor, Bishopstone and Mansel Lacy, was held this year in the rectory grounds at Bishopstone on Thursday. The weather, although threatening, was propitious for the first part of the day, but at six o'clock the rain began to fall, and the storm increased till it broke over the neighbourhood in a complete deluge. Although the floral exhibition was fully up to the high standard of excellence to which it has of late years attained, we cannot say as much of the vegetable classes. This may be accounted for to some extent by the disease now so prevalent in the potato crops. No collections were exhibited by professional gardeners, but these were amply compensated by the gentry of the neighbourhood, several of whom sent liberal contributions of ferns and cut flowers to grace the exhibition, and which greatly enhanced the attractiveness of the show. Of these the Rev. B. L. S. Stanhope, of Byford Rectory, contributed a magnificent collection of ferns, of which the Adantivm and the Caladium Houletta, meeting the eye of everyone at the extremity of the tent, elicited many expressions of admiration. The same gentleman also exhibited twelve splendid specimens of the most popular roses of the season, which, being also placed in an advantageous position drew forth the encomiums they well merited. In the other classes the competition, as may be seen from the prize list, was not very spirited, and all that can be done is to hope for a better collection next year. Tea was served out on the grounds at a rate of 6d. per head, and while some listened to the inspiriting strains of the Herefordshire Militia Band, or admired the beautiful scenery to be met with in this neighbourhood, others wended their way to the old churchyard, and amused themselves by reading the various inscriptions upon the tombstones, or admired the exterior of the fine old edifice there. There was a large and fashionable company present, among whom we noticed the Rev. Sir George Cornewall, Bart, and Lady Cornewall (Moccas), Rev. W. B. S. Stanhope, Mrs Giles and party, Lady Cotterell and party, Miss Newton, and Mrs Hall and family; the Revs. G H Davenport, R. C. Robinson, R. Cooper Key, C. H. Palmer, H. Peploe, G. A. Robbins, and F. Burr.

The different classes consisted of Flowers, Fruit, Vegetables, Honey and Miscellaneous. Bishopstone school children entered the classes of Best nosegay of wild flowers, Best nosegay of garden flowers and Best article of needlework.
The annual show was usually held on the Foxley Estate. Because the county was in the middle of an epidemic of Foot and Mouth disease the show was moved to Bishopstone Rectory
The Hereford Journal reported in the week ending August 3rd 1872 that 1,514 cattle, 365 sheep and 60 pigs were ill and 7 cattle had died.
The School children who provided the core members of the church choir were rewarded for their attendance with special treats as stated on August 14th 1872, *"the choir children were taken to Llangorse Lake on their summer trip".*

The Orphanage children were always in trouble at school for arriving late thus losing their attendance marks. Later in the book there is a section that covers Bishopstone Orphanage in full. The orphans came from a wide area, on July 13th 1874 Joseph Potter an orphan from Hallow was registered into the school. Some children were sponsored by the clergy,
April 6th 1876 "Rev G. P. Palmer came to school he brings an orphan", another entry on *July 5th 1876 "Rev Davenport stops at school to see his little orphan".*
The association with the school came to an end with a final entry on January 19th 1877 *"8 orphans removed to Wales".*
(Rev Robins and his wife were the benefactors of the Orphanage, after they moved Rev Ridley was not interested in taking on the Orphanage so he made other arrangements for the children, moving them to live in Wales.)

Discipline in the School

Discipline at the school was controlled with the use of the cane, overall the discipline at the school appears to have been generally good; there are a few entries in the logbook recording the usual children's pranks and some of a more serious nature where children were expelled.
February 16th 1881 *"elastic taken from the children hats during school hours",*
February 18th *"Policeman calls at School", "George Boucher two strips with the cane for thieving and lying".* (It appears George was the culprit who had taken the elastic from the hats possibly as a bit of fun. He was the blacksmith's son aged 10 and lived at Forge Cottage)
March 10th 1886 *"Ash Wednesday ten children absent through some untruthful boys".*
(These boys had told others that this Ash Wednesday was a School holiday)
The few children expelled from the school: December 7th 1875 *"three Goughs dismissed from this school and gone to Byford."*
James (Jim) Gough who lived in Bishopstone until the 1970's was a descendant.
December 1st 1887 *"John Lewis sent home for bad behaviour"*
December 2nd *"John Lewis forbidden by the Rector to attend this school again."*

In the year 1892 discipline became a main concern according to the log book entries; Isobel James resigned from the school as mistress on March 17th of that year: she was the fifth female teacher in less than four years to resign from Bishopstone School following the formidable Miss Drane. On March 19th Samuel William Rogers, a certified Master took charge of the school.
May 9th 1892 *"Rhoda Francis, Jessie Hyde and Annie Bywater kept in school till 5.30 for rebellious conduct. Mr Bywater objected to his children receiving any punishment whatsoever."*
(Fredrick Bywater from the Nelson Inn was not a great believer in education and he was continually keeping his seven children from school even after numerous visits from Mr Lloyd the attendance officer, who threatened court action. When his eldest daughter Annie, a 12 year old, did not return home from school on time to carry out her daily chores, Fredrick walked across the field and confronted Mr Rogers the School Master.)
May 13th 1892 *"I had occasion to punish Sydney Howells for disobedience, he ran home on being let out, I sent his brother home for him neither have returned".*
May 20th *"Sidney and Allan Howells have left to go to Kenchester School. The mother had called twice to complain of their disobedience at home".*
(Sidney Howells was 11 years old and his brother Allan aged 7, they lived with their father and mother John and Maria at the Townsend Farm. John was a farm labourer and rented the farmhouse which was in a state of decay; they were the last family to live in this old house which was pulled down around 1905. The family had come from Monmouth and the children had never settled in the schools; they first attended Bishopstone School, left and went to Byford School, then back to Bishopstone and finally Kenchester.)
Sidney died in 1919, his grave is marked with the only war grave headstone in Bishopstone Churchyard.
July 29th 1892 *"I punished Jessica Hyde for positive disobedience".*
August 12th *"a tough week owing to influence outside school little work done beyond maintaining discipline."*
August 22nd *Catherine Haines ran home at afternoon recreation, I sent for her but her grandmother refused to let her come. The girl had been told to stand on seat for talking.*
(Catherine who was aged 11 lived with her extended family at Stonehouse opposite the school. Her story brings home the tragedies that beheld many rural families in the Victorian era as she had lost both her parents. Jonathan Haines her stepfather worked for the railway as a platelayer. He married Emily and moved to Stonehouse, Bishopstone in 1870. They had four children Alfred, William, Henry and Isabella, Emily his wife died and was buried in Bishopstone church in August 1883 at the young age of 27.

They had already lost two children, Alfred died in 1878 aged 3 and William in 1881 aged 5 as recorded in the logbook, June 16th 1881 *"William Haines absent through illness."* July 7th *"William Haines removed by death."* Jonathan struggled on to bring up his other two children; he then lost his last son Henry in 1885 aged 5 years. Having lost all his sons before they reached the age of six, Jonathan remarried in 1887 to Harriet Lewis, a widow with two young children, Catherine aged 5 and Albert aged 2; this marriage produced another child they called Jonathan named after his father. Jonathan lost his second wife Harriett on March 27th 1891 who died in child birth, the same fate as his first wife, he had suffered five deaths in the family in twelve years. Ann Lewis, Harriet's mother moved into Stonehouse to look after the family.)

Summary of the inspectors report received on January 5th 1893 from the Education Department.

"Reading usually passes, the handwriting and style of the upper standard are good and spelling, reading is very fair average on the whole, arithmetic is exceptionally weak in all standards except the second, and the discipline of the school is lax, there is not at the present time a satisfactory relationship between the master and the scholars, and it is mainly owing to the constant and careful supervision of the principal manager that the work proceeds smoothly. The grant under Article 105 cannot be recommended."

(The manager was normally the Rector but on this occasion Mr J Kress from Downshill House, land agent for Garnons Estate held the post.)

January 9th 1893 *"S W Rogers resigned from this School."*

(Mr Roger, even with his stern discipline, became another failure at the School: he lasted only ten months, resigning before the inspector's report was received).

The next teacher Florence Robinace still struggled with the children's disciple, she records the following entries in the logbook, January 9th 1893 *"commenced duty here as mistress under very unfavourable circumstances the weather sufficiently cold and stormy to prevent children from attending, present 16."*

January 13th *"the behaviour of the children is far from satisfactory the infants have a habit of talking aloud and shouting while the elder scholars convulse with laughter without the least provocation. I sincerely trust that affairs will not continue in this state very long."*

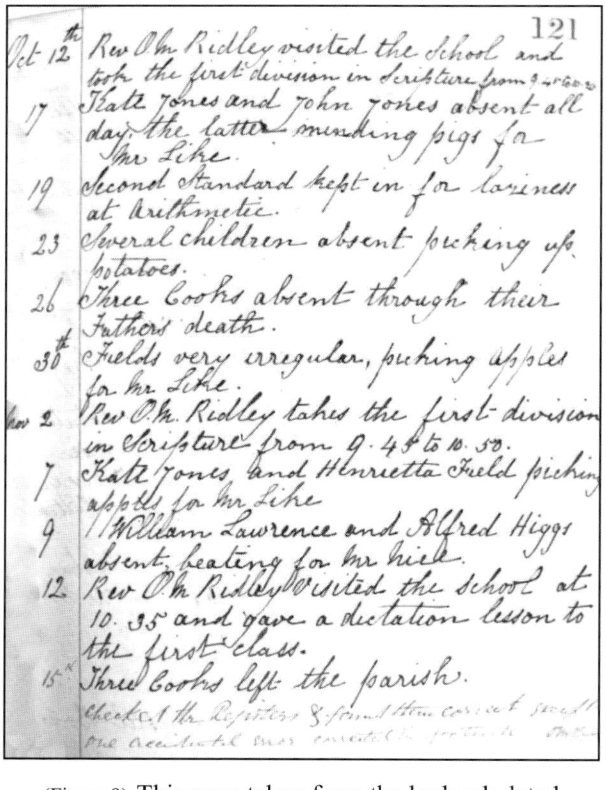
121

Oct 12th Rev O M Ridley visited the School and took the first division in Scripture from 9.40 to ...
17 Kate Jones and John Jones absent all day, the latter minding pigs for Mr Like.
19 Second Standard kept in for laziness at Arithmetic.
23 Several children absent picking up potatoes.
26 Three Cooks absent through their Father's death.
30th Fields very irregular, picking apples for Mr Like.
Nov 2 Rev O.M. Ridley takes the first division in Scripture from 9.45 to 10.50.
7 Kate Jones and Henrietta Field picking apples for Mr Like
9 William Lawrence and Alfred Higgs absent beating for Mr Hill.
12 Rev O M Ridley visited the school at 10.35 and gave a dictation lesson to the first class.
15th Three Cooks left the parish.

(Figure 9) This page taken from the logbook dated Oct-Nov 1882 records many entries of the children working on the land and beating.

January 20th *"this week I have had a hard struggle with the bad discipline, which seems to be the order of the day here."*

January 26th *"the children taught the song The Owl and the Pussycat."*

February 15th *"attendance better than ever 34, the children have commenced their examination garments. Rev Griffith has attended school daily over last month and taken religious Scriptures, the behaviour is gradually improving."*

Child Labour

Children missing school to work in the fields were regularly reported in the logbook,

November 9th 1874 *"Five boys away beating for Sir Henry"*, (This was a yearly entry, the boys would be off school beating for Garnons estate shoot, on Bishopstone hill). January 31st 1874 *"Aaron Lloyd away this week bird watching."* (This was a centuries old job carried out by children watching the newly planted cornfield and driving away any birds eating the seeds. If crows or other birds landed in the newly planted field Aaron would rush about banging on a home made drum, triangle or wooden rattle, similar to the rattles used at football matches in later years, to frighten away the birds. Every day from dawn to dark, starting at 4 o'clock on summer mornings, he would be trudging about the fields in all weather for a miserly sum of 6d per week. Sometimes in the logbook bird watching was referred to by the more specific name of crow watching. Aaron was only 8 years old). It would have been more important to the family for Aaron to earn a few pence than attend school. February 2nd 1876 *"Aaron Lloyd back to school after bird watching for ten weeks."* Aaron's sister Margaret missed even more schooling, January 22nd 1877 *"Margaret Lloyd readmitted into school after 5 year absence."*

This followed the November 16th 1876 school report; "*one boy who appears on the schedule had been employed contrary to the provisions of the Elementary Education Act 1876.*" Guess who? Aaron Lloyd. A visit from the inspector to his home on Bishon Common discovered his non-attending sister who was ordered back to school, hence the January entry.

This did not stop the traditional way of children working to help out their parents, November 8th 1881 "*Alfred Higgs away cider making, last week away beating at Garnons.*" (Alfred was aged 10 years and lived at Swiss Cottage on the hill, the Higgs family occupied the cottage for the next 80 years), March 13th 1883 *"Albert Vaughan watching crows for Mr Luther (not Lawful)"* April 10th 1883 *"Albert Vaughan back at school after watching birds nearly 5 weeks)"*

(After the last Education Act in 1870 it was against the law for children not to attend school)

Sometimes the children worked under the pretence of illness, January 25th 1889 *"J Hyde returned to school on Monday after a month's illness, the manual work has been done."*

On September 15th 1872 "*the school closed for the five weeks harvest holiday*". An entry similar to this was recorded every year, August 29th 1883 *"School closed for harvest holiday"* October 9th *"School opened day after hop picking was finished"* October 15th 1888 *"School opened this morning only 16 children the remainder gone hop picking."*

The teachers thought they had the authority to reopen the school after the harvest holiday on a specified day, several entries made in the logbook dismissed this, October 1st 1890 *"closed the school for the remainder of week not been able to get children to school as hop picking not finished,"* September 28th 1891, *"reopened school this morning no children attending owing to hop picking not being finished."*

(Hop picking was looked upon as essential work; if the school opened before the picking was finished, no children would attend, some clear evidence of how agriculture still depended on child labour. Nearly every week the teacher would record children not attending school because they were working. In this year alone the children were absent through beating, singling swedes, apple picking, cider making, bird scaring, minding pigs, pigeon shooting, carrying wood, binding, haymaking, gathering mushrooms, gathering acorns, absent through their parents' or grandparents' illness. In all cases the children are aged between 8-11 years old.)

Sickness in the School

The children's illnesses were often recorded, September 26th 1874 *"six boys away with ringworm."* October 14th 1876 *"twelve children absent with whooping cough."* February 27th 1884 *"half the school absent with mumps"* April 21st 1886 *"School closed on account of whooping cough."* May 3rd 1886 *"School reopens several children still very poorly."* Three serious epidemics hit the parish, diphtheria in 1878, scarlet fever in 1882 and measles in 1885; all claimed the lives of children.

The diphtheria epidemic started in February 1878, the teacher recorded on February 6th *"children away with sore throats."* This quickly turned into something more serious February 14th *"School closed through sickness."* March 4th *"School reopens by Doctor's permission."* March 6th *"16 children absence through illness."* March 18th *"Dr Sandford visits school, orders it to be closed till further notice."* April 15th *"School reopens after one month."* April 26th *"average very small as Dr Sandford will not allow any child to come back where a house has been infected. The children have been running wild these last 14 weeks."*

This outbreak of diphtheria claimed the lives of three children, Alfred Haines age 3 who lived at Stonehouse, Alfred Pewtress from the Steps Farm and Rebecca Watkins aged 13 from The Cottage on Bishon Lane. The epidemic spread throughout the school due to the slow response of the authorities in closing the school, children's lives were put at risk and some died through their incompetence. Complaints were made against these officers; they were called to appear before the newly formed Weobley Rural Sanitary Authority to answer this charge.

A report in the Hereford Times dated March 23rd 1878 describes the outcome of this enquiry.

The chairman of the authority was the Reverend G H Davenport. Dr. Sandford was a medical officer of health and Mr Lloyd the Inspector of Nuisances, both were questioned by the board on the outbreak of diphtheria in Bishopstone but the officers blamed each other for not acting on information received.

Reverend Ridley, rector of Bishopstone had written a letter, which was read out at the enquiry, saying that a lot of children were suffering from ulcerated sore throats undoubtedly of a highly contagious form. This letter prompted Mr. Lloyd to visit Bishopstone School on February 27th 1878 but he thought that there was no epidemic. Dr Sandford said he believed this disease had been raging for some time, the school had been shut and reopened by a private doctor without his knowledge, and Dr Sandford then produced a death certificate signed by Peter Giles Jr. the local doctor. The vice chairman asked Dr. Sandford *"do these private doctors think they know how to treat the cases or do you know better than they*." (Laughter), Dr. Sandford replies "*I am much obliged to you but I must with respect fully decline to answer the question*." (Renewed laughter) the Weobley Rural Sanitary Authority acted swiftly at the end of this enquiry by dispatching Dr. Sandford immediately after the meeting to Bishopstone with instructions to close the school, which he did.

The board went on to deal with other business, outbreaks of scarlet fever in Weobley and typhoid fever at Upperton.

The year of 1882 will be remembered as the year scarlet fever came to the parish; it would leave its tragic mark on two families, the Evans and the Haines. The Evans family's year had started badly, with the death of their baby Annie. George Evans worked for the Weobley Highway Board as a highway labourer. In the middle of March the fever arrived with seven children off school. The school log entry dated March 30th states that three Evans children were away due to the illness of their brother; the school was closed on April 5th for a fortnight due to scarlet fever. On the April 5th John Evans aged 14 died, 2 days later his elder brother George died, he was 17 years old. A gravestone in Bishopstone Churchyard remembers the three Evans children.

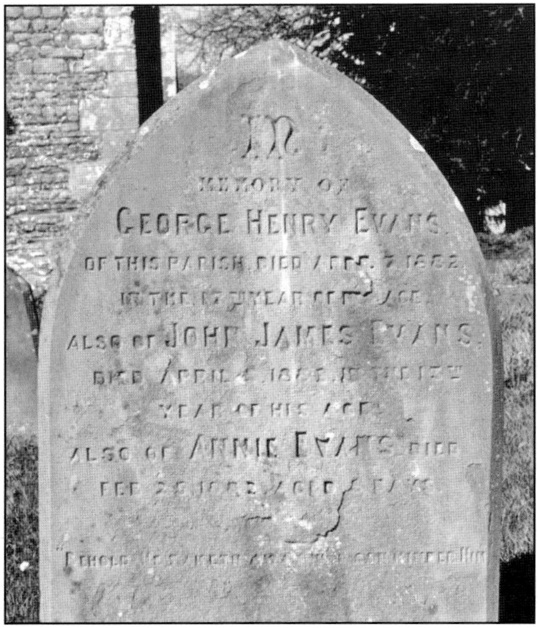

(Figure 10) Headstone of the three Evans children who died from scarlet fever

The school reopened, but the scarlet fever was still contagious with some children off school to look after their parents. On July 7th little William Haines aged 5 from Stonehouse also died from the fever. To his father and mother it was a tragedy as they had already lost two children when typhoid fever had visited the parish 4 years earlier. The contagious fever did not only leave its devastation on the parishioners as a travelling family of gypsies called Smith passing through the village lost their twins Elick and Ettie who were just 1 year old. Five young people and children were buried in Bishopstone churchyard before the scarlet fever finally left the parish.

The next epidemic, of measles, spread throughout the parish in the summer of 1885 recorded in the logbook as simply, August 10th *"several children absent with measles."* (This measles outbreak claimed the lives of two children, Sarah Alice Barnett on September 2nd aged 7, and little Henry Haines (Stonehouse) aged 6 on September 23rd. The Barnett family lived at the lodge and the father was the coachman for Rev Ridley. Exactly one month after Sarah was buried her mother Margaret died aged 44 years; the father Daniel must have been distraught because twelve months earlier on June 21st 1884 he had buried his eldest son Henry aged just 14 reducing his family of six to just three, himself and two sons Fredrick and George.)

Day Holidays.

Hereford's May Fair always caused some absentees, May 6th 1874 *"several children absent May Fair"*, May 5th 1880 *"13 children gone to May fair"* children visited the fair with their parents, some years the school closed for a day's holiday May 6th 1891 *"School closed May Fair".*

The logbook records that the school gave very few day holidays, some were given on religious days, for example February 23rd 1887 *"Ash Wednesday whole holiday",* some days to view the military, August 6th 1883 *"whole holiday given (review at Monnington)"*

If the day holiday was not given the children missed school, as on June 20th 1879 *"children not in till ten past ten as soldiers passing on turnpike road",* July 4th 1879 *"all children gone to see the soldiers".* On other odd days the school closed for various reasons, August 16th 1889 *"half a day's holiday given on account of Garnons Flower Show".* August 6th 1891 *"holiday given so children can attend Moccas flower show",* October 29th 1891 *"holiday given today (Thursday) in order for the mistress to attend drawing examination at the School of Art Hereford",* January 12th 1892 *"closed holiday, as the schoolroom was required for concert".* Any major event in the parish would also mean many children skipped school April 30th 1891 *"Attendance poor today due to a sale at neighbouring farm.(Bishon Farm)".*

Weather

The weather featured in many entries as the reason for non-attendance of pupils. The Yazor brook flooded, a problem we still have today and flood water would surround the cottages on Bishon Common as on November 10th 1875 *"Children from common sent home at 3 o'clock in consequence of the water rising so high they would not be able to get through",* December 8th 1876 *"children from common sent home rising water",* May 14th 1886 *"Common and other places flooded".*

For many years the school closed because of deep snow, this was a period of severe winters January 18th 1881 *"Snow drifted so children could not get to school"*, March 9th 1883 *"Frost and snow so severe children could not get to school"*, February 14th 1889 *"School closed three days no children could come on account of snow"*, March 10th 1891 *"no children came Tuesday and Wednesday due to heavy fall of snow"*. The most severe winter recorded was in 1892 when snow lay on the ground from January until April: January 19th *"closed, heavy fall of snow"* February 19th *"attendance poor owing to heavy snowstorm"* April 15th *"a continuous snow all day on Wednesday brought down the average attendance figure"*

(Figure 11) Volunteers' review at Garnons August 1st 1887, the children were given a day's holiday to attend.

Visitors to the School

Important visitors were always recorded in the logbook with clergy visitors given the most prominence; the rector of Bishopstone would attend the school often to give his one-hour scripture lesson and often bring with him one of his clergy friends

"Mrs Lane Freer came to school on August 16th 1872 and gave children little presents," the logbook records, although Mrs Freer now lived in Malvern she still made regular visits to her little school.

July 7th 1875 *"Sir George Cornwell came to the school",.*

(Sir George was M. P. for Herefordshire, he would have been an important visitor)

A mysterious episode in 1876, regarding the change of rectors in Bishopstone is well documented in the school logbook, it started on February 9th 1876 *"Rev M E Welby and Mrs Welby came to School"*. The Rev Welby, the school thought, was to be the new incoming rector because on March 7th Rev G A Robins called to say goodbye and take up his new post as rector of Hedson in Bucks. On March 17th the Rev Welby came to school but it does not say why he came. Mr Welby was offered the living of Bishopstone, a position he appears to have accepted and then declined, as he never came to live in the parish, contrary to the entry in the Kelly's Directory of 1876, which lists Rev Welby as Rector of Bishopstone. Another entry in the Church Times February 1876 reads "The Bishopstone parish has been offered to the Reverend Montague Welby of Magdalen College Oxford and has been accepted by him".

By July 1876 the Reverend Oliver Ridley of Cobham had accepted the living of Bishopstone and was instituted on Sunday 8th October by the Bishop at the morning service in Bishopstone Church. I cannot find out any reason why Mr Welby never took up his position so it remains a mystery. Yet fourteen years later he did accept the living at Mansel Lacy. Rev Welby who was the son of Sir William Earle Welby 1st baronet married Mary Dilwyn a well-known amateur photographer in 1857.

On November 1st 1876 Rev Ridley is recorded as taking his first scripture lesson at the school and in the July of 1877 he brought Lord Darnby's daughter to see the school.

The daughters of the Reverend Robins, who were born and brought up in Bishopstone Rectory, would often return by train from Bucks to visit the school; the entry on October 18th *"Miss Beryl and Miss Monica Robins visit the school their favourable spot once again"*.

The Rev Ridley's wife and daughters, like the previous rector's family also helped out with needlework and reading lessons at the school. Other visitors recorded, on February 10th 1885 *"Mrs Nice visits school, bought several presents for children"*. (Mr Nice was the new agent for Garnons who had just moved into Downshill House.). Queen Victoria's birthday was celebrated in the school, May 24th 1887 *"Queen's birthday the Miss Ridleys called to give children a copy of the life of her Majesty"*.

September 30th 1889, *"Rev Ridley calls at school to say goodbye"*.

(Rev Ridley leaves parish after being Rector of Bishopstone for thirteen years).
November 1st 1889, *"Mrs Davenport brings Rev Griffiths to School"*.
(Mrs Davenport, wife of Rev Davenport introduced the new Rector of Bishopstone, Rev C E S Griffiths to the school)

Demise of the School

The school started to go downhill from 1883, Miss Drane the old school mistress had fallen ill and left soon afterwards and reading through the reports it becomes evident that Rev Davenport as landlord would not continue giving his support to the school.
H M school inspector L W Colt-Williams Esq. visited the school on December 3rd 1883.
He wrote this report.
The condition of the school is fair only, weakness in spelling fluently, and in arithmetic in the first and forth, Infants well taught, the children of six are not taught any subtraction, handwriting poor, grammar is a failure, Miss Drane must attend much more carefully to circular 217 as alterations are frequent in her attendance register. I do not for a moment suspect fraud, but the rules laid down on circular 217 are so clear that no carelessness ought to occur in registration.
As if to reinforce this report on the children's failings an entry appeared on February 9th 1884 *"Admitted Agnes Walter between 8-9years does not know her A.B.C. admitted brother over 7 never been to school at all"*. The constant movement of farm labourers between farms would mean in some areas the children did not receive any schooling.
March 27th 1884 *"Temporary change today by M Morris who has been engaged for three months in order to give Miss Drane a rest for that period"*.
(Miss Drane had been suffering from health problems for the last twelve months; now aged 51 she had been in charge of the school for the last twenty one years. Leonora Drane never taught again at the school, she moved to Stretton Sugwas where she continued teaching till 1901. She could see the uncertainty of keeping the school open and it was never the same after she left, with a continual change of staff and the children playing up.)
June 17th 1887, *"M Morris resigns this afternoon"*. (Miss C E Phillips became the next temporary teacher)
On January 2nd 1888 Miss Martha E Johnson was succeeded by Miss C E Philips
Report from Education Authority from visit December 20th 1887. School year broken through Miss Drane's illness, Answering out of turn should be checked. The infants of five are backward and could write better if not allowed to shout out as much. English (Fail). A board-separating fence between the offices (toilets) *needs replacing.*
February 3rd 1888, "*Ada, Agnes, Jessie and Florence Like have gone to Mansel school"*.
(John Like of Court Farm moved his children to Mansel Lacy School, possibly because he did not agree with the continual changes of teachers at Bishopstone School, but more likely to please the Reverend Davenport his landlord. Mansel Lacy School was purpose built to hold 160 scholars, it was under-subscribed with around half that number of pupils registered, and two teachers to support.)
The School Inspector reported on March 1st 1889, "*The condition of the office* (toilets) *as to the repair and cleanliness is most unsatisfactory and requires attention"*.
The Rev Ridley replied that "the offices were cleaned before I left home in February. It is now repaired and will not occur again."
February 6th 1890 School Report after Dec visit:- *offices need attention it is scanty and ill constructed, the boy's offices open directly onto a public footpath, to this fact is attributed the very foul conditions. Plans of any new building (or alterations) that may be proposed, drawn in accordance with the enclosed rules, must be submitted to the department for approval, before work is begun.*
June 20th 1890 *"Resigned from this school M E Johnson, succeeded by Miss M B Lowe"*.
October 1st 1890*"The school has been whitewashed and cleaned during harvest holiday and the alternations required by the Education Department to be made to the offices have been corrected"*.
January 20th 1891 School inspectors report from visit in Dec:-*The school has experienced a change of teacher since the last inspection, not withstanding this circumstance it continue modestly and passes a highly successful examination, especially in reading and writing, arithmetic is good in the lower standard but falls off in the fourth and fifth standard, English is good, all the children speak with fluency, accuracy and have fair expression. Counting on the fingers should be discouraged.*
A deduction has been necessary under article 82 from the grant for the months during which the school has been in charge of Miss M B Lowe who is not qualified for recognition under Article 52.
(On receiving the report Miss M B Lowe resigned, it's not known if she gave any indication that she was not a qualified teacher, but the school could not operate without the grant money to pay the teacher's wages and the running costs of the school)
January 28th 1891, "*School closed on absent of teachers"*. February 2nd 1891, *Miss Isabel James succeeded Miss M B Lowe as teacher.*

February 13th 1891, *Visit without notice, register tested quite correct, the school premise would be better for a general clean up.* The school inspector visited the school unannounced.
January 21st 1892, Report received from Education Authority:-*The grant under article 105 can hardly be recommended next year unless the results of examination give greater evidence of the efficiency of the teacher.*
(It appears that teachers from the late 19th century were even then expected to produce good results from exams just like our modern day teachers)
March 29th 1893, *Easter Holidays commence, I have taken down maps to prepare school for a general clean, walls limed and paintwork renewed, the room could do with a general scrubbing, it has not been cleaned since the 12 weeks since my advent here.*
April 14th 1893, *reopened school today, the school is still in a most disgusting state, it has not been touched. If all my efforts are going to be checked at every turn, I shall certainly give up the work. It is not much good to work night and day for the advancement of the school if the building is allowed to fall into such a state of dirtiness and decay.*
April 27th 1893, *No of children present 27, on books 41, besides 4 babies, making in all 45 on the register.* The authorities asked the teacher to record how many children were on the schools books.
March 3rd 1894 School report, *H M Inspector reports that the school premises are not in good repair that the premises are built of half brick and half timber. That the room is very draughty as the doors fit badly and the cloakroom and offices* (toilets) *is insufficient. My lords will be unable to continue the recognition of the premises after the end of the current school year unless plans are submitted of satisfactory premises (Article 85(a) of the code). The special attention of the manager is requested to the form 69.* (The landlord, the Reverend Davenport was certainly not going to build a purpose built school for Bishopstone parish when the school at Mansel Lacy could easily accommodate all the Bishopstone children.)

The last few months the school remained open became a continual struggle for Miss James the schoolteacher, she records on March 19th 1894 *"ordinary work will be taken instead of needlework because material has run out".* June 25th *"5 dozen new books arrive".* July 12th *"books have been returned as necessary as the school will close this year".* July 20th *this day the school will not open as the teacher is away on important business. Average for week 13.5.*
This was the last entry in the Bishopstone School logbook, so I presume the school closed on July 20th 1894 after 45 years of providing schooling for the children of Bishopstone parish. At the 1896 vestry meeting it was proposed to move the balance from the school account, £14 9s 1d, to the church account. This was the final transaction and record of Bishopstone's Church of England School.
Prices of Foxley had built the school at Mansel Lacy to accommodate the children from all the three parishes under their lordship of Mansel Lacy, Yazor and Bishopstone thus explaining why the school was so large. After Bishopstone School closed some of the children went to Mansel Lacy School, but the majority of the children attended Kenchester School, much to the annoyance of Rev Davenport because it was a nonconformist chapel school.

1861-70

From 1851-73 Bishopstone like the rest of England prospered in what was called the "Victorian prosperity" period, 1860-62 saw the building of the Hereford to Hay railway, part of a national railway building programme resulting from the new wealth experienced by Victorian Britain. Although the Hereford to Hay railway did not pass through the parish it did signal the start of the industrial revolution in the area. Social reform had also started; labourers' children had been attending the village school since 1849 and this new experience gave them far more opportunities than their parents, whose only outlook was working a lifetime on the land. Agriculture was going through a boom period; this fact alone became the main influence in the prosperity of the parish.
Bishopstone as recorded in the 1861 census, supported the highest population of people ever recorded in its history, 288 individuals were living or staying in the parish that night, comprising 147 males and 141 females. The census returns list only three people living in the parish on relief, besides the six inmates occupying the Hospital, these were the lowest figures ever shown on any parish records. The parish's prosperity was in part helped by the fact that Archdeacon Lane Freer was a great benefactor to the parish, he paid the rent on cottages for the poor and covered all the running expenses of the church, which would have normally fallen on to the parishioners. The Archdeacon also provided the school free of charge for the parish children, plus a choirmaster and organist.
For the first time in the Bishopstone census, Bunshill was included, listing the farmhouse, one labourer's house in the farm buildings and three cottages attached to the farm situated on Bishon common. Bunshill was officially part of Mansel Lacy parish, although it did become part of Bishopstone in 1884.

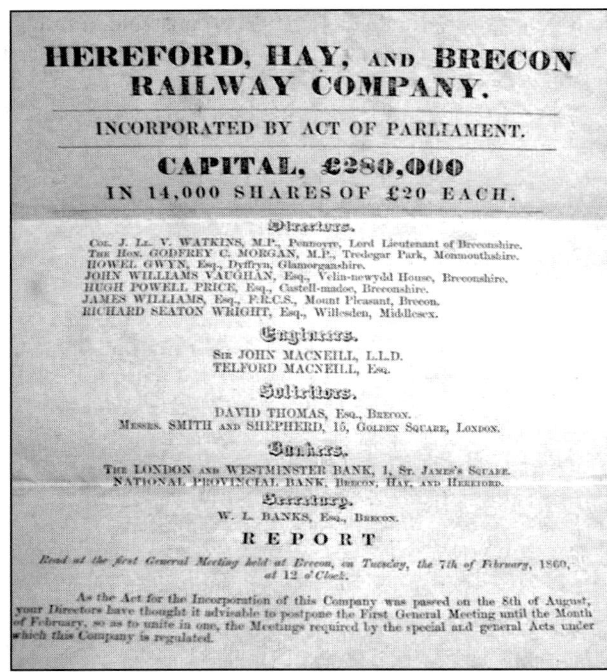

HEREFORD, HAY, AND BRECON RAILWAY COMPANY.

INCORPORATED BY ACT OF PARLIAMENT.

CAPITAL, £280,000

IN 14,000 SHARES OF £20 EACH.

Directors.

COL. J. LL. V. WATKINS, M.P., Pennoyre, Lord Lieutenant of Breconshire.
THE HON. GODFREY C. MORGAN, M.P., Tredegar Park, Monmouthshire.
HOWEL GWYN, Esq., Dyffryn, Glamorganshire.
JOHN WILLIAMS VAUGHAN, Esq., Velin-newydd House, Breconshire.
HUGH POWELL PRICE, Esq., Castell-madoc, Breconshire.
JAMES WILLIAMS, Esq., F.R.C.S., Mount Pleasant, Brecon.
RICHARD SEATON WRIGHT, Esq., Willesden, Middlesex.

Engineers.

SIR JOHN MACNEILL, L.L.D.
TELFORD MACNEILL, Esq.

Solicitors.

DAVID THOMAS, Esq., BRECON.
MESSRS. SMITH AND SHEPHERD, 15, GOLDEN SQUARE, LONDON.

Bankers.

THE LONDON AND WESTMINSTER BANK, 1, ST. JAMES'S SQUARE.
NATIONAL PROVINCIAL BANK, BRECON, HAY, AND HEREFORD.

Secretary.

W. L. BANKS, Esq., BRECON.

REPORT

Read at the first General Meeting held at Brecon, on Tuesday, the 7th of February, 1860, at 12 o'Clock.

As the Act for the Incorporation of this Company was passed on the 8th of August, your Directors have thought it advisable to postpone the First General Meeting until the Month of February, so as to unite in one, the Meetings required by the special and general Acts under which this Company is regulated.

(Figure 12) Railway Company report on their first general meeting held on February 7th 1860.

The census also shows there were 62 houses in Bishopstone, two of them uninhabited, fifty scholars were on the registration books of Bishopstone School aged between 4-12 years, with Susan Charlton the resident teacher living in the School House. Only eleven heads of households were born in Bishopstone. The main employment came from agriculture which lists 43 farm labourers living in the parish, although some of these were now recorded as carrying out more specific skills, - there were four waggoners, three waggoner's boys and a cowman.

William King was the first resident in the parish, according to the 1861 census, who came as a direct result of the industrial revolution; he lived on Bishon common with his family and they originated from Leicestershire. William was a railway guardsman; he was the first manual worker to live in Bishopstone directly employed by a company. In 1861 the railway was being built but not finished, the regular goods service did not start until August 1862. It poses the question how did William get to work? The normal means for labourers would be walking, but the distance to Hereford station would have been a very long walk there and back every day; the bicycle or hobbyhorse had just been invented, but they were not affordable for the working class. I suspect William was possibly a guard on the train used to bring materials up the track as it was being built; good evidence that the railway had reached Bishon common by 1861.

The Hereford, Hay and Brecon Railway was opened in sections:[6]

Hereford to Moorhampton, October 24th 1862	Goods only,
Hereford to Eardisley, June 30th 1863	Passengers and Goods.
Eardisley to Hay, July 11th 1864	Passengers and Goods.
Hay to Brecon, September 19th 1864	Passengers and Goods.

Another person who came to live in the parish as a direct consequence of the railway was William Smith from Birmingham, a brick maker. He met Sarah, daughter of Thomas Lewis the local mason and they married on June 27th 1860 in Bishopstone church; after the wedding the newly-weds lived with their in-laws in a cottage on the hill. Thomas Lewis would have worked on building the railway like many other local masons and labourers.

This was a busy period within the parish: it was suddenly transformed from a sleepy tranquil countryside parish, to a busy construction site with hundreds of navvies and workers in the area who pushed the railway through in less than two years.

The only other person employed outside the local vicinity was John Christy the former tailor who lived at Scaldback cottage with his wife and six children; he had just joined the Herefordshire Constabulary to become a county constable. He had served as the parish constable since 1850. His service records with the police still exist;[7] the Herefordshire Constabulary was formed in March 1857 and John Christy was the eighteenth person to join the force so his warrant number was 18. His application form states, age 35 years, height 5 foot 7 inches, pale complexion, grey eyes, brown hair and a stout figure and that he was formerly a tailor, married with six children. Formal police service was recorded as none, only experience gained from being elected parish constable for Bishopstone. His new appointment started on March 16th 1857.

In April 1858 he was reported for receiving money for his assistance in watching the Wye. For working privately he was fined 20s by the Police Authority.

(John would have been paid by Sir Henry Cotterell's agents to watch for poachers operating on the river. Landowners in this part of the Wye took salmon by rod and nets and records show the rewards could be great. In May 1846 a royal sturgeon 8ft 6 inches, weighing 182 lbs was captured near the Old Weir; in 1887 a salmon weighing 51 lb was caught at Cannon Bridge. John worked with the estate ghillie before he was the parish constable so presumably he just carried on helping out after he had joined the Police Force, until some jealous parishioner reported him to the authorities, possibly the local poacher.)

This little episode did him no harm because in June 1858 he was promoted to first class constable; a further promotion came in 1861 when he was made up to a second-class sergeant. John served with the Hereford division from 1857 to 1862, when his wife Ann died suddenly; she is buried in Bishopstone churchyard. After Ann died Sergeant Christy left Bishopstone and moved to live in the Weobley police house; his final move within the force came in 1865 when he was given charge of the Dilwyn section.
Sergeant Christy retired early on October 1st 1876 after suffering a ruptured muscle in his left leg and collected a pension of 10s 6d a week. After he retired from the Police Force John Christy became the publican of the Anchor Inn Leominster where he died on December 21st 1898.

Things were still tough for some of the poor families. In 1861 Elizabeth Gardener whose husband George had died in 1853, (no relations to the Gardiners of Bishopstone court) was forced to live on relief in Berrington Hospital with her five children aged between eight and sixteen. The Gardener's family story is intriguing because it illustrates both the opportunity it gave to some of the poor living in Victorian society and the utter devastation it could inflict on others. Their story started in the early part of the 19th century in a cottage on Bishopstone Hill, with two brothers from this very poor family, Richard born in 1809 and his younger brother George born in 1811, they both started their working life as farm labourers at twelve years old. After getting married they both lived in cottages on Bishopstone Hill. George, who married Elizabeth, had seven surviving children, he died in 1853 aged 45 years old, and this left his wife Elizabeth to bring up the children alone. Their youngest was only six months old when George died; Elizabeth asked for help from the Berrington charity, her plea was accepted, and she was given one of the almshouses to live in. Elizabeth subsidised her Berrington charity money by working as a washerwoman. The 1871 census revealed that Fanny, Elizabeth's daughter who was only two when her father died, was working as a maid for the Clerk to the Bank of England in a large house, at 19 Devonshire Road, Lambeth, London. How she made the move from Bishopstone to London is a mystery.
Fanny's uncle Richard and his family were involved in most remarkable travels around the country thanks mainly to the industrial revolution. Richard had married Mary Ann Parlour from Bishopstone and their marriage produced eight children. The 1881 census reveals the extent of their travels, because it lists where all the children were born, Sarah the eldest was born in 1848 in Bishopstone, Mary Ann followed, born in Stoke on Trent in 1852; by 1853 the family were in Shropshire where Thomas was born. The family then moved to Sedgley Staffordshire from 1854-57 where Louisa and Ann were born, during 1858-63 the family lived in Bewdley Shropshire where they saw the arrival of Elizabeth and John, by 1865 they were back in Sedgley where Henry James was born. The 1871 census shows the family were back in Herefordshire living in a cottage called Charing Cross in Weobley, Richard was then working back on the land as a farm labourer. The 1881 census records that the family were now living at Blatchinworth and Calderbrook in Lancashire, residing in a mill terrace house and working in a cotton mill. Richard although 72 years old was labouring at the mill and all the children worked in the mill, Mary Ann and Elizabeth as cotton winders, Ann, John and Henry James as cotton weavers.

One explanation could be that the family fell into poor relief on a number of occasions and entered the workhouse, Weobley workhouse had a tradition of sending their paupers to work in far off mills. The overseers paid for the train fares because they thought that it would be cheaper in the long run to pay for the family to move away and find work than have the whole family claiming relief from the overseers. Because Richard and Mary Ann were illiterate some of the census records are not consistent in stating where each child was born and although all the same place names do appear on every census form they are in different orders. What a change for a family from starting off married life living on Bishopstone Hill looking over the Herefordshire countryside to ending up living in a Lancashire mill town with its back to back houses and cobbled streets.

The Rectory lodge was occupied by William Cogan head gardener for Archdeacon Freer. His census entry records that he put up two young boarders, Edward Walton and Herbert Hadley who came from Worcester, they were the children of the Archdeacon's friends, and both lodged in Bishopstone so they could attend the school. Also lodging with William was John Whitney organist of Bishopstone church and a Professor of Music. Archdeacon Freer was very proud of the church's Father Smith organ and the church choir, so he employed John, a professional, to keep up the high standards he expected.

John Price was the oldest person recorded on the census at 106 years, he was a former miller from Michaelchurch and also an old soldier, he died in 1864 in his 110th year and was buried in Bishopstone churchyard where his gravestone can still be found.
This poses the questions why was he living in Bishopstone, how could he afford to live alone in a cottage, did he have relatives in the parish?

An article in the Hereford Times dated February 20th 1864 gives all the answers.

Death of John Price, the centenarian. This old man, who is said to have attained the patriarchal age of 109 years, a native of Michaelchurch, in this county, died on Saturday morning last, soon after nine o'clock, at 113 Widemarsh-Street, where he had been living with his son-in-law. What, perhaps was most remarkable about this extraordinary specimen of longevity was the clearness of his mental faculties to within a very few days of his death. When walking along the streets of the city, more erect in his bearing than many a quarter of a century younger. Indeed, externally, the only indications that he was a man of great age were his shrivelled features. To use his own expression, he never drank more alcohol than served his turn, nor smoked tobacco; for before he commenced the habit he saw a man's stomach opened by the doctor of the regiment in which he was serving, who was a confirmed smoker, and the blackened state of the stomach deterred him from ever indulging in the habit. Price served about 14 years in the army; he was a carpenter and millwright by trade; and for some years in the more advanced period of his life he lived at Bishopstone, under the kind care of the late benevolent Ven. Archdeacon Lane Freer, whose philanthropy Price long experienced. Frequently, after he had passed the bounds of a century, he walked from Bishopstone to this city to have another look at the "ancient city" and to hold a bit of a chat with some of its aged inhabitants, who were as children compared with him; but since the death of his best friend, the late Archdeacon, he has lived with his son-in-law. About eight months ago, he began to think of having his coffin made, and many of the tradesmen in that line appeared desirous of having the job, but this venerable dweller on earth, hearing of the excellent workmanship which was generally sent out from Mr Merrick's shop, Offa-street, called upon him, and gave an order to make a coffin. The veteran stood up against the door to be measured, and his height then was 5ft 8in; and when the coffin was completed he examined it carefully and expressed himself perfectly satisfied with the workmanship. The old man often remarked to Mr Merrick that he thought he should not reach his 109th birthday, and that if he did he should not live long after. Before his death he was confined to his room for about a month, and he breathed his last quietly on Saturday morning. Much doubt has been entertained respecting Price's age. His benevolent friend, the late Archdeacon, was some few years ago at some pains to inquire into the evidence, for it is well known that in the last century parish registers were loosely kept. After careful investigation the Archdeacon arrived at the conclusion that Price was really within two or three years of the age he represented himself, and, therefore, it is pretty certain that he was 106 at the time of his death.

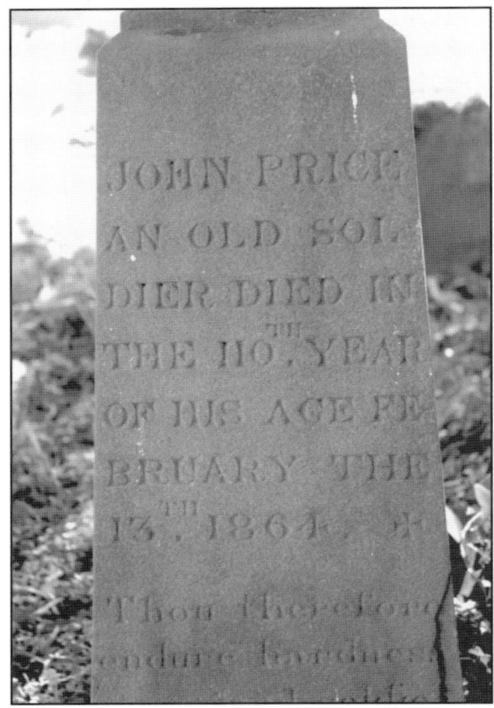

(Figure 13) John Price's headstone

The first village grocery shop in Bishon had opened by 1861; this shop was in direct competition with Hancocks the long established shop situated at Bridge Ash on the main turnpike road. Mary Davies from a black and white cottage across the road from the Lodge operated Bishon shop; the shop traded for about five years until the cottage fell into disrepair and the Davies's left. The cottage had completely disappeared by 1871.

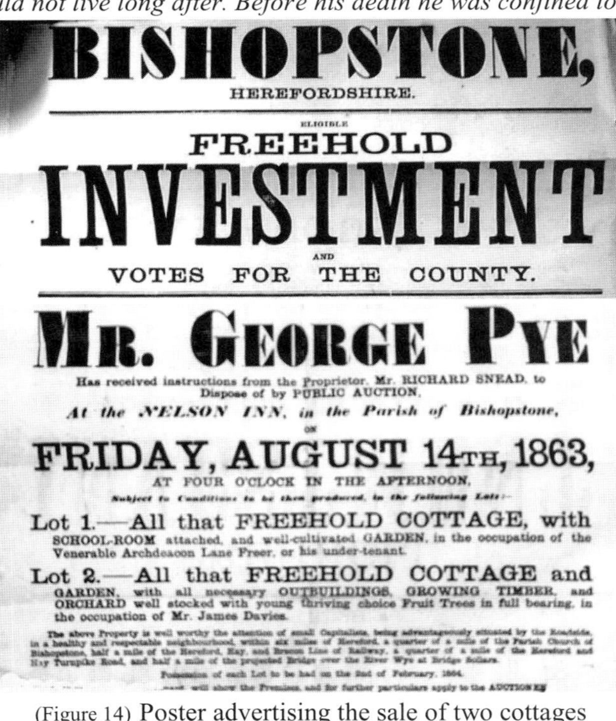

(Figure 14) Poster advertising the sale of two cottages one a with School attached the other Davies' Shop

Mary's husband James was the parish clerk and sexton for many years. Rev Davenport had purchased this cottage with the school at an auction[8] held at the Lord Nelson Inn on Friday August 14th 1863 for £350 from owner John Snead, who had only just acquired the freehold of the two properties after a long court case. Written evidence from the court case revealed that Sarah Williams whose husband built the original cottage was addicted to snuff; to fund her addiction this timber frame cottage was built at the other end of the plot, and the rent money used to pay for her snuff. Rev Davenport the new landlord showed no interest in keeping the cottage habitable, the deeds registered at the court case accurately date the cottage, part of which was now transformed into a school, as being built in 1733.

The blacksmith in 1861 was William Powell the nephew of Barnaby Hancock the former blacksmith. He grew up at Forge Cottage with his widowed mother who was housekeeper to her brother Barnaby. William died around 1865 and his wife Elizabeth was then listed as blacksmith of Bishopstone. Whether she was actually manually carrying out blacksmithing we have no indication but there are records of other women blacksmiths working in Herefordshire during this period. In 1867 Elizabeth married her employee blacksmith Richard Boucher; her eldest son William was then 10 years old.

There was a butcher's Shop operating out of one of the cottages in Burcott Row in 1861, run by Joseph Pritchard and his son. The Pritchard family had owned the property for many years it was usually let out to tenants, normally the farm labourers. Joseph had decided to open up a new butcher's shop but it was not very successful only lasting four years he then moved on to Much Birch to open a shop there. The name Burcott Row, could have derived from the fact there was a butcher's cottage located here at this time, of that I am not sure but the name only appears on documents after this date.

William Magness my great great grandfather a farm labourer worked for Joseph Plant of Court Farm he lived in the other half of Burcott Row with his wife and seven children, all aged under 13 years, they were the largest family in the parish in 1861.

The Rectory, home of Archdeacon Lane Freer was the only household in the parish run as a gentleman's residence. Henry Merton was the butler; James Apperley the pageboy was a local lad born in the Clovers, he was the son of John Apperley the wheelwright and he was destined to go on to greater things as reported on later in the book; Emily Summers was the ladies maid, Ellen Meredith held the position of cook, Ann Hughes who was born in Bishopstone was the kitchen maid. Also visiting as a houseguest, was Mary Macmichael from Middlesex who was a niece of the Archdeacon, she had brought her maid Susan Delarnere with her. They were staying in readiness for Mary's forthcoming marriage to John Cheese; this ceremony was officiated by the Archdeacon on August 22nd 1861 in Bishopstone church.

With agriculture now in a prosperous period there were eight farms and small holdings listed in the 1861 census, the largest being Bishopstone Court of 355 acres, still farmed by Joseph Plant, who employed seven labourers and two boys. Joseph was a bachelor, his cousin Ann Spender looked after him as housekeeper. He now employed John Arnold as a bailiff to run the farm, he also employed a dairymaid Elizabeth Hoity, and Charlotte Christy, daughter of John Christy the policeman, as housemaid; they all lived in. Joseph was a gentleman farmer who took his parish duties very seriously; over the years he held the duties of all the parish officials, as church warden, overseer of the poor and highway surveyor and also represented Bishopstone on the board of Weobley workhouse.

William Lloyd farmed Bishon farm covering 247 acres, he employed four labourers and two boys; ten years earlier the farm employed eight labourers, improved farming techniques had cut the workforce in half. These farm labourers were employed on a yearly contract and cottages were provided; depending on the agreement made between the two parties, some paid rent others did not. At busy times day labourers were still employed on the farms.

Parish Church (*St. Lawrence*).—Rev. George Augustus Robins, M.A., *Rector*. James Davis, *Parish Clerk*.
Village School (mixed).—Miss Leonora Drane, *Mistress*.
Almshouses.—Founded and endowed by Anne Berrington, A.D. 1723.

PRIVATE RESIDENTS.

Lloyd Mr. William, The Cottage
Robins Rev. George Augustus, M.A. (rector), The Rectory

COMMERCIAL.

Apperley John, wheelwright
Barnett Thomas, farmer, Bishon
Blashill Henry, farmer, agricultural implement, and manure agent, Steps farm, and at Hereford
Blashill Thomas, land steward to Sir Henry Geers Cotterell, Bart., Downshill
Davis James, shopkeeper and parish clerk
Gunter Miss Emma, *Nelson Inn*
Gunter Thomas, tailor
Hancock Mrs. Mary, shopkpr., Bridge Ash
Higgins William, shoemaker
Plant Joseph, farmer and churchwarden, Bishopstone court
Powell Mrs. Elizabeth, blacksmith, Bishon
Pritchard Joseph, farmer

(Figure 15) 1867 Kelly's Directory entry for Bishopstone

William a gentleman farmer purchased a lot of properties in Bishopstone over the years. It started when he attended an auction held at the Nelson on July 27th 1855 where he purchased his first acquisitions. Henry Edwards' widow ex Bunshill Farm had just died, her executors put up for sale three of her properties: "The Cottage" (tithe map no 159) on Bishon lane and two more cottages on Bishon Common (tithe map no's 142-143). The cottages on the common William was already renting to house his workmen, John Jenks and William Hall. On January 28th 1856 he bought the Nelson Inn and land from William Bythel, also on the same date he purchased a cottage on Bishon Common (tithe map no 135) for £200, and in 1860 he purchased one more cottage on Bishon Common (tithe map no 144) to house his workmen, John Jinks and William Hall. On March 6th 1861 he purchased another cottage and land on the common (130,136 on tithe map) on June 23rd 1862 he purchased a cottage in Bishon (tithe map no 167 now called the Old Post Office) for £250. He then built a new brick cottage attached to the cottage now called Mitres Rock. William's first wife died in 1862 aged 89 (he was 22 years younger), then in 1863 he married Caroline Withers, a local girl, who was only 28 years old. After the marriage he left Bishon Farm and moved into his first purchase, a large cottage on Bishon Lane (158,160 on tithe map), which still carries the name The Cottage today. William was also a good servant to Bishopstone, he always held one official parish position until he died in 1867. In his will[9] he left the Nelson Inn to his brother and brother-in-law who were his executors; they sold the premises with other cottages to Reverend Davenport of Foxley for £800 on April 18th 1868. Other properties owned by William were left for his new wife Caroline who continued to live in The Cottage on Bishon Lane.

ELIGIBLE SMALL FREEHOLD INVESTMENTS.

MR. J. H. SUNDERLAND will SELL by AUCTION, at the NELSON INN, BRIDGE SOLLARS, on FRIDAY, the 27th of JULY inst., at Four o'clock in the Afternoon, subject to conditions of Sale, all that substantially Brick-built COTTAGE RESIDENCE, with good Garden, Yard, Barn, Stable, and Outhouses, with about 3½ Acres (more or less) of highly productive Orcharding, the whole in a compact Ring Fence, and situate in the Parish of BISHOPSTONE, 5½ miles from Hereford, and within 100 yards of the Road leading from the Old Weir to Bishopstone, now in the occupation of Mr. George Gardiner. The House is in good repair, pleasantly situated, has good underground Cellaring throughout, two comfortable Sitting-rooms, three Bed-rooms, and one Dressing-room, with usual Offices and convenient Arrangements. The Fruit Trees are in their prime, and the Land in good condition.

Also, all those TWO stone-built LABOURERS' COTTAGES, with good Gardens attached, situate below the above-named Lot on the same Road, and now occupied by Jenks and another, the same being FREEHOLD and offering a good investment for small Capital.

For particulars, apply to WM. HUMFRYS, Esq., Solicitor, or to the AUCTIONEER, Hereford; and for a view, to the respective Tenants.

Hereford, July 6th, 1855.

(Figure 16) Auction advert Hereford Times 1855

Samuel Elliott farmed the 250 acres of Bunshill Farm. He employed five men and two boys, and lived with his wife Margaret and daughter Harriett, with a general servant and two farm workers living in.

Henry Blashill farmed the Steps Farm of 65 acres with his wife Mary, new baby daughter Eva and three servants living in. The Blashills are remembered for their work in the Woolhope Club, serving as chairmen a number of times.

Thomas Bailey aged 73 farmed Kenowley farm, with just 9 acres in Bishopstone parish and 20 acres in Mansel Gamage. His bachelor son Samuel helped out on the farm, also living in the farmhouse was his younger son John who operated a carrier business from the farm; he was married to Ann and they had a young daughter Emily aged five who attended Bishopstone school, quite a long trek each day to school for a five year old. Also living in was their farm servant Richard Thomas aged 56 years.

Just east of Kenowley round the hill lived Thomas and Mary Powell and their farm servant, they farmed Buckwell with its 17 acres.

Finally Stonehouse, the former New Inn with its 6 acres, was farmed by Mary Owen aged 86 and her daughter another Mary.

Other tradespersons operating in the parish in 1861 included Thomas Gunter innkeeper and tailor trading from the Nelson Inn, he employed James Morrissey a tailor journeyman who lived above the shop. Thomas died in 1862. Emma his wife struggled on running the Inn for the next five years; she then married William Taylor from Bridge Sollars. The Apperley family were wheelwrights operating from the Clovers, while John Stephens, another wheelwright, traded from his workshop behind a cottage now called the Old Post Office. John Payne occupied a cottage on the hill and gave his occupation as a hurdle maker. The only boot and shoemakers left in the parish were the Higgins family from the Stocks, their business had shrunk over the years as previously they had employed three shoemakers

Chapter 11
1870-1900

(Figure 1) Bishopstone Church.
Note! Rev Lane Freer's new tomb on the left
Remains of stone tithe barn on the right 1866

On November 26th 1863 George Robins the new incumbent with his new wife Harriet moved into the rectory to start a new family. All their children Muriel, Allen, Beryl, William and Monica were born in the rectory, creating a different atmosphere in the house to when the previous incumbent, the childless Archdeacon Lane Freer, occupied the property. The number of indoor servants employed by Rev George Robins was considerably fewer than Archdeacon Lane Freer, consisting of Susannah Hudson from London the children's governess, Sarah Price cook, Sarah Taylor and Mary Litchbridge kitchen servants, Elizabeth Thomas nursery maid, and Fanny Pember domestic servant. To celebrate the life of his children George Robins commissioned and installed a new font in Bishopstone church, with a brass plaque inset into the base recording four of the children's names. This helps date the font to the year 1870 because George Robins' fifth child Monica was born in 1871 and is not included. The children grew up with fond memories of the parish and the village school; Muriel and Beryl were frequent visitors to Bishopstone School until it closed in 1894, travelling by train from Hedson, Bucks and later from Eccleston, Chester. Beryl married Frank Gott of Leeds[1]. She became a very wealthy lady; the Gott family were industrial barons and became major figures in the history of Leeds and the wool industry in general. The Gotts built many of the public buildings in Leeds. Beryl died childless in Westwood house in 1941, and having no heirs she left large legacies to public funds and universities. George Robins was a young, enthusiastic, ambitious rector, so when the living of the large parish of Hedson Bucks was offered in the Church Times he applied and was accepted: he left Bishopstone in January 1876. An entry in the Church Times in July 1880 shows a further move: "The Duke of Westminster has conferred the Rectory of Eccleston at Chester vacant by the resignation of the Rev Ge de Longueville who held it since 1854 onto the Reverend George Augustus Robins MA. rector of Hedson Bucks".

Orphanage.

George Robins had a great interest in the welfare of children, and he opened a small orphanage in Bishopstone in 1873. George purchased a double cottage on Bishon lane, now called Cherry Trees, from Walter Morris for £210 in June 1871, and he then converted the building into an orphanage for eight children. The orphans, who were maintained, clothed and educated were overseen by a matron, Mrs Cottrell. The orphanage was completely financed by George Robins who paid for everything out of his own pocket. After he left the parish in 1876, the new rector, the Reverend Oliver Matthew Ridley, was not interested in supporting the orphanage so it closed in January 1877; the eight orphans were sent to Wales. George Robins sold the orphanage to G H Davenport of Foxley for £232.[2]

Bishopstone

Parish Church (St. Lawrence's).—Rev. Montague Earle Welby, M.A., *Rector*; Mr. Joseph Plant, *Churchwarden*; James Davis, *Parish Clerk*.
National School (boys and girls).—Miss Leonora Drane, *Mistress*.
Almshouses (for six poor persons).
Orphanage.—Mrs. Cottrell, *Matron*.

PRIVATE RESIDENTS.

Lloyd Mrs., The Cottage
Welby Rev. Montague Earle, M.A. (rector), The Rectory

COMMERCIAL.

Abberley William, shopkeeper and sub-postmaster
Apperley John, wheelwright
Barnett Thomas, farmer, Bishon farm
Boucher Richard, blacksmith
Davis James, shopkeeper & parish clerk
Drane Miss Leonora, schoolmistress
Higgins William, boot and shoe maker
James Miss A., *Nelson Inn*, and farmer
Nice George, land agent and surveyor; steward to Sir Henry Geers Cotterell, Bart.; agent for the Sun fire insurance office, Downshill house
Plant Joseph, farmer, Bishopstone court

(Figure 2) Kelly's Directory 1876 naming Rev Welby who never became Rector and Mrs Cottrell Matron of the Orphanage.

New Rector

Rev Oliver Matthew Ridley was a completely different character from his predecessor, Oliver was a wealthy man; he also appears to have been a strict disciplinarian. Born on May 12th 1824 Oliver married Lousia Pole Smart on August 3rd 1852, she was the daughter and heiress of Sir William Smart MP who lived at Aldenham Abbey. His wife died giving birth to their second child on January 7th 1858. Mr Ridley remarried Frances Eliza Keane in 1860 by whom he had three children. His wealth certainly helped the economy of Bishopstone as the 1881 census records the rector employing nine house servants to wait on his family, consisting of his wife and daughters, Mary aged 26, Solitude aged 17 and the twins Alice and Helen aged 14. A total number of 15 individuals were recorded as living in the rectory, fourteen females plus the rector. Whether Oliver Ridley had a phobia about having male servants living in the house is unclear, interestingly Phoebe Price from Tenby held the position of a parlour maid. Using females in this way as front servants, taking over the duties of the more traditional footmen, was a new trend in the 1880s that became acceptable though not fashionable. Phoebe would have worn a purple afternoon frock rather than black to distinguish her from the housemaids.
Housemaid Maria Fielder and her sister Mary, the school maid, came up with the family from Cobham in Kent, cook Susie Jacklin came from Gretton in Gloucestershire, nurse Sarah Digby came from Buxham in Norfolk, while governess Ellen Martin came from Greenock in Scotland. The Rector also employed three local girls as dairymaid, housemaid and kitchen maid. This census taken in 1881 highlights the Victorian trend of recruiting servants from all over the country.

The rector also provided employment outside the house: coachman Daniel Barnett lived in the lodge with his family and Cambrian Cottages was rented by Ridley as homes for his gardener George Taylor, and groom George Higgs. Detailed records of the grooms employed by George H Davenport of Foxley still exists, so we can presume George Higgs would have been employed by Rev Ridley on a similar basis with wages of £28 per annum, roughly the same wage as a farm labourer, to include two suits of livery, two black coats and gaiters, one stable suit, one pair of boots, one great coat every second year and three hats in two years. George would have ridden on the rector's coach with the coachman Daniel Barrett and on these occasions George Higgs would wear his fine livery, or a great coat in the winter. On a cold winter's morning, it is easy to imagine the rector's splendid four-horse coach adorned with Daniel and George all dressed in their livery, speeding down through the village in the 1880s.

John James was employed as a under gardener, he lived with his parents in a cottage on Bishon Common; John Stephen aged 16 was employed as a houseboy at the rectory, he also came from the parish. Six families in the parish had some financial dependency on Oliver Ridley.

Mary Hastings was another village person who benefited from the rector's household budget, she kept the washing under control for the rectory; Mary operated a small cottage laundry from the Post Office to supplement her sub postmistress income, she also washed all the church laundry, a service she provided until she died in 1899. This cottage is now called the Old Post Office, derived from Mary's occupancy.

The history of the mail service in Bishopstone started around 1830 when postbags were dropped off and picked up at the Nelson Inn, three times a week; they were delivered and collected by the Hereford to Hay coach service. Archdeacon Freer waived the tithe payment due from the Nelson Inn in return for carrying out this service. After this a more organized system started when Susan Chalton took on the dual role of schoolmistress and sub postmistress as previously described. Mary Owen of Stonehouse became the new sub postmistress in 1876, a job she carried out for the next eight years until 1884 after which William Abberley, who had taken over the shop at Bridge Ash became the next sub postmaster and grocer. He was a young married man with a family. Letters arrived by messenger from Hereford at 8.30am, and were collected at 6pm. After 1884 there were two post offices in the parish, Mary Hastings in Bishopstone, and William Abberley at Bridge Ash; both these post offices stayed operational until the 1920s. Bishopstone's sub post office dealt only with mail; whereas Bridge Ash offered the complete service including telegrams, savings etc.

In a 3 year period, between 1869-72 the two main farms in Bishopstone underwent a remarkable transformation. Rev Davenport followed the trend set by many other large estates, where the landowners were encouraged by the prosperity of agriculture to undertake a major rebuilding programme on their farms. G H Davenport rebuilt three farms on the estate to what the period press called model farms. These were Shetton Court in Mansel Gamage, Bishopstone Court and Bishon Farm in Bishopstone. To finance the building the estate took out a thirty-year loan of £2,000 on each farm, the repayments were £120 5s 5d per annum per farm.

(Figure 3) Court Farm's new stone buildings of 1872 are shown on this 1950s photo. The Dutch barn and the white roofed building were added later.

Bishopstone Court Farm, had undergone a rebuild in the 1770s, Rev Davenport decided that the buildings were not up to the modern standards of 1870. As Roy Brigden states, at that time "farms were commonly made up of an amalgam of buildings that had accumulated over the centuries to no logical plan, were unsuited to present conditions and were, in any case, falling into disrepair." Court Farm's new buildings included stabling for 8 carthorses, gig house with granaries over, large cider cellar, nag stable with three stalls and loose box, piggeries, two boxes for bulls, cattle sheds and yards, wagon and implement sheds, chaff house, root house with loft over, cowsheds for 26 with feeding gangways, calve cots and timber and tile barn. Completed in 1872 at a cost of £2,300, Davenport had hoped to raise the rent by £120 per year but because another depression in agriculture had just started the 308 acre Court Farm was let to Mr Joseph Plant at the old rent of £570 per year.

(Figure 4) Bishon Farm showing the E layout of the 1870 buildings, photo taken 1970.

Bishon Farm had barns and buildings that were originally attached to the two medieval farms of Bishon and Bishton. These old buildings were demolished, and replaced by a new set of modern brick buildings, and even the farmhouse had a new brick extension built containing a new kitchen and diary. Thomas Barnett his wife and their three grown up sons Thomas, Charles and George were the tenants. The Barnett family were previously farming in Clifford, and had taken over Bishon in 1865. The family moved into the Steps Farm for two years whilst the rebuilding work was carried out they farmed both farms throughout this period. In 1870 when they returned, the new farm buildings[3] included a large cider cellar with granary over, stabling for 6 carthorses, loose box, fodder store, 2 stall nag stable, harness room, coach house, large barn, root house with chaff room over, cowshed for 28 cows with feeding gangways, calves cots, loose boxes, cattle sheds and yards, bull box, spacious implement sheds, poultry, pigeon house and piggeries. The farm layout and building are still basically the same today (2010) after 140 years. After the rebuilding the rent was raised to £400 per year on the 227 acres farm.

(Figure 5) Date plaque Bishon Farm George Horatio Davenport

(Figure 6)
Cambria Cottages 1930s

When the building work was being carried out at Bishon Farm, Rev Davenport built a pair of brick and tile cottages in the front orchard called Cambria Cottages. These were built at the request of the rector of Bishopstone Mr Robins, who had complained about the lack of modern accommodation to house his employees, so Davenport built the cottages and charged Robins a rent of £7 per year. The cottages were used for many years as tied cottages for the use of the rectors of Bishopstone.

From Bishon the builders moved down to the Nelson Inn and again transformed the building, a brick cross wing was attached to the original timber building, the thatched roof was removed and the whole inn covered in slate tiles. This created six bedrooms for letting, a bar, bar parlour, two sitting rooms, kitchen dairy and cellar. They also built a range of new brick outbuildings a cow house, a loose box, yard and cart shed with loft over, nag stable and piggeries. Rev Davenport transferred an extra 25 acres of agriculture land from Bishon Farm, to make the Nelson a more viable farm of 31 acres.

(Figure 7) Nelson Inn 1928.

(Figure 8) Date plaque Nelson Inn

After this extensive rebuilding and modernisation the farm and inn was let to a new tenant, Miss Ann James, at a rent of £94 per year, Ann's elderly mother Sarah and two brothers lived with her at the Nelson, they all helped in running the business.

Land Exchange.

On December 21st 1871 there was an exchange of land between the Trustees of Rev Davenport (Foxley) and G H Cotterell (Garnons)

After the railway was built in 1862 the two estates were left with some isolated parts of land and so it was decided to exchange land to tidy up their common boundaries, which extended through the parishes of Bishopstone, Mansel Gamage, Norton Canon and Bridge Sollers. With the interest in shooting game becoming more popular in the Victorian era, Sir G H Cotterell was keen to gain ownership of the whole of Bishopstone Hill so more woodland could be planted as cover for game. Over the years the purchase of the Townsend farm, Pugh's land, and William Watkins' lands by the Garnons Estate had left them with the ownership of isolated blocks of land in Bishopstone as shown in section B of the map.

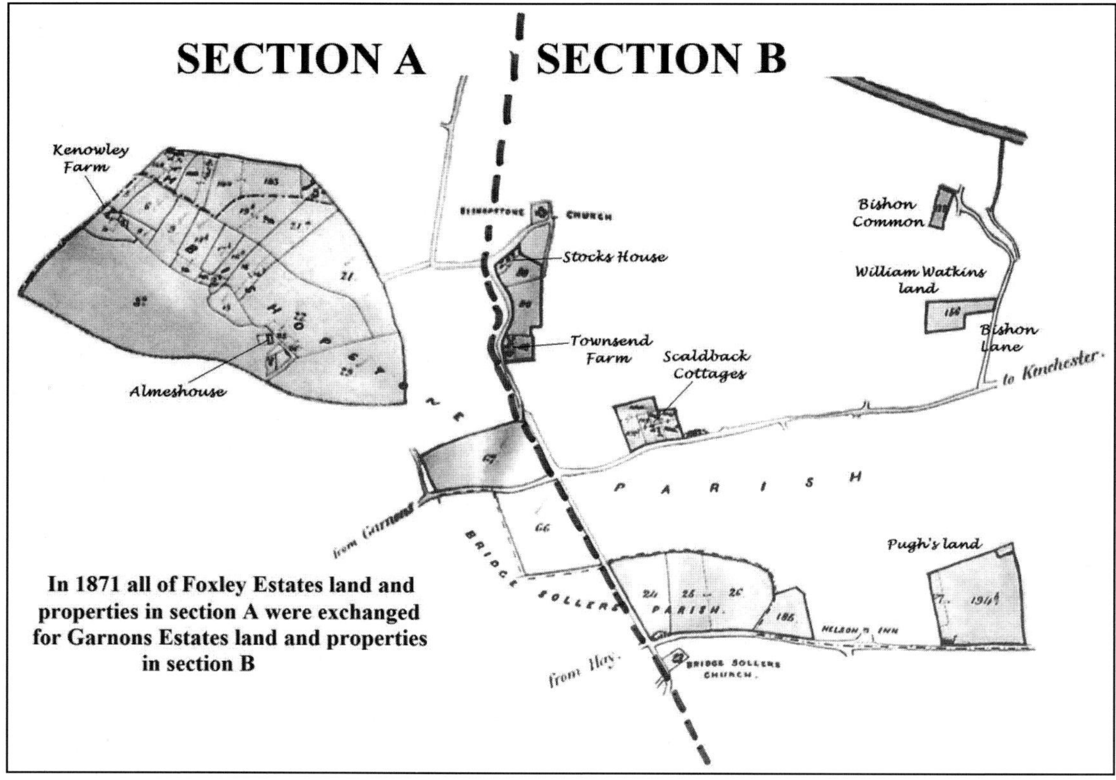

The exchange involves Kenowly Farm and Buckwell Farm exchanged for part of Smiths land including Townsend Farm, Stocks House, Lena lodge and Scaldback cottages, and is far easier to understand by looking at the map which I have sectioned for easy identification.

The total area owned in Bishopstone parish by Garnons after the exchange had now grown to 229 acres; it was the beginning of the end for the three freehold cottages and the almshouse situated on the hill, now completely surrounded by the estate's woodland with no recognized access road to the properties, only footpaths. Caroline Grove was also included in the exchange, some of the mature oaks from this wood were used in the restoration of Windsor Castle after the fire in the 1990s. This exchange between the estates was the last major transfer of land ownership in Bishopstone and it had created and set new boundaries between Foxley and Garnons.

The shooting of game became a more important social pastime for Victorian landowners. A more professional approach was taken in protecting and breeding game birds so gamekeepers were employed. New woodland was planted to provide cover for the game and this new planting slowly enveloped the whole of Bishopstone's hilltop. Well Cottage which had originally stood on the open common was now surrounded by trees and the cottage was extended and made into a shooting lodge in the style of a Swiss chalet.

The 1871 census shows two gamekeepers living in the parish; they marked a new type of occupation not seen on a Bishopstone census previously. They were not popular with the villagers as many families still relied on poaching the odd rabbit or game bird; in many cases it provided the only meat they could put on the table as buying meat was beyond the means of the average farm labourers.

The census also marks the start of the decline in Bishopstone's population, listing 127 females and 119 males, a drop of 42 persons from the census taken ten years earlier. Housing numbers had also dropped by seven homes; two double cottages on the hill plus one double cottage on Bishon Common had become derelict and fallen down. John Apperley's hundred-year-old timber and thatch cottage on Bishon common burnt down in 1867 and was never replaced. Bishopstone school had 52 scholars on their register. The census recorded 35 males and 2 females who listed their occupation as agricultural labourers, while for the first time on any Bishopstone census two shepherds were listed as a specific job; they were paid 12s a week against the 10s of normal farm labourers. There was only one person employed by a company - George Vaughan who was a platelayer working for the Railway Company.

At this point in the parish history it helps to include a few interesting statistics on labour movements. The 1851 census of England and Wales lists 177 people who stated they were born in Bishopstone. Of these, only nine were living outside the county, two in London both listed as married women, and the other seven all living within a forty mile radius of Bishopstone including three in Wales.

By 1861 this had increased to twelve living outside the county, ten years later in 1871 the numbers were nine in England and ten in Wales including one seaman, George Turner, he was recorded as being on board a ship in a Glamorganshire harbour.

Weobley Workhouse[4]

(Figure 9) The Workhouse and dreaded road leading to the separated entrance doors that many of Bishopstone's paupers walked, some for the last time.

George Wilkinson who was responsible for designing and building workhouses at Leominster, Ledbury and Bromyard also built the new workhouse at Weobley. His design followed the popular cruciform or "square" plan with an entrance block at the front, behind which lay the four accommodation wings radiating from a central hub, creating yards for the different classes of pauper (male/female, young/old). Entry to the workhouse was a voluntary decision, but one that was born out of necessity and desperation. People ended up in the workhouse for a variety of reasons. They may have been too elderly or ill to work and therefore unable to support themselves. Unmarried mothers were often disowned by their families and forced to enter the workhouse in order to survive. Orphans and people who were mentally ill or physically disabled would be entered into the workhouse, as there were no medical institutions to cater for them at this time.

Because of the Berrington charity Bishopstone was in a more advantageous position to look after its poor than many of the surrounding villages. The charitiy's facilities provided for the majority of Bishopstone paupers but if the almshouses were full the poor were sent to the workhouse.

In 1874 the Weobley Board of Guardians were awarded £900 to build sick wards on the southeast end of the workhouse. The 1881 census list 95 residents living in the workhouse split between patients and inmates. Between 1836 and the opening of the new sick wards three former Bishopstone residents, had died in the workhouse they were Thomas Morgan, Thomas Christy and Mary Mosley, all were buried in Bishopstone churchyard.

One of the conditions imposed by the Weobley Union on those entering the workhouse was that individual parishes were responsible for the pauper burials of their own parishioners. In some cases the paupers had only just arrived in the parish with no real associations with the rest of the parishioners, but the parish still had to pay out for their burials, although sometimes reluctantly.

Thomas Morgan and Thomas Christy were typical inmates too old and ill unable to support themselves. Mary Mosley, the other person buried within this period, represents the other end of the spectrum regarding age and circumstance as she was only 25 years old and possibly suffering from clinical depression or a form of mental illness not recognizable at this time. If the doctor had certified Mary as insane the Board of Guardians would have sent her to the newly built lunatic asylum at Burghill. The Mosley family lived in Burcott Row and the head of the family was Benjamin, a farm labourer working for Joseph Plant at Court Farm. This particular family had suffered many problems. Benjamin and his wife Catherine produced six children and their misfortunes started in February 1860 when a fever hit the parish. Three of the children died: James aged 23 and Liza aged 7 were buried together on February 17th, while little Alfred, aged 4, was buried eleven days later on February 28th. Their next eldest son Benjamin died in September 1864 aged 24. Their only surviving son, Charles, married Mary Jenks in 1868, both being Bishopstoneions, they moved into a tied cottage on Bishon Common and Charles like his father worked for Joseph Plant. The marriage produced a little girl called Emily born in September 1870, but disaster struck again in November 1873 when Charles died aged only 25 years, the longest living of the four brothers. Mary with Emily aged four moved in with her in-laws, the norm on these occasions where families supported each other. Benjamin her father in law was also suffering with ill heath and could not work, Mary could not cope with the loss of her husband and suffered some form of mental breakdown. The family struggling to cope with Mary, asked for help from their Guardian the Reverend George Robins. He arranged an interview with the Relieving Officer who visited the parishes on a regular basis. Mary entered the workhouse but she died shortly after, aged 25, ten months after her husband. Benjamin her father-in-law also died, leaving Catherine his wife living with her only surviving granddaughter in a cottage on the Common, scraping a living by taking in lodgers, the male line of Mosley family wiped out in one generation.

The number of workhouse deaths listed in the Bishopstone church burial records increased drastically after the sick wards were built in 1874: most of the deaths after this date were recorded as patients.

Records show that Charles Lawrence from the workhouse was buried on April 7th 1879 aged 17 as was William Davies on April 29th aged 69.

Poor little Emily Pritchard was buried on December 10th 1884 aged 10. This little girl's story I have used as a background to give a picture of life in the workhouse.

Emily was baptized in Bishopstone church on January 9th 1874 by the Rev George Robins, and instead of writing "bastard child" in the register like his predecessors, George filled in that part of the record in Latin so it could not be understood by the local people. Emily's mother, Eliza Pritchard, had married William Pritchard from Madley who had worked as a farm labourer in Mansel Lacy and latterly in Bishopstone. It appears at first to have been a normal marriage that produced four children but William suddenly died leaving Eliza alone with the four small children the eldest, Sarah, was 5 years old. Eliza gave birth to two more children who were bastards, Emily and Eliza. Such events, whatever the circumstances, were frowned upon by Victorian society. There is probably little doubt that Eliza like a lot of other young women in her predicament had been seduced by the promise of marriage. After the birth of her last baby she was forced to seek help from the relieving officer to enter the workhouse with her six children all under nine. Once Eliza and her children entered the workhouse as paupers they were stripped, bathed and given a workhouse uniform. Their own clothes would be kept in store until the day they decided to leave. Entry into the workhouse was a distressing and undesirable event. Eliza would have to undergo an interview to determine her circumstances and ensure that she was eligible for state help.

The workhouse uniforms were very uncomfortable: for the men they included jackets of 'fernought' cloth and for Eliza there were 'grogam' gowns and petticoats of linsey-wooley. Fernought was a strong woollen cloth mainly used by men on ships in times of bad weather. Linsey-wooley was a fabric made of linen, or cotton, and wool. Grogam was a very coarse mixture of silk, or mohair, and wool, which was sometimes stiffened with gum. [5]

Eliza would have been placed within a ward with her newborn child, separated from her other children, and she was also forbidden to talk to her children, they would often go for weeks without even seeing each other. Eliza would have to sleep in a huge dormitory on a simple wooden or iron-framed bed. The bedding would often be a straw-filled mattress and cover. Emily with her brother and sisters slept in a separate dormitory sharing a bed. Emily Pritchard was an inmate of the workhouse for over six years until her death when she was only ten years old.

Weobley Workhouse had one central dining room where all meals were eaten in silence with the inmates in rows facing the same way to deter interaction. It has often been said that the diet of those in the workhouse was no better than that of the lowest paid labourer, but at least those in the workhouse had it cooked and provided for them. As a point of interest I have included this article written about the standard of food within all the workhouses in Herefordshire. The food supplied inside the workhouse was regulated according to a strict official diet and three meals a day were provided.

Breakfast was usually one and a half pints of gruel and 5-6 ounces of bread.

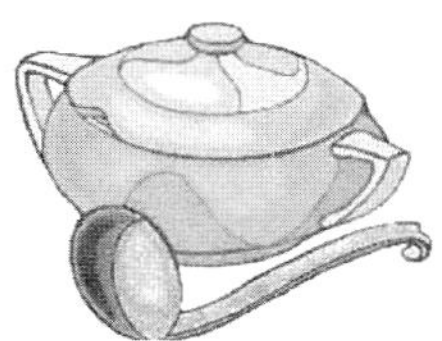

On Sundays and Wednesdays dinner consisted of 5 ounces of cooked meat and one pound of potatoes. On Mondays, Thursdays and Saturdays half a pound of potatoes and half a pint of soup and on the remaining two days there was only suet or rice pudding. Supper was 5-6 ounces of bread and either one and a half ounces of cheese or one pint of broth. The elderly and the young were usually allowed some tea, sugar and butter in addition to the normal diet to perhaps keep their strength up and ward off illness.

The diet of the children in the Herefordshire workhouses was considerably better than the adult diet.

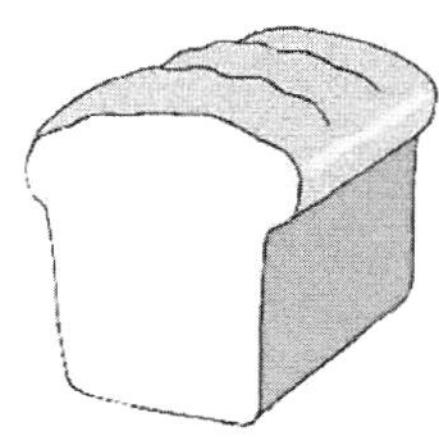

Between the ages of 5 and 9 years children were allowed 8 ounces of bread, 4 ounces of meat and 1ounce of cheese per day. For children up to five years the bread and meat were reduced by one ounce.

The main ingredient of the workhouse diet was bread and many workhouses had their own bakeries on site to produce the large amounts required and to cut costs. At breakfast time gruel or porridge - both made from watered down oatmeal - was served with the bread. The sick and the children would often have a broth that was made from water that had been used to boil the meat for dinner with a few vegetables.

Within the workhouse there where two separate schoolrooms for girls and boys, where Emily and her siblings attended lessons. In the 1881 census of the workhouse all the Pritchard children are listed as scholars. Eliza the youngest was now aged four. The responsibility of educating the children fell to the chaplain who was to instruct children 'in their moral and religious duties' two to three times a week. The schoolmaster taught the boys a trade and the schoolmistress was to teach the girls to knit and sew.

School hours in the workhouse were 9-12 and 2-5 Monday to Saturday. On each school day the children would be separated into boys and girls and be taken for an hours walk. They were to avoid the town and not cause any mischief. They were also required to salute people that they passed

When Emily died in the workhouse at the beginning of December 1884, she was taken in a workhouse coffin back to Bishopstone to be buried in the church in which she was baptized. It is not known if her mother Eliza or any of her siblings attended the funeral, possibly not.

Many of the Bishopstone entrants in the workhouse who died and were subsequently buried in Bishopstone churchyard could carry similar stories, but for record purposes I have written only brief accounts on these remaining people. William Davies buried on October 2nd 1889 was aged 51 years. He was born in Bridge Sollers and had worked as a general labourer at Lower Farm Byford before he entered the workhouse.

Celia Beavan buried on May 11th 1889 was 83 years old; Celia lived in a cottage on Bishopstone Hill employed as a housekeeper for William Pember before becoming unable to look after herself.

Bayham Leonard Mosley a toddler aged 19 months was buried August 3rd 1895.

William Pember aged 77 buried on July 24th 1896. William lived on Bishopstone Hill for many years, a carpenter by trade like so many of his family. When his workhouse coffin was carried up the path to the church it would have passed all the large tombs marking the graves of his more prosperous ancestors - what a contrast. John Pember his great nephew who was the last member of the Pember family to live in Bishopstone, held the unfortunate distinction of being one of the last Bishopstone parishioners to die in Weobley workhouse in 1935.

An entry in the account records for Bishopstone church in 1873 records William's brother James Pember a mason paid £3 2s for repairing tiles and putting up a brick coal yard. The walls of the yard he built on the north side of the church still stand today (2010). The corrugated tin roof was added in 1903 to protect the coke. Three tons of coal was used to heat the church in 1874 costing £2 14s. In 1880 to reduce the cost of heating, coke from the new gas works in Hereford was used for the first time and that year's heating costs were reduced to £1 14s. Other running costs paid by the church in 1880, were as follows. John Collins sexton and clerk was paid £4 per year; Mrs Collins for cleaning the church for 52 weeks was paid £1 14s 8d; Mary Hastings for washing linen for the year 8s 2d. The insurance cost £1 4s 3d, Gurneys for candles £1 3s 4d and bread and wine cost 1s 9d per month.[6]

Death of Joseph Plant.

Joseph Plant the tenant of Bishopstone Court Farm died on February 12th 1880 at the age of 79; he had been one of the most important people in the parish for the last thirty-one years. Joseph had taken out the tenancy of Court Farm in 1849 and had been the main employer in the parish; he had held the positions of churchwarden and overseer of the poor and roads for most of that period. Joseph had never married, he left his inheritance to his sister and nephews. All his business papers, bankbook, will, inventory and details of the farm sale are held at Hereford Record Office. Reading through his paperwork gives you a feel of the life style that Joseph enjoyed as a yeoman farmer. In his will dated 1875 he called himself a Gentleman of Court Farm Bishopstone, but in reality he was a hard drinking yeoman farmer who had made money over the good years in agriculture. At the time of his death Joseph employed six farm labourers living in tied cottages, four indoor servants and two live-in farm servants plus boys. All his employees lived in the parish, it must have been a worrying time for them all. Within five days of his death a valuer, Alfred Edwards, was called in by the executors to make a inventory of all the live and dead farming stock, household furniture and effects and when totalled up this came to a value of £1522. A simple debts list totalling £479 3s 8d was made out by the executors. The main items owed consisted of £256 4s 6d balance of rent owed to Rev Davenport plus £24 2s 0d owed to Rev Ridley for glebe land.

Edwards & Weaver arranged the auction, advertised in the Hereford Journal to be held at the farm on Monday March 8th 1880, to sell all the house contents, including silver plate, china, furniture from six bedrooms some of which contained capital goose feather beds, 20 ewes, a bay gelding, and a 4 wheel phaeton equal to new. That Monday in March 1880 would have caused much excitement in the parish: the school records show children skipping school and all the locals would have flocked down to the auction to see if they could pick up any bargains.

The new tenant James Like took on all the farming stock. The bay gelding and phaeton advertised for sale at the auction, consisted of a very fancy spring market cart with a matching smart horse, which Joseph had used both to carry out his business and to show off his wealth. Mrs Stanley, (Joseph's sister), attended the funeral and employed John Apperley the local carpenter to pack up and send items of furniture that she wanted to keep back to her home.

John's bill dated March 6th 1880 to Mrs Stanley

Finding material and making two packing frames for furniture and boxes	*8s 3d*
30 yards of packing cord	*1s 3d*
Hauling to Credenhill station	*4s 0d.*

Some of Joseph Plant's debts taken from the inventory after his death make interesting reading: J W Bulmers, wine merchants owed £27 19s 6d, pantry inventory lists; one gallon of sherry, four bottles of port, one gallon of whiskey, one gallon of gin, half a gallon of brandy and odd wines.

George Pearman Innkeeper is listed as being owed £31. George was the innkeeper at the Old Harp, 126 Widemarsh Street where Joseph would call in after market on a Wednesday and sometimes he would not make it back home to Bishopstone so would book a room. These two accounts indicate that Joseph liked a drink or two right up until he died. To put these two debts into perspective, the total of £57 19s 6d is more than a farm labourer could earn in two years.

Other items of interest from the debt list: Hereford Times bill £1 5s 6d; William Yeal labourer one weeks wages 10s; Jones and Symonds tailors £2 12s 6d (Symonds gents outfitters shop is still selling men's clothes today in Hereford); P B Giles doctor £11 19s 6d (this figure illustrates how the doctor's services were well beyond the means of ordinary parishioners). Peter Giles from New House, Staunton on Wye who practised with his son Peter Giles Junior was the local doctor for Bishopstone. The doctors from Staunton covered a large area as they do today. Francis Kilvert, the diarist, when he lived in Bredwardine, often writes of sending his servant to Dr. Giles for his cough mixture. Peter Giles was the original doctor who set up the practice that is still in business today. Joseph also owed money to the local village tradesmen. Richard Boucher blacksmith was owed £5, and John Apperley wheelwright and carpenter £21 3s 11d. For milling his corn Joseph used William James of Hereford. He used Mr Barnett of Abbey Sheep Cott Farm, Clehonger for threshing the corn, a mechanical thresher would be towed to farms with a steam traction engine and this in turn was used to drive the belts to operate the thresher. This leads to another story. Mr Barnett of Clehonger put in his bill to the executors for the previous year's threshing, which was disputed. By luck the twenty ewes put into the farm sale did not sell, so the next Wednesday they were walked to Hereford market; Mr Barnett knew this so he bid and bought the sheep but refused to pay the auctioneers and said that he would take the sheep against the bill for threshing.

Just a couple of other items which caught my eye from the inventory: the dairy lists a lot of equipment that would have produced a large quantity of cheese and butter; in the back kitchen stood a Dutch oven this was a modern invention, a large cast iron sphere on legs with an open front, which was stood in front of a open fire to roast meat turning on a spit. The other unusual utensil in the back kitchen was a maslin kettle that was used to mix wheat and rye to make a rough form of bread.

Maslin Kettle

It's worth remembering that the kitchen and other utility rooms were housed in a separate block detached from the main house. The dining room was filled with expensive furniture but of more interest were the portraits hanging on the wall which were of the three most influential people in his life, his landlord G H Davenport, the Reverend Lane Freer his old rector, and Sir Velters Cornwall his M P.

The inventory named one interesting implement, a "Mooter" which was a horse drawn device used to raise potatoes. Finally his capacity to store over 5000 gallons of cider and beer is amazing, I know he would have paid his labourers around a quart a day each in cider and this alone could amount to 600 gallons a year plus extra at harvest, so the farm could easily consume 1000 gallons a year. The daily allowance of cider for labourers was traditionally one quart and it would be collected in their own casks from the cellar daily. Owning two of these old casks, I can tell you they can hold nearer three pints. Joseph also sold some cider as shown on the tithe payment account to Rev Ridley.

Joseph Plant Tithe payment to Rev Ridley.

1878 Dec 24th	one load of straw		£2 10s 00d
1879 Feb 22nd	two loads of straw		£5 00s 00d
Feb 24th	one bushel of barley		4s 00d
Mar 1st	five bushels of barley		£1 00s 00d
April 3rd	four bushels of barley		16s 00d
May 2nd	two cwt of potatoes		12s 00d
May 6th	four bushels of barley		16s 00d
		Total	£10 18s 00d
	May 20th by cheque		£13 14s 00d
	Half year Total		£24 02s 00d
1879 June 24th	55gallons of cider		£1 14s 08d
July 14th	two loads of straw		£4 00s 00d
Oct 25th	two loads of straw		£4 00s 00d
		Total	£9 16s 08d
	Dec 31st paid cheque		£14 05s 04d
	Half year total		£24 02s 00d[7]

Rev Ridley retained a few small paddocks around the house for grazing his horses; Joseph Plant rented the rest of the glebe land. The straw and barley supplied were for the upkeep of the Rector's horses, plus potatoes and cider for his workers, these essential goods were supplied by Joseph who deducted their value from his tithe payment as shown in the account above.

Joseph Plant's comfortable lifestyle cannot be compared with the plight of the farm labourers he employed in 1880. Although a union had been formed and many parts of the country were facing unrest over low wages, the labourers of Bishopstone just had to put up with it.

Enoch Lloyd who was one of Joseph's six labourers is worthy of further investigation because he illustrates a typical example of a labourer's lifestyle in the 1880s. Enoch and his family lived in a timber framed thatched cottage on Bishon Common which was tied to the job, the rent charge of 1s per week was deducted from his wages. Enoch, a Welshman was 40 years old in 1881. He lived with his wife Elizabeth and ten children. Margaret the eldest, aged 18, was still living at home, Aaron and William the eldest boys were both working on the land, four children attended school and three were under school age. The children were frequently away from school, pig watching or bird watching at Court Farm; Aaron had been expelled from Bishopstone School some years earlier for non attendance. Margaret did attend school until she was 10 years old, and then only after intervention by the school inspectors. Enoch, who appears to have been illiterate, fell out with Bishopstone school over this so he promptly removed his children from the school and sent them to Kenchester school.

The cottage occupied by the Lloyd family had fallen down by 1885, so it must have been in a poor state of repair, with only two rooms and a space under the thatch: it is hard to imagine twelve people living and sleeping in such a tight environment. The family had moved seven times in their married life with two separate visits to Bishopstone. Enoch and Elizabeth had started married life in Brecon and over a period of sixteen years had worked their way down the Wye Valley. The question is how did they exist on their father's 10s a week wages plus the 2s 6d a week brought in by each of their boys? Records show that nearly all year round there was a chance of piecework for labourers, their wives and children, so Elizabeth and the younger children would single swedes, pick hops, stone pick or carry out any labouring job offered on the neighbouring farms. Like all their farm-labouring neighbours, Enoch would have kept a pig and some chickens while potatoes and green stuff were grown in the garden that surrounded the cottage. So far as bread was concerned Joseph Plant allowed his labourers to glean after harvest, which is to pick up all the grains of wheat or barley left on the ground in the fields after the harvest had been taken in. Elizabeth and the children could easily glean the equivalent of a sack of flour, or ninety quarter loaves, the bread supply for three months. Every household would bake their own bread. The gleaned corn would have been taken to Hereford where charities offered free milling to poor families; the sacks of grain would possibly have been pushed to town on a wheelbarrow. But no doubt there were hungry times when the family reverted back to a bit of poaching.

There was no great variation in the work on the farm, which followed a yearly pattern established over many years. Ploughing was done with an iron plough, and the corn was sown with a drill. Both the hay and corn were still cut with a scythe on Court Farm. Joseph Plant's inventory lists a horse drawn drill but no mechanical reaper .It was expected that Enoch Lloyd along with two other labourers at Court Farm, working together, should scythe 10 acres of wheat in one long summer's day, working sunrise to sunset.

Mechanical thrashers were now used but winnowing was still a separate operation. Labour was plentiful and cheap, and it had not yet occurred to some farmers that it was desirable to save labour. Enoch Lloyd was not an unusual case in the 1880's but I cannot help feeling sorry for the family when James Like, the new tenant of Court farm, evicted the family. They should have left on February 1st but with Enoch not securing a job at the Candlemas Fair he stayed on at the cottage until he was forcibly evicted on March 7th 1882. They must have looked a sorry sight, the twelve of them standing outside the cottage gate in Bishon Lane with their few possessions. Enoch eventually found a job labouring on a farm in Eardisley. He was forty one years old when he left Bishopstone parish but he never lived to see his 50th birthday.

It's understandable that those who could leave the land did so: the temptation to emigrate was great as farm workers in America and Australia could earn in a day the equivalent of an English labourer's wages for a week. The other way to escape such evictions was to set up a cottage agreement with the estate. Rev Davenport was a keen advocate of this system setting up thirteen such agreements in Bishopstone, the ten tied cottages in the parish was split between the two main farms. Two people to take up a small tenancy direct with Foxley estate were John Howells, and Jonathan Haines, both worked for the Railway Company and could afford to rent a smallholding. John Howells rented the Townsend Farm with 6 acres of land, plus two cottages and a further 6 acres of land on Bishon Common for £41 per year. Jonathan Haines rented Stonehouse plus its 6 acres for £20 per year.

Other small tenant holders were Elizabeth Watkins who farmed The Pleck with 4 acres, paying £18 per year. William Higgs the boot maker rented the Stock House for £12 a year, and farm worker Richard Collins paid £5 10s a year for the old post office. Henry Francis rented the Orphanage for £9 a year; he was a labourer at the chemical works in Kenchester.

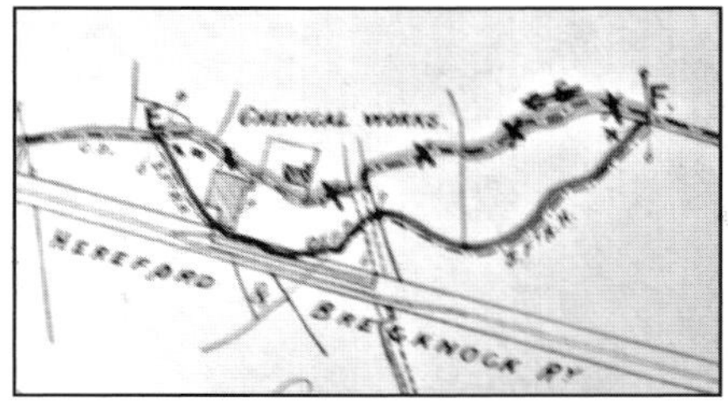

(Figure 10) Chemical works Kenchester and railway siding 1884.

(Figure 11) 1897 Sales brochure photo of a wagon from the Chemical works.

Around 1879 John Jacob started the chemical works in Kenchester; he had a railway siding installed into the works branching from the main Hereford-Hay line. This followed the 18th century idea to build these works away from populated areas so if an explosion occurred there would be a limited loss of life. One of the products produced was sulphur used by the military in making shells. The local economy benefited, with a lot of wood purchased from Garnons Hill, Foxley and other local sources. Even into the 1920's the Hamers from The Cottage, Bishon Lane still hauled timber out of Garnons Hill to supply the works.

Court Farm

When Joseph Plant was taken ill, James Like approached Rev Davenport about the tenancy of Court Farm and while searching the records I discovered a small handwritten piece of paper on which Rev Davenport had written out the agreement. A copy of it follows; it was signed by James Like and dated September 1879. They both must have thought Joseph would not live much longer but in fact he did not die until February 12th 1880, fifteen days after the date when James Like should have taken over the tenancy of the Court.

Court Farm Agreement.

Court Farm Rent £570 per annum, to include Townsend house, garden and orchard (acreage 4.3.35 value £15 per annum) to be retained by Mr Like until a new cottage is built upon the farm. No allowance will be made for the land required for this new cottage with garden nor for the land (not to exceed half an acre) that may be required if the new Almshouses are rebuilt on any part of the Bishopstone Farm. The old barn opposite the church would be removed before two years dating from February 2nd 1880. £20 to be allowed for the first two years from February 2nd 1880 till February 2nd 1882 if Mr Like produces vouchers to show that this amount has been expended on the farm to purchase bone-manure, lime and oilcake. I agree to that new terms and old ones under which I hold my present farm. Signed James Like.

In a letter dated January 21st 1882 addressed to Rev Davenport, James Like writes to say that he has not taken the barn down yet, but he will do so at any time now.

This barn appears on earlier maps, the south wall can be seen on the 1866 photo of the church, it was all that remains of the original tithe barn standing on glebe land.

This agreement indicates that moving the almshouse had already been discussed and also the building of new farm cottages to house the Court's workers. Both these buildings were not built for another 20 years, the cottages by the farm were built in 1907 and the new almshouses in 1910.

James Like was married to Mary Ann with whom he had six children. Previously James had farmed the smaller Upperton Farm on the Foxley Estate so he had a proven record of his farming credentials before moving to the larger Court Farm. James was a very keen hare courser and a steward, who ran yearly events, firstly at Upperton farm and then from Court Farm, the reports of which were published in the Hereford Times. The dogs came from all over the country, with hares in plentiful supply (hares are very rarely seen in Bishopstone today). When a hare was found in a field it would be put up, a slipper holding two dogs would release the dogs simultaneously and the dogs chased the hare over fences, hedges and occasionally the road. The dog that caught the hare was declared the winner. The Foxley Stakes prize money in 1878 was advertised as winner £12 10s, second £3 10s, third and fourth £1 10s each. Fourteen dogs entered the event and following the above procedure a dog would be knocked out in each round until you ended up with a winner. The 1878 event held at Upperton Farm was won by P W James from the Rhonda with his dog called "Greek Slave Boat".

The 1881 census reveals a Bishopstone population of 246 persons, had remained static over the previous ten years.

Small Freeholders

The small freeholders listed in Bishopstone in 1880 had now been reduced to five: William Abberley from Bridge Ash who was a grocer (owner of land marked on the tithes map as no's 186-187); John Apperley the wheelwright from the Clovers (161,162,164,165,138); John Caldcutt, a labourer who owned cottages on Bishon common (134-133); Caroline Lloyd a widow, the Cottage on Bishon lane (159,158,163); and William Lucas two cottages on hill (27). The only other land not estate owned belonged to the Berrington Trust containing the Almshouses situated on Bishopstone Hill (24), and Rev Ridley's, Rectory house and Glebe land (85,86,87,95, 96, 97,98,99,100).

The Reverend G H Davenport and Sir Henry Cotterell between them purchased every freehold cottage and land in Bishopstone that came up for sale in the period 1860-80. I have listed all the properties below; for easy recognition the tithe map numbers are included in brackets followed by the price paid.

Rev Davenport purchased his acquisitions from his own personnel funds.

August 11th 1863 from Richard Snead, cottage and School House (174-175) £350.

January 28th 1865 from Joseph Pritchard and Mortgages, Burcott Row 3 cottages (169) £800

April 18th 1868 from Executors of William Lloyd, Nelson Inn (188-189-190) £800

October 28th 1868 from William Abbett, Peartree cottage (170) £150

August 17th 1869 from Thomas Price, plot of ground on common (134) £23

October 16th 1869 from Caroline Lloyd, two cottages and land situated at Bishon Common (130-136-135) £200.

November 2nd 1870 from Mary Apperley and John Apperley, land at Bishon Common (133) £32.

July 22nd 1873 from Caroline Lloyd, two cottages at Bishon Common (143-144) plus Old Post Office and Panteg cottage (167) £1150.

April 22nd 1874 from descendants of Mary Bayham nee Foote, land in Mansel Lacy plus the Pleck and land in Bishopstone (153-154) £460.

December 1st 1876 from Mary Lewis, cottage on common (141) £150

April 1st 1878 from Henry Gibbons & Co, two stone cottages and land Bishon Common (142) £240

Purchases by Sir Henry Geers Cotterell

1868 from George Pember, Banbury Hall (64-65) £215

1878 from David Mortimer, cottage next to Almshouses (25) price not found.

Note! The cottages above standing on the following tithes numbers on Bishon Common 130, 135, 136, 141, 143 and 144 had disappeared by 1884 so are not included in the following sale list.

PARISH OF BISHOPSTONE.

89 and 90	House, Garden and Orchard...	Wm. Higgins ...	2	0	16	12	0	0
92, 93 and 94	Townsend House, Orchards, &c.	John Howells ...	4	3	38	15	0	0
100 and 102	Scaldback Allotments... ...	Various	2	2	29	5	0	0
104, 109, 110, 111, 113, Pt. 174, and 175	Double Tenement Cottage with Gardens ...	Jonathan Haines ...	6	1	19	21	0	0
Pt. 174	Snead Cottage and School Garden	Miss Brain	0	0	8	10	0	0
Pt. 172	Double Tenement Cottage with Gardens ...	Rev. O. M. Ridley...	0	0	33	10	0	0
171	House, Garden and Smith's Shop...	R. Boucher ...	0	0	29	7	0	0
168, 169 and 170	Two Cottages and Gardens Ditto ditto	Mr. James Like ... Mr. Thomas Barnett James Stephens ...	0	2	10	Let with Farm 4 5	 10 0	 0 0
167	Double Tenement Cottage and Gardens ...	John Hastings ... Richard Collins ...	0	1	19	5 5	10 10	0 0
153 and 154	House, Cottage, Buildings, Orchard, &c. ...	Mrs. Watkins ...	2	2	4	18	0	0
157	The Orphanage Cottage, Garden, and Orcharding	Henry Francis ...	0	3	22	9	0	0
142	Double Tenement Cottage, and Gardens ...	Thomas Watkins John Howells	0	0	29	4 5	0 0	0 0
130, 141, 143 and 144	Gardens, Orchard, &c. ...	John Howells ...	1	0	35	2	10	0
133, 134, 135 and 136	Pasture and Orchard ...	Thomas Watkins ...	0	3	3	2	10	0
		TOTAL.............. A.	23	0	14	£141	10	0

(Figure 12) The small properties in Bishopstone owned by Foxley Estate as recorded in the 1884 sales brochure, listing tenants, tithe map numbers, size of landholdings and rent payments.

Highways

The Weobley Highways Board was formed around 1865 to take over all the road maintenance in their district including the turnpikes. The vestry meeting would appoint a Way Warden who would report to the Highways Board in Weobley, this system continued until 1894 when it would be the newly formed parish council who would appoint a Way Warden. George Evans the parish roadman since 1868 had progressed in 1882 to a higher paid highway labourer, his job as parish roadman was taken over by Thomas Watkins who would have kept the ditches and waterway clear, repair small potholes and help the highway gang on major repairs in his area. This system of a single road man looking after an individual parish carried on for the next hundred years. The last Bishopstone parish roadman was Mr Hale who lived on Bishon Common, he retired in the 1970s.

A report from the Hereford times October 1885 reveals how the road maintenance system worked. Weobley Highway Board in 1884 purchased 1,712 tons of stone and due to wet weather conditions 200 tons of stone were delivered on March 25th to Moorhampton station. The only object of this exercise according to the Hereford Times was to keep breakers employed, as there was a saving of 5d a ton by breaking on the side of the road against purchasing stone already broken. The paupers of Weobley Workhouse carried out some of the stone breaking. Vagrants were entitled to seek one night's lodging at any workhouse and could not be turned away, even if they had no money to pay for it. Males who were deemed to be in reasonable health were expected to break stone for one hour before breakfast and two hours afterwards before going on their way.

(Figure 13) Weobley Rural Districts steamroller and road repairing gang 19th century

George Evans would walk up to twelve miles within the Weobley district to work on repairing its roads and if the work was too far away for a comfortable walk home he would live on site in a caravan pulled by the steamroller. The steamroller was one benefit that came from working together as a large group of parishes as no single parish could afford to purchase these modern expensive machines.

The roads were taken over by the newly formed Herefordshire County Council in 1889, although Weobley continued to operate as Rural District Council under the Herefordshire County Council's umbrella.

Sale of Foxley Estate.[8]

In 1884 the Rev G H Davenport decided to sell Foxley Estate. He had moved to Westwood Hall in Staffordshire in 1882 and only occasionally visited Foxley. The arrears of £2200 owing from the tenants of Foxley would have influenced his decision. Agriculture was going through another recession and in Bishopstone parish, Thomas Barnett of Bishon Farm was owing a full year's rent of £404 and James Like, Court Farm £100, while Miss Ann James from the Nelson owed over a years rent totalling £104 with an entry in the rent book saying "She cannot pay rent as she has taken nothing" presumably talking about the inn's takings. The running of the estate was put into the hands of R L Bamford land agent and surveyor of 138 Widemarsh Street Hereford for a fee of £150 per year.

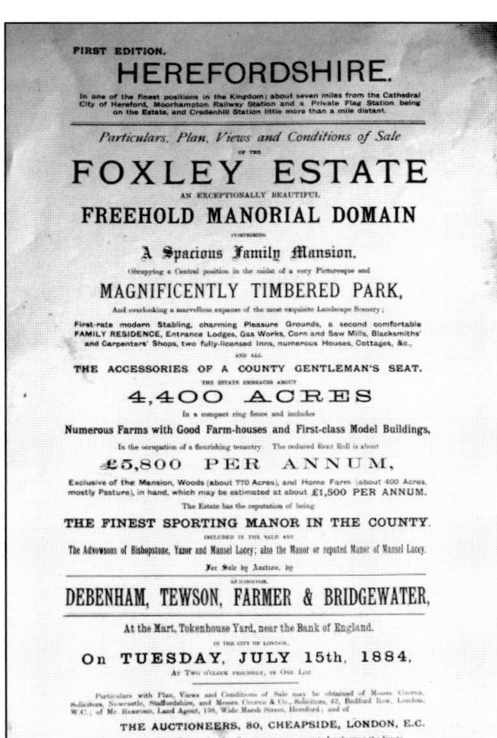

FIRST EDITION.

HEREFORDSHIRE.

In one of the finest positions in the Kingdom; about seven miles from the Cathedral City of Hereford, Moorhampton Railway Station and a Private Flag Station being on the Estate, and Credenhill Station little more than a mile distant.

Particulars, Plan, Views and Conditions of Sale

OF THE

FOXLEY ESTATE

AN EXCEPTIONALLY BEAUTIFUL

FREEHOLD MANORIAL DOMAIN

COMPRISING

A Spacious Family Mansion,

Occupying a Central position in the midst of a very Picturesque and

MAGNIFICENTLY TIMBERED PARK,

And overlooking a marvellous expanse of the most exquisite Landscape Scenery;

First-rate modern Stabling, charming Pleasure Grounds, a second comfortable FAMILY RESIDENCE, Entrance Lodges, Gas Works, Corn and Saw Mills, Blacksmiths' and Carpenters' Shops, two fully-licensed Inns, numerous Houses, Cottages, &c.,

AND ALL

THE ACCESSORIES OF A COUNTY GENTLEMAN'S SEAT.

THE ESTATE EMBRACES ABOUT

4,400 ACRES

In a compact ring fence and includes

Numerous Farms with Good Farm-houses and First-class Model Buildings,

In the occupation of a flourishing tenantry. The reduced Rent Roll is about

£5,800 PER ANNUM,

Exclusive of the Mansion, Woods (about 770 Acres), and Home Farm (about 400 Acres, mostly Pasture), in hand, which may be estimated at about £1,500 PER ANNUM.

The Estate has the reputation of being

THE FINEST SPORTING MANOR IN THE COUNTY.

INCLUDED IN THE SALE ARE

The Advowsons of Bishopstone, Yazor and Mansel Lacey; also the Manor or reputed Manor of Mansel Lacey.

For Sale by Auction, by

DEBENHAM, TEWSON, FARMER & BRIDGEWATER,

At the Mart, Tokenhouse Yard, near the Bank of England.

IN THE CITY OF LONDON,

On TUESDAY, JULY 15th, 1884,

AT TWO O'CLOCK PRECISELY, IN ONE LOT.

Particulars with Plan, Views and Conditions of Sale may be obtained of Messrs. Cooper, Solicitors, Newcastle, Staffordshire, and Messrs. Cooper & Co., Solicitors, 42, Bedford Row, London, W.C.; of Mr. Bamford, Land Agent, 138, Wide Marsh Street, Hereford; and of

THE AUCTIONEERS, 80, CHEAPSIDE, LONDON, E.C.

Who will give Cards to View, and make all necessary arrangements for showing the Estate.

Debenham and Turner were commissioned to sell the estate and it went up for sale by public auction on July 15th 1884.

The sale fell through because the new purchaser, Fredrick Charsley, claimed there had been misrepresentation in the printed sale documents and Davenport had to take Charsley to court. The case was proved and Charsley lost his deposit of £20,000. I have summarised a few of the main points in the case, which extended to over 20 pages.

Judgement came from Justice Kay delivered February 6th 1886.

The defendant has been largely engaged in buying and selling land, he was well known to the agent. He was expected to come into £28,000 a year as a successor of a peer who is thought not to live long. He arrived late at the sale, did not examine papers and bid up to £160,000 but because it did not meet reserve of £200,000 the estate was not sold.

Next morning he went to the agent's offices and agreed a purchase of £205,000, and paid a deposit of two cheques one for £5,000 and the other £15,000. There was some delay in payment of the large cheque by the bank. He visited the estate on August 1st 1884, the next day he inspected the estate. On September 27th he revisited again and met the agent Mr Bamford on October 7th. After this date nothing was seen of the defendant till a court date had been set.

When the court examined the sale documents there were some small discrepancies, which were put down to printing errors, and the agents had not known all the reductions of some farm rents. The verdict and the expenses were awarded to the Rev Davenport.

(Figure 14) **Bishopstone sale map of 1884**. All the dark grey areas carrying tithes numbers were part of Foxley Estate. Bishopstone Court 308 acres, Bishon Farm 227 acres, Nelson Inn and Farm 31 acres all three were advertised as having "newly erected farm buildings". The small properties as recorded earlier made up 23 acres, the light grey sections contain mostly glebe land, leaving only a few private freeholders, Hancocks Bridge Ash, Watkins section and a couple on Bishon Common the remainer of Bishopstone's 131 acres were part of Garnons Estate.

After much deliberation and seeking advice Davenport decided to keep the estate. To make it more economically viable he reduced the rents charged on farms and cottages to make them more affordable, but to make up the deficiency in yearly returns, he tried to rent out the mansion and shooting rights for an estimated £350 per year, plus the land in hand for an additional £385 per year.

Although extensively advertised the mansion does not appear to have been let out. Reduction in rent charges from September 3rd 1886: Bishon Farm £404 to £340 per year, Court Farm £570 to £539 per year, Nelson £94 to £86 10s per year and all the cottage rents were reduced by 10%.

The diarist Rev Francis Kilvert preached at a Lent service held in Yazor church on March 14th 1878 and although I have seen no evidence of his presence in Bishopstone he possibly visited Rev Ridley at some point of time. Francis Kilvert was a frequent visitor to the Rectory at Monnington-on-Wye to visit his sister Thermuthis who had married the Reverend W R Smith; this leads nicely into introducing the Rev Francis Kilvert's niece Francis Theodora who was born in 1880 at Monnington-on-Wye Rectory, she recalled her childhood in a talk on the BBC Woman's Hour in 1952. Although she had no direct involvement in Bishopstone's history I have included parts from her talk because of the close proximity of the parishes and it gives a little insight into parish life in the period 1886-89. Because of her father's premature death, she left the rectory at the age of nine. She describes seeing the first penny-farthing, the first bicycle to be seen in the village. That period saw the start of weekly deliveries by the butcher, and the baker whose big crusty loaves were said to be sweeter on the seventh day than on the first. Then each Saturday a bent woman in a donkey cart accompanied by a boy with a dinner bell delivered the Hereford Times to the local villages. She sat huddled up in the cart, a bright red shawl drawn tightly round her beaky face, while the boy rang the dinner bell to announce her approach.

She describes an old soldier who had fought in the Crimea who now travelled the countryside with his peddlar's pack. On Good Friday a service was always held in the evening so that the villagers, following an age long local tradition, could plant their potatoes in the daytime. Sometimes gypsies came to church on Easter Day. I am sure most of the previously described events could easily have applied to Bishopstone parish.

A new rector's arrival in the parish was always a big event. In 1889, after thirteen years, Oliver Matthew Ridley decided to take up the living of Charminster in Dorset. All the six household staff moved with the family down to Charminster including three local girls, and his coachman William Robuck. Charles Bodvel Griffith a forty seven year old Welshman became the new rector of Bishopstone, accompanied by his wife Wilhelmina and only daughter Marjorie aged seven. Three servants came with the family: a cook, ladies maid and housemaid. Charles's previous residence, the vicarage at Stork, was a lot smaller than Bishopstone's rectory although he never ran Bishopstone rectory with a large staff. Besides the indoor servants he employed a groom and a coachman. The coachman William Roberts, lived in the Lodge.

Fredrick Bywater became the new tenant of the Nelson Inn in February 1889; he was born in Leintwardine but had kept an inn in Bristol for twelve years previously. Fred and Rosana his wife brought four children with them and within two years they had added another two. Fred was an active church supporter and was elected overseer of the poor in the years 1892-93. When the church went through a cash crisis in 1900-05 Fredrick paid into the church funds each year with five others to keep the church afloat. Fredrick died at the age of fifty in 1908 this left Rosana to run the pub and farm; interestingly 1889 was the first time the Nelson was referred to as a public house before that date it was always an inn.

(Figure 15) John Collins parish clerk and sexton standing outside the church, next to Miss Wontnor the retiring organist and the new organist Miss Abberley. 1905

The 1890 Kelly's directory of Herefordshire contains a list of Bishopstone residents, John Collins, parish clerk and sexton. John, a former farmer labourer, had taken on the job in 1878, a position he held for thirty years until 1908 when he retired at the age of 79. He was paid £4 a year from the church for his position as clerk and sexton. John lived in No 2 Cambrian Cottages and worked at the rectory as a gardener and labourer. Born in 1829 he, like a few others in the parish, had benefited from the education system and his book-keeping and minutes are easy to read and understand even today. John died in 1919 aged 89 and his two daughters, who never married, stayed living in Cambrian Cottage until the 1930s.

George Nice, Bishopstone's churchwarden at this time, was the land agent for Garnons Estate, he lived at Downshill House and was also an agent for Royal Fire and Life Insurance. In 1878 Downshill House had been extensively altered with new gardens laid out and a new cross wing built on the west end, while kitchens and sanitary arrangements were brought up to the latest standards including flush toilets. The 1890 directory also lists William Abberley as a proprietor of a grocery shop operating from Bridge Ash house. Not to be confused with Apperley the wheelwright.

The Apperley family in Bishopstone

The Apperley family lived in Bishopstone, for over one hundred and seventy five years, 1770-1945. During my many years studying the parish records it became apparent that very few family names were recorded as being resident in Bishopstone for longer than a century. (If you follow the female lineage there are many candidates, it appears girls returned to their home parish if possible.) Since the seventeenth century three other families have recorded this achievement Gardiner, Pember, Hancocks and now the Apperley name could join this exclusive club. All families carry their own distinct story but I have covered the Apperley family in some depth because many were born and bred Bishopstonians and their story also illustrates the opportunities, which had arisen in the Victorian Age, not always possible before that time for the working class.

The Apperleys had always been either the carpenters or wheelwrights of the parish, and they also served as parish officers at different times, in the capacity of constable or overseer.

In 1870 John Apperley wrote a statement of ownership on a one quarter plot on Bishon common pending the sale of the land to Rev Davenport. This written statement tells the life story of the family. His father Jeremiah, came to Bishopstone with his parents William and Ann in 1770, shortly after he was born, according to his son's statement, they claimed a piece of wasteland on Bishon common by Ivors brook and William built a house on the plot. John says in his statement that as far as he could remember up to 50 years ago, neither his father nor he ever paid any rent on the ground. The enclosure map shows the plot surrounded by common. Although claiming a plot of common land and building a house on it was not unusual in many parishes throughout the county, this was definitely the last land obtained in this manner within the parish of Bishopstone.
In 1802 Jeremiah married Elizabeth Hancock in Bishopstone Church. The Hancock family had been resident in the parish for over a century, they were industrious small farmers, shopkeepers and freeholders. This must have rubbed off on Elizabeth as she encouraged Jeremiah to purchase several plots of land at the 1814 sale of William Watkins' land. Elizabeth's brother John Hancock, the shopkeeper from Bridge Ash, also purchased several plots at the same sale. Jeremiah's wheelwright business had become very successful and he expanded by building a new house and wheelwright's shop on one of the new plots he had purchased by the Roman road, moving the business up from Bishon common. The original house Jeremiah built in 1815 is still standing today, now the middle house in the Clovers Row. Jeremiah's sudden death in 1820 put his wife Elizabeth in a dilemma; she had a business but no tradesman to run the workshop. The children were still young, Thomas was aged 11, and his younger brother John just 9 years old. To overcome this problem Elizabeth employed master wheelwright John Barnes from Worcester, building a new timber framed cottage to house his family on the eastern side of their plot. He was needed to run the workshop and later on to train her son John in the wheelwright's craft.
William Apperley died aged 80 in 1817 followed two years later by Ann his wife. They left all the property on the common to Jeremiah, their only son.
In Jeremiah's will dated December 7th 1820 it states that he had left all his houses, land and carpenter's tools to his wife Elizabeth for her lifetime and after her death to his three children Susannah, Thomas and John. In the 1841 census Elizabeth is listed as an annuitant, a person who receives a private income, possibly the rent money from the two cottages on the common.
Elizabeth, died in 1857 and after her death the properties passed to Thomas and John. The elder son, Thomas, never followed his father's trade as a carpenter, he always worked as a farm labourer. John sold his share in his father's house on the common to Thomas for £30. Thomas died in Hereford Infirmary in June 1865 and in his will he left the two houses on the Common to his widow Mary for her lifetime and then to their only son John. One of the houses burnt down in 1868.
John Barnes died in 1847, after which John Apperley took over running the business and moved into John Barnes's cottage. John Apperley became a well-respected member of the community who held the position of parish constable from 1855 until the system ended in 1873. John had married twice; his first wife was Rebecca with whom he had six children, all boys, she died in 1858 four weeks after giving birth to Edmund who lived for only 3 days. John's second marriage was to Sarah Rogers in July 1860; she already had a child called Alfred from a previous marriage and Henry who was John Apperley's son born out of wedlock. Both these boys adopted the Apperley surname after the marriage; two more children were born, Elizabeth and Catherine.
James Apperley, John's eldest son, left Bishopstone school at the age of 12 to begin his new career as a pageboy to Archdeacon Lane Freer. After the death of Archdeacon Freer, James used his experience gained at the rectory to move up the domestic servants' ladder. The 1871 census reveals that James held the position of under butler to Lord Hylton at his residence, Merstham House in Surrey. Ten years later in 1881 we find that James is now married with a daughter Laura. James had progressed further in his career as he was now a lodging housekeeper of a very large house, Number Eleven Portland Place, Marylebone, London. He died soon afterwards in 1884 aged just forty.
John, the second son, became a wheelwright/carpenter like his father. Born in 1846 he attended Bishopstone school like all his siblings and after leaving school at twelve he served his apprenticeship in the family business. By 1871, aged 22, he had become a fully time served carpenter working for his father. The reason for what happened next is unclear; there could have been a family fallout or shortage of work but nothing is known except the fact John and his younger brother Charles turn up in New Zealand in 1874. In 1873 the New Zealand government had dropped the £5 assisted passage scheme and were aggressively advertising in newspapers and on posters, a free passage to New Zealand for tradespersons associated with agriculture.
Both were qualified craftsmen, John as a wheelwright and Charles as a blacksmith he had just finished his apprenticeship with a blacksmith in Burghill.

The family's emigration did not stop there, Alfred, their younger brother, who must have been encouraged by letters from John and Charles about their new way of life, decided to emigrate as well. By 1879 John, appears to have been well established in Masterton, New Zealand and he stood as guarantor to his brother by offering him a job as a wheelwright on his arrival. Unlike his brothers who remained bachelors, Alfred married Elizabeth Baskerville from Dinedor on July 19th 1879.

Alfred and Elizabeth emigrated to New Zealand on the ship Arethusa, which left Plymouth on September 3rd 1879 arriving in Wellington New Zealand on December 7th 1879. The three-month voyage was very hazardous with many ships lost. (On the internet there is a copy of a diary written by a passenger who travelled on the same voyage.) Alfred appears on the Depot Masters Book of 1879 as no 3205, (Alfred Apperley aged 24 and Elizabeth Apperley aged 22, of Hereford, occupation; wheelwright; employer; John Apperley). The three brothers never returned to the U K.[9]

Sketch of the Arethusa drawn 1899
Tonnage 950
Sunk by German Submarine 1917

William, the only son left in England from John's first marriage, returned home after his brothers had emigrated, to help his father who was now 70 years old, run the business. William was also a carpenter. Henry, John's first son from his second marriage to Sarah was described in the 1881 census as serving as an apprentice. William left the family firm soon afterwards and started farming in Breinton. John Apperley died in 1887; Sarah his wife died six years later in 1893 after which the family and properties were broken up.

No 1 The Clovers, which was originally called Bone House was built around 1875 to provide a home for John Apperley junior, the son of Thomas Apperley the farm labourer.

No 3 The Clovers was built around 1895 and immediately let to William Davies as a wheelwright shop and grocers in direct competition to Henry's wheelwright business next door. The row of three houses was called Morgan Row, later Shop Terrace and finally The Clovers; the three houses were sold to Frank Martz for £420.

Henry took over the wheelwright business after his mother's death, working from the old cottage next door to The Clovers where he lived with his spinster sisters Elizabeth and Catherine. Under Henry's guidance the formerly prosperous business started to fail, it could have been that there was a general downturn in trade, but for whatever reasons the wheelwright shop finally closed. Elizabeth married Richard Boucher the blacksmith in 1905, and Catherine, the other sister, ended up in the Almshouse. Henry then sold the cottage and land to Sir John Cotterell; he rented it back for one year in 1907 for the princely sum of £7.

Sir John had purchased the site hoping to move the almshouses from Bishopstone hill, down to the village but this never materialised. After this Henry moved back into the old family thatched cottage on Bishon Common, working as a general carpenter until 1919. After the First World War he concentrated on his passion of making cider and drinking it. He was an expert at making cider from his cottage; he also owned mobile cider making equipment, which was hauled around the local farms, where he was paid to make their cider for them. The old cottage was little more than a shack, not registered for rates because it had a rateable value under £10, the only cottage in the parish so listed. The cottage is still standing today, extensively modernized and now called Greentrees.

(Figure 16) Catherine (Kate) Apperley working in the rectory garden late 1920s

Henry was buried on December 3rd 1938 aged 77 years. Tom Prosser remembers it well, Henry had requested for his coffin to be carried to the church by motorcar, my grandfather Albert Macklin as funeral director used his own Jowett car; the problem being it only had two doors with a dickey seat in the boot. Henry's coffin was duly stuck in the boot, which meant it was hanging out the back of the car at a 45-degree angle. Tom remembers the funeral procession passing through the village in a bizarre way, my grandfather walking in front wearing his full mourning coat complete with a black top hat, the Jowett following with Henry's coffin sticking out of the boot and the rest of the mourners walking behind on the journey down to the church. Tom remarked that nobody seemed to mind. Kate died on December 30th 1943, the last of the born and bred Bishopstone Apperleys; no headstone marks Henry's or Kate's burial spots.

The 1891 census records the population of Bishopstone as 219, which was twenty-seven less than ten years previous. Twenty-two of the cottages' occupiers are recorded as farm labourers out of a housing stock of fifty-three. James Like, tenant of Court Farm had no arrears in rent so it appears that he was keeping a good profitable farm, a similar story with Elizabeth Elliott at Bunshill Farm. The same could not be said about Bishon Farm. By 1881 it was going through a tough time, Harriett Barnett was struggling, already a year's rent in arrears she decided to sell up and a farm sale was arranged. Harriett was 82 years old; two of her sons Thomas and William were still living at home. When Harriet first moved into the farm with her husband Thomas, their four boys had helped work the farm. Charles had left home, George had married and immigrated to Canada as a land agent in 1860, his son Reginald aged 5 died on a trip home to Bishopstone in March 1865 and is buried in Bishopstone churchyard with a grave stone stating these facts. George eventually returned to England in 1867 and set up a home in Liverpool.The farm sale as advertised in the Hereford Times on Thursday 30th April 1891.

Mrs Barnett who is retiring, the whole of farming stock dead or alive to include 10 powerful working horses and 3 capital nags, 47 head of cattle including 15 breeding Hereford cows and calves, a healthy stock of 260 black faced sheep, 16 pigs, also a collection of agricultural implements.

Parish Council.[10]

The Parish Council Act of 1894 provided for the establishment of a parish council in every parish of 300 inhabitants or more, and enabled smaller parishes to establish them also. Although Bishopstone's population was well under 300 it was decided to hold a meeting.

Minutes of first meeting.

Parish of Bishopstone

The parish meeting of the parochial election under the local government Act 1894 was held on December 4th 1894 at 6.30 pm at Bishopstone School. The following being present Messrs Abberley, Bywater, Like, Kerss, Pewtress, Boucher, Barnett, Elliott, Lewis, Collins and Haines. Proposed by Mr J J Kerss and seconded by Mr F Bywater that Mr J Like be Chairman. This was carried unanimously. Mr J J Kerss was nominated as Rural District Councilr. *Signed James Like Chairman.*

Just for the record, William Abberley (Shopkeeper, Bridge Ash), Fred Bywater (Publican and farmer, Nelson), James Like (Farmer, Court Farm), John Kerss (Land agent, Downshill House), George Pewtress (Shepherd, Stepps Farm), Richard Boucher (Blacksmith, Forge Cottage), Charles Barnett (Farmer, Bishon Farm), Elizabeth Elliott (Farmer, Bunshill Farm), John Lewis (Farm Labourer, Panteg Cottage), John Collins (Gardener and Parish Clerk, Cambrian Cottage), Jonathan Haines (Plate layer railway, Stonehouse) attended the first meeting.

This meeting was historic and significant because for the first time the administration of the parish was taken away from the church. 1893 was the last Easter Vestry meeting in Bishopstone Church to elect parish officers, from that point onwards only church wardens were elected.

It maybe of some significance that the Reverend Griffith did not attend the first two yearly meetings, possibly he was objecting to this shift of power away from the church. At the 1896 meeting he was elected chairman, a position he held till he left the parish in 1907.

In 1896 the long saga of the lane to Bishon Common began: *"A ditch on the lane was requested to be cleared that is causing great injury to traffic"*. 1897 *"that the road leading to Bishon Common be repaired"*. 1898 *"Weobley Rural District Council refused to take road over unless it was put in proper repair"*. Also recorded in 1898 was this little item *"attention drawn to the insanitary condition of this road by reason of the washes swimming into it from laundry"*.

In 1899 a meeting was arranged with Mr Bamford, land agent for Foxley Estate, to clear the brook and watercourses and ask Rev Davenport to repair the road. Nothing came of this and it was a thorn in the side of the Parish Council for the next sixty years until eventually the council adopted the road in the 1960s.

(Figure 17) Bridge Sollers 1869. note the old wharf entrance.

Bridge Sollers Bridge

Fording the river at Bridge Sollers had always been hazardous without local knowledge. If you were fording from the east bank it was straight to the middle and then turn at an angle upstream; if you did not follow these instruction you could end up in the deep holes either side. Bridge Sollers bridge was built in 1895-6; after many public meetings over where to build the new bridge it was finally decided on Bridge Sollers although it could easily have been built over the river at Canon Bridge with the north end landing in Bunshill just upstream of the New Weir. The first ordnance map of 1814 shows the public road fording the river at Canon Bridge; this ancient river crossing was used until the opening of the new bridge in 1896. The 1906 estate map of Bunshill still shows the hand operated ferry boat attached to a cable over the river it could be accessed from both banks by pulling the appropriate rope. It is unclear when it ceased to operate, it was possibly washed away by a winter flood and never replaced. If the new bridge had been built over the river at this point, the northern end of the bridge plus the new access road would have ended up in Bishopstone parish.

(Figure 18) View down river before the bridge was built, showing the Horse Infantry watering their horses, the regular passenger ferryboat in the foreground.

The bridge debate began in the 1850s before the railway was built. In an open letter in the Hereford Times in 1859 the writer asks for a public meeting because

"We are inclined to believe that it mainly results from the uncertainty that exists as to there being a station on the Hereford, Hay, and Brecon railway, at Ivor's Brook, which in a geographical sense, would at once determine the site of the proposed bridge. There will certainly be a station at Kenchester; a reference to the map will at once show how important it must be to the districts of Kingstone, Tiberton, Madley, Blakemere, Moccas, etc., to communicate with the railway at that place, even if the more favourable site of Ivor's Brook cannot be obtained. The worthy baronet of Moccas is, as every one in Herefordshire well knows, not prone to officious interference in public matters; but, as a gentleman largely interested in this question, we believe that he would be doing good service to his neighbourhood if he were to convene a meeting to test local and public feeling on the propriety of attempting the construction of a bridge over the Wye at Bridge Sollers or its vicinity."

Note "The Ivor's Brook station never materialised. If it had, the station would have been built on the Bishopstone to Mansel Lacy lane where the current railway bridge now stands".

Hereford Times May 2nd 1896. Bridge Sollers Bridge nearing completion.

"The Battle of the Bridges" - that memorable fight between Canon Bridge and Bridge Sollers for the new bridge, which was proposed to be erected across the Wye, was, as our readers will well remember, severe and prolonged. Not only in the districts more immediately concerned was the contest waged, but in the County Council and out of it, and eventually the palm of victory fell to Bridge Sollers.

The new bridge is entirely of iron, resting at either end on stone abutments, and supported in the middle by two pairs of cylindrical columns, the lattice girders and superstructure thus forming three spans. The distance between the abutments is 188ft, the spans between the cylinders and abutments 61ft, and the central span 64ft. The iron columns about 4ft 6in in diameter, weigh about 15 tons each, are sunk into the riverbed to a depth of 4ft 6in, and are filled with cement concrete.

These are topped with ornamental stone caps, and the whole surmounted by the superstructure in the shape of the roadway and the lattice work sides, the latter being 4ft 6in deep, weighing in all something like 97 tons. The height of the girders, taking the underside, from the bed of the river is 29ft, as the highest known flood was 23ft above the bed, there is 6ft to spare, thus putting the bridge well out of the way of the water. The width of the roadway will be 15ft. Each pair of the columns is tied with braces, while the measurements have worked out to a nicety, thus rendering the workmanship perfect and solid. Resting as it does on a splendid foundation and built with such rigidity, the bridge will be found capable of sustaining the heaviest traffic, a 20 ton traction engine being able to cross it without the slightest fear.

(Figure 19) Photo taken on February 27th 1896, Rev Davenport inspecting the progress of work on the west cylindrical columns. Mr Preece the contractor standing in front and the foreman to the rear.

The stone for the abutments comes off the Foxley estate, out of the Darkhill quarry, being the gift of Rev G H Davenport, the chief promoter, who has also given a handsome donation to the fund; and the capstones, copings, and string courses is Forest of Dean stone, out of David and Sants' quarry.

The land for the approaches on both sides has been given, that on the north side by Sir Henry Cotterell and that on south side by Mr Large, who is the owner of the adjoining farm. Some fault perhaps might be found by some with the northern approach, and many no doubt will feel inclined to criticise the gradient; but owing to existing circumstances this cannot be improved, and the present arrangement is entirely in accordance with scientific teaching.

The contract stipulates that the bridge should be erected by August, but it is confidently hoped that the work will be completed by the latter end of July.

The joint engineers engaged are Mr Stephen Williams, and Mr R L Bamford, the latter being the resident engineer, supervising the work. Stephen Williams of Rhayader had already designed and built two bridges over the Wye one at Erwood in 1877 another at Brynwern in 1885, all of lattice-girder design. The Horsehay Company, Shropshire made and supplied the superstructure.

The cost of the bridge will be something over £3000. Towards this sum, it will be remembered, the County Council consented to give a grant of £1200, while over £2000 has been obtained by voluntary subscription, and there yet remains between £300 and £400 to be raised. The payments on account to the contractors have exhausted the subscriptions in hand, and as none of the £1200 from the County Council can be received until the work has been finished the bridge passed and certified by the county surveyor, urgent appeals are being made in order to provide the needed sum of nearly £400. The successful completion of the bridge is now assured, and it is sincerely hoped that the promoters in this, what might be turned a County undertaking, will be relieved of any embarrassment, and have the satisfaction, when the bridge is opened and dedicated to public service, of declaring it to be free from debt.

Hereford Journal August 8th 1896.

The new bridge over the Wye, opening ceremony on Thursday last August 6th.

The original project started in the 1860s by Mr. J. Rankin MP representing the Madley people for a bridge at Canon Bridge connecting Madley with Credenhill. Ultimately Bridge Sollers was decided upon as having good communications with a larger number of parishes. Reverend Davenport was chairman of the Bridge committee who had subscribed handsomely to the fund.

The Wye is a river marked by many fords and as the traveller of the future crosses the new bridge at Bridge Sollers perhaps gliding swiftly along on the silent motorcar, little will he think of the inconvenience and danger, which his predecessors experienced in negotiating the primitive passage of the river at this spot. Besides the fact that a most intricate course has to be followed to negotiate the stream at this point, and that the traveller unless extremely careful often finds himself with his horse and vehicle undergoing and unexpected and wholly unappreciated not to say dangerous immersion in the water, the Wye is very liable to rise suddenly, and the passenger of the morning has frequently found himself as evening upon his return hopelessly cut off from his kith and kin.

The opening ceremony took place shortly after half past one in the presence of a large number of people.

The structure had been gaily decorated by Mrs Bamford and Mrs J J Kerss, altogether the scene was a very animated one. A barrier fastened by a silver bolt had been erected across the bridge at the north end, as architects Mr Bamford and Mr Williams had stationed themselves by this barrier. The approach was lined with an orderly crowd of spectators and many people had also congregated on the other side of the river. The band of the first Herefordshire Rifle Volunteers meanwhile discoursed selections of music on my awards below.
A stir among the company denoted that the event of the day was about to take place and amid the throng was soon discerned an interesting procession. The chief figure in the train was the wife of the gentleman who as recorded above, had been so instrumental in bringing the scheme to a successful issue. Mrs. Davenport had been appropriately asked to declare the bridge open. When Mrs. Davenport reached the barrier, Mr Bamford addressing her, said he begged to present her with the silver bolt on behalf of Mr. Williams and himself as a small memento of that occasion, adding that he trusted that although it was a little heavy it was worthy of her acceptance.
Mrs Davenport then declared "The Bridge open and toll-free to the issue of the public forever". The barriers were thrown open and the procession passed over the bridge, the band striking up the national anthem.
The procession included Reverend and Mrs. Davenport their son Mr. R Tichboure Hinckes, Mr. Rankin MP, Reverend Sir George and Lady Cornwell and many others.
Bishopstone people included in the procession were Reverend C B Griffiths (Bishopstone Rectory), Mr. and Mr. J J Kerss,(agent Downshill House), Mr. and Mrs. J H Yeomans (Bishon Farm).
The company proceeded to a field on the south bank of the river where a fete and public lunch were to be held. The lunch was held in a marquee where Reverend Davenport gave a speech.
The visitors to the ground during the afternoon and evening were numbered by the thousands and seldom were such a large company seen in the Herefordshire rural district. A varied program of sports had been arranged.

(Figure 20) 1896 Bridge demolished in 2003

Most of the Bishopstone parishioners would have attended the evening celebrations
Although the bridge was outside the parish I think it was worth recording because it had such an impact on the whole area. The journalist's view on the motorcar was very farsighted as the number of motorcars or horseless carriages in Herefordshire at that time could be listed on one hand. The 1896 Highways Act had just been passed, this was the first motoring law to encourage motor vehicles and the speed limit was raised to 14mph. Before 1896 a man holding a red flag had to walk 60 yards in front of the vehicle to warn other road users.

Cotterell Family[11]

John Cotterell was born in 1729 who originated from Broadway, Worcester; he married Ann Geers the only daughter and heiress of John Geers of Garnons, in 1756. The Geers family also owned the Marsh at Bridge Sollers and Hatfield Court estate near Leominster. John Geers died in 1762 settling his estates on his only surviving child Ann. While holding the office of sheriff in 1761, John Cotterell had the honour of presenting an address of congratulation to the king on his accession, and later in the same year he was given a knighthood. He died at Garnons in 1790 and was succeeded by his only son, John Geers Cotterell, who in 1791 married Frances Isabella Evans; another heiress whose marriage settlement brought a large sum of money. Henry Michael Evans, Frances' father, had obtained huge wealth made from trade with the South Seas, and in 1790 he was listed as owner of a London brewery and over one hundred public houses in central London.
Sir John Geers Cotterell was Colonel of the Herefordshire militia from 1796 to 1803, under his command the regiment saw active service during the outbreak of a 1798 rebellion in Ireland. He raised two battalions of infantry consisting of 1,937 men in 1803, called the First Herefordshire Volunteers. For these services he was created a baronet in 1805, he was also M P for Herefordshire from 1802 until 1831. Sir John and Anne marriage produced ten children, four boys and six girls, but three of his sons died before him. His eldest son, John Henry, died on 4th January 1834 aged 34 years old.
In 1828 he had married Lord Dacre's eldest daughter, by whom he had two sons, John Henry and Geers Henry. At the time of his death he was residing at his house in Hertford Street London, and his body was returned to Mansel Gamage for burial; the arrangements and journey were to take 14 days.

The Hereford Times reports, *"The remains of John Henry Cotterell passed through the city, shops and houses were closed and in the evening the bells of the Cathedral rang a muffled peal."*
Sir John's second son, Henry, died in 1825 aged 24, his youngest son died as an infant and the remaining son Thomas never married. Sir John Geers Cotterell was responsible for building up the estate with many acquisitions of lands in the surrounding areas. He ran the estate hands-on until his death making all payments personally and recording the accounts in his own hand. He died at Garnons on January 26th 1845 in his eighty-eighth year. On his death his grandson John became 2nd Baronet. He was fifteen years old and attending Eton College where he tragically died from a fever two years later at the age of seventeen. His younger brother, Henry Geers Cotterell succeeded as 3rd Baronet; he was only thirteen years old. It was during this period that Thomas Blashill was employed as a land agent to look after the estate. Sir Henry Geers Cotterell was M.P for Herefordshire 1857-59, he was 23 years old when elected. In 1865 he married Katherine Margaret Airey the heiress and only surviving child of Lord Airey. Lord Airey or General Airey as he was then known, served as Quarter Master General to the British army during the Crimean War and gained notoriety as the man who wrote down and signed the order for the Charge of the Light Brigade as dictated to him by Lord Raglan. Katherine brought a large marriage settlement with her to the estate. Lady Katherine was a very wealthy lady in her own right as her father left her over £100,000, and on her death she left all her fortune which amounted to more than £200,000 to her son the 4th Baronet. Sir Henry Geers Cotterell 3rd Baronet died on March 17th 1899 aged 65, in his will published in the Hereford Times it states that he left an estate valued at £118,660 12s 10d gross. He left £100 to the Hereford Infirmary, £1000 each to his daughters Alice and Louise, and his personal and household effects to his son the new 4th Baronet Captain Sir John Richard Geers Cotterell together with the residue of his property including estates in Herefordshire and his town houses in Mayfair London. Throughout the 19th century the Cotterell family had a growing influence on Bishopstone parish, by the end of the century they owned nearly a third of the parish, providing jobs and employment. Their portfolio of properties gained in the 19th century consisted of The Stepps, Kenowley, Downshill House, Swiss Cottage, Banbury Hall, Lena Cottage and an unnamed cottage on Bishopstone hill.

Sir Henry

Parish snippets

In 1884 the third reform "Act for Voters" bill was passed. Those eligible to vote were men who lived in properties valued at over £10 per annum, plus lodgers irrespective of where they lived urban or rural. This increased the voters' list for Bishopstone from sixteen to forty. In 1892 this was increased further when Bishopstone women listed as head of households were eligible to vote. These were: five from the Almshouses on Bishopstone Hill, Elizabeth Bayliss, Elizabeth Evans, Catherine Jones, Hilda Preece and Jane Waith; Sarah Apperley (Clovers), Elizabeth Parry, Martha Vaughn (Lena Cottage), Elizabeth Watkins (Pleck Cottage) and finally Elizabeth Elliott (Bunshill Farm).

In 1896 Edward Preece started the first regular passenger-carrying service from Bishopstone to Hereford, operating on Mondays, Wednesdays and Saturdays terminating at the Horse and Groom and returning at 3.00pm. Edward and his wife Catherine were the last family to live at the Stocks, the old house standing on the turn down to the church which was demolished by 1908. The Preece family then moved into "The Pleck," vacant after the death of Elizabeth Watkins. A single horse and trap carrying a maximum of four persons was used to provide this service. Edward was sent to Burghill Lunatic Asylum in 1910 but Catherine carried on the three times a week service assisted by Hawthorn Preece, her lodger. Edward died in Burghill Asylum on December 10th 1912 aged 58.

Hereford Times March 13th 1897

A COUNTRY RECTOR'S METHOD:- A contempary is responsible for the following:- An odd custom prevailed in the village of Bishopstone Herefordshire, until within comparatively recent years. The two bells now hanging in the western gable of the church were hung on a horizontal pole between two of the old yew trees, the parish clerk used to hoist a flag on another pole close by on Sunday morning when the congregation numbered four persons. This flag could be seen from the rectory, a quarter of a mile away; but if it was not in evidence at the proper time, the clergyman understood that the congregation did not reach that number and consequently did not think it worth his while to leave the rectory that morning.

In the same year that Sir Henry died, Marian Payne died in Hereford Infirmary of tuberculosis. She was 27 years old, a domestic servant, her gravestone states that she was the adopted daughter of Richard Collins, who was living in Burcott Row, she was buried in Bishopstone churchyard on April 24th 1899. The other reason I have mentioned Marian is that she was legally adopted; very few children of the working class in this period were legally adopted, although many children were raised by their extended family.

Chapter 12

Bunshill

The Manor of Bunshill had been attached to Mansel Lacy parish since the 12th century; on March 25th 1884 it was transferred by statute to the civil parish of Bishopstone while the ecclesiastical status continued with Mansel Lacy. This was part of a government Act where detached parts of parishes (having no common boundary) were attached to parishes with which they shared a boundary, to help simplify local administration.

From the 13th century the ancient manor of Bunshill formed part of the Priory of Aconbury Estates and the comprehensive records made by the Priory still survive, including many court rolls from the 14th, 15th and 16th century. These really do deserve a more detailed history written on their contents. I have dedicated just one chapter to this Old Saxon manor. Documents recording the Black Death and suppression of the religious houses have survived for Bunshill Manor whereas I have not discovered any for its neighbouring Manor of Bishopstone.

Bunshill has witnessed a colourful history in the last 1000 years. It straddles a pre Saxon trade route leading from the direction of what is now Mansel Lacy to the river crossing at Canon Bridge.

Bunesulle is recorded in the Domesday Book of 1086 as belonging to a free Saxon called Godrick, it appears he was more interested in having control of the trade route and river crossing than farming. One hide (120acres of land) was used for farming and it was valued at 10s. It contained 3 villagers and one smallholder with one plough. A note added states that there was enough land for 3 ploughs.

Godrick who never appears to have lived in Bunshill passed it to (Prince) Griffin son of Mariadoc.

The lands of Griffin passed to Walter de Laci, and were attached to the honour of Weobley. Walter de Laci came over with William the Conqueror and fought in the battle of Hastings in 1066; in return for his efforts he was granted large estates in the West of England including many in what is now Herefordshire. In this turbulent time Walter de Laci decided that Bunshill Manor would form part of his ecclesiastical parish of Mansel Lacy. Walter de Laci's son married Margaret de Braose who founded the nunnery at Aconbury in the early 13th century. Their daughter Katherine is named in the oldest deed[1] I have found with reference to Bunshill *"Release by Hugh, son of Peter de Bunneshulle to Dame Katherine de Laci, of a house and croft in the vill of Bunneshulle (Bunsell). Witnesses:Robert de Laci, Hugh de Labrocke, Robert the bailiff, and others (named)."*

Dame Katherine de Laci (Lacy) was born circ 1198 and died some time after 1267. In the tax return for the Grimsworth Hundred dated 1242 Katherine De Laci is recorded as holding lands, with no reference in the 1242 document to Hugh Bunneshulle, so this undated deed must have been drawn up in the early 13th century. The only other record of a Bunshill family name, is in the Pipe Rolls[2] 1185-6 when Rogerus de Bunehilla is recorded as in dispute with the Kings Exchequer but whether he was related to Hugh is not clear, it could just be the case that they both lived and held land in Bunshill. These documents were written before surnames were in common use, so the manor name would be used for identification purposes.

Mansel Lacy passed from the de Lacy family to Sir Peter de Genevile through his marriage to Maud, niece and co-heir of Walter de Lacy. Sir Peter de Genevile's daughter Matilda became prioress of Aconbury. If it was the Lacy family or the Genevile who built the church in Mansel Lacy is not recorded, but Sir Peter de Genevile is the first recorded patron of the church followed by seven resident Prioresses of Aconbury over the next 220 years.

Katherine Genevile, Sir Peter's other daughter inherited land in Bunshill, a transcript of her will made in 1285 is shown below.

Katherine Genevil gave to God and to the Church of the Victorious Cross of Aconbury, and to the nuns serving therein, a virgate and half of land, with two acres of pasture and two dwellings in the vill of Boneshill, providing that the profits accruing therefrom should be expended on the purchase of shoes and vestments for the nuns, and not for other uses, and that such articles should be distributed by two nuns chosen by the Aconbury chapter; and should these funds be perverted to any other purposes, the gift to become void.

Phillip Rufus who was a canon in Hereford gave a virgate of land in Bunshill to support a chaplain to celebrate masses for his soul and that of his ancestors.

Roger de Chandos gave lands in Bunshill to the Abbey of Llanthony at Gloucester.

By the end of the 13th century Aconbury Priory owned most of the land in Bunshill and some land in Mansel Lacy. Bunshill was a manor in its own right, holding manorial courts, detached from its ecclesiastical parish of Mansel Lacy; the parishioners of Bunshill had to attend Mansel Lacy church, a long trek on a cold winter's day.

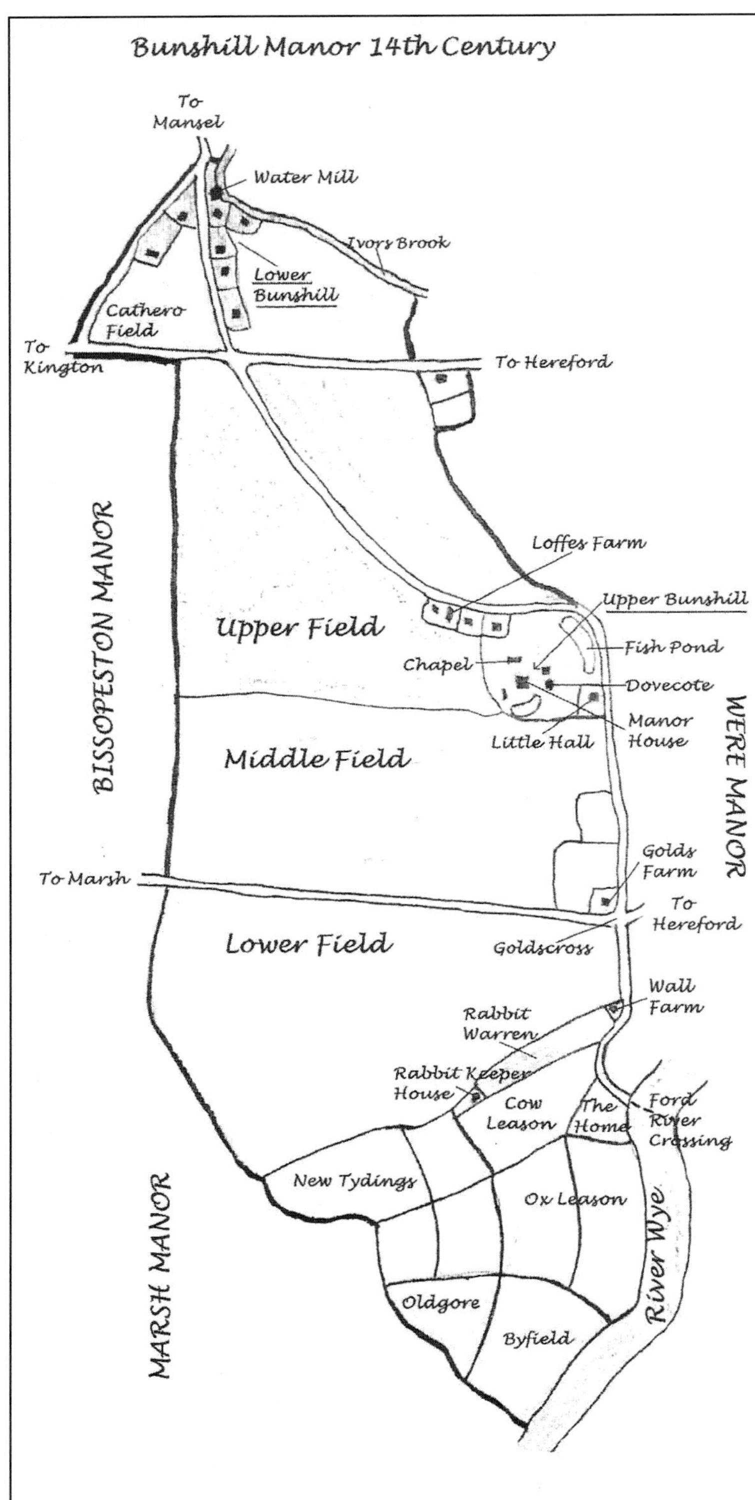

Bunshill slowly began to develop into a monastic site, an under prioress and nuns lived on site to oversee cloth and shoe production and to cater for their worship needs a permanent separate chapel was built. A reeve employed by the Prioress carried out the day to day running of the estate lands. He would make all the farming decisions on the sale of livestock and crops, ploughing and planting on the demesne land and collecting rent from tenants and freeholders; he kept a detailed record of these accounts. Bunshill was split into two parts Lower Bunshill which comprised of a row of tenements and a mill down by the brook or by the river. I have not been able to establish where this settlement stood. Crop marks from aerial photographs reveal rectangular patterns following Bishon lane, similar to other sites in other parts of the country with proven 13th century allotments. There are also ridges and lumps in the meadow with a definite flat area where a house possibly stood down by the original brook. This area today is still called "The Catherers," a name which has medieval origins. So I favour the idea that this is the site of the settlement called Lower Bunshill. Upper Bunshill and the main manor house occupied the site where the farm stands today and there were also a few tenements sitting beside the Roman road the main throughway between Hereford and Kington.

This is an example of a Reeve's account[3], covering the period 1336-1337.

Accounts of Ralph, the reeve of Bunshill

Rents; *44s at Michaelmas, 43s 6d at Lady Day, 26s 8d at Pentecost, 6s 3d in arrears*

(This rent was collected from the smallholding tenants)

Perquisites of court; *6d from court held Monday the Morrow of Michaelmas*

14s 10d from court held Sunday after St Bartholomew

6s 8d from the Great court at Mansel

(The following accounts relate to the Manor Farm)

Sale of crops; *31 seams of wheat, £5-2-6* [a seam is a horse load]*; 3 seams of peas, 7s 6d; 2 seams of beans, 5s 3d; 6 seams of oats, 24s 10d*
Sale of livestock; *1 bullock 7s, 1 cow 9s, 1 cow 6s, 1 calf. 2s 2d, 1 calf 10d, 3 pigs 10s 4d, 1 horse 12s.*
Purchases; *1 ploughshare 11d. 2 pieces of iron 6d. Paid the blacksmith 6d. Horse whips 12d. 4 clouts for the* wagon [iron patches to protect the woodwork] *12d. 2 spades 6d. Reaping hooks 3d. 7 waxed 11d. 1 mare 10s 8d. 1 cow and calf 11s. 21 lambs 15s 4d*
Expenses; *Threshing corn 13s 4d. Weeding the corn 9s 1d. Mowing 8½d. Harvesting 12s 2d*
Household expenses in autumn 3s; Paid to the household servants 14s 6d
Paid to the Lady's clerk 6s 8d. For sums owed on the Lady's orders 40s

An account record made four years later for Dame Joan de La Galesch of Bunshill dated September 30th 1341 confirms that Bunshill had grown into a well organized community. The shoes made at Bunshill for the nuns had leather soles with cloth uppers made from either flax or hemp grown on the Manor lands. The busy site would have contained a large hall, a workshop for the shoemakers, sewers and tailors, cottages to house the workers plus a barn, stables and other buildings needed for a working farm. These buildings encircled a central courtyard as referred to in the following accounts. There was also a chapel separated from the main building where the nuns would carry out their daily prayers and a resident Friar would have lived on site as he was needed to give communion to the nuns and parishioners, because only a man could carry out this duty. The hemp and flax were grown in the area called the Catherers (the name means a field used to grow hemp), convenient to Ivors brook which ran through the end of the fields so providing water to wet the flax and hemp as it was hung over the hedges surrounding the small fields This method of watering was essential to produce good thread for cloth making, The brook was diverted in the 19th century to its present course

This is only part of a very comprehensive list[4] of the Bunshill accounts made in 1341.

Paid for 34 rods (verges) bought at Hereford fair in summer for coats for the Convent	*26s 6d*
Paid for 5 yards of blanket for the shoes of the Convent	*3s 9d*
Paid for cutting out and making 30 pairs of shoes	*2s 6d*
Paid for freshening the leather. 8 hides	*2d*
In meat bought for the sewers and tailors	*9d*
And for women who watered the flax	*8d*
Paid for one household loaf	*3d*
In 8 gallons of ale	*7d*
In eggs	*2d*
In cheese	*2d*
In bread	*1d*
Paid for herring bought in lent	*4d*
Paid to tend the geese	*6d*
Paid to the boy who tends the cows	*12d*
Paid for 3 iron nails	*9d*
Paid for a Kneeler for the Friars room	*1d*
Paid for an Ox	*13s 4d*
For making 2 ditches in the courtyard of the chamber	*10d*
Paid for a sheath (Iron point) to the plough	

Also one pyx for Corpus Domini and a chalice for mass, plus Two gilt crosses
The new shoes were issued to the nuns at the convent in Holy Week and the old pairs given to the poor by the almoner.
The purchase of a chalice to use in the celebration of Mass, and a pyx (a small box usually very ornate, possibly made from a rare material such as ivory in which the bread for the Eucharist was kept) plus two gilt crosses, would indicate that the chapel was in daily use. The chapel appears to have been fully used up to the time of the Black Death, but after 1349 I have found only two further references, one in the period 1398-1400 when the chapel with a toft was let out for 2s 8d per annum, the other in 1401 when the overseer only collected 16d for the chapel and toft in that year's accounts, indicating that the building had fallen into disrepair.
Bunshill was the second largest estate owned by the Priory after the manor of Aconbury, Bunshill had a rental value of £8 15s 11d against Aconbury's £19 19s 4d. The Priory owned many other properties spread over a large area as recorded in their rental accounts [5]Barowe 26s 5d, Peterchurch and Vowchurch 33s 3d, Lulham 10s, Brugge (Bridge Sollers) 18d, Mansel Lacy 6s, Foy 4s 2d, Blakestone 13s 5d, Stoke Bliss 42s 2d, City of Hereford 100s 8d, Ludlow £4 7s 2d, In Shropshire 94s 3d, In Monmouthshire 29s 4d, In Gloucestershire 26s 9d making a total yearly rental income of £52 10s 5d.

Historians at this point usually talk generally about the peasants in their medieval village, this is not the case with Bunshill where the peasants and tenants are known by name. The court rolls of the manor of which many have survived in good condition (now in the keeping of the National Archives) tell us in great detail the lives of those tenants. I find it very interesting because it is not a fictional account; these named people lived and worked in Bunshill in the 14th century.

Roger the Miller operated the mill, Roger le Muleward (Mill Keeper) looked after the mechanical parts of the mill. John Gold, William Ayleward (his surname meaning a servant of a noble man), John Cobbe (he is possibly the son of John Cobbe who made a hasty departure from Bishopstone in 1308), Roger Alayn, Ralph Jones and John Tulletree were all serfs born in the Manor and bound to the Prioress of Aconbury for life. There were also several smallholders owning either a half or one virgate of land in Bunshill. A virgate of land is equal to one quarter of a hide (one hide in Herefordshire is 120 acres, the size varies according to region, and is used for the purposes of taxation only) therefore a virgate equals roughly 30 acres.

The Bunshill land was divided into three huge common fields amounting to over 100 acres plus some enclosed fields and meadows. The main Manor Farm was located within the 2 acre present day farm site. Bunshill also contained one larger tenement of 40 acres occupied by Roger Alayn; 500m north of the present farm it sat by the side of Bunshill lane. Most of Roger Alayn's land would have been made up of strips in the common fields plus up to 5 acres of land enclosed around the homestead. Roger was an important person in the village and held the position of tallyman, he kept an account of the work the tenants had done and measured out the seed they used. There were also six smaller tenements of between 10 and 20 acres occupied by the smallholders recorded. Besides the mill at least four of these small farms were situated in Lower Bunshill. Dotted about between these farms were the cruck houses of the peasants, William James, Walter Hughes, Roger le Smythes just to mention a few. Each would have strips of land in each of the common fields. Most owned either an ox or a bullock, each family would put their beast with others to make up the team needed to pull a plough. Bullocks were the poor man's oxen. After ploughing the land was sown. Men sowed grain and women planted peas and beans.

(Figure 1) Site of Lower Bunshill. 2010

Some also owned a few cows, goats and sheep as can be seen from the following court rolls. Most peasants also kept chickens for eggs. They also kept pigs. Peasants were allowed to graze their livestock on common land. In the autumn they let their pigs roam in the woods to eat acorns and beechnuts; Bunshill's pig wood like Bishopstone's was situated at Wormsley a few miles walk away. Boys were paid to pig watch, living out in the woods. However the peasants did not have enough food to keep many animals through the winter so most of the livestock was slaughtered in autumn and the meat was salted to preserve it.

All the previously named people were copyholders, so called because the holder had a copy of the record of his holding in the manorial roll. This came with many restrictions and rules common to that manor, most were leftovers from the Anglo Saxon period. Many of these restriction and rules appear in the court rolls. There were also three freehold messuages in Bunshill, although they still came under the manorial court they were subject to less rules but they did carry a service to the King to provide military fighting men.

The lives of children would have been very different to today. They would not have attended school for a start. Many died before they were six months old as disease would have been very common. As soon as possible, children joined their parents working on the land. They could not do any major physical work but they could clear stones off the land (which might damage farming tools) and they could chase birds away during the time when seeds were sown, a practice carried on for the next 500 years in Bishopstone. It was said that a peasant could expect to be fully bathed just twice in their life; once, when they were born and when they died! Face and hand washing was more common but knowledge of hygiene was non-existent. No-one knew that germs could be spread by dirty hands.

The peasants lived in cruck houses; the roof was thatched and they had a wooden frame which was plastered wattle and daub. This was a mixture of mud, straw and manure. The straw added insulation to the walls while the manure was considered good for binding the whole mixture together giving it strength. The mixture was left to dry in the sun and formed a strong building material. These houses were not big and repairs were quite cheap and easy to do. There would be little furniture within the houses and straw would be used for lining the floor, at night any animal you owned would be brought inside for safety. There were a number of reasons for this. If left outside at night the wild animals which roamed the countryside could easily have killed a pig, cow or chickens; or they could have been stolen or simply wandered off. The loss of any animal could be a disaster but the loss of valuable animals such as an ox would be a calamity. If they were inside your house, none of these would happen and they were safe, in winter they acted as central heating as well! They would have also brought in fleas and flies etc. increasing the unhygienic nature of the house. After you had paid your taxes, you could keep what was left, which would not be a great deal. If you had to give away seeds for the next growing season, this could be especially hard as you might end up with not having enough to grow let alone to feed yourself.

(Figure 2) My interpretation of how Lower Bunshill could have looked before the Black Death.

People were allowed to rest on Holy days (from which we get our word holiday). Religion was of immense importance to 14th century society, the parish priest, or in Bunshill's case the chaplain played a significant part in the lives of the parishioners. There was a great deal of magic in 14th century orthodox religion, and many pagan beliefs survived, these beliefs and practices were resorted to when they heard of the approaching plague. The court rolls cover the six years 1343-49 before the Black Death hit Bunshill in May 1349. The villagers were going about their normal business unaware of the tragedy that would befall them.

Although historians dispute the precise origins of the Black Death; there is fairly common agreement that it must have originated among rodents in the high steppe of the Central Asiatic Plateau. During 1346 it was raging around the shores of the Caspian Sea and it had reached Constantinople in late spring 1347. By early summer 1348, the pestilence was raging throughout the Mediterranean; it had reached the coastal towns of Normandy by summer 1348. When the pestilence reached England is disputed, according to Geoffrey le Baker's chronicle, on August 15th 1348 the pestilence erupted in Bristol, England's second city. The Black Death spread very quickly, nine months after it arrived in this country it hit our parishes; four months later it had gone leaving up to half the people dead. The people believed that faith was the only way to combat the approaching plague. In addition to the powers attributed to saints and holy relics, in the minds of theologians as well as simple folk, God was called on to bless the holy bread that was given away on Sundays in place of the Eucharist, "so that all who consume it shall receive health of body as well as soul", and thus it was regarded as providing a medicine for the sick as well as protection against the plague. It was commonly thought appropriate for the faithful to sprinkle holy water to drive away evil spirits or pestilential vapours, as well as to drink it as a cure for disease or a protection against it.

Priests alone had the power to administer the seven sacraments, of which penance assumed particular significance at the time of the Black Death. Three conditions were necessary for the forgiveness of mortal sins; penitents had to be truly contrite, confess their sins to a priest, and perform the penance, they were given, which was appropriate to the sin that had been committed. Those who died with sins that were unconfessed and unrepented would go to hell. The pyx and chalices purchased by Joan de la Galesch in 1341 would have been well used during the Black Death, they were carried to the homes of the dying to give them the Eucharist.

A record of the accounts of Bunshill Manor made in the year 1343-44[6] by William the Bailiff still survives. These early accounts were written in highly abbreviated Latin making them sometimes difficult to read. I have left in the whole transcription of this document because it helps explain exactly how a medieval Manor works.

A few odd Latin words like "famuli" have been left in, according to the reference books about manors the famuli were the body of servants who usually had no land of their own and were primarily used by the lord of the manor to farm his demesne land and to tend his flocks and herds.

They were lodged in the "curia", buildings that formed part of what we would call the home farm. They were paid a regular wage as well as board and lodging and if they did hold any land their rents were reduced. The prioress's bailiff lived in the old Bunshill manor house, which acted as a home farm with a suite of rooms set aside for the Prioress or supervisor when she visited. Judging by these accounts, the Prioress seems to have brought her own personal servants (the "household" mentioned in the accounts) when they came. In the few years after this account, a small detachment of nuns occupied the site hence the building of the chapel; the reasons for this change are unclear but possibly the idea was to expand the site into a form of sub priory. What can be deduced by comparing these accounts with the later 1394-7 accounts is that Bunshill was run by two different systems. Before Black Death the prioress of Aconbury was farming the demesne land through her bailiff, but afterwards, when the Prioress stopped farming the land, the demesne lands were leased out (hence the "tenant of the demesne" mentioned in 1394-7) and the tenant occupied the Manor House. The Black Death had a far-reaching effect on Bunshill as recorded later in this chapter.

Account of William de Lugwardine bailiff of Dame Joan Walsche for her manor of Bounshull viz from the Vigil of St Michael 17 Edward III to the same Vigil 18 Ed III [September 28th 1343-September 28th 1344]

He accounts for 7s 11¾d arrears from last year *Total 7s 11¾d*

Rents of assise; *He accounts for 24s 5½d in rents received from Mansel at Michaelmas. And 19s 8½d for rents from Bunshill at the same time. And 23s 11d from Mansel at Annunciation and 19s 7½d from Bunshill at the same. And 10s from Mansel at Christmas and 16s 8d from Bunshill at the same.* *Total 114s 4½d*

Sale of wheat; *He accounts for 32s from the sale of 8 qrs sold at All Saints, price 4s per qr. And 7s 2d from sale of 2 qrs sold after harvest, price 3s 7d per qr. And 7s 4d for 2 qrs sold at the same time, price 3s 8d per qr.* *Total 46s 6d*

Beans; *He accounts for 6s 7¾d for 1 qr 6½ bs sold around St Andrew's Day, price 3s 8d per qr* *Total 6s 7¾d*

White and black peas; *He accounts for 9d from sale of 1½ bs 2 pecks of white peas. And 18d from sale of ½ qr of black peas at St Andrew's Day. And 22d from sale of 7 bs 2 ps of black peas sold after Easter price 3d per bushel.* *Total 3s 1d*

Oats; *He accounts for 2s 6¼d for 1 qr oats sold at the feast of St Nicholas. And 6s for 4 qrs sold after the Nativity of St Mary the Virgin, price 18d per qr* *Total 8s 6¼ d*

Livestock; *He accounts for 12d for 4 geese sold price 3d each. And 12d for squabs sold. And 3s for 1 boar and 3s for 1 colt and 2s 1d for 1 calf* *Total 10s 1d*

Income from the manor; *He accounts for 4d for 6 cheeses sold. And 16d for 1 bushel of dung. And 12d for sale of straw* *Total 2s 8d*

Plough services; *He accounts for 5s for 20 plough services sold this year, price 3d each* *Total 5s*

Pleas and perquisites of court; *He accounts for 20d from 1 court held there on Friday the feast of St Gregory the Pope; and 2d from 1 court held there on Friday after the feast of St Mark the Evangelist; and 7s 7d from 1 court held on Monday after the Translation of St Thomas the Martyr; and 2s from a fine on Roger Aleyn's daughter for a licence for her marriage; and 2s 6d from rents of assise of tenants in Mansel and Bunshill* *Total 13s 11d*

Outside receipts; *He accounts for 19s received from the Lady for making linen cloth and other cloth And 6s 8d from the Lady for hay for herself and others, Sales on account; He accounts for 3s 3d received for various sales on the account recorded elsewhere* *Total 3s 3d*

Total receipts £12-5-8¼

Expenditure; *Upkeep of Ploughs; He accounts for large iron bought for the plough 13d for the year; paid to the blacksmith 13d; for 1 ploughshare 11d; for 1 plough sheath 3d* *Total 3s 3d* *and more this year because William Dews land was ploughed*

Farrier; *Paid for farrier's work for the plough team 12d* *Total 12d*

Upkeep of Wagons; *For 1 metal catch bought for the wagon 1d; for cloutnails 1d; for 2 hemp ropes for the wagon, the bigger one 9 cubits long 15d; for 4 pounds of grease and tallow for them 4d; for 4 metal catches for the same wagon 4d* *Total 2s 1d*

Expenses of the manor; *½ qr of salt bought for salting down the meat and for use for the famuli 16d; 1 shackle for a fastener 4d; 1 hemp halter 1d; 1 pair of hooks and hinges for the store room door 3d; board nails for the same 1d; board nails to repair the gate 1d; for sawing 5 boards and 1 curved piece for the gate 3d; paid to 4 women brought in for 1 day to plant beans 4d viz 1d each per day. Paid for the Easter candle at Mansel ½d; for consecrated bread for Mansel church 2½d. Paid the king's bailiff for hidage 1¾d; paid to a cooper brought in for a day to repair various vessels 2d; paid to Roger Aleyn for expenses of 1 mare 5s* *Total 8s 8d*

Building supervisor; *1 roofer for 1 week repairing various houses 6d* *Total 6d*
Purchase of grain; *For 6 seams of wheat bought for making malt 2s 6d; for 1 quarter of oats bought for making malt* *Total 2s*
Stores purchased; *For 1 bullock bought for the larder 5s 6d* *Total 5s 6d*
Weeding and mowing; *For weeding all the corn this year 5s 4¼ by the view of John the ploughholder; For mowing flax 7d; for 6 women brought in for 2 days to wash and cut the said flax 9d viz ¾d each per day. The cost of 2 meals for them 4d. For mowing the meadow called Rudmedowe 9d. For lifting the hay 1d. For mowing John Tullitree's meadow 1¼d* *Total 6s 11½d*
Item for threshing 32 qrs 1 b.of wheat, beans and white peas and going to the stack 5s 4¼d, giving 2d per qr and no more because the famuli threshed 4 seams of wheat. For threshing 14qrs 1 b of oats at the stack 14d, giving 1d per qr. For threshing 9 qrs of wheat, 3 bs of new grain and 8 qrs 3 bs of wheat from external land of William de Weston and 2 bs of oats, 1 qr 1 b of white peas and 1 qr 6bs of black peas at the stack 3s 5¾ d giving 2d per seam. For threshing 4 qrs 6 bs 1 trug of oats and 4 qrs 7 bs 1 trug from the external land of William de Weston 9¼d *Total 10s 9¼d*
Harvest; *For all kinds of corn reaped this year 12s by the tally contra the Lady. For the cost of various men eating at the Lady's table for 3 weeks in harvest 17d, the price of 1 qr 2 bs of wheat for extra bread and other things from the storeroom by the same tally. Nothing recorded here for gloves for the harvesters because they were a gift from the Lady.*
Wages; *For the wages of William the bailiff 10s pa paid at Lady Day for the preceding year. The pay of the ploughholder; 5s 6d; pay of the driver 3s 6d; cowherd 2s 6d; dairymaid/dairyman 3s; the Lady's maid servant 2s at Michaelmas; Roger the poultryman 6s pa. Paid William de Weston in part payment of his wages 2s. Wages of Adam Godale for his service for the year 4s 8d for making shoes for the convent. Leaky's pay in Ladyday quarter 12d* *Total 40s 2d*
Storeroom; *For 25 ells of linen cloth bought for the Lady 10s viz 5d per ell. For 26 ells of linen cloth bought 9s viz 4½d per ell less 2d. For 8 ells of linen cloth bought 3s viz 4½d per ell. For 12 ells of thick linen cloth bought 3s 2d viz 3¼d per ell minus 1d. For 3 ells of linen cloth bought 12d viz 4d per ell. For 6 ells of linen cloth bought 2s 6d viz 5d per ell. For weaving 5 ells of woollen cloth for "soccis" for the Lady 4d. For fulling the same 4d. For 1 lb of woollen thread bought 4d. For 26 ells of linen cloth 10s 8d viz 5d per ell less 2d. For 21 ells of linen cloth bought 9s 4d viz 5½d per ell less 3½d. For dyeing and shearing 19 ells of woollen cloth 2s 11½d. For 2 stones of tallow bought for making candles 21d. For dyeing 4 ells of white woollen cloth black 6d; for shearing the same cloth 2d*
Item for lambskin for shoes 2s 6½d; for curing the same 9d. For 6 goat skins 2s 4d, for 2 goat skins 10d, for 6 goat skins 2s 4d, for 6 goat skins 2s 2d. For white tawed leather for shoes 5d. For tanning 22 goat skins 2s 10d viz 1½d per skin and 1d as a tip. For dressing the same skins 2s 9d, viz 1½d per skin. For 1 dressed lamb skin 2s, for dressing two lambskins for shoes 12d. For eyelets bought for shoes 1d.
Item paid for a pittance on the feast of Saints Crispin and Crispianus half a mark [the patron saints of shoemakers]; for a pittance on St Katherine's day half a mark; for a pittance on All Saints Day 6s; for a pittance on the feast of Circumcision half a mark. Item for a "caste" bought for the Lady 3d. For payment to the Lady's maid servant coming out to Bunshill at the time of cutting and wetting the flax from Monday next after the feast of St Barnabas to Monday the vigil of the Apostles Peter and Paul [10 June – 20 June] 13d. For a pittance at the beginning of Lent 4s. Item paid for meat bought for a pittance around the Nativity of St Mary the Virgin 2s *Total 103s 5d*
Item for the costs of Dame Joan le Walsche and others coming on Monday before the feast of St Barnabas the Apostle viz for purchase of bread 2d, for ale 8d, for beef, pork and mutton 6d. Total 16d
Purchase of hay; *For 1 wagon load of hay bought for the Lady's sheep at Aconbury* *Total 3s 4d*
Money paid over; *Delivered to Dame Joan le Walsche for Church Silver 6s* [12s] *by tally; delivered to the same 4s without tally at Easter. Delivered to John Tullitree 2s 8d for rent of William de Weston's land on the Lady's orders. Delivered to the Lady 3s for 1 boar sold, 3s for 1 colt sold, 2s 1d for 1 calf sold. Delivered to the Lady 8s 6d for wheat, oats and new grain sold.* *Total 32s 3d*
Total of expenses and money paid over £11-13 4½. The total is in arrears by 12s 3½d of which 40d is allowed to the bailiff for an amercement placed upon him; and 40d is respited for an amercement on Roger Aleyn. And allowed to the bailiff 2s for his expenses in various all debts against anyone touching this account

Produce of the grange in the 18th year of Edward III (1344)
Wheat; *He accounts for 1 qr 3 bs 1 peck brought forward. And for 26 qrs 1½ bs received from the grange by tally against Roger Alayn, from which 4 qs were used by the famuli. And he accounts for ½ qr received from Mansel. And for 1qr received as a rent from Mansel. And for ½ qr purchased as in the account for making malt. And for 9½ qrs 1 trug received from -----[fold in document] by tally against John Gold and threshed at the stack. And for 7 qrs 5 bs from the external [outside the manor?] land of William Weston* *Total 46 qs 2½ bs*

From which 5½ qrs were used for sowing in the field called Rodfield by tally against William the ploughholder and 1½ qrs for sowing the land of William de Weston by tally against the same ploughholder; Used for making maslin for the famuli 14½ qrs. Paid to the vicar of Mansel for his rent 2 qrs. Used for baking bread for Dame Joan de Walsche and other visitors at Bunshill around the feast of Purification 1 b. Delivered at Aconbury ½ qr. Used for malt as in the account ½ qr. 1 qr of new grain. Item used for bread provided for the Lady and various men who ate at her table for 3 weeks in harvest time 1 qr 2 bs. And sold as in the account 8qr, and also 4 qrs of new grain sold

Total 38 qrs 7bs and carried over 7 qrs 3½ bs of wheat

And he accounts for 3 qrs 2 bs received from the grange by tally against Roger Alayn that was threshed at the stack. And for 2 bs received William de Weston *Total 3½ qrs.*

***Beans;** He accounts for 3½ bs sown in the garden by the view of William the ploughholder; And ½ qr used for fattening the pigs for the larder. Delivered at Aconbury ½ qr; sold as in the account 1qr 6½bs.*

Total 3qr 2 bs and there remain 2 bs of beans

And he accounts for ½ peck brought forward. And for 3 ½ bs from the produce of the grange threshed at the stack by tally against the said Roger Alayn and 1 b 1 trug from the external land of William

Total 5½ bs ½ peck

***White peas;** He accounts for 1b sowed on land of William de Weston by tally against William the ploughholder;; 1 trug delivered to Aconbury and 1½ bs 2 pecks sold as in the account Total 3½ bs and carried over1½ bs 1½ pecks of white peas And for 1 b brought forward And for 6 qrs 2½ bs from the profits of the grange by tally against Roger Alayn threshed at the stack and for 5bs from the land of William de Weston* *Total 7 qrs ½ b*

***Black peas;** 1 qr 3 bs sowed by tally against the said ploughholder; sowed on the land of William de Weston ½ qr by tally as above in the account of white peas sowed. And 2 bs for fattening 3 pigs for the larder and 2 bs for feeding 3 pigs from the stock. And used to make horse cake as fodder for the mare used to pull the harrow 6 bs at each sowing more this year because the hay was ruined by a flood while it was being mowed .(Used for making maslin as detailed elsewhere) 1qr 6 bs 1 trug. And sold as in the account 1 qr 3 bs 2 pecks 5 bushels carried over* *Total 6 qrs 3½ bs*

And there was 1 bushel brought forward. And 14 qrs 2 bs received from the produce of the grange by tally against Roger Alayn, threshed at the stack; and 2 qrs from the rent of William the driver; ~~and 1 qr as listed elsewhere purchased to make malt~~ and 4 qrs 7 bs 1 trug from the produce of the demesne by tally against John Gold; and 3 qrs 5½ bs 1 peck from the produce of William de Weston's land.

Total ~~18qrs 2 bs; 16qrs 5 bs~~ *Total 25qrs 2 pecks*

***Oats;** For sowing in the field called Guddefelde/Ruddefelde 7 qrs by tally against the ploughholder. For sowing on William de Weston's land 1 qr by tally against the sower. For flour for pottage for the bailiff, 2 plough servants and 1 cowherd 2 qrs at the costs of the Lady. Allowed to the vicar of Mansel for his rent 4qrs. Used for making malt 1qr as in the account. And 2 qrs of new grain. Used to feed geese at nesting time and in the summer 2 bs. Sold as in the account 1qr 1 b of old grain and 4 qrs of new grain.* *Total 22 qrs 3 bs and carried over 2 qrs 5 bs 2 pecks*

He accounts for 14½ qrs received from the above wheat for the allowance of the famuli as in the account and 1 qr 6 bs 1 trug of peas for the same purpose. *Total 16 qrs 2 bs 1 trug*

***Allowances to the famuli;** To William the bailiff 4 qrs 1 trug of wheat during the year taken at the rate of 1 trug each week, and no more because he ate at the Lady's table for 3 weeks at harvest time. Allowed to 1 ploughholder and 1 driver for the same period 1 trug of wheat with sometimes an allowance of peas as well, making in all 6 qrs 2 bs 1 trug of wheat and 1 qr 6 bs 1 trug of peas, and no more for the same reason. Allowed to 1 dairyman/dairymaid and 1 cowherd for the same period 1 trug each of wheat every 3 weeks making in all 4 qrs 1 trug and no more because they ate at the Lady's table for 3 weeks. And 1½ bs brought forward And ½ qr excess And 1 qr received as wort from the new grain*

***First grade malt;** 1½ bs 1 peck delivered to Aconbury. And ½ b used for brewing ale for the use of Dame Joan le Walsche and others at the Feast of Purification; and 2 bs for brewing ale for the Lady and her household at harvest. Sold 1 b 2 pecks.* *Total 5½ bs And 1 qr carried over*

And 4 bs brought forward and 1 qr excess and 2 qrs received from the wort of new grain (de fuso de novo grano)

***Second grade malt;** 3 bs delivered to Aconbury; used for brewing ale for the Lady 1½ bs; used for brewing ale for the Lady and her household at harvest time 5 bs; and 2 bs sold.*

Total 1 qr 2½ bs and 2 qrs ½ b of second grade malt carried over

***Ordinary malt;** 1½ bs brought forward which was used for brewing for the Lady's use during the above period and so nothing is left.*

***Mares;** 1 mare received from Roger Alayn in exchange for a colt as below. Carried over 1*

Colts; *1 2½ year old colt brought forward from last year and exchanged with Roger Alayn for the said mare Carried over none*

Yearling colts; *1 brought forward and sold as recorded below. None carried over*

Oxen; *6 brought forward and 6 carried over*

Cows; *2 brought forward and 2 carried over*

Bullocks; *1 brought forward, 1 bought in – total 2; 1 carried over and 1 in the larder*

Calves; *2 brought forward from the 2 cows; 1 sold and 1 carried over*

Boar; *1 brought forward; sold as in the account*

Sow; *1 brought into this age group; carried over 1*

Pigs; *2 brought forward and 2 upgraded total 4*

2 sent to the Lady's larder and 1 upgraded as above, total 3, carried over 1

Hoggets; *1 brought forward and 6 upgraded from the 1 year old pigs. Total 7*

2 moved up into the next age group as above and 1 butchered for the Lady's store room and the bailiff has the carcass Total 3 and 4 carried over

Piglets; *2 brought forward and the young sow had 6 in June*

1 went to the Lady's larder on Monday after the Translation of St Thomas the Martyr [7 July], 1 sent to Aconbury for the use of the Lady, 4 upgraded to hoggets as above. None carried over.

Geese; *25 brought forward of which 1 is a gander and 5 are unmated. 35 hatched Total 60*

Of which 14 by tally went to the hospice at Aconbury for various pittances, 2 goslings were given as a gift to Dame Joan de Wylynton in the summer, 2 goslings went to Aconbury in the summer for the use of the Lady, 1 goose used for the famuli at harvest time for their reaping feast 11 died, 5 used by the Lady at harvest and 6 went to Aconbury for the feast of the Assumption. ~~5 were sold for 10d~~ 4 sold ---[faded] and 1 sold for 2d Total 46 and 14 carried over of which 1 is a gander and 5 are ---[faded]

Ducks; *4 brought forward of which 1 is a drake. 1 died and 3 carried over including the drake. No increase this year because they are young.*

Capons; *17 brought forward and 11 brought up from lower age group. Total 28.*

13 sent to Aconbury, 3 used for the Lady and other occasional visitors, 3 given to Dame Joan de Welynton,. Total 19 and 9 carried over

Cocks and hens; *23 brought forward of which 4 are cocks. 1 cock and 9 hens set aside for breeding Total 23 11 sent to Aconbury, 2 died. Total 13 and 9 hens and 1 cock carried over*

Pullets; *5 brought forward and an increase of 90 and 24 received from customary tenants at Michaelmas. Total 119*

Of which 11 upgraded to capons as above, 6 given to Dame Joan de Wyelinton, 6 at Aconbury, 61 died as attested by everyone in the manor, 5 used for the Lady at harvest and 22 sold Total 111 and 8 carried over

Eggs; *240 received from ducks and hens as above.*

Of which 60 were used for the Lady on her visits and 220 at Aconbury. None carried over

Dovecote; *Nothing from the dovecote for the most part because the Lady had the key in her possession. But the income received from the squabs is recorded in the account.*

The Prioress it appears deals with the doves and their eggs herself, for whatever reason she did not trust William with the key.

Orchards; *34 gallons of cider made from the produce of the orchards this year, of which 24 were sold for 12d. Total 24 and 10 gallons carried over*

Meat; *4 quarters and 2 shoulders from 1 heifer butchered for the larder as above. And 4 hams from 2 pigs as above. All used in the house as testified by the Lady. None carried over*

And no offal from the pig because it was used for the Lady's household as witnessed in her account. And there was 1 stone of tallow from the heifer and it was delivered to the Lady for making Paris candles. And nothing for the pig's tallow because the Lady ---[faded]

Hides; *1 from 1 heifer and it was tanned for ----[faded]*

Skins; *20 bought in and 2 from the Lady's store and --- to the Lady for making shoes --- [entry partly illegible]*

Plough services; *25 received from customary tenants –[faded] virgate[s] of customary land 6d. Each customary tenant –[faded] will plough 2 acres in the winter season and 2 acres at the Lent season and at the fallow season [1 acre?] – [faded]. Each plough service is worth 3d. And they are sold as in the account Total 25*

Of which 5 acres to be ploughed are of William de Weston's land. And 20 sold as in the account

Even in the 14th century Bunshill Manor was run, in many ways similar to a modern day business based on a very comprehensive profit and loss ledger.

The regular Manor court hearings were held in the courtyard of Bunshill Manor House, following a tradition left by the Anglo-Saxons, who always held open-air meetings for Manorial and Hundred courts. All the residents of the manor had to attend the court or they were fined for non-attendance; on the plus side everyone had their say, the majority ruled and the system worked fine for hundreds of years. William the bailiff of Bunshill held the Manorial Courts on behalf of the Prioress. The court dealt with the tenants' grievances, and issued fines to anyone who broke the rules of the manor. These early courts appear to be an easy way for the prioress to collect money from her tenants, as these fines for wrongdoing were paid to William the Bailiff who acted as the Prioress's agent.

With the heading faded and some of the document missing, the following transcript is from the oldest surviving Court Roll for Bunshill[7]. It was written in the years 1343 and 1344 on the same piece of parchment.The first legible part refers to the Court dealing with the villagers who were charged with wrongdoing.

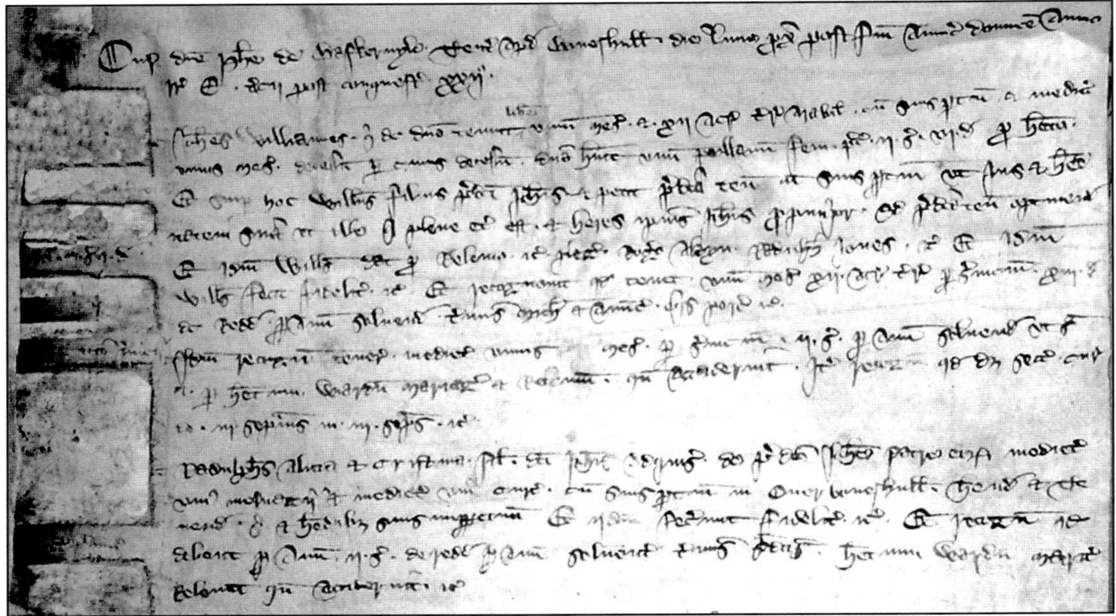

(Figure 3) 14th century Bunshill court roll

Walter Robines *for 2 oxen in the corn surety* ***Ralph Jones***
Alice de Straddel *for 12 sheep in the corn surety* ***John Williams***
Richard le Hemere *from the Weir [de la Were] for 1 cow in the corn surety* ***Roger Aleyn***
Walter Hughes *for 3 lambs in the oats pledge* ***John Williams***
The same ***Walter*** *for another 3 lambs in the oats pledge* ***John Jamyes***
John Walens *for 1 bullock in the Lady's oats pledge* ***John Jamyes***
Walter de la Marshe *for 1 bullock in the oats pledge* ***John Gold***
William Aylward *for 1 bullock in the oats pledge* ***John Gold***
All the above amerced (fined) 1d

The Prioress through the control of the bailiff would have farmed the largest proportion of the common fields called demesne land. Livestock were not allowed into the common field until after the harvest, in1343 the field had been planted with oats and corn and all the named parishioners had let their stock run into these crops causing damage. Parishioners like Roger Alayn could and did in court, offer surety to pay the fine if the offender did not.

It was presented by the court that ***Alice*** *(4d) daughter of* ***Roger Alayn*** *didn't do her boon reaping. Also* ***Ralph*** *son of the said* ***Roger***. *So they are in mercy.* ***Roger Cobbe*** *is presented for the same as is his brother* ***John, a charcoal burner.***

Ralph Jones *(2d) and* ***John Gold*** *(12d) presented because their sons did not do the work they owed in the cornfield; the bailiff is to make sure they do in future.*

As well as the tenant giving their time to work in the fields for the Prioress, their families were also expected to help; the above fines were imposed to ensure they carried out their duty in the future. Nothing changes; even today teenagers can rebel against work.

The next court held on Friday the feast of St Gregory March 3rd 1344 records how the court dealt with disputes, all the tenants had to attend the court so a dispute could be discussed and an agreement reached.

It records how Roger the Miller had a dispute with John de Tulletree, this could have been over the cost Roger charged John to mill his corn or the quality of the flour produced. In any case they agreed their differences and it was recorded so in the court record.
John Piersson son of John Pier (Pier surname of a man who grew and sold pears), stood surety for William Ayleward who was charged with having six of his pigs in the Prioress's peas. Some of these surnames were first generation so the clerk had to deal with the problems of identifying two or three generations of families the best way he could, one roll even records John the son of John Piersson who was the grandson of the original John Pier. This eventually settled down to just a forename and surname, so it reverted back to John Pier the grandson who is recorded as the alehouse keeper in Bishopstone in 1385. Confused? I am.
Roger de Muleward was accused in the Court of gaining ground by encroachment, it could be he was overstepping the boundary marks or moving the marks himself which was a common ploy. There were literally hundreds of boundaries in the large common fields, many of these boundaries were marked by a balk (narrow strip of turf), other boundaries were marked by large mere stones, and in others cases the boundary could be even an imaginary line between two bushes. Some encroachments could be accidental, working before daylight or after dusk, using a wobbly plough or an oxen team that would not be driven in a straight line. These oxen teams were led by a boy, usually bare footed, what a terrible job on a freezing winter morning. Roger was also in trouble with the court for selling a willow and a poplar tree. Trees were held in high esteem because they were looked upon as valuable assets to an estate; Roger was lucky to get away with the 21d fine.
On August 10th 1345[8] a Court was held at Aconbury in the presence of Matilda de Grandison Prioress and Treasurer of Aconbury to deal with a serious incident that had occurred in Bunshill. John Gold a serf who was born in Bunshill and held a copyhold farm in the Manor, was accused of assaulting the Lady's steward and stabbing him with his knife. The reason for this assault is not recorded but there must have been more to it than a personal dispute, because all the villagers in Bunshill supported John Gold in court. It appears that the steward called at the farm where the assault took place, whether to collect money or deal with some other business it is not clear, but John with the assistance of his son John, attacked the steward and stabbed him. Roger Alayn witnessed the assault and was reprimanded by the court for not going to help the steward. John Gold fled the scene initially but afterwards he surrendered himself to the Prioress. The whole community in Bunshill stood together and put up a surety of £10 to help secure his release. The farm he held in Bunshill plus his goods and chattels were taken from him by the Prioress. Neither John Gold nor his son appeared in the court records after this date. The court jury was made up from people who seem to represent all the tenants of land the Priory owned in Herefordshire. There must have been a special reason why the new prioress Matilda de Grandison decided to deal with John Gold and his son through the manorial court system, possibly to suppress a conflict of interest.
There is no doubt if the law of the land had dealt with John, the punishment would have involved prison or the gallows. Lucky for him the whole village supported him even though he lost his land holding he still retained his life. The farm located on the crossroads with the now A438, referred to as Goldcross, was called Gold's Farm for the next 200 years.
John Piersson died in 1347, the court records illustrates how the manor system worked; firstly a heriot was due, similar to a death duty, to the lord of the Manor, in this case the Prioress. Because the family did not have a cow worth 6s 8d to give, the Prioress was offered one iron bound wagon, and a brass pot. His son John put himself forward as his offspring to take over the smallholding. The court demanded payment of eight and half marks as an entry fine plus 40s at All Saints day, 20s at the following Feast of the Purification, 40s on the following feast of St Peter ad Vincula and 13s 4d at the feast of St Dionysius, and only after he did fealty and formally acknowledged what he owed, was he allowed to take possession of the smallholding. Why the odd monetary figures of 13s.4d? This dates back to when the mark was the accepted currency (One mark is equal to 13s 4d, half a mark 6s 8d)
Ralph Jones' son was also in trouble with the same court for planting a hedge without permission, so he was fined. John Cobbe, Roger and Ralph his brothers plus Roger Alayn were before the court for not carrying out the work in the fields to help gather in the Prioress's harvest. Was this the start of serfs complaining about the villeinage system? The Peasant's Revolt did not break out until 1386, but it is clear that revolt had been brewing for a long time before, in the villages of England.
Margaret the daughter of Roger the Miller had left the parish so breaking her bail, as a serf she was not permitted to live outside the parish. Margaret could have become a freewoman by making a payment of money to the Prioress and only then if the court agreed it; she would have lost all the benefits and rights that came with being bonded to a parish. The Court put a restraining order on her brother to encourage her to return; also they found out that Margaret had left a chest worth 3d behind in the house of John Cobbe, which the Court seized.

Copyholders of Bunshill 1348

Roger the Miller held the large mill.
John son of Roger the Miller held a messuage and half a virgate of land (15acres)
Roger Alayn held a messuage and one virgate of land (30acres), his son called Ralph and daughter Alice lived with him.
John Piers held a messuage and half a virgate of land. He lived with Margery his wife and daughter Joan
John Piers Son held a messuage and half a virgate of land, he had a son also called John.
John Gold a messuage and half a virgate of land. (The prioress held the land on his behalf after the court case in 1345
John le Muleward (mill engineer) held a messuage and half a virgate of land, from his father Roger who had just died. William and Margery his brother and sister lived with him. They paid a rent of 6s per year.
William Ayleward and his wife Juliana held a croft.
William James held his father's croft, he had married Christina Williams by 1349.
John Cobbe held a messuage with a house and half a virgate of land rent 5s per year. John lived with his brother Roger who was a charcoal burner and another brother Ralph a serf.
Ralph Jones held a messuage and half a virgate of land, his son John was a chaplain.
Ralph, Alice and Christina Williams children of John Williams held a messuage and one curtilage of land in Overbonshill.
William Williams son of John Williams held a messuage and 12 acres of arable and the moiety of a messuage.
John Tulltree held a messuage and half a virgate of land rent 6s. The Tulltree's came into the Manor through marriage as recorded in the 1339 court rolls. William Ostebarne held half a virgate of land in Bunshill. After his death, William his son surrendered it to his brother John who died without heirs. After the death of William and John it came to Juliana their sister, she had a licence to marry Geoffrey de Tulltree from an outside fee. After the marriage they gave a fine to Lady Alice de Sutton to gain entry to the land for the duration of their lives, and after their death the legal right for the farm to pass down through their heirs for three generations. John Tulltree as grandson of William Ostebarne now held the farm.
There were fourteen copyholders living in Bunshill plus the famuli.
We have now reached the year 1349 when the Black Death reached Bunshill, the manor court sat four times in that year to try and deal with its disastrous consequences, I have included the full transcript of each Court held because of its historic content.

Court of Philippa de Baskervyle held at Bunshull Monday after St Mark the Evangelist 23 Ed III [April 27 1349] [9]Note! all the Court Rolls up until 1350 are covered in footnote 9
Richard Ode** for 1 horse in the corn, surety **Ralph Jones
Roger Adames** for 1 mare in the same, surety **Ralph Jones
Waiter Ede (Gilbertes)** for 8 sheep in the same, surety **Roger Alayn
William Ayleward** for 1 sheep in the same, surety the said **Roger
Juliana Ayleward** for 12 sheep in the same, surety the said **Roger
Waiter de Straddel** for 12 sheep in the same, surety the said **Roger
William Bannde** for 20 sheep in the same, surety the said **Roger
*The homage present that **William James** made default of suit of court, therefore he is distrained. He came afterwards.*
*It is presented by the **bailiff** that **Roger le Shepherd** allowed a ram to be killed by dogs for lack of guarding it, therefore he is amerced*
Many historians have the opinion that the villagers knew the Black Death was spreading throughout the country, so law and order started to break down.

Bunshull Court held there Tuesday next after the feast of St James, 23 Ed III [July 28 1349]
***John Cobbe** who held 1 messuage with a house and half a virgate of land has died. There is no heriot because he held nothing of value when he died. He was accustomed to pay 5s pa rent. The property has returned to the hands of the Lady. There have been two proclamations for his heir.*
*Death of **John son of Roger the miller** who held 1 messuage with a house and half a virgate of land. There is no heriot because he held nothing of value when he died. The property has returned to the hands of the Lady. There have been two proclamations for his heir*

*Death of **William son of John** who held a messuage and 12 acres of land, and the moiety of a messuage for which there is due as heriot one ewe lamb worth 2d. He was accustomed to pay 4s rent. The property has returned to the hands of the Lady as it was proclaimed three times and no one came.*
*Deaths of **Ralph, Alice and Cristina Williams** who held the moiety of a messuage and lands paying 2s pa for which a heriot of a cow is due. Ordered to be taken into the Lady's hands*
*Death of **Margery la Pere** who held 1 messuage and half a virgate of land, paying 5s pa rent. A heriot of a cow is due. Her daughter **Joan** is her heir.*
*Death of **Roger Alayn** who held 1 messuage and 1 virgate of land for which the heriot due is an ox worth 11 shillings, one iron bound wagon, an iron with its fittings, and a brass pot worth 10s 4d, and the property has been taken into the Lady's hands.*
*Death of **Ralph Jones** who held 1 messuage and half a virgate of land for which a heriot of an ox is due.*

The Black Death arrived in Bunshill during May or early June 1349, on July 28th the court asked three times if there were any heirs of Ralph, Alice and Christina Williams, John Cobbe, Roger Alayn, John Miller and his son William, no one came to claim their holding so we can only presume all these families had died from the Black Death or run away, so these tenements were legally taken back in the hands of the Prioress.

I would like to move the reader away from these factual Court Rolls into a fictional account of the deaths suffered by the Jones family as a way of explaining what happened in Bunshill, Bishopstone and the other surrounding villages. Ralph Jones a serf had lived all his life in Lower Bunshill as a smallholder, he was married and his children were now grown up.

Ralph Jones Story

"Ralph peers out from the opening of his house, behind him low moaning sounds can be heard, coming from his wife and daughter who are lying on sack bedding in the interior gloom, already showing symptoms of the dreaded plague with large swellings in the neck, armpits, or groin. The swellings were intensely painful, he slowly walks back in to them and offers water but they do not respond, merely rolling around in agony. He looks at the swellings which are bright red: he knows if they turn a dark purple, or black they will be certain to die. Ralph moves back to the door and looks out anxiously; he is waiting for his son, John a chaplain to arrive so his wife and daughter can confess their sins and receive absolution, he worries that John will not arrive in time and his wife and daughter will go to hell. Ralph reflects on how proud he is of his son who is the chaplain of Winforton, all those years of studying helped by the nuns had certainly paid off, without their help he would have never achieved his vocation. He opens the door on which hangs a cross, a sign that the pestilence has come to this house. All is deadly quiet outside. He had helped to bury four of his neighbours within the last week, Ralph, Alice and Christina Williams, and John the miller's son. What a struggle that had been, there were only a few adults left in the Manor who were fit enough to dig the graves up by the chapel. Ralph worries who will bury him if he falls victim to the plague; he looks out again to see his son hurrying toward him dressed in his clergy robes, what a relief, at the same moment Ralph notices pain under his arm and feeling down he finds a hard lump. He realises his time left on this earth will be short but he is pleased to see John who can now set their minds at rest and maybe death will take them to a better place."

On a warm summer's evening when walking the dog across the Cathero field, I often reflect on the tragedy and suffering of Ralph Jones and others who lost their lives to the Black Death here in July 1349. How different the area would have looked then, with half a dozen enclosures containing houses and the mill standing down by the brook.

***Bunshull. Court of Lady Phillipa de Baskervyle held there Wednesday after the Exaltation of the Holy Cross* (September 15th 1349).**
Joan la Pere *was granted 1 messuage with a house and close to hold by rents and services accustomed. Her sureties were **John Piersone** and **John Williams***
John *the chaplain son of **Ralph Jones** surrendered 1 messuage and half a virgate of land to use of **Stephen le Palmer** who was granted entry according to the custom of the manor.He did fealty. Entry fine 2 marks, one to be paid at Michaelmas next and one at Ladyday. Sureties **John de Tulletree** and **John Piersone***

*There are still remaining in the hands of the Lady 1 messuage and half a virgate formerly held by **John Cobbe** for rent of 5s pa; 1 messuage and half a virgate formerly held by **John le Muleward** for rent of 6s pa; 1 messuage and 1 virgate formerly held by **Roger Aleyn** for rent of 10s*

The Court tried to carry on with business as usual, traditionally after the death of a tenant their landholdings would be passed down to their heirs, but now three farms, totaling over 100 acres, remained empty with no living members of the family left to take them on. Interestingly the son of Ralph Jones had become a chaplain, this was one route to take you out of poverty. Peasants could rise through the ranks of the church and also receive an education. John Welsh's son from Bishopstone followed a similar route and became a chaplain of Bishopstone Church.

Court held at Bunshull Friday after the feast of St Nothelmus 23 Edward III (October 23 1349).

There are tenements still in the hand of the Lady because no tenant came

It a poignant entry because no one came to the Court Meeting, those who had survived were possibly afraid to meet in a group because of the fear they could catch the pestilence.

John son of Roger the Miller plus his family, Roger Alayn and family, Ralph Jones, Margery La Pier, John Le Muleward and his family, Ralph, Alice and Cristina Jones, John Cobbe and his brother Ralph had all died from the Black Death, it had reduced the number of tenants in Bunshill from 14 to 6 between May and October 1349.

How many others died in the Manor House household is unknown but it was the end of what had been a short period of an expanding monastic way of life at Bunshill, the nuns had died or returned to Aconbury, and the complex reverted back to a farm. Evidence associated with the monastic way of life still survived into the 18th century: the carp pond by the roadside, the rabbit warren on the river escarpment, and a dovecote by the farmhouse

John de Tulletree survived the plague: he was the only copyholder to continue farming in Bunshill. John Piers' son also survived but he moved on to pastures new by taking over the alehouse in Bishopstone. Who was left in Bunshill can be identified from the "Rental of Lady Eva de Seymour 1353"

Bunshill	**Lady Day**	**Pentecost**	**Michaelmas**
Joan la Pier	20d	20d	20d
Sir William de Stoketon	20d	20d	20d
Stephen le Palmer	20d	20d	20d
John de Tulletre	20d	20d	20d
Sir William de Stoketon	20d	20d	20d
Roger Lussone	20d	20d	20d
Richard Nicholas	1½d		1½d
John Hokyns	1½d		1½d
William Perkyns	1½d		1½d

The bottom three were the freeholders in the Manor, Sir William de Stoketon could have been a member of the clergy taking advantage of cheap land to rent or the friar left after the nuns departed; over half the smallholdings were left empty because there were not enough living left to work the land. The plague also closed down Bunshill's mill, after its closure the mill at Mansel Lacy, also under the ownership of the prioress of Aconbury, was used by the tenants of Bunshill Manor.

In a deed[10] dated May 12th 1359, Roger Comyn purchased one messuage and 14 acres of land in Overbonshill, Lowerbonehill and Were(Weir) from Richard Nicholas and his wife Sybil for 20 marks of silver. Shortly after purchasing this messuage Roger Comyn secured the lease on the manor of Bunshill. Roger also held by tenancy the mill at Aconbury

In 1351 an Act of Parliament set a standard for the measurement of cloth. In 1366 Roger Comyn of Bunshill was appointed the Kings Aulnegeour for Herefordshire, as an officer representing the king he would travel between markets and fairs checking cloth sizes. He produced cloth at Bunshill capitalising on the few cloth makers who survived the Black Death and using the facilities which already existed at the Manor farm.

A Chancery record in 1361 records that Roger the son of William le Young of Lower Bunshill owed £10 to Edmund le Parker of Byford; the only interest to the reader is that at least one of the smallholdings in Lower Bunshill was still occupied after the Black Death.

The 1377 poll tax record lists Roger Comyn occupying Bunshill with 20 other persons over the age of fourteen living in the Manor. Roger's tenancy of the Manor came to an abrupt end in 1394 for some unknown reason, the making of cloth at Bunshill finished with his departure after a hundred years of continuous production.

The demesne land of the manor of Bunshill was leased in the short term to Richard Jones and John Alton who both failed to keep up the rent payments. In 1398 a farmer named Robert Taylor took a long-term lease on the manor which by then had fallen into disrepair. He agreed to repair the houses in the manor and bring the land back up to scratch by hedging, clearing ditches and ploughing the demesne lands in the common fields. The accounts[11] covering the period January 21st 1394-1397 reveal that the manor had suffered years of neglect.

Roger Comyn left Bunshill owing the Prioress money. When he held the manor he had taken 3 oxen as heriots (payment to the Lord of the Manor on the death of a tenant within the manor): a price of 38s 8d was agreed between the parties as the value of the oxen, the accounts record he paid up his arrears.

Richard Jones paid four pounds for the crops on the land when he started his lease, six pounds rent for three years and nothing for the fourth year. We can only presume that weather played a part as from 1394-1411 England suffered a mini ice age with very cold winters. This matches the accounts' records of poor returns during this period with many tenants not paying their rent on their yardlands (an early English word meaning an area of land usually in common fields).

Richard Jones received money from Aconbury to repair the manor house.

Paid to Richard Jones tenant of Bunshill for repair of the house there 30s. And various costs for the repair there for the period of this account viz for carpenters and tilers brought in and nails, stone and tiles bought for the same as itemised in an agreement with the said Matilda £4 12s 9d.

Cost of the repair of the manor house for the period of this account as detailed in the roll 58s 7d.

For purchase of stone tiles 66d; for moss 5d; for carriage of 2 wagon loads of wattle and daub 12d

This gives some nice information on the structure of the manor house, it was timber framed with panels of wattle and daub and a stone tile roof, which matches the description of the house that was pulled down in 1754 although by then it had been extensively enlarged. The moss listed in the account was used as a form of insulation above the ceilings.

Isabel the widow of Richard Dewale chaplain and tenant of a Hereford Cathedral smallholding in Bunshill, appears to be the only person who prospered through these accounts. In 1398 the chapel with its toft (homestead) was let out for 3 years for 2s 8d per annum possibly to a chaplain.

For sums distributed and paid, to eight nuns 2s each and to 3 nuns 16d each, and paid to all 11 nuns an additional 3s 4d, Total 36s 8d. Paid for pittances for the period of this account at two feasts of All Saints 4s 8d.

The number of nuns receiving payment from Bunshill varies between nine and eleven, the accounts covering the years 1398-1401[12] list the names of the nuns receiving their part of the rent income from Bunshill.

Note! Each nun held the title of "Lady" similar to the male clergy being addressed as "Sir."

Prioress, Lady Matilda Heynre, Lady Katherine Markley, Lady Elizabeth Bardolf, Lady Agnes Barry, Lady Margaret Churgrym, Lady Beatrice Chetwyn, Lady Margaret Plowfeld, Lady Elena Pope, Lady Margery Bayly all received 15s 4d

A manor court held in 1394 records the death of Roger Loffe; Roger his son takes over the tenancy on his father's farm for his own life and that of his son John. Loffe's farm was situated on the right-hand side of the lane leading to the present day farm, it became the farm at the centre of a legal battle in 1608 when Richard Savaker held the tenancy. The court records three generations living within this enclosure, it follows a natural progression where a father would go to the manorial court to obtain permission to build a new house next door for his son and family.

Robert Taillour (Taylor) had taken a lease on the manor in 1413, as part of this lease Robert had agreed to repair all the houses within the manor cut the hedges and clear the ditches. He had left Bunshill by 1430 without completing his agreement the houses were still in a poor state of repair, after his departure there appear to have been a few years of uncertainty in the manor.

The court held on Tuesday before the Feast of St Ethelbert king and martyr 15 Hen VI (May 1437) deals mainly with repairs to houses in the manor and the death of Roger Loffe whose holding passed to Thomas Horsnett.

The homage present that John Godfrey has not repaired his house as ordered at last court under a pain of 40d. Richard Smith has not repaired his house as ordered at last court under a pain of 40d.

Roger Loffe has died since last court and he held 2 messuages and half a virgate of customary land by services etc. A sheep is due as heriot to the Lady and is in the custody of Thomas Horsnett. Roger Loffe's house is ruinous and he was ordered to repair it at the last court under a pain of 40d for which pain the said Thomas Horsnett, who is the executor of Loffe's will, holds himself responsible.

John Godfrey, Richard Smyth and Thomas Horsnett are ordered to repair their houses before the next court under the same pain.

A lease dated April 10th 1446 held at the Augmentation Office helps fill in the gap of who rented Bunshill in the middle part of the 15th century. It is a lease from Ann Barry, Prioress of Aconbury to William Horsnet of Bunshill and Joan his wife and to John Smyth of Bunshill and Alice his wife of the whole manor of Bunshill with the appurtenances during their lives under the annual rent of 40 shillings payable half yearly. The Horsnet and Smyth families were already tenants in the manor but with a new lease now up for grabs the families combined to take on a new lease for the whole of Bunshill.

From its court rolls Bunshill always appeared to have a fairly law-abiding society living within the Manor with very little reference to any misdoings, although it could be that they dealt with any problems themselves rather than have anything recorded. But in a court held on April 18th 1448 we have the first report of bad behaviour, Margery Mors is reported as a common scold, a woman, who, in consequence of her boisterous, disorderly and quarrelsome tongue, is a public nuisance to the neighbourhood, and also that she took 3 lambs worth 16d from Maurice Sawyer.

The next section features the 15th -16th century court rolls[13] leading up to Henry VIII's dissolution of the monasteries in 1539 which included the nunnery of Aconbury and its lands including Bunshill. We have 12 court rolls, the last one dated September 27th 1535. Historically they are great and make it easy to follow through the succession of tenants and where they lived. The court dealt with all the problems associated with running a manor such as cleaning ditches, cutting hedges and repairs to houses. If a ditch was not cleaned out, the court established who should be responsible for that ditch and ordered the offending party to clean it out or they would be fined. The farmer in the 16th century knew land drainage was an important part of farming and all the water was channeled through ditches to the river or brook, a lesson that we could learn from today.
The other item recorded in most of the court rolls was the problem of stray animals; I find it hard to understand considering the value villagers placed on their livestock, no one came to claim the animal so it was sold with the money going to the court. These are a few examples,
1490; *They present a stray boar above one year in age, which is in the custody of John Savacer and it is worth 16d. They order 8d to be allocated to Savacer to pay for its keep.*
1503*; They report a stray black horse in the keeping of John Savacer and a stray heifer, which has been in the bailiff's custody since 3 July.*
1509*; There are 2 white sheep as strays and David Wheth is looking after them.*
1530*; They present 1 white sheep as a stray since Michaelmas, now in custody of John Wenland.*
1535*; The homage present 1 white sheep as a stray at Lady Day, which is in the custody of John Wenland*
Most of Bunshill's court rolls from 1489 start with the heading "*Court with view of frankpledge"* which means a community pledge whereby all men over 12 living within the manor of Bunshill, were jointly held responsible for the reporting of any crime within their group. An example on how it worked can be found in the court held on Monday the feast of St Matthews 5 Hen V11 [September 21st 1489] *They present an affray between John Savacer (2d) and Richard Smith (4d) for which Smith was most to blame.* The court settled this dispute with both parties fined in proportion of blame.
Also in the 1489 Court we learn that John Smyth the bailiff held the Manor farm with its demesne land at a £2 a year rent, John Smyth's death was recorded in the 1491 court *The homage present the death of John Smyth the Lady's "farmer", on whose death there is due to the Lady the best beast as heriot.*

John Wenland married Katherine, the daughter of John Smyth; the old bailiff, then moved into the manor house in 1509 after negotiating a new lease for Bunshill. He also took on the customary farm called Little Hall. The Jurors on all these Court rolls numbered only 3 or 4 persons, representing the five main farms left in the manor, Golds Farm, Loffes Farm, Mors Farm, Little Hall and Manor Farm.
The Savacer family had held a tenancy on at least one of these farms since 1472. In 1504 John Savacer transfers his farm holdings to his son William and daughter-in-law Elizabeth.
This forward planning by John to surrender his farms to his son failed because William died suddenly, Elizabeth remarried David Whethe in 1507, much to the annoyance of John who accused him of trespass and destroying a crop of corn valued at 12d. David was granted the tenancy of Golds Farm and Loffes Farm through Elizabeth his wife. Remember John had just passed the tenancies over to his son just before he died, and as John was still living in Golds Farm he could have been facing eviction. John who was born within the manor and had lived there all his life, managed to persuade the court to hand the tenancy of Gold's farm back to him and his wife Margery for their life time. In 1529 John surrendered the tenancy of Golds Farm to his other son Thomas, and his wife Elizabeth, as recorded in the court rolls for Michaelmas 21 Henry V111 [1530]. Thomas Savacre was ordered to repair the kitchen and barn at Gold's Farm in the same roll. Interestingly Golds farmhouse had a separate building housing the kitchen, normally only found in larger houses. Bishopstone Court had a similar arrangement.

Bunshill rent; customary tenants for the years 1534-35

William Rolles, John Pember, Thomas Savacre	*£4 10s 04d*
Bunshill rent freeland and land	*£0 10s 03d*
Bunshill farm one messuage (Manor) John Wenland	*£2 00s 00d*

The above rental list the tenants of the four main farms, John Wenland's Manor Farm contained approx 60 acres plus buildings including a large barn. Loffes Farm and Golds Farm together totalled 60 acres, they were both farmed by Thomas Savacre for a rent of 28s per year. The 30 acre Little Hall Farm was farmed by Thomas Wenland at a rent of 8s 8d per year. Mors Farm had been in the tenancy of John Pember since 1515, it contained 30 acres at a rent of 7s. Remember, most of the lands attached to the farms lay in strips within the three common open fields plus each farm contained a few acres enclosed around the homestead. All these farms and their tenants can be traced back into the 14th century through the court rolls, making an interesting exercise although they changed tenants regularly, sometimes moving between different farms within the manor. Little Hall Farm for example had five different tenants between 1472 and 1535. Besides the main farms Bunshill manor contained three other customary cottages standing in small plocks of ground, plus the freeland of John Savacre called Libes the Querelem, and John Olivers freeland; all these plocks contained a cottage.

John Wenland became the Lady's Farmer in 1509 by leasing the whole manor of Bunshill for 40s per annum; he also leased the priory land in Mansel Lacy including the water mill. This also included looking after the customary farms and cottages. John Wenland appears to have been a very formidable individual; his son Thomas followed his father's attitude and they caused many problems with other tenants within the Manor that resulted in five court cases and a threat on Thomas's life. This bad feeling started in 1509 when John Wenland in his first year as the tenant of Bunshill claimed that a three-acre meadow called "The Home" on the riverbank was common land. The other tenants in Bunshill opposed this claim and issued the following statement in the 1509 Court Rolls.

They declare on oath that a pasture called the Home has been held in private ownerships not in common for the last 18 years

This niggling continued for the next 20 years with many claims in the court rolls against John Wenland for not carrying out his duties, by failing to repair the customary houses and barns, not cleaning out his ditches and overburdening the common pasture.

In 1530 his son Thomas was awarded the customary farm called Little Hall by his father. Elizabeth, Thomas's mother died shortly after; whether this was a factor in what followed is unknown but Thomas tried to renew his claim on the "The Home," initially through the manor court, but failed. Much to the annoyance of the other tenants, he then appealed to the Chancery Court naming his fellow tenants of Bunshill as wrongdoers. Thomas must presumably have had a reasonable amount of money to be able to afford to take this action.

These were uncertain times, with monastery and priory lands under threat of being confiscated by the king. It appears that John and his son Thomas tried to take advantage of the situation to increase their own wealth. They tried to interfere with the glebe land in Mansel Lacy, offered land for sale that they did not own, and tried to stop customary tenants from using the mill, all these actions resulted in Chancery Court cases. John Wenland left the Manor House in 1536, forced out by the other tenants; his son Thomas left Little Hall at the same time. Now it gets confusing as they both always refer to themselves as living in Bunshill although according to the tax records neither lived in Bunshill, they also aligned themselves with the parish church of Kenchester.

This was certainly stated in a case[14] brought by Thomas in the Court of Requests and Star Chamber, when the petition he sent to the court was addressed To the King our Sovereign Lord from your true and faithful subject Thomas Wenland of Bunshill.

This is my interpretation of the events as recorded in a letter to the Court.

In August last year he stated, he was attending divine service in his church at Kenchester as he ought to, when the church door opened and 16 persons carrying swords, bills and spears and other weapons entered. Anyone who has attended a service at the small church at Kenchester could easily imagine the scene: the large church door creakily swinging open whilst the service was in progress, I bet the look on the Rector's face was a picture as 16 heavily armed persons came in and dragged Thomas outside. I thought that the church was a place of sanctuary where you could shelter in safety but it appears not so in the 16th century. He writes, that *"this put him in danger of his life if he had not made a better shift of himself."* So I presume Thomas fancied himself as a bit of a swordsman, you can picture the scene in the churchyard, with Thomas surrounded by attackers, defending himself with his sword then leaping on his horse and high-tailing back to Bunshill You can imagine the grins on their face as he disappeared up the lane. I think they only wanted to frighten him. His petition goes on to say that he could not now attend divine service in his church, as he should do by law because he was in danger of his life as they were trying to kill him.

He named the leading offenders and asked for them to be brought to court; John Smyth, Maud his wife, Thomas Smyth and Alison. The Smyths were a powerful local family, descended from the family who lived in the Townsend Farm Bishopstone in the 14th century, John from the Weir (Kenchester) and his cousin Thomas from the manor of Credenhill (later owner of Foxley).

John Wenland died in 1549, and in his will dated March 22nd he states John Wenland of Bunshill within the parish of Kenchester. The will also reveals that he had lost most of his wealth, but also interestingly he and his son appear to have made up their differences with Thomas Symth who was named as an executor of his will[15].

On the suppression of the religious houses by Henry VIII in 1539, the Crown claimed all the lands of Aconbury Priory including Bunshill from Lady Eva le Seymour (Prioress of Aconbury). The tenants of the manor were not evicted their tenancies were simple transferred from Aconbury to the new lessee, William Caldecott.

A document[16] dated March 10th 1540 under the seal of the Court of Augmentation states that Bunshill Manor formerly belonging to the monastery of Aconbury was leased to William Caldecott, yeoman, of Holme Lacy, with all houses land etc belonging to the said manor, then lately in the tenure of John Wenland, except great trees and woods for 21 years at a yearly rent of 40s.

William never lived at Bunshill, and he sublet the manor comprising three main farms to Thomas Savacre, William Savacre and Thomas Barroll who by 1539, according to the tax assessments, occupied the old manor house vacated by John Wenland.

Bunshill had five taxable holdings in the 1543 tax assessment list. Surprisingly Thomas Barroll (Manor Farm) and Thomas Savacre (Gold's House and Loffes Farm) were both assessed at £4 8d which indicates the farms at this time were of similar sizes in terms of landholdings, the slightly smaller farm occupied by William Rolles paid £3 6d followed by John Pember (20s 2d) and Thomas Howell (11s 11d).

The will of Thomas Savacre[17] who died in 1569 indicates that he was a fairly wealthy man, from him the tenancy of Looffes Farm passed to his eldest son William. Such wills are worthy of a read and this one shows the effort that Thomas, who would have made the will on his death bed, had taken to list all his posessions and to whom he wished to leave them.

In Dei nomine Amen, the last day of October in the year of our Lord God 1569 I Thomas Savacre of Buncell in the parish of Maunsell Lacy being sick in body and whole in mind and of good and perfect remembrance do make my last will and testament in manner and form following. First I bequeath my soul to Almighty God and my body to be buried in the churchyard of Maunsell aforesaid. Item I give and bequeath my iron bound wain, my dung cribbe, my plough, my yokes, my harrows, my cor--les and my other implements to the team to John my son. Item I give and bequeath all my bedding and implements to the same, as feather beds, flock beds, mattresses, coverlets, blankets, bolsters and pillows, to my daughter Anne, except one pair of Welsh yarn sheets of the second sort which I give and bequeath to my daughter Katherin. Item I give and bequeath the rest of my linen stuff to my said daughter Anne. Item I give and bequeath my great pan to my daughter Anne. Item I give and bequeath my second pan to my son John. Item I give and bequeath my third pan to Katherin my daughter. Item I give and bequeath my gawne skellet to Anne my daughter. Item I give and bequeath my other skellet to Katherin my daughter. Item I give and bequeath my posnet to Katherin my daughter. Item I give and bequeath all my pewter to Anne my daughter except two platters and two pottingers of the second sort which I give and bequeath to Katherin my daughter. Item I give and bequeath my best candlestick to Anne my daughter. Item I give and bequeath my second candlestick to John my son. Item I give and bequeath my third candlestick to Katherin my daughter. Item I give and bequeath my fourth candlestick to William my son. Item I give and bequeath my fifth candlestick to Elizabeth, daughter to William my son. Item I give and bequeath my second coffer, my whiche and my boulting trough to William my son. Item I give and bequeath my wife's coffer and forcet with all that is in them to Anne my daughter. Item I give and bequeath my three stundes, my hogset, my tankards and my other vessels and sieves to Anne my daughter. Item I give and bequeath my biggest broche to William my son during his life and after his death to John my son. Item I give and bequeath my other broche, my cobberds, my frying pan and my gridiron to Anne my daughter. Item where I owe to John my son three pounds, I do give and bequeath three of my oxen viz two of the best and one of the worst oxen to the same John my son in recompense of the said debt. Item I give and bequeath my best cow to Katherin my daughter. Item I give and bequeath my other cow to John, son to William my son. Item I give and bequeath my heifer to Anne my daughter. Item I give and bequeath my bull to John my son. Item I give and bequeath one sheep to my godson Thomas, son to William my son. Item I give and bequeath one sheep to John Sadler, son to Katherin my daughter. Item I give and bequeath one sheep to Margaret, daughter to John my son. Item I give and bequeath one sheep to Anne, daughter to William my son. Item I give and bequeath to John my son and Anne my daughter all my corn on the ground.

Item I give and bequeath to William my son ten bushels of rye, four bushels of wheat and six bushels of winter barley out of the same to be yielded and paid to him by the said John and Anne after harvest next. Item I give and bequeath to Katherin my daughter twenty bushels of rye out of my said corn on the ground to be yielded and paid unto her by the said John and Anne after harvest next. Item I give and bequeath 12d to the reparation of the parish church of Maunsell Lacy. Item I give and bequeath 12d to the reparation of the church of Kenchester. Item I give and bequeath to Margery Brayne two bushels of rye after harvest. Item I give and bequeath my mare to Anne my daughter. Item I give and bequeath my colt to John my son. Item I give and bequeath my geese and poultry to Anne my daughter. Item I give and bequeath my biggest brandert and pothooks to Anne my daughter. Item I give and bequeath my other brandert to John my son. Item I give and bequeath the rest of my goods and cattells unbequeathed to John my son and Anne my daughter to see me honestly buried, whom I do make and appoint mine executors to fulfil and accomplish this my last will and testament. These being witnesses, William Gomond, John Foote and Thomas Clerk.

In 1554 the main lessee for the Manor was John Waters, who in 1571 sold his interest to Thomas and William Barroll, a father and son who were the sitting tenants. The Barroll's were an old Hereforshire family who were already wealthy landowners, Thomas who was the fifth son of Robert from Allensmore who had already acquired land in Bodenham and Byford; they were now the outright owners of Bunshill and Lord of the Manor. They appeared to be very good farmers, increasing their wealth from farming. When Thomas died in 1577 at Bunshill he was a wealthy man as recorded in his following will[18].

Jesus 1577 will of Thomas Barrol

In the name of God the 11th day of November in the year of our Lord one thousand five hundred seventy and seven. I Thomas Barrol of Bunshill sick in body but whole in mind and of good and perfect memory, thanks be unto my Lord God, do make, constitute and ordain this my testament and last will in manner and form following. First I give and bequeath my soul unto God my maker and redeemer and my body to be buried in the parish Church of Much Maunsell.

Item I give and bequeath unto the Cathedral Church of Hereford 12d. Item I give and bequeath unto the said parish church of Much Maunsell 3s 4d.Item I give and bequeath unto the parish church of Kenchester 12d.Item I give and bequeath unto my son William a yoke of oxen which I bought at Bodenham, my best brass pot, my best brass pan, my best broachs (Spits made from silver because it was the custom to take them to the table with the joint or fowl that had been cooked still on them), *my best pair of cobirons*, (pair of iron supports for roasting spit) *my best coffer* (wooden chest, an important article of furniture), *my best treen vessels* (platters made from wood), *with all the residue of my pipes and hogsheads (excepting three of the said hogsheads). Item I give and bequeath unto my son Richard a yoke of my best oxen, and my best bullock at Bodenham and one of my calves weaned. Item I give and bequeath unto my son John three oxen and two yearling bullocks at Bodenham, a weaned calf, twenty bushels of rye in the barn, four acres of wheat and barley stretching upon Sugmeare being of the farm land, three acres of rye lying at the corner of the farm ground, paying the tithe thereof, a pair of wain wheels iron bound at Byford. Item I give and bequeath unto Maunde my daughter, three bushels of rye* (crossed out in original will) *and an ox, if God send her a safe delivery of her child, and if it please God that she die thereof, then I give and bequeath the said ox called Lightfoot unto my son John Item I give and bequeath unto Elizabeth my daughter six bushels of rye, Item I give and bequeath unto Rolland the son of John Eclye an ox now in the keeping of the said John his father. Item I give and bequeath unto Sybill the daughter of the said John Eclye a black yearling heifer now being at Bodenham. Item I give and bequeath unto Joan my daughter four kine (cows) and two heifers with calf, all the residue of my household stuff unbequeathed, twenty sheep and the corn unbequeathed growing on the farm ground. Item all the residue of my corn growing upon the copyhold ground. I give and bequeath unto William my son. Item I give and bequeath unto Thomas Ferowe and Elizabeth Floyd my servants 3 bushells of rye equally divided betwixt them. Item I give and bequeath unto Margerye Barrol an heifer with calf, and a calf, two sheep and a swine. Item I give and bequeath unto Joan my daughter my grey mare and the brocked colt. Item I give and bequeath unto John my son my best colt, and the little mare colt. Item I give and bequeath unto Richard Welshe my servant my colt now in the valet. Item I give and bequeath unto the use of the poor at the sickmens in Hereford a bushel of rye. Item I give to Sislye Pember 12d. Item all kind of corn unbequeathed and grain at the barn and a recke (rick) of peas I give and bequeath unto William my son and Joan my daughter to be equally divided betwixt them. Item I give and bequeath unto the said William and Joan 30 of my swine unbequeathed with geese, ducks, hens and all other kind of poultry. Item I give and bequeath unto Richard my son a three-year-old heifer. Item I give and bequeath unto Joan my daughter a yearling bullock. Item I will have bestowed on me the day of my burial £6 to be paid by my daughter Joan, Item all my money, and debts owing unto me I give and bequeath unto Joan my daughter.*

Item the residue of all my goods and cattles not already bequeathed and given, I give and bequeath to William my son whom I make, constitute and ordain the sole and whole executor of this my last will and testament, and Robert Barrol and John Eclye the younger overseers thereof, these being witnesses, Robert Barrol, John Eclye and James Piggin with others.

Debts owing to the testator

Imprimis with Thomas Clerke	*20s*
Item with William Watkyns	*20s*
Item with Jenkyn Lewis of Hereford	*20s 14d*
Item with John Phelpotts of Byford	*7s*
Item with Thomas Welshe of Bishopston	*3s*

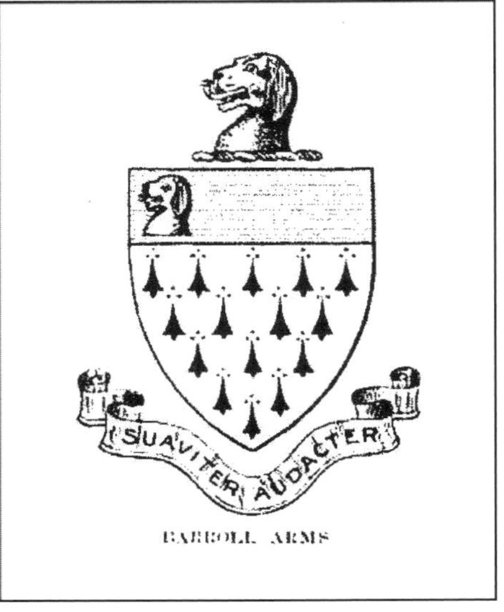

BARROLL ARMS

The ox was the most valuable animal on the farm they were used to plough, work the land and pull wains, carthorses had not yet arrived on the farming scene. Hence the reasons why in Thomas's will he left teams of oxen to his children, as a wealthy man he had made provisions for all his children in the will.
One of the witnesses to the will was his brother Robert.
William his son and heir, now Lord of the Manor, had his coat of arms entered in the Heralds College in 1585 as "Barroll of Bunshill".

William carried out a controversial policy of removing all the rights of the ten copyholders on the manor. By threats, payments in money or offering other land he owned in other parishes in exchange for their copyholdings he succeeded in removing all the rights from nine copyholders. He enclosed all their lands, which measured around 100 acres into his demesne land, keeping the vacated houses and cottages to house his own farm workers or lease back to the poor unfortunate copyholders. Only the Savacer family refused to move: they were reasonably wealthy and so could afford to make a stand against William Barroll. This historic action by William can be taken as evidence as the reason why Bunshill farm is today an isolated farm, for if William had not removed the copyholders Bunshill would have developed over a period of time into a small village.
William died in 1585 without heirs; he gave all his land in Byford to his brother John, and all of Bunshill manor to his other brother Richard. John's grandson, Colonel James Barroll, became famous in the Civil War when he was the gallant defender of Canon Frome against the Scottish Army in 1646. He was killed in battle 12 months later.

When Richard died in 1600 he left Bunshill to his three daughters as co-heiresses, Joan the eldest was already married to William Traunter, whom she had married at Titley Church on December 17th 1594. They lived at Oakcroft part of Titley Manor. Bridget, who was unmarried at the time of her father's death, married William's younger brother Simon Traunter again at Titley Church on June 8th 1601. Sybil, the youngest sister, married Roger Henyns.

Late in life Richard was married for a second time to Elizabeth in 1593; he left the manor to his three daughters, with the proviso that Elizabeth could remain living in the manor house as long as she did not remarry. Richards's only son and heir William had died before his father. Elizabeth remarried William Sollers around 1605 and moved out. Bridget and Simon moved into the vacated house; once married Bridget's inheritance passed to her husband, who by purchase of some land and negotiation over other interests with the other heiresses gained sole ownership of Bunshill manor.
One of the interesting outcomes was the giving of the great tithes of Bunshill to Pryce's Almshouses in Hereford. William Pryce citizen and merchant tailor of London, who died in 1604 was a wealthy man, he was a cousin to the Traunter's of Oakcroft who were named as beneficiaries in his will. He also left money to Joan, the wife of William Traunter. From the money gained by the sale of the Saracens Head in Watling Street London, and other lands he owned the Almshouses were built on Whitecross Road, still in use today. It appears that as part of the deal with Joan for her share of Bunshill the great tithes money was reallocated to these Almshouses.

The will of William Savacre

April 28th 1592[19]

In the name of God Amen. I William Savacre of Bunsell in the parish of Mauncellacy being sick in body but of whole and perfect memory do make my last will and testament in manner and form following. Inprimis I give and bequeath my soul to almighty God my Maker and Redeemer and my body to be buried in the parish churchyard of Mauncellacy

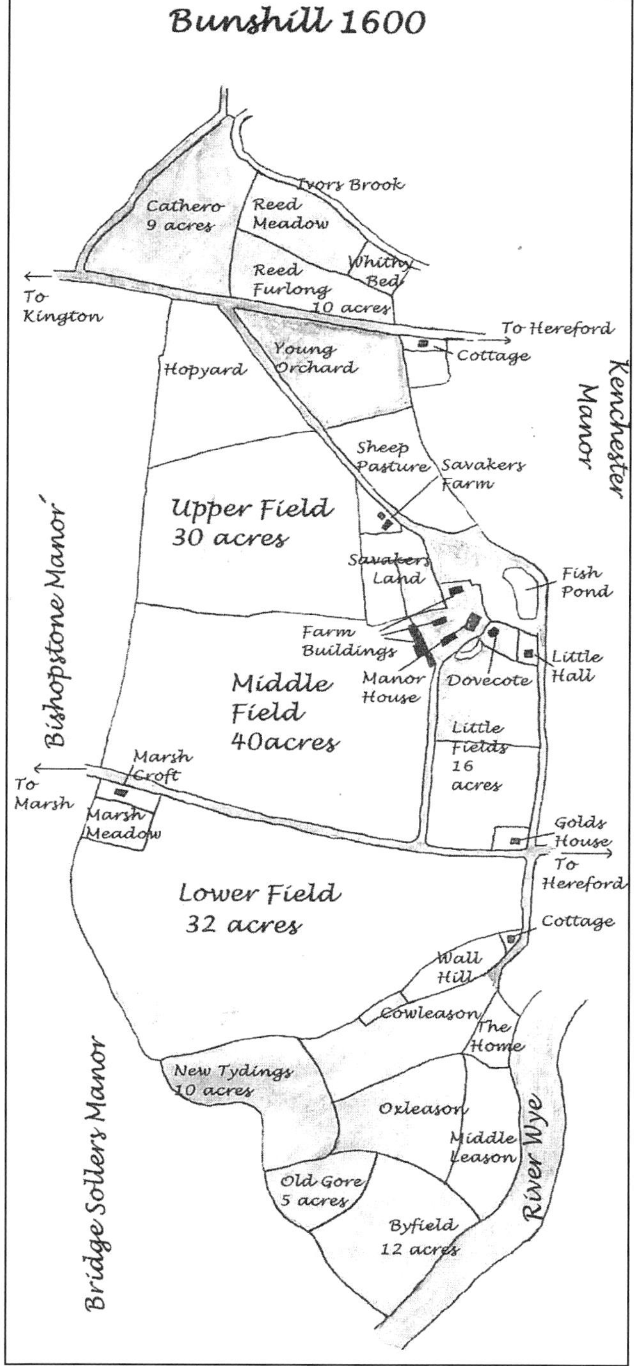

Item I give and bequeath one red ox with a white face to my daughter Anne, lying and being in the hands of Richard my son. Item I give and bequeath unto my daughter Anne one red ox named Samson being at my house at Bouncell. Item I give and bequeath a black brown bullock unto my daughter Anne, the bullock being named Browne. Item I give and bequeath another black bullock named Mighty unto my daughter Anne. Item I give and bequeath unto Anne my daughter one yearling calf being white with some black named Blossom. Item I give and bequeath unto Anne my daughter one brass pan the which I bought at Leominster. Item I give and bequeath unto Anne my daughter the best brass pot in my house with pot hooks. Item I give and bequeath unto Anne my daughter a little broche and a great one with coubardes. Item I give and bequeath unto Anne my daughter all my sheep. Item I give and bequeath one pan of a gallon to Anne my daughter. Item I give and bequeath unto my daughter Anne 24s being in the hands of Richard my son. Item I give and bequeath unto my daughter Anne one wain bound with iron being in the keeping of Richard my son. Item I give and bequeath all my beds, pewter and all household stuff to my wife and my daughter Anne. Item I give and bequeath unto my daughter Anne two best colts, the one a horse colt and the other a mare colt. Item I give the mare and the other colt to my wife. Item I give and bequeath the one half of the boards in the barn to my wife and the other to Anne my daughter. Item I give and bequeath the one half of the swine to my wife and the other to my daughter Anne. Item I give and bequeath a black cow and a sucking calf to my wife, Item I give and bequeath half the corn on the ground to my wife and the other half to my daughter Anne. Item I give half the corn in the barn to my wife and the other half to my daughter Anne. Item I give all the edge tools to my daughter Anne. Item I give and bequeath all the valies to Richard my son. Item I give and bequeath one great chest to Anne my daughter after the decease of her mother. Item I give and bequeath one trowe and one borde to Richard my son after the decease of his mother. Item I give and bequeath two ewes and two lambs to my daughter Elizabeth. Item I give the wain strakes to Richard my son. Item I do make my daughter Anne my full executrix and John Saduler alias Evanes to be overseer.

Witnesses at the making hereof, William Pylkington, Thomas Pember, Richard Pember

Proved in the Cathedral church of Hereford 2 September 1592.

William Traunter and Elizabeth Barroll tried to remove the Savacer family from Looffes Farm, Bunshill, in 1603, but they were unsuccessful; the jury at the Assizes found for Richard Savacer.
Simon Traunter the new lord of the manor tried again in 1608 to remove the Savacer family from Bunshill by taking Richard Savacer to court. The statements for Simon Traunter were taken in Hereford and Richard Savacer's statements were taken in Weobley.

Depositions taken in case brought by Simon Traunter against Richard Savacer. Taken at Hereford (For Simon Traunter)[20]

John Blether of Sarnesfield aged 50
He knows the plaintiff and the property in dispute very well
Elizabeth, now wife of William Solers in the time when she was a widow, before she married Sollers, leased to Richard Knight a messuage and lands late of Katherine Savacer, widow. Blether was a witness to that lease.
William Traunter of Oatcroft aged 37
He knows the plaintiff and the property in dispute very well
He confirms the lease by Elizabeth Solers to which he was also a witness
In 1603 there was an Assize case between Richard Savacer plaintiff and Elizabeth Barroll and William Traunter defendants. The evidence was in favour of the defendants but the jury wanted to find for Savacer so the judge stopped the case and suggested that the parties should go to arbitration. They did this and Savacer chose Sir James Scudamore to act for him while Barroll and Traunter chose John Seaborne Esq.
Roger Herring of Burghill aged 36
He knows the plaintiff and the property in dispute very well
All the copyholds in the manor of Bunshill apart from that now in dispute have been reduced into the demesne and are enjoyed by the lord of the manor in demesne and lease. After the assize case he spoke with Roger Pitt who told him that the jury should have found against Savacer
Oswald Knight of Eywood aged 26
He knows the plaintiff and the property in dispute very well
He repeats the story about the assize case
Thomas Carpenter of Kinnersley aged 64
He knows the plaintiff and the property in dispute very well
There was a settlement of the manor in 1593, by licence from Queen Elizabeth I, when Richard Barroll, on his marriage to his wife Elizabeth granted it to John Barroll of Byford and Walter Bithell of Ayley to hold in trust for Richard and Elizabeth. He was a witness to that settlement along with John Pritchard and James [document faded]
Richard Knight of Lyonshall aged 38
He knows the plaintiff and the property in dispute very well
Elizabeth Barroll leased the lands in dispute to Knight before her marriage to Sollers, and he assigned them to Simon Traunter.
The jury at the Assize were all copyholders and that is why they found for Savacer
All the above witnesses spoke in favour of Simon Traunter by saying the court case held in 1603 was flawed because all the witnesses who spoke for Richard Savacer were the copyholders that had been removed by William Barrell so they were biased.

E134/6 Jas 1/Trin 5 [1608] Depositions taken in case brought by Simon Traunter against Richard Savacer. Taken at Weobley (For Richard Savacer)

Savacer Davies of Mansel Lacy aged 60
He knows the defendant and the property in dispute very well
He was at the Assize case and he heard read out as part of the evidence a grant of the disputed lands to the defendant's grandfather, father and mother for the term of their lives
Thomas Welshe of Fusters Moor aged 40
He knows the defendant and the property in dispute very well
Copyholds in the manor of Bunshill were always made for 3 lives and the entry fine was one year's rent. He saw such grants being made by John Scudamore who was then the steward of the manor
Thomas Caldicott of Dinedor yeoman aged 76
He knows the defendant and the property in dispute very well
In the time of Henry VIII there was a copyhold in the manor of Bunshill granted to William Caldicott (Thomas's father), William's wife Elizabeth and Thomas himself as their son. Copyholds were always granted for 3 lives like that.

Five or six years after Thomas entered into his copyhold William Barroll , Lord of Bunshill, compounded for his tenement and granted him a tenement and lands in Dinedor where he now dwells. The lands at Bunshill contained 35 acres in a field, those at Dinedor only contain 10 acres in a field and the meadow and pasture in Bunshill were far better than at Dinedor. When he left he had only his own life left on the Bunshill land.

This evidence given by Thomas Caldicott I think is magical because as well as explaining how the manor court system worked, it shows how William Barroll as Lord of the Manor had forced him from his copyhold farm by an offer of a smaller holding in Dinedor. Plus the fact that Thomas had lived through many of the great events in English history. Henry VIII's dissolution of the monasteries, Mary Tudor, the whole reign of Elizabeth 1, Francis Drake's circumnavigation of the world and the defeat of the Spanish armada by the English fleet.

Further evidence given in answer to questions from Savacer

Savacer Davies of Mansel Lacy aged 60

He doesn't know if Edward VI was seised of the property or not but he remembers hearing a deed read out at the Assize. William Savacer and his wife Katherine held the lands for life and the defendant has held them since their deaths.

John Dyggas of Bishopstone yeoman [no age given]

William and Katherine Savacer held the land and after their deaths Richard held it until he was interrupted.

John Dyggas from Bishton farm also gave evidence in the Bishopstone tithes court case of the same period. Welshe and Caldicott were also interviewed again but didn't add anything extra

The results of the court case are unclear but the Savacers farm had lost its copyhold rights by 1630 according to the valuation carried out on Bunshill in the November of that year.

Simon Traunter died in 1630 aged 54 and Francis the eldest son inherited Bunshill as his heir. In his will Simon left legacies to his other children Christopher, Arthur and Eleanor; he also left 40s to the people of Mansell Lacy.

Francis registered himself as the new Lord of the Manor, and was required by law to give a valuation of the manor through the Court of Wards; the court outcome was as follows with written agreement.[21]

"The king is prepared to grant general livery of the manor inherited following a valuation of the estates by an auditor of the court of wards and liveries." The Manor of Bunshill held of the King in Chief by service of one quarter of a knight's fee

The Manor contained 10 messuages (dwelling house), 2 tofts, (land once occupied as a messuage, on which the building has decayed) *90 acres of arable land, 60 acres of meadow ground, 30 acres of pasture land, plus a 6 acre wood in Wormsley. The taxable value £4.13s.4d per annum. The court agreement on the new value dated November 26th 1630.*

On October 1st 1633 Francis married Elynor the youngest daughter of Richard Evans Gent of Hereford. A marriage settlement[22] of £600 was made between Bridget Traunter widow, and Francis her son whereby he held the manor of Bunshill with all lands and houses held in trust by Richard Evans and Thomas Traunter of Oatecroft for Elynor.

These 17th century marriage settlements were normal practice when landowning gentry married; the £600 that Elynor brought into the marriage together with Francis's Bunshill manor lands were held by trustee's for the benefit of the husband wife and children.

I have found no record of Francis's involvement in any activity throughout the civil war period; I believe he would have been a royalist as were all the other local lords of the manors. The civil war appears to have left Francis in some debt; in 1657 he started raising money through mortgages on land in Bunshill, £100 from 35 acres straddling the Roman Road, then in the next year £350 for 65 acres on land down by the river and a messuage and land in Moccas.

By Easter 1663 Francis's wife Elynor had died, and he legally regained the freehold of Bunshill from the trustees who had held the manor under the marriage settlement. The manor consisted of seven dwelling houses, nine tofts, one dovecot, six gardens and orchards, six were occupied cottages or smallholdings with gardens and orchards. The land holdings of 70 acres arable, 56 acres meadow, 104 acres pasture, 16 acres wood and 20 acres of fern and heath all belonged to the manor although some land Francis owned lay outside the manor boundaries. In the previous 30 years four dwelling houses had fallen down and had not been replaced.

Simon, the eldest son and heir of Francis, studied law and became a practicing lawyer in Hereford, he married Margaret the youngest daughter of Nicholas Taylor, Esq. of Presteign, and they lived in All Saints, Hereford. Francis died and was buried in Mansel Lacy churchyard on March 2nd 1670. Simon now inherited the title of Lord of the Manor of Bunshill, he also held the high social position of Clerk of the Peace for the County of Hereford from 1671-88.

(Figure 4) Marble tablet in Mansel Lacy church to celebrate the lives of Simon Traunter's children

As a qualified lawyer he was responsible for all the Quarters Sessions courts held in the county. He lived mostly at his town house in Hereford using Bunshill as his country residence. William his eldest son attended Wadham College Oxford and then the Middle Temple London; he also qualified as a lawyer like his father. Two of Williams brother's died in childhood and a magnificent marble tablet was commissioned by their father to celebrate their young lives, still to be seen affixed to the south wall of the chancel in Mansel Lacy church. Samuel was five years old, Simon ten weeks, they were the second and fourth sons of Simon: Simon died in March, 1675 and Samuel in April 1676. This is part of the lovely verse written on the tablet.

A child most lovely to behold
And super-wise for one of five years old

William married Mary Philpot granddaughter and heiress of Nicholas Philpot, at St Nicholas Church Hereford on April 23rd 1685 and moved into Bunshill but sadly Mary died later that year when she was only 18 years old. William inherited his wife's possessions including £400 left by her grandfather and Ploughfield Farm Preston-on-Wye which was valued at £600. Mary was buried in Turnastone Church where there are two memorials, one a large stone tomb slab on the nave wall plus a wall tablet on the opposite wall of the nave

Many people think that the wall tablet tells a romantic poetic tale from the 17th century but I'm not sure.

Mary Traunter of Bunshill, only daughter of Nicholas Philpot and Penelope his wife.
Died June 26th 1685 aged 18.

The good, the Faire, the witty and the Just
Lyes crumbled here into her pristine Dust
How can we then enough her death be moane
In whom all virtues were comprised alone
Soe sweet a humour, such a grace did shine.
Throughout her life that she was all Divine.
Propitious Heaven decred Yt she should prove
The wonder of her sex in faith and love
Then immaturely snatched her from our eyes
Least to too high a pitch our joy should rise.
The Best of Husbands here she did confess
His friends and He made up her Happyness
And they thought all ye actions of their life
Well blessed in such a daughter and a wife.
To tell you further Who and What she was
Does all Poetic numbers far surpass.

William married his second wife Ann Thomas, daughter of Edward Thomas of Michaelchurch Court; Ann was the niece of Eleanor who was married to Humphrey Digges of Bishton Bishopstone. The Traunters and Digges families would have known each other well as neighbours and their long association with the law courts in Hereford.

William Traunter gent of Bunshill died in 1691, aged 28 leaving behind his wife Ann, 24 years old, and his only child and heir Simon aged 4.

I William Traunter of Bunshill in the county of Hereford being sick in body but of perfect mind and memory thanks be to God do make this my last will and testament in manner following. First I give my soul to Almighty God hoping through the merits of Jesus Christ my Saviour to be saved and my body to be buried in Christian burial at the discretion of my executor and executrix hereafter named.
Imprimis I do appoint and order all my debts to be justly and honestly paid.
Item my will is that my executor and executrix shall have the tuition and take care of the education of my dear son Simon Traunter. And I do nominate my dear brother Simon Traunter and my beloved wife joint executor and executrix of this my last will and testament. In witness whereof I have put my hand and seal the 11th day of June 1691. *William Traunter*

The probate inventory was made on the 22nd June 1691 by Humphrey Thomas (Simon's brother in law), William Llywelyn and Henry Allen

A true and perfect inventory of the goods, cattels and chattell of William Traunter of the parish of Mansell Lacye in the county of Hereford, gent, taken and appraised the two and twentieth day of June 1691 by those names are underwritten.

Imprimis the decedents wearing apparel	*£10.00.00*
The decedents two saddle horses and furniture	*£20.00.00*
Three other horses	*£10.00.00*
Eight cows and one cow and calf	*£21.05.00*
Two heifers	*£02.10.00*
One bullock	*£01.10.00*
Seven calves	*£02.10.00*
Four oxen	*£15.00.00*
Six bullocks	*£10.00.00*
Fifty five acres of hard corn one with other	*£41.04.00*
Fifty five acres of lent grain of all sorts	*£22.00.00*
A hundred sheep	*£13.18.08*
Forty six lambs	*£03.16.08*
Five yearling cattle, three two year old cattle	*£08.10.00*
Twenty three swine of all sorts	*£06.16.00*
***Upper Garretts** goods in the upper garrets; two beds and two bedsteads, one set of curtains and valence, three rugs, one blanket, two bolsters, one side table and three bushels of wheat.*	*£03.09.00*
***Mens Chamber** In the mens chamber, three beds and bolsters with ordinary coverings, three bedsteads, one press.*	*£01.15.00*
***Middle Chamber** In the middle chamber over the great palour, one bed and bolster with the curtains, valance, and hangings of the room and other appurtenances therein.*	*£07.00.00*
***Blue Chamber** In the blue chamber, one bed and bolster with the bedstead, curtains, valance, hangings of the room and other appurtenances therein*	*£06.00.00*
***Two Parlours** In the two parlours, eighteen Turkey-work chairs, two table boards, two stands, one Chippendale table, two stands, one large looking glass, one brass and irons with a pair of tongs, fire shovel and* bellows	£19.00.00
***The Hall**; In the hall one drawing table, one other table, seven old chairs, one malt mill and one bench.*	*£01.00.00*
***Little Parlour and the room next to the kitchen;** Three tables, nine leather chairs, one couch, one stand, one looking glass, two shelves, one chimney piece, one pair of andirons, one pair of tongs and one clock.*	*£04.11.00*
***Closet;** In the closet next to the little parlour, one side table and one bench.*	*£00.00.06*
***Kitchen;** In the kitchen; brass and pewter of all sorts with fire tools and all other appurtenance there unto belonging*	*£10.08.00*
***Rawett Chamber** In the Rawett chamber, one bed and bolster with the curtains, valance, hangings of the room and other appurtenance therein.*	*£09.00.00*
One large sestern and ring	*£01.00.00*
One rich furniture for a bed	*£25.00.00*
***Maids Chamber;** In the maids chamber, two beds and bolsters, two bedsteads with the appurtenances thereunto belonging.*	*£02.10.00*
***Chamber over Kitchen;** In the chamber over kitchen, one bed and bolster with the bedstead, curtains, valance, hangings of the room and other appurtenances thereunto.*	*£06.11.00*

Linen of all sorts		*£13.09.00*
Silver plate of all sorts		*£25.16.06*
Great Cellar*; In the great cellar thirteen hogsheads of cider, whereof six of redstreak*		*£15.15.00*
Two hogshead of strong beer		*£02.00.00*
Twenty three hogshead		*£08.00.00*
Little Cellar; *In the little cellar six hogsheads, three half hogsheads, Two hogshead of harvest beer.*		*£02.12.06*
Brewhouse and Bakehouse*; In the brewhouse and Bakehouse, one furnace, Four tubs, one trin, one vat, two hogsheads, one cheesecoule and one churn.*		*£02.17.00*
Dairy House; *In the dairy house, two cheese tubs with other utensils thereunto belonging with two hundred and a half of cheese and four stone butter.*		*£03.04.00*
Kill House; *In the kill house bacon and beef.*		*£01.15.00*
Fifteen bushels of malt.		*£01.10.00*
Eight bushels of rye.		*£00.16.00*
Twenty acres of clover hay		*£10.00.00*
Implements of husbandry of all sorts.		*£08.00.00*
Old lumber not apprised		£01.00.00
	Total	£380.04.04
Due to the deceased by specialty		£200.00.00
	Total	£580.04.04

Humfrey Thomas, William Llywelyn, Henry Allen. November 2nd 1691.[23]

To help visualize the size of the old Bunshill Manor House, it could be compared with the Ley in Weobley, an inventory taken in 1676 for William Bridges of the Ley Weobley totaled £472, which lists a similar number of rooms and items.

William's probate inventory gives a good idea of the rambling old manor house with its great hall, 3 parlors, 6 bedchambers, closet, attics, and kitchen. The bed furniture in the Rawett bedroom valued at £25 and the Chippendale table are a good indicator to the wealth of the family. There were two large cellars whose contents included 13 hogsheads of cider (6 of them Redstreak), 2 hogsheads of harvest beer; there was bacon and beef hanging in the kill house, and the dairy held 250 cheeses and 4 stones of butter.

Simon commissioned another marble tablet inscribed in Latin to mark his eldest son's death, remarking on how he loved his two wives' and was well respected by all who knew him; this was fixed to the church wall opposite his brother's monument. Simon died in 1699 when he was 65 years old. Simon his grandson and heir aged 12 years old had to wait another 9 years before he inherited the estate in 1708 on his 21st birthday. Ann, William's widow married Thomas Duppa, son of Sir Thomas Duppa usher to James II, and they moved to Haywood, the Duppa family home, where little Simon Traunter grew up. Bunshill Manor was let out to the Jones family. Thomas Duppa died in 1704 aged 31, and Ann died in 1710 aged 43 years. This left young Simon with two properties, one in Bunshill and the other in Haywood; he decided to keep Haywood Estate and sell Bunshill, so in 1712 he sold the manor to James Brydges, Duke of Chandos who already owned large Herefordshire estates. The Traunters were the last owner-occupiers of Bunshill manor. The conveyance dated February 21st 1712 states that Simon Traunter of Haywood sold the manor of Bunshill and other lands to James Brydges of Westminster for £2,250, of which £773.00 was paid to Catherine Carew to pay off one mortgage and £400 to Hugh Russell to pay off another mortgage; the remaining £1076.10s was paid to Simon. The conveyance lists Bunshill as lands and two cottages.

Simon died shortly after in 1713, in his 28th year, two years are inscribed on his flat gravestone inside Mansel Lacy church, as he died in 1713 and was buried in 1714.

Brydges had financial problems and in 1731 sold his estates to the Governors of Guys Hospital although they did not obtain full possession until 1754. A report commissioned just prior to their purchase on November 11th 1729 described[24]

"Bunshill Farm containing a large old manor house in very bad condition and must be pulled down, the outbuildings also bad save a long barn, pretty tight. There were some stacks of hay and two of corn. The farm contains 237 acres of all kinds. The tenant one Weaver married the farm tenant's daughter and held it above 30 years, the rent £96 per annum, on this farm are a good number of very old elm trees. The tenant seems industrious and indicated that he would advance some more rent to have the building put in good order".

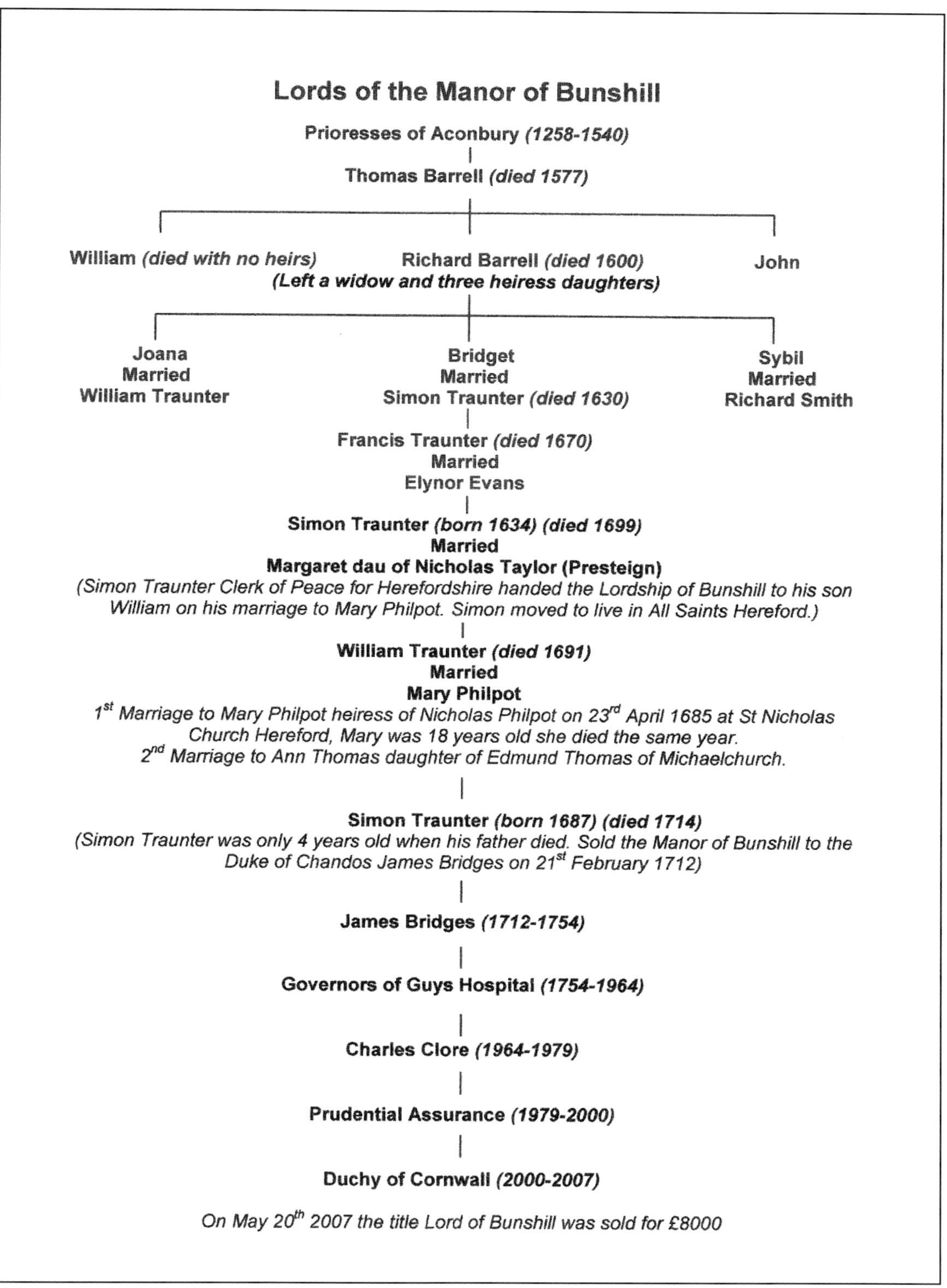

Weaver family of Bunshill

In 1715 William Weaver married Margaret Jones in Hereford Cathedral, she was the daughter of John Jones who had held the tenancy of Bunshill from the Traunter family since 1699. John died the year before his daughter's marriage and was buried in Mansel Lacy churchyard. William, on his marriage to Margaret had taken over the tenancy of Bunshill.

With the negotiations still going on with Guys hospital over the purchase of the Duke of Chandos' estate in Herefordshire, William obtained a new 21year lease on Bunshill in 1730 at £100 per year. The conditions attached to the lease are interesting,

William had to supply 2 fat hens and 2 fat capons at Christmas and he also had to keep a greyhound and a fighting cock at his own expense to support the Duke's sporting interests. To plant yearly 10 grubb stock and graft the same with good cyder fruit. To fill up dead gapps in hedges with good stock of thorn, to keep ditches clean. Not to plough up any hop land, meadow or pasture without consent, to plough all the land in usual course of husbandry. To deliver at the end of term, house and buildings in good repair, with all land and ditches clean.

The Weavers held the tenancy of Bunshill for the next 100 years over three lives. And confusingly father, son, grandson, and great-grandson all carried the name William, the first William born at Bunshill was baptized on October 1st 1716, he married Ann and their son and heir William, the third William Weaver, was born in 1745. This William Weaver married Elizabeth Powell at Mansel Lacy church on March 12th 1772, and their son, yet another William, was born in 1774. In 1779 William and Elizabeth started a new 21 year lease with Guy's Hospital for Bunshill Farm. They were among the forerunners of breeding Hereford cattle. William died on May 11th 1801 when he was 56 years old, Elizabeth died in 1821 aged 68 years. William left just over £1000.00 in his will proved on September 10th 1801; he left £200 to his wife Elizabeth. The lease of Bunshill, his plate, silver, china, household goods, furniture, implements, stock and personal estate could be used by Elizabeth during the term of her natural life providing she remained sole and unmarried, after which it passed to his eldest son William. William was left a £200 legacy, Thomas his other son was left £150 and there were legacies of £100 each to his four daughters Majorie, Mary, Elizabeth and Ann. A fine wall tablet in Mansel Lacy Church was commissioned to record his life.

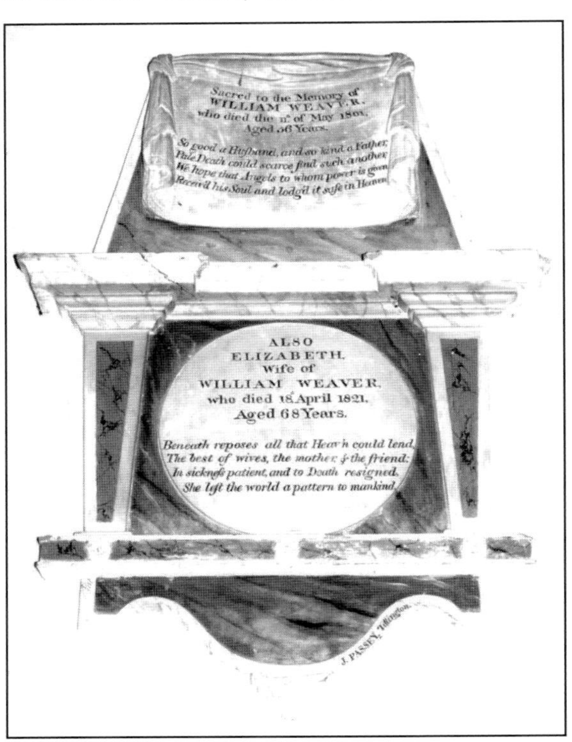

(Figure 5) Spectacular wall mounted tablet in Mansel Lacy church to celebrate the lives of William and Elizabeth Weaver who died in 1801 and 1821

An audit commissioned by Guys Hospital in 1800 to record the bad debt on its Herefordshire estates reveals that William Weaver had started a new lease in 1800, when the rent for Bunshill was increased from £140 per year to £185; he was also in arrears of £70 due to the fact that he only paid half the rent in 1797.

The entire field names were listed in this lease, some were listed in math not acres, the earlier form of measurement of field size. i.e. Marsh meadow 6 days math - the time taken by a single man to cut the meadow with a scythe.

The field names included the three old medieval common fields, Lower Field 50 acres, Upper Field 40 acres, Middle Field 30 acres, Lower and Middle Field straddled the now A438. They were later subdivided into smaller field as illustrated in the 1842 tithe map. The only other name worthy of mention is Bricking Field later called "The Long 15 Acres". Originally I thought the name referred to the brick kilns built in 1756-7 to supply bricks for the new farm house, but this lease made 24 years earlier seems to imply that brick making was going on in the field in 1730. The first major use of bricks for building in the area began in 1715 when Robert Price commissioned the building of the new mansion at Foxley in brick, so maybe some of these bricks were supplied from this field as we know that John Sneads from Bishopstone hauled bricks to the construction site at Foxley. Brick Kiln Field is where the bricks for the new farmhouse were made on the other side of the lane; the clay for making these bricks was gathered from a pit within this field still visible today the whole area must have contained good brick making clay.

Things were no better in 1754, a report[25] made by the Guys Hospital agent after they gained full possession said *"the buildings which are prodigiously large we found extremely out of repair and the greatest part must be taken down and a new house built. A part of the farm lying in Mansel Lacy was let to Thomas Morgan of Whitehouse Farm, Bishopstone as a under tenant at £8 10s a year. There is a small tenement in the same parish very near the same farm let to one Hord, we apprehend this should be laid to Bunshill farm, Weaver is willing to have it comprised in his lease, it is worth £4 to £5 a year especially as it lies handy for Bishopstone Common."*

The small farm referred to in this report as let out to Mr Hord, became part of Bunshill Farm soon after, it stood on Bishon Common north of the brook. The farmhouse was used to house the farm workers from Bunshill for the next 200 years and was pulled down in the 1970s

(Figure 6) Bunshill farmhouse taken in 2000 built in 1757-58 from bricks made on site by Samuel Bach

The Governors decided to act and over the next three years they demolished the old house and some of the farm buildings, and built new. The boards for the scaffolding were cut from "stoggle" (pollard) trees on the farm. The bills for the work carried out at Bunshill makes interesting reading, though confusing at times because the Governors of Guys Hospital decided to rebuild Stretton Court at the same time. The same master tradesmen, John Nicolas bricklayer mason, Francis Thomas carpenter and Benjamin Davies tiler carried out the work on both houses. A large number of trees on Bunshill Farm appear to have been felled and used on other estates owned by the hospital, because in July 1756 Francis Wood was paid 4s 6d[26] for making a crane for loading timber, the same Francis was paid £2 2s on the same bill for making plans and estimates for the proposed new house at Bunshill. The plans must have been accepted promptly because in the following month, Francis Powell made new gates for the brickyard and the commissioner paid 4s 6d for a pair of ironmoulds to make bricks. Samuel Bach the brickmaker arrived and by October was paid £39 4s for making the bricks in Brick Kiln Field.

On March 19th 1757 Francis Thomas was paid £10 17s 10d for taking down the old house. It appears that the new house was built partly on the site of the old house, because in a later entry in 1758 it refers to taking down the malt house and the rest of the dwelling house, so we presume William Weaver lived in the part left standing until he could move into his new house.

(Figure 7) The Granary Bunshill Farm, built by John Nicholas in March 1757 the original brick piers are easily identified. The original wood framed granary was built on top of ten brick piers; the stone infill between the piers and brick infill above were added later.

Francis Thomas the carpenter was paid £12 9s for taking down the sheepcote and rebuilding it, £3 17s for repairing the barley barn, £4 17s for repairing the wheat barn and £8 18s for building a new cow house. As well as bricklaying on the house John Nicolas built piers on which the granary was to be erected. Glazing the house cost £9 17s 8d, the bill paid for this was dated April 1758

A new cider mill was installed, the mill and runner cost £10 10s purchased from Richard Adams, and the new cider press and screw was made on site by the carpenter Francis Thomas at a cost of £4 5s 9d. All this cost the Governors £599-02-05, a pretty hefty investment for that time.

The towing path marked on the map along the river bank through Bunshill is of interest, we know from the Berrington Almshouse account book, that coal was purchased in the 1700s from barges moored at Bridge Sollers. These early barges were hauled upstream by teams of up to 12 men called bow hauliers. It was tough, hard, dangerous work that required team work. For centuries the river had been used as a route for transport, early on as a way of moving timber and rafts carrying stone floating downstream, and after the River Wye and Lugg Navigation Acts of 1662 and 1695 a more organized form of river transportation system was formed with upstream traffic as well as downstream.

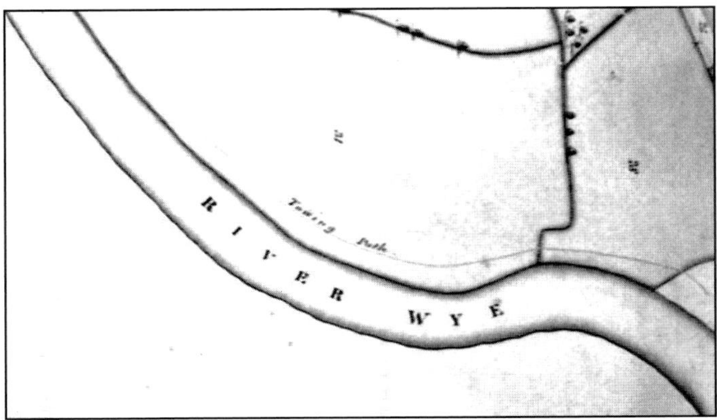

(Figure 8) 1819 map of the river meadows, Bunshill showing the horse towing path.

In 1809 a further Navigation Act on the Wye was passed which made provision for a "Horse Towing-path" evidence of which we see on the Bunshill map. 1811 was the first year that a barge hauled by horses on the Wye was recorded. River traffic increased the wharf at Canon Bridge across the river, which appears as a place from where many loads of timber and goods were sent. An entry in the ledger book of the Liverpool and Bristol Company (deposited in Hereford Library) lists a barge named James which left Canon Bridge on January 16th 1828 carrying a cargo of timber, planks and 3,000 tree nails.
On a 1906 map of Bunshill a footpath down to the ferry over to Canon Bridge is still indicated, a self operated ferry where the boat was attached to a wire suspended above the river by a slip rope so that it could be retrieved from both banks. This was used regularly up to just before the 2nd World War when a flood washed the equipment away.
In March 1819 the farm was "in pretty good tenantable repair"[27] with a good dove house and buildings although several of the fields needed draining, as recorded in a survey of Bunshill farm. The rent charge was worked out on each parcel of land making interesting reading.
Bunshill's rent was now £260 17s 6d per annum, a huge increase over the £100 paid in 1730. Elizabeth carried on farming Bunshill after her husband's death with son William, they were breeding Hereford cattle, and the programme for the Hereford Spring Show in 1804 lists William Weaver of Bunshill entering a yearling Hereford bull. After Elizabeth's death in 1821 the three-life tenancy on Bunshill finished, William was not eligible to take on the new tenancy, but he was offered and accepted a tenancy on Stretton Court, another farm owned by Guys Hospital. William went on to be a very successful Hereford cattle breeder

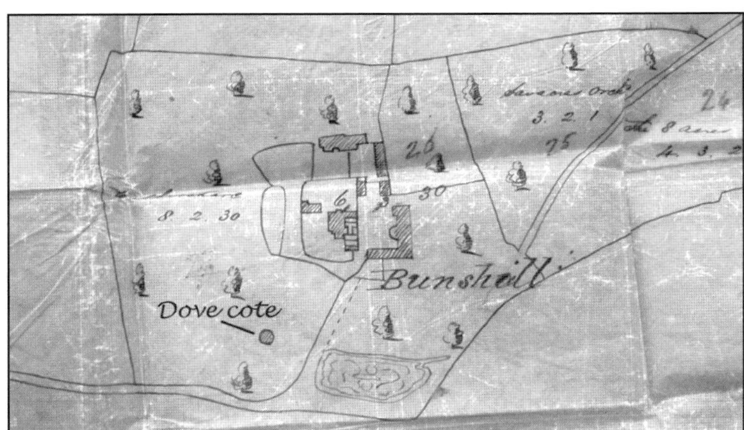

(Figure 9) Early 19th Century map shows layout of farm and position of dovecote.

The new tenant of Bunshill in 1821 was Mr Henry Edwards, a 40-year-old gentleman with his wife Margaret. Henry became a very influential man in the area and a man of some wealth. He purchased two of Bishopstone's enclosure lots on Bishon Common and built two pairs of double cottages for his workers with his own money, he financed the building of the Cottage on Bishon Lane and he also appears to have had interest in growing fruit. An extract from the Gardener's Magazine, Hereford Horticultural Show September 24th 1834 states "*Mr Edwards of Bunshill exhibited six plates of pears, he would have won all the prizes in the pear classes if he had been a subscribing member.*"
Henry died July 31st 1851 aged 75; he had been the tenant of Bunshill for 30 years, his wife Margaret carried on with the tenancy until her death in 1854.

The tithe map of 1841 was the first legally recognized document showing the layout of the farm and accurate measurements of each field.

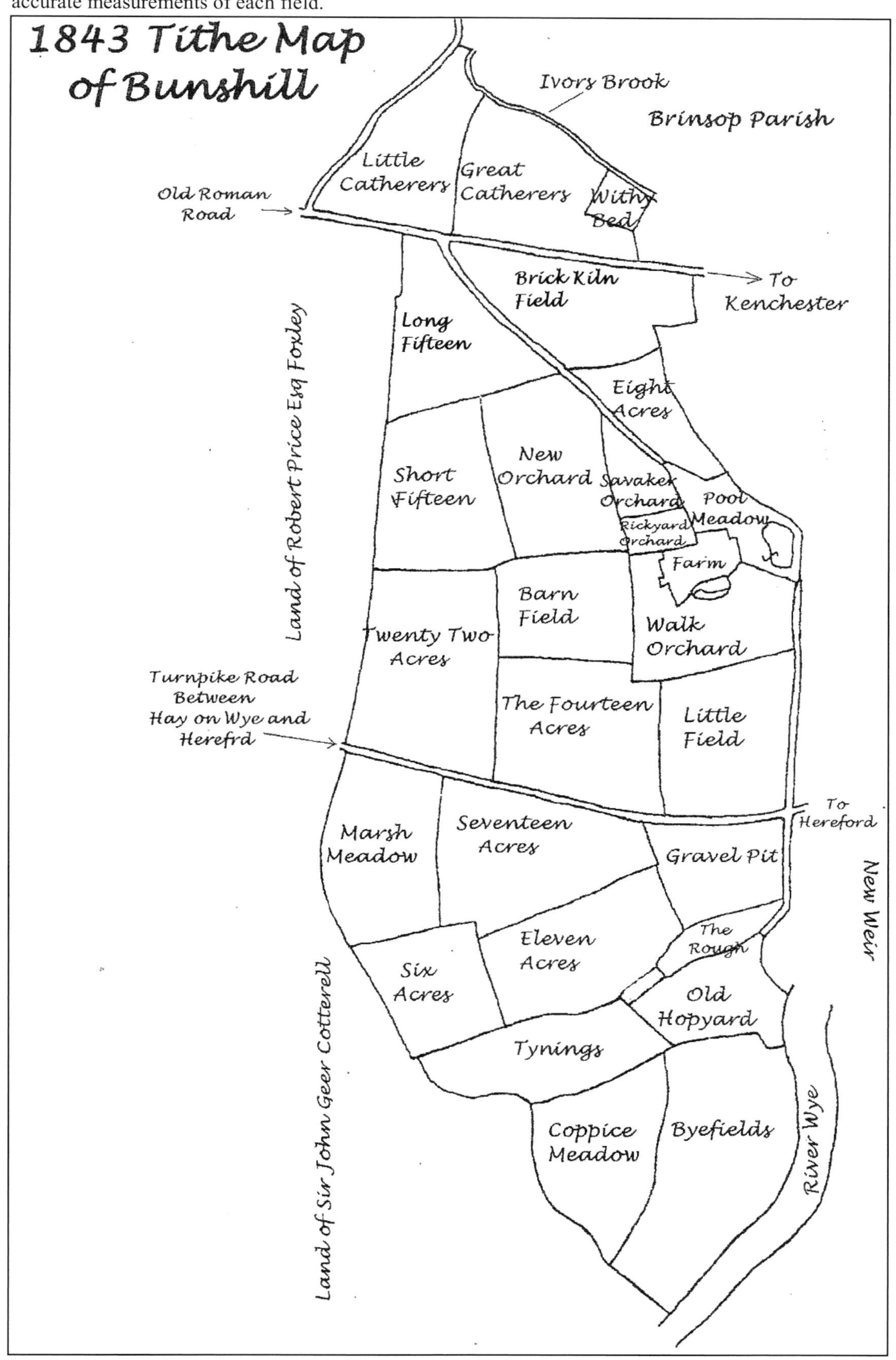

In 1855-6 the roof had to be stripped for the incoming tenant Mr Parry, a retired grocer from Hereford who rather fancied himself as a gentleman farmer and, as the report said, "spares neither money nor trouble inside and out and keeps his place quite a model of order and careful management." The 21 year lease[28] to John Burdett Parry signed on September 16th 1857 for Bunshill reads: Messuage or farmhouse, buildings, cottages, closes and pieces of land in schedule 250 acres, 3 roods, 13 perches called Bunshill Farm, Rent £375 per year. also £20 for every acre converted to tillage, £5 per year for the last four years for every acre not cultivated.

Mr Parry lost his sight after a few years and had to give up his farming hobby.

On July 27th 1859 the Elliots, father and son, Samuel and James succeeded him, they paid Parry £140 for the assignment of the lease. They had previously farmed in Credenhill. The father did well but his son James was not quite as successful; although a good farmer he had a timid disposition, he didn't like trying new things and hadn't got quite enough capital to make the best of the farm.

The 1861 census return on Bunshill lists Samuel Elliott and Margaret his wife with son and daughter John and Harriett.

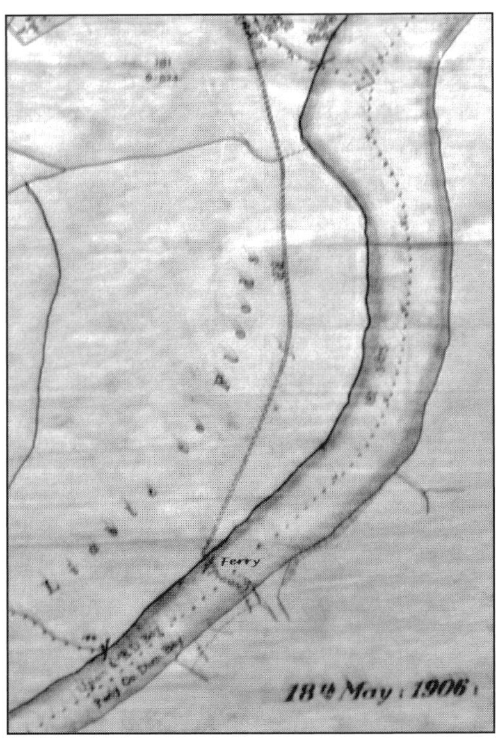

(Figure 10) Map showing the ferry at Bunshill was still operating in 1906

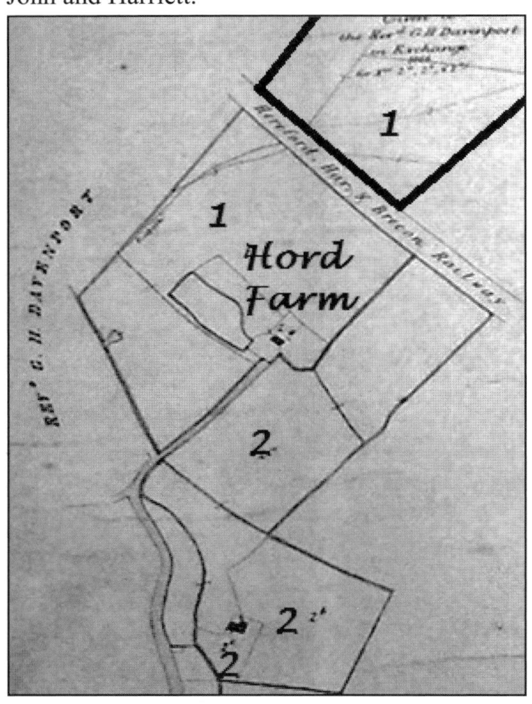

(Figure 11) The railway cut Hord Farm in half. (no 1 on the map) the land on the other side of the railway line was exchanged in 1866 with Rev Davenport for no.2 (on the map) which was described as land with a mud and lime walled thatched cottage. This cottage was demolished soon after and replaced with a new brick double dwelling.

Samuel farmed 250 acres employing 5 men and 2 boys. Listed as living in Bunshill cottage was agriculture labourer John Roberts, and family. Interestingly the census lists one house situated within the farmstead.

Ten years later in 1871 the census shows that the son John Elliott had taken over the farm with his wife Elizabeth and two young children, also living in were Mary Francis a domestic servant, Alice Solfice nurse to the two children plus groom William Crump.

John's death was reported in the Hereford Times dated April 27th 1878 "John Elliot aged 36 of Bunshill Farm died on April 14th after a short illness".

His wife Elizabeth took over the tenancy of Bunshill Farm which she held for the next 27 years.

On March 25th 1884 Bunshill was transferred to Bishopstone parish for civil reasons.

The decline in agriculture at the end of the 19th century resulted in a lack of investment by the board of Guys Hospital in their farms, by 1905 when Elizabeth Elliott surrendered her tenancy on the farm, a survey describes the farm buildings as *"a ragged lot of premises, worn out and badly arranged that will need replacing with new ones more suited to modern farming methods."* Tenants in the 20th century included Mrs Elliott, John Lewis and Thomas Smith who are covered in the next chapter.

Chapter 13
Parish Houses 1900

This chapter covers all the properties standing in the parish at the turn of the 20th century and their inhabitants thereafter. Many of the older parish houses were in need of repair in 1900 and some of these were thought not worthy of saving so they were demolished.

To establish duties on land values for the 1910 Finance Act the Inland Revenue Commissioners, produced a map and field books[1], often referred to as the modern domesday book. Information recorded in the field books included location of the property, marked on the accompanying map, a market value of the property, plus notes made at the time of inspection, listing materials from which the property was constructed and a description of all rooms and outbuildings. From these records, together with memories of the older generation, I have been able to put together a description of the properties in Bishopstone and their inhabitants.

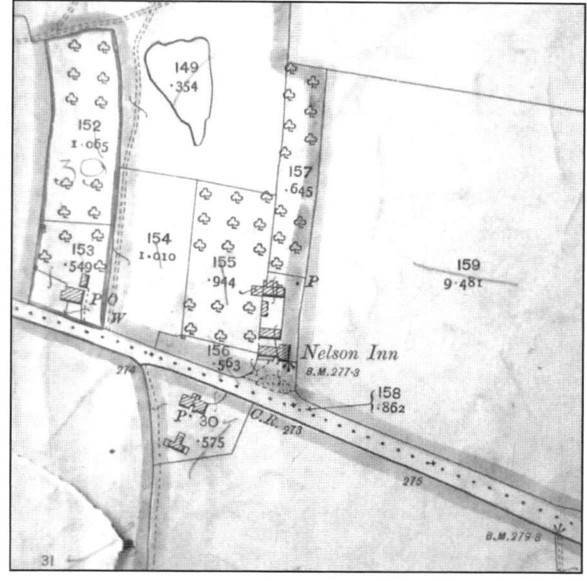

(Figure 1) Sample of 1910 valuer's map showing Bridge Ash numbered 39 and the Nelson Inn

The Nelson Inn was opened around 1809 by William Bethell who had converted part of his timber-framed cottage into an inn. It was extended and modernised in 1871 by Rev Davenport. The 1901 census records it as a farm of 31 acres and a public house, Fred Bywater was the head of the family, living with Rosanna his wife and five of his six children. The younger three children attended Kenchester School, Annie and Elsie the two eldest girls worked for their father. Rosie their 17-year daughter was an invalid and was living in an institution. Fred was a strong character as we know from his earlier run-ins with the schoolmaster of Bishopstone School; he sat on the Parish Council, and was a regular churchgoer, he contributed every year to keep the church open until he died on May 22nd 1907 at the age of 50. Rosanna his wife took over the business helped by her children. In the 1910 survey it states that the market value of the Nelson was £1575 for which Rosanna paid a rent of £60 a year to Rev G. H. Davenport, this represents a drop to 33% on the original rent of £90. The house was built of brick with a slate and tile roof, containing two sitting rooms, liquor bar, tap room, cellar, private kitchen, larder, three family bedrooms and four smaller bedrooms in poor condition. Outbuildings were listed as a three bay barn, lumber, cow house for four, brick and tile loose box and loft, stable for two, cart shed and loft, feeding shed and dairy. The 1911 census lists Rosanna as head of the family, occupation innkeeper, living with five of her adult children; Rosie the invalid daughter now aged 27 had returned to the family home. Ernest the eldest son was farming the smallholding helped by his younger brother William while the daughters Amy and Elsie were helping their mother in the pub.

(Figure 2) Nelson Inn 1965

In 1926 Mr Charlie Tompkins and his wife Hannah acquired the freehold of the inn from Rosanna Bywater. Charlie was a keen sportsman, he started up and ran a local football team from the late 1920s. Charlie made one of his own meadows behind the Nelson into a football pitch; the team recruited players from surrounding villages and played in the old Herefordshire League. The team was disbanded on the outbreak of war in 1939. The war saw an influx of American and Canadian service personnel using the pub, they would walk over from Foxley camp to use the facilities. One little bit of information on the pub during the war years came from Vera Peat a member of the Timber Corps who was billeted at Scaldback.

She remembers her uncle and aunt from Liverpool coming to visit her over a weekend in 1943. They took Vera for a drink at the Nelson, but the ladies were not allowed to drink inside the bar, it was men only, so they had to stand and drink outside, much to the annoyance of a horrified aunt.

After the war, in February 1948, Alton Court Brewery based in Ross-on-Wye purchased the Nelson from the Tompkins family; they sold the 31 acres of land attached to the Nelson Inn to Stanley Lewis of Bishopstone Court Farm. Alton Court Brewery was taken over by Stroud Brewery in 1956, which was in turn taken over by West Country Brewery in 1958.

In 1949 Flo Collins became the landlady of the Nelson, she was helped by her husband Bill, they had previously run the White Lion in Kington. In those days The Nelson had a bar and a lounge each entered by separate external doors. Bill, a Londoner, had always worked on the railway, eventually ending up as a train driver for G.W.R. In the evenings he ran the bar and Flo, who had learnt the trade as barmaid at the Black Swan on Aylestone Hill, had another set of customers in the lounge and neither were seen very often in the other's domain.

Courtesy of the Hereford Times

BILL and FLO COLLINS . The Nelson Inn

In August 1977 Bill suddenly died, Flo carried on until October 1978 when she gave up the tenancy. Bert and Ivy Griffiths became the next tenants but due to a downturn in trade West Country Brewery sold the freehold of the pub in 1982 to Roy and Jo Edwards who rebuilt the pub. They removed the ceiling in the lounge and part of the bar to create an open area, they also built a new large kitchen and the Trafalgar function room and extended the car park. The Nelson turned from a small drinking pub into a modern business catering for people to "eat out," one of the first pubs in the area to do so. There was even a church fete held there for two years.

In 1988 the Nelson was sold to Margaret and Bob Eden, when Roy and Jo Edwards moved to live in Spain.

For the next sixteen years Margaret and Bob ran the Nelson serving food and drink, a place where the locals could hold their meetings, play pool, darts and boules.

(Figure 3) Nelson Inn 2000

Bridge Ash was listed as part of the Digges estate in the 17th century, parts of the house could date back to this period. John Hancocks in 1860 used the premises as a grocers shop, forty years later it was still a grocery shop and now also the post office. William Abberley ran the shop and P O in 1900, he lived with his postmistress wife Martha and three of their adult children who were still living at home. Andrew Charles their youngest son ran his own separate business from a workshop at the rear of the premises as a coachbuilder and wheelwright[2]. Samuel the eldest was the local postman while the two daughters Eliza and Sarah worked at home as assistants in the shop. William Abberley sat on the parish council and was overseer of the poor for seven years from 1907-14. The property was valued at £400 in 1910; Rev Davenport purchased Bridge Ash for £700 on March 16th 1899 a good illustration of the decline in property prices over this period.

(Figure 4) Bridge Ash 2000

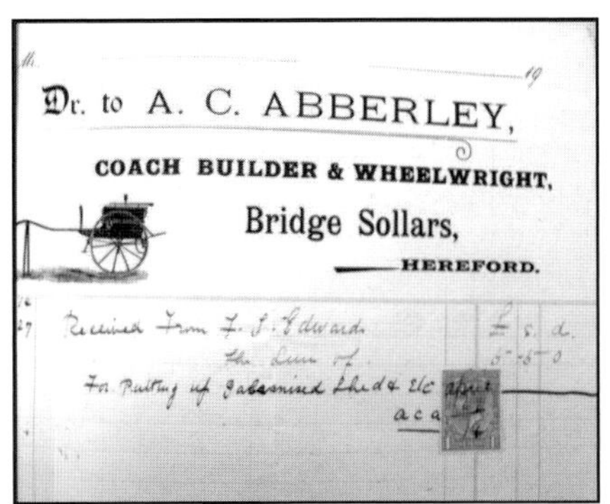

Dr. to A. C. ABBERLEY,

COACH BUILDER & WHEELWRIGHT,

Bridge Sollars,

HEREFORD.

William paid £20 a year rent. The house was built of brick and stone with a slate roof, four rooms up, and four rooms down with a passage, and the outbuildings consisted of a workshop and wheelwright shop. William also rented the 11 acre Little Park field from Sir John Cotterell for £13 a year, the field was valued at £68. In the 1911 census William lists himself as a grocer and corn merchant; he had been married to his wife Martha for 41 years. William's 38 year old son Samuel helped with his father's business and the two spinster daughters Eliza and Sarah, now in their thirties, were still assisting in the shop and post office.

Interestingly, for the two boys, Andrew Charles and Samuel, to register as voters in 1914 they were listed as lodgers occupying rooms at Bridge Ash.

"Post Office," BRIDGE SOLLARS,
HEREFORD, Mch 1914
Church Wardens
Bought of W. ABBERLEY,
Grocer and Provision Dealer.

Oil 10 " Oil 10	1 8
Oil 1/8 Oil 1/8	3 4
Oil 10	10
Oil 1/10½ Candles 1/-	2 10½
Oil 1/8	1 8
Oil 1/8	1 8
	12 0½

Paid with thanks
Mch 31/14
S Abberley

At the 1920 Foxley sale Mrs Abberley purchased the freehold of Bridge Ash; William had passed away. The family ran the post office throughout the twenties and thirties. The late Eleanor English remembers that at that time "*Bridge Ash was a sweet post office with a big front door, on the right was the P O counter.*" Samuel is listed in Kelly's Directory in 1922 as sub postmaster and his sister Sarah as a shopkeeper.

By 1926 Sarah was running the shop and post office, she was also the telephonist, in what was described as a Post Telephone call office, and for a time the only telephone in the parish. The first allocation of telephone numbers given out for the exchange were one to twenty, Bridge Ash P O was given the number Bridge Sollars 1[3], Sir John Cotterell B S 2, Garnons Land Agent B S 3, Captain Hinkes Foxley B S 4, Captain Gilbert B S 6, Fred Edwards Marsh Farm B S 8, Mr Parr New Weir B S 9, Rev Roberts Kenchester Rectory B S 10, my grandfather Albert Macklin's B S 11, Mr Hollis Downshill B S 13, Mr Edwards Sub Postmaster Mansel Lacy B S 15, Rev Hughes Kenchester Chapel B S 18. As more demand came for the telephone all the numbers jumped by twenty and 11 became 31. Telephone calls came down a single line into the post office where Sarah would answer personally; she would then dial the requested number to see if anyone was at home and if all was well Sarah could connect the two by pushing the appropriate plug into a numbered socket. It may seem antiquated in our modern digital age but in 1926 it was the cutting edge of technology with Bridge Sollars one of the first call offices in the county, although in theory it should have been called Bishopstone exchange as Bridge Ash is within the parish boundary.

(Figure 5) Percy and Hilda Alderton standing next to their 1957 Austin Westminster

The post office moved in the late 1930s to the cottages over the main road although Sarah is still listed as a shopkeeper in the 1941 Kelly's directory. During the war years Percy Alderton, proprietor of the Nelson Garage, moved down from Lena Cottage with his family to live in Bridge Ash with Martha and he eventually purchased the property. Martha Elizabeth Abberley was the last of the Abberley family to live at Bridge Ash, she died in 1956. After Percy sold the garage in the late 1950s Hilda, Percy's wife, started up a bed and breakfast business from the house. Bridge Ash was sold to Ivor Johnson in the 1980s when Percy and Hilda moved up to the bungalow Deanswood in the village.

Banbury Hall, first listed on the 1811 survey as part of Foxley estate, was built in the early part of the 18th century. In 1901 Samuel Painter, his wife Margaret, son Samuel and daughters Emily and Eva occupied the cottage. Samuel worked on the Garnons estate as a gardener, and the children attended Kenchester School. Eva the youngest daughter must have been a very bright student as on reaching 12 years old, instead of leaving school Rev Hughes offered her a teaching position. Miss Painter taught the primary class at the school for the next 40 years and many Bishopstonians from the older generations have fond memories of her. Eva's brother Samuel joined the Herefordshire Constabulary as P C 79 before the First World War; his son Geoffrey also joined the Police Force and ended up as Chief Superintendent at Hereford in the 1970s. The Painter family moved from Banbury to a thatched cottage next to the Chapel at Kenchester. Old Mr Painter was a renowned gardener and I can just remember his combined apple and pear tree that he had grown by grafting both cuttings on to a single thorn root stock; this unusual apple and pear tree had matured to a large tree in the front garden and became a talking point amongst the locals. The 1910 value of Banbury Hall was £110.00 for the cottage, garden and orchard. The 1910 survey lists Arthur Parry renting the cottage for £6 a year from Sir John Cotterell, a brick, slate and stone cottage with a tile roof, two rooms up, two rooms down, a passage, shed, pigscot and privy in fair repair. According to the 1911 census Arthur was one of Garnons estate carpenters and was married to Elizabeth. In 1915 George Holder rented Banbury from Garnons estate for £6 per year, he had married Ethel Violet Burborough in 1912, she was the daughter of the last ferryman to work the ferry at Bridge Sollers before the bridge was built; they lived in Banbury Hall for the next forty two years. George, although living in Bishopstone parish was the parish clerk for Bridge Sollers for many years and also attended their church. In their old age they eventually moved into one of the Berrington Almshouses. The next tenants of Banbury Hall were Gilbert and Dorothy Hicks, he worked on the estate. In the August of 1991 when Gilbert Hicks died he had lived in Banbury Hall with his wife for 36 years: only two families had occupied the cottage in 77 years.

(Figure 6) Miss Painter 1921

(Figure 7) Banbury Hall 2000

(Figure 8) Gilbert and Dolly Hicks

The Village News 1992 reported, "*Mrs Hicks will be moving to Hereford after spending all her life in the Bishopstone area. She was born on Bishopstone Hill, christened at Bishopstone Church in 1911, her father William Saunders was a gamekeeper on Ganons Estate. Dolly attended Byford school she remembers the community spirit was very strong in her early days, there were frequent concerts and dances held at the school, and she, with friends, walked to nearby villages for whist drives, most of the villagers were agriculture workers who rarely had a day off work. With amusement she recalls how, on their wedding day, her husband was still expected to look after the dairy cattle. He did in fact, do the morning milking but was let off the evening milking by a kindly Mr Turner.*"

Downshill House

William Turner of Weobley built Downshill House in 1812 on a parcel of ground called Downset Close, hence the name. Downshill House was occupied in 1901 by John Kerss, land agent for Sir John Cotterell, he lived there with his wife Ada and their daughters Isobel and May. Also in the house lived two servants Alice Merrick a housemaid and Thomas Handley a 17-year old groom. John Kerss was Scottish, he was an agent to Sir Henry in 1890 replacing George Nice. He was also previously employed as a clerk of works for Earl Somers at Eastnor Castle. John immediately became involved with parish affairs and held the position of overseer and wayward guardian from 1890-93, he became Bishopstone's first rural district councillor in 1894 and was churchwarden from 1896-1902.

(Figure 9) Downshill House 1908

He resigned his position in 1907 and another Scot, James Ramage, became the next land agent living in Downshill House. In 1910 the property was valued at £882, rent free, built of brick with a slate roof, comprising of sitting room, drawing room, office, morning room, two servant rooms, five bedrooms, box room, attic room, back stairs, entrance hall, kitchen, laundry, pantry and cellar. Outside were a workhouse, granary, stable with two loose boxes, cow house for two, and pigscot, standing in 8 acres of orchards and gardens.

The 1911 census lists James Lindsay Ramage land agent, married to Agnes, living with their 20-year-old daughter Helen plus one domestic servant, Annie James.

After James Ramage left Downshill, the next land agent Peter Murray Thomson occupied the house from 1920 until 1932, followed by John Hollis and his wife Polly. They lived in Downshill throughout the Second World War during which time Major John played an important part as Company Commander over several local platoons of the Home Guard. John Phillips, Victor Hoare, and John Duberley were all land agents who occupied the house at different times between 1951 and 1975. Sun Valley rented Downshill for a period as a home for their American managing director, and from the late 1900s Sir John and Lady Cotterell occupied the house.

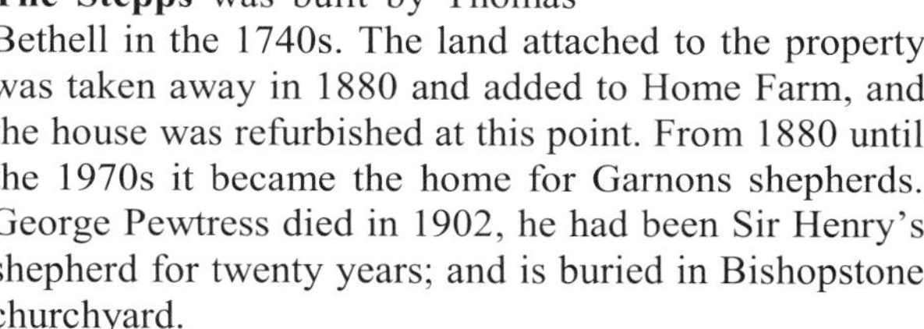

(Figure 10) John Hollis

(Figure 11) Stepps 2000

The Stepps was built by Thomas Bethell in the 1740s. The land attached to the property was taken away in 1880 and added to Home Farm, and the house was refurbished at this point. From 1880 until the 1970s it became the home for Garnons shepherds. George Pewtress died in 1902, he had been Sir Henry's shepherd for twenty years; and is buried in Bishopstone churchyard.

James Humphries the new shepherd, aged 49, his wife Margaret and their five children became the next occupiers. No separate value was given for the property in 1910 as it was added into the Home farm valuation, but it was described as "*A brick timber stone house with a slate roof, parlour, kitchen, pantry, back dairy, three large bedrooms, three small bedrooms, cellar, barn and implement shed*".

The 1911 census lists William James shepherd, living with his wife Annie, son Reginald and daughter Elizabeth, plus a lodger John Hall, a herdsman. Tragically both the boys living in the house died in or from the effects of the Great War. Between 1920 and the Second-World-War; Edward and Mary Lewis farmed The Stepps as a smallholding, while their son also lived in the parish in a cottage on Bishon Common. After the war Robert (Bob) and Iris Jones moved into The Stepps, Bob was the shepherd on Garnons estate for many years. The Stepps was sold by Garnons estate to Mr and Mrs Evan-Bevans in the early 1980s, they in turn sold the house to Mrs A Lawrence the widow of a former vicar in1992.

(Figure 12) Shepherd Bob Jones outside the Stepps in the 1950s with son David and daughter Muriel, and hand shearing the sheep on Garnons estate.

(Figure 13) Swiss Cottage 2010

Swiss Cottage is so named because in the 1880s Sir Henry Cotterell renovated the original Well Cottage with a new high-pitched roof and timber decorations to make it appear like a Swiss chalet. A new large timber panelled room was added to accommodate shooting parties, a far cry from when the original cottage stood on open common land; it was now completely enclosed by woodland. The 1910 value of the cottage was £110, rent-free, a stone cottage with a tile roof, two rooms up two rooms down and a privy, in fair repair.

In 1901 Richard Higgs and his wife Anna occupied the cottage with Richard their son, who worked as a cowman at Home Farm in Byford, and Nellie his unmarried sister who was still living at home. Richard and Nellie had attended Bishopstone School when younger but they were always absent, wood picking, stone picking or cider making. Members of the Higgs family lived in Swiss Cottage up until the late 1950s. Elizabeth the daughter-in-law of Richard and Anna, who died in 1960, was the last person to live there. I can remember her from my childhood days as being a rather scary person who lived in the house in the wood.

(Figure 14) Overgrown Site of Lucas Cottages in 2010

Lucas Cottages, a double dwelling on Bishopstone Hill next to the Almshouse were built in 1818, were owned by the two Lucas brothers who had inherited a cottage each from their father. On the turn of the 20th century this pair of privately owned freehold cottages was one of only five privately owned properties left in the parish, all the other properties were owned by either the Garnons or Foxley estates. In 1901 William Parker rented one of the cottages; he was head of the family and his occupation is listed as a rabbit catcher working from home. He lived with his wife Emma and their four daughters; the two eldest daughters both worked in Garnons House, Ellen as a housemaid and Emily as a general servant. The family had lived in Bishopstone since 1895.

By 1911 the Parkers had moved on and this half of the cottage was now empty.

Next door lived William Davies a general labourer who was born in Bishopstone, and his wife Elizabeth who was a charwoman, they lived with their daughter and two sons. The 1910 value for the pair of cottages was £303 including half an acre garden. Built of brick and stone with a slate and tile roof, each cottage contained two bedrooms, kitchen, back kitchen, shed, pigscot and privy and was in fair repair. Garnons Estate purchased the cottages just before the First World War, they were demolished soon afterwards.

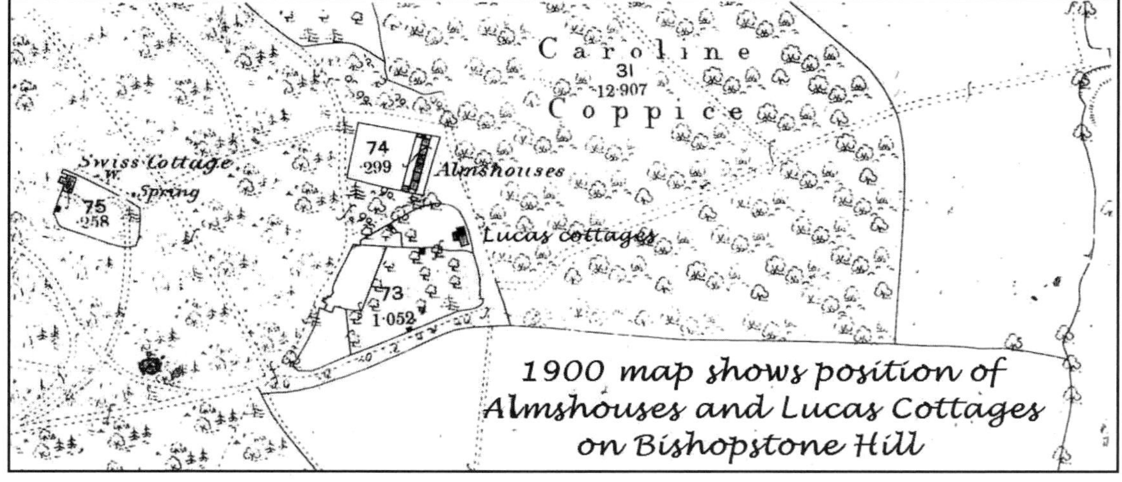

Berrington Almshouses on Bishopstone hill were of a terrace design, built of brick with a common stone tile roof divided into six individual Almshouses each having two rooms, one in the front and one at the back.

At either end of the main almshouse stood two separate buildings, one a communal wash room, the other the coal store. Each almshouse had a back garden, and the front doors opened on to a common yard. Their condition was described as poor by 1910, the building work on the new almshouses had already started, but the 1911 census shows the old building on the hill still in use.

Number one was occupied by Ann Vaughan, who was a 57-year-old widow. Ann had lived all her married life in Bishopstone, she had been married to John Vaughan who was twenty five years her senior; they had three children, two girls and a boy who they brought up in the parish. For many years they lived in a small cottage situated between Lucas Cottages and the almshouses but after John died in 1897 it was pulled down. Both Ann's daughters had died before their 25th birthday, Mary in 1894 and Rose in 1900, also her granddaughter died in 1898. She applied to the trust and was admitted and given living quarters. Ann died in 1915 aged 74. All five Vaughan girls are buried in one common grave in Bishopstone churchyard. This was not an uncommon tale in working class families, normally Ann would have expected her daughters to look after her in old age, but with her two daughters dead she had to turn to the charity or it would have meant entering the workhouse at Weobley.

Number two, in 1901 was occupied by John Hastings, a 68-year-old widower; he had lived in the village all his adult life and was postmaster from 1884 until 1899, living at Bishon Post Office. The 1911 census lists John Apperley aged 69, formerly living in the Clovers Bishopstone, as occupying number two.

Number Three had been the home of Jane Waithe for the last 35 years**,** now aged 62 in 1911. Born in Bishopstone and possibly retarded, she was accepted into the Hospital for her own safekeeping after her mother had died. She occasionally worked "labouring outdoors for the farmhouses" as stated in the 1881 census.

Number four was occupied by William Waithe in 1901, he was Jane's brother they were both born within 100 yards of the almshouse in Lucas Cottages. William's wife Emma, died in 1900 at Weobley Workhouse; there is no record of why she had entered the workhouse, he died in September 1903.

This Almshouse was listed as unoccupied in 1911 in readiness for the move down to the new almshouses, which could only accommodate four persons.

Number five in 1901was occupied by Elizabeth Probert, a 72 year old widow who came to the parish in the late 1870s with her daughter. By 1881 she was a widow and in 1891 she was living with Richard Collins as a housekeeper.

This almshouse was also listed as unoccupied in 1911.

Number six was the home of Richard Collins in 1900; a widower aged 77 years, he had lived all his life in Bishopstone working as a farm labourer for most of the time living in Burcott Row and working for different tenants of Bishon Farm. He was the elder brother of John Collins the parish clerk and sexton who lived at Cambria Cottage. He and his wife Eliza had one daughter, Mary, who died in 1872. After Mary's death Richard and Eliza adopted a child called Marian Payne from Bath who was under a year old. How this came about is a mystery but under the Public Health Bill 1872 a section was passed called Protection of Infant Life & Legislation, this was introduced to stop baby farms, which had become a lucrative business selling babies. In the 1881 census Marian then aged nine was called a "receiving child". Marian died from T B in 1899 as previously recorded. The death of Marian seemed to have had some effect on Richard's mental state and in 1912 he was admitted into Burghill Asylum where he died in 1914. On Marian's headstone the inscription reads *"the adopted daughter of Richard Collins",* unusual because adoption held no legal status until 1926.

The almshouses on the Hill were demolished around 1913 after the completion of the new almshouses in the village.

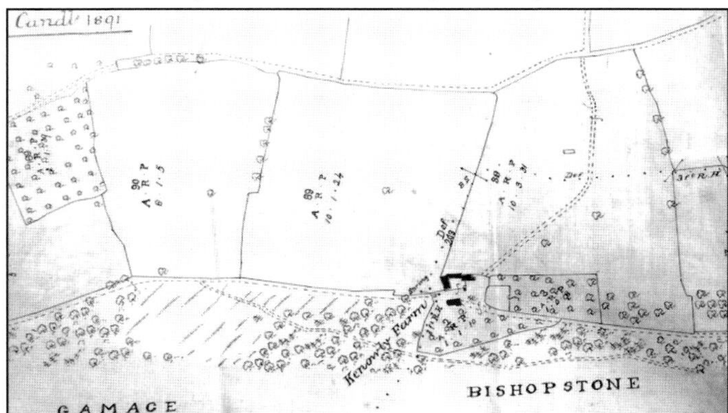

(Figure 15) Estate letting map for Kenowly Farm in 1891 features House, Farm buildings and land.

Kenowly Farm: A farm has stood on the site since records began, blessed with a natural spring. Most parts of the buildings dated back to the 17th century, ownership passed from Foxley to Garnons in the 1871 exchange of lands. After the exchange Kenowly was let out as a small farm containing 40 acres. Just before the turn of the 20th century Kenowly was integrated into the Home Farm lands and the house was used to provide a home for the farm workers.

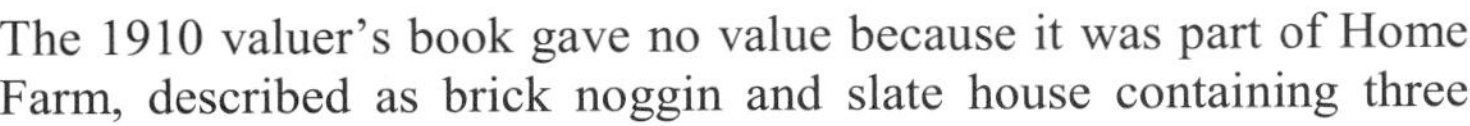

The 1910 valuer's book gave no value because it was part of Home Farm, described as brick noggin and slate house containing three bedrooms two box rooms four living rooms, in fair repair. Outbuildings: brick and tile cider mill, pigscot and granary, timber and tile two bay open shed, disused workhouse, stone and tile stable, cowshed, loft room.

(Figure 16) Sarah Jones

In 1901 William Price a farm labourer lived at Kenowly with his wife Mary and daughter Elizabeth. The 1911 census records the farm's occupiers as Anne Lawrence, a widow, and her son George who was a farm labourer working on Home Farm.

(Figure 17) Teddy Jones who died at the farm in 1918

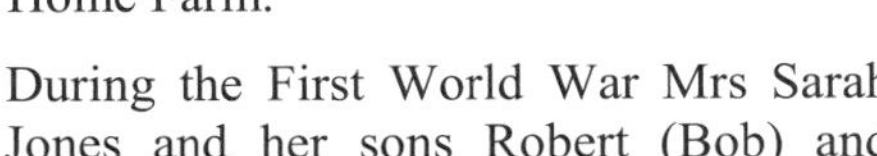

During the First World War Mrs Sarah Jones and her sons Robert (Bob) and Teddy moved from Burcott Row in the village up to Kenowly, Bob had secured a job as shepherd for Garnons estate. Teddy died in 1918 but Bob and his mother lived on at Kenowly until 1933.

The Wadleys moved in after the Jones family and stayed until after the Second World War.

The last family to occupy the farm were the Heaths, Harry and Kathleen and their two daughters, who left in around 1957, soon after that the old timber framed farmhouse was demolished.

(Figure 18) Ruins of Kenowly Farm 2010

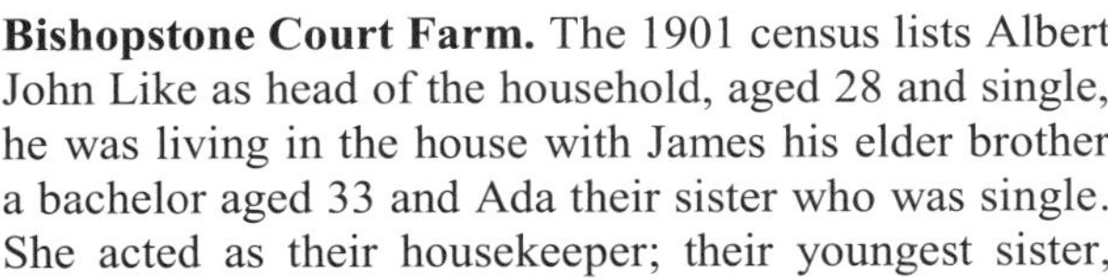

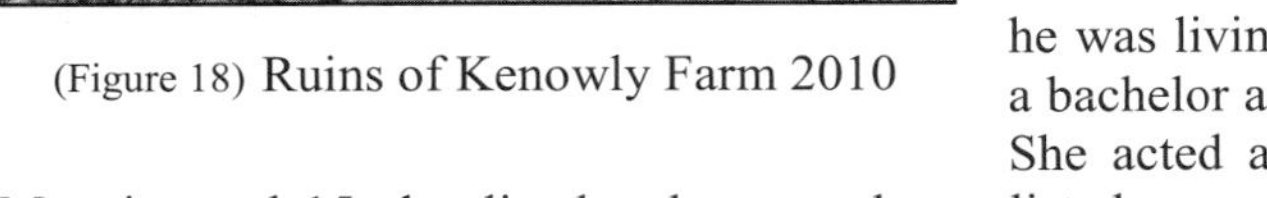

Bishopstone Court Farm. The 1901 census lists Albert John Like as head of the household, aged 28 and single, he was living in the house with James his elder brother a bachelor aged 33 and Ada their sister who was single. She acted as their housekeeper; their youngest sister, Maggie aged 15 also lived at home and was listed as an apprentice in a music book warehouse. A different state of affairs from ten years earlier, when the 1891 census records James Like senior and Mary his wife, living with their seven children, two boys and five girls; then the house was buzzing with two servants and all those children. Mary died in 1892 when her youngest child Maggie was only 7 years old. James senior died in 1900 and as his eldest son James never took on the tenancy of the farm, Albert John his younger son became the next tenant. This seems a bit odd but maybe James did not want to take a risk at farming or was in some way incapable. Farming was going through a tough time during this period so they did not employ any live-in servants and the house was run on just the basic needs. James did not get involved in any parish activity but Albert John, who liked to be called John, took over where his father had left off, he attended his first parish council meeting with his father in 1896. After his father's death John was overseer to the poor from 1901-2 and churchwarden from 1903-11. He was the largest farmer in the parish, employing four full time farm labourers and extra men and women at harvest. John married Frances Ann Westlake from Warwick in October 1907, by 1911 John and Francis were living alone in the Court employing one house servant Gertrude Ellenor. The 1911 census lists 12 rooms in the house and that John was only employing two workers. One of these workers, John Clark lived in the outbuildings on the farm.

(Figure 19) Early photo of entrance gates.

The 1911 census form was the first to be filled in by John in person and signed by his own hand, so we presume the information is correct. John was a founder member of the Farmers Union in Herefordshire. With the war looming tough times lay ahead, the farm size was reduced to 206 acres throughout the First World War years due to the government's compulsory acquisition system. Because of this his rent was reduced to £258.00 per year.

In 1910 Court Farm contained 311 acres of land and was valued at £9,192. A J Like paid a rent of £392 a year to Rev Davenport, which included three cottages. Out of this rent Rev Davenport paid £50 13s 3d tithes, £12 4s 5d land tax, £19 12s rates, £2 7s 10d insurance, 10s charity payments to the "Penner Acre Charity" and a payment to the 1703 Poor of Bishopstone charity of £2 2s leaving a net total of £304 a year. To find the value of the farm for the 1910 Finance Act, this figure was multiplied by 25, then by adding on the tithes' value of £1266 plus charity £66 and the value of footpaths £100 giving the total £9,192: it was from this formula that all the values were worked out.

The entry in the 1910 field book describes the farmhouse as being built of stone walls with a slate roof containing sitting and drawing rooms, kitchen, three bedrooms and servants room, two box rooms on the first floor, four disused rooms on the second floor, no attic, very defective sanitary arrangement, in fair repair. Detached a timber frame brick and noggin building with a tile roof containing back kitchen, dairy, washroom and servant's room. Stone and tile six bay open front shed, stone and tile seven bay open front shed, two-stall houses, seven bay open feed shed and foal, stone and tile workman's room and six pigscots, stone and tile four loose boxes, cider cellar and granary. Stone and tile three bay wainhouse, three straw bays, four bay implement shed, loosebox, still shelter for three draft horses and loft. New six bay French barn. Stone and tile cowshed, chaff house, workhouse, cutting loft, cow house for twenty-six cattle, two bull boxes.

The farmhouse started to deteriorate after the 1914-18 war; the stone tile roof had partly fallen in and was leaking. John Like of Bishopstone Court died suddenly in October 1927, he was 56 years old. John was a popular farmer and at the time of his death he was serving on the Weobley Rural District Council, Weobley Board of Guardians, trustee of Berrington charity, executive of the National Farmers Union, chairman of the Parish Council and had been a churchwarden for the last twenty years. He left a widow Frances, they had no children. Mrs English remembers him as a kind, stocky man who cared about his workmen. At the funeral service in Bishopstone Church the choir led the singing and Miss Phyllis Jones was the organist. The list of neighbours and friends who gave wreaths includes most of the families living in Bishopstone: Wall (Stonehouse), Cassell (Post Office), Amos (Pleck), Macklin (The Knoll), Kitching (Lodge), Stinton (Scalback), Dunn (Burcott), Jones (Clovers), Preece (Lena Cottage), Powell (Burcott), Pugh (Scaldback), Morgan (Clovers), Cartwright (Clovers), Kate Apperley (Almshouse). Other wreaths came from Tom Watkins, wife and boys, (Bishon Farm); Mr and Mrs T Smith (Bunshill Farm), Employees, Rawlings (Cambria Cottage), Daws (Burcott), Morris (Church Cottage), Lloyd (Church Cottage), Rounds (lodger at 3 the Clovers), Mr and Mrs Hopkins (servants who lived in).

(Figure 20) Bishopstone Court 1932 unoccupied.

Mrs Like moved to a Bungalow in Kenchester and was always a willing helper at Rev Roberts' fetes.

Captain Hinckes rented the farm from the Foxley Trustees and incorporated the land with his Mansel Lacy farms. The house was now in a very poor condition and left empty, the roof leaked and plaster fell from the walls. During this period both the farmhouses of Bishopstone Court and Bishon Farm stood unoccupied.

In April 1934 Captain Hinckes wrote to Alfred Watkins, the well-known local historian, asking him to visit Bishopstone Court as they had just discovered a large original Elizabethan fireplace hidden behind a smaller one. Alfred Watkins met Captain Hinckes on site on April 13th 1934 and what follows are extracts from the report Watkins wrote on April 23rd 1934[4].

(Figure 21) Alfred Watkins' photo of the Elizabethan fireplace taken in 1934

Invited to Bishopstone court to meet Captain Hinckes who is having alterations made to the house having let it to a farmer called Lewis. In the large room they have found a fireplace about 7 foot across, a curved top, stonework in good repair, surround perfect and two very substantial hooks for utensils. The house had undergone a dramatic reconstruction in the beginning of the 18th century when apparently the top two floors have been enclosed in stone. I think from examination of the structure and the way beams and timber has been built in, I conclude the original house had stonewalls to the first floor and timberwork above. The roof trusses appear original, as are the very large timber beams supporting the 1st floor. The house in places seems to be built on piles for a number of holes were found in the repair of the staircase, the timbers all rotted, but you can put your arm down the holes, where only a few pieces of timber can be found, of course they may have belonged to a still earlier building. The ordinary slate roof was put on by Rev. Davenport forty years earlier, the doors on the second floor are plain ledger doors the first floor doors are 1860, the main alterations dates from the mid 1860s. The windows are also 1860, all around the house there is a plain chamfered base course about 2 foot off the ground, this is early Elizabethan as is the fireplace which dates to the time the Berringtons built the house in the 16th century. The joint to the top floors are not original, giving to the theory that the house had been severely burned by fire; otherwise it is difficult to visualize the reason for some of the alterations. The house stands on a rectangle island, the island has a dry stone retaining wall, vehicle access is over the original stone bridge. The original 16th-century gateway way was taken down in the 1890s for safety reasons, a secondary access is via a more modern two arched brick bridge with a stone central pier situated on the west. The moat is approximately 30-35 foot wide and 10 foot deep; the water is controlled by a modern sluice gate. This ties up with the theory of damage sustained in the Civil War, and repairs carried out by Baron Price and the later rebuilding programme of Rev Davenport in the 1860's.

(Figure 22) William and Matilda Lewis tenants of Bishopstone Court 1934-43

Part of the 1934 restoration programme was to install a new water supply; the water came from the spring on the hill filling a holding tank, the water was then gravity fed through lead pipes into water tanks in the roofs, giving an endless supply of water to both Church Cottages and the Court.

In 1934 William Lewis who was farming the Batch at Weobley moved into the Court with his wife Matilda and their five children, Stanley, Florence, Betty, Elise and Edith. Stanley had lost a leg in a farming accident as a boy, he used a wooden leg and the local community knew him as Peg Leg Lewis. William began his parish duties by becoming churchwarden in 1935; the parish council meetings started again in 1937 and he was elected chairman. According to the minutes no parish council meetings had been held for seven years. He decided to combine the parish meeting with the vestry meeting, holding both on the same evening and electing his daughter Betty as clerk. William served as chairman of the parish council for six years, and churchwarden for eight years till his death in 1943 at the age of 84. Stanley secured the tenancy of the Court after William's death; he was forty years old and now married to Joyce, with a son David and daughter Beth. Ruth their other daughter was born in 1945. In 1948 Stanley purchased the 31 acres formerly attached to the Nelson Inn that included the pond into which Charlie Kitching had put the excess fish from Captain Gilbert's ornamental pond. According to local gossip, shortly after he purchased the land Stanley contacted a Birmingham ornamental fish dealer who took away most of the goldfish. The price paid by the dealer for the fish covered the purchase cost of the land and from then on Stanley always kept tanks of goldfish at the Court, which could be purchased by the public. Stanley died from cancer in 1954 at the young age of 51.

(Figure 23) Stanley Lewis and family tenant Bishopstone Court 1943-54

The funeral of Stanley William Baker Lewis was held on May 27th 1954 at Bishopstone Church, he was a prominent seed grower, and also a pioneer in grass seed growing having connections with the Aberystwyth Welsh plant experimental station, demonstrations were frequently given at Bishopstone Court. Most of Bishopstone parishioners attended the funeral; the coffin bearers were his six workmen Mr. G. Reynolds, Mr C Kitching, Mr. D. Burton, Mr B Gullick, Mr J Carless, and Mr. C. Davies. His son David was only 15 years old so he could not take over the lease of the farm. Stanley's four spinster sisters were affectionately known by the older members of the community as the Lewis girls. Two of them, Betty and Edith, played a big part in parish activity from 1935 until the 1970s. Edith was the parish clerk and Betty church secretary, while Edith played the organ in the church; she was also the Sunday School teacher and the driver of their Morris 1000 car. Even after they left the parish in 1955 to live at Kemeys at Swainshill they played a major role in the running of parish affairs, helping to organise fetes and the Best Kept Village competition. Between them they held a number of prominent positions throughout the years in various farming organizations and the Conservative party, and their efforts were recognized by a personal thank you and visit by Prince Michael of Kent. They spent their last few years together in the Weir Nursing Home. The members of the Lewis family are all buried in their own plot in Bishopstone churchyard.

(Figure 24) Left to right Elise and Edith meet Prince Michael of Kent

Mr Bob Carrington took on the tenancy of Court Farm after the death of Stanley Lewis; he worked the land from August 1955 and moved into the farm on February 2nd 1956. Bob came from Hill Top Farm Wormsley, another farm on the Foxley Estate; he walked his livestock to Court Farm including his Wye herd of pedigree Herefords that he had started in 1949. Bob employed five men and a boy. Unlike Bishon and Bunshill farms Bob never used any working horses on Court Farm or made any cider. His father was a gamekeeper on Foxley Estate and an expert on partridge. Bob Carrington had experienced the two extremes of farming practice, from farm labourer to the owner of two farms. Born in 1915 he started work at the age of 14 on a farm near Eardisley where he lived in and was paid 6s a week. He had to attend the hiring fairs where the workers were not treated any better than animals and at one of these he was hired to work on a farm in Moccas for 7s a week. In 1940 when working at Green Farm Norton Canon as a waggoner, his employer John Hughes was killed in an accident by his horses when they bolted; Bob who was working in the same field witnessed this. Afterwards Bob ran the farm for the widow of John Hughes, hence excluding him from war service. He managed to save up and buy a tractor; this started him off as he rented the tractor out all through the war years, which as Bob said earned him *"a few quid."*

(Figure 25) Bob and Hazel Carrington

(Figure 26) Bishopstone Court 1960s

In 1960 Court Farm won the Best Farm over 300 acres in the Hereford Corn Exchange competition, and Fisons Fertiliser Best Farm. Bob had just started his breeding of polled Herefords, and with two others farmers had bought the polled bull "Harnhill 1 Tim" for 2000gns at the Herd Book Society April sale. He called the new herd B.C. and quickly built up a worldwide reputation for the quality of his Hereford cattle and selling bulls around the world.

(Figure 27) Prize bull B C 1 Nicola

(Figure 28) Stock Herefords 1965

His most expensive bull went to South Africa for 5000 gns and many others were sold for over 3000 gns. He became an expert on the breed and for many years travelled the world judging. Bob talks about his workmen: *"In Church Cottages Ben Lloyd lived one side and Ben Stevens the other, they had eleven children between them but there was never any trouble. I lost three good men to the Henry Wiggins factory in Hereford in the 60s; I don't blame them, as the money was so much better than farm workers' wages."* He carries on *" Ben Stevens died in the field collecting hedge trimmings with a pitch fork, he asked me in the morning if he could finish early to go to the pictures, when he didn't return home at tea time his wife sent out the two boys who found him dead on the field edge. I was in the doctor's surgery in Hereford when I received a phone call to return home, I could not believe he was dead."* Bob rented 35 acres from Garnons Estate, the old Kenowly Farm, he also purchased a farm in Carmarthenshire in 1963. Bob and Hazel held a dispersal sale on 9th November 1981 where they sold a large proportion of their pedigree Hereford cattle herd; from the proceeds they purchased the freehold of Bishopstone Court Farm from Mrs Davenport of Foxley. The Foxley estate had owned the farm for 270 years.

(Figure 29) In 1990 David and Ginny Carrington with their children Russell and Nicola occupied Bishopstone Court.

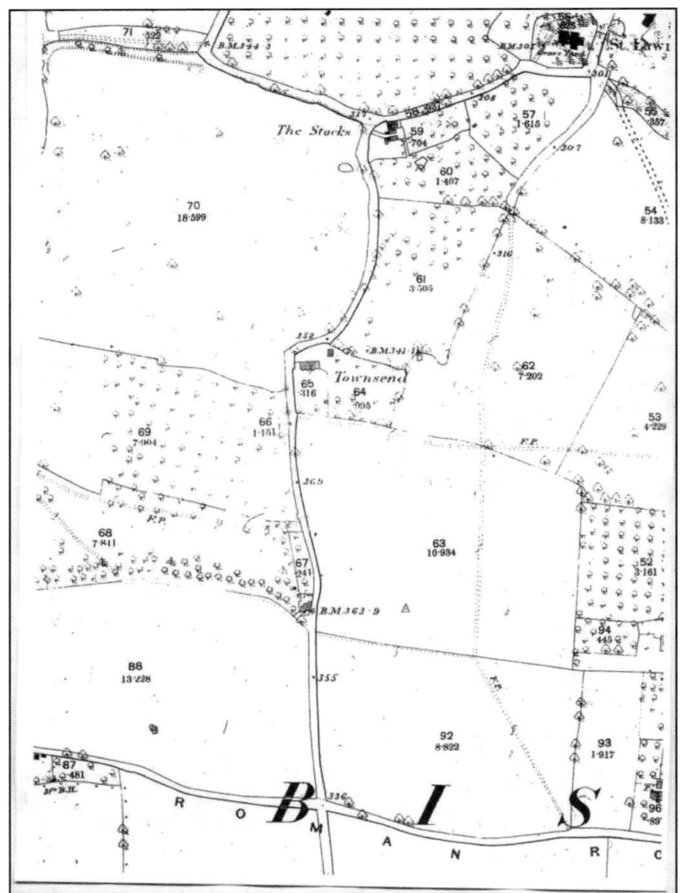

(Figure 30) 1905 map showing positions of Stocks House and Townsend

Stocks House dates back to the 14th-15th century, although the site itself could date back to the Anglo Saxon era. The name stock usually means the site of the village stocks although after much research I have found no record of any stocks in Bishopstone.

As part of the Foxley Estate, Stocks House in 1901 was the home to husband and wife Edward and Catherine Preece.

They had started the three times a week passenger carrying service from Bishopstone to Hereford in 1896, terminating in the Horse and Groom yard. Previously they had lived and operated their carrier business from Ivors Brook, Mansel Lacy. Their business was on the decline by 1901 so Edward was working as a general labourer on the railway and Catherine had taken over the reins, operating the carrying service herself. They also had taken in two lodgers, the wonderfully named Hawthorn Preece and Arthur Jinks: both were general labourers working on the railway with Edward. Also living in the house was Elizabeth Price aged 13, a servant and William Green aged 7 years a boarder who was attending Mansel Lacy School.

From 1902 Edward increasingly started to suffer from mental problems; the family and business moved up to "The Pleck" in that year. The house and barns were demolished by 1905; from deeds we know the house was of large timber frame structure standing on low stonewalls. The north gable end formed the boundary with the lane going down to the church and stone forming part of this wall can still be seen in the bank around 30 yards from the turn. A large timber framed barn built at right angles to the house made an enclosed yard; the entrance to this yard is now the gateway into the field.

(Figure 31) The entrance to Stocks House today a gateway into a meadow

Townsend Farm, the name meaning the last house in the medieval village, the farm was first recorded in 1345 as occupied by the Smith family (blacksmiths). Purchased by John Crow in the 17th century, it was then a large timber framed house with barns stables etc. A cottage was built at right angles to the main house in the 1700s. John Smith who inherited the farm sold it to Garnons estate in 1828. The stone cottage was demolished in the late 1860s, the stone used to build the wall can still be seen today on the S bend in the lane leading down to the church. The garden gate opening to the house is still clearly visible in the hedgerow. The ownership of Townsend Farm and Stocks House passed to Rev Davenport in the 1871 exchange.

John Howells, his wife Maria and Allen their 15-year-old son occupied Townsend in 1901 and in the Kelly's Directory of that year, John advertised himself as a cottage farmer and carrier. As well as farming Townsend he rented several small orchards on Bishon Common from Rev Davenport.

He also worked as a platelayer for the railway. The 1900 rental returns show John paying £33 16s per year rent for Townsend Farm with its 6 acres and the two orchards on Bishon common. Townsend was never occupied after 1905, possibly because of low returns on the rental, Rev Davenport decided it was not economic to repair the farm house, and it had been demolished by the time of the 1910 valuation.

(Figure 32) Lena Cottage in 2010 now called Fiddle Cottage. Left; date stone positioned bottom of the East wall

Lena Cottage was built in 1828, originally called Lane Lodge it was built to guard the end of the proposed east drive to Garnons new mansion. Although the drive is shown sweeping through parkland on the original grand plan, the project was abandoned after the lodge was built. How the lodge name changed to Lena is unclear unless at some point the a and e were misinterpreted by a clerk. The 1910 value of Lena Cottage was £85 and the estate charged £4 per year rent. It was listed as a stone and tile cottage, two bedrooms, kitchen, back kitchen, pigscot and privy in fair repair. The 1901 census also listed the cottage as having three rooms occupied. The occupiers in 1901 were William Preece and his family; he was a gardener working for Sir John Cotterell. William lived with his wife Annie; sons John, Frank and little Stanley aged 4 years. He shared the job of sexton to Bishopstone Church with John Collins from 1895 until John retired in 1908, they were paid £4 per annum between them. William then became full time clerk and sexton. He was a parish councillor from 1902 until 1921 and overseer for the poor on several occasions. Although heavily involved with Bishopstone church, William, his wife Annie and their children are not recorded in any of the church records of baptisms, marriages or burials.

The 1911 census lists all the same occupants, John (Jack) and Frank who had both joined their father working as gardeners at Garnons. All three boys served in the 1st World War and miraculously all survived.

After the war the boys returned to their jobs as gardeners on the estate. The family lived in the cottage until the mid 1930's although Jack Preece moved jobs and went to work at the New Weir as a gardener. Mrs Hybert and her son Ernest, a tailor, were the next occupiers. After the war Ellen Lawrence lived in the cottage with her daughter and son in-law Percy Alderton and family.

Harry Jones and his wife Jane followed Mrs Lawrence; Harry had lived in various properties within the parish since 1911, including Kenowly Farm. Harry and Jane lived in the cottage throughout the 1950s into the 60s. The estate sold the cottage in the mid 1970s to Mr and Mrs Budd who changed the name of Lena Cottage to Fiddle Cottage.

(Figure 33) Harry and Jane Jones outside Lena Cottage 1950s

Scaldback Cottages (Scaldback is an Anglo Saxon name for small hollow valley). The original enclosure held a smallholding throughout the medieval period this was purchased in the early 1600s by John Crow "Bishon Farm" who let the dwelling house fall down. In the 17th century deeds these small enclosed parcels of land carried the name Scaldback hence the present name of the cottages. The new cottages were built by the Garnons estate in the early 1830s to house estate workers. They were called model cottages; estate owners were just starting to build better housing for their workers, they were built from drawings and plans using stone to match the other cottages on Garnons estate.

The ownership passed to Rev Davenport in the 1871 exchange. On the 1910 Valuer's field book it lists the original cost to build the cottages as £100 for the erection of the cottage No 1, and £125 for building cottage No 2 with outbuildings. The market value for Scaldback cottages and land in 1910 was £480, being two stone and tile cottages, each containing three bedrooms, three living rooms, pigscot and privy.

(Figure 34) Scaldback Cottages 2000

No 1. The 1900 voters list records that James Whiting my great grandfather, a nurseryman, lived in Scaldback for a year, he later moved down to live on Bishon Common. Richard Lloyd, a shepherd working for Mr Like at Court Farm followed James into the cottage. 12 months later Richard and family moved down to the Clovers so relieving him of the restrictions of living in a tied cottage. Afterwards he worked as a casual on many local farms including Bunshill, the family lived in the Clovers until the 1920s.

This yearly movement of farm workers caused many restless nights for families, worrying if work and accommodation could be secured for the next year. Court Farm was placing yearly adverts in the Hereford Times for a cowman during this period. Thomas Dixon was hired in 1904 and moved into Scaldback where he stayed for two years, tragic circumstance befell his family as reported in the Hereford Times on December 22nd 1906[5].

Child's Sufferings, Pitiful tale of Herefordshire cottage life.

A distressing case was investigated on Monday at the Herefordshire General Hospital by the City Coroner (Mr J Lamb) who, with a jury, assembled to hold an inquiry relative to the death of a child named Frank Edward Dixon, aged one year and nine months, son of a farm labourer named Thomas Dixon, of Bishopstone.

Mr F H Swallow (Messrs Corner & Co represented the Hereford branch of the National Society for the Prevention of Cruelty to Children) and the Chief Constable (Mr Frank Richardson) was also present.

Mr H J Getting was foreman of the jury.

The father of the child stated that he was cowman for Mr Like and lived at Scaldback. The child had good health up till about three months ago, when it began to "fall off" and its food was changed from solid food to milk. The child began to sink and get thinner without any apparent cause. A doctor was called in.

The Coroner; How did the child go on after the change of food? – Witness; The children were put away from me for a time- for a month or five weeks.

Were you convicted? -Only bound over, Sir

What about the children? What became of them? –They were sent to Weobley Workhouse, and when they came back this child was not so well.
You were charged before the magistrates with neglecting the children. How long ago was that? –I think it was on the 9th of November, but I am not sure.
Mr Swallow; The 29th of October was the date of the hearing, He was convicted, and bound over in the sum of £10 to come up for judgment when called upon.
Witness, continuing, said his wife was in a very bad state of health. She was suffering with consumption and had sunk to a shadow. Dr Hounsell saw her in August, and said he could not do her any good. She was so weak that when she came out of the bedroom she had to put her hand against the wall to hold herself up.
The Coroner; The child's right arm was broken. When did that happen? –Witness; I cannot account for it. The children were taken from me. I did not know that the child's arm was broken or injured at all till I came here today.
You saw the child when it came back from Weobley? – Yes, and I noticed a mark on the forehead and another on the jaw.
What kind of mark was it? –It was blue. I said to my daughter, "Strip the child, and let us see what other marks there are." The child was stripped, but there were no other bruises to be found. There were no bruises on the child when he went to Weobley, but there were when he came back.
The Coroner asked the house surgeon (Dr Taylor) what sort of a fracture it was.
Dr Taylor replied that it was a simple fracture.
The Coroner; One of your children died in November 1905, rather more than a year ago? –Witness; Yes.
And it was considered then that it was a natural death, the child being a weakly one? –Yes Sir
Continuing, witness said when Dr Hounsell was sent to see Frank, he told the wife that they had better get the child into hospital at once as it was born with rickets. The child was sent the following Wednesday by a Mansell Lacy carrier, his daughter Beatrice, who is 14 years of age, going with it.
Beatrice Dixon said she had helped look after the children, as her mother was very ill. She was one of the children who were sent to Weobley Workhouse. The bruise on the child's forehead was caused by falling against the fireguard, and that on the chin by a kick from her little brother. She could not account for the broken arm.
Inspector Merchant, of the N. S. .P. C. C., stated that on the 29th of October he went to Weobley to prosecute the father for neglecting the children, who were in a deplorable state when taken to the workhouse. The mother had been able to get about the house up until a month ago.
Dixon (warmly) She does nothing at all in the house, and has not for three months.
Witness, proceeding, said he knew the mother was suffering from consumption, but in October she was about the house. The deceased child was only 16lbs in weight, when it should have weighed 31lbs. Its emaciation was caused by want of proper nourishment and attention. One child - one older than the deceased – was suffering from curvature of the spine. When witness and a constable went to the house there was no food there.
Dixon There was food in the house when you took the children away.
Witness said he went on two occasions – two consecutive days. The father would not let him take the children away on the first day, and when he went on the second (the 18th October) they (he, a constable and Supt. Williams) had to force the garden gate. There was no food in the house on the first day, but there was on the second, when the children were removed. In February last, when Dixon lived in Catherine Street Hereford, the parents were cautioned about their treatment of the children, and also prior to that – in July last year.
The Inspector, on being asked about the bruises on the child, said Dixon had made a statement about them being received while the child was in Weobley Workhouse, and he thought the Guardians ought to be given the opportunity of saying whether they occurred in the Workhouse or not.
The Coroner replied that he did not think that was necessary, because what the girl had said accounted for the bruises.
In answer to questions by jurors, it was stated that the other children were now back at home, and that there was only the girl Beatrice, 14 years of age, to look after them and the mother.
Dixon said his brother's wife sometimes went in to assist.
A juror; I think somebody ought to see to the children and the poor woman, and not leave them there like that – (hear, hear). The girl is not able to look after them all.
The Coroner; I agree with you.
A juror; It is a shame.
Mr Taylor, the house surgeon, said the child was admitted on December 5th extremely ill, wasted and rickety. It might have been born with rickets, which probably developed from the want of proper food.

What the child said about the bruises was sufficient to account for their presence. He discovered the fracture to the arm, halfway between the elbow and the shoulder, when it was in bed, He did not think that it was done in the Workhouse. It was possible for the child to do it tumbling about. The child died on December 15th the cause of death being pneumonia.
The foreman: What is your opinion about the nourishment of the child?
Witness; The child did not look well nourished, but how much of that was due to lack of feeding or its illness it was difficult to say.
A juror: A broken arm would be very painful?
Witness: It must have been very painful for the first week, and that must have had a bad effect on the health of the child.
Mr Swallow: It is not possible that the arm was broken after the 26th of November?.
Witness: It must have been done a fortnight or three weeks from the day of the post-mortem.
The children were taken to the Workhouse on the 19th October. Is it possible that the arm was broken then? – I put the limit at a month.
Asked if the doctor would not have noticed a fracture of the arm, Dr Taylor replied that it might have been overlooked if the child was not stripped, but it would have been obvious to anyone who saw the child stripped.
Inspector Merchant: The children, on admission to Weobley Workhouse on the 19th October, were stripped and examined by Dr Hounsell.
A juror said he thought it would have been much better if the child had been kept in the Workhouse than sent away to Hereford to the hospital.
Mr Swallow replied that the guardians said they could not keep it there the father being in regular work.
A juror inquired if he could ask Dixon what were his wages? He thought it was a fair question.
Dixon: My wages are eleven shillings a week and a cottage and garden.
Inspector Merchant: His wages altogether are worth about 17s per week.
Dixon Excuse me sir. The cottage is not worth eighteen pence per week. Some gentlemen were there a few days ago, and said to me, "You best not think about stopping here. The place is condemned."
A juror: Who owns the farm and cottage.
Dixon: Mr Davenport, sir.
Another juror remarked that Dixon's wages were not a lot to keep a large family on and also an invalid wife.
The Coroner in asking the jury to agree to a verdict of "Death from pneumonia" said he hoped the publicity, which would be given to the case, would have a good effect in some way. There was some satisfaction in thinking that it would.
A juror said he thought a rider to the effect the death was accelerated by neglect should be added.
A second juror: What I think is that the man did not have enough to keep his family of eight children and poor wife on.
The foreman (to Dixon): What sort of sanitary condition is your house in?
Dixon replied that it was very bad, adding that there was no bedroom window. When he went there he was promised that the house should be "done up" but it had never been touched. The rent of the cottage, he explained, was treated, as part of his wages, but Mr Davenport was responsible for the repairs. He (Dixon) had spoken to Mr Like about the cottage, and he had promised to see about it for him, but nothing had been done to the house. Mr Hudson had been down there.
A juror: I should think the Sanitary Inspector ought to go round there.
In answer to a juror, Dixon stated that the cottage, which had a fan-tile roof, was not far off the Vicarage.
The Coroner remarked that he did not see that the jury could make any representation to anyone, but hoped the publicity given to the case would have some effect.
Dixon added that Mr Like gave him a quantity of skimmed milk every day, milk skimmed by hand, not with the separator.
The jury agreed to a verdict of "Death from pneumonia" no rider of any kind being added.
R A Hudson who was mentioned in the coroner's inquest was the agent for Foxley Estate. On 22nd December he wrote to the editor of the Hereford Journal.
Sir,- The evidence of Thomas Dixon, as given on Monday, the 17th inst., in your report of the inquest on his child is misleading and untruthful, as to the state of the cottage he occupies at Bishopstone. He is reported to have said that "there was no bedroom window," There is a window frame, but when I visited the cottage the glass in it was broken; this should have been kept in repair by the tenant. It is not customary for landlords to repair windowpanes after the tenant has held the cottage for some years.

In other respects I found the cottage in repair, the roof being quite good, and the doors and window frames in repair, but it was in a most filthy state inside, and I noticed that while the parents had a bed to sleep in, the children had no beds, but lay on the floor of a room upstairs.
I shall be much obliged if you could find room to insert this letter in the next issue of the "Journal" as Dixon's evidence is calculated to give a wrong impression of the circumstances of the case.
Yours faithfully R A HUDSON. Foxley Estate Office, Yazor.

The 1910 field book records Edward Lawrence as the tenant paying Rev Davenport £9 per year for the cottage with a 1 acre orchard and garden. Edward who was married to Julia, a Londoner, lived in Scaldback cottage with their five children all under nine years old. Edward Lawrence was a charcoal burner employed in the chemical works at Kenchester.
Mr J Fisher, a bricklayer, occupied no 1 Scaldback throughout the 1920s; the Hill family followed the Fishers in 1933. Frank Hill and his wife Mary and their three young boys Francis, Lionel and Douglas had from 1925 lived in No 15 Bishon Common, the cottage was tied to his job as waggoner on Bunshill Farm. In 1933 Frank started working as a platelayer on the railway, so enforcing the move from the tied cottage on the common up to Scaldback. By now the family had grown by three more children, Dennis, Eric and finally a girl Molly who was born in 1933. At the outbreak of war Frank Hill was directed to work in the munitions factory at Rotherwas. After a few years of cycling to the factory and working long shifts during the war years, Frank decided it would be best to move the family into Hereford. All the boys entered the services during the war; Douglas was killed in France and his story is covered in the war section. Francis the eldest son moved back into Bishopstone with his wife Violet after the war and lived in Burcott Row for many years. After the war the cottage was used to house Bishopstone Court farm workers, and many families lived in No 1 over the next 60 years. In the early 1970s Dennis and Christine Morgan purchased the cottage from Foxley estate.

(Figure 35) Sarah Montague standing outside the cottage 1936

No 2 Scaldback, William Stinton the carrier had taken on the tenancy by 1902, besides the cottage there were outbuildings consisting of a timber frame stable, cow house, loose shed and loft and 2 acres of land for which he paid £20 per year rent to Rev Davenport. William Stinton operated a passenger carrying service to Hereford every Wednesday and Saturday; in the early years he competed for the village business with the more established carrier run by Catherine Preece from the Pleck. From 1915 to 1928 they were the only regular passenger carrier service into Hereford. William Stinton and his wife Susan eventually moved into an almshouse, both were suffering from ill heath and old age and finally packed in their carrier business. William Stinton died in 1930

William Montague and family who previously lived in Clifford, moved into No 2 Scaldback at Candlemas 1928, they lived there until 1937. During this period William worked as a farm labourer firstly for Captain Hinckes and later William Lewis at Court Farm. In 1937 he became a tenant of Captain Gilbert, farming the 20 acres attached to the Old Rectory, and William swapped houses with Charlie Kitching, the Montague family moving into the Lodge, now renamed Bishopstone Lodge Farm. William Montague, whilst farming, was also the village postman. Two of the Montague's children, Bill and Fred, made Bishopstone their home after they married. Bill with his wife Mary moved into one of the new council houses built down by the Nelson as a first tenant in 1945, they lived in the house for over thirty years. Bill was a renowned and expert hedge layer who charged by the yard, he worked for all the local farmers. Fred, who like Bill was short in stature, married Nora who came from the Whitfield estate, home of the Clive family to work for the Gilberts in the Second World War. Fred and Nora lived in a caravan on Court Farm when they were first married, then they moved to Burcott Row where they lived for many years, before finally moving into No 14 Council Houses. Bill and Fred both served in the Home Guard throughout the war.

(Figure 36) William and Sarah Montague

Charlie and Rose Kitching moved into Scaldback in 1939 where they lived for the next 26 years, Charlie was a churchwarden at Bishopstone church for many years. No 2 Scaldback was purchased from the Foxley Estate by Joe and Maureen Baker in the mid 1970s.

(Figure 37) The Lodge with Old School House in the distance 1947.

(Figure 38) Charlie Kitching 1961

The Lodge was built by the Reverend Lane Freer in 1842. The 1901 census shows it was occupied by William Roberts and family; he was coachman to the Rev Griffith. The 1911 census reveals Herbert Roper and his wife Elizabeth, who were both Londoners, now living in the Lodge with their two young children. Herbert worked as a domestic servant and gardener for Rev Wilmot. In 1922 Captain Gilbert and his mother purchased the Lodge as part of the Rectory Estate, the Captain brought with him his chauffeur and handyman Charlie Kitching, who with his wife Rose and twin sons Albert and Ralf moved into the Lodge: Rose also worked for the Gilberts as their domestic help. The Captain had previously rented the rectory at Canon Frome, the parish from which the Kitching's family originated. Charlie and Rose lived in the Lodge until 1937 when the Montague and Kitching families swapped homes. William Montague and family lived in the Lodge for the next ten years throughout the war years. Dennis and Edith Johnson became the next occupiers when they became the new tenants of Rectory Farm in 1947-48. Captain and Mrs Gilbert swapped houses in 1957 with the Johnsons who moved into part of the Rectory, the Captain and Mrs Gilbert left the Rectory and occupied the Lodge. After the death of Captain and Mrs Gilbert's several tenants occupied the Lodge, before it was sold in the late 1990s to Richard Fishbourne and partner. Richard renovated the Lodge and built an extension on the north side.

(Figure 39) Kitching Twins outside the Lodge in the late 1930s

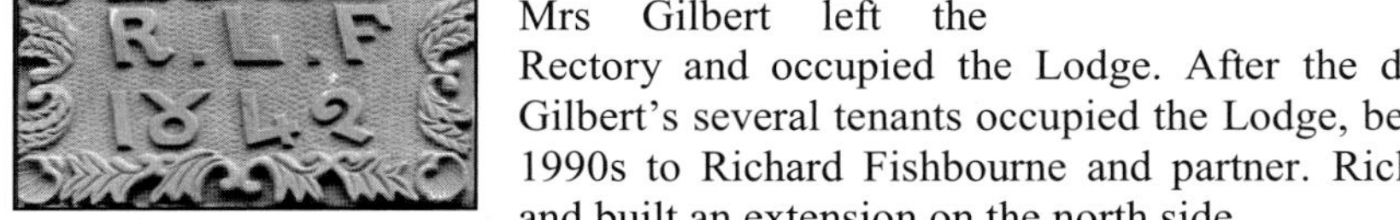

The date plaque on the front of the Lodge carries the same design and date as the two collection boxes in Bishopstone Church.

The Rectory was built in 1811 by the Rev Adam Walker and extensively enlarged by Rev Lane Freer in 1841. Rev Charles Bodvel Griffith aged 60 was the rector of Bishopstone in 1901, he lived in the Rectory with his wife Wilhelmina Dells Owena, daughter Marjorie Ruthven aged 17 and her German governess L V Vorthwaith. Also living in the house were the servants, Mary Wager the cook, Ellen Benfield the housemaid and Agnes Jay the parlour maid.

(Figure 40) Rectory 1939

Rev Griffith had married Wilhelmina, the granddaughter of Baroness Ruthven on June 19th 1879. Her eldest brother Walter was the 8th Lord Ruthven. An historically famous family Saxon by descent, they were very wealthy with estates in Scotland, Ireland, Herefordshire and houses in London. The family were regular visitors to Bishopstone Rectory, the 1891 census list Frederica Hore Ruthven and Charles Ruthven as visitors to the Rectory, these were Wilhelmina's brother and sister. Wilhelmina Griffith presented a large brass altar cross to Bishopstone church in memory of her sister Frederica. It carries the inscription *"To the Glory of God and in loving memory of my beloved sister Freddie Aug. 14th 1897"* and it is still used today. On October 30th 1907 Marjorie married Lionel Owen R Ashley at St Paul's church Knightsbridge, Lionel Ashley was a cricketer who played for Dorset. He was the grandson of George Ashley, rector of Stretton Sugwas, who died in 1904 leaving all his estate to Lionel; it was a large estate including The Lakes at Stretton, Railway Terrace consisting of six cottages, Clifford House, Kings Acre plus, in Wales, the Groes and Caer Groes estates which consisted of twenty two farms with cottages.

(Figure 41) Inscription on the base of altar cross Bishopstone church.

(Figure 42) Marjorie Griffith 1907.

What happened to Marjorie in her lifetime I do not know, but she must have had fond memories of Bishopstone because on May 30th 1974 the church records list the burial of the ashes of Marjorie Ruthven Bodvil Ashley aged 90 years who had lived at 10 Offington Court Worthing Sussex.

After Marjorie's wedding Rev Griffith resigned from his position as rector. The Reverend Richard Hurt Wilmot, who came from Gloucester, became the new rector to take over the living of Bishopstone. In 1911 he is recorded as living in the Rectory with his wife Charlotte, and servants Ethel Garbett the cook and Emily Gilbon the house parlour maid.

The value of the Rectory House, Lodge and outbuildings in 1910 was given at £1225 plus £700 for the 20 acres of land. Described as a stone and slate house with two morning rooms, drawing and large dining room with ante room, kitchen, scullery, servants' hall, larder, four bedrooms, cellar, butler's pantry, housekeeper's room, two dressing rooms, two dark rooms, two W Cs, back hob, three servants' rooms and laundry.

Outbuildings were listed as: stable for four, harness room, coach house and granary, cow house, milking shed, two pigscots, calves house, barn, double cradle and a lodge containing three rooms up and three down.

When Rev Wilmot resigned in 1916, the position of rector for Bishopstone was advertised in the Church Times. Isaac Robinson Timperley applied and was offered the living; he was previously the rector of Christleton in Cheshire. Isaac was inducted as rector of Bishopstone in May 1917 and moved into the Rectory with his wife Mary. Rev Timperley was not a farming man so the glebe land was let out to John Like of Bishopstone Court. Rev Timperley was appointed chairman of the parish council in 1918 and started the Guild of St Lawrence Church in the same year. The guild appears to be a forerunner of a Sunday school, the war had just finished and Isaac perhaps thought that religious guidance was needed for the children aged up to 12 years old who lived in the parish. He kept a register listing 34 children from the parish when he started. The Walls from Stonehouse were the largest family, sending six of their children, followed by the Amos family from the Pleck who sent their five. The Fishers from Burcott Row sent four children, the Rawlings from Panteg Cottage three, and the Jones family who kept The Shop at the Clovers sent their two children. The final entry in this register was March 21st 1920 when there was still a regular attendance of 29 children.

(Figure 43) Wall children 1919

In 1920 Edward Bettington, who had designed several replacement rectories carried out alterations to the rectory, since Rev Timperley had complained about its poor state of repair. On August 2nd 1921 Mr Timperley resigned as rector of Bishopstone, he was the last designated parish priest and also the last rector to live in the rectory. After much debate the diocese committee decided to join the living of Bishopstone to Kenchester and Bridge Sollars, the rectory was to be sold off by the Church Commissioners and the sale money held on account to build a new rectory if required. Bishopstone Rectory was one of the largest in the Hereford Diocese's rural area and the upkeep too expensive for such a small parish. The Rectory with farm building, land and lodge sold for around £3000, the diocesan board invested the money, and the interest was paid quarterly to the rector of Bishopstone. On February 27th 1923 The Rev T M Roberts from Kenchester Rectory was admitted and instituted to the parish church of Bishopstone.

(Figure 44) Captain Gilbert and family 1928.

The following information came from my talks to Eleanor English nee Gilbert in 2008. At the age of 90 she still had a remarkable memory of her childhood in Bishopstone, from when she arrived aged 4 years old in 1922 until she left at the age of 12 to attend boarding school.

"The Rectory was advertised and was purchased by Gertrude Gilbert, her son Captain Humphrey Adam Gilbert and his wife Margaret, in the summer of 1922. Gertrude Gilbert known in Bishopstone as Granny Gilbert was the daughter of General Adams, Gertrude was born when his regiment was on the march in India, her mother was following the line by carriage, when she went into premature labour at seven months and was carried into a native hut on the side of the road where Gertrude was born. Gertrude was sent back to Europe where she was educated and brought up by an aunt in Boulogne, France. She returned to Bombay where she met and married Reggie Gilbert, a lawyer whose family came from Norfolk. Humphrey, her only child, was born in Bombay. Sadly Reggie died in Bombay while Humphrey was back in England training to become a barrister. Gertrude moved back and lived in Nellworth Hall, Builth Wells. Humphrey joined the South Wales Borderers as a full time soldier before the war. He married Margaret Money-Kyrle on November 3rd 1915. The Money-Kyrles owned two estates: The Homme, Much Marcle and the Whetham Estate near Calne in Wiltshire. Both were inherited by Margaret's brother Roger when he was still at school .He joined the Royal Air Corps and fought throughout the 1914-18 war; after the war he could not afford to run both estates so he sold off the farms on the Homme Estate but kept the main house and park. Most of the tenants bought their farms including Westons Cider. This is why we always drink Westons cider" explained Eleanor. *"After the war Captain Gilbert rented Canon Frome Rectory while he looked for a permanent home to buy in the Wye Valley with his mother, this needed to be both near the Wye for the fishing and the ancestral home of his wife. Gertrude also wanted a home big enough for herself and Humphrey's family so they bought Bishopstone Rectory. In the summer of 1922 the Gilbert family moved to Bishopstone bringing the Kitchings with them. Gertrude, Captain Gilbert, his wife Margaret and their children myself Eleanor aged 4, John aged 3 and Ernle just 1 year old moved into the Old Rectory. Gertrude spent time between Bishopstone and Ramsgate in the early years. In the 1920s the Captain farmed the land with the help of Charlie Kitching. Two Jersey cows were milked daily for butter and milk, pigs and chickens were also kept. Haymaking in the summer was carried out with the help of old Samuel Gwilliam,"* (my great grandfather) who Eleanor remembers would not go anywhere without his cider costrel and drinking horn. Because there were a number of poor people in the parish, skimmed milk was left in the dairy for any villager who wanted it, she often remembered children coming up the drive with their billy tins to fetch milk while any milk left over was fed to the pigs. Eleanor remembers having two governesses who taught her at home. The first was Renee Roberts, daughter of the Rev Roberts from Kenchester, who only stayed until she was old enough to take up nursing at St Thomas' Hospital in London.

(Figure 45) Gertrude Gilbert 1939.

The next governess was Miss Turley the daughter of the Rector of Madley, who rode over every day on her motorcycle wearing leather helmet and breeches. Eleanor remembers the Miss Collins sisters who lived at 2 Cambria Cottages "*they always had a very nice flower garden full of polyanthus. Kate Apperley and Jane Waithe from the Almshouses were given little jobs by father in the summer weeding and clearing paths; Jane wore a summer bonnet and Kate always a black straw boater hat that she would decorate with a cake frill. Every person wore hats and caps; men would tilt their hats when meeting women on the road. One Sunday afternoon whilst walking down the village with my mother and brother John, we met Mrs Amos, a large women from the Pleck Cottage. John tilted his hat to her, mother was very pleased because he had remembered without being told, he was only four years old. We would take our pony to the blacksmith shop to be shoed; the blacksmith came from Byford to work in the forge on only a few set days a month. Bridge Ash was a sweet Post Office with a big front door, on the right was the Post Office, and the passage was lined with shelves filled with big bottles full of sweets.*

(Figure 46) Eleanor English 2008.

Mrs Hinckes was a great friend of my mother we would be driven over in the Morris Cowley for afternoon tea in Foxley House. It was set in a beautiful park and there were many servants. Captain Hinckes always appeared to be a rather gruff man to me as a child. My father liked Captain Hinckes, who had given father's batman from the First World War a job as a gamekeeper; his name was Offa, a Welshman. Mrs Holder from Banberry Cottage came to work for my mother as a housekeeper, her husband George was a gardener at Garnons estate. Mr Preece from Lena cottage would carry two pails of water on a yoke from the waterspout on church lane back up to his cottage every day.

Frank Hill was a young man who lived on the common, he worked at Bunshill Farm as a waggoner's boy and worked part time in the garden looking after the roses, we always gave him a good breakfast. He was also very good with ponies."

In 1957 the Rectory was divided into two separate living accommodations. Dennis Johnson, as the tenant of the farm lived in one half. Dennis had developed his milking herd of cows and was now operating a full-blown dairy complete with bottling plant. The business had increased dramatically because his milk round included Foxley Camp, which was now the home to hundreds of ex-servicemen and their families awaiting new housing. After the death of Stanley Lewis from Court Farm, Dennis purchased the old Nelson fields from the Lewis family. In 1960 Captain Gilbert had plans drawn up to convert the house into four flats but it never materialized. Mr and Mrs Seaborne became the next tenants of Rectory Farm they built large sheds on the farm to house thousands of chickens.

Captain Gilbert's son, Major Ernle Gilbert became a career soldier after the war, returning to Bishopstone in 1963 after he had retired from full-time soldiering. During the war he had married Helena who was an Austrian national. Ernle carried on soldiering part time in the T A where he rose to the rank of Lt Colonel and Commander in Chief of Herefordshire Light Infantry. Like his father he was a keen naturalist and fisherman. At different times Ernle was chairman of Hereford Nature Trust, chairman of the parish council, and churchwarden; he also carried out many other public duties. He was the main instigator in making Bishon Common an S.S.S I. site so protecting its natural flora.

(Figure 47)
Ernle Gilbert 1981.

Burke's Peerage entry on Ernle Gilbert.

LT.-COL. ERNLE REGINALD FORESTER GILBERT, of Chedgrave Manor, Norfolk, and Bishopstone, Herefordshire, Maj RA (ret), Hon Lt-Col Herefordshire, L.I. (T. and A.V.R.), served in WW II; *born* 1 June, 1921; *educated* Marlborough; *married* .6 December 1946

The Old Rectory remains in the hands of the Gilbert Family in 2010.

(Figure 48) Old School House 1975.

The Old Schoolhouse was originally a timber framed cottage built in 1753 by Simon Williams, it was enlarged by Rev Lane Freer in 1854 when he built a schoolroom extension on the cottage.

Thomas Watkins a road labourer, and his grandson Henry Francis occupied the Schoolhouse in 1901. Thomas had come to Bishopstone in 1870 to work at Court Farm as a farm labourer, living firstly in a cottage on Bishon Common where he and his wife Mary brought up their five children. Mary had just passed away so Thomas was living with his grandson. In 1902 Miss Mary Wootton, organist for Bishopstone church became the new tenant, the 1905 photo shown in chapter 11 shows Mary standing outside the church.

My grandfather John Wall married Sarah Gwilliam on March 5th 1905 and moved into the schoolhouse on a one-year agreement before moving over the road to Stonehouse. In 1906 the new tenant was also newly married, John "James" Gough listed in the 1911 census as a domestic gardener was originally from Birmingham. James worked in the kitchen garden at Garnons where he met and married Naomi from Byford. By 1911 they had been married for 5 years with two children Vera and John. John junior like his father used the name James which became shortened to "Jim". Jim lived in Bishopstone for the rest of his life mostly at Panteg Cottage, he was a character who will be remembered by many of the older generation.

The value of the Schoolhouse in 1910 was £120, listed as brick noggin and slate roof two rooms up and two rooms down plus classroom.

The Schoolhouse was purchased at the Foxley sale in 1920 by Rosanna Bywater licensee of the Nelson Inn. Rosanna extensively rebuilt the cottage and the two separate buildings were made into one dwelling. Rosanna died in 1939 and the property passed to Amy and Ernest her children. The deeds changed hands on February 15th 1944 when Fred Bywater paid Amy £500 for the house and grounds. Fred had been farming Wistaston Farm , Kings Pyon and when he moved to the School House he changed the name to Wiston House. In 1964 Fred Bywater had to go into Hampton Grange Home for the Blind and Mr and Mrs J Farrell purchased the property. Eight months later in October 1964 John and Florence Farrell sold the house and grounds to Mr Ivor Johnson of Knapp Farm, Bridge Sollers for £2800; Chris Stevens who worked for Ivor Johnson and his family lived in Winston for several years. In November 1972 Ivor sold the house to Mrs Lillian Dufty wife of Robert or Bob as we knew him. Over the years the original orchard attached to the cottage has been sold off to provide six building plots, the last two Hill Crest and Kimberley were sold in 1975. Mr and Mrs R Thrupp purchased the house in 1999.

Stonehouse was built in 1590 by Paul Delahay as the New Inn and was acquired by the Berringtons of Bishopstone Court before the Civil War. It ceased operating as an inn in 1825 when a new stone face was built on the front of the original timber framed house.

(Figure 49) Stonehouse with members of the Wall family 1930.

The 1901 census reveals that a Welshman William Ball a widower, was renting the smallholding. William had moved down from Kenowly Farm after his wife Harriet had died in January 1900, his niece Elizabeth Powell was living with him as a housekeeper. In February 1906 John and Sarah Wall took on the tenancy of Stonehouse and its attached four acres of land. The Wall family were an old Herefordshire family; prominent landowners and farmers during the Civil War they owned a forge and several mills on the river Arrow. Over the centuries the family farmed all over north Herefordshire ending up at Upper Farm Eardisley where a lot of the family are buried inside the church. With the demise of agriculture at the end of the 19th century the family slipped back into labouring. John was working at Marsh Farm, Bridge Sollers for Mr Fred Edwards. This was the start of a long association between the Wall family and Bishopstone, the family would live in Stonehouse for the next ninety years.

Tragedy befell John and Sarah Wall in July 1907 when John their two-year-old son fell into the open well at the rear of Stonehouse and drowned. Afterwards the well was capped and a pump installed over the kitchen sink.

(Figure 50) Lena, George, Kitty, Edgar and Molly Wall outside Stonehouse 1930.

The 1910 value of Stonehouse was £290, described as a stone and tile cottage containing three bedrooms, kitchen, back kitchen dairy, cellar, brick noggin and tile cow house for two, barn, loose shed, pigscot and privy. John paid £12 16s a year rent.

(Figure 51) George Wall on his Douglas motorcycle en route to his wedding at Bishopstone church, his passenger is Artie Preece 1935.

The 1911 census lists the occupants of Stonehouse as John Wall, his wife Sarah, and children Doris, Kathleen and Edgar, also a lodger John Pember. John and Sarah went on to have a further four children, twins George and Mary, Lena, and finally Molly.

John Wall purchased Stone house in 1920. Although the property was listed on the 1920 sale brochure, John negotiated directly with Foxley as a sitting tenant and purchased the smallholding for £300. At different times John Wall was chairman of the parish council, overseer of the poor, and for a period held the office of parish clerk. He died in 1948.

My father in the year 2000 wrote about his memories of John Wall.

As a boy about 10 years old, (1925) I would, with my mother and most mothers and children in the village, go to the Marsh Farm at Bridge Sollars for the annual event of hop picking, usually a happy time for all when the weather was good. The farm was owned by a bachelor farmer Mr Fred Edwards, considered a gentleman farmer, who employed about six farm workers including John Wall.

(Figure 52) Fred Edwards and Miss Clark

John Wall did not have anything to do with hop picking or drying because he was in charge of the corn threshing machine operated by a steam engine and at this time of year would be busy going from farm to farm threshing corn.

Sometimes we would see him walking back home to Stonehouse at the same time as the hoppickers. He was a tall man very quiet, never heard him raise his voice to noisy children. Mr Edwards thought a lot of him, because I was told, (later in life) that he loaned John Wall £200 to help pay for Stonehouse, when it was put up for sale.

A very rare event for a farm worker to buy his own house, but John was a very careful man with money, never spending time or money at the Nelson Public House, like lots of his fellow workers.

He had about 5 acres of land attached to the Stonehouse so he always had 2 or 3 milking cows, a pig or 2 and a flock of chickens. Sarah his wife would sell the milk, butter and eggs, to the village folk, also pig meat when pig killing season came round. On market day she would fill a large basket with produce and take it to Hereford Market travelling in Bill Stinton's horse drawn "carrier" cart.

That went on until the Second World War, during the war one of the jobs my wife Kitty had was to deliver milk and eggs to the villagers. I well remember coming on leave and helping with the hay making both at Stone house and at the ground at Kenchester Rectory that John Wall used to rent. John Wall was a gentle man and enjoyed having his grandchildren sitting on his knee when they visited.

(Figure 53) John and Sarah Wall 1940.

(Figure 54) Sarah, John and Rose Wall 1958.

After the war Sarah Wall purchased an Austin Seven car from the money she made selling produce throughout the war years to the locals. She never learnt to drive, it was used by Edgar her son and other members of the family.
I well remember going for Sunday rides in the car during the 1950s, when we would all have to get out of the car at the bottom of steep hills, and walk to the top while Dad drove the Austin up the hill by himself. There was not enough power in the car to carry all the family up the hill, at the top we would then all get back into the car and carry on with the journey.

(Figure 55) Edgar and Mary Wall 1975

After being demobbed from the army in 1947 Edgar Wall, Mary his wife and their children Rose, Sarah and John lived with Granny Wall in Stonehouse.
Edgar died in 1996 and the house was sold soon after to Ian and Hillary Robinson.

Cambrai Cottages were built in the early 1870s by Foxley estate. Rev Davenport commissioned the build, possibly influenced by Rev Ridley who required two cottages for his gardeners. Rev Ridley rented both cottages after they were built until he left the parish in 1889. They were still occupied by the rectory gardeners in 1901 but now they paid their rent to Rev Davenport.
The 1910 value for both cottages was £300, described as two brick and tile cottages, three rooms up, two down, pantry, passage, pigscot and privy each. Good repair, area 1acre 30 perches.
No 1 Cambrai Cottage. In 1901 this half of the cottage was occupied by Albert Lawrence a gardener who worked for Rev Griffith. He lived with his wife Jane and niece Helen Stevens. Albert was a Bishopstone lad who was born and raised in the parish and had attended Bishopstone School. When Rev Griffith left the rectory in 1907 Albert lost his job and moved out. Henry Francis took over the tenancy on November 2nd 1908, he paid £7 16s rent per year. Henry was employed at the Chemical Works at Kenchester as a fireman; he lived with his wife Kayla and son Henry who was a farm labourer. After the First World War George Rawlings moved into No 1 Cambrai Cottage, he had married Lizzie Gwilliam, sister of Sarah Wall. George worked as a waggoner for John Like "Court Farm"; Sam Gwilliam, Lizzie's father also lived with them. This was George's second marriage, his first wife had died in childbirth; George and Lizzie had three children Albert, Wilfred and Joyce who all grew up in the village. Lizzie lived in this cottage for over 60 years until she died in 1981. Soon afterwards Foxley sold the cottage to Stuart and Pauline Jordan.

(Figure 56) Left Lizzie Rawlings standing next to her father Sam Gwilliam, husband George in the background; Right their three children Albert, Wilfred and Joyce

(Figure 57) Cambrai Cottages with sisters Sarah Wall and Lizzie Rawlings 1936.

(Figure 58) John Collins headstone Bishopstone church

No 2 Cambrai Cottage. was occupied by John Collins, parish sexton and clerk, who lived with his wife Elizabeth and daughter Harriett, who never married. John retired as sexton and clerk in 1908 a position he had held for thirty years. He can be seen on the 1905 photo, standing outside the church with Miss Abberley and Miss Wootton. He was a short man with a huge white beard. He had occupied the cottage since February 2nd 1877, after securing the job as the rectory gardener.

(Figure 59) Miss Harriett Collins

The 1911 census reveals that he had retired from gardening, not surprising as he was 82 years old and now a widower having lost his wife Elizabeth. Harriett his daughter still lived with him working from home as a dressmaker; he paid £4 16s rent per year. After John Collins died his other daughter who lived and worked in London as a ladies maid retired to Bishopstone to live with her sister Harriett. Harriett outlived her sister and occupied the cottage until the early 1950s.

In 1955 Bob Carrington leased Court Farm; this cottage was tied to the farm and used by his workmen including Bill Jones, Ben Lloyd and John Kingston. Bob Carrington purchased the freehold of the cottage along with Court Farm in 1977, he sold the cottage in the early 1990s.

Bishon Farm. Humphrey Digges built the farmhouse in the 1670s it was purchased by Uvedale Price of Foxley in 1718. Rev Davenport, putting in a new range of farm buildings and adding a new east wing to the farmhouse extensively rebuilt the farm in 1870. The bricks used for this and the Nelson Inn came from Foxley's own brick works.

The 1910 value of Bishon Farm was entered at £6020 a farm of 226 acres, with dwelling house, new farm buildings and three cottages known as Burcott Row. Mr Yeoman was the tenant paying a rent of £307 per year. (note! The rent in 1884 was £400 per year). Expenditure recorded as spent in the last year 1909, £160 on new Dutch hay barns, £80 on water supply, charity payments attached to the farm £5 to the poor of Burghill and £10 to the poor of All Saints Hereford.

(Figure 60) Bishon Farmhouse 1929

Description: stone, brick noggin with a stone tile roof, containing hall, two sitting rooms, kitchen, dairy, storeroom, two box rooms, three bedrooms, clothes closet (used as bedroom), two attic rooms and one large room, fair repair. Outbuildings; tile and thatch fowl house, brick and tile double pigscot, brick and pan tile stables and tack room, stalls for two horses, loose boxes for six horses, two four bay French barns, lower engine house, turnip and chaff house with cutting loft over, cellar with granary over, brick and pan tile five bay open feed shed and implement shed, two bay open feed shed and bull house, brick and tile four bay open feed shed, cow house for twenty eight and calves cote.

In 1901 Charles D Barnett a bachelor was the tenant of Bishon farm, he lived with his sister-in-law Ellen Price who was recorded as his housekeeper. Charles employed one domestic servant, Kate Wall aged 17. She was the sister of John Wall from Stonehouse, Kate was one of the reasons why John came to settle in the village, to keep an eye out for his younger sister. Charles Barnett was reported as being a strange man, who was always behind with his rent and never involved himself in any parish duties, unlike his father who held the tenancy before him, although Charles was one of the five people who were paying out yearly to keep the church afloat at the beginning of the 20th century

R L Bamford was a land agent who ran the affairs of Foxley estate from 1882 until 1905, his record of correspondence with Rev Davenport gives an insight of the problem with collecting the rent from Charles Barnett. On July 25th 1895 R L Bamford writes *"Mr Barnett of Bishon Farm did not come today with settlement. So I have given him notice to quit. I shall have no difficulty in letting the farm. Complications may arise as he is a very peculiar man to do business with."*

(Figure 61) Bishon Farmhouse rear view 1929

Sept 12th 1904 R L Bamford writes *"Mr Paske has agreed to take on Bishon Farm at £300 a year."*

Mr Paske did not take up the tenancy for some unknown reason.

Joseph Yeoman was the new tenant from February 2nd 1905; they had finally managed to persuade Charles Barnett to leave although he still owed two years rent.

Joseph Yeoman was a very different kind of farmer who took his parish duties seriously, he was chairman of the parish council and a prominent church member.

In the 1911 census Joseph Yeoman is listed as a 41-year-old farmer, who had been married to Edith for seven years, they had four children John, Herbert, James and Florence. Joseph was the first person in the village to own a car, in 1918 he purchased an "ALLDAY" car, described as having two brass headlamps, which he polished every time the car was taken out. It had a hood covering the two front seats with a dickey seat that opened out of the back for two passengers, with no protection from the weather. Joseph also possessed the first wireless in the parish, a crystal set that he purchased in 1917 to keep up with the progress of the war. Joseph lost all his working horses to the war effort; they were sent to France with a million other horses, he hired steam tractors from the war agricultural committee to help with the ploughing on the farm. The principle was that two steam tractors were stationed one at either end of the field, and the plough was drawn from one to the other by means of a wire rope.

(Figure 62) Harry and Dora Watkins

The farm was put up for sale in 1920 by Foxley estate. Tom Watkins purchased Bishon Farm and several cottages in the 1920 auction, the family moved into the farm on February 2nd 1921. Tom with his wife Marion and young family had moved from a rented farm at Canon Bridge, two of the Watkins boys, Russell and Harold, are shown on the 1921 Kenchester school photo. The farm was reportedly bought on money borrowed from his father but with the agriculture depression taking a tighter grip the farm failed. Sadly the pressure was too great for Marion who took her own life. John Watkins senior put the farm up for sale as the mortgagee on Wednesday September 26th 1928 at the Law Society's rooms in Hereford. Edward, Russell & Baldwin advertised and conducted the auction, billed as Bishon, Brick House, Seven Cottages, Set of Farm Buildings, 209 acres.[6]

The farm failed to meet the reserve of £6,000 so John senior, a widower, decided to run the farm himself. Peter Watkins his grandson takes up the story: *"My grandfather John Watkins had 14 children and seven different farms in his lifetime including Ballingham Court and Moccas Court. After grandmother died he lived with his daughter Mrs Wood of Swainshill and he travelled up to Bishon everyday in his Buick 8 until his eyesight went. He then moved to live with father at Church Farm Madley. Macklin would fetch him every day in his Jowett car and take him home in the evening."* After Tom Watkins and his family moved out of the farmhouse it lay empty for the next eleven years, only used by workmen and by John Watkins as a bait room. On Wednesday January 19th 1938, Edwards, Russell & Baldwin at the Law Society's Rooms Hereford, put up Bishon Farm 209 acres and seven cottages to auction again on the instructions of John Watkins. The bidding failed to reach the reserve of £7,000. Bob Carrington remembers a local farmer went the highest with a bid of £6,000.

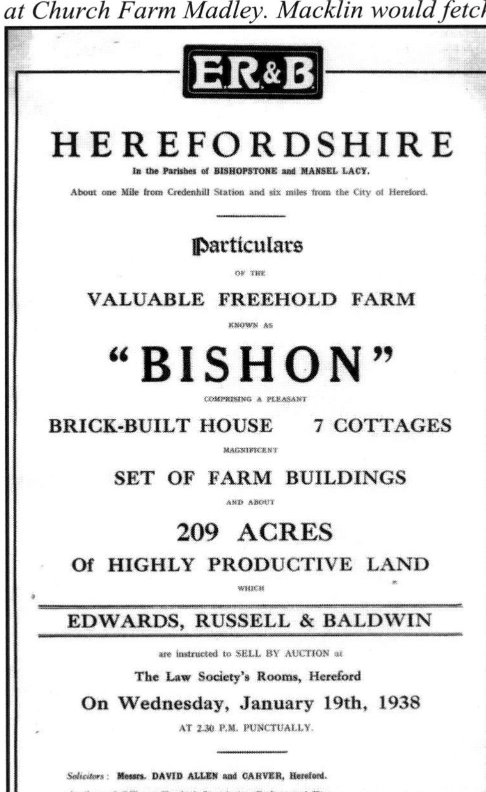

ER&B
HEREFORDSHIRE
In the Parishes of BISHOPSTONE and MANSEL LACY.
About one Mile from Credenhill Station and six miles from the City of Hereford.
Particulars
OF THE
VALUABLE FREEHOLD FARM
KNOWN AS
"BISHON"
COMPRISING A PLEASANT
BRICK-BUILT HOUSE 7 COTTAGES
MAGNIFICENT
SET OF FARM BUILDINGS
AND ABOUT
209 ACRES
Of HIGHLY PRODUCTIVE LAND
WHICH
EDWARDS, RUSSELL & BALDWIN
are instructed to SELL BY AUCTION at
The Law Society's Rooms, Hereford
On Wednesday, January 19th, 1938
AT 2.30 P.M. PUNCTUALLY.
Solicitors: Messrs. DAVID ALLEN and CARVER, Hereford.
Auctioneers' Offices: Hereford, Leominster, Tenbury and Hay.

Peter continues *"Grandfather died November 1938, he left Bishon Farm to father, plus seven cottages and three draw wells. We moved to Bishon from Church Farm Madley on February 2nd 1939, I was 14 years old and had just left school, Donald had his 10th birthday two weeks after we arrived. We brought with us 15 horses, eight were working, no tractor. We ordered our first tractor, an orange Fordson with rubber wheels, it came in the spring 1939. Father always had a car; in 1920 he owned a Scrips Booth, an American car very unusual, this was followed by a brand new Bullnosed Morris. Grandfather employed George Rawlings to look after the cattle, Edgar Wall worked on the farm before he moved to Wyevale Nurseries, Tom Spencer, he was a waggoner, Henry Roberts from the Pleck, he was a farm labourer. When we came to the farm father took all the workes on."*

Henry (Harry) and Dora Watkins with their sons Peter and Donald occupied the farm throughout the war but after the war Peter moved on to his own farm, leaving Donald at home to help his parents. The Watkins were always very supportive and interested in village affairs, they always allowed the villagers to hold their celebrations on the farm: in 1937 the coronation of George V1, in 1944 the Homecoming celebration at the end of the Second World War, in 1953 the coronation of Elizabeth II, in 1958 the Best Kept Village celebrations, in 1978 the Silver Jubilee, in 1981 the marriage of Prince Charles and Lady Diana, the 2000 Millennium Celebrations and many other fund raising events for Bishopstone church. Harry Watkins, who was short in stature, always talked through his nose, an old fashioned farmer who used working horses on the farm until he died in 1963. I can picture him now scything the wheat around the edge of the field that the binder had missed. Dora his wife died in 1981 leaving Donald the farm.

Jim Roberts, the last fulltime farm worker on Bishon Farm recalls his time working on the farm, *"When I started in 1958 my wages were £3 5s per week, overtime 1s 3d an hour, I worked a 47 hour week including a couple of hours on a Sunday feeding livestock. I would earn extra money for piece work hoeing swedes, for a row 1650 yards long I would get 3s 6d. Bishon Farm made 1000 gallons of cider every year until I left in 1974. Donald bought eight new rum casks to store the cider in, he threw 18lb of meat into each cask, the cider sometimes turned out black in colour. He gave men still cider rations every day. Donald liked to test out the strength of his cider on the village boys; I remember young John Roberts drinking nine horns of cider. He did not reach the top of the drive before he had to drop his trousers, next morning Dan Roberts his father came down to see Donald as John had spent all night on the loo but nobody admitted anything. Mr Watkins still had a couple of working horses on the farm when I came. Donald hired his broad wheel wagon out to the filmmakers for the film Cider with Rosie."*

(Figure 63) Jim and Kathleen Roberts 1960

(Figure 64) Donald Watkins 1981

In the early 1990s Donald donated all his cider making equipment to the Hereford Cider Museum. For years he employed local women to pick up his cider apples. Donald served as a churchwarden for Bishopstone church. In later life he suffered from poor health and became wheel-chair bound. In 1989 Donald sold 180 acres of his farm; 100 acres was purchased by Mr Hobby from Madley, and 80 acres by F Price & Sons Magna Castra Farm, Kenchester. I will always remember Donald when he was younger as a big strong man, carrying 2 cwt sacks up the steps to the granary on his shoulders. Donald would have a competition with his workman Jim Roberts to see who could hang upside down for the longest with their legs wrapped around a beam in the barn - the competition seemed to go on for hours.

(Figure 65) The Pleck cottage 1929

The Pleck house was built around 1575 by John Eckley, it replaced a much older dwelling that had previously stood on the site. John purchased the land from the Crown after it had been seized by King Henry VIII on the dissolution of the monasteries, because it was endowed to St Mary's Chapel in Bishopstone Church. It had many owners throughout the years until Rev Davenport purchased the smallholding in 1874.

(Figure 66) rear garden 1929

Henry Francis rented The Pleck in 1901, he worked at the Chemical Works at Kenchester where he had been employed for twenty five years. During his employment at the works Henry lived in Bishopstone.

The 1910 assessor valued the Pleck at £260 which he lists as a brick noggin and stone tile cottage with four living rooms, four bedrooms, shed, pigscot, privy in fair repair, outbuildings, garden, grassland and 2 acres.

Edward Preece had held the tenancy since February 2nd 1908 paying £13 rent per year. Edward had moved up from The Stocks in 1908 bringing with him his carrier business. Soon after the move the doctor admitted him to Burghill Asylum where he died in 1912. In the 1911 census Catherine his wife had three lodgers, Hawthorne Preece, William Walker who was a cooper, and George Parker a roadman. Catherine operated the three times weekly carrier service to Hereford from Bishopstone, until 1916. Whilst Edward was in the Asylum, Catherine had to pay for his care costing her 9s 2d a week which was one of the reasons she needed to take in lodgers.

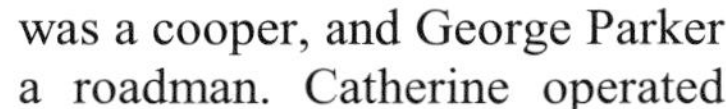

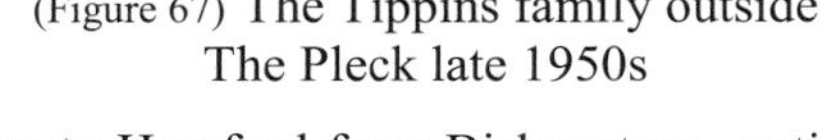

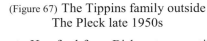

(Figure 67) The Tippins family outside The Pleck late 1950s

(Figure 68) Mrs Bradley, Mrs Tippins and Janet Bradley

The Pleck was purchased by Tom Watkins in the 1920 Foxley sale. Fred (Coddy) Amos was the sitting tenant who had moved into the Pleck during the First World War. The Amos's remained tenants until 1931. Helen Matthews recalls *"Mrs Lizzie Amos died of cancer after being diagnosed by Dr Stead shortly after leaving Bishopstone to live in Dorstone".* Elizabeth Amos is buried in Bridge Sollers churchyard.

In 1932 my grandfather's building firm A Macklin & Son carried out a conversion on Pleck Cottage for John Watkins Bishon Farm, changing it from a single dwelling to a double. No 1 using the front door and front garden, No 2 using the back door and rear garden.

(Figure 69) Wat Tippins

No 1 the Pleck had a high turnover of workmen including Helmer, Statham, Inns and Lambert. Henry and Gladys Roberts lived with their daughter Joyce throughout the 2nd World War in No 1. Les Spencer can remember Joyce as a member of the Palladium Playtime Theatre Group who entertained the troops, he can remember seeing Joyce on stage at the theatre at Foxley Camp. In 1946 Walter and Annie Tippins and their children, Tony and Silvia, moved into No 1 the Pleck. Walter was employed on Bishon Farm, they were the last family to live in No 1. After a period living down at the Marsh Farm, Bridge Sollers, Walter and family moved into No 6 the Council Houses in 1965.

(Figure 70) George and Dolly Wall

No 2 was the home of George and Dolly Wall in the mid 1930s, they were followed by Percy and Catherine Bradley and their children, Nora and Gerald, they moved in just before the Second World War started. Janet their youngest daughter came along later, they were the last occupiers of No 2 The Pleck and left in October 1961. The male members of the Bradley family were remembered in the village as motorcyclists throughout the 1950s, Percy riding a 350cc B S A and later on son Gerald on a 500cc B S A.

(Figure 71) Percy Bradley on his B S A motorcycle

The cottage has slowly become derelict over the years even though it is a Grade 2 listed building.

(Figure 72) Forge Cottage 1960s

Forge Cottage was built by the blacksmith John Snead in the 1730s.

In 1901 Richard Boucher the blacksmith lived with his wife Elizabeth and their employee, striker William Lucas. Richard continued working the Smithy until his death in 1928. My father remembers him still working in the early 1920s; he thought he was in his seventies when he was actually over eighty years old. After his death his wife Elizabeth moved into an almshouse with her sister Catherine Apperley.

The 1910 assessor valued the house and blacksmith shop at £85. Described as a brick noggin thatch cottage, two rooms up, two rooms down, blacksmith shop, privy, shed and pigscot in poor condition. Owned by Rev Davenport, Richard paid £6 16s a year rent. He had occupied Forge Cottage since August 2nd 1867. Thomas Watkins of Bishon Farm purchased the cottage in the 1920s sale, with sitting tenant Richard Boucher, he was the last resident blacksmith to live in Forge Cottage. With the decline in the farrier side of blacksmithing in the 1930s, the horses left in the parish were catered for by the regular visits to the forge by Bill Reece who cycled from Kings Acre; his own forge was sited behind the Bay Horse public house. After the Second World War the power required on the farm moved from horseflesh to the horsepower of the internal combustion engine in the form of a tractor, and the forge became redundant. Donald Watkins told me the last person to use the forge was Jones of Eaton Bishop.

(Figure 73) Joe Haines

(Figure 74) George Haines

John Gilbert and family rented the cottage for a short period after Richard Boucher, then George Haines a carpenter agreed to rent Forge Cottage from John Watkins, Bishon Farm, but firstly the family lived at No 2 the Clovers while the thatch roof on Forge Cottage was being replaced with slate. This was the last thatched roof house in Bishopstone. In 1933 the Haines family, George, Bessie and son Joe moved in and shortly afterwards a new addition to the family was born, Helen. The family lived in Forge Cottage for the next 38 years. After George Haines died Donald Watkins sold the cottage to D&J Cooke Builders who partly demolished and then extended and modernized the property, it was then sold to Mr and Mrs R Allport in 1974.

(Figure 75) Helen Haines

(Figure 76) 1974 Forge Cottage before and after renovation

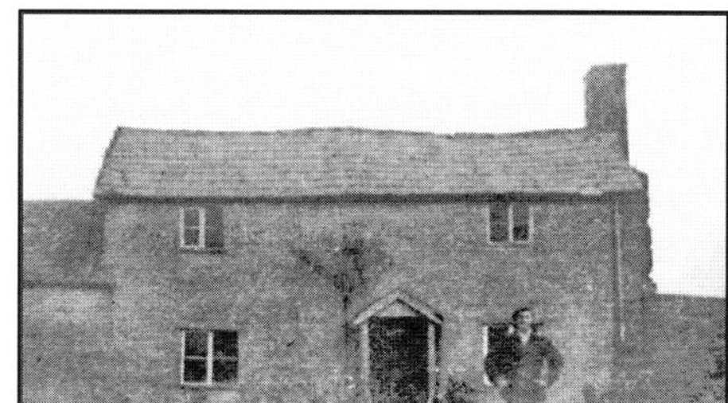

(Figure 77) Jim Roberts standing in front of Peartree Cottage, Jim and his wife Kathleen were the last occupiers of the cottage before it was demolished.

Peartree Cottage was originally called Rose Cottage, Samuel Powell built the cottage in 1834 on part of Burcott Row garden. It was purchased by William Abbott for £50 in 1863. He was a cabinet maker from 33 Skinner Street Birmingham and he in turn sold the cottage in 1868 to Rev Davenport for £140, nice profit in five years. Rev Davenport attached the cottage to the lease of Court Farm who used it as a tied cottage for farm labourers. There was a high turnover of occupiers during this period as the workers were employed on a yearly contract. These labourers were treated not much better than the livestock they tended; they were hired and fired on a whim.

John Like's farm labourer, David Price and his son George lived in the cottage in 1901, both worked at Court Farm. Also living in the cottage was Arthur Webb, a road labourer, and David's daughter Ada Webb who cooked and kept house. There was no value put on the property in 1910 as it was valued as part of Court Farm but the description was a stone, brick and tile cottage two rooms up, two rooms down lodgers room, cellar, pigscot and privy.

The cellar was also used as a lodger's room, because the cottage was built on a bank with a separate external door leading into the cellar. Called the Badger's Hole this was the home of the Bethell family for a time after the First World War.

(Figure 78) Rear view of Peartree Cottage 1950s

In the 1920 sale Peartree Cottage was sold as part of Bishon Farm and so housed many of their workers up until the Second World War. After the war the Thomas family lived in Peartree for many years.

Donald Watkins recalls an incident, *"Ted and Betty Thomas had a lodger called Tom George who was a postman and also a gardener at Stretton House. One evening while smoking his pipe under the pear tree he started to walk in circles, small at first and getting larger; after half an hour they called in a policeman who was staying with Jim Gough. He stopped him and recognized that he had a mental problem so father fetched the Wolseley Fourteen, and took him to hospital. Father left him at the door with the doctor. That was the last he was seen in Bishopstone."*

The Jenkins family followed the Thomas family in the 1950's. The last person to live in the cottage was Jim Roberts, a farm worker employed by Harry Watkins Bishon Farm. He helped pull down the cottage in 1962-3 with a tractor and chain, he said the rubble left on the site after it was demolished was pushed in the cellar. Robin and Helen Matthews soon afterwards purchased the site along with Burcott Row.

(Figure 79) Burcott Row just before it was demolished in the 1970s

Burcott Row had become a terrace of three cottages by 1900. Parts of the structure dated back to before the Interregnum 1649-60 and the first records of a house on the site are found in the will of David Pugh who died in 1679, a soldier and farmer who owned the freehold, when it was then possibly a Herefordshire long house with the family living at one end and the livestock the other. From his will and inventory in 1679 it was shown to be a large house. It was firstly converted to two cottages by Joseph Pritchard, and then extensively rebuilt to make three cottages by Rev Davenport in the 1870s. The row of cottages formed part of the tenancy on Bishon farm, providing tied cottages for their farm labourers. The 1910 survey describes Burcott Row as three stone brick and tile cottages each containing two rooms up, two rooms down a pigscot and privy each in poor repair, no value given because it was part of Bishon Farm. Tom Watkins purchased Burcott Row as part of Bishon farm in the 1920 sale, the Row in the late 1960s was condemned as unfit for human habitation and stood derelict for a number of years before finally being demolished in the 1970s.

(Figure 80) Bishopstone children outside the Knoll. Back row L to R Cecil Macklin, Steve Jancey Arthur Portman 1924.

No 1. Burcott Row. Ben Lawrence an agricultural labourer, his wife Sarah, and their six children occupied No 1 in 1901. Around 1904 Amos and Sarah Jones moved in, Amos had secured a farm labourer's job on Bishon Farm. They had a new baby son called Teddy in 1905. In 1906 Amos and Sarah contracted a life threatening illness; Sarah was so ill it was thought she would not survive, then her husband suddenly took a turn for the worse and he died. This left Sarah a widow with three small children, she was lucky not to be evicted from the cottage. By 1909 Harry the eldest aged 12 was working on Bishon Farm as the main breadwinner. Harry was serving in the First World War when the family moved to Kenowly. Harry and his brother Robert lived most of their lives in Bishopstone, Harry at different times occupied Kenowly Farm, Lena cottage and lastly one of the almshouses. Robert worked for Garnons estate all his working life as a shepherd.

My grandfather Albert Macklin rented the cottage from 1923 until 1925, during this period he built his new bungalow called The Knoll. My father Cecil Macklin wrote this next article in 1987, when he was 72 years old. It's about the people who lived in the village during the time he lived at Burcott.

Cecil Macklin's memories of the village in the 1920s.

It's a Wednesday morning, as we pass Scaldback, Mr and Mrs Stinton are backing their horse into the shafts of the carrier brake, preparing for the 9 o'clock twice weekly trip to Hereford.

The brake will carry about eight persons facing each other, with Mrs Stinton sitting beside her husband, acting as eyes and ears for he is about 70 years of age, he is both deaf and very short sighted.

Passing the lodge to the Rectory we can see Mr & Mrs Kitching hurrying down the drive, he to his job as chauffeur/gardener and his wife as cook to Captain H A Gilbert at the Rectory.

There coming towards us is one of the two cars in the village, a bull nosed Morris, driven by Captain H A Gilbert making an early start for a day's bird watching in some remote part of Wales. At the Old School House Mrs Price will be waiting for the carrier, on the opposite side, Mrs Wall with a couple of large baskets laden with fresh butter, eggs and dressed chickens. Along comes Mr Will Stinton with his brake picking up passengers and produce, now followed by a group of children on their way to Kenchester School. The older and more energetic boys will trot behind, watching out for Will's long whip. About 24 children age ranging from 4 to 14 will walk to Lady Southhampton School at Kenchester, built with the Methodist Chapel some 100 years ago, being the first free school in the area.

(Figure 81) Ernle standing in front of Captain Gilberts' Bullnose Morris 1927

Walking past Cambria Cottages, Miss Harriett Collins is weeding the garden, a polite, chatty person in her late 50s who has never left the village, looking after her father, past gardener at the Rectory and one time verger of Bishopstone Church.

She lives with her elder sister Sarah, a more remote person always dressed in black with white lace around her throat, very much the retired ladies maid.

As we approach the Almshouses there is a lot of chatter going on around the "well" where the most active resident is drawing the day's supply of drinking water. She is Kate Apperley, a slight chirpy person in her fifties, with thick glasses and frizzy red hair always wearing a straw boater hat with a large hatpin. A generous soul fetching and carrying for her older and less active neighbours, she is the daughter of the last wheelwright in the village, her bachelor brother living alone in a little black and white house on the common, no longer a wheelwright but making a few shillings in the cider making season with his own mill and press.

Before we get near the smithy we can hear iron striking iron and voices raised above the sound of the bellows. It is Mr. Boucher the blacksmith with his "boy" Bill Lucas, a likable character. A tall man with a pink face a white fringe "gaffer" beard about 70 years old he has a north eye, never quite sure whether he is looking at you or the person alongside.

There are a couple of horses tied up in the open ended "prentice", so it will be worthwhile waiting until the red-hot iron shoes have been tried for size to get the smell of the burning "hoof-horn".

While Mr. Boucher is fitting the shoes with those special shaped nails, Bill Lucas is standing by the horse's head quietly smoothing the fears of the smell of its burning feet.

Coming up the drive from Bishon farm is Mr. and Mrs. Tom Watkins (uncle of Mr. Donald Watkins) in a spring trap and pony on their way to Hereford market. As they move away another smart "turn out" comes up the orchard from the Pleck, a well-known character "Coddy" Amos, a heavily built man, of swarthy complexion wearing a muffler, bit of a mystery man. Horse-dealer, cum trainer, ladies man, but no one can dispute he owns the smartest trotting outfit in the district and fast too, it is a thrilling sight to see them "go" on the open road.

Standing by the gate of the next row of cottages is a tall heavily built man wearing dark glasses with a chair on his shoulder. He is "Blind Fred" to everyone around and is about to deliver the chair whose basketwork seat he had recently replaced. With his keen sense of hearing and good memory he can identify all his acquaintances, often by their footsteps, always as soon as they speak. In constant demand at small social functions with his melodeon, anytime you can hum it, he can play it. He is the son of Mrs. Evans, mother of a large family all grown up and away from home. A great field worker and snuff taker, always the mouthpiece of the pickers at the annual hop picking at the Marsh Farm, Bridge Sollers.

The last of the cottages is the Post Office, Postal Orders and stamps only, run by Mrs. Castle, sister-in-law of the owner Tom Gore, a stocky man, with a fascinating habit of blowing out his cheeks at the slightest exertion. He earned a precarious living hedge laying, swede hoeing and stone "knapping".

In the next row of cottages called "The Clovers" lives Mrs. Reade widow of the late Rector of Kenchester with Bridge Sollers, the Rev Compton Reade, late of Kenchester Rectory now residing in Bridge Sollers churchyard. She is rarely seen about during the day, but a solitary ghost like figure, heavily veiled in a white frilly dress can often be seen walking the road or around her tiny garden soon after day-break.

The Hamer family, comprising mother age 80-ish, two sons and two daughters all unmarried, occupies, turning down towards the common, the first house called the Cottage. A musical family, Nora a qualified organist teaches piano and organ, also plays the Father Smyth organ at St. Lawrence Church. Both sons have good singing voices, Fred a tenor and Josh a baritone, he lost a leg when a boy, always walks with a crutch, never had an artificial leg fitted. They have been known to give a family evening's entertainment of singing around the piano. The Hamers were the local timber hauliers. At least one load a day passing from Garnons Estate to either Credenhill Railway Station or Kenchester Chemical Works. The heavy timber carriage with its shaft horse and two or three trace horses depending on the size of the load causing endless damage the water-bound macadam road, making a constant demand for poor old Tom Gore's knapped stone to repair the potholes.

Passing down the lane we are overtaken by a man on a bike with a short four-rung pig ladder strapped to his back. It is Harry Parton, the pig butcher from Mansel Lacy, he turned into the next cottage called "The Orphanage" occupied by Bill Oliver a bachelor living with his mother. After the usual chat and a horn of cider, Harry is shown the pig in its sty. He approaches with his short length of rope with a loop on the end, and as the pig is "barking" at him, very smartly passes the loop over its snout and pulls tight. Harry calls for assistance to pull a strongly protesting pig over the pig bench. Once alongside the bench we all give a heave, pulling the pig's legs from the ground and lying on its side. Kicking and squealing like mad. Harry takes a turn of the rope around the end of the bench, everyone available holding on to its legs with their knees against its back.Harry very expertly carries out the slaughter and soon the kicking and squealing dies away. The cider costrel is produced and everyone partakes of a horn of cider. Next, a bed of straw is laid on the ground and the corpse is carried on to it with lots of straw placed on and around. The whole thing is set alight and burns furiously but Harry is in control and deftly shifts the burning straw around the carcass with a forked beanstick to make sure the flesh is not scorched. Mrs Oliver will have the furnace going to produce buckets of hot water. Harry is stripped off and now comes the hard work of scraping off the bristles. Sometimes he uses a butcher's knife and sometimes a "scraper," a piece of metal punched like a nutmeg grater to form a very rough surface. The carcass is now tied onto the pig ladder and carried into the house where the rope around the snout is pulled over the pig hook, which is fixed into a beam running across the ceiling. The ladder is removed. Harry, washed and cleaned up approaches, "steeling" his knife ready for the opening up. He calls for the tip bath to receive the contents of the belly and with a few professional strokes it all tumbles into the bath. Bill takes the bath away for his mother to start cleaning the "chitlings". Harry delves in and cuts out the bladder, always in great demand by small boys, to be blown up and hung up to dry and used as a football. Harry now removes the "fry", liver and lungs called "lights". Bill produces the "belly stick" which is placed about halfway up the carcass to allow cool air to circulate. After a final clean with his mutton cloth, the veil is stretched over the front legs. It all looks very clean and clinical and as Harry always says, "there's only two parts of a pig you can't eat, that's its eyes and its squeal".

(Figure 82)
Frank and Violet Hill

Tom and Lena Spencer came to Bishopstone in 1933, they lived at No 1 for a while before moving next door. George Hybart and his family followed them into the Row. Frank Hill and his wife Violet occupied No 1 from 1947 until 1965, Frank will be remembered for his expertise in growing roses, he exhibited and won many prizes at local shows. They were the last people to live in the cottage.

No 2 Burcott Row. On the turn of the century George Windsor agricultural labourer lived here with his wife Jane and their three sons. Between the wars Tom and Lena Spencer and family occupied No 2, Tom worked as a waggoner at Bishon Farm, Les his son takes up the story. *"We first lived in No 1 Burcott, when we came to Bishopstone, we moved into the middle house after Mrs Evans left. It had a back and a front door, a real luxury, No 1 only had the one front door. On the outbreak of war in 1939 we left, dad was sent to work for the War Ags so we had to give up the house because it was tied to the job at Bishon Farm. I will always remember walking to Kenchester School, up to eight of us from Bishopstone in a gang, sometimes Dennis Hill from Scaldback would give me a lift on the crossbar of his bike."*

After the war No 2 became the home of many families including the Jenkins family, Robin and Helen Matthews and Frank and Val Betambeau just to name a few.

(Figure 83) Fred Monty outside No 3 Burcott Row 1958

No 3 Burcott Row. John Pember the shepherd from Bunshill Farm with his housekeeper Sarah Cadwell lived in this end cottage in 1901, John was the last of the Bishopstone Pembers. Before 1910 he had moved into Stonehouse as a lodger to John Wall where he stayed for the next 20 years, he is still remembered by a few as an old man shuffling through the village on his way home from Bunshill. John made a final move into Weobley Workhouse where he died in 1935.

By 1911 William Evans, a 56-year-old farm labourer lived in No3 with Charlotte his wife and 8 children. The family was made up of Evans and Griffiths children, some from previous marriages. Two of William's boys, Thomas and John, were killed in the war. Fred Griffiths, Charlotte's son was born blind. He was well remembered in the village by the older residents as a player of a melodeon and accompanying singer. He also taught Jo Haines how to play the church organ. Tom Prosser remembers he had a good singing voice and also a braille watch, the children always asked the time on meeting him to see him use his watch. Fred later married and moved to Byford from where he would walk every day along the A438 to the Nelson Inn and back, sometimes in the dark, a feat that would be very dangerous today because of the heavy volume of traffic. In the 1930s and up until the start of the war Charlotte lived in the cottage alone, her one son George was a career soldier and only visited his mother when on leave although for voting purposes he was registered to that address. During the Second World War Mrs Pickles, a relative of the Holder family lived in the cottage, she was an evacuee from London, bombed out of her home.

(Figure 84) Gillian, Joyce and Kathy Montague

(Figure 85) Fred and Nora Montague

Just after the war Fred and Nora Montague moved into No 3, their three children all girls Gillian, Joyce and Kathy they were all raised in the cottage, the last family to occupy Burcott Row before it was demolished.

Panteg Cottage. William Lloyd of Bishon Farm built Panteg Cottage in the early 1860s on a roadway between the now Old Post Office and Burcott Row, the cottage was purchased by Rev Davenport along with other cottages from Caroline Lloyd in 1873. Built of brick and attached to the Post Office it appears out of place with its mismatch in roof heights. In 1901 Thomas Gore a 39-year-old bachelor lived in Panteg Cottage with his widowed mother Catherine; he had taken the tenancy on in 1899. Thomas was the parish roadman at this time.

(Figure 86) Panteg Cottage

At the 1920 Foxley sale Miss Hughes, the schoolmistress from Kenchester School, purchased Panteg. She only lived in the cottage for a short period of time, before letting the property to George Morgan a roadman and his wife Rose, who after a few years moved down to No 2 The Clovers. In 1927 Mrs Matthews, a widow whose husband was killed in the First World War, became the next tenant, she lived with her son and two daughters. After Miss Hughes died in 1937 Jim and Rose Gough purchased the freehold, they lived in the cottage until the 1970s. Jim was an interesting character, a Bishopstonian born and bred he was an expert beekeeper and gardener. Before the war he was a roadman but on the outbreak of war he was sent to the munitions factory at Rotherwas where he worked on the gate as a policeman. Throughout the war Jim was one of the air raid wardens for Bishopstone. He always kept a beautiful front garden full of flowers which also featured a magnificent topiary of a peacock.

(Figure 87) Jim Gough drawing water from his well. Note his topiary in the background

Always interested in village affairs, Jim was a parish councillor and one of the main instigators of Bishopstone's entry into the Best Kept Village Competition in the 1950s. In later life Jim bought a Triumph Tiger Cub motorcycle, which he used for transport to work. After Jim died, Rose moved into an almshouse, Robin and Ann James purchased the cottage, they in turn sold the property to Heather Kennard.

The Post Office of 1900 is now called The Old Post Office, a cottage that was built in the 17th century. One record I have found dated 1681 refers to the tenant John Snead the blacksmith, purchasing elm timbers from Byford to repair the cottage and charging the cost of the timbers to the then lord of the manor Thomas Berrington.

(Figure 88) The Old P. O. was a village shop in 1965

Mary Ann Lewis a 60-year-old widow was the post mistress in 1901. In 1909 she asked Rev Davenport for permission to make an interior door thus joining the Post Office with Panteg Cottage. Mary had started to suffer from ill heath and had needed the help of her neighbours, Thomas Gore and his mother Catherine to run the Post Office. The 1910 assessor valued the two cottages put together at £130. Described as a stone, brick and tile cottage containing 5 bedrooms, 5 living rooms, pigscot, privy, two cottages newly made into one, fair condition.

(Figure 89) Rosanna Britten; Note! The timber framed Burcott Row in the background. 1930s

When Mary Lewis died in 1912 Thomas Gore and his mother moved into the Post Office and the internal doorway was blocked up. Thomas married Mary Jane Griffiths in 1912 and between them they are listed in Kelly's Directory as either post master or post mistress living in the Post Office for the next 14 years.

Thomas Gore purchased The Post Office in the 1920 Foxley Sale. When he died in 1928 the cottage was inherited by Mr Millichip, who rented the cottage to Mrs Rosanna Britten, a widow. Her daughter Jessie Prosser had just lost her husband Charlie to consumption, he had worked for John Like Bishopstone Court. With her young son Tom, Jessie moved in with her mother. The shop at No 3 The Clovers closed in 1931 and seeing an opportunity, Mrs Britten with her daughter Jessie opened their village shop in the Old Post Office selling sweets and cigarettes etc. The shop ran for the next 32 years until 1963. Mrs Britten's other daughter Bessie was married to George Haines, they lived in Forge Cottage. Jessie also delivered the mail around the villages of Bishopstone, Byford and Bridge Sollers on her post bike throughout the 1950s; she would start from Bishopstone Post Office at 6am timed to arrive at Garnons House for 7am the latest time expected for their mail delivery.

Jessie sold the property to Mr and Mrs Vidler in 1967, they in turn sold it on to Jeff Smith the builder who built a new house in the garden and he then sold the cottage to Clive and Jo Jones.

(Figure 90) Jessie Prosser

The Clovers are three cottages in a row with an interesting history. In 1812 Jeremiah Apperley who was a wheelwright from Bishon Common bought three plots of land at auction. On the one plot he built a new brick house, the middle cottage of today's row and then moved his business up from the common. Jeremiah died in 1820. The Apperley family built an attached brick cottage nearer the road in around 1870. Then finally in the late 1890s built on the opposite end of the row a cottage and wheelwright shop.

(Figure 91) The Clovers in the early 1970s

The cottages were known by several names over the years: in 1870 the cottage nearest the road was called "Bone House", in the early 1900s they became "Morgans Row", this changed in 1920 to "The Row", then in 1930 "Shop Terrace" and finally in 1940 "The Clovers". In the early 1900s Frank Martz of 30 Commercial Street, Hereford purchased the three cottages for £420.

The assessor's book in 1910 describes No1 and 2 as two brick and tile cottages, two rooms up, two rooms down, pigscot and privy each and No 3 The Shop as two bedrooms, two box rooms, parlour kitchen, back kitchen, timber and tile cider mill, pigscot and privy. Market value of the three cottages was £440

(Figure 92) No.1 The Clovers

No 1 (nearest the road) was occupied in 1901 by Joseph Price, a farm labourer working at Bunshill Farm who lived with his wife Alice and their son Joseph. By 1910 Richard Lloyd, a farm labourer and his family lived in No 1. Richard's son Thomas rented the cottage after his father's death. During the First World War (Jack) his brother who is listed on the 1911 census, was sent from Bishopstone to work in the South Wales coalfields as a miner. The Lloyd family lived in the cottage until 1927. The next tenant was William Cartwright a bricklayer's labourer. He moved in with his wife May and son George, two other children were born at the Clovers including a daughter Joan born in 1935. Joan remembers walking to Kenchester School, and also fetching the rations of orange juice and cod-liver oil from Kenchester Rectory during the war; the Rector distributed the children's rations on behalf of the government. She can also remember walking up the village to collect fresh milk from the Walls, who always left a billy can of milk under the seat in their porch, Joan also collected her father's cigarettes from Mrs Prosser's shop.

(Figure 93) William Cartwright

At the start of the war William Cartwright was directed to work at the Munitions Works at Rotherwas; after many war years of cycling to work day and night he got fed up and moved the family to Park Street in 1943.

William's brother-in-law Bill Meadham and his wife Hilda followed the Cartwrights into No 1.

After the Second World War the house became vacant. Mrs Eagling takes up the story: *"The house was offered to Joyce and Arthur Portman but they didn't want it. We were living at Kenchester with the in-laws. Granny Mac told us about the house so we jumped at the chance as there were no houses available to rent after the war, we came in 1948 and stayed 18 years. The landlord of the Clovers was a man called Bradford, he bought the Row as an investment, the rent was £14 per year. I remember Rev Arrantash, he was an Australian, he came with a wife and a couple of children and after leaving the parish he moved back to Perth where he died. Clive repaired the Eagle's beak on the reader in the church and also made several book holders."* Clive and Maud Eagling were very active members of the community during their stay in Bishopstone. Clive ran the youth club from 1960-65, and his father Jack was the station master at Credenhill railway station for many years until its closure. Clive commuted to work in the 1960s riding a 150cc Francis Barnet motorcycle. After the Eaglings left the row was put up for sale.

No 2. In 1901 a widow named Harriet Baynham lived here; she was a dressmaker supporting herself by working from home. By 1910 John Samuel Simcock who worked as a platelayer on the railway lived in No 2, he died in Weobley Workhouse in August 1914, the unfortunate route of many poor people when they could no longer work and afford to pay the rent. Mrs Reade the widow of the Rev Compton-Reade, ex vicar of Kenchester and Bridge Sollers, then rented the property until 1925. Ray Jenkins who worked as a gardener at the Old Rectory followed her. George and Rose Morgan, in laws to Jim Gough followed Ray Jenkins, they lived in No 2 from 1927 until George died in February 1945. For a short period at the end of the Second World War Mr Ben Nation from London and his family rented the house; he was a conscientious objector, and not liked by the parishioners.

After the war No 2 became the home to ex R A F serviceman Albert(Abby) Kitching and his wife Barbara, they were tenants for the next 17 years until 1965. During this period Abbey worked as a stoker on the R A F camp Credenhill.

(Figure 94) Albert & Barbara Kitching

No 3 was occupied by William Davies in 1901, a wheelwright living with his wife Ellen, niece Ellen Smith and the apprentice wheelwright Alfred Lawrence aged 17 also lodged with them. The 1905 Kelly's Directory lists William Davies as operating a wheelwright and grocer's shop; his wheelwright business was failing, so he tried selling groceries and tobacco to help the finances but it did not work because by 1907 he had given up the lease. John Richard Jakeman became the new tenant, he too sold groceries, tobacco and homemade cider, which he produced from the cider mill in the outbuildings. In the 1911 census John and his wife Emily had taken in three lodgers to help pay the rent. They kept the shop going until 1919 when William Jones tried his hand at shop keeping for a couple of years.
John and Phoebe Jones were the next tenants in 1925, Phoebe ran the shop mostly as a tobacconist, it's hard nowadays to understand how a shop that sold mostly cigarettes and tobacco could survive but in the 1920's most adults smoked in one form or other. John(Jack) Jones came originally from Kenchester Mill, he was a miller and his wife Phoebe nee Jancey was a Bishopstonian. Jack died in 1931 enforcing the closure of the shop and Phoebe moved into the Almshouses.
Freddy Rounds lodged with the Jones family, he came to Bishopstone to work as a waggoner for Hamer's the Cottage Bishon Lane, they hauled timber from Garnons woods to Credenhill station or the Chemical works at Kenchester. Dad often told the story of how the children in the village were frightened by Fred bringing the horses home at dusk, riding the lead horse he would gallop at high speed through the village followed by six very large draught horses, the dust and the noise made by the horses making the children run to take cover. Fred married Phyllis, Jack's daughter, who was the organist at Bishopstone Church and they lived for many years afterwards in Bunshill Cottage.
Jim and Rose Gough lived in No 3 after the Jones, they were followed by Herbert and Winifred Payne and family who occupied the house just before the Second World War. Herbert Payne was a carpenter by trade; the Paynes had three children, Ruth, John and Margaret.The family lived in no 3 until 1969, when they left to live in Withington
The Clovers was advertised in the Hereford Times for sale in 1967, three cottages, one with a sitting tenant, plus 1 acre of orchard for £1200. It was purchased by Mr Davies who owned Green's the paper shop in Commercial Road. Herbert Payne and family moved out. Mr Davies sold the cottages on to the Verry brothers from Kings Thorne in the early 1970s. Firstly No 3 was purchased by John and Carol Verry, shortly after Nos 1 and 2 were purchased by Dave and Viv Verry. Mr Davies retained the ownership of the two orchards originally attached to the properties.

(Figure 95) No 3 The Clovers 1970s

Apperley's Cottage. Elizabeth Apperley built this cottage in 1820 to house her workman John Barnes after her husband died.
In 1901 Henry Apperley a bachelor lived in the cottage with his two unmarried sisters Elizabeth and Catherine; in 1906 he sold the one-acre plot to Sir John Cotterell who intended putting the new almshouses on the site but Rev Davenport had other ideas and donated a piece of ground in 1910 to the Berrington Trust to built the new almshouses on.
In 1907 Henry rented the cottage and workshop back from Sir John for £7 per year but the cottage and wheelwright workshop was falling into disrepair, so he moved down to the small cottage he owned on Bishon Common.
The 1910 assessor's value on the property was £118, land £88, cottage £30, described as stone and timber cottage with a tile roof, two rooms up, two rooms down, pigscot and privy in a decayed condition. The cottage was not lived in after 1908 and left abandoned, the garden and orchard turned into a scrubby wasteland. The one-acre site was purchased in 1925 by my grandfather Albert Macklin from the Garnons Estate, he cleared the land and built a new bungalow on it, known as The Knoll.
In 1977 this bungalow was demolished and a new house was built called Jolin, occupied by John and Jo Macklin.

The Cottage on Bishon lane was built by George Procter in 1837 with money loaned from Henry Edwards of Bunshill Farm; unable to repay the loan he sold his part for £100 to Henry Edwards who gained full possession. William Lloyd from Bishon Farm bought the house in 1855 at auction, after Henry Edwards death and named it "The Cottage".

(Figure 96) The Cottage in 2000

In 1900 The Cottage was still in the ownership of Caroline Lloyd, William's young second wife, who let out the house with four acres to old Henry Bowen who lived with his daughter Lucinda. The Cottage was recorded as a smallholding during the 25 years of Henry's occupancy, he also employed a farm labourer to help out. When Henry died in 1904 his daughter Lucinda kept on the tenancy until 1912 after which she moved into the new almshouses.

The value of the house in 1910 was £540, described as brick and slate roofed house, three rooms up, three rooms down and store. Brick noggin barn, cow house for three, stalls, stable for two, pigscot and privy in good repair.

Caroline Lloyd found a new tenant, Henry Hamer, a hauler and carrier and it became a very busy site with four men and boys operating carriages and working horses, and piles of timber and materials stacked on the surrounding land. The Hamers' main business was the haulage of large loads of timber. By 1920 Mrs Hamer now in her 80's lived with her two unmarried sons both in their 40s, and two unmarried daughters. Fred ran the timber haulage business and smallholding. Josh who had his leg amputated as a boy, never used an artificial leg but always walked with a crutch, he was trained as a tailor. Fred and Josh had good singing voices and both sang in the Hereford Three Choirs Festival. Nora was a music teacher and church organist and their sister Jane was the housekeeper.

(Figure 97) Arthur Haimes "standing on the left" as Chairman of the Parish Council accepting the award for the Best Kept Village award· 1958

When Caroline Lloyd died in 1925, Arthur Haimes purchased the property for £550 from her executors, and rented The Cottage out to Mr John Hartland and his wife Mary, he was a retired corn merchant and the original partner in the Hereford firm called Griffith & Hartland. My father remembers them as a couple in their 70s. Donald Watkins recalls *"They would serve afternoon tea on request, you had to pay"*. They left in the spring of 1939 when Arthur Haimes decided to live in the Cottage himself; he was the head gamekeeper for Sir John Cotterell, a job he had held since 1920, Arthur had previously lived in a tied house in Mansell Gamage. With him came his two sons and a stepdaughter Edith Bailey. Alec the eldest son was a schoolmaster, his other son Cecil died in the war, he was a carpenter. Edith was the housekeeper and post delivery girl throughout the war. Mr Arthur Haimes was chairman of Bishopstone's parish council from 1952-60, throughout the glory years of winning the Best Kept Village Competition; he also represented the parish on Weobley Rural District Council. Arthur became wheelchair bound just before he died in 1960. Edith had a new bungalow built called Tamarisk on a small meadow behind the Clovers. Edith and Alex sold The Cottage to Mr and Mrs Maund who came to Bishopstone with their son John. They also sold the orchard next to the house on the corner of Bishon Lane to Williams of Kings Acre Road, a builder who developed Canon Rise over a period of years building eight new bungalows. The Maund family held many memorable fund raising whist drives in their house. After Mr Maund died in 1972 their son John continued to live in the Cottage until his sudden death in 1993. The house was put up for sale and purchased by Mr and Mrs Smith. The Maund family retained the land attached to the Cottage.

(Figure 98) Audrey Smith sitting on the wing of Arthur Haines' Morris 8 car. Note! The pheasant mascot he used on the car. Audrey was born in Stone cottage Bishon Common

(Figure 99) Orphanage 1960

The Orphanage was built in 1731 by a carpenter named William Powell. For many years it had been a double dwelling until Rev Robbins purchased the property in 1870 and converted it into an orphanage for seven children and a matron, hence the name. When Rev Robbins left the parish in 1876 he sold the cottage to Rev Davenport.
The 1901 tenant was John Jones a miller who worked at Kenchester Mill. His wife Phoebe was formerly a Jancey, her family lived in a cottage on Bishon Common. Phoebe was a laundress working from home taking in other people's washing. Remember earlier from the parish council report, *"of washing water running down the lane"*, this had come from Phoebe's laundry.
The 1910 assessor put a value of £130 on the cottage, garden, meadow and orchard, total area 3 acres, occupied by John Jones since 1896, he paid £8 per year rent. Described as stone and slate roof house containing three bedrooms, two living rooms, two back kitchens, pigscot and privy in fair repair.
The 1911 census records that John Jones was now a farm labourer living with his wife Phoebe and their children, Christopher an apprentice blacksmith, Elsie, Phyllis and Marjorie who were all attending Kenchester School. After Christopher had served in the 1st World War he moved to Staunton on Wye, where he worked as the village blacksmith. The cottage was sold in the 1920 Foxley sale forcing the Jones family to move up to the shop at No 3 the Clovers.

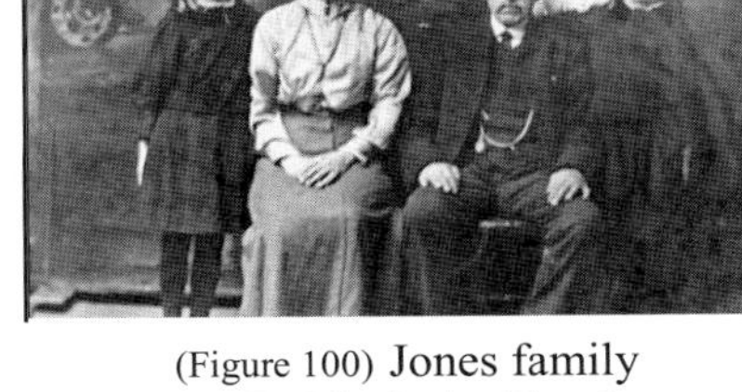

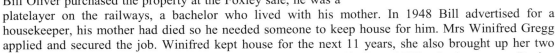

(Figure 100) Jones family L to R; Marjorie, Phoebe, Christopher, John, Elsie and Phyllis 1916

Bill Oliver purchased the property at the Foxley sale, he was a platelayer on the railways, a bachelor who lived with his mother. In 1948 Bill advertised for a housekeeper, his mother had died so he needed someone to keep house for him. Mrs Winifred Gregg applied and secured the job. Winifred kept house for the next 11 years, she also brought up her two granddaughters Sheila and Jillian in the cottage. During this period Winifred made cider and homemade spirits on the premises, she would also take by bus on a Wednesday any surplus eggs and garden produce to sell at the market. Bill had one straight finger caused by a wasp sting when he was young man; he also had a great liking for "tripe and onions". He died in 1956 and was buried in Stretton Sugwas churchyard. Mrs Gregg left the cottage in 1959. She died in 1973 aged 86 and was buried in Bishopstone churchyard.
In 1960 Mr Wintour a retired farmer with his son and two daughters Audrey and Nora became the new owners of the Orphanage and changed the name of the property to Cherry Trees.

(Figure 101) Cherry Trees 2000

Stone House Bishon Common was built in 1820 by Henry Edwards of Bunshill Farm to house his workmen; it was built on plot 29 awarded in the Enclosures of Commons Act. At some point before 1873 the barn on the side of the house was made into a cottage, making a double dwelling. Rev Davenport purchased the cottages from Caroline Lloyd in 1873. Stone House in 1901 was the home of Caroline Phipps a widow who lived with her daughter Olive and two bachelor sons, William who worked for the railway as a platelayer and Benjamin a carpenter. Walter, Caroline's husband had died in 1895. The family had worked and lived in Bishopstone since 1875, living at one time in Scaldback Cottage before moving to this cottage on the common. They rented 2 acres of land with the cottage in 1910 paying £9 per year to Rev Davenport. The value for the cottages in 1910 was £130 described as two stone and slate roofed cottages joined together, containing two rooms up, two rooms down, pigscot and privy each.

(Figure 102) Stone house 1952

The 1911 census lists Caroline as head of the family living with William and daughter Olive. William (Bill) Phipps worked on the railways until his premature death in 1928. My father remembered Bill, as being a larger than life character and well known at attending all the social events held in the parish.
Mrs Caroline Phipps purchased the cottages and 2 acres of land in the 1920 Foxley sale as a sitting tenant, she died in 1921 leaving the freehold to Bill her eldest son. After Bill died, the ownership of the cottages passed to Benjamin his brother who lived in Derby. Benjamin rented out the cottage to many different tenants, including Robert (Bob) Duffy who later in life returned to live in the village, and Tom Lewis whose father lived at The Stepps House.
In 1948, James (Jim) Suff who was living at the Mill Kenchester bought the two cottages and 2 acres of land for £600. He moved in with his wife Dorothy and four daughters, Dorothy, Gladys, Patricia and Frances. Jim worked on the R A F camp Credenhill; he was the most influential figure in having Bishon Lane accepted as a public road by the Herefordshire council by hauling tons of building rubble from Credenhill camp to make a solid base for the road. After the Suff family left in the 1980s the house had several owners before being purchased by Mr and Mrs David Scott.

(Figure 103) Stone Cottage 1950s

Stone Cottage, the other half of the cottage was occupied in 1901 by William Watkins, a general labourer working in the building trade who lived there with his wife Elizabeth. By 1910 Sarah Davies a widow was living in this half of the cottage paying a rent of £3 16s for a year.
This cottage had many tenants over the years. After the Second World War William (Bill) Bowen a builder's labourer with his wife and son Freddy lived in the property, followed by Muriel Linquist whose husband served in the R A F. The cottage became derelict for a period before being purchased and renovated by Martin and Diane Powell who sold the cottage in 1987 to Jim and Wyn Fisk.

Greentrees, was built in 1830 by John Clayton on enclosure award plot 35. It contained only two rooms, a timber framed structure with a thatch roof. It was not on the rating book because it was valued at under £20. Purchased by John Apperley soon after it was built, the property had passed through inheritance to Henry Apperley. In 1901 James Hargest a 73 year old was renting the cottage, he worked as a farm labourer on Bunshill Farm. He was living with his wife Eliza and daughters Ester and Edith.
Henry Apperley moved into the cottage in 1908 with his sister after selling the family home in Bishon. Henry enlarged the cottage and added his cider mill and the 1911 census records Henry aged 49 a wheelwright living with his sister Katherine. In 1925 the cottage was finally added to the rating list with the note *"not listed before under entry value."* After Henry Apperley died, Leslie and Phyllis Evans and family lived in the cottage, the thatch roof had been removed and replaced with a corrugated tin roof. In 1962 the Evans family took advantage of the £10 assisted emigration scheme and moved to Australia.

(Figure 104) Schoolgirls from the common L to R Annita Linquist, Frances Suff, Doreen Evans and Pat Suff. mid 1950s.

The next occupiers were Leonard and Edna Hill, who renovated the cottage and called it Green Trees, Mr and Mrs Eric Bone were the next owners, Eric was a retired chemist.

(Figure 105) Greentrees 2000

Cottage, the last cottage on the left down Bishon Lane in Bishopstone parish was a timber and thatch cottage, two rooms up and two rooms down. Elizabeth Williams built the cottage around 1820 on the enclosure award plot 36 and her descendant Mr R Withed "The Ridge" Staunton on Wye owned the freehold in 1900.

In 1901 William Jancey rented the cottage, he worked on the railway as a platelayer. William was the brother of Phoebe Jones who lived at the Orphanage. He lived with his wife Sarah and their two sons Francis and William, paying a rent of £3 per year. They were the last people to occupy the cottage.
By 1910 the cottage had fallen down, the assessor valued the property as being worth £20 and described it as an old tumble down cottage unfit for habitation. It was demolished soon after.

There were four other cottages on Bishon Common in 1900 although not in Bishopstone, three were attached to Bunshill Farm and owned by Guys Hospital, the other was a freehold cottage. Only a very small area of Bishon Common is in Bishopstone, the majority is in Mansel Lacy Parish with the rest in Brinsop parish. Before the Enclosure Act it was called Lower Mansel Common. Historically these cottages have always been associated with Bishopstone, more so after the railway was built, cutting them off from their respective parishes. One pair of cottages, nos 17 and 18 were in Brinsop and the other two cottages nos 15 and 16 in Mansel Lacy. Who numbered the cottages and when, I'm not sure, but they were certainly used as postal addresses after the Second World War. .

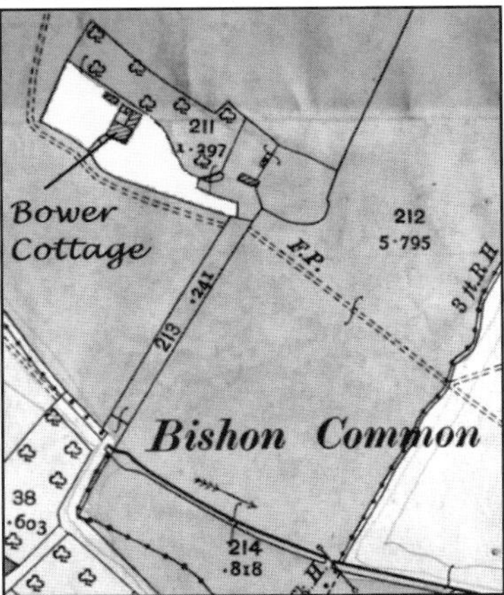

No 15 was called Bower Cottage in 1900, it was a cottage enclosed out of Bishon Common in the parish of Mansel Lacy owned by George Evans a gardener. In 1907 George Evans, then aged 84, sold Bower Cottage for an annuity of 6s per week, a popular practice at the time because it gave the elderly a regular income since there was as yet no old age pension. Bill Lucas the blacksmith lodged with George until he died on December 15th 1914 and the cottage and land were sold to Guys Hospital for £110[7]. After Guy's Hospital purchased the cottage it was used to house Bunshill's farm workers. Alfred and Mary Thomas were the first tenants, followed by Frank and Mary Ellen Hill who lived there from 1925-1933 when Frank gave up his job as a waggoner to work for the railway they moved up to Scaldback. Henry and Elizabeth Symonds spent some of the Second World War years in the cottage.

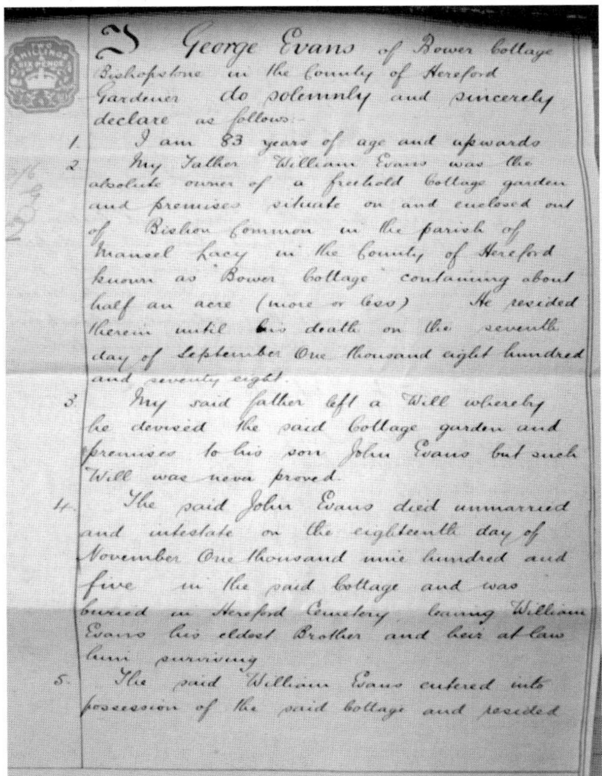
George Evans of Bower Cottage Bishopstone in the County of Hereford Gardener do solemnly and sincerely declare as follows:

1. I am 83 years of age and upwards
2. My Father William Evans was the absolute owner of a freehold Cottage garden and premises situate on and enclosed out of Bishon Common in the parish of Mansel Lacy in the County of Hereford known as "Bower Cottage" containing about half an acre (more or less) He resided therein until his death on the seventh day of September One thousand eight hundred and seventy eight.
3. My said father left a Will whereby he devised the said Cottage garden and premises to his son John Evans but such Will was never proved.
4. The said John Evans died unmarried and intestate on the eighteenth day of November One thousand nine hundred and five in the said Cottage and was buried in Hereford Cemetery leaving William Evans his eldest Brother and heir at law him surviving
5. The said William Evans entered into possession of the said Cottage and resided

(Figure 106) Part of the hand written deed of Bower Cottage a common practice on cottage properties that had never carried any deeds

Dan Carpenter came to work at Bunshill farm in May 1947 with his wife Frances and five children, they lived in No 16 for a short period before moving to No 15, described by Rose their youngest daughter as a larger cottage with an orchard. The children, Phyllis, Davey, Bill, Edward and Rose all grew up in No 15. Bill, Eddy and Rose all worked in the bread trade; Bill was a baker for Meredith Bakery at Credenhill, Eddy and Rose were on the delivery.
Davey their eldest brother was a character; he worked for Ivor Johnson at the Knapp farm and was a regular frequenter of the Nelson Inn where many tales of his antics were recalled. He once featured in the national press, because he fell off his bike "under the influence" in front of a police car and was arrested for his own safekeeping. His excuse was that his left pocket was full of walnuts and the weight of the nuts made him fall off his bike. He also fell into a potato-raising machine, and to everyone's amazement was expelled out of the back of the machine completely naked except for his leather belt, much to the amusement of the lady potato picker who witnessed the event. The machine had torn his clothes off, but because he was completely relaxed he escaped unharmed.

Another tale happened one winter's night. In his usual haunt he asked Ian Astley who was building his new bungalow in the village how he came to the pub. *"Walked along the main road"* was the reply. *"No need to walk that long way home"* says Davey *"I will show you a short cut up to the village".* Leaving the bar after Davey had drunk a good few pints of rough cider, he says *"follow me"* making his way up through the back orchard of the pub. It was a pitch-black night. Davey struggled over the first stile and staggered on up the field. Fifty paces further on he let out a shriek *"Stop Ian! Water has just touched my boll---s I've walked into the bloody pond".*

Another tale Rose told me about her brother, when they lived on Bishon Common Davey would often arrive home with his trousers wet up to the knees and his mother would say to him, *"You've seen three bridges over the brook and picked the wrong one to cross again."* Davey passed away in June 1989.

The Carpenters left the cottage in March 1964 and moved to Breinton, they were the last occupiers of Bower Cottage before it was demolished.

(Figure 107) Frances Carpenter outside No 15.

(Figure 108) Rudd brothers;
L to R. Ron, Frank, Ernie, Jo and Eddy.1940s

No 16 was originally the site of a small farm, which was integrated with Bunshill Farm in 1754. A small two up and two down brick cottage, was built on the site around the beginning of the 19th century.

Walter and Elizabeth Rudd came to live in No 16 in 1914. Walter worked as a platelayer on the railway and when he was conscripted into the Royal Engineers in 1916 Elizabeth moved back to Stretton Sugwas for the duration of the war. On Walter's return from the war the family moved back into No 16 and lived in the cottage until 1935. Walter and Elizabeth had seven children while living on the common, they all attended Kenchester School and the boys Eddy, Ron, Frank, Ernie and Jo served in the 2nd World War. Charles and Ada Weaver occupied this cottage in 1945. After the war there were many occupiers including John and Phyllis (nee Carpenter) Simpson followed by Bill and Ruth Mitchell who were the last occupiers, they moved out in 1965 to a new council house in the village. The cottage was demolished soon afterwards.

No 17; George Powell railway platelayer, moved into No 17 with his wife Mary and children William, Edith and Ada in 1915, he was conscripted in 1916 and served as a sapper in Royal Engineers like his neighbour Walter Rudd. The family lived in the cottage until 1934 when George and Mary moved to Abergavenny. In 1945 Howard and Catherine Hale move in to No 17, Howard became the parish roadman a job he carried out for the next twenty years. A lot of parishioners, especially the school children when on their way to and from school will remember him sat in the hedge drinking cold tea from a bottle. Mrs Hale died in 1965.

(Figure 109) No 17 & 18. 1950s

(Figure 110) Alice Gregory

No 18; William Roberts, a farm labourer lived in the cottage before the First World War. James Whiting, my great grandfather, a nursery man who worked for Kings Acre Nurseries, rented No 18 from 1919-23. James was joined in January 1920 by Albert Macklin my grandfather a plumber, painter and decorator, his wife Alice and their son Cecil, my father. In 1922 Albert's nephew Arthur Portman joined the family before they moved up to Burcott Row. In 1938 Cyril and Alice Gregory moved into No 18 with their children Irene, John, Harold and Marian, Cyril was a gardener at Edgecomb Swainshill and died when his children were young.

Alice lived on the common before she was married, her parents the Potts had moved onto the common in 1929, she lived in No 18 for the next 27 years, finally moving to a new council house in the village in 1965

No's 17 and 18 were purchased by David and Sue Scott in the 1970's; they had the cottages rebuilt, extended and renamed Bishon House

Bunshill Farm can trace its history back to the Domesday Book, when it was a manor under its own right. In 1901 the tenant of the farm was Elizabeth Elliott aged 61, she lived with her son Walter and daughter Bertha having taken over the tenancy when her husband John died. John was not quite as successful as his father, although a good farmer he had a timid disposition. Elizabeth Elliott did not suffer the same attitudes as her husband; she attended the first parish council meeting in 1894 and served as overseer to the poor for the following two years. Elizabeth Elliot vacated the farm in 1905. The new tenant in 1906 was John Edward Lewis; the 1910 survey shows a new barn, but not much else had changed.

(Figure 111) Granary

In 1910 the assessor's value for the farm was £9,593; the tenant John Edward Lewis paid a rent of £395 a year to Guy's Hospital and it was listed as a farm with house, buildings and five workmen's cottages plus 249 acres of land. The three storey brick farm house had a slate roof, containing hall, dining room, sitting room, kitchen, scullery, dairy, wash room, underground cellar, on the first floor five bedrooms, on the second floor five bedrooms; in fair repair.

Outbuildings: pan tile and brick feeding shed, three pigscots, timber and pan tile granary, 6 bay corn barn, brick and tile barn and mixing house, stock house, wood and slate stables with loft over, brick and timber wainhouse and feeding house, cow house. *"Bunshill Farm in 1910 had a team of twelve horses to farm the 250 acres. Before the first war the land was mainly farmed for the production of milk, which was sold to the Cheese Factory at the Knapp Farm, Bridge Sollers. During the first war women were employed on this farm at the rate of 3d and 4d per hour".* Extract from the W I book of local memories[8].

The 1911 census of Bunshill Farm reveals John Lewis a farmer aged 52 living with Elizabeth his wife to whom he had only been married for 4 years. The household staff consisted of Thomas Worthing, a groom, and Francis Bethell, a general servant. Elizabeth, whose maiden name was Smith, started a family line of tenants who still occupy the farm today. John Lewis of Bunshill Farm gave up his tenancy with Guy's Hospital in 1919. John had served on the parish council and held the position of overseer for five years. The new tenant to take on the farm was his brother in law Thomas Smith with his wife Gertrude. Tom became the new overseer of the poor for four years from 1920-24 and was also appointed trustee to the Ann Berrington Charity in 1928.

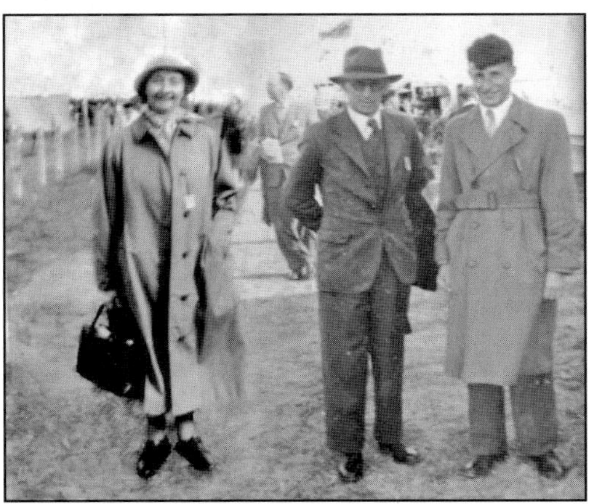

(Figure 112) 1956 Herbert & Hilda Smith and their son Geoffrey at the last Three County Show held on Hereford racecourse.

Thomas held the tenancy until 1944, Herbert his younger brother became the next tenant.

Geoff Smith recalls *"We came in 1944, Uncle Tom and Aunty retired to a house on Kings Acre Road, he left behind a blue Fordson tractor. We only used it for ploughing, all the other farm work was carried out by our four working horse. Dad thought that the tractor was too heavy and compacted the ground. Dad came from the "Batch" farm near Weobley, I was born there. Grandad had seven children, Mrs Lewis who first rented the farm in 1910 was dad's eldest sister, her brother Tom took over the tenancy followed by my father who was the youngest of the family."*

Herbert Smith died in January 1969, he had been the tenant of Bunshill for over 30 years. Geoff married Margaret Barrell and are now the tenants of Bunshill they have two children Anthony and Alison.

In 1961 Guys Hospital put all their Herefordshire estates up for sale including Bunshill. Charles Clore purchased all the Herefordshire Estate; since then the estate ownership has changed twice , firstly they passed to the Prudential, and now to the Duchy of Cornwall.

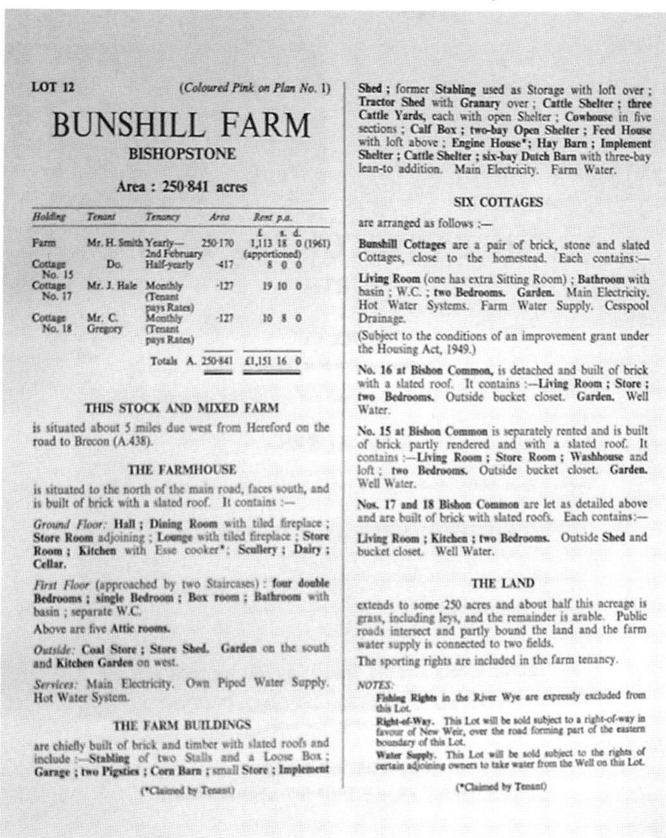

LOT 12 *(Coloured Pink on Plan No. 1)*

BUNSHILL FARM

BISHOPSTONE

Area : 250·841 acres

Holding	*Tenant*	*Tenancy*	*Area*	*Rent p.a.* £ s. d.
Farm	Mr. H. Smith	Yearly— 2nd February	250·170	1,113 18 0 (1961) (apportioned)
Cottage No. 15	Do.	Half-yearly	·417	8 0 0
Cottage No. 17	Mr. J. Hale	Monthly (Tenant pays Rates)	·127	19 10 0
Cottage No. 18	Mr. C. Gregory	Monthly (Tenant pays Rates)	·127	10 8 0
		Totals A.	250·841	£1,151 16 0

THIS STOCK AND MIXED FARM

is situated about 5 miles due west from Hereford on the road to Brecon (A.438).

THE FARMHOUSE

is situated to the north of the main road, faces south, and is built of brick with a slated roof. It contains :—

Ground Floor: **Hall ; Dining Room** with tiled fireplace ; **Store Room** adjoining ; **Lounge** with tiled fireplace ; **Store Room ; Kitchen** with Esse cooker*; **Scullery ; Dairy ; Cellar.**

First Floor (approached by two Staircases) : **four double Bedrooms ; single Bedroom ; Box room ; Bathroom** with basin ; separate W.C.

Above are five **Attic rooms.**

Outside: **Coal Store ; Store Shed. Garden** on the south and **Kitchen Garden** on west.

Services: Main Electricity. Own Piped Water Supply. Hot Water System.

THE FARM BUILDINGS

are chiefly built of brick and timber with slated roofs and include :—**Stabling** of two Stalls and a Loose Box ; **Garage ; two Pigsties ; Corn Barn ;** small **Store ; Implement Shed ;** former **Stabling** used as Storage with loft over ; **Tractor Shed** with **Granary** over ; **Cattle Shelter ; three Cattle Yards,** each with open Shelter ; **Cowhouse** in five sections ; **Calf Box ; two-bay Open Shelter ; Feed House** with loft above ; **Engine House*; Hay Barn ; Implement Shelter ; Cattle Shelter ; six-bay Dutch Barn** with three-bay lean-to addition. Main Electricity. Farm Water.

SIX COTTAGES

are arranged as follows :—

Bunshill Cottages are a pair of brick, stone and slated Cottages, close to the homestead. Each contains:—

Living Room (one has extra Sitting Room) ; **Bathroom** with basin ; W.C. ; **two Bedrooms. Garden.** Main Electricity. Hot Water Systems. Farm Water Supply. Cesspool Drainage.

(Subject to the conditions of an improvement grant under the Housing Act, 1949.)

No. 16 at Bishon Common, is detached and built of brick with a slated roof. It contains :—**Living Room ; Store ; two Bedrooms.** Outside bucket closet. **Garden.** Well Water.

No. 15 at Bishon Common is separately rented and is built of brick partly rendered and with a slated roof. It contains :—**Living Room ; Store Room ; Washhouse** and loft ; **two Bedrooms.** Outside bucket closet. **Garden.** Well Water.

Nos. 17 and 18 Bishon Common are let as detailed above and are built of brick with slated roofs. Each contains:—

Living Room ; Kitchen ; two Bedrooms. Outside **Shed** and bucket closet. Well Water.

THE LAND

extends to some 250 acres and about half this acreage is grass, including leys, and the remainder is arable. Public roads intersect and partly bound the land and the farm water supply is connected to two fields.

The sporting rights are included in the farm tenancy.

NOTES:

Fishing Rights in the River Wye are expressly excluded from this Lot.

Right-of-Way. This Lot will be sold subject to a right-of-way in favour of New Weir, over the road forming part of the eastern boundary of this Lot.

Water Supply. This Lot will be sold subject to the rights of certain adjoining owners to take water from the Well on this Lot.

(*Claimed by Tenant)

(Figure 113) Page of the 1961 sale brochure

Bunshill Cottages were built in the 1850s by Guys Hospital, to house Bunshill's farm workers. In the 1901 census James Crump a shepherd lived there with his wife Elizabeth and their son Alfred. James worked at Bunshill farm and the other half of the double dwelling was unoccupied. The 1910 value was not listed, as the cottages were part of the farm value. Described as a double dwelling cottage, stone with a tile roof containing two rooms up and two rooms down, privy and pigscot each. In 1911 the cottages were both fully occupied, one by Charles Skyrme, a waggoner on the farm and his wife Mary who lived with their five young children. Next door lived Edward Neath, a cowman, with his wife Jeannie and young daughter Emily.

No 1 Bunshill cottage: In 1930 Alfred Rounds married Phyllis Jones who lived at the Clovers Shop, they moved into No 1 Bunshill Cottage where the family lived on and off for the next thirty years.

Shirley Wadley, daughter of Fred and Phyllis remembers *"My granny ran the shop at the Clovers, grandfather was a miller, mum went to the high school, she played the organ at Bishopstone Church from the age of 16. Dad worked on the railway, in the war it was a protected occupation so he never joined the military but he was in the Stretton Sugwas Home Guard. Mr Peake lodged with us for as long as I can remember. The Moffat's lived next door; Jimmy Moffat joined the Army as a career soldier and rose rapidly through the ranks, he has now retired after years of service. Your mother and mine were at the High School together, I will always remember your mum laughing at this tale: when my mum was at school she sat on some pig fat, Granny washed the tunic and hung it on the line, when she returned the pig had eaten the tunic whole."*

(Figure 114) Rounds family L to R Shirley, Fred, Steve, Margary and Phillis

Mr Peake who lived with the Round family had mysterious air about him, we would meet him on the road wearing fine clothes, rolled umbrella and bowler hat. As children we always thought it rather strange dress for a farm labourer, explained now by the fact he was an official of the Order of Foresters and was always attending meetings in Hereford.

No 2 Bunshill Cottages was the home of many farm labourers who worked on Bunshill Farm throughout the 1920s and 30s, including the Baugh and Harris families. James Thomas lived in the cottage throughout the Second World War; his daughter Ethel was one of only two women from Bishopstone who served in the military during the war, they retired to the Almshouses in the village. The Moffats came to Bunshill in 1947 the same time as Ben Carpenter, both worked on the farm.

Chapter 14
1900 to 1950

At the beginning of the 20th century Bishopstone's farmers were still suffering from the grip of the long depression which had started in the 1870s, huge quantities of grain from America and Canada flooded onto the market and the price of corn fell. New advances in refrigeration also affected the livestock price, cheaper meat could now be imported from as far away as New Zealand. Although the parish was suffering financially, Great Britain as a country was booming at the turn of the 20th century Queen Victoria was monarch of an empire where the sun never set.

This agricultural depression marked a change in traditional agricultural ways, with a decline in the number of people working the fields, especially the younger generation; many of the young men had left agriculture for new careers in workshops and factories. This is clearly evident by the population returns of Bishopstone parish, in 1901, 181 persons were registered as living in the parish, 108 less than in the farming prosperity boom of the 1860s. This decline in Bishopstone's population continued in 1911 with 165 persons living in the parish, while by 1931 this figure had dropped to an all-time low of 130.

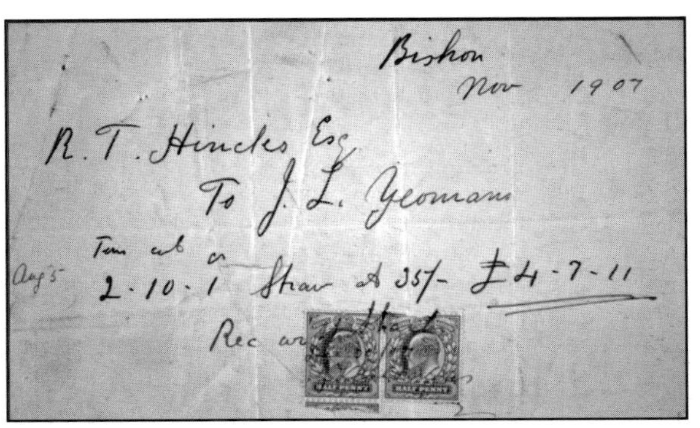
Bishon
Nov 1907
R.T. Hinckes Esq
To J.L. Yeomans
Tons cwt qr
Aug 5 2.10.1 Straw at 35/- £4-7-11
Rec

(Figure 1) Straw bill Bishon Farm 1907

The 1911 census confirmed the decline in the parish's dependence on agriculture: 19 farm workers were listed, including shepherds, waggoners, cowmen and labourers. 12 farm workers were heads of households, all living in tied cottages, the other 7 farm workers were either sons of the above or lodgers.

The occupations of the other parishioners were wide and varied: 8 worked as domestic gardeners either at the Rectory or on Garnons Estate, the railway company employed 6 parishioners and 3 others were employed at the chemical factory Kenchester.

The tradespersons living in Bishopstone parish in 1911 were two carriers, a blacksmith, wheelwright, carpenter, innkeeper, grocer and post mistress plus a land agent and a clergyman, the last two listed as gentry.

Bishopstone was not an isolated case. Herefordshire as a whole was suffering from this agricultural depression which had started a decline in the English country house estates, with many being broken up and sold off. The evidence of the demise of these large estates can be found in a Hereford Times issue for January 1900, which lists Herefordshire properties for sale: there were 20 estates, 24 farms, 75 country houses and 200 houses and cottages.

Foxley estate managed to remain intact until the death of Rev Davenport in 1919. Ralph Davenport who was Reverend Davenport's only son changed his name by licence to Hinckes in 1895 so he could take the inheritance of his father's brother, Harry Hinckes. Harry Hinckes himself had changed his name to Hinckes by licence in 1890 in compliance with the will of Miss Theodosia Hinckes. Harry died in 1895. Miss Theodosia Hinckes in her will of 1874 stated that only a person with the surname Hinckes could inherit her estates. The Davenport family were through marriage the rightful beneficiaries of her estates, so to overcome this clause in the will it was simpler to change the surname. Theodosia Hinckes left in her will Tettenhall Wood mansion house in Staffordshire and estates in Shropshire and Herefordshire plus two coal collieries.

Ralph Hinckes travelled extensively to many parts of the world to study farming methods, he wrote several books and papers on the subject. Ralph was committed to the military and served as a Captain in the Herefordshire Regiment as a volunteer.

The Hereford Journal in 1900 reported Captain Hinckes of Foxley being with the Hay Volunteers D Company, who were part of the Herefordshire Regiment. On July 14th 1900 Captain Hinckes and 88 men left Hay on the 4.30 train for a camp in Salisbury where they were preparing for action in the Boer War. The ladies of Hay had collected money and as a memento each man was given a belt, a purse, a briar pipe and a sum of money varying between £4 and £4 10s.

In 1902 Captain Hinckes purchased a petrol engined Star motorcar made in Wolverhampton to replace his first motor vehicle that had been steam driven, this was the first petrol car to be seen regularly in the area. The Star was part exchanged in 1907 against a new 18/24 HP Peugeot, a luxury car of the time which cost a staggering £948 10s 8d with all the accessories. An allowance of £200 was given for the old Star car. (In 1910 £900 could purchase three pairs of cottages similar to Cambrai Cottage in Bishopstone). As well as the initial cost these early cars carried extremely expensive running costs, the Peugeot needed an engine rebuild after 3 years costing £104.

By 1913 the value of the Peugeot reg no LN908 had dropped to £200. A chauffeur called Harrison was hired to drive the car for the first few days after its purchase at a cost of £1 1s a day, petrol cost £1 0s 4d a gallon bought in cans. Both these figures represent more than a weeks wages for an average farm worker. The laying of Gore Macadam on the main road (A438) was first used in 1915 at a cost of 7s 4d a ton; at the same time James Fryer, motor engineers, were advertising in the Hereford Times a Ford Universal car with two seats £115, five seats £125. A new B S A gents bicycle cost £14 in 1905, well out of the reach of most labourers. A Gurneys' grocery bill dated 1905 shows 2lb of butter cost 3s, tin of coca 9d, leg of lamb 6s 10d, Peamans oats 6d lb.

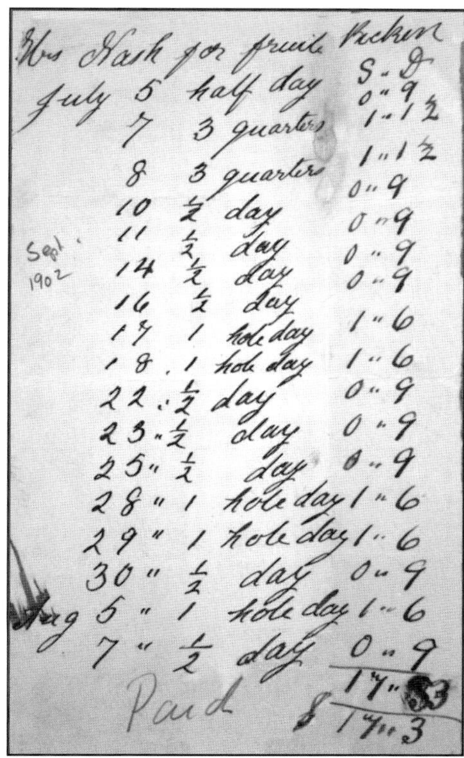

Mrs Nash for fruit Pickin

			S - d
July	5	half day	0 " 9
	7	3 quarters	1 " 1½
	8	3 quarters	1 " 1½
	10	½ day	0 " 9
	11	½ day	0 " 9
	14	½ day	0 " 9
	16	½ day	0 " 9
	17	1 hole day	1 " 6
	18	1 hole day	1 " 6
	22	½ day	0 " 9
	23	½ day	0 " 9
	25	½ day	0 " 9
	28	1 hole day	1 " 6
	29	1 hole day	1 " 6
	30	½ day	0 " 9
Aug	5	1 hole day	1 " 6
	7	½ day	0 " 9
			17 " 3

Paid £ 17 " 3

Sept 1902

(Figure 2) 1902 fruit picking bill

The wages paid by Joseph Yeomans, "Bishon Farm" in 1910, were: labourers 2s 6d a day, top rate "waggoner" 3s a day, boy 8d a day, fruit picking day rate 1s 6d. The farm workers' wives or any other person in the village could earn a few shillings fruit picking, mostly apples for cider in the autumn.

The Old Age Pension Act was introduced in 1908

David Lloyd George was an opponent of the poor law in Britain; he was determined to take action that would in his words "lift the shadow of the workhouse from the homes of the poor". He believed the best way of doing this was to guarantee an income to those people who were too old to work. In 1908 Lloyd George introduced the Old Age Pensions Act that provided between 1s and 5s a week to people over seventy. These pensions were only paid to citizens on incomes that were not over 12s a week.

Bishopstone's records suggest it is possible that this Act had the reverse effect on the poor of the parish; many more elderly residents were institutionalised into the workhouse and asylum after the Act, where they were readily accepted because their pension money would pay for their keep. Between 1849 and 1906, ten Bishopstone parishioners died in the workhouse or asylum, after the Act was introduced between 1913 and 1917 eight died in these institutions.

At the 1907 Bishopstone parish council[1] meeting the chairman read a circular from the county council asking how many smallholdings were in the parish and if there was a need for any more. After the meeting a report sent back to the council, stated that in Bishopstone parish there were eleven smallholdings; The Stepps Farm, Kenowly, Townsend, Scaldback, The Rectory, Bridge Ash, The Nelson, Stonehouse (Bishon), The Pleck, The Cottage Bishon lane and Stonehouse on the common. No formal demand had been received by the parish council for any further holdings and there was no unoccupied land available. In order to provide housing for John Like's (Court Farm) workers Rev Davenport built two new three-bedroom farm workers cottages in 1907 next to Bishopstone Church. The first occupiers were George Griffiths, a waggoner with his wife and three children in No 1, and George Gladwyn a cowman, his wife and four children occupying No 2.

(Figure 3) Church Cottages

(Figure 4) Church Cottages plaques

Many farm workers lived in the cottages over the years, Henry Warburton and Cyril Bevan before the Second World War, and Jim Careless and Harry Heath after the war, they were all employees of the Lewis family. With a new tenant of the farm, Bob Carrington in 1955, new workers came to live in the cottages including Ben Stevens and Ben Lloyd. Ben Lloyd was a trusted employee of Bob Carrington who moved to Carmarthenshire to manage Bob's newly purchased farm in 1963. Ben Stevens died suddenly whilst working in the fields leaving a wife and five children. Mrs Stevens left the cottage in 1969 to live in Hereford.

(Figure 5) Ben Lloyd and Margaret Carrington leading a Hereford bull 1958

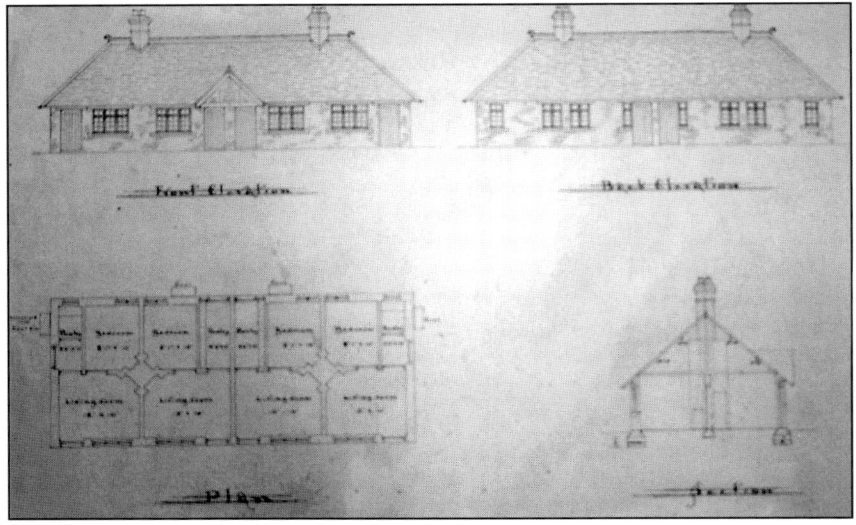

(Figure 6) Original plans of the proposed new Almshouses

C W Preece Builders started work on the new almshouses on September 23rd 1910, plans for the building were drawn up under the guidance of Sir John Cotterell[2]. The land on which the new almshouses were built was donated by Rev Davenport and his son, it was valued at £12. The almshouses were built over a period of three years, completion was held up by financial problems until Rev Davenport stepped in to complete the project. The old almshouses were pulled down in the summer of 1913, and care was taken to retrieve the original commemorative stone from its front gable so it could be built into the new almshouses.

The cost of building the almshouses was £417 10s; this money was raised by the sale of the original site and buildings to Sir John Cotterell who paid a generous £200, together with a gift of money from Rev Davenport. Each house contained one living room, one bedroom, pantry, a privy at the bottom of garden and a communal washhouse and shed for all to use. A communal washhouse was part of the original almshouses design, built in the rear gardens to provide amenities for clothes washing.

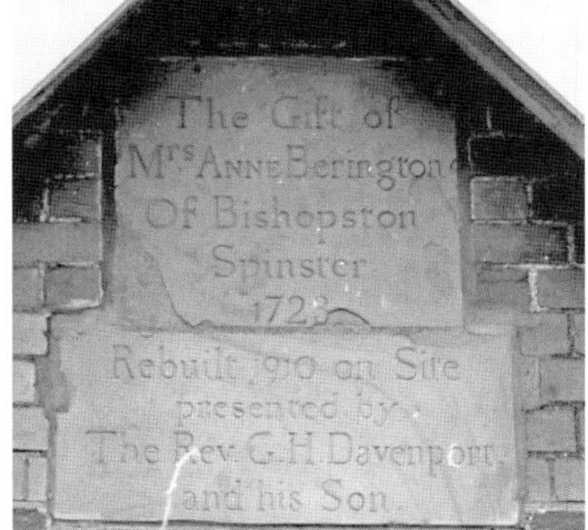

(Figure 7) Stone plaque

The rules to qualify for a place in the almshouses were also changed for the new occupiers. "The houses are for aged men or women who from old age, ill heath, accident or infirmity are unable to maintain themselves; each occupier must be a member of the Church of England and have lived in the parish of Bishopstone for at least two years. Each occupant lives rent free and receives a small pension and a Christmas gift of coal, boots, beef and dress allowance". Note! The Christmas gifts of goods were slowly replaced over the years by giving a small amount of money.

(Figure 8) Almshouses 1940s

After the building was completed Ann Vaughan, Jane Waithe, Richard Collins, the three original residents from the old almshouses moved in, with one new person Lucretia Bowen who formerly lived in The Cottage, Bishon Lane.

John Apperley, a resident of the old almshouse had died in May 1913 just before they moved down from the hill. Richard Collins lived in the new almshouses for only a few months before he was sectioned to the Lunatic Asylum where he died shortly afterwards in February 1914.

The occupiers of the almshouse would receive two loaves of bread free every month as part of the Ann Martin Bread charity attached to Bishon Farm.

To name the occupiers of the new almshouses over the twentieth century would be to compile a list of over 30 people but it is safe to say that the Ann Berrington Almshouses provided a safe home for many elderly, mostly widowed Bishopstonians throughout these years.

(Figure 9) Harry Jones standing in the doorway of No 2 the Almshouses in 1960

The Berrington Trust re-registered the new almshouses with the Charity Commission in 1911 so replacing the original charity first registered with the commissioners in 1877.

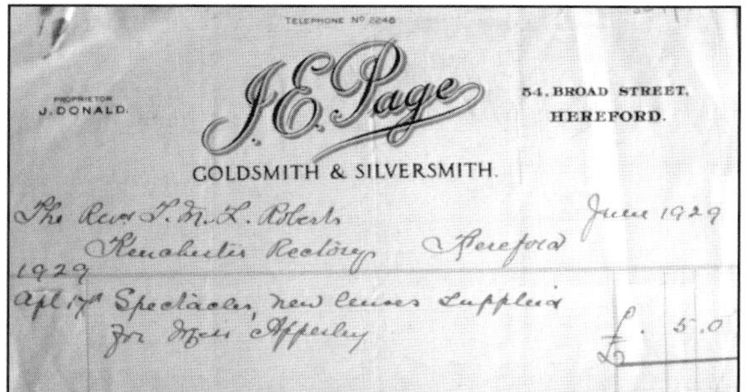

TELEPHONE No 2248

PROPRIETOR J. DONALD.

J. E. Page

54, BROAD STREET, HEREFORD.

GOLDSMITH & SILVERSMITH.

June 1929

1929 Apl 17th Spectacles, new lenses supplied for Mrs Apperley £ 5.0

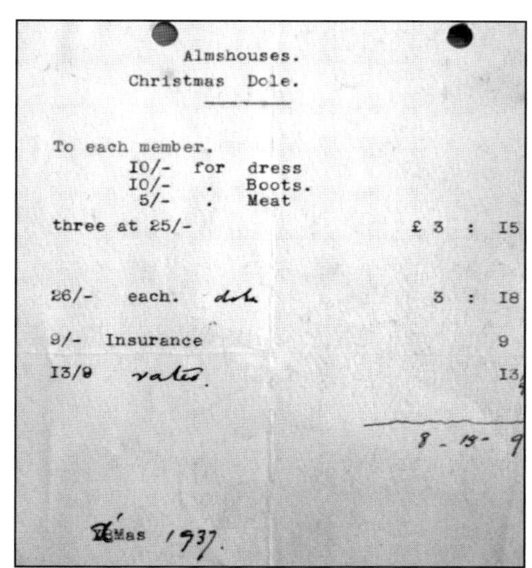

Almshouses.
Christmas Dole.

To each member.
10/- for dress
10/- . Boots.
5/- . Meat

three at 25/-	£ 3 : 15
26/- each. dole	3 : 18
9/- Insurance	9
13/9 rates.	13
	8 - 15 - 9

Xmas 1937.

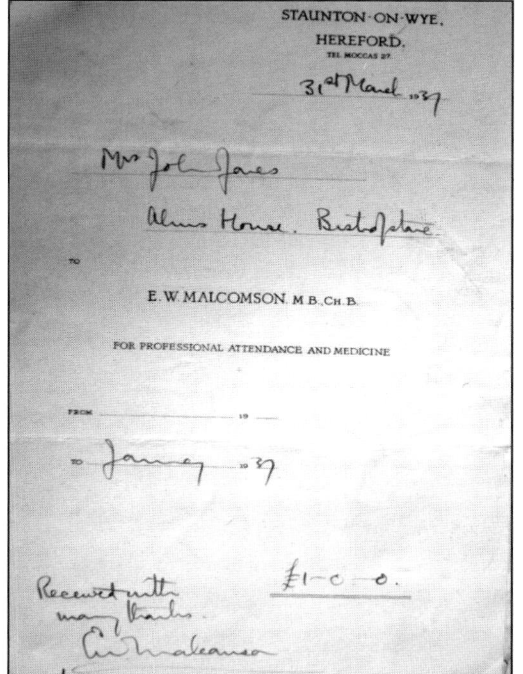

STAUNTON-ON-WYE,
HEREFORD.
TEL. MOCCAS 27

31st March 1937

Mrs John Jones
Alms House. Bishopstone

TO E.W. MALCOMSON M.B., CH.B.

FOR PROFESSIONAL ATTENDANCE AND MEDICINE

FROM ... 19 ...

TO January 1937

£1-0-0.

Received with many thanks
E.W. Malcomson

Ann Berrington's Charity.
Xmas 1943

Mrs Watkins 1-5-0 Christmas Gift
1-6-0 Quarter's Income

Mrs Jones. 1-5-0 + 1-6-0

Mrs Stinton 1-5-0 + 1-6-0

Miss Apperley 1-5-0 Christmas Gift

1-6-0 to be returned to Bank

Miss Apperley died on Dec. 28th

CREDENHILL, Oct 1st 1928

Bishopstone Almshouses

Bought of A. REESE & Co.
(Late D. PEARCE).

COAL, COKE, AND LIME MERCHANTS.

TERMS—CASH MONTHLY.

	T.	C.	Q.	Description	£	s.	d.
1927 Dec 23	10-0			Stinton Coal Hauling			
	10-0			Apperley " "			
1928 Jan 31	10-0			Stinton " "			
March 20	10-0			Apperley " "			
	2 0 0			Tons. 40/-	4	0	0

Paid H Reese Dec 10 1928 With thanks

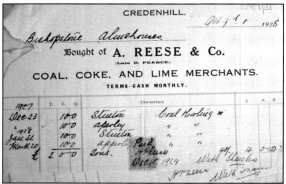

(Figure 10) A few bills from the Almshouses from 1920s to 1940s. Top left; new glasses for Kate Apperley, below a doctors bill both before the N H S. Above right, Christmas dole and a Reese coal bill at 40s a ton.

Woolhope Club visit to Bishopstone[3] and surrounding villages.

On Thursday, June 26th 1913 the Woolhope Naturalists' Field Club, held their second field meeting, a walk from Credenhill Station through Kenchester, Bishopstone and Mansell Gamage before catching the evening train back to Hereford from Moorhampton Station. I have abbreviated the full report from their 1913 year book, but it does include some interesting bits on Bishopstone and the travel arrangements.

70 people disembarked at Credenhill station at 9.30 and headed for the site of Magna Castra a quarter mile away. We were on the site of Magna Castra well before 10 o'clock and inspected the excavation of Mr G H Jack and Mr. H. E. Jones who have been working on the site for the last 18 months, the most interesting features of this buried city laid bare for inspection. A vote of thanks was given by Mr. Jack to the owner of the site Mr. Hardwick and his tenant Mr. A J Whiting for affording the club facilities for excavating on this historic spot. After inspecting the site for half an hour the visitors moved off on foot in the direction of Bishopstone, traversing an old Roman roadway adorned at intervals by cottage gardens displaying a wealth of old-fashioned flowers very pleasing to the eye. The Rectory was the next place of call, by invitation of the Reverend R H Wilmot, whose charming old house with its quaint chimneys occupies the site of a Roman villa. Here we were on Wordsworthian ground, and the Rector besides entertaining us with light refreshments, treated us to an admirable paper recounting the historic associations of Bishopstone and Wordsworth's connection with it. He read it standing just in front of the window where a hawk pounced on a dove as recorded by the poet in a sonnet that is perhaps little known. The lady to whom the poet gave the name of Lesbia in the poem was Loveday Walker, daughter of the Rector of Bishopstone at the time. Mr. Hutchinson had with him a copy of the sonnet and read it to the assembled company. Mention was made in Mr. Wilmot's paper of the unearthing of a Roman pavement in the parish in 1812, a discovery which prompted Wordsworth to write a sonnet on "Roman antiquities discovered at Bishopstone" which had a special significance for those participating in this outing in view of the visit just paid to Magna Castra:-

(Figure 11) Excavation Kenchester 1912

(Figure 12) Exavation Kenchester 1912

While poring antiquarians search the ground
Upturned with curious pains, the Bard, a Seer,
Takes fire:-The men that have been re-appear;
Romans for travel girt, for business gowned,
In festal glee: Why not? For fresh and clear
As if its hues were of the passing year,
Dawns this time-buried pavement. From that mound
Hoards may come forth of Trajans, Maximins,
Shrunk into coins with all their warlike toil;
Or a fierce impress issues with its foil
Of tenderness - the wolf, whose suckling Twins
The unlettered ploughboy pities when he wins
The casual treasure from the furrowed soil.

The parish church nearby was next visited, and Mr Mines tested the qualities of the fine old organ of rich tone, which is one of its main features, an organ that was built by the celebrated Father Smith and was formerly in Eton College. In the churchyard is the grave of Archdeacon Freer, who restored the church in 1841, and among the visitors on this occasion were one or two gentlemen who remember attending his funeral in 1863. In the orchard the other side of the road opposite the church, a portion of what experts say is a paved Roman road was seen, and Mr. Jack, perhaps the club's best authority on Roman antiquities, thinks it was probably a private way to the Roman villa erected where the Rectory now stands. Very plainly the wheel tracks are to be seen, showing that Roman roads of old were not entirely devoid of ruts. [I think they were possibly looking at the old village road closed in 1820]

Mr.and Mrs. A J Like kindly showed the party around Bishopstone Court, once the seat of the ancient Berrington family. It is still moated to a large extent, and there are some interesting remains of an old gateway at the entrance.

The house is of grey stone with mullioned windows, and in its spacious rooms are a couple of Queen Anne grates. Giving a glance to the modern for a moment, as we quitted this old world residence, we could not help noting the almost palatial farm buildings, with stone columns and stone arches. Bishopstone Court Farm is on the Foxley estate. From Bishopstone our objective was Garnons, the residence of Sir John Cotterell Bart., and between us and it lay Bishopstone Hill. Those who through disinclination or age, and there were several septuagenarians and at least one octogenarian in the company, preferred an easy route kept to the roadway which skirts the base of the hill; but be it said to the credit of the members that nearly all chose the bee-line over the summit. And a delightful walk it was, through lovely glades, along with Frederick Payne (Sir John's head gamekeeper) who led the way. When we reached the brow, after a stiff climb, and began to traverse a downward path on the southwest side we now and again obtained glimpses of the beautiful countryside as far as the Black Mountains and the Graig, in Monmouthshire; the Rev H B D Marshall pointed out a section of Offa's Dyke. From here we descended to Garnons, and were graciously received by Sir. John and Lady Evelyn Cotterell, who entertained us to sumptuous light refreshments daintily served in their handsome dining room. Sir John was good enough to conduct his numerous visitors through the main apartments of his castellated mansion, pointing out the main objects of artistic or other interest. The west wing of Garnons was built on the site of the old residence, and the present building was erected in 1813. Afterwards Sir John and Lady Evelyn piloted us through the beautiful gardens, where in the exquisite floral colour schemes there is ample evidence of the artistic temperament. During a convenient pause in the tour, the President, in sentiments delicately expressed, thanked Sir John and Lady Evelyn for the kind manner in which they had received the club and for their generous hospitality.

(Figure 13) Garnons 1905

From Garnons Sir John's agent (Mr J L Ramage) acted as a guide to Mansell Gamage Church,and our last call of antiquarian interest.

From Mansell Gamage, the party, or those of us who had not chartered a vehicle, walked to Moorhampton Hotel, where we found that host Perlman had prepared a bountiful spread. After dinner a toast to the King, then the party made its way to Moorhampton station for the homeward journey to Hereford.

First World War 1914-1918

(Figure 14) Weobley & District T. A. Volunteers training in Pembrokeshire.
Note! B S A motorcycle and B Jones & Son of Weobley steam lorry both driven to Pembrokeshire.

Britain's declaration of war with Germany was made on Tuesday August 4th 1914; who first heard the news in Bishopstone is not known, but as communication was only by word of mouth or newspapers, possibly Thomas Gore or Miss Abberley owners of the two post offices may have been the first to hear.

The volunteers from Bishopstone at the beginning of the war were all young men from agricultural backgrounds; within two weeks of the declaration of war five youngsters John Hall, Frank James, John Evans, Jack Preece and Arthur Preece left the parish as volunteers. This was followed by conscription of single men on January 2nd 1916, and finally on May 4th 1916 conscription came in for all men married or single between the ages of 18 and 41. The only exemptions were workers in essential work.
The 1911 census reveals there were 21 male parishioners living in Bishopstone who would have been eligible to fight at the start of the war in 1914. The roll hanging in Bishopstone church lists 19 names from the parish who contributed to the war effort.
The Hereford Times reports on the first two years of the war were full of optimism, printing the full size paper of ten pages with stories of locals on the front, and carrying hundreds of adverts for farm labourers, but by year three of the war, it was reduced to a single sheet with lists of the dead and injured but with no stories attached.
A book called "Herefordshire and the Great War" published by Collins lists the names of the men killed in the war, their service units and from which parish in the county they came from, the Bishopstone entry lists five names.

IN GRATEFUL MEMORY OF THE MEN
OF BISHOPSTONE WHO GAVE THEIR LIVES
IN DEFENCE OF KING AND COUNTRY IN
THE GREAT WAR 1914-1918.
JOHN EVANS.
JOHN HALL.
THOMAS EVANS.
FRANK JAMES.
ARTHUR PREECE.
(Figure 15) Brass plaque on the wall of the church.

Private John Hall in the 1911 census was recorded as a 22-year-old herdsman who lodged with William James of the Stepps Bishopstone and was born in Withington. John volunteered to serve his country after a recruiting campaign in Hereford by the Kings Shropshire Light Infantry. In September 1914 he travelled to Blackdown Barracks Shrewsbury and joined the newly formed 5th Battalion of the Kings Shropshire Light Infantry, at the age of 25 years he was given a service number 11674. After training he arrived in France on May 23rd 1915 and fought in many of the great battles of trench warfare including the Battles of the Somme in 1916. On February 2nd 1918 the 5th Battalion was immediately disbanded; after nearly three years it had simply run out of men, 667 had lost their lives on the battlefield. The remaining men were moved to other battalions within the K.S.L.I John was moved to the 7th Battalion. On March 28th 1918 the First Battle of Arras began with the first attack at 5.15 a.m. The Germans succeeded in entering our trenches, fierce fighting started and John Hall from Bishopstone was killed along with 47 others. There is no known grave; his body was never identified, like so many other soldiers. His name is inscribed on the Arras Memorial, he was 29 years old when he died and was officially listed as' Killed in Action, Remembered with Honour! John's parents Isaac and Mary Hall were living at Lower Green End Withington when they received the telegram informing them of his death.

William and Charlotte Evans of Burcott Row Bishopstone had three boys who served their country in the Great War; two lost their lives, Thomas and John. George Evans the youngest son joined up when conscription came into force in 1916. George survived the war and stayed on in the army afterward as a career soldier.

Private Thomas Evans was working as a wagoner at Lloyndu Farm Abergavenny in 1911, he was 20 years old; Thomas volunteered for service on the declaration of war. Because he was living in Monmouthshire he joined the 3rd battalion Monmouthshire Regiment as they were up and ready to leave for the front, his service number was 1738.
He arrived in Flanders on February 13th 1915. The Second Battle of Ypres began in April 1915 when the Germans released poison gas into the Allied lines for the first time. In the fighting to hold the line on May 11th 1915 Thomas lost his life at the battle of Frezenberg Ridge which took place over the period May 8-15 1915. The 3rd Monmouth's (in 83 Brigade) shared the Brigade boundary line, running from Westhoek to Bellewaarde, with Princess Patricia's Light Infantry (80 Brigade). Frezenberg was the last high ground before Ypres and if the Germans had been able to take it they would have had a clear run to Ypres and then on to the sea. The Allies were shelled and machine-gunned to bits and an awful lot of bodies were never identified including Thomas's.

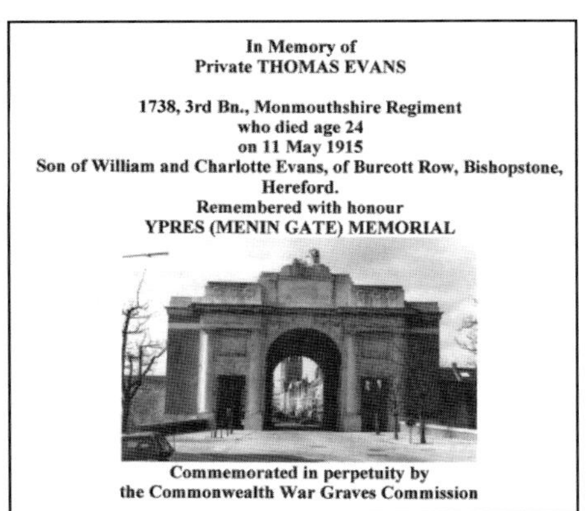
In Memory of
Private THOMAS EVANS
1738, 3rd Bn., Monmouthshire Regiment
who died age 24
on 11 May 1915
Son of William and Charlotte Evans, of Burcott Row, Bishopstone, Hereford.
Remembered with honour
YPRES (MENIN GATE) MEMORIAL
Commemorated in perpetuity by
the Commonwealth War Graves Commission

The Monmouths were driven back to their support trench, and out of the whole battalion (about 800 men) only two officers and 120 men survived. Thomas is commemorated on the Ypres (Menin Gate) Memorial as "Killed in Action".
A telegram arrived at Burcott Row informing of his death, the second to arrive in the parish.

Lance Corporal John Evans, their second son, joined the 1st Battalion Herefordshire Regiment in August 1914, his service number was 235997. The battalion of 700 men was made up entirely of volunteers consisting of new and old fighting men of the militia and regulars. They travelled by train to their war training camp at Pembroke Dock after marching through Hereford to the station to a continuous roar of cheering, interspersed with many a "Good-bye" and "God bless you" from mothers, wives, sisters, and sweet-hearts. On July 16th 1915 John with his battalion left Southampton for Gallipoli, arriving at Suvla Bay in August. The 1st Herefordshire Battalion received its baptism of fire on August 10th at the Dardanelles, landing in small boats, many were cut down by the Turks' machine guns. John survived this battle, and then went on to fight in Egypt and Palestine. In 1918 the 1st Herefordshire Battalion moved to the war in France. John was promoted to lance corporal and on July 23rd 1918 the victorious advance of Villemontoire began, John lost his life on that first day with one other soldier from the Herefordshire Battalion, he is buried in the Hereford Section of the Raperie British Cemetery plot 111A, row E, grave 3 Villemontoire. William and Charlotte Evans received another telegram to confirm the loss of a second son.

In Memory of
Lance Corporal J EVANS

235997, 1st/1st Bn., Herefordshire Regiment
who died
on 23 July 1918
Son of Mr. W. Evans, of Burcott Row, Bishopstone, Hereford.
Remembered with honour
RAPERIE BRITISH CEMETERY, VILLEMONTOIRE

Commemorated in perpetuity by
the Commonwealth War Graves Commission

John enlisted in Hereford and had given his residential address at Bishopstone, yet he also appears to be remembered on a war memorial in St Mary's Church Abbeycwmhir Radnorshire so it's possible he was working as a farm labourer in that parish when war was declared.

Private Frank James 10283 1st Battalion King's Shropshire Light Infantry was the eldest son of William and Annie James from The Stepps Farm Bishopstone. He Joined the K.S.L.I. with the other Bishopstone boys in August 1914. They went to France in September 1914 and fought in the Flanders trenches all through the first and second battles of Ypres which ended in May 1915. This major attack by the Germans failed to take the town, even though they used chlorine gas for the first time. In December 1915 at La Brique the enemy launched a gas attack using the new phosgene gas for the first time, and Frank was caught in the gas cloud. He was brought back to a hospital in England suffering from gas poisoning but died on April 24th 1916 from the effects of the gas at the age of 22 years. He is buried in Bishopstone Churchyard.

(Figure 16) James brothers headstone in Bishopstone churchyard

Private Arthur Preece 10172. 1st Battalion King's Shropshire Light Infantry. Arthur was born in Holmer in 1896, the 1911 census shows he was working as a nurseryman, how he came to be listed on our roll of honour is a mystery. Possibly he was lodging in the parish working for Garnons Estate, and to reinforce this idea an Arthur Preece appears on Byford's church plaque of war dead who appears to be the same person. Arthur, like Frank James whom he must have known, joined the Ist Bn K S L I and travelled to France in August 1914. He fought in the same trenches as Frank right through the first and second battle of Ypres. Ironically he was killed in a relatively quiet period, Arthur is listed as "Killed in Action", July 26th 1915 aged 19, son of Samuel and Sarah Ann Preece of 8, Priory Place, Widemarsh Common, Hereford. Remembered with Honour! He was buried in Grave 1P, Row 31, La Brique Military Cemetery.

ROLL OF HONOUR
Men of Bishopstone who served their King & Country in the ·Great War 1914 - 1918·
G.DAVIES, F.JAMES,
J.HALL, A.PREECE,
C.JONES, T.EVANS,
J.EVANS, G.EVANS,
J.S.PREECE, J.RUDD,
A.GWILLIAM, W.GWILLIAM,
F.W.PREECE, S.G.PREECE,
H.B.JONES, W.WILLIAMS,
G.HOLDER, R.S.JAMES,
E.G.THOMAS.

While John Hall, John and Thomas Evans, Frank James and Arthur Preece had all lost their lives in the war, the other 14 men named on the roll all suffered in the conflict. Two of them, Edgar Thomas and Reggie James died young as a direct result of warfare. There are also a couple of other names associated with the parish who were not put on the roll.

George Davies who was born in 1888 on Bishopstone hill in Lucas Cottage, he was still living at home with his widowed mother Elizabeth when he received his call up papers in 1916. Although George Davies served in the war, I have not been able to identify his regiment or service number due the large number of men with the same name.

George Evans, born in 1897; lived with his large family in Burcott Row; he was working on Bishon Farm as a farm labourer when the war began. George was possibly influenced by his older brothers to sign up; he was the only one to survive the war, and became a career soldier after the conflict. For the same reason as George Davies, I was unable to trace his service medal record, there were 838 George Evans's who served in the First World War. The Luftwaffe destroyed most of the First World War records during the bombing on London in the Second World War, leaving only the medal record cards to search through by name.

(Figure 17) Charles Gwilliam

In Memory of
Private CHARLES HENRY GWILLIAM

10362, 1st Bn., King's Shropshire Light Infantry
who died age 21
on 02 January 1915
Son of Samuel Gwilliam, of Bishopstone, Bridge Sollars
Remembered with honour
PLOEGSTEERT MEMORIAL

Commemorated in perpetuity by
the Commonwealth War Graves Commission

The first person in Bishopstone to receive the telegram to say his son had been killed on the frontline in France was Samuel Gwilliam my great grandfather, it arrived in early January 1915, six months after the war had started.
Samuel Gwilliam was a widower who moved to Bishopstone to live with his daughter Sarah Wall (my grandmother) at Stonehouse in 1914 at the start of the war, together with his son Alfred and grandson William. To make room in the house Sarah's two eldest daughters, Doris and Kitty, were sent to their grandparents' house in Clifford. Samuel spent the rest of his life in Bishopstone, he died in January 1945 at the age of 86 years. His daughter Elizabeth married George Rawlings in the autumn of 1920, after which he lived with them in Cambrai cottage. Samuel was a typical Herefordshire farm labourer, a hard working cider drinker, who became a well-known character in Bishopstone, Samuel fathered thirteen children and also brought up a grandson as his own.
Four of Samuel's five sons, Samuel, George, Charles, and Alfred served in the Great War, plus William his grandson; only John (Jack) his eldest was retained for agriculture work. He was a renowned ploughing expert who won many ploughing awards.

Charles Gwilliam who joined the army from Stretton Sugwas is remembered on their war memorial. He died on January 2nd 1915, the company records state *"On January 2nd 1915 the battalion moved into billets in Armentieres for a week's rest after a month in water logged trenches"*. The story told within the family is that he was killed by a single shot to the head by a German sniper, witnessed by his brother Fred, who was serving alongside him in the trenches. This story was possibly fabricated to ease the suffering at home, Charles was probably blown to pieces by a shell as his body could not be identified; hence he was not buried in a registered grave.

(Figure 18) Jack Gwilliam

Alfred Gwilliam

Private Alfred (Fred) Gwilliam 10223, joined up in August 1914 with the other volunteers from Bishopstone, he was 19 years old when he entered France on September 10th 1914 with the 1st Battalion K.S.L.I. He served with the same battalion throughout the war taking part in all the great battles on the Western Front. Fred returned home on April 18th 1919 after nearly five years of trench warfare.

William Gwilliam

Corporal William Gwilliam 25009, joined the K.S.L.I. in 1916 after receiving his conscription papers. He was soon promoted to corporal and was then transferred to the Devonshire Regiment where he stayed until he was discharged in 1919. William saw action in France for 3 years. William was Alfred's nephew, although a year older than Alfred; he was the illegitimate son of Agnes Gwilliam, Alfred's eldest sister. His father was the son of John Hall of Lulham Farm who employed Samuel Gwilliam as a farm worker. As was common practice in the late 19th century, he had taken advantage of his position and Agnes had to suffer having two children by him, which her father kept quiet in fear of his job. Samuel brought William up and passed him off as his son.

Private George Henry Holder DM2/223808 lived in Banbury Hall with his wife Ethel, he was a gardener employed by Garnons estate. As a married man he was conscripted after May 1916 making him 34 years old when he was called up. George was born in Staunton on Wye, and after leaving school he moved up to Birmingham where he trained as an apprentice gold ring maker under his uncle. During the war he served in the Army Service Corps as a driver taking supplies up to the front line. George Holder served in the Home Guard during the 2nd World War. George and Ethel lived out the rest of their lives in Bishopstone, he died in 1957 and is buried in Bridge Sollers churchyard.

Private Reginald Stanley James 116957, Reg was the younger brother of Frank James he was the youngest boy from Bishopstone to serve his country, only sixteen when he went to war in France as a member of the Royal Army Medical Corps. Reginald was demobbed from the army in 1919 but died on December 17th 1920 aged 20 years; suffering from the effects of serving in the war. Three young men who called The Stepps their home had lost their lives to the war effort. After Reg's death his parents William and Annie moved out from The Stepps to Hacton Villas, Preston-on-Wye. The two brothers Frank and Reg are buried in Bishopstone churchyard under one headstone.

Chris Jones

Shoeing Smith Christopher Jones 4677 was the son of John and Phoebe Jones, The Orphanage Bishon Lane. Christopher was 21 years old at the outbreak of war, he was a blacksmith working in Brinsop. He joined the Royal Field Artillery as a shoeing smith and arrived in France on August 22nd 1915. Because of his profession Christopher did not see any front line action, he worked in the main base camp shoeing horses. Towards the end of the war when the army were running out of horses, Christopher carried out labouring duties for the regiment. After the war he carried on his blacksmith trade working out of the forge at Staunton on Wye.

Private Harry B Jones 2707 aged 17 years old in 1914, was working on Bishon Farm when war was declared; living in Burcott Row with his widowed mother and two younger brothers, Harry was the only wage earner in the family. When conscription forced him into service in January 1916, Harry was directed into the Monmouthshire Regiment, and not long after arriving in the front lines he was caught in a gas attack. After he recovered he was transferred into the South Wales Borderers no 39513, and finally finished up in the Army Service Corps before being discharged in 1919. Harry always suffered from the effects of being gassed in the war, this left him with respiratory problems for the rest of his life. After the war Harry married Jane and they lived firstly in Kenowly and then Lena Cottage, eventually ending up in an almshouse. Harry died in 1971.

Harry Jones

William Preece and his wife Catherine who had lived in Lena Cottage since 1890, saw three of their boys go to war, John, Frank and Stan. They all survived the war but the worry was too much for their mother Catherine who died in November 1916 and never saw her sons return home.

Private John (Jack) Sidney Preece 3154 was the first of the brothers to volunteer, he joined the Herefordshire regiment in August 1914, possibly attending the recruiting campaign with John Evans from Burcott Row. Both the families had lived in the village for over ten years. William Preece as sexton would have seen Mrs Evans every Sunday in church. Jack would have fought alongside John Evans in the Dardanelles where many from the regiment landing in small boats were cut down by the Turks' machine guns. John survived this battle then went on to fight in Egypt and Palestine before being transferred to the Royal Defence Corps later in the war. Jack Preece was one of the lucky ones who survived, after the war he worked for many years as a gardener at the New Weir Kenchester.

Private Francis (Frank) William Preece 148308 volunteered and joined the Army Service Corps in 1915, arriving in France on December 21st, he was 20 years old. The Corps were responsible for bringing up supplies to the front line, its soldiers survival rate were higher than the soldiers fighting in the front line trenches. Frank returned home in 1919.

Stanley George Preece was working as a cowman for the Reverend Wilmot throughout the first two years of the war; he joined up in 1916 when he received his conscription papers. I have been unable to identify his records except for the fact that his conscription papers ruffled the feathers of his employer and caused a court case as reported on later in this chapter.

J Rudd is one name on the list I have not been able to positively identify, but he could be Joseph Rudd, brother of Walter Rudd who lived in Bishopstone.

Private Edgar George Thomas 62748 volunteered in 1915, and for some unknown reason was enlisted into the Royal Army Medical Corps. He arrived in France on November 22nd 1915; what happened to him during the conflict is unrecorded but his records show that he was discharged wounded on July 12th 1917. Edgar died on February 6th 1918 aged 21 years and is buried in Bishopstone churchyard. Why he was not recorded on the Roll of Honour in the church is a mystery. He was the son of Ted and Emily Thomas who had lived in Bishopstone during the First World War and returned to the parish to live at Peartree Cottage during the 1940s and 50s.

(Figure 19) War Grave headstone of S T Howells Bishopstone churchyard

William Williams, who lived at Scaldback Cottage, worked as a farm labourer for John Like, Bishopstone Court. William, a married man, received his conscription papers in May 1916, when he was 23 years old. I could not identify William in the medal records.

There were several other men living in Bishopstone who contributed to the war but are not recorded on the church plaque.

Driver S.T Howells 61496 Royal Engineers who died November 5th 1919, "Remembered with Honour". Sidney is buried in the only war grave in Bishopstone churchyard, maintained by the War Graves Commission who pay the church to keep the grave tidy and periodically replace the headstone.

It is surprising that Sidney in not recorded on the church roll because he was born in Bishopstone at Townsend Farm and baptised in Bishopstone Church on March 26th 1882, he also attended Bishopstone School. After the war had finished, Sidney stayed on in the army and he died in an accident at Brecon. Sidney was buried in Bishopstone churchyard on November 9th 1919 and it appears that it was too much for his father John who died a few days later and was buried next to him on November 20th 1919.

Corporal Walter William Rudd 96610, was living in Bishopstone in 1914. The parish records show his son Edwin was baptised in the church on August 9th of that year and was living in a cottage on Bishon Common. Walter was born in Tiverton, Devon in 1886. The 1911 census records that he was working as an iron founder in Cardiff, and by 1914 he had married and was now working as a platelayer for the Midland Railway Company. Walter joined up by conscription in May 1916 and because of his engineering background was enlisted to the Royal Engineers; he served in France for three years. After the war Walter and his family lived for many years in No 16 Bishon Common.

Sapper George Powell appears in the Kenchester school records as a parent, where it lists his occupation as a soldier; he was a married man, working as a platelayer on the railway before the war. George joined by conscription like his neighbour Walter Rudd and ended up in the Royal Engineers; the family lived in No 17 Bishon Common for many years after the War. Both Walter and George's names are missing from the roll

Opposition to the war.

Not everyone agreed with the war. Mrs Wilmot, the Bishopstone rector's wife, appears to have been a formidable woman; she questioned the authorities when appearing at a tribunal in Hereford. She wanted to keep her cowman Stan Preece, who lived at Lena Cottage. He was called up by conscription but she refused to let him go; Stan appeared before a tribunal where he was ordered to comply and enter military service. Extract from the Hereford Times,

Mrs Wilmot was obviously disappointed by the decision and seemed aggrieved that her request to retain one man was refused. She argued that she herself worked hard, not only on the farm, but also in patriotic work outside chiefly with women taking up war duties, she had moreover been teaching women dairying and poultry keeping, from morning to night for years and she was denied this minimal of necessary assistance.

The chairman, "Are you sure it is not possible to employ someone above the Military age."

Mrs Wilmot, "There is not a dairyman to be found".

The chairman suggested that women might be available, but Mrs Wilmot pointed out that they could not lift the heavy weights incidental to the work, she also argued that conscription would have avoided much of the unfairness that now existed if it had been established at the beginning of the war.

Mrs Wilmot exclaimed, Lord Selborne has broken his word to me which he repeated in parliament, she said she would travel the country from top to bottom protesting against this decision, this is not only a loss to her but to the county as she supplied the district around Bishopstone with milk.

Mrs Wilmot declared that she was ruined if she could not keep this man.

I don't know if this was the case but within a month of the tribunal Rev Wilmot resigned as rector of Bishopstone and they both left the Rectory by September 1916.

Housing in the parish

After the 1914-18 War the annual parish meeting of 1919 held at the Old School Room discussed a questionnaire received from the District Council about housing needs and the parish's response to the questions asked.

(1) How many houses have been erected since the census of 1911 of rateable value up to £8.

Answered four: (These were the four new almshouses)

(2) Rateable value between £8 and £16.

Answered none.

(3) How many houses have been demolished or closed in the same period.

Answered Ten; (Six old almshouses on the hill, Pair of cottages on the hill ex Lucas Bros, Pair of cottages on Bishon Common)

(4) How many houses now vacant.

Answered; none.

(5) Number of new houses your Council considers is required in the Parish

Answered; Eight

Two council houses were built 26 years later in 1945, next to the Nelson Inn, but the parish would have to wait another 36 years to have their full allotment of council houses. Two new properties were built in the parish between the wars, a bungalow called The Knoll and the Nelson Garage which included living accommodation, both built in the late 1920s.

Death of Bishopstone's "Lord of the Manor"

(Figure 20) George Horatio

At 9.00 o'clock on the morning of Thursday October 16th 1919 Bishopstone's lord of the manor, Rev. George Horatio Davenport breathed his last breath, he was 87 years old. After his death the Foxley Estate passed to the trustees of his will, Mr Phillip Dashwood and Mr Harvey Barnster. Up until a month before his death, he was in his usual health carrying out his duties. Rev. Davenport was the last of his generation of this prominent family, three sisters and a brother predeceasing him Mrs Arkwright (Hampton Court), the Hon Mrs Hanbury (Shobdon Rectory), Lady Longley and Mr Harry Davenport, for sometime MP for Leek in Staffordshire who died in 1895.

The death of his wife had preceded his by 19 months; Rev. Davenport's express wish was to be buried beside her at Stanford-on-Soar, near Loughborough. On Tuesday October 19th 1919, while a simultaneous memorial service was held at Yazor Church, he was buried at St John the Baptist Stanford-on Soar. His body was taken up the previous day by motor hearse; Capt R T Hinckes his only son was the sole mourner who attended the interment from Foxley.

Rev Davenport was born at Tettenhall Staffs on August 1st 1832, was educated at Rugby School and Oriel College, Oxford, graduating MA in 1857; in that year he was ordained Deacon in the diocese of London. He was the eldest surviving son of Mr John Davenport of Westwood Hall, Leek Staffordshire, and Foxley Herefordshire. At the age of 30 he inherited the estates on the death of his father in 1862. Ordained in 1863 by the Bishop of Hereford Dr Hampden, he was vicar of Mansel Lacy with Yazor, of which he was the patron, from 1863-1881. He was married in 1866 to Sophie Diana Dashwood, third daughter of the Rev S Vere Dashwood of Stanford Hill, Notts. Rev Davenport was an alderman and founder member of Herefordshire County Council, Justice of the Peace, and a member of the Weobley Board of Guardians and District Council for many years. Rev Davenport was devoted to country life and as a landlord took a great pride in his estates and particularly Foxley, where over a period of years he rebuilt most of the estate farms and put up numerous cottages. His chief hobby was genealogy.

(Figure 21) Foxley House 1910

Foxley dispersal sale 1920[4]

After the death of Reverend G H Davenport auctioneers Edwards, Russell & Baldwin from Hereford, held a sale at the City Arms Hotel on January 14th 1920 consisting of ten lots. The trustees of Foxley Estate had decided to sell most of its holdings in Bishopstone except for Court Farm, to raise money for death duties.

Lot 1 A highly desirable farm know as Bishon

A pleasant, brick-built house with a tile roof

Containing hall, dining and drawing rooms, store room, kitchen, dairy, five bedrooms and bathroom, with a small lawn and vegetable garden.

Three cottages and gardens (Burcott Row). A splendid set of farm buildings, which are nearly new. Totals 206 acres, 2 roods. 16 perches

In the occupation of Mr. Joseph Yeomans, whose tenancy expires at Candlemas next owing to his having purchased another farm in Vowchurch.

Mr. Tom Watkins of Canon Bridge purchased this lot for a reported £9000.

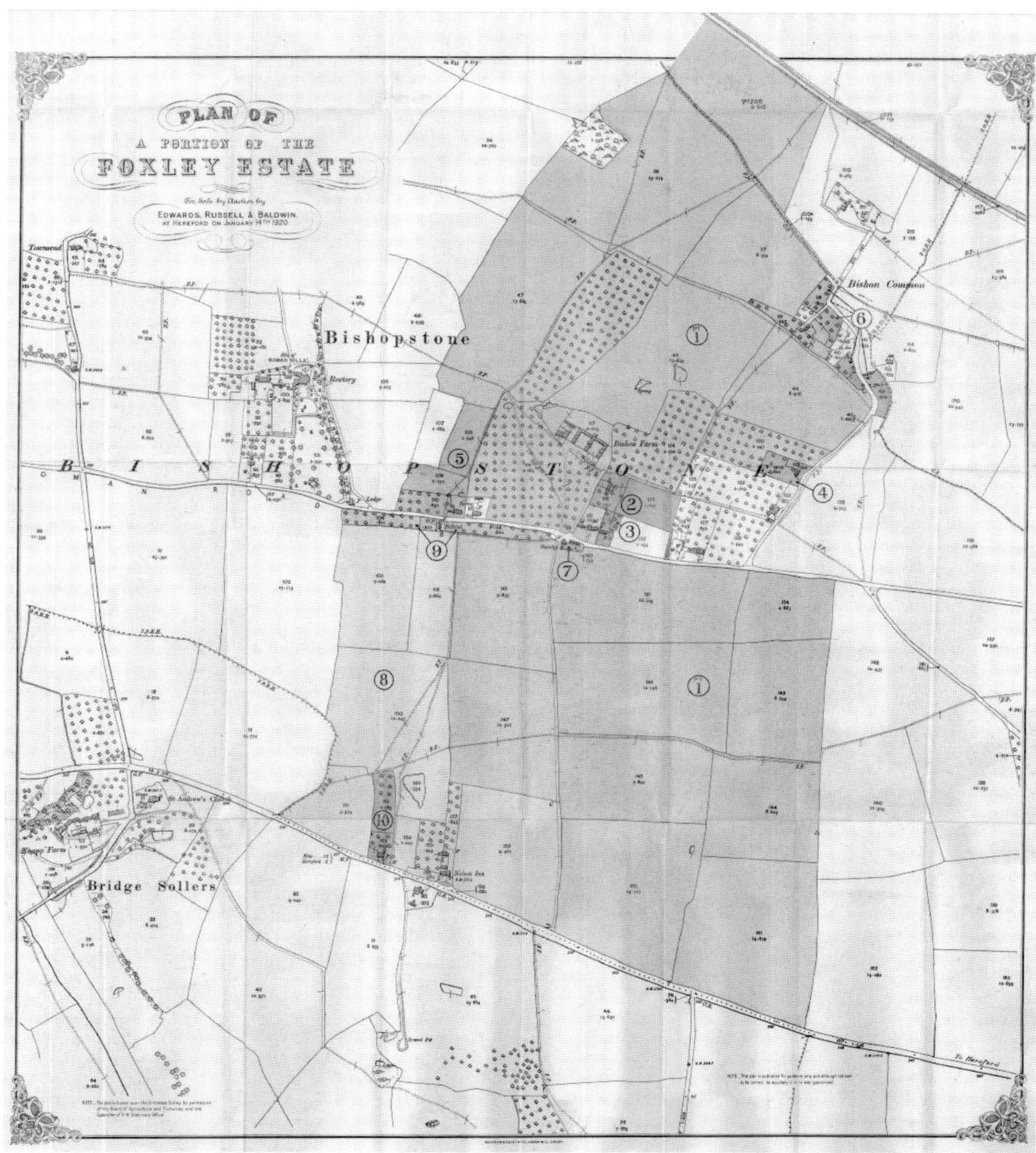

Lot 2 A half-timber house with a tile roof. (Pleck cottage) and 2 acres, 1 rood 27 perches, containing sitting room, kitchen, two back kitchens, pantry and four bedrooms, out buildings, large garden, orchard on a piece of pasture land. Let to Mr. Alfred John Amos at £16 per annum

Mr. Tom Watkins of Canon Bridge purchased this lot for £300

Lot 3 Two brick and slate cottages with gardens. (Panteg Cottage, Old Post Office)

Let to Mr. George Rawlings and Mr. Thomas Gore upon quarterly tenancies at rents amounting to £11 per annum.

Mr Thomas Gore purchased the Old Post Office for an undisclosed sum

Miss Hughes, teacher at Kenchester School purchased Panteg Cottage for an undisclosed sum.

Lot 4 A good stone-built cottage, (Orphanage) with outbuildings, garden and a piece of orchard land. Water is supplied by a pump in the house.

Mr John Jones is the occupant paying £9 per annum rent.

Mr Bill Oliver purchased the Orphanage for £250

Lot 5 A capital small holding (Stonehouse) comprising a stone-built house, buildings and several pieces of pasture and orchard land, containing in the whole about 4 acres.

Let to Mr John Wall on a yearly candlemas tenancy of £13 per annum.

Mr John Wall purchased Stone house for £300

Lot 6 A small holding (Stone house on Bishon Common) comprising two cottages with gardens, outbuildings, and several pieces of pasture and orchard land, containing in the whole about 2 acres. Let in part to Mrs Phipps and Mr Hamer at an aggregate rent of £12 per annum.
Mrs Phipps purchased this lot for an undisclosed sum.
Lot 7 A cottage, garden and blacksmith's shop (Forge Cottage). In the occupation of Mr Richard Boucher quarterly tenancy at a rental of £7 per annum.
Mr Tom Watkins purchased Forge Cottage for £150.
Lot 8 A very valuable fully-licensed Inn known as "The Nelson" farm buildings, several pieces of excellent pasture, orchard and arable land, the whole containing about 30 acres 2 roods 26 perches. The foregoing is let to Mrs Bywater at an apportioned rent of £93 per annum.
Also an adjoining field of very productive arable land, of 9 acres in tenancy of Mr Joseph Yeomans, making a total lot of 40 acres.
Mrs Bywater purchased the Nelson for an undisclosed sum.
Lot 9 The Old School House with a good garden and 2 pieces of orchard land, 1 acre 3 roods 25 perches. House let to Mr Joseph Price at a rental of £5 per annum.
Mrs Bywater purchased The Old School House for £320.
Lot 10 A brick and stone-built slate-covered house with Post Office and Grocer's Shop known as Bridge Ash. 1 acre 2 roods 18 perches. Let to Mrs Abberley at a rental of £20 per annum.
Mrs Abberley purchased Bridge Ash for an undisclosed sum.

Bits and Pieces

Early in 1922 Mrs Rosanna Bywater from the Nelson Inn employed Tracy Read Contractors to enlarge the pond behind the Nelson, this was a spectacle witnessed by many parishioners and children who had never before seen this engineering feat. Two steam engines were positioned either side of the pond, they pulled a dredger bucket between them attached on to a wire winch rope, creating the pond we see today. Rosanna sold the Nelson in 1926, where she had been the landlady for nearly 50 years and moved up to the Old School House in the village, altering the house, making what was the school room into a living room with a bedroom above. She died in 1939.

With the schoolroom no longer available, the 1926 parish council annual meeting was held at Bishopstone Court, the parish council had used the schoolroom for its meetings for the last 31 years.
The sudden death of Mr John Like of Bishopstone Court in 1927 meant that the parish had lost the chairman of the council and their district councillor. The 1928 parish council meeting was held at Bishopstone Rectory by kind permission of Captain Gilbert. Reverend Roberts as chairman proposed that a letter be sent to Weobley District Council stating that for the last 30 years the parish council had written and complained about the poor state of the roadway down to the common and pointing out that the condition was such that children going to school had to remove their boots or shoes in order to get through the water. A copy of the letter was also sent to the Director of Education and the Medical Officer of Health.
From 1929 until 1937 no parish council meetings were held, the reasons for this are unclear. William Lewis of Court Farm was elected chairman in 1937. At the annual parish meeting held in Bishopstone vestry on April 29th 1939 it was proposed that a telephone kiosk should be positioned in Bishopstone together with a stamp machine.
Only two parish meetings were held during the Second World War. At the May meeting in 1944 Captain H A Gilbert was still away on active service so Major Hollis from Downshill House was appointed the new chairman. The new Rector Max Benjamin told the meeting that Mr. H. G. Watkins had offered a piece of ground for the purpose of building a parish hall, a vote of thanks was proposed by Mrs. Gilbert. (This piece of land fronted onto the main road lying west of the bridle path; this offer was held open until Harry Watkins died in 1963 but was never taken up by the parish council).
At the 1945 parish meeting Captain Gilbert, having returned from active service, was reappointed as chairman. The question of the telephone kiosk was again discussed but it was ultimately decided that the matter should be left in abeyance until after the war.
The next parish meeting was not held until March 12th 1948 but as no parishioners attended the meeting except the Rector and Captain Gilbert, it was adjourned in hope that at a later date more parishioners would attend. Twelve days later on March 24th a parish meeting was called again, this time 33 parishioners attended, a representative from nearly every house in the parish. Two representatives from the parish to serve on the rating authority of the Rural District Council were appointed, Mr. J. Haimes and Mr. S Lewis. A letter was written to Herefordshire County Council about repairs to the road leading to the common which stated, "That the seven cottages on Bishopstone Common are entitled to have reasonable access to the roads of the county."

In 1948 the Birmingham and Midland Red Omnibus Co started a bus service that ran daily through the village; before the Second World War the Midland Red ran a bus service along the main road, replacing Darling's buses that had run a limited service between Hereford and Eardisley in the 1920s and 30s. Darling Buses charged 4d return for a journey from the Nelson to Hereford.
The secretary wrote to the Midland Red bus company asking if the 8:30 a.m. bus to Hereford and the 9:15 p.m. bus from Hereford could run through Bishopstone.
The very first regular refuse collection was started by the Weobley Rural District Council in 1948, the collection took place every three weeks.

Macklin Family

In 1920 Albert Macklin with his wife Alice, my grandfather and grandmother, and their 5 year old son Cecil (my father) moved into Bishopstone to live with Alice's father James Whiting who rented a cottage on Bishon common: Alice wanted to look after her ageing widowed father. Albert Macklin was a high-class decorator who as an apprentice had learnt his trade working on many of Herefordshire's mansions.

BUILDER ♦ PLUMBER ♦ PAINTER ♦ DECORATOR

Pumps, Bells, Lead Lights, Hot and Cold Water.

A. MACKLIN,
BISHOPSTONE,
BRIDGE SOLLARS,
HEREFORD.

Painting, Paper-hanging and Distempering.

1925	To work at Alms houses as per Estimate	£ 13	0	0
	To Repairing brick entry to store House & Galv. Lavatory Pail		6	6
	Self 7 hrs. mortar & cement		18	10
	Total	£ 14	5	4

Received with thanks
8/2/26 A. Macklin

He was bought up in the Working Boy's Home in Hereford after his father had lost the family business through an addiction to the amber nectar: the family broke up and the children were placed into care. Because of ill health he was refused entry into military service and at the start of the war he was sent to Peterborough to work in an aircraft factory as part of the movement of labour supporting the war effort. Working as part of the factory maintenance team he learnt pipefitting, which stood him in good stead in later years. In 1924 Albert purchased a plot of land from Garnons estate where formerly stood the Apperley's old Wheelwrights shop and timber framed cottage. This was derelict with the roof fallen in, the cottage had not been occupied for 17 years. Albert Macklin worked from home and in 1926 secured a large contract to paint the main dining room in Foxley House, which included painting murals on the walls depicting the four seasons of the year and applying gold leafing to the coving around the ceiling. This gold leafing, of which I still have a few samples, could only be purchased through a bank. By now the family business was expanding employing two local men.

(Figure 22) The Knoll

Albert finished building his new bungalow on the old Apperley site in 1926, which he named "The Knoll", the first bungalow in Bishopstone, in the same year he and Alice adopted a baby girl Edith. Albert used a horse and cart to move his building materials, the only route he ever used going to Hereford to collect supplies was down the old Roman road, now a disused lane by Magna Castra farm, as this was the most direct route to town.

After 1930 the building side of the business specialised in building wells and piping water from the well to a small lift pump in the kitchen, a modern idea. There are still cast iron well covers today with the name "A Macklin Builder Bishopstone" on them, there is one at Bishon Farm and another at the Orphanage. Albert Macklin brought his son Cecil, my father, into the family business in 1932 and called it "A Macklin & Son". The business was expanding and now employed six men from the parish: Bill Montague, Fred Jancey, George Rawling's son George, Charlie Cartwright and one of the Spencer boys from Burcott Row. Arthur Portman, Albert's nephew whom Albert had brought up from the age of nine after Arthur's mother had died, also worked for the business.

(Figure 23) Macklin family 1928
L to R Arthur Portman, Edith, Alice, Albert, Darkie the horse and Cecil

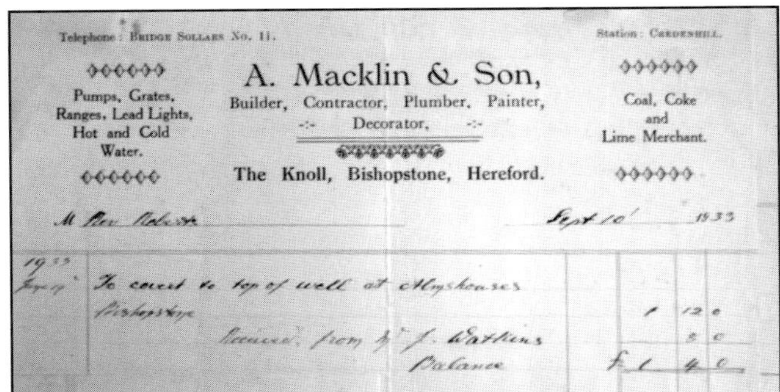

Telephone: Bridge Sollars No. 11.
Station: Credenhill.

Pumps, Grates, Ranges, Lead Lights, Hot and Cold Water.

A. Macklin & Son,
Builder, Contractor, Plumber, Painter, Decorator,
The Knoll, Bishopstone, Hereford.

Coal, Coke and Lime Merchant.

Next to The Knoll was a large yard which was used to stock coal, coke, logs, and lime, this was sold as a supplement to their main business as builders. The coal was purchased in twenty ton railway trucks which were shunted into the sidings at Credenhill station, it was then hauled by Darkie the horse pulling a dray up to the yard in Bishopstone. Fred Jancey from Burcott Row carried out the local delivery of coal and logs on Saturdays. The logs were cut on site by a large unguarded circular saw driven by a petrol engine; the logs were sold at 2s a basket. Paraffin and lighting oil in 45 gallon drums were kept in a large shed made from WW1 shell cases filled with clay, this was sold to the villagers by the pint, a service that carried on for the next 35 years until the 1960s, many parishioners used paraffin and oil for cooking and lighting before electricity came to the village.

"A Macklin & Son" also became undertakers, arranging funerals for local people. Dad remembered their first job on April 20th 1932 when he was sent over to Upton Court Holme Lacy to fetch the body of Charlie Evans. Mrs Evans lived at Burcott Row, her son Charlie aged 25 had worked in the stables at Upton Court where he had been kicked in the head by a horse that killed him. Dad fetched the body by horse and cart, measured up, and made the coffin. The coffin was placed on the bier (which is now in Bishopstone church and owned jointly by the three churches). My grandfather Albert led the funeral procession from Burcott Row to the church walking at a slow funereal pace. He was smartly dressed in his mourning suit and wearing his black top hat, which I still have to this day. The next job in August 1932 was Alice Emily Davies aged 31 who had died from a fever in Hereford General Hospital, she was a sister to the Bethell family who lived in the cellar under Peartree Cottage called Badgers Hole. It was the same routine again, except the horse and cart journey was to fetch the body from Hereford morgue.

The three parish's bier outside Bishopstone church with my grandfather's funeral hat

The final and largest funeral carried out by my grandfather was that of Gertrude (Granny) Gilbert on April 2nd 1946 when he led a very large funeral procession down the New Road to Bridge Sollers church, the coffin was carried on the village bier.

(Figure 24) Albert and Alice Macklin 1947

By 1935 the depression had hit Bishopstone, and A Macklin & Son were down to employing only one working man; the work had dried up so my father and his cousin Arthur Portman travelled to Worcester and signed up to join the Royal Air Force on March 4th 1936. Albert started to suffer from arthritis. It was always said by the family that this was caused by digging out too many wells and working for hours in knee high water. It became very severe during the Second World War, and after many trips to different hospitals and hot spring resorts he became bedridden in 1947. To make ends meet my grandmother became the Postmistress for Bishopstone, running the Post Office from the Knoll with the help of her daughter Edith, for 16 years until 1964. My father built the bungalow Greenwalls on part of the site between 1952 and 1957.

The Knoll was demolished in 1977 and a new house called Jolin was built on the site.

Cecil Macklin on his Velocette motorcycle Bridge Sollers 1937

Rev Roberts, Church fetes and the District Nurse.

In the late 1920s Reverend Roberts purchased a sectional wooden building and had it erected in his courtyard at Kenchester Rectory to use as a day school for their children. Rev and Mrs Roberts allowed the building to be used by both Bishopstone and Kenchester villagers for social and parish activities. One evening a week throughout the 1930s a working men's club made use of this building, the children of the parishes also used it for their Sunday School, it provided a venue for many whist drives and socials events, and was used regularly by the Mothers' Union.

(Figure 25) Ex Roberts hut in 2010

Every Christmas Mrs Roberts arranged three parties, children's party, one for the cottagers and their families and one for the farmers of the parishes and their families; these were held in the hut on three consecutive days. The sectional building was sold off when Rev. Roberts retired in 1943. Greenlands the auctioneers held a house sale at the Rectory, where the timber building fetched £110. Among the other things sold at the sale I noticed a hive of bees fetched £6, which represented over two weeks' wages for a farm worker.

This very building is still in use today as a café at the rear of the bus station. If this building had been kept until the end of the war and moved onto the site offered by Mr Harry Watkins, a parish hall for Bishopstone would have become a reality.

Mrs Roberts also held an annual fete on August Bank Holiday at Kenchester Rectory to raise money for the needs of the parishes and the Nurses Association.

This event was always reported in the Hereford Times, as taken from the August 1936 edition:

(Figure 26) Three parishes Church Fete held at Kenchester Rectory 1936. The only people I can identify in the line up are "Granny" Sidney Evans (centre with veil) Kitty Wall on his left next to the convict, far left Sarah Wall.

"The Annual August Bank Holiday Garden Fete took place as usual at Kenchester Rectory on Monday, although the absence of the rector who is at the present time in a London hospital left a gap, Mrs. Roberts ably filled his place.

The usual attractions were provided on the Rectory lawn in beautiful weather the parishioners attended in large numbers. The stalls were, Fancy stall Mrs. Hartland, China stall Mrs and Miss Lewis, Sweet stall Mrs A Matthews and Miss Vallender; ice-cream stall Mrs Kitching, Mrs Holder, Mrs Macklin; buffet tea stall Mrs. Roper, Mrs. Warbuton, Miss Hewer and Miss Iris Roper. Mrs Rawling, Mrs Marpole, Mrs and Miss Scamell and Mrs Evans served drawing room teas. The amusements included hoop-la managed by Mr J. Roberts, Mr. E. Gilbert and Mr. A Greenland; bowling for good money prizes, Mr Fred Edwards and Mr. Frank Edwards; Fortune-telling by Mrs G W Baker and games of croquet.

There was a cake competition, which drew excellent entries. Mrs. H P Lindsay judged the cakes; the winners were 1st Mrs Rawling, 2nd Mrs Holder, and 3rd Mrs W Roper. The fancy dress for children and adults was an interesting feature of the afternoon. The winners were: - Children: most outstanding costume, Glyn Marpole (Gipsy Man); prettiest costumes, Vera and Raymond Lewis (Spanish girl and Bedtime); most original, Sidney Evans (Grannie). Adults 1st Mrs. Rawlings and Mrs. Wall, (ancient and modern), 2nd Mrs Kitching (French Fisherwoman). In the evening a whist drive was held in the parish room."

(Figure 27) Sam Gwilliam and Helen Haines fete 1937

Some of the money raised at the fete went to the Nurses Association, the history of the district nurses in Bishopstone are worthy of recording. There are no records of district nursing in the parish prior to 1860 but shortly after that two elderly ladies who resided in Preston-on-Wye covered the district on foot. Their main workload was attending to confinements, if their services were required at night they were fetched by horse and trap. In 1904 the County Nursing Association was formed and the people were asked to contribute a penny a week. As this was rather a lot, it was decided that a shilling a year would cover the running of the Association, although extra charges applied if their services were called upon, such as 10s 6d for a confinement.

In 1907 Mrs. Day, the sister of Sir Geoffrey Cornewall became interested in district nursing of this area, and she persuaded a certified midwife named Miss Bannister, to come and live in this area with a view to doing all the nursing required. She was provided with a bicycle, in 1933 she acquired a car that she used for a couple of years before retiring in 1935. During her time she nursed the sick, attended midwifery cases, visited the school and monitored the children under five years of age.

(Figure 28) Back Row, L to R. Arthur Hughes, George Cartwright, Wilf Rawlings, Leslie Holder, Tom Prosser, Glyn Marpole, ?? Front Row, Winnie Phillips, Margaret Davies, Helen Haines, Ernie Phillips, ??, Joyce Britten

In 1935 Miss Wiggin took over the nursing and by this time the voluntary contribution was raised to 4s 4d a year. The contributions were collected by a very good band of collectors. Mrs Roberts the Rector's wife did a tremendous amount of voluntary work to raise funds to pay for the nurse and her equipment. She held jumble sales and a whist drive every year.

Between 1938 and 1948 a Queen's nursing sister covered the parish. She had her own car and received a car allowance as well as a salary. In 1948 the National Health Service came into being and the District Nursing Association was taken over by the county council so there were no more voluntary subscriptions.

(Figure 29) Percy on his Orc motorcycle 1920s.

Nelson Garage.

In 1929 Percival H Alderton formed an ambitious plan to open a garage next to the Nelson Inn. Known to everyone as "Percy" he came from Abergavenny in 1927 to work for and "live in" with Mr Arthur Williams, the Byford village blacksmith.

Permission to build was at first refused by Weobley Dristrict Council, the chairman Sir John Cotterell, being the main objector.

But Percy had a friendly voice backing him in the shape of Mr. Archer Matthews of Bridge Farm, Bridge Sollers, also a councillor and a well known forthright fellow. One day he made contact with Percy to let him know that Sir John would be away for the next council meeting and to get his application in again. Percy did so, and this time it was approved.

It was said that Sir John was not pleased when he heard of it, but was powerless to reverse the council's decision. So the Nelson Garage was built with accommodation in the form of a small metal clad bungalow alongside the garage. Percy also had other important plans, he had courted Miss Hilda Lawrence for some time and they decided to marry that same year.

(Figure 30) Record of building the Nelson Garage in 1929

(Figure 31) Left; Percy filling a 1925 Clyno owner R Teaque, Villa Store, Brecon. Above, Percy's first car a 1922 Morris bullnosed Cowley.

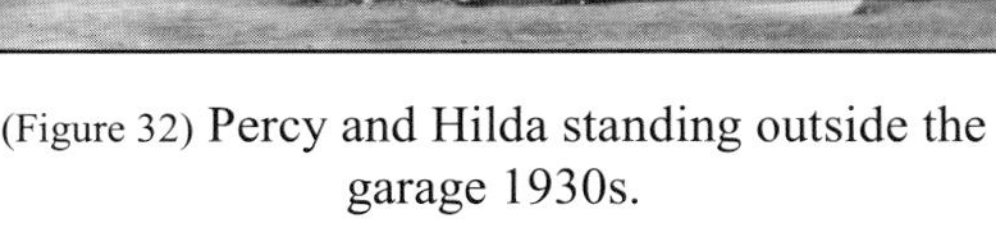

(Figure 32) Percy and Hilda standing outside the garage 1930s.

(Figure 33) Percy nursing his son sitting on the bumper of his 1930 Morris Oxford

My father remembers first meeting Percy in January 1929 when the active members of the village congregated at the pond behind the Nelson to ice skate on the frozen water.
In due course children came along, sadly they lost Peter in 1934 and Brian in 1935 both in infancy, they are buried in Bridge Sollers churchyard. Two daughters followed, Jean and Vivian. Percy and Hilda attended Bridge Sollers church on a regular basis for the next 50 years.
During the 1939-45 war, Percy was joined by his brother-in-law and the garage business concentrated on the repairs of agricultural machinery. At this time Percy was running a motorcar and providing a taxi service, which was in great demand for weddings and funerals, also for meeting visitors and collecting returning servicemen from Hereford railway station.
Becoming a well known reliable man, his garage business expanded and to cater for more vehicles on the road he installed an underground tank and petrol pump; by 1955 that had expanded to five pumps. When he first started Percy sold petrol from two-gallon tins at 18d per gallon.
During the war Percy and his family moved up to Lena cottage to live with Mrs Lawrence, Hilda's mother; the family was enlarged further when Mrs Alderton senior joined them. Percy purchased Bridge Ash in 1952 from Miss Abberley and the whole family moved into Bridge Ash.

(Figure 34) Nelson Garage in the 1950s.

In 1960 Percy sold the garage to Texaco, the petrol retailers. Royston Jones who had worked previously at the County Garage in Hereford, became Texaco's first tenant of the garage. Don Ellerton rented the back workshop, he was a racing car mechanic and for several years the high-pitched scream of testing racing engines could be heard echoing across the Bishopstone fields. Texaco built the new service station around 1966 employing Dennis Murphy as manager.
Percy became a part-time postman for a while delivering mail to Bishopstone and the surrounding area in the early 1970s. When Byford School closed, he bought a mini bus and had a contract to transport children to Staunton on Wye school.
Hilda started doing bed and breakfast at Bridge Ash, and enjoyed the company of visitors from all over the country. Their eldest daughter Jean married and went live on the Isle of Skye in Scotland. Daughter Vivian also married and moved to South Africa. Eventually Hilda's health deteriorated, she found the stairs difficult, so Bridge Ash was sold and Deanswood, a bungalow in the village was purchased. Hilda, always known to the villagers as "Mrs Alderton," passed away in March 1989. Percy died on August 4th 1993 in Stretton Nursing Home and as my father commented at the time, a piece of Bishopstone history died with him.

Kenchester School[5]

After the closure of Bishopstone School in 1894 the majority of the parish children attended Kenchester School, the only exception being the families occupying the few cottages and farms belonging to Garnons Estate, whose children attended Byford school.
In 1821 Lady Southhampton who lived at that time in the New Weir, gave an endowment of money for a chapel and school at Kenchester. By 1826 the chapel was built. A religious enthusiast and pioneer, Lady Southampton had a great urge to give education to the poor so before her death in 1838 she had not only established the evangelical ministry of the Word by founding the chapel but had built a Boys' and girls' school to accommodate 100 pupils with teachers residences adjoining.
Later, owing to a dwindling population and the fact other schools were being established in the neighbourhood the boys' and girls' schools were combined.
In the early 1920s my father remembers eleven children from Bishon Common walking to school along the footpath that then ran beside the Yazor Brook.
In 1920 the school children were very interested in drama, with the school taking second prize in a drama competition at the Community Council festival in Hereford. They presented the play Darby and Joan and the adjudicator remarked on the excellence of the performance.
Mr Griffiths, owner of The Weir, offered yearly scholarships to the Girls High School.
He paid all the school charges, Phyllis Jones and my mother Kathleen Wall were two who won the scholarships in September 1920. They both remembered those long school days, leaving Bishopstone at 7 o'clock in the morning to walk to Credenhill Station to catch the train into Hereford, while after school the train timetable meant they would not arrive home until 7 o'clock at night.

This higher level of education for girls in the 1920s gave no greater job opportunities, unless your parents were well off. My mother and Phyllis after their High School education could only find work by going into the service of large households as maids. The only benefits they both achieved from attending the High School was learning to play the piano. Phyllis was the organist at Bishopstone for many years starting at the young age of seventeen; it was no mean achievement to play the Father Smith organ in Bishopstone church that was reputed to be difficult to play. My mother was the organist at Kenchester church 1947-64 and also organist for Bishopstone church from 1957-82.

(Figure 35) **Miss Painter's Class Kenchester School 1921**
Back Row Miss Painter (Teacher) Albert Walker, Eddy Rudd, Bill Thomas, Cecil Macklin, William Watkins.
Middle Row Dolly Gwilliam, Ada Powell, Ethel Williams, ??, Dorothy Morgan, Lucy Hill, ??.
Front Row Russell Watkins, Frank Portman, Molly Wall, Grace Walker, Joyce Walker, ??, ??, ??
Launa Jones, Vera Rutherford, Tom Bethel. **Front** Harold Watkins.

The 1932 records show that there were 57 pupils on the Kenchester School register. Miss Hughes was the certified teacher with Miss Eva Painter as the supplementary teacher. (Eva was born in Bishopstone at Banbury Cottage) Miss Hughes was the sister of the Reverend Hughes, minister of Lady Southampton Chapel. By 1934 the average attendance was down to 39. On February 9th 1934 Miss Hughes resigned as head mistress of Kenchester School after 43 years of filling the post, her total service to the school was 51 years, which constituted a record for the county. She lived for a period at Panteg Cottage in Bishopstone before moving back to live with her brother at the Residence in Kenchester. Three years after her retirement Miss Hughes died. Her funeral was held on February 18th 1937 and the school was closed for the day in respect. After Miss Hughes retired Miss Olive Ferris was the head mistress for two years, until she moved to take up a new post as Head of Kington Primary School. Mrs Griffiths who followed Miss Ferris as head mistress lived in the Chapel House.

A few log book entries in 1934.
June 13th; School closed today for the visit of the Duke and Duchess of York at the Three Counties Show at Hereford. August 28th the school annual outing went to Malvern by coach. November 29th School closed by royal command in honour of the wedding of Prince George and Princess Marina of Greece.
November 30th The parents of the girls object to their daughters changing into gym kit on the grounds of indecency, I have therefore decided to run two separate gym classes, the boys only in the boys yard, the girls in the girls yard, the girls are then able to do their exercise in navy knickers without being indecent.
December 6th six travellers left Bishopstone for Cheltenham they are clean and well-behaved children.
This entry refers to the Smith family who were a proud Romany gipsy family; they left Bishon Common on the December 6th 1934 after selling their plot of land on the Common to Ernest Hybart.

My father remembers seeing them leave the parish, their brightly painted caravan heading down the road towards Kenchester followed by a dray and several pinto ponies. After this the visiting gipsies parked their caravan on the road verges, either at the junction of Bunshill lane or yearly by the willow tree by the five gates, using the willow to make their pegs.
An entry in the school logbook made on January 6th 1938 records the first warning of the impending war: School practiced gas-mask drill.

(Figure 36) **Kenchester School 1938**
Back Row. Mrs Griffith (Teacher), Betty Spencer, Lorna Scammell, Violet Synnock, Molly Caunsell, Joyce Rawlings, Nancy Watkins, Rosie Rudd, Edith Macklin, Joyce Roberts, Margery Cartwright, Miss Painter (Infant Teacher).
Middle Row. Eric Davies, Leslie Spencer, Mary Davies, Norah Griffiths, Helen Haines, John Griffiths, Molly Hill, Phyllis Rudd, Gyn Lewis, Trevor Watkins, Eric Hill.
Front Row. Tom Prosser, George Bullock, Geoff Clark, Dennis Hill, Earnest Rudd, Steve Rounds, Ken Davies, Wilf Rawling.

The logbook records that the children spent many lessons gardening in the school garden, this garden is now the grassed triangle of land outside Kenchester chapel but then a tall perimeter hedge protected it. The sports field for the school was in the small meadow on the west of the five gates.
Miss Heep became the head mistress during the war period, followed in 1948 by Miss Sedman who became the last head mistress of the school; Miss Painter taught the infants. In the W I History of 1955 it records, “The school is not modern, but improvements of a central heating plant and electricity in 1945 did help” but on the downside it records, “The lavatories are flushed once a week”.
School dinners started in 1942 with the food brought from a canteen in Hereford. The new kitchen was built onto the school in 1952, where a paid helper prepared the food and washed up. The children paid for their dinners, except for those in poor circumstances who had them issued free.
The records show that pupils were taken each week for outside study, including forestry studies in Garnons woods. A party of children searched for traces of Offa’s Dyke and also visited the New Weir gardens and glass house.
The school had regular visits by the School Medical Officer, and district nurse, a logbook entry records that the standard of cleanliness and dress was beyond reproach for many years, a real tribute to the wonderful care given to the children by their parents. The dental service also visited the school regularly in their van.
The main domestic subjects taught were cookery, needlework and gardening in the school garden.
In the 1965 W I Scrapbook is a list, naming the following subjects taught at the school: Arithmetic, English, Nature, Find out, Painting, Handwork Modelling, P E and Spelling. Adding *“sometimes we listen to French records and the school radio”.*

(Figure 37) **Kenchester School 1949**

Back Row. Freddy Bowen, John Payne, Nora Bradley, Evelyn Stinton, Margery Rudd, John Gregory, Tony Tippins.

Standing. Bill Carpenter, Rhoda Jones, Rita Thomas, Irene Gregory, Betty Price, Sylvia Tippins, Michael Stinton.

Sitting. John Bullock, Joyce Reynolds, Sylvia Baugh, David Macklin, John Clark.

Front. Harry Gregory, Ken Montague, Edward Carpenter.

Kenchester School closed on March 18th 1970 having provided the main schooling for Bishopstone children since 1894. All the children still attending the school in 1970 were transferred to Credenhill School which is still today the designated primary school for the parish.

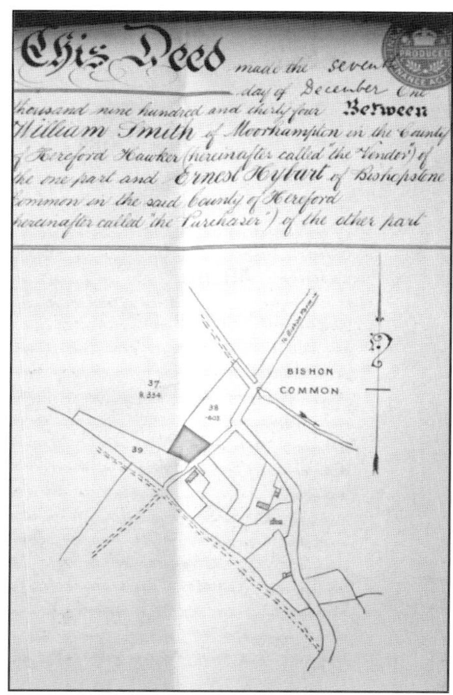

This Deed made the seven
day of December One
thousand nine hundred and thirty four Between
William Smith of Moorhampton in the County
of Hereford Hawker (hereinafter called "the Vendor") of
the one part and Ernest Hybart of Bishopstone
Common in the said County of Hereford
(hereinafter called "the Purchaser") of the other part

In 1932 William Smith a hawker from Moorhampton[6] purchased the old enclosure plot 41 on Bishon Common. In 1826 James Lewis had built a cottage on the site; James his son who worked for Rev Lane Freer as a pageboy inherited the cottage after his father's death. In the 1850s he emigrated to Australia and the cottage fell into disrepair. Arthur Lawrence gave a written statement attached to the sale paperwork, as no deeds existed for the quarter acre site.

"The land formerly belonged to my mother's brother James Lewis who many years ago went to Australia and was never heard of again. The said James purported to give the property to my mother Harriet Lawrence, on her death on November 23rd 1917, I took possession of the said land."

The gypsies used the site as winter quarters for a couple of years, living in their brightly painted horse drawn caravan. Guy's Hospital wanted to buy the ground but seemed unwilling to deal directly with William Smith, so an intermediary, Ernest Hybart the tailor who lived in Lena Cottage, acted on their behalf. He paid William Smith £24 for the land on December 7th 1934, and then sold it on to Guy's Hospital the next day for the same price.

From March 28th 1934 all new drivers had to take a driving test. There were four vehicle owners in Bishopstone at this time Percy Alderton, Captain Gilbert, Albert Macklin and Peter Thomson. Any drivers who had a licence before this date never needed to take a test as they were exempt. My father possessed one of these licences although he went through a voluntary driving test whilst in the R A F.

Geoffrey Morgan Jones told me a story about Bishopstone *"As a boy in the mid 1930s, I was great friends with John Roberts, the rector's son. Captain Gilbert bred fancy cockerels so he could use the feathers for fly-fishing. One particular cockerel he could never catch, so he said to John Roberts that if he could catch him, he could keep him. We managed to catch the cockerel with the help of grain and a fishing net. I took it back to the farm and let him run with the hens, he soon fought and killed the old Rhode Island Red cockerel. Thinking I was on to a good thing I arranged a cockfight with Stanley Lewis of Court Farm for a wager of 1s, on my cockerel to win. We put the pair together at Court Farm and soon my cockerel had killed their prize Rhode Island Red. We boys who were watching soon scattered on the arrival of a very angry Mrs Lewis, Stanley's mother, a very formidable lady. I never collected my winnings"*

On November 25th 1935 John Pember was buried in Bishopstone churchyard. He died in Weobley Workhouse as a pauper, John had worked as a shepherd at Bunshill farm he had lodged with John and Sarah Wall (my grandparents) at Stonehouse since 1910. Dad remembers John Pember as an old man shuffling along the road crippled with arthritis but still working at lambing time on Bunshill farm.

The Pembers were the parish masons in Bishopstone all through the 19th century, their burial plots in front of the church door contain three large chest monuments, evidence of their wealth; John was buried in an unmarked grave on the edge of the churchyard.

(Figure 38)
Sir John Cotterell

On November 13th 1937 Sir John Cotterell died, he was the 4th Baronet. During his lifetime he had been a captain in the Life Guards and High Sheriff of Hereford in 1879. On his death Sir Richard became the 5th Baronet.

The parishioners celebrated the coronation of King George VI and Queen Elizabeth on May 12th 1937. To mark the occasion the children were given a day off school, and festivities for the children and adults were held at Bishon Farm. In the wainhouse everyone had a sit down meal at lunchtime, consisting of cold beef, ham, jelly and fruit, and plenty of beer for all. Games followed the lunch and were enjoyed by both the children and adults. Then everyone sat down for tea followed by the presentation of a coronation mug to each child. A firework display organised by my grandfather Albert Macklin in the evening provided the finale. The china and glass purchased for the event was afterwards presented to the parish. The cost of the activities was covered by house-to-house collections. George Phillips now living in Orchard Close can remember the evening display of fireworks as a ten year old. This was the first recorded time Bishon Farm was used as a venue for any village event, after this the farm was used for royal celebrations and fundraising events on numerous occasions.

Second World War 1939-45

War was declared with Germany on September 3rd 1939, and on January 1st 1940 two million 19 to 27 year olds were called up for military service, and food rationing started a week later. Bishopstone already had two career service men, Cecil Macklin and Arthur Portman. The war changed Bishopstone, like many other parishes forever. The pre war class system still had a place in parish society, Peter Watkins remembers attending church on Sundays after war was declared, *"The Gilberts' pew was the first in the south transept, Bishon Farm was the second row, it was all very formal.*

(Figure 39) Captain Gilbert with his wartime pony

As a member of the farming class I could only say "Good morning Miss Olyffe" "Good Morning Miss Eleanor", you couldn't chat them up or anything." Bishopstone Court occupied the front pew in the north transept, all the labourers and workers sat in the aisle pews, this class system gradually disappeared after the war."

"Everyone had two jobs" Tom Prosser said, *"if you were on a protected occupation being an agricultural worker you had to join the Home Guard. Other wartime directives sent some people like Fred Rounds from agricultural to work on the railways".* The under seventeens joined the ATS at Weobley, which as Tom said would mean changing when you came home from work and then riding over to Weobley on your bicycle to learn drill, route marching and map reading. Every weekend trainees practised on the firing range at Credenhill Camp.

Dennis Johnson and his father were the local special constables, checking the movement of people. Jim Gough and Mr. Haimes were the air raid wardens, patrolling the village at night looking for any chink of light showing through the blackout curtains. If there was, it meant a harsh rap on the door, they were both very conscientious about their job. We had a few evacuees in the parish: one, a young girl called Veronica, was put up by my grandmother for a while. George Holder's brother and family were bombed out from their home in London, so they moved into the middle house of Burcott Row. George's sister-in-law brought her mother, Mrs Fanny Pickle and a boy called Alan Row, about 15 years old, said to be Mrs Pickle's son. A couple of conscientious objectors fled London and moved into the middle house of the Clovers, they were called Benjamin and Edith Nation.

The two eldest Wall girls returned home from service in London after their employers' houses were bombed out. They joined their youngest sister Molly working at the Munitions Factory, Rotherwas. Jim Gough was given a war directive from gardening to working as a policeman on the gates of the Munitions Factory. Captain Gilbert was called up again thus serving in both World Wars, he was sent to Brecon; all his servants were called up for war duties. With petrol rationed the Gilberts' car was stored away and out came the pony and trap again. Mrs. Gilbert and her daughter Olyffe went hop picking at Marsh Farm as part of their contribution to the war effort, such a contrast from her childhood when she was looked after by many servants. Towards the end of the war a Catholic Irish lady by the name of Maggie O'Reilly from Bartestree Convent came to help out at the rectory.

(Figure 40) Mrs Gilbert watching Harry Stinton bushelling the hops Marsh Farm.

(Figure 41) Above. L to R. Mrs Jones, Mrs Meadham and Mrs May Cartwright who lived at No 1 The Clovers and an unknown girl. Marsh Farm
Left the Alderton family hop picking just before the war. Marsh Farm

The Canadians started the building of Foxley Camp on January 27th 1940, work ceased due to the worst storm of the century sweeping the country. Major Davenport recalls seeing birds frozen in the trees. The driving rain had turned overnight to freezing rain encapsulating the poor birds as they perched.

In 1942 the Americans started to build their sector of Foxley Camp. Tom Prosser and Joe Haines from the village worked on this sector as carpenters. When the building work finished in 1943 Tom and Joe now aged 17 travelled by train to Worcester to join up, Tom into the R A F and Joe into the Royal Marines.

(Figure 42) Building Foxley camp in the winter of 1940.

Every Saturday night trucks were sent to the villages, including Bishopstone, from Foxley Camp to pick up local girls for the weekly dance. At these dances two of the Wall girls from the parish met and eventually married service men stationed at Foxley. Molly Wall married an American, John Martin, a private in the U S Army on May 29th 1945 by special licence at Bishopstone Church. Her eldest sister Doris travelled to Canada and married Wilfred Forget in Orilla Ontario in 1950.

(Figure 43) Gathering hay at Stonehouse in 1943 Canadian serviceman Wilf Forget left, local helpers centre, Sam Gwilliam far right. Bishon Farm's Fordson tractor and hay cart

(Figure 44) Molly Wall, G I John Martin and his friend standing outside what today would be the driveway to "The Lindens".

Tragedy came to Bishopstone on Thursday June 4th 1942. The Hereford Times dated June 6th reported that the river was being dragged at Bridge Sollers after receiving a report a lad had been drowned there whilst bathing on Thursday evening around 7.30 pm. The boy's name was stated as Leslie Derek Henry Holder aged 17 years of Banbury Cottage Bishopstone. Leslie had gone with a group of lads, some from Bishopstone including Joe Haines, to cool off in the river after a hot summer's day. They had gone to a then popular bathing area called the Saltbox just up river of Bridge Sollers Bridge and whilst crossing the river he stepped into a deep hole and disappeared under the surface. The boys dived down but could not find him, Mr Compton from the Marsh Farm was fetched and he dived late into the night into the river but nothing was found. Police dragged the river all day Friday with no result. The body was discovered on Sunday by a serviceman going down for an early morning dip. The inquest held at Madley, heard evidence from his father George Holder and Miss Betty Lewis to say that as far as they knew Leslie could not swim. The funeral was held at Bridge Sollers church on Tuesday afternoon. It was attended by the Weobley Flight and Kington Flight of the Air Training Corps of which Leslie was a member. They provided the bearer party; Tom Prosser, also a member of the Corps remembers it well as being too tall to march with the other bearers he marched in front of the coffin. Two flights of Corps marched behind the wheeled bier from Banbury Cottage down the New Road to the church. The last post and reveille were sounded at the graveside, then the Air Training Corps saluted and marched away. Lt P B Compton represented the Home Guard for whom Leslie acted as a messenger.

Photograph by VIVIANS

Lawrence, R. W. Handley, G. Hicks, G. Stinton, W. H. Mills, A. Stinton, J. Humphries, I. J.
Montague, W. Black, J. H. Reynolds, G. Hughes, G. Peake, H. Holder, G. Bayliss, H. Montague, F.
Langford, R. Lewis, J. R. Portman, W. Skyrme, T. Price, G. J. (L/Cpl.) Hart, A. C. Davies, R. Hamer, D. Evans, F.
Eacock, R. (L/Cpl.) Baugh, S. (L/Cpl.) Haines, G. (Sgt.) Lawrence, G.S. (Lt) (Coy. Q M.) Hollis, J A. (Major) (Coy Cmdr.) Compton, P.B. (Capt) (Pl. Cmdr.) Powell, A J. (Sgt.) Jones, R.G. (Cpl.) Alderton, P.H. (L/Cpl.)

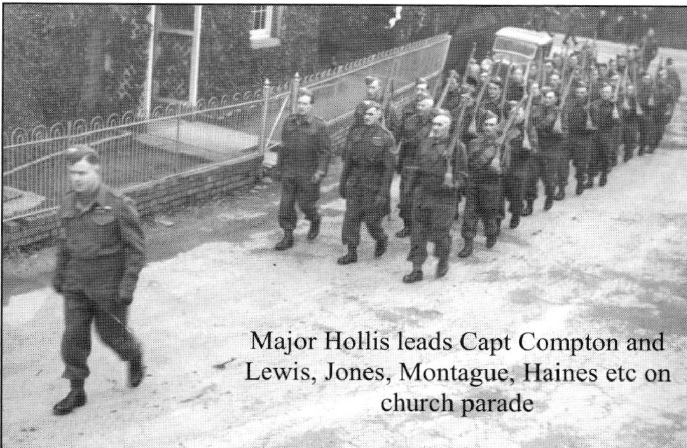

Major Hollis leads Capt Compton and Lewis, Jones, Montague, Haines etc on church parade

The local Home Guard was formed on July 23rd 1940, made up from local volunteers living in the parishes of Bridge Sollers, Byford and Bishopstone, aged between 17 and 65. They were called 22 Platoon, "F" Company 4th Herefordshire Battalion. Captain Basil Compton, tenant of the Marsh Farm Bridge Sollers was made Platoon Commander. Major Hollis land agent for Garnons Estate who lived at Downshill House was made Company Commander over several local platoons. Beside Major Hollis the other Bishopstonians who served in the Home Guard were Sergeant George Haines, Corporal Bob Jones, Lance Corporal Percy Alderton, Private George Reynolds, Private George Holder, Private Fred Montague, Private Bill Montague, Private Henry Peake and Private Fred Rounds who served with the Stretton Sugwas Platoon.

The Home Guard headquarters was in the wooden bungalow overlooking Bridge Sollers Bridge, with a pillbox containing a machine gun on top of the bank across the road, which they manned. One exercise involved the Americans from Foxley Camp acting as the enemy trying to capture the bridge; the Home Guard using local knowledge soon rounded up the Americans and locked then up as prisoners in the bungalow, leaving their commander wandering around looking for his men.

A Secret Service was operating within Bishopstone parish during the war, unknown to its parishioners. In June 1940 after the Dunkirk evacuation undercover volunteer units were formed in the area. With a real threat of invasion from the Germans, secret resistance organisations were formed all over the country. The idea was to fight the Germans by means of sabotage after the invasion, the instructions given to each group were to slow down their advance through the country by blowing up bridges, road and rail, and carrying out guerrilla warfare. The local group covering this area was called Adam Patrol and a permanent underground operational base was built on Bishopstone Hill.

One of Adam Patrol's members was Geoffrey Morgan Jones of Sugwas who told me about this secret organization and he recently contributed to a book written about their operations in Herefordshire during the war.

Geoffrey said the operation base on Bishopstone Hill was built underground and had a corrugated iron roof, a small disguised entry trapdoor and a small-boarded escape tunnel. The Royal Engineers had done a brilliant job in its construction especially as there was no sign of any spoil; the vent-breathing pipe was hidden in a large tree 30 feet away. Near the operational base was a separate underground explosives store, entered via a hidden trap door, which contained timer, grenades, nitro-glycerine, and phosphorous, and some plastic explosive. *"We never approached the operational base in daylight and always used a different route to approach the base."* Their operational role was as he said, *"to be a bloody nuisance to the Gerrys"* the main targets in the area were the bridges on the Hereford to Brecon railway line, Bridge Sollers bridge and several road bridges on the main A438, "they had all been recced in secret by us, to work out what explosive were needed to bring them down, hence the positioning of the base on Bishopstone Hill." After D-Day the threat became less so the group was disbanded. The Royal Engineers removed the operational base after the war.

Several land girls were employed on Bunshill Farm in the war years including Margaret Hopkins of Wembley London, who went on to marry Frank Price of Magna Castra Farm, Kenchester in 1944. Court Farm were said to have used land girls in the war, but I have been unable to find out their names. Vera Peat, a 17 year old from Liverpool was billeted in Bishopstone for a short period during the war, her memories of the time were sent to me by her daughter Bev.

"I joined the Timber Corps when I was 17 yrs old, very exciting, but also rather daunting. I remember standing in the railway station (Lime St), with other girls looking as lost as I myself felt; had I done the right thing?

Our first posting was Bury St Edmunds working in a sawmill for the first 6 weeks, a rather frightening experience at first, handling those huge circular saws. I could not see the sense in that part of it really, working alongside the men, I don't suppose they liked the idea either. We lived in huge huts with big fires in the middle. The men were not service men. I could never understand the point of that part of the training, but still, it was part of the job.

After 6 weeks, we were all split up, rather sad really, and sent to different parts of the country. My friend, Sylvia and I were sent to Hereford. As soon as I stepped from the train I loved it. We were taken to live with Mr and Mrs Kitching, two of the nicest people I had ever known.

The house was called Scaldback Cottage in Bishopstone. It was an old cottage with a well in the front garden from where we drew the water. There was a big field at the back where Mr Kitching had 2 cows and a couple of pigs. One was huge and chased us everywhere. At the back of the cottage was a huge house with tennis lawns. Ralph and Abby took Syl and I there for a game of tennis but said we were rubbish. Mrs Kitching had worked for years as a cook. We met the son but not the rest of the family.

I was very impressed with it all. The cottage was lovely, with oil lamps for lighting. After a while Ralph and Abby came home on leave and taunted the life out of us. They thought it was great having two young girls living there. When we were having a bath in the kitchen in the tin bath, they would rattle the door latch as if they were coming through. Mrs Kitching would be shouting "leave the girls alone, stop tormenting them". I remember vividly getting out of the bath and into my silky pyjamas that stuck to every part of my body. (far too much information for her daughter, thank you very much!), Ralph picked me up, dashed across the back field and dumped me into the cow trough. Mrs Kitching going mad and Mr Kitching sucking on his pipe and grinning. (I can't imagine why!?)

Once a week, Syl and I would walk to Credenhill to catch the RAF bus to Hereford for the cinema. Then we had to stand in a huge queue for a bus back to the camp. We had offers of their company from the camp home, but thought that we'd rather face the ghosts of the Roman soldiers that haunted that lane than the passions of the service men.

Mrs Kitching would be waiting for us by the fire with her knitting, always with a hot drink ready for us before bed. She really was a second mum.

The countryside around about was beautiful. Mrs Kitching would make Syl and me a picnic to eat by the river. We loved it

Our work was very hard. We always suffered with blisters on our hands. We would cut pit props, then take them by wagon to the railway sidings.

I remember finding 3 baby mice amongst the timber and taking them home. Mrs Kitching gave me a shoebox to keep them above my bed. Sylvia hated them. I can't remember what happened to them. Ralph probably dumped them while I was at work. Must admit, those boys nearly drove us mad for that fortnight, but I think on the whole, we enjoyed them being there, we missed them when they went back.

Again, Hereford is a wonderful place, I really loved it. Then it was alive. Full of Americans, Canadians and of course English, all vying with one another.
After a few months, Syl and I were moved to other parts of the country. I missed Mr and Mrs Kitching, nowhere else was quite the same and I was sorry I lost touch with them."
The timber was cut from the local woods and hauled to the sidings at Credenhill station, the locals had frightened the girls by telling tales of the ghosts of Roman soldiers supposedly haunting the road around Magna Castra field.

Getting a meal ready at Bishopstone Court, Rugby School.

(Figure 45) 1943 Bishopstone Court, Mrs Stanley Lewis and Betty Lewis standing behind the table

Another little known event that happened locally throughout the war years was the Harvest Camp held at Bishopstone Court Farm. Every year from 1940 until 1945 the boys from the public school of Rugby camped on the farm to help gather in the harvest from the Court and surrounding farms.
In 1940 the County War Agricultural Committee under the Ministry of Agriculture were given the task of increasing farm production as a vital contribution to the war effort. They doubled the amount of land under the plough in Herefordshire by 1944.
But how were they going to be able to gather in this extra production in crops, with many farm labourers away fighting in the war? Land Army girls helped but willing though they were, couldn't make up the difference alone.
The answer was to recruit an army of boys and girls from schools and youth groups, set up camp in the county for a few weeks and help with the harvest. Many of these groups came from public schools. In 1945 thirty eight of these camps were held throughout Herefordshire. The master in charge of the Rugby School boys in Bishopstone was Mr R M Carey, what follows is his report on the camp.

Rugby School Bishopstone Farming Camp.[7]
This year the number in the camp was reduced to 20, and in many ways this proved an extremely pleasant number; we supplied many of the farmers within 2 miles of Bishopstone, and as usual, the boys were very much struck by the cordiality and kindliness of both farmers and labourers. Many of them, on leaving, said how they had enjoyed the camp, and hoped to come next year and put in a plea to work at the same farm, for they had got to like their fellow workers. Of course the work at one Camp very much resembles that of another, and in common with other camps we stoked, pitched and carried bales, threshed and cut thistles in wet weather; and at the end of the camp were able to look at a considerable area of farm land completely cleared- a most satisfactory sight.

(Figure 46) Boys loading a cart Bishopstone Court 1943

We shall be glad if the Hereford W A E C could add to its efficient record by eliminating all queen wasps next May, as we had two nests within 100 yards of our dining room! However we fairly soon learnt how to take them; normally the powder was arid, but once or twice the nest was destroyed with a spade and a bucket of water as the only offensive weapons. In fact bathing and wasp destruction were our main relaxations. The Camp were unanimous in their feeling of grateful thanks to Mr Lewis, who was a most kind and hospitable host.

We must not forget our local children attending Kenchester School, the logbook records the older children throughout the war years helping out at Bunshill Farm, Magna Castra Farm and the Old Weir, where they spent many school hours singling mangolds, hay hauling and bringing in the harvest.
The logbook also records that on July 24th 1939 five weeks before war was declared "I gave first instruction on Scatter and Cover as suggested by Education Committee, It takes 2 mins to assemble the whole School ready dressed and a further 5 mins to Scatter and Cover."

Bishopstones service personnel World War 11.

This brass plaque in the church lists three names John Gilbert, Cecil Haimes and John Williams who died in the 2nd World War, in fact there were four men associated with the parish who died. The missing name is Douglas Hill who was living with his parents in Scaldback cottage when he received his conscription papers.

John Gilbert 6144734 East Surrey Regiment.

John Gilbert

John was the first Bishopstone resident to be killed in the war; he was the eldest son of Humphrey and Margaret Gilbert from the Old Rectory. John Humphrey Kyrle Gilbert was killed on May 20th 1940, he was only 21 years old. John was Company Quartermaster Sergeant for the East Surrey Regiment. Regimental records state that the Brigade had been retreating from Belgium towards Dunkirk. They had set up headquarters in a farmhouse near Amiens. On May 20th 1940 German armoury overran the headquarters. As Company Quartermaster John would have been in or by the farmhouse, he was possibly killed in the defence of the building. The company commander escaped from the farmhouse but was left behind enemy lines, the French farming community hid him and he arrived home after many months having escaped through Spain. John is buried in Plot 9, Row G; Grave 13 in the Abbeville Communal Cemetery Extension France.

Cecil Haimes

Cecil Haimes 14389065 7bn Leicester Regiment.
Cecil was the son of Arthur and Ella Haimes, head gamekeeper for Garnons estate. The family had lived in Mansell Gamage before purchasing the cottage on Bishon Lane just before the outbreak of war. Bevan and Hodges, a Hereford building company, employed Cecil as a carpenter; my father could remember him cycling to work in Hereford. He was conscripted in 1940 as a 30 year old, after basic training he was posted to the South Staffordshire Regiment and afterward transferred to the 7th Battalion Leicestershire Regiment where he trained for the special forces called the "Chindits" specializing in jungle warfare against the Japanese. He left Liverpool by ship in early 1943 bound for India. On their arrival in Bombay they were flown straight into the jungle. Cecil spent some months of jungle fighting in an operation to take Malaysia, called Operation Thursday. After fierce fighting and the loss of 73 soldiers the battalion was disbanded and the men were attached to the Indian 3rd Army. The Chindits used mules to carry their equipment through the jungle, and were famous for never leaving a man behind. Cecil was transferred to the large military hospital in Maynamat suffering from neuritis of the hands. Just prior to hearing that Cecil had died from malaria in hospital Mr & Mrs Haimes had received a cablegram saying he was in hospital but doing well. Cecil is buried in the Maynamat War Cemetery in Bangladesh, Plot 10, Row E, Grave 3.

Douglas Hill 14506120 6th Airborne Divisions.
Douglas was the second son of Francis and Ellen Mary Hill from Scaldback Cottages, his eldest brother Frank lived for many years in Burcott Row. On his 17th birthday in 1941 Douglas's conscription papers arrived. Peter Watkins of Bishon Farm remembers bumping into Douglas in Hereford one Saturday and going for a drink with him, he told Peter that he was trying to get into the Parachute Regiment, this was the last time anyone from Bishopstone saw him. Douglas landed in France on D-Day June 6th 1944 and died 19 days later in the battle to take Caen. He was 20 years old. Douglas was buried in Ranville War Cemetery Plot 11a, Row 6, Grave 2; Ranville was the first village liberated after the Normandy landings.

John Williams 4105028 46th Regt. Reconnaissance Corps, R. A. C.
John was the brother of Catherine Hale who lived on Bishon Common, her husband Howard was the roadman in Bishopstone for many years. John, whose full name was Felix Rhyddach Jack Williams, was aged 17 and living with his sister and her husband when he received his conscription papers. John served with the Herefordshire Regiment until he moved to the Reconnaissance Corps and was attached to the 46th Regt; he sailed from Liverpool on the liner Duchess of Bedford on January 10th 1943 arriving in Algiers on January 17th. John took part in the army's advance through Tunisia pushing the Germans back. The Germans sent reinforcements from Sicily to Northern Tunisia and in the battle to stop the advance just outside the town of Beja, on February 28th 1943 John Williams was killed. He was 22 years old. He is buried in the Beja War Cemetery, Plot 1, Row D, Grave 9.

After the First World War a roll naming all the men from the parish who served their country was commissioned and hung in the church but unfortunately no similar roll was made of the persons who served in the Second World War. I found it fairly difficult to trace the people who served in the forces, as many did not appear on Bishopstone's voters' list because they were mostly under 21, so I have had to rely on the memories of the older residents, although I am sure there will be someone I have missed. The four killed in action were easy to find, as comprehensive records exist for the war dead. Of the others who served their country and survived the war, for some I was able to obtain a lot of information, while for others I have just a name.

Percy Bradley

Percy Bradley
Percy and Catherine Bradley came to live in Pleck Cottage in spring 1939 just before the declaration of war. He was called up by conscription in December 1941. Percy was in the REME that was attached to the Eighth Army fighting up through Italy and into Germany, Janet his daughter recalls her mother saying "she never heard from him for four years"; he saw his son Gerald for the first time when he returned home after the war, he was aged four.

(Figure 47) Percy who was fighting with the Eighth Army reaches Capannori Italy

Gwendoline Bryan
Gwendoline is recorded as living in Bunshill Cottages during the war, she was one of only two women holding a service vote, listed on the 1946 voters list for Bishopstone, I have found no other record for Gwendoline.

George Cartwright
George had grown up in No 1 The Clovers. He had wanted to join the Navy, but was turned down because of a sight problem, and so he joined the REME. Because he was underage George lied about his age to get in, he passed out in February 1943 with No. 2 Section, "D" Company L.T.B.R.E. George was stationed in the north of Scotland during the War, after the war he stayed on in the Army for about five years helping with the clear up in Germany.

George Cartwright

Ernle Gilbert

Ernle Gilbert Army
One of the three Gilberts who entered service in the Second World War, Ernle like his brother John fell into the catchment of the 17 to 21 conscription introduced in April 1939. After 6 months training he graduated as a corporal. He was attached to a gunner troop and by 1942 he was promoted to Major. Ernle fought up through Italy into Austria before ending up in Germany.

Humphrey Gilbert

Captain Humphrey Gilbert Army
Captain Gilbert was one of the few who served in both World Wars, although not sent abroad he served in logistics for a pioneer corps in the Knighton area from their depot in Brecon.

Joe Haines

Joe Haines Royal Marine.
Joe was born and brought up in the parish, son of George and Bessie Haines from Forge Cottage. In August 1943 he travelled with his cousin Tom Prosser to Worcester to join up. Joe had his eighteenth birthday on the beach of the D-day landings and then fought up through France and Germany.

Abby Kitching

Albert (Abby) Kitching R A F
One of the Kitching twins who lived with their parents Charlie and Rose at Scaldback Cottage, born and brought up in Bishopstone. Aged 17 when conscription was first introduced in April 1939, they were among the first parishioners to leave the village.

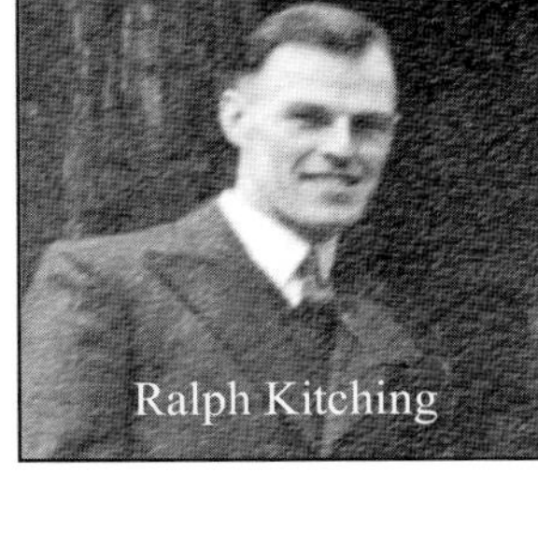
Ralph Kitching

Ralph Kitching R A F
After serving throughout the war, Ralph stayed on and became a career serviceman, as a Military Policeman in the R A F.

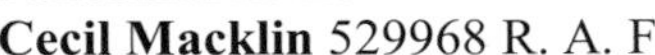

Cecil Macklin

Cecil Macklin 529968 R. A. F.
Cecil joined the R. A. F. on March 4th 1936; after training he was posted to 214 Squadron, Felton, under Bomber Command. The squadron were equipped with the old "Harrow" bombers; a timber-framed aircraft, and Cecil's carpentry skills were used on their maintenance. With the onset of war his role changed and during much of the war he was stationed in various parts of Scotland in charge of a Barrage Balloon Unit protecting vital infrastructure such as the Forth Bridge. Later in the war he returned to wooden airframe maintenance this time on the very successful twin engined Mosquito. Cecil was promoted to Flight Sergeant during the war; he was demobbed on October 24th 1945.

Arthur Portman

Arthur Portman R A F
Arthur was a career serviceman with the R A F, joining in March 1936 with his cousin Cecil Macklin. He moved over to France after D-day helping set up airfields where he stayed for the rest of the war.

Tom Prosser

Tom Prosser R A F VR 3214755
Tom Prosser lived at the Old Post Office, which was then the village shop, with his mother Jessie, and his grandmother Mrs Britten. Tom was seventeen when he went by train to Worcester in August 1943 with his cousin Joe Haines to join up. He joined the R A F and trained as a ground crewman. Tom was posted overseas in October 1944, he landed in India in the November. Posted to 62 Squadron working with Dakota aircraft, Tom moved down through Burma and ended up in Rangoon in January 1946.

Wilf Rawlings

Albert Rawlings

Albert & Wilf Rawlings Army
Both the brothers were born and brought up in Bishopstone they lived at home with their parents George and Lizzy and sister Joyce at No 1 Cambrai cottage. Albert, the eldest, was conscripted in April 1939. Wilf was still a teenager when he took part in the D-day landings, he served with the Kings Own Yorkshire Light Infantry fighting up through France, Belgium, Holland, Austria and finally into Germany.

Steve Rounds. No 14910031.

Steve Rounds

Steve lived in Bunshill Cottages. He joined up in 1943, wanting to join the Herefordshire Regiment but ended up in the K.S.L.I. Steve was later transferred into the Engineering Corps. He entered the war in Belgium, and fought up through Germany. When the war ended he signed up for extra service and stayed in Germany until he was dispatched home in February 1947. On the boat home he asked for a pint at the bar; another voice behind shouted for a pint and the barman said *"from the accent you both must be from the same place."* he looked round and saw it was Wilf Rawlings.

Ethel Thomas Ethel was the other woman serving in the military; her family came to live at Bunshill in the war. Her father worked at Bunshill Farm, her parents stayed after the war eventually ending up in the Almshouses.

Edward Tomkins Edward, son of Charlie Tomkins from the Nelson, had been bought up in the parish from the age of five. He was conscripted in August 1939 on his seventeenth birthday.

Edgar Wall

Edgar Wall Army R.E.M.E. No 7643858

As part of the conscription programme Edgar received his call up papers to report to St Peters Church Hall Hereford on July 26th 1940 where he passed his medical. He had married Mary Bridges at Bishopstone church in 1938 and as a married person his call up to the services would have been delayed. His entry documents state his occupation as van driver, at the time he was driving for Wilson's the florist. Edgar trained with the R.E.M.E. as a mechanic between 1940-42 at Donnington Camp. On April 11th 1942 Edgar set sail on a troop ship from Portsmouth for Bombay in India to fight in the Burma campaign. On April 23rd the ship docked in Capetown where Edgar spent two days exploring and going to the top of Table Mountain by cable car. On May 19th 1942 the ship docked in Bombay and after disembarking and sorting out the kit he moved up to Baceilly on June 5th 1942. This was followed by 30 months of jungle warfare against the Japanese. By Christmas 1945 Edgar had reached Rangoon, the capital of Burma, and as a treat the troops watched live the Tommy Trinder Show, which Edgar enjoyed. In February 1946 Edgar returned home on leave; a happy event followed with the birth of their first child Rosemary on November 10th 1946. Edgar signed up to extend his time in the army and went back to India to help with the clear up, he was finally released from the army on December 3rd 1947. Edgar Wall kept a very comprehensive war diary, thank you to the family for letting me view the diary and extract the above information.

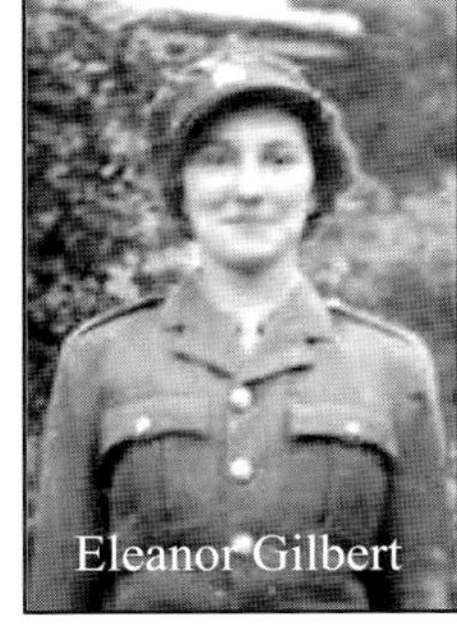
Eleanor Gilbert

Eleanor Gilbert

Eleanor joined the ATS at the start of the war but suffered an injury and was invalided out; she went to work for the Red Cross at Garnstone House which had been converted into a children's hospital during the war. In the later part of the war Eleanor went to Portsmouth and worked for the Navy. She saw the fleet leaving for D Day, and recalls *"It was a Sunday when I was walking on the Downs and looked down on the fleet, there were so many vessels it looked as if you couldn't put a pin between them."*

Bishopstone, Bridge Sollars, Byford,
Kenchester and Mansel Gamage
Welcome Home

Marsh Court,
Bridge Sollars,
Herefordshire.

Dear

The Committee of the above Fund desire me to express to you on their behalf their deep gratitude for the services you have rendered to our country in H.M. Forces during the World War 1939-1945.

The enclosed cheque is sent to you from the five parishes as a small token of appreciation for these services.

Yours sincerely,

Chairman.

A Welcome Home Committee was formed in 1944 to consider the collection of funds as a thank-you offering to the men of the villages who served their country in the war. Bishopstone and Kenchester were joined in this effort by three other parishes, namely Bridge Sollers, Byford and Mansell Gamage.

The chairman of the committee was Mr P B Compton, Marsh Court Farm, Bridge Sollers, the secretary was Miss E K Lewis of Bishopstone Court, and the treasurer, Mr G Lawrence of Byford. There was no parish hall (still the same over sixty years later) so all the meetings were held in the back of the Nelson Inn.

The events held to raise funds included sheep dog trials, gymkhana and other sports to be held on September 30th 1944. There was an auction of a calf and a ram in Hereford Cattle Market, also a whist drive was held at Byford School on November 17th. In the Granary at the Old Weir on December 18th a dance and raffle was held. The total amount raised was £1195, so the seventy four beneficiaries were each given £16 10s 00d on their return home, or in the case of those who lost their lives, the next-of-kin were handed the money as a gift. The war in Europe ended officially on May 8th 1945; Bishopstone held a service of thanksgiving in the church at 4.00pm, which was attended by a large number of parishioners. Three months later on August 15th another service was held to celebrate V J day (Victory over Japan) the official end to all hostilities. It was many months before all the service men and women returned as many were serving in the Far East.

Death of our Patron

Captain R Hinckes

Captain Hinckes of Foxley died on Thursday March 21st 1944 he had been suffering from ill heath for some time. His son Major John Davenport at the time of his father's death was serving in the Mediterranean. In 1931 Major Davenport had changed his name by deed poll from Hinckes back to Davenport, the original family name. Captain Ralf Hinckes served with the Herefordshire Regiment until May 1916 when he was found medically unfit for active foreign service and was posted to the recruiting staff. He will be well remembered for the success he achieved in breeding pedigree Hereford cattle, called the Mansel Court Herd, his Herefords sold worldwide. Throughout his life he travelled extensively and held many prominent public duty posts within Herefordshire.

Rectors, Bishopstone Church and the Father Smith Organ

Rev Roberts Bishon Farm 1937

Rev Thomas Mark Foulkes Roberts MA was instituted to the benefice of Bishopstone on February 27th 1923. He lived in Kenchester Rectory, as he already held the positions of Vicar of Bridge Sollers and Rector of Kenchester. Rev Roberts was rector of Bishopstone for 21 years, he was well liked but not averse to controversy. In the early 1930s he was attending a sale at Hile-Smith the auctioneers in Hereford when he was tackled by a Mr Field from Swainshill who accused him of interfering with his business and said that if he had not been wearing his dog collar he would "knock his block off". The rector instantly took off his dog collar and jacket and laid them on the ground, stood up and held an excellent boxing stance in front of Mr Field. With that Field said no more and hurried off, little did he know Rev Roberts had been a boxing blue at university. He also taught at the Cathedral School. At the beginning of the war Mr Parr from the New Weir purchased a new Rover car for Rev Roberts, sending him up to the factory in Solihull to choose a car off the assembly lines. The Roberts had 5 children, four boys and a girl, three of whom saw service in the war; Captain John Roberts, Lieutenant Michael Roberts and Major Eric Roberts. Although he suffered ill health his wife died before him; after her death he lodged at Bunshill as all his children were away in the war. Rev. Roberts died in October 1943 and was buried next to his wife in Kenchester churchyard. It was the wish of his family that instead of flowers at his funeral a subscription should be given to the local branch of the Nursing Association and a total of £15 11s 00d was raised. They returned the money for local use and in 1948 it was used to purchase an invalid chair for the use of elderly and invalid people of the parish. Leslie Roberts, his eldest son, lost his life in a tragic motor cycle accident on September 8th 1945.

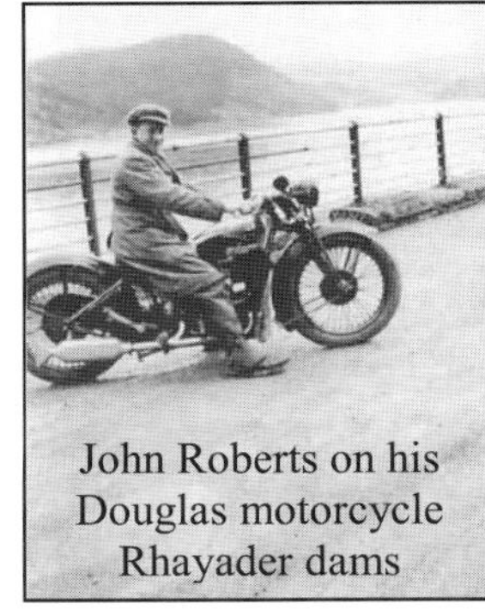
John Roberts on his Douglas motorcycle Rhayader dams

The new rector was Rev Stanley Max Benjamin who was described as a very keen energetic man whose particular interest was in music. He was a friend of Miss Elsie Lewis of Bishopstone Court, and previously a minor canon and chaplain of St Woolas Cathedral Newport. He married in February 1944 and was instituted into the church on March 11th of the same year. He immediately set about trying to restore the Father Smith organ in Bishopstone Church[8]. As proof to his effort in trying to restore the organ over twenty items of correspondence dated between 1944-48 are deposited in Hereford Record Office. The final letter dated January 30th 1948 from Ingram & Co quoted that it could cost anything from £500 to £600 to restore the organ. Because the Father Smith had stopped working a small harmonium was placed at the front of the church to provide music for services.

(Figure 48) Father Smith organ and gallery Bishopstone church. Access to the gallery was by a stairs on the right 1940.

The history of this ancient organ is interesting. It was built by Father (Bernard) Smith in 1700-1 for Eton College, where it resided until it was purchased by Robert Price in 1844 and presented to Rev Lane Freer.
Father Smith who built the organ was born in 1630 and was brought to England by Charles II, he built organs for the Chapel Royal, Whitehall, Westminster Abbey, St Margaret's Westminster and St Paul's Cathedral. The organ was modernized when fitted to Bishopstone church and some of the largest wooden pipes were replaced with metal ones. It had the original keyboard with keys that are black, which in more modern instruments are white. My mother played the organ on numerous occasions. From 1926-43 the organist was paid £5 per year, the organ blowers 15s a year. A door at the back left hand side let the boys into a compartment where a lever was pulled up and down to operate the bellows. Phyllis Rounds was the regular organist from 1926 till 1943. The organ blowers were young lads from the parish.
In a letter, dated September 28th 1955, Rev Benjamin Rector of Stretton Grandison writes, *"When I went to Bishopstone in 1944, I found the organ in an appalling state, rotten and unplayable. However, I had advice from the Archdeacon and approached Eton College to ask whether they would like the organ back. After some uncertainty the College thought they would like it, and sent a man down to see about packing it up etc. He spent three day with us and then decided that the College really did not want the organ, not worth the effort. The next move was to offer it to Hereford Museum, but they simply hadn't room for it. After this it was advertised with absolutely no result, in the end, eventually I persuaded Ingrams, very reluctantly, to remove the whole thing and gallery".* The Church account book records: *"£15 received for the organ from Ingrams".* It seems the organ was removed early in 1948 after the Easter meeting; what a pity; it would have been such an asset to the church nowadays.
This is not the end of the organ saga, the 1983 reference book by James Boeringer of organs made between 1601 and 1854 contains a surprise entry, Lytchett-Minster parish church organ, *"Ex Herefordshire Bishopstone parish church of St Lawrence".* Whether it is the complete organ or only part I do not know but the photo on the internet shows a large gallery organ.

(Figure 49) The church lost two other prominent features when it was redecorated in the 1940s. Above the very ornate ceiling decoration above the nave and chancel Right; the large tin plate scripture scrolls hanging either side of the East window.

The other work carried out in the church in 1946 was the installation of a new heating system paid for by the nephew of Rev Lane Freer on condition that the church wardens maintained his grave.

The Rev Max Benjamin's replacement Rev Arrantash arrived in late 1948. Although born in London, Rev Arrantash was brought up in Australia, he came with his wife and two children. He wrote many letters asking to have a new rectory built using the £3,113 14s 11d held by the Church Commissioners from the sale of Bishopstone Rectory. The Church Commissioners refused to release the money and to add insult to injury moved the money into their general fund losing it from the parish forever. Rev Arrantash resigned over this action in April 1952 and returned to Perth in Australia where he lived out the rest of his days.

Rev Arrantash

1947 will be remembered for the big freeze, snow had covered the ground on January 22nd but it did not thaw and on February 12th a very heavy snowfall overnight combined with a high easterly wind drifted the snow, filling in the roads to hedgerow level. After a few days with no sign of a thaw in sight, the villagers started to dig out to the main road. On March 6th there was another heavy fall of snow blocking the roads, then after six weeks a sudden thaw brought flooding to the area.

(Figure 50) Above villagers clearing the snow at the end of Bunshill Lane L to R Gerald Bradley, Percy Bradley, Norah Bradley, Mrs Bradley, Hilda Meadham, Ruth Payne, Jessie Prosser, Helen Haines, Mrs Payne, Joyce Rawlings, Boys unknown.
Top Right: Skating on Nelson Pond. Right: Crossroads

(Figure 51) Above new Council Houses built in 1944, Photo 2000, Left Bill and Mary Montague who moved in when the houses were first built

The December 1st 1943 edition of the Hereford Times carried a report on the November Weobley District Council meeting regarding the supply of power to the two new cottages the council were about to build in Bishopstone (these are the two cottages next door to the Nelson). The Shropshire, Worcestershire and Staffordshire Electric Power Company would soon be bringing the power line to the parish and this led to the question of whether the cottages should be wired for power, lighting and provision of a hot-water cylinder, which would add an extra cost of £35 per home. It was decided that if the council were erecting modern cottages, the council should give them modern services. From the above it appears the main electricity lines passed through the parish in 1944, although the local line to the village appeared sometime after. The first evidence of the electricity supply reaching Bishopstone is a pole agreement I have dated May 28th 1948 between my grandfather Albert Macklin and The Shropshire, Worcestershire and Staffordshire Electric Power Company for pole No 31 for which they paid a ground rent of 1s per year. Not all the houses were connected immediately; some cottages did not connect to the electric supply until the mid 1950s. Bishopstone church records show that electricity was installed into the church in spring 1950 when the Midland Electricity Board charged £7 14s 00d to bring in the supply. This was equivalent to over two weeks' wages for an agricultural worker. Harding Bros fitted all the lighting and power points in the church for a charge of £90 0s 5d.

Chapter 15
1950-2000

(Figure 1) School field day. circ 1950.
Back Row. John Clark, Edward Carpenter, Rhoda Jones, Michael Stinton, Joyce Reynolds.
Middle Row. Gerald Bradley, John Evans, John Bullock, David Macklin Sylvia Baugh.
Front Row. Margaret Payne

Parish Council

Captain Gilbert stepped down as chairman of the parish council at the 1951 parish meeting and Mr. D. Johnson was elected chairman. The secretary Miss B Lewis was asked to write to the Midland Red Bus Co asking for a 6:15 p.m. and 9:15 p.m. bus to be sent to Bishopstone daily.

A letter was received from the Boundaries Commission about moving boundaries and joining other parishes; after discussion the meeting desired that the district boundary remained as it was and should not be united with any other urban or rural authorities. Housing was again discussed, the reply to the Rural District Council read; *"That in view of the fact that Bishopstone is a compact village centre, possessing both an ample water supply from springs and electricity supply to pump the same, and also good communications, eight new houses should be built in the parish."*

The 1952 parish meeting was held on April 8th when 20 parishioners attended plus Mr H Long, a representative from Weobley Rural District Council. After formal business the main discussion centred on the parish footpaths. The National Parks and Access to the Countryside Act 1949 ordered local authorities to produce a map of the footpaths in their area which the locals wanted to be made into public rights of way, and the Bishopstone parishioners were requested to record these paths on to a definitive map. I don't think the councillors or parishioners realised at the time how important this meeting was and what far-reaching effects it would have on the future parishioners. Dr Malcolmson from Staunton on Wye did realise this and recorded every footpath in that parish on their map. Bishopstone lost some of its traditional paths i.e. from Bishon Common to the church, from Bishon Common to Kenchester church and the footpath that followed the river bank from Bunshill to Bridge Sollers. A few parish representatives had considered the footpaths before the parish council meeting and recommended that the following five footpaths should be kept open.

1. Bishopstone Lodge to the church.
2. The continuation of the path from Bishopstone Court through Moat Meadows to the Bridge Sollers-Mansel Lacy road opposite Shetton Lane.
3. From Bishopstone Smithy to the Bridge Sollers-Hereford main road(Bridle path).
4. Lena Cottage to Swiss Cottage.
5. From a point on the Kenchester-Bishopstone road opposite Bunshill Lane to Bishopstone Common.

On the proposition of Mr J Gough It was agreed that the following three paths should also be kept open.

1. A point on the Bridge Sollers road opposite Bunshill Lane down to the river.
2. From Old School House Bishopstone to a point on the Bridge Sollers-Hereford road between the crossroads and Bridge Ash House.
3. From Kenchester Rectory to Bridge Sollers across Bunshill Farm.

On the proposition of Mr P Bradley seconded by Mr S Lewis it was unanimously agreed that the eight paths noted should be marked on the map to remain open.

Since 1952, Weobley Rural District Council along with later local authorities have closed the following paths, nos 1, 2 and 4 from the first list, and no 1 from the second list. We have gained the bridle path around Bishopstone Hill, this was entered on to the definitive map by the kind permission of Sir John Cotterell in the early 1970.

Alice Macklin Post Mistress 1948-1964

Throughout the war the delivery of mail had been from Swainshill Post Office; at the 1953 parish council meeting it was requested that Bishopstone Post Office should now deal with it. From the summer of 1953 the deliveries were made from Bishopstone Post Office (The Knoll).

(Figure 2) Marley built 1955circ.

Postal bikes were provided; Mrs. Jessie Prosser as previously recorded covered the villages of Byford, Mansel Gamage and Bridge Sollers, Mrs Reynolds the other post Lady delivered to Bishon Common, Bunshill and Kenchester. This system carried on until the post office operating out of The Knoll closed in 1964, the post office then moved up the village to Mrs. Reynolds' bungalow called Marley.

Fetes were the main events used to raise money for the churches. The 1951 fete held at the Old Weir Kenchester on 28th July attracted a huge crowd of parishioners.

(Figure 3) 1951 Fete Children's fancy dress. Stepping forward David Macklin, standing behind in spotted dress Rose Wall. Three ladies standing in the line Mrs Price holding her daughter's hand, Kitty Macklin holding my hand and far right Nora Montague

Bishopstone, Bridge Sollers & Kenchester

A

GARDEN FETE

will be held at

The Old Weir, Kenchester

(By kind permission of Mr. and Mrs. J. Hewer)

on SATURDAY, JULY 28th, 1951

to be opened at 2-30 p.m. by

The Lord Bishop of Hereford

Jumble, Produce and Other Stalls
Various Attractions including Hoop-la, Skittling for a Pig :: Children's Fancy Dress Parade
Folk Dancing by the Credenhill Troupe

Buffet : Teas : Ices and Lemonade
Music Supplied by W. R. Gregg, Weobley

ADMISSION FREE

Come and Spent an Enjoyable Day in the Country

DONATIONS OR GIFTS for the Stalls would be appreciated and may be sent to Miss B. L. Lewis, Bishopstone Court, Hereford.

Proceeds in aid of Church Funds

David Greig Ltd 04149- 1

Name: Mrs Watkins
Address: Bishopston
Date: 23-6-1951

No.	Description	Provision
1	Bacon 1½ lbs	4 0
1	Sugar 3 lbs	1 3
1	Cheese 2 lbs	2 4
1	¾ Tea	2 9
1	3 lb Flour	1 2
1	Hp Sauce	1 3
1	1 lb Chivers Marmalade	1 4½
1	½ Sultanas	7½
	2 lb Syrup	None
1	8 ozs Bovril	4 0
1	Butter 1½ lbs	3 9
1	Marg 1½ lbs	1 9
1	Lard 12 ozs	1 0
	Sugar 3 lbs	£1-5-3

(Figure 4) Grocer Bill 1951 due to the food shortages after the war syrup and sugar were both omitted from the order

Rev Arrantash introduced the Lord Bishop of Hereford to open the fete. There was the usual children's fancy dress, the winner being Josephine Arrantash, 2nd place Rhoda Jones, and 3rd place Ruth Lewis. Walter Tippins won the skittles for the live pig on display by the side of the alley, donated by Mr Wright, Bridge Farm, Bridge Sollers. Walter walked the pig home to the Pleck after the event. Other attractions included folk dancing by the Credenhill Troup, Hoopla, Jumble, Produce and other stalls.

The Coronation of Queen Elizabeth II on June 2nd 1953.

For the first time many of the parishioners were able to watch the event on TV. There were only two televisions in the parish, one belonging to Percy Alderton and the other to my grandfather Albert Macklin. I can remember watching the event with twenty to thirty others villagers, children and adults crammed into the front room, looking at proceedings on a hazy 9 inch screen. I believe a similar situation occurred in the Alderton household.

Bishopstone held their village celebration of the coronation at Bishon Farm, by kind permission of Mr and Mrs Harry Watkins. A combined service was conducted before the event at Bishon Farm by the Rev D Stewart and Rev A Williams from Kenchester Chapel.

There were various games and entertainments such as Fancy Dress Carnival for the children, a boys and girls race, a tiny tots race and a ladies and gents race; there was also an obstacle race which included crawling under a lorry sheet, which was won by Dennis Johnson with Clive Eagling second.

Competitions included the best ladies ankles, gents knobbly knees and also gurning, the pulling of the ugliest face through a horse collar. Plenty of beer and soft drinks were available through out the day. The children sat down to a good tea at gaily decorated tables packed with food. The grown-ups sat down for their tea afterwards and then the children were each presented with an inscribed commemorative spoon.

1953 Commemorative spoon

A comical football match followed, which caused great amusement. The teams were ladies v gents, fancy dress costumes were worn, the Rev Stewart was the referee and he carried a real revolver from which he shot blank cartridges to announce each goal. At the start of the match my father Cecil Macklin dressed as a policeman was chasing the ball around for about 5 mins when he was shot by Rev Stewart, he collapsed to the ground and was carried off on a stretcher; it appeared to everyone watching, like a film from the silent movies. A film of this football match was taken by Mr Godfrey Davies of Wyeval Hereford and was shown to the village later at a Christmas party. The day festivities concluded with a bonfire in Mr Watkins' field by the Nelson.
A house to house collection was made in the three parishes to buy trees to plant in the villages as a memento of the occasion, the total collected came to £91 16s 00d, out of which money four flowering cherry trees were purchased and planted, one in Kenchester churchyard, one in Bishopstone churchyard, one in Bridge Sollers churchyard and the last one on Kenchester Chapel garden. Fifty years later Bridge Sollars still have their tree, which is in a very poor state, but the one planted outside the Chapel at Kenchester still gives a magnificent show in the spring. The commemorative spoons were also purchased from this collection. The small surplus of money left was used to purchase table cloths and extra china for the three parishes.

S Buckley wrote a series of articles for the Hereford Times in 1953 called Herefordshire Journey. No IV was titled *"I meet Mr & Mrs Ted Thomas of Bishopstone"*.
Perhaps it is true to say that Herefordshire has almost everything that we associate with the English country life, woodlands, clear running rivers, in summertime a warm genial climate and hedges rich in bird life.
Even on this cold November day as I make my way to Bishopstone the hedgerows were alive with noisy, chattering birds. For the country lovers this is indeed a county of their choice, and a beauty and tranquillity that the modern world has not destroyed. Yet to appreciate it in full we must have watched the landscape through all the seasons of the year. Those who have seen the same branches weighed down with snow in winter appreciate the beauty of green trees in summer more. The swirling rivers in November have a particular beauty to those who have watched them flowing gently in summer.
Here at Bishopstone, we find all these things, the bracken-covered hillsides, the woods are not far away or the swirling Wye. Here too, I was walking where the Romans walked, for they brought a road from Kenchester to this tiny village under the woods of Mansell Hill. Here was found fragment of a Roman patterned pavement, which can now be seen in the Hereford museum. This was the home of the Berrington family who founded the Almshouses here two centuries ago. They lived at the moated house Bishopstone Court, and their monuments can be seen in the church close by. Standing aloof among the orchards this can almost be called a miniature church. Cross shaped and having a west turret rising from its stone roof this fine old church is mostly 13th century.
The Normans left their mark here, for the masonry in the nave is theirs. The timbered porch is 14th century, and in the rather overcrowded interior are many interesting carvings from the past. Over the nave with a small head on a wall plate, is an old barrel roof. Over the chancel, with its 600-year-old piscina, are 17th-century beams painted with texts. Two men with folded arms stand at the sides of the Jacobean reredos, and another two stand by the post of the pulpit's stairway.

Bishopstone Church 1955

Dressed in ruffs and quilted sleeves, typical of Jacobean dress, are the sculptured figures of John Berrington and his wife. There is also a monument sculptured by Peter Hollis of Sarah Freer whose son was once the rector here.

A Dutch alms dish in 17th century brass shows two spies of Canaan carrying a huge bunch of grapes. Pictured in the six glass panels all about 300 years ago are scenes of the return of the Prodigal Son.
To find the vicar of this beautiful church I had over a mile to walk, but the walk was well worth it. The Reverend David Stewart is a genial middle-aged man, who has the problem of looking after two other parishes besides that of Bishopstone. Before he came here he had spent a number of years as an Army Padre and did much good work at the notorious "Belsen" camp. It was his ministrations that helped to bring the inmates of a terrible place back to normal health. "But those things are best forgotten" he said.
It was from him that I heard of Mr. and Mrs. Ted Thomas "You'll find them a kindly old couple," he told me, and indeed I did.

(Figure 5) Bishopstone Church Dutch Alms plate 1641 now in the safe keeping of Hereford Catherdral.

In the tiny Pear Tree cottage I find them, 80-year-old Mrs. Thomas and 86-year-old Ted. They are a cheery couple, a real "Darby and Joan." "That's quite an age Mr. Thomas" I said "yes" he answered, "and I've never had a doctor in my life, except for broken bones."
Ted was born in Llanwarne and except for a few years he spent as a collier in Wales, has never been out of Hereford. A healthy looking old man, he spent most of his life working on the land and started work when he was ten. His main interest now is his garden. "It helps out," he told me. "When we get all our vegetables from it." Tending this garden must be quite a job too, for it is no small one. In spite of this he wishes he could be back working on the land. "Time passes too slowly at home" he remarked. I asked them how they would like to live in a town. "Ah, no," said Mrs. Thomas "we've lived in this house 13 years, and we wouldn't like to leave it now." Ted agreed "Its too smoky in the town anyhow; too many people all crowded together."
Mrs Thomas's main worry is the rationing. "We don't get much for two, but we always manage somehow." Although her sight is not as good as it was Mrs Thomas does all her own housework and cooking. She was born not far away at Preston-on-Wye, and went to work at Bristol as a children's nursemaid. She, too, has done her share of farmwork, for she has helped many times during the harvests.
I could have spent hours listening to them talking of the past. Married 60 years, what memories they must have and what changes they must have seen, this kindly couple whose door is always open. They always have a kindly word for a stranger, and they talked to me in a manner I shall always remember. In this journey of mine, I shall probably meet many such Mr. and Mrs. Thomas's, but never a Mr. and Mrs. Ted Thomas. Good luck to you both!

Dennis Johnson purchased the old Nelson fields from the Lewis family of Bishopstone Court Farm in 1955, four fields including the small field bordering the Roman road running from the Old School House up to the Almshouses. This small field now contains five bungalows. A letter was sent to Bishopstone Parish Council in 1955 from the Trustees of Lady Southampton Chapel offering the lecture room at Kenchester as a parish hall for the use of the three parishes (Bishopstone, Bridge Sollars and Kenchester). Bishopstone Parish Council agreed in principle, so long as events could be held to raise money towards building a new parish hall of their own in the future. The water supply for the cottages on the common again became an issue for the parish council in 1956; the water was traditionally collected by bucket from a spring fed waterspout, which emptied into the Yazor Brook. Any small rise in the water level meant there was insufficient room for the bucket to be placed under the spout and in the case of a flood no fresh water was available at all. As a temporary solution the Weobley District Council dropped two concrete rings over the spring and installed a hand pump; the cattle and frost soon put paid to this, and the cottagers returned to catch water in a bucket. In the same year 1956 a request was made to the Rural District Council to pipe and fill in the ditches between Bishopstone and Kenchester Rectory, this was completed by 1957.
A tragedy came to Bishopstone on February 9th 1956 when Sandra Kitching, aged five, was run over and killed by a milk lorry on her way home from Kenchester School. She was the youngest child of Abby and Barbara Kitching who lived at 2 The Clovers Bishopstone. The inquest heard how a group of children were walking home after school towards Bishopstone and when hearing the lorry approach, stood on the grass verge; but Sandra ran out between them and under the rear wheels of the lorry. The children ran and fetched the Reverend David Stewart from the rectory; he rose from his sick bed and raced down to the accident.

Sandra's funeral was held at Bridge Sollers church on February 14th over which the Reverend David Stewart officiated. It is thought locally that he never got over the shock of the accident, because he died four days later on February 18th at home, aged only 66. It must have deeply affected him, he wrote in Bridge Sollers burial register "killed on the way home from school by a milk lorry."

Rev and Mrs Stewart

Reverend David Stewart's funeral service was held at Bridge Sollers Church and most of the parishioners from the three parishes attended, plus the churchwardens from his three churches. Churchwardens, Mr. C Kitching and Mrs B Reynolds, represented Bishopstone church. Following the service the cortege left for the interment in the churchyard of Silian church in Cardiganshire; the service preceding the internment was taken in Welsh.

Reverend David Stewart was highly regarded by the parishioners although he was our rector for only four years from 1952-56.

In the Second World War Mr Stewart served as an Army Padre in the 35th C.C.S. He was one of the first people to enter Belsen camp after Germany surrendered and what he saw had a profound effect on him for the rest of his life. He wrote a book called "The Crime of Belsen." On entering the camp there were over 10,000 dead bodies lying around, he writes, and in the month of March alone 17,000 people had been gassed in Belsen; there were only 1870 survivors. The photographs he had taken he used as illustrations in his book. Rev Stewart never forgot what he saw. His book makes the reader almost live through the horror that these unfortunate beings endured.

Coming-of-Age Celebrations

JOHN HENRY GEERS COTTERELL

at Garnons

8th May, 1956

(Figure 6) Three legged race led on the left by Peter and Beryl Jones from the Stepps, John Cotterell partnered with his sister Rose appear to be in second place far right

On May 8th 1956 the parishioners who were tenants and employees of Garnons estate were all invited to attended the Coming-of-Age Celebrations of John Cotterell. In the afternoon fun races were held in front of the house.

After many years of requests the parish finally had it own telephone kiosk, which was installed by the blacksmith's shop in the autumn 1956.

Best Kept Village Competition

At the annual parish council meeting held on April 4th 1956 the particulars of the Best Kept Village Competition were considered and it was agreed that an entry should be made. The competition was organised by Herefordshire Community Council. There was great activity in the village that summer, volunteers tidied up the churchyard, they levelled graves and some of the older headstones were moved to the edge of the churchyard. Meanwhile everyone became a little more conscious, tidying outside their house, growing flowers and picking up litter. The village was awarded second prize and a cherry tree, which now stands next to the telephone kiosk, was planted to commemorate the event on November 17th 1956 at 3pm by Mrs Alderton the parish's oldest resident, helped by Miss E K Lewis the clerk.

1957 New telephone kiosk and 2nd prize commemorative tree

The competition bug had now bitten the parishioners: for the next year all the stops were pulled out, fences were painted, churchyard grass cut like a lawn, houses whitewashed, flowers in front gardens planted to give beautiful displays. All this work was worthwhile in the end when Bishopstone won 1st place out of the 28 villages taking part. The parish council received a telegram on July 12th 1957 as notification that they were winners.

NO LITTER WAS FOUND ANYWHERE

BEST-KEPT VILLAGE AWARD FOR BISHOPSTONE

NOTABLE EXAMPLE OF COMBINED EFFORT IN SCATTERED AREA

EARDISLAND PLACED SECOND IN COUNTY COMPETITION

The Hereford Times Report of July 19th 1957.

Bishopstone which has no village hall, no war memorial, no school and a population of only 164 people has won this year's Best Kept Village competition organized by Herefordshire Community Council.

The first three finalists of the 28 villages taking part in the competition were from Weobley rural district. Following Bishopstone, which is 7 miles west of Hereford and north of the Hereford Hay road, were last year's winners of the competition, Eardisland with Weobley in third place.

Bishopstone, this year's best-kept village.

Both the number of entries and the standards are higher than last year, Miss M A Fildes, assistant secretary of the Council, told a Hereford Times reporter on Monday that the judges were particularly impressed by the decrease in the amount of litter during the past year.

Preliminary judging was carried out by a team consisting of representatives of the W I Federation, the Community Council and the Council for the Preservation of Rural England.

Marks were awarded for absence of litter, the condition of hedges, fences and walls, the condition of the village centre, green and playing fields; tidiness of gardens and allotments, condition of churchyards; the cleanliness of churchyard, cleanliness of verges, ponds and streams; the surrounds of halls, schools, war memorial, bus stops and shelters; the scarcity and orderliness of advertisements; and the external appearances of outhouses, sheds and gardens. Bonus points were also awarded for the general appearance of the village.

The final selection between the first four villages chosen in the preliminary judging was carried out by Commander the Hon. Humphrey Pakington R.N. Chairman of the Worcestershire Community Council who is also closely associated with the Council for the Preservation of Rural England and the National Playing Fields Association.

In his report on Bishopstone he said this is a case of a scattered village or rather a group of hamlets whose inhabitants have overcome the difficulties of being scattered with a triumphant result.

Perhaps the first thing that strikes the visitor is the beauty of the gardens and evidence of the care expended on them.

This might be attributed to the personal pride of the owners. But one finds that wherever a community effort is needed the same care is lavished. The churchyard is very well kept. I was particularly struck by the treatment of the turf and the paths around the telephone box and the prize tree planted last year when the village recorded a second in the competition.

The same pride is used on properties fronting the main road, I would particularity commend the trim appearance of the garage and inn.

It was noteworthy, that no litter could be found on the road. I saw one advertisement only, a square of blue and white fixed over a cottage door like a coat of arms. The effect is very pleasant.

Altogether Bishopstone is a notable example of what a joint effort can do in a scattered village.

Commander Pakington said of Eardisland that though it was a beautiful village and the general standard extremely high, there were criticisms; of the churchyard could have been better kept; there were unnecessary advertisements; the surroundings of the small building used by the W. I. could have been tidier; and there was some clutter behind a gate.

Led by members of the parish meetings under the chairmanship of Mr. A. J. Haimes, head gamekeeper on the Garnons estate and parish representative on the Weobley District Council the villagers made every effort to appeal to the judges.

Volunteer teams cut the churchyard and moved a rubbish dump with the help of local farmers and approval of the church council. The final results were first Bishopstone 92%, second Eardisland 82%, third Weobley with 81%.

A formal event was held at 4.30pm on September 7th 1957 where Mr. A J Haimes as chairman of the parish council received the trophy on behalf of the village. Miss Edith Lewis clerk to the parish council standing on his left. Bishop of Hereford far right. Afterwards everyone went to Bishon Farm, where by invitation of Mr H G Watkins, tea had been laid out in the wain house, the cost of it met by a collection in the village. The afternoon closed with folk dancing to the sound of amplified records on a neatly mown square of grass bordered with straw bales, and a comic cricket match in fancy dress.

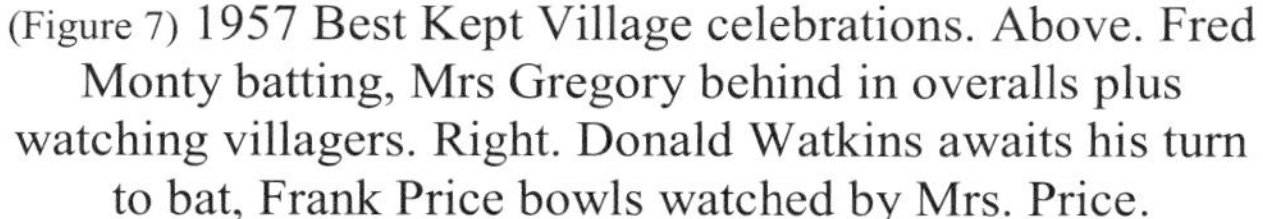

(Figure 7) 1957 Best Kept Village celebrations. Above. Fred Monty batting, Mrs Gregory behind in overalls plus watching villagers. Right. Donald Watkins awaits his turn to bat, Frank Price bowls watched by Mrs. Price.

Residents of Bishopstone for the second year in succession turned out in force on Saturday August 23rd 1958 at 6pm to receive their plaque for winning the Best Kept Village competition. But at the presentation they were informed by the chairman of the organisers Capt. Bengough they must stand down for a year as potential winners, for no village is allowed to hold the plaque more than two years running. Extending his congratulations Capt Bengough spoke of Bishopstone's splendid record in the competition: second in 1956 and first in each of the two following years. This he said showed the wonderful sense of pride they had in their village, and it was the right sort of pride. The village contained neat and colourful gardens, clipped hedges and grass verges

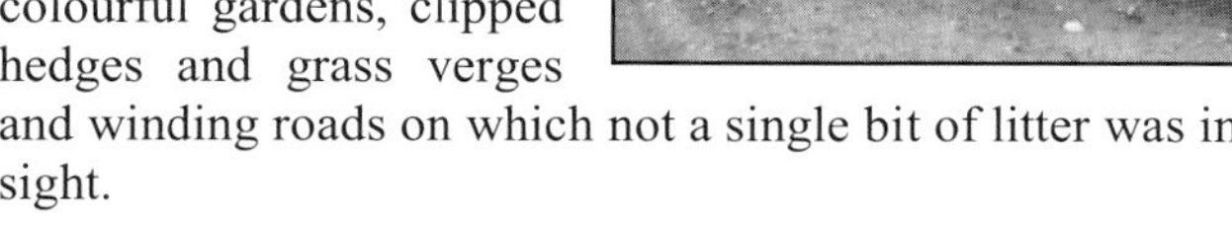

and winding roads on which not a single bit of litter was in sight.

(Figure 35) Above, the Trophy that could only be held for two years. Left 1958 presentation, Mr Arthur Haimes is in a wheel chair with Mr W H Gifford (wearing a bow tie) Secretary for the Coucil for the Preservation of Rural England who unveiled the trophy, on his left Dennis Johnson acting chair parish council and Edith Lewis parish clerk

The effort was all the more commendable because of the straggling nature of the village. Bishopstone residents had made a supreme effort and he thought their village was "almost immaculate". They had beaten 60 other villages that had entries in the competition this year.
Mr Gifford representing the Preservation of Rural England unveiled the plaque.
The acting chairman of the parish meeting, Mr H D Johnson receiving the plaque on behalf of the village said that everyone in the area had earned the award. After the award ceremony the villagers watched a film show in the wainhouse on Bishon farm. The presentation was preceded in the afternoon by a sports event arranged for all Bishopstone children, which was held between 3.00-4.30pm, in the orchard in front of Bishon Farm.

(Figure 8) Hereford Times July 25th 1958 outside Burcott Row L to R Cathy and Gillian Montague, Alice Gregory, Nora Montague

(Figure 9) August 23rd 1958 Bishopstone residents and guest who were watching the unveiling ceremony across the road, (1) Cecil Macklin (2) ? (3) Mrs Morgan (4) Susan Macklin (5) Roger Kitching (6) Doris Carless (7) Mr Morgan (8) Margaret Carless (9) ? (10) Jim Gough (11, 12, 13) ? (14) Clive Eagling (15) John Macklin (16, 17) ?. (18) Maud Eagling (19) Abbey Kitching (20) Colin Campbell (21) Lynette Eagling (22) Edith Campbell (23) Jennifer Campbell (24) Ann Campbell (25) ? (26) Viv Jenkins (27) Eirwin Jenkins (28) Paul Eagling (29) Royston Jones (30) Mary Wall (31) Joyce Montague (32) Marian Gregory (33) Sarah Wall (34) Irene Gregory (35) Pat Campbell (36) Janet Johnson (37) Kitty Macklin (38) ? (39) John Simpson (40)? (41) Janet Bradley (42) Rose Carpenter (43) Gillian Montague (44) Sandra Holder (45) Nora Montague (46) Phyllis Simpson (47) John Simpson Jnr (48) Vivian Alterton (49) Winifred Gregg (50) Dawn Caine (51) Fred Montague (52) Richard Carpenter (53) Jill Gregg (54) Sheila Gregg (55) Helen Matthews (56) Terry Matthews

Hereford Evening News Tuesday June 21st 1960

Bishopstone is back in the fight and wary of spies

"There's really nothing very special about our village" that's the sort of remark likely to greet a stranger who starts asking to many questions in the tiny village of Bishopstone.

And, after a single drive through the main street you might be quite justified in believing that to be true.

Tucked away from the main Hereford-Hay road, the village is kept at a respectful arm's length even by its own church and public house.

But if members of the 160 strong community would seem to be somewhat disparaging in their description of the place they call home, remember that it could be all a matter of strategy. The fact is that they just don't want to tell too much at this moment. Something of an unofficial Secrets Act.

Truth is that Bishopstone is anything but a run of the mill community. Village centre "battle honours" speak volumes for the village formidable reputation in the Herefordshire Community Council's Best-Kept Village Competition.

After warming up with a second place several years ago, they took the first prize in two consecutive years. Last year they were banned from entry on account of this very prowess.

Now they are swinging into action for the current competition with customary efficiency. Tempered with an element of secrecy. For they are not going to allow their opponents to be panicked into special efforts by leakage of the news "Bishopstone is rearming".

Here a newly painted gate, there a freshly trimmed verge. One minute a village storekeeper snipping away at the lovely hedge the next minute slipping unobtrusively through her cottage door to dodge our cameraman.

Bishopstone is certainly not seeking publicity, and many of its modest folk were anything but anxious to talk or be photographed; yet they were kind and hospitable while modestly declining to be "in the picture". What sort of people occupy this delightful snippet of the Herefordshire scene basking so unobtrusively beneath the woods of Mansell Hill.

A leading figure is Mr. Henry Dennis Johnson, a Farmer who makes his home at the Rectory. "Not too much about what we are doing now," he urges, concentrate on the seat we put up at the village centre to mark winning the competition two years running. "We call it the village centre because the telephone kiosk is there".

He explained that the lovely stone seat adorning the tiny village green was built to incorporate the 2 "Best-Kept Village" plaques. The stone was given by Sir Richard Cotterell.

For in the words of Mr. Johnson "We are very conscious of our community life".

And the tidy village tag has had outside repercussions, apart from merely stimulating opponents to a higher standard. Tourist traffic has increased since the community became known for its rural pride, Mr Johnson revealed.

This does not go down too well with James John Gough who has occupied his old world cottage in Bishopstone for 26 years. He gives unstinting support to the part the village is playing in tidying up the countryside, but he deplores the influx of weekend sightseers.

(Figure 10) Neat and tidy verge and wall outside Panteg Cottage and Burcott Row in readiness for the inspectors. 1960

But James John is a cheery fellow and he hasn't allowed a little disturbance from inquisitive outsiders to dampen his enthusiasm for his garden, a garden which I can safely say is outstandingly lovely in a truly lovely village.

Looking back over the happy years spent in his cottage, he recalled that Bishopstone was a very different place in his earlier days there. Economic circumstances of the countryside at that time forced cottagers to plant potatoes and other food where now lovely scented roses grow.

Mentioning that the village has no craftsman, the Forge stands, but its furnace embers have long since died, he remarked "We have nothing of importance to write about". I chuckled and left.

Putting in an eight-hour day at the age of 73 is Mr. Charles Kitching, whom I found using a billhook to good effect on the verge leading to the rectory.

Charlie Kitching

For a good many years after World War I he was chauffeur-gardener for Captain H. A. Gilbert who now lives at the Lodge. (Everyone I've found had a good word for Captain Gilbert).
Later, Mr Kitching took on the postal delivery, he knows what it is to cycle around the four parishes on an uninviting winter's morning.
A regular occupant of the new seat at the village centre is 79 year-old George Cooper who saw quite a bit of the world before putting down his roots in his Almshouse at Bishopstone 13 years ago.
From the seat, and between puffs of baccy, he wages anew many a World War I campaign. Regular work he left behind him when he passed the 74 mark and though he still does the odd job or two, he has ample time to reflect on the good and bad days.
Of the times when he helped lay new roads out of London, and of Army service before the 1914-18 war. "That I shouldn't say too much about because I slipped 'em," he said.
At the parish church, tucked in a quiet corner, well away from the village, there was further signs of activity. The churchyard has been levelled to present a more tidy setting for the handsome church with its magnificent roof.

George Cooper

The spiritual needs of Bishopstone with the neighbouring Bridge Sollers and Kenchester are cared for by the Reverend W. R. Saunders.
Mr. Saunders pointed out that levelling and moving of the old gravestones was not actually a best-kept village effort, but was a church project with the same end in view.
In fact, the whole aura of this lovely Norman building and its surrounding display a neatness reflecting creditably on the unflagging interest of the parishioners.
Of them, Mr. Saunders had this to say, "They support their church wholeheartedly. Bishopstone people are exceptionally keen church workers".
Lying close to the church is Bishopstone Court, a fine stone building approached through a lovely entrance straddling a moat. And all around are signs of neat, good farming. The tidiness that abounds speaks well for the industry of the present occupier, Mr R Carrington who has lived there over five years.
The Nelson Inn, on the main road is a tidy step from the village, but the villagers, and a good many motorists from other parts, find it a step well worth taking. A quaint building, with the date 1871 imprinted on the wall, it offers a traveller snacks, bed and breakfast, and by order full meals, as well of course as its primary commodity.

Bill Collins

The licensee, Mrs. F. G. Collins, has been mine host for eight years.
Bishopstone is not without its young folk, and if the opinions of youngsters I spoke to are any criterion, they are not anxious to abandon country life for the supposedly more exciting pastimes of the city.
Grandma is Mrs. Sarah Ann Wall, a widow, who was looking after the children while mother was cleaning the church. Since 1905 she has lived in the same cottage, Stonehouse. Six of her 15 grandchildren live in the village, while three are in America, and one is in Canada.
At approaching 77, Mrs Wall is not so set in her ways that she would resist a change. "I would like a new cottage," she confirmed.
And the hub of all this is not some central village hall, where noisy Saturday night dances and midweek whist drives are all the go. This is a village revolving around a parish church that, to go back to Mr. Johnson is "The axle from which all other village activities spring."
The village meeting place is the vestry.

The Romans it was who pushed through the road from Kenchester and, I understand, the Roman lived in his villa on the very spot where Bishopstone Rectory stands.
And this, they told me, was a village about which there was nothing to write.
Bishopstone won 2nd place in the 1960 Best Kept village competition this was the last year the village entered the competition.

My Memories of Bishopstone 50 years ago.

I suppose I am lucky enough to remember the village before any development had taken place, when Bishon Farm was still worked in an old traditional way using workhorses. A memory of a village and its folk can easily appear wonderful and romantic looking through young eyes. Frank Betambeau said to me one day, that when he first came to the live in the village in the early 1960s everyone seemed to be related. True is the fact that out of Bishopstone's population of 160 in 1960 we could account for 23 in four related families, the Macklins, Campbells, Walls and Gwilliams.

In these memories you may find too many references to vehicles, it's because, as a young man I was always fascinated with the internal combustion engine, something that has stayed with me all my life; from this interest I went on to earn a living in the garage business. The transport used by the people of the parish was always of interest to me. Even at the age of ten with Paul Eagling my mate, we would go down the bridle path to the main road and sit on the bank in the summer holidays and spot registration plates on cars, mostly VJ and CJ the Herefordshire allotted plates, occasionally FO the Radnorshire number. In a morning we would hardly fill in one page of an exercise book, I can remember looking longingly up the road for the next car to come along, it seemed like an age, today the traffic count on this road would be in the thousands per day.

We came to live in Greenwalls, Bishopstone, permanently in 1957, I was ten years old. Because both grand parents lived in Bishopstone and the building of Greenwalls had taken 5 years I was a constant visitor. Granny Mac ran the post office and Grandad Mac was bedridden, the post office originally built as a bungalow was now a house. Before the war Grandad Mac had decided to raise the whole roof by six feet and fit four bedrooms in the roof space.

(Figure 11) Greenwalls 1959

There was a resemblance to a builder's yard to the side of the house still, with stacks of bricks, tiles and a large shed contained two large drums of paraffin, which the villagers would buy for heating and lighting, I can remember filling the quart measure using a stirrup pump, before pouring it into the customers utensils. Also humming away in the shed was a charger used to charge customers' accumulators (batteries used to power their wireless sets). Stuck in the orchard stood the remains of a Bradford truck, a relic of happier times when it was used as the firm's transport, and a patch of ground used by Frank Hill to grow his prize-winning roses.

The post office was located in a front room of the house, it had a high counter which as children we could not see over. Behind this counter, a no go area for us, there were letter racks, mail bags and various articles of post office clothing such as hats and overcoats hanging on a rack and standing at the back was the large post office safe where all the stamps, postal orders etc were kept. In the hall the public telephone stood on a stand for the use of the villagers. Living in the house with Grandad and Granny were Aunty Edith and her children, Derek, Pat, Colin, Jenny, Ann and Christine.

A blackened fire range stood in the grate of the back room, it may seem strange now but every day the fire was lit, even in the summer, it was used for cooking. There was an oven on the one side with a hot plate, over the open fire hung a black kettle, that always appearing to be singing. On the side a large frying pan which Granny would soon pull over and start frying a huge amount of sausages to feed the large family.

Although the well was in the yard outside the back door, water was pumped by hand to a tank in the roof. The house was built with the luxury of having flushing toilets up and down stairs and a bathroom "what you would expect from a builder". In the back kitchen was the furnace. Every Monday morning the fire was lit to heat the water for washing; after being boiled in the furnace the washing was carried outside into the yard, and put through a large cast iron mangle which must have stood over five foot tall.

There was no such problem next door at home in Greenwalls, we had all the mod cons, even a washing machine we brought with us from Kenchester which had its own wringer attached to the side. The only down side, we had the same system as Granny, having to hand pump the water into the roof, later Dad converted it to an electric pump.

We walked or rode a pushbike everywhere as we had no car, Dad cycled to work at the RAF camp at Credenhill, Mum who played the organ at two or three services on a Sunday usually had a lift with the Rector.

(Figure 12) Nelson Garage 1950s

Rev Saunders was a man of firm religious beliefs; I never saw him laugh and he smiled very infrequently. He was a stout man, slightly overweight and always wore a thick leather belt around his midriff over his cassock; his wife was a small person with large darting eyes. I can see him now driving up through the village in the Wolseley 6/90 with regal elegance, not appearing to notice anything or anybody. Every Saturday morning he would drive down to the Nelson Garage and buy ½ gallon of 5 star petrol costing 2s 6¼d. How do I know this? Well, because I had a Saturday job at the Nelson Garage and would often serve him. No getting out of the car in 1960, when he pulled up my job would entail running out to ask what was wanted, putting in the petrol, taking the money, bringing the change, and carrying out any other jobs required, tyre pressures, cleaning the windscreen, all part of the service, the driver never left his seat.

The garage had been purchased by Texaco, Roy Jones was the manager. It was just as Percy Alderton had sold it with 5 petrol pumps alongside the road, 4 containing petrol, 2star 4s 5d, 3star 4s 8d, 4 star 4s 10½d, 5 star 5s ½d and a TVO pump, but I cannot remember the price. These pump prices will be imprinted in my brain forever, they say you never forget your first job. The office was in a tin hut that was also a shop, which sold cigarettes, drinks and all types of spare parts for cars, fan belts, spark plugs, contact breakers etc.

(Figure 13) New Nelson Service Station

Percy would call in at the garage for petrol in his Austin A95 Westminster, the smartest car in the parish I thought. Percy would always crack a joke and Mrs Alderton would sit in the car all smiles.

Around the back in a shed was a workshop, as a thirteen year old it was my dream come true. This is where Don Ellerton worked on racing and hill climb cars and occasionally I was allowed to clean and polish parts from the engines. The noise was spellbinding as Don test revved the engines to full capacity. I particular remember a Cooper built single seater with a Triumph Bonneville engine. A regular visitor to the garage was Innes Ireland the racing driver. Don after packing in the workshop went on to become a commercial airline pilot.

(Figure 14) Flo Collins with one of her poodles outside the Nelson

Next door at the Nelson Inn lived Bill and Flo Collins. Bill was nearly as round as he was tall and struck me as being a bit gruff to us boys, Flo wore a lot of makeup and always appeared a bit glamorous and sophisticated with her toy poodle dog. Children were not allowed into the pub then, you had to be over sixteen years old. Although it was our ambition as young teenagers to drink beer we never had the means or money to get any, no supermarkets or four-packs then. But the smell of beer coming out of the half-opened bar window on a summers day was like nectar to us, so we would sit at the table outside and take it in until Bill came out and chased us off. The Nelson seemed to us the liveliest place in the parish to hang out in the summer holidays, the noise coming from the bar window was of people enjoying themselves, no drinking and driving to worry about.

(Figure 15) inside the Nelson, Flo the landlady's arm over the back of the settle, sat L to R. Mr Birch, George Haines and Bob Jones 1950s.

It would be a few more years before I could frequent the pub but one thing that does stick in my mind, always parked outside the pub was a Black Humber Hawk, the preferred car for the local farmer, it belonged to Ben Lloyd of Kenchester Court a regular frequenter of Flo's snug.
Summer holidays as with all school children of our era hold fond memories of long hot days seemingly to go on forever. The three highlights of those holidays I most remember, fifty odd years ago, were swimming in the river, Sunday School trips and the harvest.

(Figure 16) Bishopstone residents swimming in the river. Above L to R; Bradley family, David and John Macklin, Gilbert family. Right; typical sunny summer Sunday afternoon with many villagers picnicking on the river bank

Swimming in the river at Bunshill will be remembered by many families from Bishopstone. Like many other children from the village I learnt to swim there, it was not just our generation, my father had learned to swim there 40 years earlier. On a hot Sunday afternoon you would find many of the families from the village sitting on the banks having picnics while the kids played in the water
Some of the antics we got up to in the river would today seem positively foolhardy. I can remember one particular day when a gang of us decided to swim down from Bridge Sollers Bridge to Bunshill a distance of three miles, our one aim was to find the deepest part of the river. At several likely spots we would test the depth by diving down and holding the person above you by the feet, hence it was two people deep or three, etc. Well, the deepest hole we found was opposite the Weir gardens, we tried to go for a four persons but could not achieve it, all I can say is it's deeper than three.
Sunday school trips for the three parishes were in some ways the highlight of the summer; we, like most of the families in Bishopstone, could not afford to go on an annual holiday. Early on a summer's morning, a crowd of between twenty to thirty of us villagers would be waiting by the telephone kiosk, eagerly looking down towards oak tree pitch. Who would be the first to spot the buses coming in convoy over the bank, would there be two or three Wye Valley buses this year? When the buses stopped out would step Betty Lewis, clipboard in hand, to try and organise the boarding but to her bemusement there would always be a clamber to try to board their latest bus identified by the big fin on the back. On the bus there would be a guessing game as to which seaside resort we were heading for, Barry Island, Porthcawl or Weston Super Mare, and on the way home there was always singing. The old favourites "She'll be coming round the mountain when she comes" "Ten green bottles hanging on the wall" and "Show me the way to go home," there must have been others but I can't remember them.

(Figure 17) 1950s Parish bus trip to Porthcawl L to R Back Row; Bill Thomas, Gerard & Percy Bradley, Jean Thomas. Front Row; Cissie Bradley, Janet Bradley, Mrs Thomas, Benard Thomas, Helen and Bob Mathews

Bishon Farm's gathering of the harvest had been virtually unchanged since the 1920s except that in the 1950s a Fordson tractor replaced the two horses needed to pull the binder although the horses were still used to fetch in the sheaves after drying in the field. The farm was owned by Mr Watkins, a man of short stature who always talked through his nose.

(Figure 18) Stooking the sheaves

The village ladies always remembered Mrs Watkins as being a lovely person. Donald their son a bachelor helped run the farm, different as chalk and cheese they were, Donald was a very tall strong man and always talked very slowly.
After we had heard on the bush telegraph that the binder had started cutting the corn, myself, and a few of the other lads would turn up at the field and help "stook" the sheaves; we were not paid for the work, it was something to do and we always hoped for some liquid reward at the end of the day. Some of the older boys were paid for their efforts. There was always excitement when the binder reached the centre square, we would stand around the outside with sticks to club the rabbits that bolted out, some years we caught loads but on other occasions we caught hardly any. One year a fox came out to everyone's surprise. Mr Watkins would be slowly working his way around the outside of the field cutting the missed bits of corn with an old scythe and tying them into sheaves. This all changed in 1958 when the Watkins's bought a second-hand combine, that required two men, one driver and another filling sacks with corn, tying the tops and dropping them off at the corners. This was soon modifying to a one man operator by having a tank fitted to collect the corn.
At the end of the day we would go back to the farm and hang about hoping for the offer of cider. Donald was either very good to us or it could have been for his own amusement, but he invariably invited us all down to the cider cellar for a few horns.

(Figure 19) Donald Watkins on his 1955 combine

This was potent farmhouse cider he made himself; if you were not careful, he would always try to give you more than was good for you, then watch and laugh as we made our wobbly way back up the drive. At the end of harvest Mr Watkins would give us a few shillings.
With this money we would go to Mrs Prosser's shop, full of all types of sweets in large jars, gobstoppers, bubble gum, sherbet fountains, Spangles and many other types of sweets whose names are long forgotten, she also sold tobacco and cigarettes. As thirteen year olds we had began to lose interest in sweets, cigarettes and smoking were of greater interest; nearly everyone smoked in those days. We would ask for 5 Woodbine cigarettes costing 10d, Mrs Prosser would ask who they were for, "a visitor" we would reply in unison, she would hand over the packet with a little wry smile on her face, she knew we were going to smoke the cigarettes ourselves.

(Figure 20) Donald Watkins and Jim Roberts hauling a heavy trailer with his new Nuffield tractor. circ 1960

In late September we would go hop picking down on Marsh Farm with the other villagers. I don't think I was much help, always leaving too many leaves in the crib, but I do remember the cockatoo who lived in a cage on the farm. "Cocky fight the Germans" he would repeat over and over.
Every Sunday at 3.00pm the children from Bishopstone attended Sunday School at the church. There were 18 on the register in 1960, split into infants and juniors; Miss Betty Lewis taught the infants and Miss Edith Lewis the juniors. Miss Betty was a forthright spinster, bossy and would stand no nonsense; she wore big round glasses and always a hat. Her sister Miss Edith was smaller and quieter and gave the appearance of missing her vocation of becoming a schoolmistress.

(Figure 21) Standing outside The Pleck, circ 1960 L to R Janet Bradley, Pat Campbell, unknown, Colin Campbell and Joyce Monty

All the children in the parish attended, we were encouraged or told to go by our parents. It was essential to have your name ticked on the register as this brought many benefits, the Sunday school trip in the summer to the seaside and the Christmas party where we were given presents of books for good attendance. The Sunday School as far as I can remember was boring and I am sorry to admit that most of the carvings of initials on the pews in the church were carried out during this time. But the memorable part was walking to and from the church in a big gang where we would mess about, play tag and the girls in the spring always picked the snowdrops and primroses along the lane to take home posies for their mothers. Occasionally Mr Carrington came by in his Vauxhall Cresta car, very impressive it was too, with American finned styling and roaring six-cylinder engine.
One day a couple of us were trying to catch goldfish in the pond behind the Nelson and also keeping a weather eye open for Mr Johnson who owned the pond when Captain Gilbert came over the stile from the Nelson. He was dressed in his country wear, I think his normal mode of transport the Ford Thames van had broken down. We knew he was interested in ornithology and pointed out a moorhen's nest, which led to a conversation about his egg collection. The Captain invited us back to the Old Rectory to see his collection: it was amazing, rows of eggs in cabinets he had collected before the 1954 Act made it illegal to take wild birds' eggs. It's difficult to imagine how birds considered rare now were commonplace in 1960. On Bishon Common and thereabouts there were hundreds of pairs of peewits, even curlew and snipe were plentiful, the common was a paradise for wild life then.

(Figure 22) Lecture Room Kenchester

Thursday night was youth club night, held in the lecture room at Kenchester and the teenagers from Bishopstone, numbering around fifteen would pushbike or walk there for a 7.30pm start. The Bishopstone contingency made up threequarters of the members. The club started up in 1960 and ran for 5 years, until Clive Eagling our youth leader moved to Credenhill. They tried a temporary leader for a few months but because a permanent leader could not be found the youth club closed. We would play chess, darts, skittles, had quizzes and played table tennis but the greatest attraction was the Dansette record player on which we played the latest 45s. The highlight of the club came in 1965 when the boys won the Hereford League Table-Tennis Tournament, held from October to April throughout the county. The cup presented at the Town Hall, Hereford, was proudly brought to the club, and each player received a medal. I can remember one particular trip when in March 1965 we went to the Regal Theatre in Gloucester to see Billy Fury, who at time was the idol of many of the girls, and the pop group The Pretty Things.
Occasionally we went on bus trips to places like Blackpool or Rhyl. We were not much different from the teenagers of today; except for the fact we had no money. Hanging about outside the club were the older boys with their motorbikes. The club finished at 9.00 pm and on the way home the boys on the motorbikes would do a bit of showing off to impress the girls, roaring by and making them squeal. One motor biking character sticks in my mind, walking home from the club one winter's evening we could hear the thump thump of a British single approaching, all you could see in the darkness was the glow of a cigarette coming towards us, it was Brian Cato on his 350cc AJS. I don't think the lights on the old bike ever worked but it never stopped him riding at night.
All the schoolchildren after taking the 11 plus left Kenchester School to attend schools in Hereford, catching the 8.30am service bus. One morning the bus stopped at oak tree pitch as there had been an accident. The bus driver got out and came back to say a guy on a motor bike had hit the milk lorry, it was Gerald Bradley but thankfully his only injury was a broken wrist; although it did cause much anguish to Janet his sister who was a passenger on the bus.

(Figure 23) Donald Watkins Ford Thames van parked outside Bishopstone church in 1963, in the foreground the flower covered grave of his father Harry Watkins Bishon Farm

I don't know what made Ford Thames vans so popular in the village, but we had three, Captain Gilbert, Edgar Wall and Donald Watkins all had one.
A centuries old daily chore of collecting clean water from the wells was still the norm in 1960, many of the cottages had their own well in the garden but there were still several communal wells in the village.

One well in Mr and Mrs Payne's garden at 3 The Clovers served all three cottages in the row, another communal well was behind Burcott, but most people would remember the well in the centre of the village, located behind the telephone kiosk which supplied the Almshouses and Forge Cottage; its still there today but now covered with a concrete pad. These wells did not have the fancy appearance of wishing wells, they had to be functional, remember most household would draw an average of two buckets a day. Both these communal wells were covered with a wooden A frame with lockable trap doors on the front for access and metal winding handle on the side attached to a galvanised bucket on a long chain to drop down the well.

(Figure 24) standing outside the Clovers. L to R, Paul Eagling, Colin Campbell, John Macklin, Peter Eagling and Robin Kitching.

Six lads from the village were in the Scouts, John Roberts, Robin Kitching, Paul and Peter Eagling, Colin Campbell and myself; we caught the 6.00pm bus on a Saturday that went up through the village and got off at Kinnersley turn. The Scouts were held in Kinnersley village hall and the rector there was the scoutmaster; it was good fun, we went camping, learnt boxing and many other skills. We caught the 9.30pm bus back to Bridge Sollers and would walk home from the crossroads or across the bridle path. The one lasting memory of the Scouts happened at Christmas when we would ring handbells around the local houses collecting for charity. We came to this one house where a lively party was in full swing. If the Rector had any sense he should have missed this house but he didn't. We rang a peal on the bells, the door opened and the Rector held out his hand. A gloved hand came out through the opening and dropped a penny into his palm, there was an immediate scream and he dropped the penny with a few choice words that should never come out of a clergyman's mouth. The partygoers had heated the penny over the fire. I will never forget seeing the perfect imprint of a penny engraved into his hand.

Stonehouse was the home of Granny Wall where I spent many an hour, she lived with uncle Edgar, aunty Mary and my three cousins Rosemary, Sarah and John. I can remember Granny Wall, Granny Mac and Mrs Kitching would occasionally meet for afternoon tea in the front room at Stonehouse, the matriarchs of the village, they would all be wearing hats even though it was summer and indoors. The conversation was always parish business, mostly the church.

Around 1960 and still fresh in my mind was the time we were called up for the killing of the pig. Granny, white haired and somewhat rotund wearing her wraparound apron came out to greet us, business like, there was work to do. A man turned up in an old car, the pig in the stye knowing what was coming started to squeal, the man leant over the stye gate, humane gun to the head and the pig dropped like a stone. Now came the difficult bit, but with many hands we hauled this huge pig out of the stye and onto a bed of straw which uncle Edgar lit to burn off his bristles. Suddenly, to every one's amazement the pig got up, walked a few paces and dropped down covered in burning straw; nerves they said, it often happens, but I'm not convinced. Again it took all of us to the haul the pig up by a rope passing over a beam in the barn. Uncle Edgar slit his stomach and his entire intestines drop into a long tin bath placed in a strategic position. Now the work started for us children, sat at the table outside we would clean out the giblets, a boring job involving pumping a lot of clean water to wash all the muck out of the tubes but it was all worthwhile when they were fried and eaten. Meanwhile the pig was brought over and butchered. There was plenty to eat for the whole family for the next few weeks, liver, heart, brains all had to be eaten but the hams and bacon sides were salted and hung for the winter. We feasted on brawn, pigs trotters and many other parts of the pig, you name it we ate it. There were always jobs to do at Granny Wall's, help milk the cows, feed the chickens and pigs, picking apples but the most monotonous job was turning the churn to make the butter. How so much food was produced from a smallholding is still a mystery to me.

(Figure 25) Granny Wall with her pigs.

I suppose my lasting memories are of the things, sights and sounds that are no longer with us, the sense of identity we gained as children from walking the mile journey to school as a gang, "we were from Bishy".

The same walk to school my parent had undertaken forty years earlier; the long summer holidays when we children explored and covered every field, meadow and hedgerow in the parish, only returning home for meals. The sight of the roadside banks through the village covered with primroses in the spring. The constant summer cry of the curlew, being dive-bombed by peewits as we walked across the field and meadows. The Yazor brook full of sticklebacks and bullyheads, the same brook now barren of fish due to climate change, some summers completely drying up. The distant sound of a steam train pulling up the valley and blowing its whistle, the thrill of standing under the small bridge on the common, when the steam train thundered overhead at full speed, and lastly the aromatic smell of the hop yard at Marsh Farm on a September morning.

Development of the Village

The new interest in parish life became very obvious throughout the 1950s, the parishioners who had experienced the hardships and terror of war, appear to have had a new-found optimism. The villagers worked very closely as a team in the Best-kept Village Competition, with up to thirty five residents regularly attending the parish meetings, something unheard of before the war.

Many of the old residents of the parish blamed the Best Kept Village competition for the influx of new bungalows, which started to spring up in the village. *"People came to look at the village liked what they saw and wanted to live here"* Jim Gough used to say. I think it was more of a general trend in many villages in Herefordshire, where you can see many 1950-60s bungalows. After the war, housing was in short supply, as with all the other commodities, food and clothes (food rationing did not finish until July 4th 1954) and the Ministry of Housing homed many hundreds of married servicemen in Foxley Camp.

(Figure 26) The above aerial photos give a graphic illustration of the growth of the village in the 1950s and 60s with five different sections of new private Bungalows plus Orchard Close.

My father Cecil Macklin was one of these returning servicemen who started the trend of building your own property after the war, he attended an auction held at Foxley Camp on July 10th 1952 and purchased a Canadian hut for £265. He dismantled the hut on site and transported it back to Bishopstone by tractor and trailer. On part of my grandfather's orchard over five years he rebuilt it into a bungalow called Greenwalls, so called because the walls were covered with hand cut, green roofing felt tiles; the family moved up to Bishopstone from School House, Kenchester in 1957.

In 1955 locals George and Adelaide Reynolds who were living at Scaldback, built a bungalow they called Marley, this was soon followed by Mr and Mrs Quinn who had a Woolaway bungalow erected called Fayre Mede on the plot next door, both these plots were purchased from Mr Bywater and were part of his orchard. Mr Quinn was a pharmacist who worked for Chave and Jackson the chemist, he was a newcomer to Herefordshire. Including these three bungalows, over the next 15 years 36 new properties were built in the village, doubling the housing stock.

Mr and Mrs Dan Roberts built a bungalow called Whipsiderry in 1959. Dan purchased the plot from Dennis Johnson at a cost of £200, this price included Dennis having to sink a well on site.

The 1958 parish council meeting was informed that demolition orders, had been served on two cottages on Bishon Common. At this meeting Mr. Frank Hill raised the question *"would it be possible to erect council houses rather than the permission given to allow a caravan site at Bishopstone. On the proposition that five cottages in the village came under category 5, unfit for human habitation"*.

Frank Hill aimed this comment at Mr and Mrs Booth who had just won an appeal to The Ministry of Housing for a permanent caravan site for their mobile home at the top of the Walls orchard; the parishioners were niggled because both the parish and district council had originally refused the application. Mr and Mrs Booth were Londoners, they were soon moved from this site to make room for the proposed new council houses, but not before they had secured a new site for their caravan behind Mr Maund's cottage in Bishon Lane where they lived for many years; both were very active in parish and church affairs.

Foxley estate advertised three building plots for sale in 1960, formerly the small paddock attached to No 2 Scaldback Cottage, these were purchased by Ian and Pat Astley and Maurice and Doris Williams. Only two bungalows were built, The Lindens on the eastern plot, and Bromleigh on the double plot.

(Figure 27) Building Lindens; L to R. Ian Astley digging first turf, putting up roof timbers, finished

Dennis Johnson continued to sell building plots west of Whipsiderry, next door a bungalow called Rosemullion was built for Edith Cockerel a friend of Dan Roberts. A pair of bungalows was built further west, Carreg Escab occupied by Zdizlaw Borakohski and family, and on the next plot Winnal, first lived in by Fred and Eyely Oakshott. Donald Watkins of Bishon Farm built a new Woolaway bungalow in 1962 called Springfield behind Forge Cottage for his worker Jim Roberts. Dennis Johnson built an agricultural bungalow called Farrington, first occupied by Robert and Thomas Nicholls who were retired farmers.

Brian Suff, nephew of Jim Suff applied for outline planning for 3 dwellings on Bishon Common in 1964; after an appeal held on November 9th 1964, he gained permission for two dwellings, Park Hill House and Greyleys.

Arthur Haimes was chairman of the parish council and the parish representative on Weobley Rural District Council from 1952-60. He and his vice chairman of the parish council Dennis Johnson promoted this fast development of the village by both selling the land they owned in the parish for development. In a small meadow which ran between The Old Post Office and the Clovers Arthur Haimes applied for and was given permission in 1959 to build a bungalow (Sunny Bank) in the centre of the patch. His health was failing and he was wheelchair bound, the idea was to sell The Cottage on Bishon Lane and move into the more convenient bungalow with his stepdaughter, Miss Bailey. He died before he could move and Miss Bailey only occupied the bungalow for a short time before it was sold to Mr and Mrs Daft, she was an ex school teacher. Before he died he sold off two building plots to the west of Sunny Bank on which the bungalows Llanfair and Magnis were built. Magnis was originally built for Major Wilson who had a disagreement with the builder and refused the bungalow but later purchased No 4 Canon Rise, one of another new development of bungalows.

Sunny Bank

1965 Llanfair

1965 Magnis

1965 Deanswood

Arthur Haimes had also sold the plot to the east of Sunny Bank to Eric and Christine Bartup who had a new timber framed bungalow erected on the site, he also sold the orchard on the corner of Bishon Lane to the builder Willdav, the builders from Kings Acre road. They developed Canon Rise and built 8 new bungalows on the site. Within a few years, twelve new bungalows had been built on land previously owned by Arthur Haimes.

1965 No7 Canon Rise

A very welcome development came in 1961 when the mains water was laid through the village. Problems had been building up for the last ten years due to the quality of the well water in the parish. Mr Morley the sanitary inspector for Weobley RDC had tested all the wells in the parish and found the water contaminated with bacteria. Cesspits were becoming popular in the late 1950s when flush toilets and bathrooms were installed in some of the cottages. Having a high water table throughout the village meant that the cesspit spreaders were contaminating the well water. Several of the wells were stripped down, and the top ten feet rebuilt laying the bricks with mortar to try and stop the contamination. With more new housing programmed Weobley Rural District Council decided to make mains water available to the parish. The pumping station at Byford had been built in the war to supply Foxley camp, and a six inch main passed over the corner of Bishopstone Hill; a small reservoir was built, fed by this pipe, the remains of which can be seen today from the bridle path over the hill.

A six-inch asbestos pipe was laid quickly through the village, mostly in the fields opposite the houses for easy installation, only a few sections were laid in the road. This gave the villagers and the common a safe supply of water that was also needed for the future development of the village.

At a council meeting on January 16th 1961 a proposal was again put to the meeting by Frank Hill, to build council houses rather than have a caravan site in Bishopstone. In April 1961 a parish council sub committee had a meeting with Weobley Rural District Council regarding land near the Nelson Inn with a view to build council houses on the site. It was reported that they had received eleven applications for council houses from parishioners. The RDC reported that they were actively trying to buy land to put the new houses on. At the March 20th 1962 parish meeting it was reported that planning permission had been sought for 16-17 council houses on land near the Nelson Inn.

This turned out to be a private initiative and was turned down by the council. Dennis Johnson lodged an appeal and on December 16th 1962 Herefordshire North Planning Committee issued a final refusal notice.

At the March 11th 1964 parish council meeting members were informed that negotiations were under way to buy an orchard in the ownership of Mrs Wall to erect 12 council houses. A final figure of £3000 was paid for the site. The meeting of April 20th 1965 reported that the council had now purchased the site. The houses would be of a prefabricated type, but because of a delay in purchasing the Staunton-on-Wye site and other sites, work did not start immediately; the council issued a statement saying it was essential to have an estimate for all the sites to obtain the most advantageous price. But an assurance was given that the building would start within twelve months and that the people living in

Orchard Close west side

Orchard Close east side

Bishopstone would be given the first opportunity to take a tenancy.
In 1966 the new tenants moved into Orchard Close: Albert and Barbara Kitching in No 3, Edmund and Dora Compton No 4, Reuben, Dorothy and George Phillips No 5, Walter, Annie and Sylvia Tippins No 6, David and Brenda Watts No 7, Reg and Dorothy Holder No 8, John and Phyllis Simpson No 9, Frank and Valerie Betambeau No 10, Bill and Ruth Mitchell No 11, Mark and Marion Turrell and Alice Gregory No 12, Edward and Kathleen Greenway No 13, Fred and Nora Montague No 14.

Reuben and Dorothy Phillips

In 1994 the Leominster Council housing stock was taken over by the Marches Housing Association. Because of concrete failure the original prefabricated houses were demolished in 1999 making way for new houses to be built on the site using traditional methods. Some of the old tenants returned to live in the new houses but many didn't.

Fred and Nora Montague

No1 & 2 Orchard Close

Reuben and Dorothy Phillips pictured on the left were celebrating their golden wedding anniversary in 1975 when this photo was taken outside No 5 Orchard Close. Reuben moved back to live in one of the newly built Bungalows in 2000, he died in 2002 aged 102 making him one of only two male centenarians recorded as living in Bishopstone parish.
George his son was still living in Orchard Close in 2010, the only original resident left from 1966.
The two bungalows Nos 1 and 2 were traditionally built in 1968 to house retired tenants.

1966

(Figure 28) Matthews' Shop, a young Terry mowing, Helen looking through the door.

Robin and Helen Matthews in 1964 built a new house called Pleasant Views on the site of the old Peartree Cottage. In 1966 they built an extension on the side for a shop and post office, it was a nice little shop. Robin and Helen kept a good stock of many goods and along with the post office it was a central part of the village and a good meeting place.
In 1974 the shop closed after falling victim to the sewage saga. From the autumn of 1972 the road through the village was closed to traffic for nearly two years, and with customers not being able to reach the shop at times and the difficulty in receiving deliveries, Robin and Helen came to a decision to close it.
They managed to keep the post office going for another 2 years finally closing its doors in September 1976, there had been a post office in the parish for the last 117 years.

Between the autumn of 1968 to spring 1969 D & J Cooke builders built our first home, a bungalow in the village now called Sheiling, the only interest to the general public would be the cost of building in the late 60's. In early 1968 the almshouse gardens were put up for sale to raise money to build bathrooms and toilets onto each almshouse: the cost of this plot including outline planning was £600, the total cost to build the two bedroom bungalow on the site with garage was £2,400 making a total outlay of £3000.

Bishopstone lost six of its oldest residents in the 1960s, Captain Gilbert, Albert Macklin, Sarah Wall, Herbert Smith and Charlie and Rose Kitching. Between them they had lived a total of 260 years in the village.

Captain H A Gilbert died on Tuesday July 19th 1960 and was buried at Bridge Sollers church three days later. He and his family had played a large part in parish life since they had moved into the Rectory in 1922.
The obituary that follows is taken from the Hereford Times July 22nd 1960.

Capt. H A Gilbert, Cricketer, Ornithologist and Angler, Well-Known Herefordshire Personality.

Capt. Humphrey Adam Gilbert who died at Bishopstone on Tuesday, aged 74 years, won for himself a national reputation in three outdoor pursuits as an ornithologist, a cricketer and an angler. A breezy personality with a keen vein of humour, he was for many years a prominent Herefordshire figure, passionately fond of the outdoor pursuits, which he followed.

He was the only child of Mr. and Mrs. Reginald Gilbert, of Glannant, Crickhowell, and was born in Bombay. His military career was spent with the 3rd South Wales Borderers, and for part of the 1939-45 war he also served with a Pioneer Battalion in the Knighton area.

In November 1915, he married into a leading Herefordshire family, his bride being Miss Margaret Vincentia Audley Money-Kyrle, eldest daughter of Major and Mrs. Audley Money-Kyrle, of the Homme Much Marcle. There were two sons and two daughters of the marriage. The elder son C. Q. M. S. John Humphrey Kyrle Gilbert, lost his life while serving with the East Surrey Regiment in 1941.

It was through cricket that Capt. Gilbert first won recognition, and he got his Oxford blue in 1907.

In the seasons for Oxford 1907-08-09 he took, in all first-class matches 142 wickets at 16 runs each. In 1908, for the gentleman v players at the Oval, he took nine wickets, including those of such immortals as Jack Holmes (twice), Tom Hayward, Hardstaff Arnold and A E Trott.

In 1909 for Oxford against M A Noble's Australian team he took eight for 71 in the first innings, the eight included Noble, Ransford, S. E. Gregory, Armstrong,Trumper and McCartney.

This feat brought him to Edgbaston as a reserve for England in the first test in 1909. He also bowled against the Players at Lords and on the Oval.

Captain Gilbert played in first-class cricket for over 25 years, putting up some fine performances for Worcestershire right up to the end of that period. Afterwards he assisted Herefordshire for a number of seasons and was always ready to encourage young players especially in the art of slow to medium bowling.

At Oxford incidentally, he gained his BA degree, and became a barrister of law in the Middle Temple, but his love for the open-air was too strong to allow him to continue in the legal profession for long.

Taking up ornithology more or less as a hobby at first, he soon became one of England's leading authorities on bird life.

With Mr Arthur Brooks of Builth Wells as his cameraman he roamed the countryside, adding much to the knowledge of the haunts and behaviour of all kinds of birds.

The pair's greatest achievement was probably the film "Secret of the Eagle and other rare birds" which caused a sensation when it was shown, particularly for the close-up scenes of a Golden Eagle's nest, which was finally discovered in May 1925 after 2000 miles of travelling.

It included a slow motion sequence of the eagle in flight, as well as shots of the old birds feeding and brooding the young, and repairing the nest.
Another outstanding film they made was "Secrets of bird life". With his films and his still pictures, Capt. Gilbert was kept busy for some years lecturing to scientific organizations and schools throughout the country. He proved himself to be a born lecturer, telling his wonderful story in a racy, refreshing manner that gained him a high reputation wherever he went.
In collaboration with Dr. C. W. Walker, he also produced a book "Herefordshire Birds" which won high praise from the highest ornithological circles. With Mr. Brook he also wrote "Watching and Wandering Amongst Birds" which dealt with bird-watching adventures on the Pembrokeshire Coast, the Hungarian marshes and the Orkneys, and "Secrets of Bird Life".

(Figure 29) Captain Gilbert, fishing in the Wye. 1935

Birds, however were by no means is only interest.
His knowledge about the Wye and its fish was widely recognized and he wrote a fascinating book "Tales of a Wye Fisherman" which will stand for all time as one of the leading works of its kind. He was incidentally, for many years a member of the Wye Board of Conservators.
In the 1920s Capt. Gilbert was a frequent broadcaster and was known as the BBC's country correspondent. Birds were naturally his chief topic and these again appeared in his activities when, with Lt-Col C. W. Mackworth-Praed, he rebuilt and operated the Orielton decoy near Pembroke.
Between 1934 and 1939 12,000 birds were ringed, and the facts were established that migratory ducks visiting the decoy had an east to west migration.
Captain Gilbert took a keen interest in the works of the Woolhope Club and was president in 1929 and again in 1948. He was secretarial editor for some years and was also a member of the executive committee of the Herefordshire branch of the Council for the Preservation of Rural England.
His activity in public life was almost confined to his membership for a few years of the Weobley Rural District Council, to which he was elected unopposed in 1938 as a representative for Bishopstone.

Albert Macklin

Albert Macklin my grandfather came to Bishopstone in 1920 he died in February 1960 after he had been bedridden for thirteen years.

Sarah Wall my grandmother died in April 1968 and she was buried in Bishopstone Church on 1st May. Sarah Wall had lived in the village for 63 years and her obituary in the Hereford Times reflects on her life.

Sarah Wall

"Mrs Sarah Ann Wall a member of Kenchester W I for over 40 years, has died at the age of 84 and leaves the rural scene in the neighbourhood the poorer, says a W I member. Mrs Wall was born at Lulham, near Madley, as one of a family of twelve. She married John Wall, steam tractor driver in 1905.
She set up house at Old School House, Bishopstone and later moved to Stone House. Possessing remarkable drive, capacity for hard work and business ability, she managed to run her smallholding, work on the land of neighbouring farms and raise seven children.
Mrs Wall was an ardent churchgoer and whether addressing the squire, parson or fellow villager, her outspoken comments on local affairs were respected by many, and rarely ignored.
In recent years, with the coming of grand and great-grandchildren, she became head of the "clan" and was always concerned about the latest arrival. Few birthdays were overlooked".

Granny Wall always believed in hard work, if we visited as children she would always give you a job to do. Turning the handle of the separator to take off the cream for butter, fetching and carrying food for the pigs, cows and feeding the chickens and ducks. Granny talking to a newspaper reporter in 1960 said *"I would have liked a modern house with its convenience as I never had a bathroom or flush toilet"* Stonehouse was a typical old fashioned cottage, tin bath in front of the fire, pump over the sink and the twin holed privy down the garden.

Michael Bowen her eldest grandson who now lives in America, lived at Stonehouse for a period during the Second World War. His memories of Granny Wall were as a lady who knew her own mind and was not afraid of voicing it, *"she loved Winston Churchill, Gilbert Harding and any other curmudgeon. During the war in the black out, he remembers going down the garden to the toilet and having to walk back in the dark passing the fence where the dead chickens hung, bumping into the dead pig hanging in the kitchen that had been killed on the quiet, and waiting for granny to come home from market every Wednesday bringing good stuff, meat pies and chocolate biscuits*". He went with her on one or two trips and said what an eye opener it was! *"Getting prime meat from the butchers, provisions from the grocer when only pounds of butter crossed hands, no money! All, of course, during rationing. Granny always managed to step out of the house on Sunday two minutes before the Rector came along in his car whereby she got a ride to church".*
Granny Wall was certainly a character remembered by family and the older parishioners.

Mr Herbert Smith of Bunshill Farm died in April 1969 aged 84, he had farmed Bunshill since 1944. His obituary in the Hereford Times states that the funeral took place at Kinnersley church as he was a native of that parish. Mr H Smith was a life member of Hereford Herd Book Society and a member of the NFU for many years. I remember Mr Smith as a tidy farmer, who always appeared smartly dressed on market day. He was using horses on the farm up until the 1960s and afterwards had a fondness for Nuffield tractors and he also owned a very nice MG Magnette car.

Herbert Smith

Charlie Kitching

Charlie Kitching was buried at Bridge Sollers church on May 20th 1969; he had lived in Bishopstone for 48 years. Why he was buried in Bridge Sollers is a mystery considering he had served as church warden for Bishopstone church from 1942-64 under four rectors. Charlie came to Bishopstone in 1922 with his wife Rose and newly born twins Albert and Ralph; Charlie and Rose were married in 1916. Charlie was a chauffeur cum handyman at the Old Rectory and Rose helped in the house; in the early days he helped the Captain farm the land attached to the rectory. The late Eleanor English could remember vividly Charlie pitching the hay on to the wagon when she was a child, together with her two brothers jumping on top of the hay to tread it down. Then Charlie would throw a rope over to tie down the load and on the way home to the barn the horse drawn wagon would pass under trees to the great delight of the children as the branches brushed over their heads while they held firmly onto the rope. During the war in 1939 Charlie and Rose moved from the lodge into No 2 Scaldback cottage where they lived for the next 26 years, later they briefly lived in the Clovers. Charlie and Rose celebrated their golden wedding anniversary in Bishopstone on September 16th 1966. In my memories of Charlie he always seemed to be cutting grass or hedges with a hook, his party trick was stalling a car engine by shorting out the sparking plugs with his hands not recommended unless you like having 10.000 volts passing through your body. I did witness him performing this once. On one occasion Charlie in his old Ford car had a collision with the rector's Wolseley. He kept his old Ford car in the paddock next to Scaldback, its entrance on to the road was blind. Charlie had for years used the method of stopping the engine and listening, and if he heard nothing he started the engine and drove straight out onto the road. This method did not cater for deafness which comes with age; on this particular day the rector was driving by and Charlie hit his car in the side, both parties were on their way to attend the church service. Rose died five months after Charlie in October 1969, she was 85 years old.

Rose Kitching

The Hereford to Hay railway line closed in 1964. Although it did not pass through the village we had a long association with it, there were always some parishioners who worked on the railways and at the time of closure we had two, Leslie Evans who lived on the common as a plateman, and Bill Collins from the Nelson who was an engine driver. We always heard the whistle in Bishopstone as the trains sounded for the crossing at Kenchester. I had the pleasure of travelling the line from Kenchester station to Hereford as a boy, but regrettably never travelled up line to Brecon. There were eight passenger trains a day using the line, the very last scheduled passenger service ran in October 1962. The line carried goods only traffic after this; the last train ever to use the track was on September 28th 1964. The line was dismantled soon after and Donald Watkins and Jim Roberts used some of the track to construct a bridge over the Yazor Brook.

To mark the Golden Jubilee of the Women's Institutes in 1965, a book was compiled covering that year, with a description of the buildings in Bishopstone their occupants and life in general. From this book I have taken the following interesting extracts.

In the centre of the village the houses lie back from the road enclosing an open area where the awards of the "Tidy Village Competition" are displayed, a tree for second prize in 1956, a stone seat for first prize in 1958 and 1959 and only this year a glass fronted notice-board was erected as a memento of winning second prize in 1960. The telephone kiosk also stands in this area.

A set of cottages well worth mentioning, is Burcott Row. Throughout the year the gardens to these cottages are brilliant with flowers. Mr. Hill in the end house is a keen rose grower, his garden offering a display of colour which at times is breathtaking. Further along lives Mr. Montague who specializes in dahlias the varieties and hues of which are beyond description. Adjacent to Burcott Row is the house of Mr. Gough, an enthusiastic beekeeper. His garden displays a sunken fish pool and such rarities as a stone salting trough and a cider millstone. In the autumn his house is a glorious sight covered with a red-leaved Virginia creeper.

Next to Mr. Gough's home is Mrs. Prosser's shop. Here in the converted hallway of her cottage essential items are kept for purchase, and a large assortment of sweets for the children to buy with their pocket money.

(Figure 30) Photographs taken at the 1965 fete held on 24th July at the Rectory Kenchester
Top left; Maurice Williams blowing up balloons for the balloon race
Top right; Betty Lewis and Mrs Booth serving at the cake stand with Mr Compton
Bottom left; Harry Jones far left talking to Sarah Wall and a group of parishioners.
Bottom right; Major Gilbert winning the rifle range prize

Bishopstone extends from the church and Bishopstone Court Farm to the boundaries of Kenchester. It consists of about 45 dwellings, mainly cottages and modern bungalows. Many of the cottages are "tied" i.e. owned by a farm and rented to the farmworkers, and are very old. One built in 1828 has part of its external wall badly dissolved away by salt, evidence of an interior pig-salting slab. This method of home-curing bacon was commonly practised.

Most of Bishopstone is built along the Roman road which in Roman days led to Magna Castra, a large camp in Kenchester. Unlike the majority of the houses built on the roadside the Old Rectory Farm now owned by Major E. Gilbert is approached via a long drive lined with splendid horse chestnut trees, a lodge is built at the entrance to the drive

Almost opposite the Rectory Lodge stands Bishopstone post office, the office is run by Mrs Reynolds who with her husband, is also postman for the area covering Bishopstone, Bridge Sollars, Byford, Mansell Gamage and Garnons.

She works from 6 to 9:30am delivering the mail, then opens the post office until 6pm with one hour for lunch. Her regular duty includes pensions, family allowance, saving stamps, postal orders and stationery, amounting to a business of roughly £150. Collections are made by post office van at 6:10am 10:30am and 4:30pm; a standard letter requires a 4d stamp the postcard needs a 3d stamp. Parcel rates are 2s 9d first 2lb, each additional pound costing 3d.

The largest farm in Bishopstone is Bishopstone Court farm, farmed by Mr. R. Carrington. The house is situated 150 yards north of the church and there is supposed to be a connecting passage between the two buildings so far not located. The house is approached via a gateway and bridge over the moat, which probably proved more useful in the days when Cromwell garrisoned his troops in the house than it does today! Mr Carrington farms 200 acres of specialised corn, grown for seed, and has nearly as many cattle, a hundred of which are Poll-Herefords (having no horns). About 50 breeding cows are kept on the farm. Besides cattle there is also a large flock of breeding ewes. This year the ewes were crossed with a new Colbred breed of sheep.

(Figure 31) Oak Tree Pitch March 1965 the village was cut off for 3 days, During 1963 the road was blocked by snow for a fortnight.

Bishon Farm of 250 acres is farmed by Mr Donald Watkins and his mother Dora, his father Harry having died in April 1963. A mixed farm of 250 acres growing corn, and providing cattle and sheep for the livestock market.

Bunshill Farm consists of 250 acres of which half is arable; since about 1900 the farm has been occupied by relatives of the present tenants, the Smith family.

The local inn, "The Lord Nelson" is situated on the main A438 road. The Nelson is a low red brick building with a lounge bar and public games bar where darts and quoits are played most evenings. There is also a shove halfpenny board, but this game is no longer very popular. Today the licence for the "Nelson" is held by Mrs. F. Collins. It has been noticed recently that more spirits have been sold than beer, gin being more popular than whisky with both ladies and gentlemen. Young people seem to find vodka the drink of the moment. The older local men still prefer their draft beer drunk by the pint, the sale of cider has decreased considerably. Besides its function as a "local pub" the Nelson also offers bed and breakfast facilities during the summer months and accommodation is available for eight people.

2nd Post Box Bishon Lane.

(Figure 32) Left Nelson Dart team 1964
Back Row L to R; Sonny Hoskins, Bob Winnie, ?, Tom Weaver, Ivor Barnfield, Bob Birch, Frank Betambeau.
Front Row; Bob Mathews, Ray Cook, Bill Heins, Bill Collins.

On July 30th 1966 while England played in the World Cup final the three parishes held their fete at Kenchester Rectory, a bit of bad planning but I suppose not many thought England would reach the final. Dan Roberts who worked for Wallis the TV shop rigged up a television in the coach house, which enabled many attending to see the final and afterwards the television was sold to the highest bidder. The total takings for the day were £94 but how much the television made is not recorded.

There were two main events in 1970, firstly the parish outing on May 28th, to the Mumbles, organised by Miss B E Lewis and Mrs I Astley, and secondly the Garden Party at The Knap Farm raising £223 to be divided between the three parishes.

On February 15th 1971 the new decimal currency came in, which many of the elderly parishioners found difficult to understand. It was goodbye to the shilling, replaced by the new 5p piece, and the half-crown coin (now12.5p). There were 240 old pennies (d) to the pound now replaced with 100 new pennies (p).

A few of the long-term residents from the parish passed away in 1971-2. The first in January 1971 was George Haines aged 77 years who had lived at Forge Cottage for nearly forty years. I remember him as a jolly fellow who always walked down the bridle path to the Nelson for his daily pint; he was a carpenter by trade until he retired. On February 15th 1971, Harry Jones aged 73, who was living in the Almshouses was buried, he had lived in Bishopstone for most of his life. Harry had left the village as a teenager to take part in the First World War. On April 30th 1972 Harry Peake was buried, he had lodged with the Rounds family since 1932, and worked for many years at Bunshill farm.

Arthur Maund aged 79 passed away, he had lived in The Cottage, Bishon lane for ten years and had been an active member of the parish council and a trustee for the Almshouses.

On July 6th 1972 Walter Tippins was buried, he was known as "Wat". The Tippins family had lived in the Pleck during the 1940s, 50s and 60s. As far as I know, Wat was the last employee of Bishon Farm to collect his daily allowance of cider from the cellar. When I worked with him as a boy helping with the haymaking, if it started to drizzle with rain, Wat would say *"it's only gnat's pee"* which I think is an old Herefordshire saying meaning its not raining heavy enough to stop working.

Mrs M Gilbert was buried at Bridge Sollers Church on August 13th 1972; she had lived at the Rectory for the last 50 years. Surprisingly, her funeral was attended by a large family of the gypsies as in her earlier years Margaret was a founder member of the Gipsy Lore Society. She was a loyal supporter of Bishopstone church and for a period between the wars almost single-handedly kept the church going, always fund raising. Margaret joined the other Bishopstonians who preferred Bridge Sollers churchyard for their burial rather than Bishopstone.

Mrs Gilbert

Between 1900 and 2000 twenty-nine Bishopstonians had been buried in Bridge Sollers churchyard, during the same period one hundred and forty eight burials had taken place in Bishopstone churchyard which equates to roughly one in five of Bishopstone residents buried at Bridge Sollers.

A meeting was held in March 1972 at Kenchester reading room to make a proposed "Village Plan" for building development in Bishopstone. There was a full house of Bishopstone parishioners. The village was expanding at an alarming rate with 36 new dwellings since 1955, with many new modern bungalows: the housing stock had doubled in just over fifteen years. Out of the meeting came five main points, which were adopted by the Council.

(a) No large-scale development, but there is a need for some, but limited.
(b) Acceptable rate: 35 dwellings spread over a period of years.
(c) Development in depth was preferred to ribbon development, infilling acceptable.
(d) Development restricted to north side of Roman road.
(e) The centre of the village is the Old Forge.

A great upheaval in the village started in autumn 1972, when the new sewerage was being laid. The contractor encountered running sand in the excavation as they were laying the pipes through the centre of the village from Pleasant Views to the Almshouses. This problem meant that the original estimate of six weeks to complete the work turned into nearly two years, the original contractor went bankrupt. After many failed attempts, including waiting for summer to see if the water table would lower, the only engineering solution was to build an underground hydraulic station where a ram pressed 3ft concrete pipes through the offending section. The six-inch sewer pipe was then laid inside the larger pipes. The village was closed for weeks causing considerable inconvenience to residents. There was no bus service for over 12 months; the parish council wrote to the district council throughout 1973 complaining of the delays in finishing the sewer and again in April 1974, this time asking for a reduction in the rates.

(Figure 33) Sewer pipes stacked in anticipation outside the forge 1972

It was finally completed in June 1974, the cost escalating from an estimated £45,000 to a final figure of over £100,000.The sewer is gravity fed running down the village to a pumping station on Bishon Common where it is pumped at high pressure through a 2 inch pipe to Credenhill.

Machinery still blocking the road, Forge Cottage totally rebuilt during this period 1974

The Hereford Times picked up on the story after three pregnant ladies, Carol Verry, Viv Verry and Jo Macklin read a poem written by Pat Peden at the 1973 Christmas W I meeting at Byford.

(1) In Autumn time of '72;
They to the village came
Bishopstone was invaded
And will never be the same.

(2) 'Six weeks is all we need they said
We watched and hoped in vain
Now fifty-eight weeks further on
'Six weeks' they've said again

(3) Yes, J.C.B's and pipes and things
And cranes and pumps for water
Are making up our daily lives
Although they didn't oughta.

(4) Now many folks complain because
The lorries are too many
And other folk are more than cross
'Cos buses there aren't any

(5) The dust depresses most of them
'Cos floor they get so dirty
And windows they can't see through
No wonder they are shirty

(6) But whilst they mostly moan and groan
Bemoan the 'status quo'
There's three of us at least
Who make the best of a poor show.

(7) 'Cos whilst its all been going on
And others have been bored
There's no doubt we have used this time
And 'bull's-eye' we have scored.

(8) So clean those windows Bishopstone
'Cos next year you will see
We're pushing prams,now there's a change
From drains and J.C.B's.

(9) And if the critics get us down
And say we should be pure
We'll look them in the eye and then
We'll blame it on the sewer.

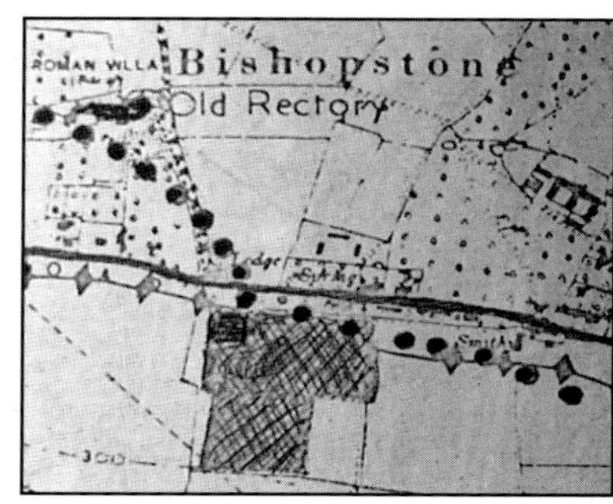

On March 14th 1974 the Council received a notification from Mr D Johnson of a large development in Bishopstone of upwards of sixty dwelling in a field between the Nelson Inn and the Roman road. (Shaded area on the map shown on the left) It was refused on the grounds of being outside the agreed village plan and an undesirable extension of the village.

In 1973 the rector of Bishopstone William Rolleston Saunders retired.

(Figure 34)
Rev Saunders' last service at Bishopstone Church 1973
L to R; Back row;
Hele Gilbert; Maurice Williams;
Erlne Gilbert; ?; Mr Lee;
Phillip Williams; Ian Astley.

Front Row
Dan Roberts; Kitty Macklin;
Alice Macklin; Betty Lewis;
Mrs Lee; Miss Lee;
Rev Saunders; Mrs Saunders;
Doris Williams;
Pat and Karen Astley;
Mr Nichols.

George Raymond Webster, the next priest in charge, was the first rector of our benefice who lived outside the three parishes. The Rectory at Kenchester was sold off by the Church Commissioners.

May 1974 recorded the start of another battle that the parish council would continue for the next twelve years concerning a travellers' encampment on the junction of Bunshill lane and Bishopstone road, where on the corner lay a triangular green area of waste land on which travellers occasionally stayed. Over a period of years this turned into a more permanent encampment with two, then three caravans and a fence appeared around the perimeter. A far cry from the Smiths' Romany caravan and ponies I can remember from the 50s who came most years, when their children would attend Kenchester School. The local Bobby from Mansel Lacy first dealt with the offenders by serving court eviction notices and became a regular visitor, but one day Fezzie their leader was said to have cast a spell on him. This caused his nose to bleed profoundly, which would not stop. He never went to the site again. After the involvement of the M.P. Peter Temple-Morris and Herefordshire Council they were eventually moved with a large police force and firemen standing by, as Fezzie had threatened to burn the caravans on site. I can see her to this day looking out of the back window of the caravan as it was loaded on to a low loader and taken away, cursing and yelling but refusing to come out of the caravan. This was transported to a site in Burghill and it is still there today. As soon as the caravans left the green was enclosed into the adjacent field by the Council so they could never return.

The parish had another bout of house building in the late 1970s, a change in the local planning officer at Leominster District spelled the death of the bungalow; now only houses were allowed, it's surprising what an influence one person can have over a district. David and Pat Peden built Pipers Croft in the garden of their bungalow the Burrows. Richard Hinksman from the Nelson filling station gained permission to build a residential dwelling behind the garage in 1975.

Alice Macklin my grandmother passed away in January 1977, she was 86 years old. The Hereford Times obituary records: Mrs Macklin who was affectionately known in the village as *"Granny Mac"* she had lived in Bishopstone for 56 years and was postmistress for 16 years. When she retired the parishioners held a social evening and presented her with a fireside chair.

(Figure 35) My father Cecil Macklin with David, Timothy, Jo and Jonathan Macklin standing outside the Knoll, demolishing the Knoll and building Jolin Autumn 1977

The Knoll was demolished and a new house was built in its place, we called it Jolin bringing the name from our old bungalow, now known as Sheiling. Mr Geoff Morgan and his wife Rose built the house called Hunters Moon in 1979 on part of her father's field and Mrs Eleanor English gained permission to build her house Glebe Cottage in 1979.

Hunters Moon

Ivor and Dennis Johnson sold the two building plots next to Pipers Croft; two houses were built on the plots, Kimberley by John Flannagan and Hill Crest by Frank Betembeau.

The five parishes of Bishopstone, Bridge Sollers, Byford, Kenchester and Mansell Gamage decided to hold a joint celebration for the Queen's Silver Jubilee on Monday June 6th 1977. A committee was formed from people representing the five parishes and £240 was raised to cover the cost. The event was held on the cricket field at Byford on a specially given bank holiday. The weather was terrible, it rained heavily all day putting a damper on the event. There were games for the children, side stalls and a pig was roasted. In the evening a large bonfire was lit on the Mansel Gamage side of Garnons park. Every child under sixteen in the five parishes was given a "Jubilee Crown" to mark the event. A tree was also planted in each parish to mark the occasion, the Bishopstone tree was planted in the field belonging to Col Gilbert in front of The Lodge.

(Figure 36) Fete held at the Old Rectory 1977 which included a Children's decorated bike competition. L to R; Gillian Austin, Jonathan Macklin, Carl White, Adrian Dickson, Anthony Smith, David Macklin, Alison Smith, Timothy Macklin, Nicola Roberts, Gary Watts

Sir Richard Cotterell

Sir Richard Cotterell resigned as chairman of the parish council in April 1978 because of ill heath. He died on December 5th of that year aged 71; he was the 5th Baronet, educated at Eton and Sandhurst. In World War II he was the commander of the 76th Shropshire Yeoman Medium Regiment RA, and during the period 1943-45 they fought in the Middle East and up through Italy. Sir John Cotterell became the 6th Baronet on the death of his father.

In 1980 Jeff Smith, a builder who was living in the Old Post Office gained permission to build a four-bedroom house in the garden, he also built three new houses on the site of old Burcott Row.

Every October in the orchards of Bishon Farm some of the village ladies would go cider apple picking, following a tradition that had been carried out by the village womenfolk on the same farm for centuries. Even in the 1980s the cider fruit was picked into buckets, on hands and knees, and emptied into sacks. Depending on how ripe the fruit was, these sack were sometimes emptied out making a huge tump to carry on ripening. In 1980 the apple picking started on October 20th and finished on 13th November; Donald paid the pickers £1.47½ per hour.

L to R; Viv Verry; Jo Macklin; Jean White; Mrs Kingstone. 1978.

If the ground was frosty it was very cold work, the ladies can remember sitting on up turned buckets for the morning and lunch breaks. Donald would bring out a big bag of sweets every day. After all the apples were picked Donald would haul the fruit down to Bulmers by tractor and trailer. Twenty years earlier in the 1960s some of this fruit was kept back to make the farm cider.

(Figure 37) Louise Macklin; Jo Macklin; Mrs Kingstone; Geraldine Matthews; Carol Verry; Jean White. Front; Jonathan Verry

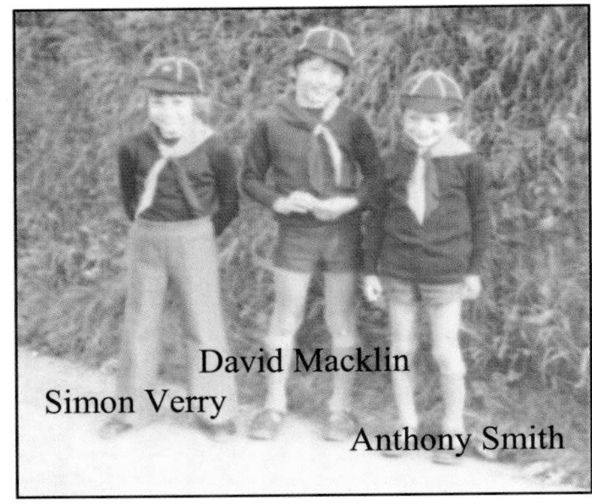

(Figure 38) Bishopstone Cubs 1978

July 29th 1981 The Royal Wedding of Prince Charles and Lady Diana Spencer.

The village celebrated with a gathering at Bishon Farm which was attended by a large crowd of residents. Competitions were held for adults' and children fancy dress, throughout the afternoon different kinds of races were held for the children including a sack and three-legged race.

A football match for the boys and a game of rounders for the girls finishing off with a tea party held in the barn.

Above left. Sitting on the throne competition. L to R; Ian Astley; Robin James; unkown; Sitting; Author; John Verry, Mr Astley; Cecil Macklin; Front. Rebecca Verry, Jonathan Verry
Centre. Splendid table of food laid out in the Wainhouse;
Right. L to R. Mrs English; Mrs Kitching; ?;? Rev Webster.

In December 1982 the parish council was asked to investigate the setting up of a youth club but nothing came to fruition; again in 1983 the parish council were asked if a recreation area could be provided for the children to play on. Leominster District council wrote to all landowners in Bishopstone asking if they would sell land for this purpose. From this Mr Donald Watkins said he was willing to sell some land behind Cambria cottages. The area was just less than one acre but large enough for a football pitch. The land was valued at £3600 plus Donald's agent fees. Leominster District Council valued the land at £2750 and offered a grant for this amount. I met up with Donald and we pegged out the site. We were just trying to organise some fund raising events to cover the difference when I received an early morning call from Donald to say he was withdrawing his offer after a disagreement with Eric Howells, the parish clerk. It was such a pity as the village would have owned a piece of land to hold their events and provide a play area for the children but it was not to be. Donald never told me what was said between them to make him change his mind. Eric Howells the parish clerk who lived at White Roses died suddenly.

January 13th 1982 after a heavy snowfall

(Figure 39) 1984 Fete Old Weir

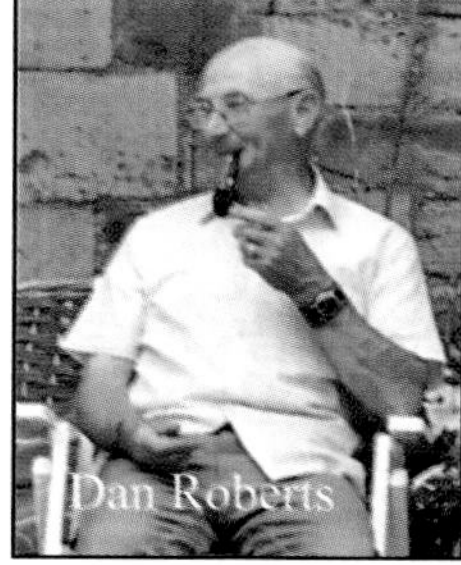
Dan Roberts

On May 15th 1985 Dan Roberts died after a short illness. Although he had moved to Byford he will always be remembered in Bishopstone. He became a churchwarden in 1967, a job he held till he left the parish in 1984. I always think of Dan when I see the gravestone of George Cooper who came to the parish with nothing and left this world with nothing. Dan found a large stone, which had been ploughed up on the Rectory Farm, he had an inscription carved on it and used it to mark George's grave. After Dan Roberts left Whipsiderry John his son, wife Margaret and their children lived in the bungalow. In 1986 John applied for outline planning to put a dwelling in the garden but it was refused because the site was too small. He then bought the building plot next to Marley and had a new bungalow built calling it "Meadow End" after his favourite football stadium at Edgar Street.

Mr Eden from the Nelson Inn put in an application in 1988 to convert the barn at the Nelson into a residential dwelling which was approved.

In 1989 Donald Watkins of Bishon Farm who was suffering from ill health decided to sell off 180 acres of his land in two lots, 80 acres north of the Roman road, which was purchased by F Price and Sons from Magna Castra Farm and another lot of 100 acres south of the road, purchased by Mr Hobby of Madley.

Sale Bishon Farm

The Optimist Raft group based at Bishopstone was formed in 1984; they ran both mens and ladies teams over the next 5 years competing in the mens 100 mile race from Hay to Chepstow and the ladies' 40 mile race from Bridge Sollers to Ross. The ladies won their 40-mile race twice, and the men won their 100-mile race twice. Over the five-year the teams raised over £3000 for charity. The men also took part in the British Championships, achieving second place

(Figure 40) September 15th 1989 Bishopstone from the South East

The 1990s saw no new development in the parish. A new footpath was opened up in 1990 to connect Church Lane with the bridle path around the hill, this link made an excellent circular walk, still enjoyed by so many parishioners today.

The Dutch almsplate dating back to the 17th century was handed in to the Cathedral Treasury on September 23rd 1991, it always looked spectacular when it was used as Bishopstone Church's altar piece, in my opinion a sad loss to the church.

Pat Astley 1981

Throughout the 1970s, 80s and 90s Pat Astley organised many coach trips from the village, the outings to Bristol and Blenheim Palace in 1992 were a typical example of Pat's enthusiasm in arranging these enjoyable days out.

Cliff Knight

The Reverend George Usher retired to Sidmouth in Devon in September 1998, a retirement town for clergymen; Mr Saunders, our previous rector had also retired to the same town. Rev Clifford Knight became the new minister, he was appointed Priest in Charge for Bishopstone on October 5th 1999 at his service of Institution held at Credenhill Church.

Cleaning out the moat at Bishopstone Court in 1995, after the water had drained away a large wooden plug was discovered in the bottom of the moat possibly Victorian. Under this plug were a number of old medieval wooden pipes that ran to a ditch, a reminder that moats had always needed the regular maintenance of clearing out the silt.

The Ann Martin's Bread Charity.

A little part of Bishopstone's history ended in 1999 with the Charity Commissioner finally closing the Ann Martin's Bread Charity. In the early 1990s the Charity Commissioners for England and Wales decided to wind up ancient charities of low value. Donald Watkins made a one-off final payment of £21 in 1994 to release the farm from the charity but it took a further five years to finalise all the paperwork. The last monies paid for bread went to two elderly residents in Orchard Close. Ann Martin purchased Bishon Farm in 1660, in part of her will dated December 19th 1683 she left 40s per year to be paid by the occupiers of Bishon Farm to buy bread for the poor of Bishopstone. The farm paid 40s into the charity for over 300 years, the amount of bread that could be bought with the money slowly decreasing over the years from 480 penny loaves a year at the start down to about 3 when it finished.

In the autumn of 1999 the villagers living on the council estate packed up and departed leaving 12 houses awaiting the demolition team.

Millennium Celebrations

A number of people from the village organised a party to be held in a marquee, with a bonfire and fireworks to celebrate the coming of the new millennium on the evening of December 31st 1999, this was held in Donald Watkins' field by the telephone box.

(Figure 41) Selection of Photos from the Millennium party where Bishopstone parishioners welcomed in the new century

Many parishioners collected or supplied wood, there was so much material that we needed Anthony Smith with his Manitou to push it into a huge bonfire.

All the villagers attending brought food which resulted in a feast, the drink flowed and it turned out to be a marvellous party that everyone attending would remember for years to come and the envy of many surrounding villages.

Big Ben rang in the year 2000 over our sound system while we toasted in the new millennium with champagne, watching our brilliant firework display and bonfire. From the elevated field fireworks could be seen in the surrounding areas, giving the impression of kinship as the whole country were celebrating this once in a lifetime event. Most villagers turned up, making it a night to remember. One parishioner Sandra Horton wrote a poem about the event part of which follows.

(1)
Oh! What a celebration
Oh1 What a great event
We had a wild millennium
Just dancing in a tent

(2)
Oh! What a celebration
With sausages rolls and booze
We had a clown with bright red nose
Who wore enormous shoes

(3)
He kept the party going
And never wore a frown
Instead of hair he should have worn
A halo or a crown

(4)
So yes it was a special night
We'll never see again
As we stood and watched the fireworks
We toasted with champagne

On March 19th 2000 Donald Watkins helped plant a commemorative oak tree watched by Bishopstone residents.

On August 12th 2000 the Bishopstone ladies group held a Duck Race on the river at Bunshill. It turned out to be a great day and to see the 1200 yellow plastic ducks come floating down the river was a sight never to be forgotten. The area down on the river bank had turned into a carnival site with tents, stalls, bunting and balloons.

A pig roast, refreshments, games and piped music all added to the atmosphere with £1400 raised for the urgent repairs needed to St Lawrence Church.

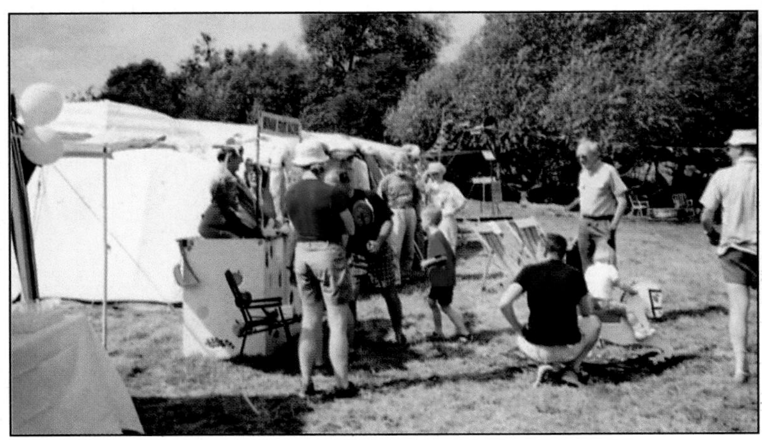

(Figure 42) Jim Fisk trying out the human fruit machine with other volunteers, L to R. Sandra Horton. John Horton and Wyn Fisk

Village Time Capsule and Millennium Summer Party- September 9th 2000

The event began with a little ceremony to bury a time capsule in the middle of the village next to the stone seat. Cecil Macklin as one of the oldest village residents, and on behalf of Mr Phillips who had just celebrated his 100th birthday but was unable to attend the party, performed this task. Placed inside the capsule were a set of coins, set of postage stamps, stock list of all current stamps, copy of a "History of Bishopstone" by C A Macklin, photographs of Hereford market, copy of Hereford Times, register of electors in Bishopstone, video tape of the village and photographs of every house in Bishopstone. The capsule was covered with a slab inscribed "Bishopstone Time Capsule 2000." Perhaps one day the capsule will be dug up and provide an historic record of life in the village at the end of the 20th century.

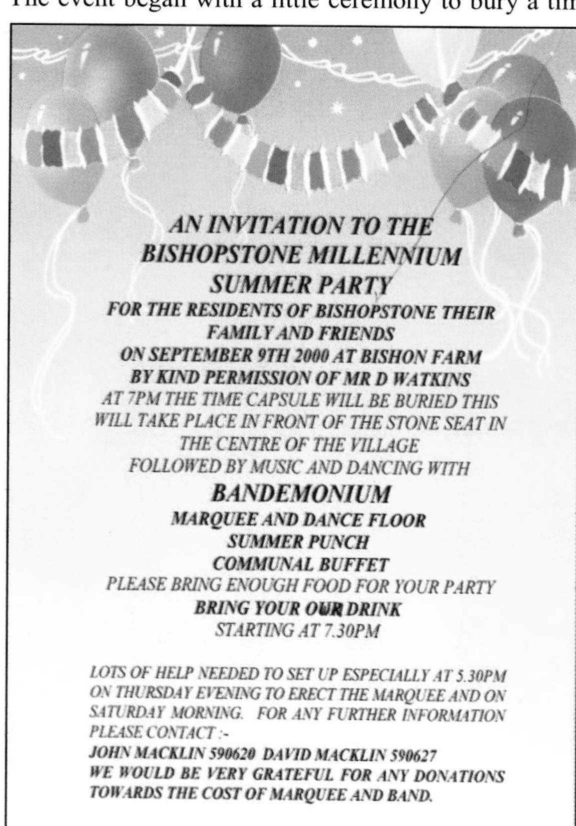

AN INVITATION TO THE
BISHOPSTONE MILLENNIUM
SUMMER PARTY
FOR THE RESIDENTS OF BISHOPSTONE THEIR
FAMILY AND FRIENDS
ON SEPTEMBER 9TH 2000 AT BISHON FARM
BY KIND PERMISSION OF MR D WATKINS
AT 7PM THE TIME CAPSULE WILL BE BURIED THIS
WILL TAKE PLACE IN FRONT OF THE STONE SEAT IN
THE CENTRE OF THE VILLAGE
FOLLOWED BY MUSIC AND DANCING WITH
BANDEMONIUM
MARQUEE AND DANCE FLOOR
SUMMER PUNCH
COMMUNAL BUFFET
PLEASE BRING ENOUGH FOOD FOR YOUR PARTY
BRING YOUR OWN DRINK
STARTING AT 7.30PM
LOTS OF HELP NEEDED TO SET UP ESPECIALLY AT 5.30PM
ON THURSDAY EVENING TO ERECT THE MARQUEE AND ON
SATURDAY MORNING. FOR ANY FURTHER INFORMATION
PLEASE CONTACT :-
JOHN MACKLIN 590620 DAVID MACKLIN 590627
WE WOULD BE VERY GRATEFUL FOR ANY DONATIONS
TOWARDS THE COST OF MARQUEE AND BAND.

A strong working party of villagers assembled in the morning to erect a marquee, down by Bishon Farm. Inside they laid down a wooden floor so a barn dance could be held in the evening. Bandemonium provided the music, and four men from the village carried out a comical performance of Morris dancing. Not to be out done some of the ladies then gave a hilarious rendition of "Old MacDonald had a Farm"

This was followed by the appearance of a surprise guest, Eddie Edwards better known as "Eddy the Eagle" who joined in the fun and presented the draw prizes.

181 Bishopstone Millennium mugs were sold by Barry Megson. The mugs featured a picture of Bishopstone Church on the front and on the back a brief history of the village.

Villagers were invited to plant daffodils outside their properties alongside the road to mark the turning of a new century. Many villagers participated, the flowers are still in evidence 10 years later and give a colourful display lining the road through the village in spring.

(Figure 43) Villagers who attended the Millennium Capsule Ceremony on September 9th 2000.

The millennium year is a good place to finish this book on Bishopstone's history, the parishioners were in a celebratory mood and prosperous. The only downside, an ageing population now occupies Bishopstone, like so many other rural villages. The history of any parish is continuous, made by the parishioners in a never-ending cycle. Since the year 2000 Bishon Farm, whose history dates back to the Anglo Saxons, has ceased to operate as a farm, and the farm buildings will be converted into 7 houses and bungalows. An example of how things can change so quickly.

I have tried to capture in this book a flavour of the people who worked and lived in our parish over the centuries.

HRO Hereford Record Office, HCL Hereford City Library, TNA The National Archives.

Chapter 1

[1] Transactions of the Woolhope Naturalists Field Club Volume XXX111 Part 11 (1950)
[2] Herefordshire S. M. R. No 8311
[3] Herefordshire S. M. R. No 6285
[4] HRO Woolhope Club 2000 Aerial Photographs of Herefordshire
[5] Herefordshire S. M. R. No 906
[6] RCHM page 17, S. M. R. No 7223
[7] Woolhope Naturalists Field Club Report, Second Field Meeting, Thursday, June 26th 1913.
[8] Herefordshire S. M. R. No 6288
[9] J Duncumb. Hundred of Grimsworth. (1892) HCL
[10] HRO AL88-46 Railway Map 1832
[11] Herefordshire S. M. R. No 30820
[12] Bishopstone Tithes Map 1839
[13] J Duncumb. Hundred of Grimsworth. (1892) HCL
[14] HRO AL2 collection. On open shelves.
[15] HRO. Both's Register. Fol 186
[16] TNA C 241/74/146
[17] J Duncumb. Hundred of Grimsworth. (1912) HCL
[18] HRO. AL 2 collection.
[19] HRO. AL 2 collection.
[20] HRO. AL 2 collection.
[21] HRO. AL 2 collection.
[22] TNA C241/127/37

Chapter 1 List of Figures

Fig 1 Woolhope Naturalists Field Club Volume XXX111
Fig 2 Author's photo Hereford Museum
Fig 3 Woolhope Naturalists Field Club Vol 54
Fig 4 Author's drawing
Fig 5 Author's photo Hereford Museum
Fig 6 HCL
Fig 7 Author's drawing
Fig 8 H C L Watkins collection
Fig 9 N L W Domesday Book
Fig 10 Author's collection
Fig 11 Royal Commission on Historical Monuments
Fig 12 Author's collection
Fig 13 T N A (Footnote 23)

Chapter 2

[1] HRO AL 2 collection, on open shelves.
[2] TNA C/131/9/23, C/131/10/6, C/241/151/115, C/241/157/147.
[3] HRO Both's Register.
[4] HRO Both's Register.
[5] Batsford. History of Everyday things in England, Vol 1, page 164.
[6] Private Records.
[7] HRO AL 2 collection.
[8] HRO AL 2 collection.
[9] J Duncumb, Hundred of Grimsworth. (c.1892) HCL
[10] HRO Open Shelve,"Visitation Returns of the Diocese of Hereford in 1397".
[11] HRO AL 2 collection.
[12] NLW Aberystwyth, IPM, Calendar of Fine Rolls.
[13] J Duncumb, Hundred of Grimsworth. (c.1892) HCL
[14] TNA C/1/132/7
[15] Private Records.

Chapter 2 List of Figures

Fig 1 Private collection
Fig 2 Internet
Fig 3 H R O
Fig 4 Internet
Fig 5 Authors drawing
Fig 6 Authors painting

Chapter 3

[1] Private Collection. (All the Rental Rolls in this chapter came from private records)
[2] J Duncumb, Hundred of Grimsworth. (c.1892) HCL
[3] HRO Open Shelve, Probate Act 1407-1581(All the Clergy in this chapter came from this reference).
[4] J Duncumb, Hundred of Grimsworth. (c.1892) HCL
[5] HRO Hereford Diocese 1546 Visitation
[6] HRO. Microfilm.
[7] HRO. The 1582 –85 visitation reports can be found in HD 2
[8] HRO. Three Glebe Terriers, HD2/6/6,-8,-9.
[9] HRO. All Wills in this Chapter are found in Herefordshire Will section unless otherwise specified.
[10] Private Records.
[11] Faraday, M.A. Herefordshire Taxes in the Reign of Henry V111.
[12] HRO. HD/AM/33-4
[13] Private Records.

Chapter 3 List of Figures

Fig 1 HCL Reference section
Fig 2 Author's photo Bishopstone Church
Fig 3 HRO (Ex Library green reference books)
Fig 4 Author's drawing
Fig 5 HCL Reference section

Chapter 4
[1] Woolhope Naturalists' Field Club, Transactions, Vol XX11 page 96.
[2] TNA.PROB 11/123.
[3] NLW.IPM section 1600-1700
[4] TNA. PROB 11/129.
[5] www.british-history.ac.uk, online Charles 1, Calendar of State Papers.

Chapter 4 List of Figures
Fig 1 Author's photo Bishopstone Church north window
Fig 2 Author's drawing
Fig 3 Woolhope Naturalists Field Club Volume ?
Fig 4 English Heritage
Fig 5 Author's photo Bishopstone Church
Fig 6 Author's photo Bishopstone Church

Chapter 5
[1] HRO. HD4/2/11.
[2] HRO.HD4/1/157-159.
[3] HRO. All wills unless stated differently can be found in the Will Section.
[4] HRO.HD2/6/8.
[5] HRO.HD2/6/9.
[6] HRO. Bishopstone Court Roll
[7] HRO.B47/H35

Chapter 5 List of Figures
Fig 1 HRO (Bustin collection)
Fig 2 HCL Reference section
Fig 3 HRO (Bishopstone Court Roll)
Fig 4 Author's photo All Saints Church

Chapter 6
[1] The dates and events are taken from "Memorials of the Civil War in Herefordshire" John Webb.
[2] HRO Quarter Sessions 1672
[3] NA C6/297/68
[4] History on Line
[5] HRO AN10
[6] Private Records
[7] TNA Prob/11/229
[8] TNA Prob/11/270
[9] TNA Prob/11/291
[10] HRO Tax in Herefordshire open shelve
[11] HRO HD4/1/200
[12] HRO All Wills unless stated differently can be found in Will Section
[13] Private Records

Chapter 6 List of Figures
Fig 1 HCL Reference section
Fig 2 Internet
Fig 3,4,5 Author's photos

Chapter 7
[1] Private Records
[2] HRO AN10
[3] HRO Bishops Transcripts of Bishopstone
[4] HRO BG11/17/5/86
[5] Private Records.
[6] HRO Charities of Herefordshire open shelves.
[7] HRO R81/1
[8] HRO HD4/3
[9] HRO Q/SO/5
[10] Private Records
[11] HRO Will Section
[12] The Allen Chronicle published by Merlin Books

Chapter 7 List of Figures
Fig 1 HCL Reference section
Fig 2 HCL Reference section
Fig 3 Private collection
Fig 4 HRO (S89)
Fig 5 Author's painting
Fig 6 Author's photo Almshouse
Fig 7 HRO (R81/1)
Fig 8 Author's photo Bishopstone Church
Fig 9 Author's photo Bishopstone Church
Fig 10 Private collection
Fig 11 Author's photo Bridge Ash

Chapter 8
[1] Private Records
[2] Private Records
[3] Internet www.absoluteastronomy com
[4] The Eighteenth-Century Land Agent by Pamela Horn
[5] HRO wills held at HRO
[6] Internet Herefordshire.greatbritishlife.co.uk
[7] HRO W69
[8] HRO Land Tax Records

Chapter 8 List of Figures
Fig 1,2,4,5,6,7 Private collection
Fig 3 Author's painting
Fig 8,9 HRO
Fig 10 HCL Reference section
Fig 11 Hereford Times
Fig 12 Internet

Chapter 9
[1] HRO 1826 Inquest
[2] Private Records
[3] HRO Ref E5/13
[4] TNA C6/297/68
[5] HRO AN10
[6] HRO look up ref
[7] HRO K42/475

Chapter 9 List of Figures
Fig 1 British Library
Fig 3 National Portrait Gallery
Fig 8,14,15,17,18,26,27,29 H R O
Fig 13 Dave Verry
Fig 21,28 HCL Reference section
Fig 24 Internet
Fig 2,19,20,23,25 Author's photos
Fig 4,5,6,7,31 Private collection
Fig 9,10,11,12 Author's paintings, drawings
Fig 16 Pat Jenkins
Fig 22 Bishopstone Church
Fig 30 Weobley Museum

Chapter 10
[1] HRO AG9 Quarter Sessions books
[2] HRO AG9 Quarter Sessions books
[3] Hereford Journal March 1853
[4] Private Records
[5] HRO AF92/2
[6] Branch Lines Around Hay-on-Wye published by Middleton Press
[7] HRO CB48 Records of Hereford Constabulary.
[8] Private Records
[9] HRO Wills

Chapter 10 List of Figures
Fig 1,2,3,6,8,9,11,14,15 HRO
Fig 5 H C C
Fig 16 HCL Reference section
Fig 4,7,12 Private collection
Fig 10,13 Author's photos

Chapter 11
[1] TNA MS193-4
[2] Private Records
[3] Private Records
[4] HRO L89
[5] Hard Times in Herefordshire by John Powell published by Logaston Press
[6] HRO BA28/2/38
[7] Private Records
[8] Private Records
[9] Internet. N Z records on line
[10] HRO S89
[11] Internet Who's Who online

Chapter 11 List of Figures
Fig 1,11,17 HCL Reference section
Fig 3 Margaret Jenkins
Fig 5,8,15 Author's photos
Fig 7 Alderton collection
Fig 10 TNA
Fig 17 Cotterell collection
Fig 2 HRO
Fig 4 Donald Watkins
Fig 6 Wall collection
Fig 9,13 Weobley Museum
Fig 12,14,18 Private collection
Fig 20 H C C records

Chapter 12
[1] NA Ancient deed series BE326/634
[2] HRO A2
[3] TNA SC6/260/10
[4] HRO A2
[5] HRO A2
[6] THA SC6/860/11
[7] THA SC2/176/37
[8] TNA SC2/176/37
[9] TNA SC2/176/40
[10] TNA CP 25/1/83/44
[11] TNA SC 6/860/12
[12] TNA SC/176/36
[13] TNA SC/176/38
[14] TNA STAR 2 19 248
[15] HRO wills
[16] TNA E326/426
[17] HRO wills
[18] HRO wills
[19] HRO wills
[20] THA E134/6JAS/East28[1608]
[21] HRO AW28/22/2
[22] HRO Aw28/22/3

[23] HRO wills
[24] HRO C99/11/1
[25] HRO C99/111/235
[26] HRO C99/111/2
[27] HRO C99/111/247
[28] HRO C99/111/161

Chapter 12 List of Figures

Fig 1,4,5,6,7 Author's photos
Fig 3 TNA
Fig 11 Private collection
Fig 2 Internet
Fig 8,9,10 HRO

Chapter 13

[1] TNA 1910 field books.
[2] HRO S90
[3] Kelly's Directory 1925
[4] Private Records
[5] Hereford library.
[6] Private records
[7] HRO AW28
[8] HRO W I Section

Chapter 13 List of Figure

Fig 1,2,9,15,28,30,88,106,113 HRO
Fig 3,4,6,7,11,13,14,18,24,31,32,34,41,46,58,76,80,86,96,101,105,111 Author,s photos
Fig 8,39,94,98 Audrey Tozer
Fig 12,16,17,33 Muriel Holmes
Fig 21 HCL Reference section
Fig 25,25 Margaret Jenkins
Fig 29 Ginny Carrington
Fig 38,47,64 Ian Astley
Fig 42 Internet
Fig 52 Geoffrey Morgan-Jones
Fig 62 Donald Watkins
Fig 67,69 Sylvia Price
Fig 72,73,74,75,79 Bob & Helen Mathews
Fig 91,95 John Verry
Fig 93 Joan Clark
Fig 100,114 Shirley Wadley
Fig 107 Rose Davies
Fig 112 Geoff & Marg Smith
Fig 5 Alderton collection
Fig 10 Sylvia Jenkins
Fig 19,20,60,61,65,66 English Heritage
Fig 22,23 Lewis collection
Fig 27 Bob Carrington
Fig 35,36,48,83,84,85,110 Joyce Bradley
Fig 37,40,44,45,81 Eleanor English
Fig 49,50,51,53,55,56,57,59,70 Wall collection
Fig 54,87,97 Hereford Times
Fig 63,77 Jim Roberts
Fig 68,71,78,82 Janet Jones
Fig 89,90 Tom Prosser
Fig 92 Dave Verry
Fig 99 Audrey & Nora Wintour
Fig 102,103,104,109 Pat Jenkins
Fig 108 Margery Webb

Chapter 14

[1] HRO Bishopstone Parish Council minute book
[2] HRO W69/111/322
[3] Woolhope Club Vol
[4] HRO sale catalogue
[5] HRO Kenchester School Logbook
[6] HRO AW28/23/11
[7] HRO K38
[8] HRO S89/17

Chapter 14 List of Figures

Fig 1,2,21 Private collection
Fig 4,7,15,16,19,22,23,24,25,26,35,37,49,51 Author,s photos
Fig 5, Hereford Times
Fig 8,27,28,36,50 Bob & Helen Mathews
Fig 14 Weobley Museum
Fig 29,31,32,33,34,41 Alderton collection
Fig 39,40,50 Eleanor English
Fig 47 Janet Jones
Fig 3 Ginny Carrington
Fig 6,10,20,45,46 HRO
Fig 11,12,13 Woolhope Library
Fig 17,18,42,43,44 Wall collection
Fig 38 Muriel Holmes
Fig 41 Joan Clark
Fig 48 Bishopstone Church

Chapter 15 List of Figures

Fig 1,3,5,11,13,16,24,34,35,36,37,38,39,41,42,43 Author's photos
Fig 2,18,22,30,31,32 HRO
Fig 6,15 Muriel Holmes
Fig 9 Hereford Times
Fig 14 Phyllis Daniels
Fig 17,21 Janet Jones
Fig 25 Wall collection
Fig 27 Ian Astley
Fig 40 Alan Knott
Fig 4,19,23 Donald Watkins
Fig 7,8,10 Joyce Bradley
Fig 12 Alderton collection
Fig 16,29 Eleanor English
Fig 20 Sylvia Price
Fig 26 English Heritage
Fig 28,32,33 Bob & Helen Matthews